IN THE HIMALAYAS

AND

ON THE INDIAN PLAINS

IN THE HIMALAYAS

AND

ON THE INDIAN PLAINS

C. F. GORDON CUMMING

GYAN

Published by

Gyan Publishing House
5, Ansari Road
Daryaganj, New Delhi-110002
Phone: 011-47034999, 9811692060
E-mail: books@gyanbooks.com

Distribution Network
gyanbooks.com
India, USA, Canada, UK, Australia, France

ISBN: 978-81-212-8822-4 (PB)
First Published, 1884

2nd Impression 2023

Printed at: Gyan Press, Delhi.

IN THE HIMALAYAS AND ON THE INDIAN PLAINS
Author: C. F. Gordon Cumming

TEMPLE AT KILBA.

IN THE HIMALAYAS

AND

ON THE INDIAN PLAINS

BY

C. F. GORDON CUMMING

AUTHOR OF

"IN THE HEBRIDES"; "AT HOME IN FIJI"
"A LADY'S CRUISE IN A FRENCH MAN OF WAR"
"GRANITE CRAGS OF CALIFORNIA"
"FIRE FOUNTAINS"
ETC.

WITH FORTY-TWO ILLUSTRATIONS

LONDON
CHATTO AND WINDUS, PICCADILLY
1884

EXPLANATORY PREFACE.

I THINK it is due to this volume to preface it with a few words of explanation, to account for half the book having appeared, some years ago, as the second part of my first publication: *From the Hebrides to the Himalayas*—a bulky work, illustrating many curiously similar customs and legends, of which I had collected notes in these two far distant countries.

Having no notion of the relative proportions of handwriting and of print, my manuscript had attained a grievously unwieldy length—a fact, however, which my publishers did not appear to have realised till the greater part of one volume was in print, and till I was on the very eve of sailing for a prolonged residence in the Pacific.

At the last moment came a sudden request for wholesale abridgment! Doubtless the wiser course would have been to have published "The Hebrides" by itself, leaving the Indian travels intact. But this would have involved sacrificing my primary idea in connecting the two countries, namely a comparison of their folk-lore; and as there really was no time for thinking out *pros* and *cons*, it seemed simplest to cut the knot by suppressing about half of my Indian manuscript.

Now, however, that I have started the Western Isles as a

separate volume,[1] it seems well that my notes on the Eastern Plains and Highlands should appear in their original form.

For although, in the meanwhile, a flood of Indian literature has made each scene familiar (and guide-books now instruct *tourists* in the way they should go !), I know that I was unusually favoured in the companionship of men who had lived long in the country, had thoroughly mastered many of its languages, and who took the deepest interest in all questions concerning the people, their religion, and their customs in general. To the unwearied kindness of these good friends I was indebted for many a lesson in the art of observing whatever was best worth studying, in the bewildering mass of novelties which distract the new comer; and also for such clues as enabled me to venture on threading even the outskirts of the perplexing labyrinths of eastern thought.

[1] *In the Hebrides*. Chatto and Windus.

INTRODUCTORY.

Facilities of travel have been so rapidly developed within the last ten or twelve years, that a pleasure-trip to India is now accounted a perfectly simple means of exchanging our wintry fogs for a spell of glorious sunlight—in fact it is simply a question of leisure and lucre.

And yet it seems but yesterday that my determination to join my sister and her husband in India, and devote a year to mere sight-seeing on a very large scale, was greeted with a chorus of amazement, not only by friends in this country, but by those whose cordial welcome to the Eastern world contributed so greatly to my enjoyment of its wonders.

These, with one accord, assured me that during their long years of exile in the Indian land, no lady, and very few gentlemen, from the old country had ever found their way thither, save as residents, bound by some tie of duty to some special station.

And no wonder, for swift steamers, and Indian railways, are creations of very recent date, and but for these distance-annihilators, assuredly few would care to face the tedium and trouble of such a journey for mere pleasure.

Besides, in pre-railway days, the accounts of Anglo-Indian existence were by no means inviting. The occasional glimpses of gorgeous Orientalism were small compensation for the dreary dulness of station-life on the burning plains all through long summer months, during which the fair fresh Western faces become paler, and more pale, as they lie gasping under the monotonous swing of the punkah, dreading heat-apoplexy, should the weary "punkah-wallah" fall asleep (as he is only too likely to do), and living from dawn to sunset in such darkness as precludes the possibility of almost any occupation—even reading—while it greatly favours the inroads of every horrible variety of creeping animal life.

This being the general impression of Indian life, and certainly my own till I found my way thither, it was pleasant to glance at it through a rosier medium, and see how those who have times and seasons at their own disposal, may now visit this wonderful land, and store their minds with its grand pictures without being subject to any of its miseries. For my own part, I can tell of a year of unmitigated enjoyment, during which my "panorama of travel" carried me over many thousand miles, full of infinite variety, and with no greater trouble or inconvenience than often attends the simplest journey across country (and such monotonous country!) in Old England.

After devoting seven months to the glories of the great mountains, and five months to exploring some of the principal cities of the plains, I returned from our Eastern Empire, having seen more of its marvels than almost any old Indian of twenty years' service, and yet had never felt one day of real heat, and rarely seen a punkah in action. Nor did I there make acquaintance with any species of venomous creature in its wild state, except three harmless snakes, much like those familiar to us on English moors.

Of course, every one who lands at Calcutta receives the homage always paid by the mosquito to the new comer; but I never suffered even from these anywhere else. My experience of Indian climate, by dint of judicious locomotion, was to prolong a balmy continuous summer, from one December till the next; and to this a second and a third might well have been added, always wandering over new ground.

Perhaps these wanderings gained an additional charm from the aimless, easy-going way in which I found myself drifting from the Western Isles to the Eastern Hills. The only mistake was, drifting homeward in like manner; and only the rude shock of finding myself once more in the bitter snows of an English spring, awakened me all too quickly from this fascinating dream, to return to the prosaic commonplaces of ordinary life.

I need scarcely say that in offering to the public the following records of a year's delightful wanderings, I am well aware that I can now have nothing new to tell, for since they were penned, Royal Princes have visited the land, and many travellers have followed in their wake, and fluent writers have recorded their experiences. So the only excuse for the publication of these pages, is the fact of their being the notes of one who claims the honour of having been a pioneer in these fresh fields of delight—one of the very first to discover the entirely "new sensation" of travelling for pleasure in India.

CONTENTS.

CHAPTER I.

CHRISTMAS IN CALCUTTA.

CHAPTER II.

A RAILWAY JOURNEY.

CHAPTER III.

MID-WINTER ON THE GANGES.

CHAPTER IV.

HINDOO PILGRIMS AND LIVING WATERS.

CHAPTER V.

CAWNPORE AND LUCKNOW.

CHAPTER VI.

AGRA.

CHAPTER VII.

WAVES OF FAITH ON THE SEA OF TIME.

CHAPTER VIII.

DELHI.

CHAPTER IX.

MEERUT.

CHAPTER X.

A GRAND DURBAR.

CHAPTER XI.

SIMLA.

CHAPTER XII.

CAMP LIFE.

CHAPTER XIII.

UNDER CANVAS.

CHAPTER XIV.

THE SACRED ARK.

CHAPTER XV.

THE CEDAR SHADE.

CHAPTER XVI.

VILLAGES ON THE CLIFFS.

CHAPTER XVII.

A PEEP INTO CHINESE TARTARY.

CHAPTER XVIII.

CHILDREN OF THE MIST.

CHAPTER XIX.

FROM UMBALLA TO MASSOURIE.

CHAPTER XX.

FROM MASSOURIE TO HARDWAR.

CHAPTER XXI.

IN THE HOLY CITY OF HARDWAR.

CHAPTER XXII.

BENARES.

IN THE HIMALAYAS
AND
ON THE INDIAN PLAINS.

CHAPTER I.

CHRISTMAS IN CALCUTTA.

The City of Kali—Her Worship—The Doorga-pooja—Sceptical Literature—The Brahm-Somaj—First Morning in Calcutta—Servants—Markets—Native Bazaars—Kites and Adjutants—Vehicles—Calcutta Races—Brown Men and White—Midnight Mass—The Evening Drive—An Indian Dinner Table—Afghan Merchants.

CHRISTMAS in Calcutta!

How strange it seemed to be shutting out the hot sun and sitting in the cool shade, with doors and windows open, while we thought of all the dear ones at home, round the blazing Yule log; [1] and of the white world that lay outside, and the busy fingers that were twining the evergreens! There were Christmas decorations here too; for the natives dearly love all tokens of feasting, and they place tall plantain leaves and bunches of fruit in the gateways, as symbols of plenty, and hang up wreaths of laurel and Indian jasmine, or strings of small lamps and of those great orange marigolds, which they offer at the shrines of all their gods.

But of the real message of Christmas, the great mass of the people know little more than they did when on the site of this

[1] When the sun rises here at 6 A.M. it is just midnight in England.

great city of palaces, there stood only a wretched village called Kali-ghat, the village of the dread goddess Kali, to whom a draught of warm human blood gives joy for a thousand years. Here grim human sacrifices were offered to her, and here, too, Hindoo mothers of old used to throw their tender babes as dainty morsels to the yawning jaws of crocodiles.

To the temple of Kali, south of the city, vast multitudes still resort, during the annual holidays known as Doorga-pooja—the worship of Doorga, "the inacessible one," by which name, as well as those of Devi, Parvati, and a score of others, Kaļi is also commonly known. As Devi, "the bright one," she is the goddess of robbers and murderers, including the Thugs, who long did her righteous pleasure in strangling unwary travellers. As Parvati, "the mountaineer," she is represented as a fair and saintly woman; as Annapūrnā, "the giver of good," she sits on a water-lily giving rice to mendicants; as the mother of Ganesha, the elephant-headed god of wisdom, she sits enthroned on a lotus blossom with the child in her arms. Under other titles she is worshipped as "the wanton-eyed" Hindoo Venus; in short, under many aspects of benignity or of terror she meets us at every turn in the complex mythology which is still the dominant feature of all life in Hindostan, the fact being that she and Siva her spouse have absorbed the characteristics of a multitude of other gods, and she is simply the feminine edition of all his attributes; hence, while he is worshipped as Mahā-devah, "the great god," she is Mahā-devi, "the great goddess."

Nonsensical as we must deem this grotesque mythology, I confess that I greatly marvelled at the contemptuous indifference displayed by the great mass of Europeans to all matters relating to the faith (and practice) of the brown multitudes around them, as to a tissue of puerile fables unworthy of the smallest attention. Yet, considering that we are here in the cradle of two of the most widely-spread faiths of the world (Brahminism and Buddhism), and that the fundamental truths of both had been thought out by men of this self-same race many centuries ere light from the East first dawned on Pagan Britain, it seems strange indeed that any can live in India, and yet give no heed to the present development of the said creeds, and their application to the daily lives of about 700,000,000 of our fellow-men in Asia, beginning with 193,000,000 in Hindostan, and including all the millions of China, Japan, Thibet, Burmah, Ceylon and all other lands where faith in Buddha still prevails.

Yet so infinitesimal is the amount of interest bestowed on native customs and traditions, by average foreigners, that an exceedingly small proportion of the inhabitants of Calcutta ever dream of turning aside from their daily routine drive in the European quarter to visit Kali-ghat, the true god-mother or goddess-mother of the great modern city; and yet an early morning in the temple affords a glimpse of the inner life of the people such as can never be obtained in the European city.

For day by day, throughout the year, these sacred courts are thronged at early dawn by a most picturesque crowd of worshippers—lightly-draped brown men, closely-veiled bejewelled women, and quaint little brown children brilliantly attired; and the sun's rays gleam on blue and orange and scarlet draperies, and are reflected by sparkling jewels—nose-rings, and ear-rings, rings on fingers and toes, silver and gold bangles—and the blaze of sunlight lends additional value to the deep, cool shadow of the temple wherein the white-robed priests move to and fro, presenting the offerings of the worshippers.

In the outer court, two forked sticks tell of the daily sacrifice of blood, not necessarily as atonement for the sins of the people, but in order to propitiate the goddess. On these rest the heads of the victims. There is a large fork for the heads of the devoted buffaloes, and a small one for those of sheep and lambs, goats and kids. Every morning at sunrise some victims are here offered, and on special days upwards of a hundred are sacrificed—an offering on so large a scale as to recall far greater sacrifices by Israelitish kings under the Mosaic dispensation. But these are exceptional occasions.

The ordinary ceremonial is very simple, though deeply suggestive. Suppose the offering to be a few kids or lambs, the officiating Brahmin lays his left hand on the head of each, marking its horns and forehead with red paint, and repeating a formula of consecration to the goddess. He sprinkles it with water and lays flowers on its head. Then an attendant of the temple seizes each poor little bleating creature by the forelegs, and holding them up over its shoulders, he lays its head in the fork, and a stick is placed so as to keep it steady. Water is then poured over the victim, whose shudder proves that the offering is accepted by the deity. The sacrificial butcher (a big brown man in the very lightest of raiment) then comes forward, with a big curved knife which has been duly consecrated, and chops off the head at a blow.

When all the victims have been slain, those who have offered them (both men and women) approach, and kneeling on the blood-stained earth, lay their own heads on these rude sacrificial altars, beseeching great Doorga to accept of this offering. Then all the heads are carried sunwise round the altar, and the worshippers—pilgrims from all parts of India—walk sunwise after them, and then make the sunwise circuit of the temple, adoring the goddess. Then the priest marks each worshipper on the forehead with her sacred symbol, and those who can afford it purchase blessed wreaths and garlands of large African marigolds. Thus shriven and adorned, they go forth to the commonplace duties of daily life, while the bodies of the victims are cut up at the temple shambles, and the meat is offered for sale, so that all men may have a chance of feasting on "things offered to idols."

The approach to the temple is through a sort of ecclesiastical bazaar, whose multitude of small booths display a wonderful assortment of brazen vessels and idols, including many clay images of most worshipful coiled snakes, with crest upreared; and perchance among the pilgrims may be seen *yogis* got up to personate the god Siva, their naked bodies smeared with ashes, their faces painted, and living snakes coiled round their necks, one resting on each shoulder, and one on the head, as a hideous substitute for a turban, crowning the unclean, uncombed elf-locks.

Resident yogis busy themselves in combing, brushing, and generally adorning their sacred white cows and oxen, while one devotes himself to the care of holy monkeys, of all ages and sizes, which come trooping down at his call to accept offerings of food, gabbling and chattering, while rapidly, with both hands, collecting the scattered grain. He speaks to them as to his children, and a chorus of holy apes and monkeys reply, and come boldly up to snatch sugared cakes from his hand. They fight and scramble, they play tricks each to his neighbour, pull one another's tails, and generally behave in a manner by no means calculated to foster feelings of reverence in their worshippers.

Indeed it is difficult to conceive how the goddess herself can inspire reverential awe in her votaries. One would even think that it must all be lost in disgust. As Kali "the black" she is generally represented with a black face, and her tongue hanging out, looking just like those Chinese pugs, whom I always feel inclined to call by her name. She is said to have been so bloodthirsty, and to have slain such myriads of victims, that in her frenzy of delight she danced upon their bodies, till her own husband, Siva the Destroyer, was sickened by the sight, and (devising how he might check her), he left his place among the gods, and lay down with the slain. Suddenly she perceived him under her feet, and in the shock of horror thrust out her tongue, and could never draw it back again.

In spite of occasional little ebullitions of temper, she seems to have been a wife after Siva's own heart, for when in an evil hour she died, her disconsolate spouse roamed to and fro upon this earth, carrying her lovely corpse upon his head, and refusing to be comforted, till at length the other gods in pity interfered, and cutting up the body into fifty-one parts, distributed them throughout India, where each part became thenceforth a centre of pilgrimage.

She is sometimes represented as a ghastly skeleton, her hair entwined with serpents, and the mystic cobra raising his hood as a protecting canopy above her. Sometimes her whole body is wrapped round with endless strings of skulls, in fact a necklace of these is an invariable adornment of her images. She wears dead bodies as ear-rings; and holds in her various hands, heads dripping with gore, a cup overflowing with blood, and divers weapons.[1] Sometimes she is represented with four arms, sometimes with twelve, and is invariably smeared with the blood of her victims. A lovable goddess truly, to be Calcutta's guardian saint! Yet this image of grotesque horror is the most popular object of worship in Eastern Bengal.

Her great festival, called the Doorga-pooja, *i.e.* worship of Doorga, occurs in the end of September, and lasts nine nights, during which all business ceases, even in Government offices, and Christians and Mohammedans rejoice in their holidays as much as the Hindoos themselves. Among the latter, every family who can afford it, provides an image of the goddess varying in size from a few inches to twenty feet in height. These are made of clay or wood, and gaudily painted. Each image is solemnly consecrated by the Brahmans, who pray that the spirit of Doorga may descend and dwell in this form. Then during several days it receives solemn worship, washings and offerings, and incessant prayer; while the worshippers prostrate themselves in the dust, lying at full length, so that their feet, thighs, hands, breast, mouth, nose, eyes, and forehead may all simultaneously touch the earth.

Then succeed dancing and revelling, until midnight, when divers animals are solemnly sacrificed; the head of each being of necessity severed at one blow, else dire disaster will ensue. The

[1] The twelve weapons of Doorga are each severally invoked in a sort of litany, of which each sentence begins with the most holy word OM, which is the concentrated essence of all worship, both in Brahminism and in Buddhism.

OM to the sword, the sharp-edged chastiser, Thee I adore, O Lord.

OM to the trident, destroyer of our enemies, Thee I adore, O Lord.

OM to the arrow, the javelin, the thunderbolt, the club (addressed severally to each), Thee I adore, O Lord.

OM to the bow, propeller of the arrow, defend us and bless us, O Lord.

OM to the noose, the goad, the shield, the bell, and the axe, defend us and bless us, O Lord.

The goad is worshipped as being, in the hand of the goddess, "Lord of the Elephant." (See *Indian Arts*, by Sir George Birdwood.)

flesh of the creatures thus sacrificed may be eaten by all. It is whispered that even the Brahmins sometimes partake of it, this however, is denied. These sacrifices are offered in the courts of private houses, and the heads and blood are then carried into an inner hall, and ranged in presence of the idol, each head being surmounted by a lighted lamp.

When atonement has thus been made for the grosser sins of the people, a small altar is erected and sprinkled with clean dry sand, whereon are offered flowers, rice, clarified butter, and sweet grass, which, being burnt with fire, are supposed to cleanse the worshippers from all remaining sin.

On the last great day of the feast, the Brahmins formally unconsecrate the images, and with divers ceremonies, dismiss the dread goddess from her multitudinous abodes, which being no longer holy, are then carried to the banks of the Ganges amid wild rejoicings. The images are broken into a thousand pieces, and the fragments are tossed into the holy river, after which the busy mercantile city resumes its ordinary round of daily life.

The annual sums expended on this festival in Calcutta alone used to be calculated at half a million of our money. It seems, however, as if the worship of Doorga was on the wane, even in this her own especial city; for whereas a very few years ago, five thousand of her images were annually made in Calcutta at the time of her great festival, now scarcely one thousand are sold. The greatest falling off of her adherents seems to have taken place in a recent year of terrible famine, when her patronage was found sadly worthless in time of need. Nevertheless she still receives her sacrifices of blood; the great sacrificial knife lies before her shrine, ready to immolate whatever victims are brought to her temple; and on the great feasts, hundreds of goats and buffaloes are slain, and her altars reek with their blood.

These sacrifices are sometimes offered by the poorest of the people, who out of their wretched penury scrape and hoard every farthing they can by any means accumulate, that they may at length be able to bring to the temple an offering worthy of acceptance. We were told of the case of one man whose earnings were only twelve shillings a month. By dint of supporting his own existence, and that of his wife and children, exclusively on rice and a little curried fish, he contrived in the course of his life to devote 50*l.* to the service of Doorga, as being the one thing needful, for the sake of which he and his family were content to deprive themselves of all that most men would deem necessaries of life. However hard pressed they might be, nothing could induce them ever to touch the money laid aside for her.

This particular instance was mentioned to us as the type of a vast number of the poor Hindoos, whose marvellous self-denial in the service of their gods does certainly put our self-indulgent practice of Christianity to the blush.

No one who studies the creed and practice of this race with unbiassed mind, can fail to be struck with their intense earnestness in living up to teaching which, however distorted, has in it rich veins of thought—perverted forms of the very doctrines which we deem most sacred. Thus, as the Christian is taught to recognise the indwelling of a Divine Presence, and to reverence his own body as being the Temple of God, so the Hindoo likewise recognises the sanctity of his whole body, because of indwelling deities, for whose sake he must guard against any ceremonial defilement. As he is bound to honour many gods, he localises their dwelling-place. Hence he believes that Brahma the Supreme deigns to dwell in his head: Siva (Mahā-devah) sits enthroned in the palm of his hand: Vishnu in certain fingers: and so every part of his body is consecrated by the presence of the gods.

So too, although we Christians are taught that, "whether we eat or drink or whatsoever we do, we should do all to the glory of God," I think it can scarcely be a transgression of charity to judge that comparatively few habitually obey this precept, whereas, the most casual observer cannot fail to see that in the daily life of the average Hindoo, this is the ruling principle. In the preparation of his food, in bathing, eating, drinking—each act that is done or left undone—none is too trifling to be endowed with religious significance, and dedicated to the gods. From the very earliest stage of his being (when the Hindoo mother attends religious rites on behalf of her unborn child) until the final hour when his body is committed to the flames of the funeral pyre, each detail is regulated with reference to the invisible celestial rulers.

There certainly can be no doubt that the apparent indifference in religious externals which characterises the white race, as distinguished from these very earnest brown men, must be a very serious stumbling-block in the way of their conversion to the faith nominally professed by white men.

They say (and not without reason) that, whereas they, the Hindoos, Mohammedans and Parsees, cease not to observe rigid fasts, and to live every hour of their lives by strict rule and in solemn observance of their fate, the English alone appear utterly unconcerned about anything, save food and rupees. Even our attendance on forms of worship one day in seven, they perceive to be of the most easy-going character, save when it ranks as a military duty; and external reverence in daily life was never a marked characteristic of the British. Of course a multitude of their educated men know much of the teaching and spirit of Christianity, and marvel that it should have so little visible influence on practice.

They read our sacred Book, and therein find commands to "show gentleness to *all* men,"—commands which too many obviously apply only to such as have not one drop of coloured blood. Then they find perpetual injunctions to self-denial and all holiness of life; and, I fear, we scarcely let our light shine before the heathen in these matters. They believe Sabbatical observance to be binding on us, and see that Sunday is the favourite day for travelling, sport, and other things that entail vast labour on the many; and so with a thousand other things. One who had been long in India and had thought much on this matter, told me that he was sure no missionaries would ever make many converts among the natives till they could rouse the mass of English to a life of Christian devotion as earnest as is that of the Hindoos to the oppressive and never-ending service required by their many gods.

At present the prominent aspect of Christianity to the native mind is that of a faith which allows its votories to eat unclean meat at all times, and do their own will in all things. I have often been positively assured by Hindoos, remarkable only for their roguery, that they were Christians, being willing to eat any meat, and drink any fermented liquor we liked to give them!

The last clause is a particularly painful one, for, whereas the world has never produced a more sober race than the people of India, while obedient to their own religious teaching, there is no doubt that the example of foreigners has done much to awaken the craving for drink. An English clergyman who worked in India for thirty years, has stated his conviction (as regards the good and evil of foreign intercourse) that for every Hindoo converted to Christianity by the missionaries, the drinking practices of the English have made a thousand drunkards. Chunder Sen, too, the great native reformer, has told us of the bitter wail of Indian widows and orphans, who curse the British Government for the introduction of licensed arrack-taverns.

As regards the more intellectual men, it is said that the unbelief of Europeans is the chief stumbling-block in their path, and that there are no sceptical books of any note published in the West, especially those of a philosophical nature, which do not find free circulation in India, where, being looked upon as types of European thought, they carry more weight than is their due. Consequently a vast number of the more thoughtful natives believe that Christianity is on the wane, having been proved by white men themselves to be false!

But lest such grievous error should not of itself spread fast enough, there are emissaries of evil in the spiritual world as in the physical: and just as these busy themselves in advancing the work of civilisation by the aid of dynamite and infernal machines, so do the promoters of free-thought in England and America make it their business to send to India large consignments of all manner of infidel publications, carefully selected to suit the tastes of the students at the colleges, and other educated natives.

And so well has the poison worked, that some of the wealthiest of these have even formed an association for the promotion of atheism, and for the gratuitous distribution of atheistic publications among such students as are too poor to purchase this precious literature for themselves. The head-quarters of this association are at Madras, but there is reason to fear that its influence is far-reaching, and it is further spread in Southern India by the regular issue of three English and Tamil free-thought journals publishing lists of the English sceptical publications on sale at their offices and elsewhere.

Calcutta has naturally proved a rich field for these zealous labourers in the cause of evil, who here publish a monthly journal purposely "to expose the absurdities of the Christian faith." Though English is so well known by the educated Hindoo, that the circulation of these works in the original might very well have satisfied less aggressive opponents, the mischief has recently been enormously increased by the translation of some of the most popular infidel books and pamphlets into the languages of the people, and these have been printed for general circulation in various parts of Bengal and the North West Provinces.

Thus has the first of all educational agencies—the printing press—been enlisted by the adversaries of Christianity; and though its advocates are now awakening to the necessity of vigorous effort in spreading their counter influence by the same penetrating agency, the poison has been widely sown and goes far to account for the fact, which would otherwise be so perplexing, namely, that the vast mass of Hindoos educated in Christian schools have hitherto become practically infidels, retaining their idol temples to please the women, and probably accompanying them there, but quite ready to laugh at the whole system of absurdity, yet without the smallest leaning to Christianity. To them in truth, this has been "an age of light—light without love," which has simply freed them from the restraint of any creed or moral law; and so it comes to pass that the clever Bengalee *baboos* are as a general body notoriously the most irreligious class to whom this nineteenth century has given birth.

It has been suggested, however, that some such dark valley

of unbelief does lie between every old religion of a noble type, and Christianity, when the lamps which lighted the darkness of past generations have burnt out, and the more perfect light of day has not yet dawned.

Of late years, a new light has dawned on the Indian horizon—a movement from within—the awakening conscience of India's own sons, feeling for some better state of things; as yet they know not what. But that the effect of Western education and Western thought is seething in the Eastern mind is certain, and it may be that the leaven now working will work, till the whole is leavened and some strange reformation is brought about. The new sect is called the Brahm-Somaj, or worship of the Supreme. Its members adore one God and profess to be for ever seeking Light, from whatever source it may reach them, whether from the Hindoo Vedas, the Koran, or the Bible. As yet they are strongly opposed to Christianity, and one of their number, who embraced it, found himself subjected to more serious persecution than seemed quite consistent with free thought. However, when it was suggested to some of them that they were undoubtedly tending thereto, their reply was, "Possibly—we cannot tell to what we may be led."

The account of the opening of their church in Calcutta reads like that of a revival meeting in Britain. From dawn till night the services continued almost without intermission. Hearty congregational singing was followed by fervent and eloquent preaching, and prayers were offered literally with "strong crying and tears." The various new members were admitted to the church by a rite somewhat akin to baptism. In fact, such forms as they adopt are mostly borrowed from Christianity, while Scriptural phraseology is freely used, though apparently without accepting its full meaning. Many of our most beautiful hymns have been adapted by them to their own use, by omitting all specially Christian allusion. Thus our evening hymns, "Abide with me," and "Glory to thee," are commonly sung with the alteration of one line in each.

This sect is a development and offshoot from one which was founded in the beginning of this century by Rajah Rammohun

Roy, who has been described as the Lüther of Brahminical Catholicism; a clever man and a deep thinker. Having in very early life revolted against the whole monstrous system of idolatry, and having detected for himself how utterly modern Brahminism is at variance with the monotheistic teaching of the Vedas, he translated an ancient Sanskrit abstract of these for gratuitous circulation among his own countrymen. He also published it in English. His power of acquiring languages was remarkable. As each new phase of religious thought presented itself to his mind, he set himself to learn the language in which its sacred books were written, that he might be fully competent to judge for himself. Thus, having first mastered the Sanskrit, which opened to him all treasures of ancient Brahminical thought, he next studied Pali that he might study the Buddhist Scriptures. Arabic unlocked the Koran, and Hebrew the Jewish Scriptures. A knowledge of Persian facilitated the study of the teaching of Zoroaster. To Hindustani and Bengalee he added a colloquial knowledge of English and French; to these he added Latin, and in later life began the study of Greek that he might read the New Testament in the original. Amongst his writings is one called "The precepts of Jesus, the Guide to Peace and Happiness," chiefly consisting of selections from the New Testament. In 1830 the first Hindoo Unitarian Church was opened in Calcutta, and Rammohun Roy, invited the attendance of all who believed in the Unity of God, whether Christians or Unitarian Hindoos or Mohammedans. This was the first meeting for public and united worship ever held by Hindoos, whose own religion is essentially one of solitary worship, each man by himself irrespective of his neighbours. Soon after having seen this practical result of his preaching, this great reformer was sent to England by the king of Delhi, to state certain grievances, and here he died in 1833, and was buried at first in a garden, and afterwards in a cemetery at Bristol, having apparently sacrificed all Hindoo prejudice in favour of burning.

His mantle descended on Baboo Khesub Chunder Sen, a name now familiar to this country, where his earnest and eloquent lectures won vast sympathy from all who care to follow the groping of human minds in search for truth; though it does seem open to question why one who was supposed to come to England to learn, should forthwith have assumed the position of a teacher!

The Brahm-Somaj now have large churches in Calcutta, Allahabad, and the other chief cities. The women are said to have meetings by themselves, as, of course, none but the lowest caste would appear in public, and there is no use in hurrying matters—when the fruit is ripe it will fall of itself. And though this movement is the declared foe to caste, the prejudice against allowing women to be seen is too great to be overcome. To such an extent is it carried that during a year's residence in India, I am not conscious of having ever set eyes on a native lady, not even the wife of a respectable tradesman.

The Brahm-Somaj also strongly condemns polygamy, and the custom of marrying children, and other Hindoo practices; more especially the perpetual seclusion of widows, some of whom have actually ventured on re-marriage. And men born in high castes have not scrupled to marry wives from the very lowest castes, and even widows, without any dire grief befalling them. The mere fact of crossing the sea, "the black water," as they call it, would effectually destroy whatever of their caste remained, and this it was which they encouraged their leader to do in coming to England. The said leader, however, subsequently fell greatly in the estimation of his followers, by sacrificing his principles to his ambition, in bestowing the hand of his child-daughter, a girl of thirteen, on the young Maharajah of Cooch-Behar, aged fifteen, when the customary idolatrous ceremonial was duly observed.

But it is high time I should return to the record of my first impressions of life in the great Anglo-Indian capital.

The first few days in an Indian home do indeed seem strange to every new-comer from Europe. The extreme publicity of life in those large rooms, each having access to the other by many doors which invariably stand open to admit free currents of air, veiled only by heavy purdahs (or curtains) from behind which swift, silent, barefooted attendants suddenly appear, and as noiselessly vanish again, like white-robed ghosts. Some one has described an Indian bedroom as "a section of a street with a bed in it!" an account which I recognised as true to the letter, when first awakened at about 5 A. M.—*i.e.* before sunrise—by seeing a couple of bearers bringing in lamps, and a curious-looking *bheestie*, or water-carrier, filling my bath from a black buffalo skin; another man bringing hot water, and a fourth with *chota hazeri*, or small breakfast of tea and fruit. Such an awakening seemed in truth like a bit of some curious dream of Arabian Nights. How to proceed with the mysteries of a morning toilette was really a serious consideration with all these brown beings flitting about, and always appearing when least expected. Before I was half dressed, in came another relay to tuck up the mosquito curtains, and stood salaaming in solemn silence, waiting for orders, which of course I was unable to give, so could only stare at them admiringly.

As there was no lady in the luxurious home of the "merchant prince" who so hospitably welcomed me on my first landing in India, there were no ayahs, or waiting-women, in attendance, which accounted for all these masculine apparitions, whereat my English maid was even more bewildered than I was myself, though life on board ship had accustomed us pretty well to sudden incursions of stewards and quarter-masters. Nor was it very long before she, like a good many white women, learnt to look on all men of colour as mere lay figures, whose sole purpose in life was to wait her good will and pleasure in all things. The number with whom she very soon contrived to share the charge of my sister's two small children, would puzzle most nurses. Not that her attendants were limited to brown men. She was a damsel of calm and comely presence, who seemed born for life in the tropics, inasmuch as she grew daily more fresh and rosy. Soon her fame went forth, and the notion of allowing such an unappropriated blessing to return to Britain was too much for the many sergeants and clerks and other officials, whose chances of wives depend on waiting for somebody's widow, or marrying a half-caste, or a soldier's orphan from the Lawrence Asylum. So it came to pass that from distant stations came letters from men well-to-do, stating their exact circumstances, the number of their rupees, various advantages in the way of carriages and servants, and the date at which they could take leave of absence and come to fetch her, should she honour them with her hand. I should be afraid to state how many such were kept in play like juggler's balls, and how many photographs were sent to and fro. For the credit of the sex, I must add that she refused to leave us till we were safely landed in England, when she returned to marry the poorest of the lot, but one whom she *had* seen and cared for.

The photograph system is largely practised. Men in out-of-the-way stations send theirs to some milliner's shop at Simla or Calcutta, and the shopwoman shows it to all her friends. Sooner or later she sends him one in return, and, should he be satisfied, he comes to fetch his bride. One of our neighbours lost her maid in this way. In short, the exportation of English servants is an expensive risk, and few degrees less troublesome than employing native ayahs, an article of which, I am happy to say, we had small experience. They are for ever prowling about, watching your every action, and immediately retailing it, with additions, in the bazaar. Few, if any, of them can do a stitch of sewing. All your work and their own must be done by a dirzé or tailor—who sits in the open verandah, mending clothes or making ball dresses for the amusement of all comers.

Of the multitude of servants entailed by the extraordinary subdivision of labour consequent on caste, I need not tell you. You know that it takes one man to set your bath, a second to fill it, and a third to empty it. And as with the servant, so with the master, the rule of life seems to be, never to do anything for yourself that you can possibly induce any one else to do for you. Thus no man dreams of shaving himself, but calmly sits in his verandah, trustfully resigning his throat to one of "those niggers"—while it is currently reported that young England will not even put on his own stockings!

Probably one-third of your household are Mohammedans, whose sole distinguishing mark is that they button the breast of their linen vest on the right side instead of the left, or *vice-versâ*. All who are in any way connected with cooking or serving your food must, of necessity, be Mohammedan, to avoid the defilement of touching beef or fowls. How they answer to their consciences for cooking bacon I do not know; but they reserve the right of loathing us for eating it and other abominable things, and look upon us as altogether gross and self-indulgent—and perhaps on the latter point they are not far wrong!

To return to our first morning in Calcutta. As new-comers we were bound to take the older inhabitants out sight-seeing, so we commenced at daybreak by going the round of the noisy markets, which, however, seemed to me less picturesque than those of Egypt. However, the fruit-market was attractive, and we experimentalised on all manner of things unknown—custard-apples and guavas, and various other fruits, good and bad. The game-market was also a point of interest, the supply of snipe, quail, floriken, chickore, black partridge, wild geese, wild duck, teal, ortolans, and such like, seeming unlimited, the countless wide mouths of the river, and the jheels, or swampy lakes, so numerous in the neighbourhood, being the favourite haunts of all manner of water-fowl, and a fruitful source of fever to the sportsmen. We next turned to the fish-market, where divers unknown fish and far-famed Hoogly prawns, fattened on the deceased Hindoo, were duly pointed out to us.

There was amusement in the mere fact of listening to all the people talking their unknown tongue, which, however, is anything but musical, for the gentlest conversation in Hindostanee always sounds as if people were quarrelling violently. Should you hear one man giving directions to another, you would think he was administering sharp rebukes, while a wrangle over a few copper pice produces a deafening Babel.

One thing that attracted our notice was the peculiar form of greeting among the people, whose morning salutation is invariably in the name of God. Two Mohammedans will commend one another to Allah—two Hindoos to Ram, Ram (*i.e.*, to Rama, who, like Krishna, was an incarnation in human form of Vishnu. Both are beloved of the people, but Rama is the god to whom most turn in the hour of death).

The impression of delightful novelty of this, my first impression of native life in India, remains indelibly stamped on my memory, as a new revelation of light and shade, form and colour. The ever-moving throng of picturesque individuals, each one a study for an artist—some loaded with fruit, some with sugar-cane; graceful women bearing on their heads one, two, perhaps three, highly polished brazen water vessels—*lotas* they are called—

BULLOCK CARRIAGE.

glittering in the sun, piled one above the other. Perhaps one graceful arm, adorned with many bangles, is raised on high to steady the topmost lota, while the other encircles a quaint brown baby, sitting astride the maternal hip. A very noteworthy figure is the water-carrier, the lean, lanky, almost naked bheestie, who is accompanied by a large-horned bull, bearing two great water-skins, which are simply buffalo-hides sewn up and resembling huge leather bottles. Holding one of these by the neck, he sprinkles a glittering water-shower to lay the dust on the parched roads, scattering the tame pigeons and crows, which alight so fearlessly among the people.

Wherever we turn, there are new combinations of colour and sunlight, blue sky, green foliage, cream-coloured houses and clear-cut shadows, with groups of brown mortals either robed in dazzling white, or almost devoid of all garments. Richer folks drive in indescribable little carriages with scarlet canopy, called "ekka," being drawn by one pony, or else in large-wheeled carriages drawn by horned oxen, and containing whole family parties of women and children veiled and draped in silk and satin, sparkling with spangles, embroidery and jewels, and only revealing tantalising glimpses of magnificent black hair and eyes, pearly white teeth, and rich brown skin.

The said rich brown hue is naturally the most impressive feature of all. It is so curious to find oneself in a great crowd all of the same general tone of colour, only varying in tinge according to caste, from the clear olive of the Brahmin to the dark brown of the lower castes, but all alike, with fine silky dark hair and dark eyes. It would seem as if the European races alone were distinguished by infinite shades of colour : hair varying from flaxen to black, eyes from light blue to grey, to deepest brown. I only saw two exceptions to the invariable dark eyes of India ; namely a blue-eyed Himalayan girl and a man, and very odd and unnatural they looked.

It is not necessary to go far off the beaten track to see native life in all its simplicity, for just behind Chowringhee (the "West End" where the merchant princes live in luxurious houses) lies the Black Town, whose squalor and poverty contrast with the wealth of the great streets as strangely as Seven Dials with Belgravia. It is a place of dingy, narrow, irregular alleys, with huts of baked mud or twisted bamboo. The inmates (all but naked) squat basking in the hot dust, like beings of a different world from those who are driving up and down the Maîdân in latest Parisian toilettes, or radiant with white linen and richest gold-brocaded silks.

Poor as they are, both they and their homes are scrupulously clean—for here cleanliness does not rank *next* to godliness, it is an essential of religion, and the purity of the kitchen must be unsullied. Of course ideas on this subject may differ, and irreverent foreigners are apt not to appreciate the purifying qualities of sacred cow-dung—the sovereign cleanser from all stain whether spiritual or physical. My attention was called to the fact that many of the rude mud floors were ornamented with elaborate geometrical patterns, drawn with red clay—a mode of decoration in which the women excel, and which they patiently renew every morning after washing the floor. Curious—is it not?—to find these Eastern women giving to their house-cleaning the identical finishing touch still practised by many a "gudewife" in Scotland. On Speyside and near Forres, in Galloway, Ayr, and Stirlingshire, almost the same patterns, though less elaborate, may be seen traced on the cottage floor with red bathbrick or pipeclay.

Another link to some remote corners of Scotland is the hand-mill, consisting of two circular stones, the lowest of which is fixed in the earth, while the upper one works on a pivot by means of a handle. The grain is poured in at the central hole, and works its way out at the edges in flour. Each family thus grinds its own corn, two women working at a time. It is exactly the old quern of Scotland, still to be found in some of the far isles.

This vision of home is quickly dispelled by the Babel which surrounds us. The cries of the kites are drowned by the constant clamour of the bazaar, and loud voices bargaining for infinitesimal coin. Others are beating cymbals and tomtoms in honour of their gods, and the atmosphere is tainted with a general smell of ghee and rancid oil, with the heavy smoke peculiar to the fuel of the country, which is simply dried cow-dung. The said ghee is a sort of butter, prepared by boiling, curdling, and churning milk till it becomes rancid, when it is packed in jars. These, on being opened, emit a vile effluvia, but are nevertheless hailed as a dainty, fragrant and delicious as a German *Sauerkraut*, and equally delectable for external or internal use! So the height of native bliss is to be well smeared with this compound, and then to sit in the sun drinking small cupfuls of it.[1]

The immense number of stalls for sweetmeats is among the most striking peculiarities of a native bazaar. The consumption thereof must be tremendous, to say nothing of the quantity of sugar-cane, which old and young seem to munch whenever they are not chewing a horrid compound of areca nut and lime, rolled up in a green leaf of the betel pepper, which stains the mouth of a hideous brick-dust colour. This unpleasant habit greatly mars the beauty of the invariably strong well-conditioned teeth, which show to such advantage when the betel is replaced by sugar-cane. Then every mouth alike displays rows of such dazzling ivory as most Europeans might well envy. Surely there can be no work for dentists in India!

In truth, every Hindoo bestows infinite care on his teeth, which he polishes vigorously with a soft flat stick, about the width of a finger. This is an important religious action, and must be preceded by ceremonially rinsing the mouth on awakening. As you pass through a native town in the early morning, it seems as if the whole population had turned out of their houses to perform this part of their toilet in public, and such an amount of scraping and polishing goes on, that you marvel how any enamel is left. They consider our use of tooth-brushes to be among our many unclean practices, inasmuch as we do not have new ones daily; for the touch of saliva is deemed utterly polluting. So they spit on the all-cleansing earth, and having scraped both teeth and tongue, the stick is thrown away as worthless. Yet as a proof of how indivi-

[1] The annual consumption of ghee in British India (exclusive of native States) is estimated at considerably over five million hundredweights, the value of which is about £14,000,000! Its price varies from 5*d.* to 1*s.* per pound, but is gradually rising, owing to the continuous decrease of grazing land, consequent on the increase of cultivation. To meet the ever-increasing demand, the Indian government have now invited the dairy farmers of Australia to commence ghee-making on a large scale, offering to send Hindoo ghee-makers to instruct them in the art. As milk yields a larger proportion of ghee than of butter, and neither time nor distance will injure this unfragrant produce, it is probable that men on remote ranches may be glad to avail themselves of this never-failing market.

dual holiness sanctifies all things, it is affirmed that the much-worshipped sacred Bo-tree of Ceylon grew from a twig which had been thus used by a noted saint (for the wood of the sacred fig-tree is that preferred by holy men). Ordinary mortals generally use the wood of the tamarind [1] or mimosa.[2]

Nor is this the only part of the morning adornment that occurs in public. The bath is either at the river or the open tank, while the bather utters a formula dedicating himself to the gods, and praying that he may be cleansed from all guilt incurred by touch, taste, deed, word, or thought, known or unknown. He ought also to repeat a hymn to the cleansing Ganges. This is the morning ceremonial, but promiscuous washing goes on in the street at all hours and seasons; as does also the work of the barber, who reduces the fine silky black hair to a very small top-knot. Some dandies allow themselves to retain three locks. This is the only moment when the lower-caste Hindoos are seen bareheaded. If, therefore, you care to mark the strange diversity of cranial development between the elongated high skulls of the upper-castes, and the low type, common to the serfs, or low-castes (in other words the descendants of the Aryans and those of the aboriginal races of India), the barber's hour will give you ample opportunity for study.

In short, but for this little celestial top-knot, you might imagine, as you glance at a group of those brown shining skulls, that you had got into a colony of the hairless men of Australia; that curious tribe of aborigines known as the Bald Men of the Flinders and Albert Rivers, who literally are destitute of any vestige of hair, and go through life from their birth to their grave as bald as a billiard ball. Certainly Mother Nature would have saved the Hindoos a great deal of trouble if she had created them with the same deficiency. Beard and whiskers are likewise scrupulously removed, only moustaches being permissible; so when you see a man with a beard you know he must be a Mohammedan, as the Koran strictly forbids shaving the beard.

After the ceremony of shaving, comes that of marking the brow

[1] Neem. [2] Baubul.

and rubbing the head and other parts of the body with ashes taken from the domestic hearth, in self-dedication to the special god to be honoured, whose mark must be imprinted on the forehead. Then, every man alone, each by himself, proceeds with his morning worship, selecting by preference a place beside a tank or stream, whence taking water in his hand, he drinks a little several times for his internal cleansing ere he begins to pray.

As regards the painting of those curious lines and marks on the brow, denoting to which of the principal religious parties the wearer belongs, it appears that although the Hindoo sects are practically innumerable, they are satisfied with about seventy distinguishing marks, one or other of which is painted on the forehead, and probably branded on their arms and breast. These marks consist of spots, circles, triangles, straight lines, curved lines, crescents, simply or in combination, and of varied colours. Thus, a simple spot symbolises Brahma the Supreme Being, while a spot in the centre of a circle, inclosed in a triangle, symbolises the Trimurti, *i.e.*, Brahma, Vishnu, and Siva, the Hindoo Trinity. Some sects adopt a mark like an eccentric cross, with the four points bent: this is called the *swastika*. Some are simply marked with three white lines, others have perpendicular stripes; a small horizontal line on the forehead denotes having bathed—in fact, being ready for society.

Other marks show at whose shrine worship has been offered; thus, the worshippers of Siva are marked on the forehead with three horizontal lines made with ashes taken from sacrificial altars, and moistened with glutinous rice-water. On those of Vishnu is impressed the symbol of his sacred footprint in curved lines of white, red, and yellow; different sects dispute as to the propriety of thus indicating one foot or two, so the sect which is in favour of only one foot, indicates it by one curved line of white between the eyes, crossed by a central red mark in honour of the goddess Laksmi, wife of Vishnu. Another sect, while indicating both feet resting on two lotus-blossoms, still does homage to Laksmi, and contrives to suggest all this by three vertical curved lines, one of which comes half way down the nose.

The disputes concerning these frontal emblems are bitter to a degree, and as both parties worship the same images in the same temples, ruinous law-suits sometimes arise between the two factions as to which mark shall be impressed on the images! Our British ritual cases have their counterpart in this far East! A third sect is distinguished by marking the central line in black with charred incense taken from Vishnu's altar.

In short, these lines and spots of divers colour, which in our eyes are so strangely disfiguring, are literally the "seal on the forehead," once common to many oriental nations, and to which such constant reference is made in Scripture, where the servants of the Most High are said to have been sealed; while of those who had forsaken His service, it is said that "their spot is not the spot of His children." Hence, too, in the Revelation, the destroying angel is bidden to stay his hand till the servants of God have been sealed on the forehead, as a mark whereby to distinguish them.

Among the Hindoos the paint used is commonly a yellow paste made from sandal-wood, sometimes mixed with vermilion. Black paint is, as we have seen, obtained from burnt incense, and white from lime. Occasionally a mixture of turmeric and sacred cow-dung is prepared, and sometimes the latter choice ingredient is mixed with the ashes from some sacrificial fire and spread over the whole body as a ceremonial purification!

Happily the Hindoo women do not indulge in the abominable use of paint or other artificial adornment, though I am told that some of them are tattooed with patterns of flowers punctured on the body, and rubbed with the juice of certain plants. The fingers, you know, are stained with henna, and the lips too often discoloured by the incessant chewing of betel.

One of the peculiarities of the race which first attracts the eye of a new-comer is the attitude of rest. A weary man seems never so comfortable as when simply poised on the *soles of his feet*, with his shoulders almost between his knees, an attitude in which few Europeans can retain their balance at all—certainly not without great fatigue. Yet this is to the native as natural as sitting is to us; and you will generally see a coachman get off his comfortable box, the moment the carriage stops anywhere, and thus squat in the dust. This constant pressure on the muscles enlarges the knees, so that in old age the knees and heels are the most prominent features of those lean lanky skeletons, whose wrinkled skin hangs on them in loose flaps.

Thus at rest, a Hindoo seems never to mind how long he remains undisturbed, for he knows as little of the value of time as a genuine Highlander; nor do our dealings with the people go far to improve their appreciation thereof. The utter indifference with which men are kept waiting hour after hour about the most trivial business, and are then desired to return next day, a distance of perhaps some miles, would sorely try the temper of any people, less patient than these, or less thoroughly schooled to conceal all irritation in presence of their superiors. While marvelling at their patience I have often thought of that Perthshire vassal, who, having thus lost half a morning, departed in high dudgeon; when at length his master called for him, and Donald was not forthcoming, a friendly bystander explained matters. Quoth the chief, "I suppose Donald was swearing at me?" "Hoot na! he was na sweering at your grace! he was jist damning at large!"

But these men, though they are clever, diligent workmen, never seem to lose their temper at this waste of their precious time. It is the Sahib's *hookum* (command), so they must wait, for the will of any white man is law, and they are as flexible in character as in body, which is saying a good deal, their lithe spare figures seeming built for such athletic games as wrestling, running, and climbing. They are wonderfully neat-fingered, and their nicety of touch and exquisite finish tell well in all manner of refined works.

In physical strength, however, they rank far below the white man, and it is said that in such work as shipbuilding, and other trades demanding great power, the work of one Englishman equals that of three Hindoos. This, however, only applies to the natives of the plains. The hill tribes are sturdy and strong as any other highlanders, and I have often marvelled to see the loads those hill men and women carry for twelve or fourteen miles—heavy blocks of timber, or sacks of grain, but especially a certain tin case of my own, which in England generally involves two porters, but which one Pahari would carry for a whole march without a murmur.

Among the most startling novelties of an Indian bazaar is the multitude of crows and kites which are for ever walking gravely about, seeking what they may devour, or, with sharp piercing cries, circling over our heads. Large numbers of these kites met us off the mouth of the Ganges hours before we sighted land, and followed the ship, as gulls are wont to do. These were but flying squadrons of the grand army, which we here find in full possession of the town. There are brown kites of all sizes, and great white Brahminy kites (brown the first year, white the second), as different one from another as a cygnet from a swan. All new-comers admire these handsome birds, but all residents, most ungratefully, loathe them, inasmuch as in this land, where drainage of any sort is utterly unknown, they are nature's appointed scavengers, whose duty and whose privilege it is to consume all carrion and other foul matter, and so preserve the city from pestilence.

(How strange it is to think that only three hundred years ago[1]

[1] Three hundred years ago! Just the time when, A.D. 1589, a company of English merchants addressed a memorial to Queen Elizabeth, craving permission to equip three ships for the purpose of trading to the East Indies. This first expedition started in 1591 and proved disastrous, but eight years later an association of "merchant adventurers" was formed in London to renew the enterprise on a larger scale, and in the year 1600 a royal charter was granted them. Trading stations were first established at Madras and Bombay; that in Bengal was of later date, and it was not till 1687 that the British merchants were compelled to abandon their first station on the Hoogly river, and intrench themselves on the present site of Calcutta.

Here they were besieged in the year 1756, and compelled to surrender to the Nawab Sooraj-oo-Dowlah, who flattered himself that he had for ever extirpated the hated English, till he was taught his mistake by the arrival of Colonel Robert Clive with true British troops. TO-DAY CALCUTTA RANKS NEXT TO LONDON AS THE SECOND CITY OF THE BRITISH EMPIRE! with a population of three-quarters of a million!

Close on Calcutta follows the city of Bombay, likewise numbering close on three-quarters of a million inhabitants. Yet when in 1661 Bombay was ceded

British kites were doing the same useful work for the City of London, where they were protected by municipal laws! Herr Schaschek, a Bohemian traveller who visited England in A.D. 1461, specially noted the multitude of kites which hovered around London Bridge, and a century later, in 1555, another traveller, Belon, records that not even in Cairo, were the kites more numerous than in London, where they fed on the garbage of the streets, and even of the Thames!)

Here in Hindoostan, the kites are ably assisted in their good and useful work by the adjutants, whose lives are protected by a fine of (I think) fifty rupees for killing one. They are a kind of great ugly crane of a dark blue-grey colour, with huge bill which opens far back into the head, and a long pouch which hangs over the breast. They stand five feet high, and a full-grown bird sometimes measures seven feet six inches from the tip of the beak to the claws, while the expanse of wing averages fourteen feet from tip to tip. A favourite amusement of the British soldier is to throw bones for the fun of seeing the adjutants catch them before they fall. Sometimes they tie two bones together with a string, and throw them to two birds, who each greedily swallow one, and then stand half choking and bowing to one another in ludicrous style, till they succeed in biting the string.

Another pleasant pastime used to be, to affix a slow match to

to Charles II. by the Portuguese, as part of the dower of his bride, it was a worthless possession, fatal to Europeans, and was made over to a company of adventurous London merchants for an annual rental of £10. Calcutta, now the world-famed "City of Palaces" was at that time represented by a cluster of mud huts in a dismal, unhealthy, swampy jungle on the low, slimy shores of the Hoogly, where a handful of sorely oppressed merchants strove to establish a footing.

Many a prolonged contest awaited them and their successors—contests both with men and nature, especially with the ever-shifting river and silting sands. The latter difficulties continue to this day, gigantic steam-dredgers being ever at work, together with every conceivable device of modern river-engineering, but for which the Hoogly would long since have ceased to be navigable.

As it is, British determination has conquered all difficulties; ships of the largest tonnage sail to and fro securely, and to-day the total import and export trade of India exceeds in value £122,000,000.

a fine large bone, and lay it in some tempting spot, where an unsuspecting adjutant was sure to pounce upon it. Then the fuse was ignited, and as the luckless bird flew high over the city with his prize, a sudden flash would carry off his head, and the huge body would come tumbling into the street, greatly to the consternation of the lieges! This amusement is now happily illegal.

Of course, among the lions of Calcutta, Fort William holds a prominent place, not by reason of its beauty, however, for it has none of the grandeur of the Mogul forts which we find further up country, being merely a low octagon built on a flat green space; a small spot ceded to British colonists about the middle of the seventeenth century, and fortified by Clive after the Battle of Plassey. It is said, first and last, to have cost the Hon. Company 2.000,000*l.*! Inside the fort is a fine church, which we saw in all the beauty of its Christmas dress.

Another lion is the big banyan tree in the Botanical Gardens, which is worthy of a visit from all lovers of curious vegetation, inasmuch as they may travel many a long mile ere they fall in with another specimen of the many-pillared tree so grand as this one.

When thoroughly wearied with sight-seeing, were turned home to the real breakfast of the day, and spent the next few hours in the cool shade of a wide verandah, content to watch the busy life in the street below; and though the European element predominated, there was no lack of novelty. Hideous gharrys, answering to our cabs, but made wholly to keep out the sun; palanquins and bearers for such as prefer them; gentlemen's buggies, which are simply gigs with a hood to them; picturesque native carriages; two-wheeled ekkas with bright curtains, drawn by the swiftest of ponies, with three or four fat baboos curled up where there seemed scarcely space for one; larger carriages with quaint double hoods of scarlet and gold, and drawn by richly-caparisoned white bullocks, trotting merrily along; hackeries without number (heavy carts, sometimes covered), whose wooden wheels being never greased, are for ever creaking and groaning, night and day, while the drivers shriek and howl at the strong patient bullocks, with the meek beautiful eyes, almost twisting off their tails as a means of gentle suasion.

The creaking of these wheels, mingling with the shrill cries of

BULLOCK CARTS.

the kites, is the most characteristic sound in India—a never-failing accompaniment to whatever scene may be passing before the eye.

These Indian bullocks, like all the other cattle here, have a great fleshy hump between the shoulders (a hump which finds great favour among beef-eating foreigners, who find it a close-grained and very delicate meat).[1] It is supposed that this hump, like that of the camel and yak, acts as a reservoir of food, being nature's provision for certain inhabitants of dry and arid lands, inasmuch as in times of starvation it will shrivel up before the rest of the body begins to suffer. A yoke laid across the necks of a pair of bullocks, and pressing against this hump, is the sole harness by which they are attached to their heavy burdens. They have only to bow the neck and they are free. So, just as the German oxen draw wholly by the forehead, these draw all weights by their hump, which too often is terribly galled. Indeed, the treatment of the sacred bullock by the reverent Hindoo is often horribly cruel. He is forced to work till his bones cut his miserable skin, and when galled and raw is still driven on. His tail is twisted till it actually breaks; and when at last the poor brute sinks exhausted, the chances are that his brutal driver will place straw and sticks round him, and light a fire to compel him to rise once more. Should even this fail to rouse the dying beast, he must on no account be killed—he is left to die at his leisure, with the assistance of the kites, vultures, and pariahs.

Where the Hindoo draws his limit in the use of all these means of gentle suasion it would be hard to define, for sometimes an obstinate sacred ox blocks up a narrow street in very inconvenient style, yet no one will venture to strike him, or use any means of forcible persuasion to move. Mr. Russell mentions that on one occasion, when native troops had been sent in pursuit of a strong party of robbers, who were encamped in a thick forest, their progress was arrested by a vast flock of half-wild cattle, who with levelled horns absolutely blocked the way, bellowing and stamping so furiously that the men dared not advance, indeed could not do so, except at the point of the bayonet. The men would rather

[1] By a very absurd misnomer, it appears on the bill of fare as "buffalo hump," whereas the Indian buffalo has none at all, being quite flat-necked.

have died than hurt the sacred bullocks, and would only try, by shouting and waving their long waist scarfs (cummerbunds), to induce them to move. The bullocks were obstinate and stood their ground, and meantime the robber troop escaped.

This being the day of the great Calcutta races, we were duly taken there, but, having no special racing instincts, I found my chief amusement in watching the intense excitement of the natives, who solaced themselves between whiles with flying paper kites,—a nice childish amusement for big men, I thought, till I was told that the strings of the kites had been rubbed with diamond dust, and that the object is to fly above your antagonist, and then, drawing down your kite sharply, cut his string, so that this becomes a favourite vehicle for gambling. Then I understood why half the population seemed to have entered their second childhood. The same game finds equal favour in Japan, where grey-haired men rejoice like children in cutting the string of a rival kite.

Here I received my first lesson in the antagonism of brown and white skins, a gentleman of our party suddenly insisting on my changing places with him, for what cause I could not divine, till he pointed out that a very handsome and beautifully dressed native lad had taken the seat next to mine—a lad whose delicately-refined hands, well chiselled features, and large, thoughtful, velvety-black eyes, would have rejoiced the heart of an artist. He was the sort of boy who, should he visit Britain, would be the petted darling of London drawing-rooms. I felt horribly annoyed at having moved, but the lad seemed to think it quite natural; his race gets accustomed to such humiliation at our hands. I remember my dismay when, speaking of a restive horse, whose prancing blocked the narrow road, I called to my friend to wait, as the beast would not let me pass, whereupon his rider, just tinged with colour, at once thought I referred to himself, and explained apologetically and most courteously that indeed it was the fault of the horse, and not his!!

As to a native travelling in the same railway carriage with you, it is a thing almost unheard of. But the unfortunate half-castes seem to occupy the most uncomfortable position, being neither flesh nor fowl as regards race. (Eurasians they are politely called, being a combination of Europe and Asia.) They are for the most part an unusually intelligent and industrious race, almost invariably well educated, and daily occupying more and more positions of trust. Fortunately for them, they are a sufficiently large and important body to form their own society, as they are socially shunned alike by brown men and white, in whose eyes a dash of the tar-brush is the worst form of evil. So there is a grievous lack of sympathy between all shades of colour, and too often the owner of a white skin seems to consider himself at liberty to address his darker brethren, no matter how highly educated, in an imperious tone of superiority painful and amazing to a new-comer. You very soon find out that the old command to "honour all men," has, like a good many other injunctions, been practically expunged from the Anglo-Indian Bible, or applies only to such as own pale faces.[1]

I have often marvelled to see English ladies returning from church, where they had been paying devout homage to the memories of saintly Syrian Jews (the tradesmen of 1,900 years ago), yet shrinking with contemptuous aversion from contact with their own servants—men differing in colour by but few shades. And socially, a man may be guilty of any enormity, rather than be suspected of having one drop of dark blood in his veins—so difficult is it to realise that black or white, coal or diamond, are all made of the same stuff.

Leaving the race-course, we followed the multitude in a round of the principal shops, all gaily decorated in honour of the season. The chief lounge seemed to be at Wilson's Hotel, the ground floor of which is a great shop, combining all trades, milliners and tailors, boots and bonnets, sugar-plums and cutlery, perfumes and wools, wines and groceries—in short, everything you can put a name upon. The great stands of Christmas cakes were worthy of

[1] The above was written before the "Ilbert Bill" had added tenfold fuel to this flame, and awakened in the brown and half-brown races a sense of irritation and antagonism which may yet prove a fruitful source of future trouble.

Gunter's, and a large Christmas tree was an additional attraction to all the little folk.

The ornamental cakes are supposed to be especially dear to the English heart, and the number of these presented to their employers on Christmas morning by the various tradesmen is startling. I saw about a dozen on one lady's table. Besides these things, trays of all manner of sweetmeats, fruits, and flowers are presented, sometimes by the servants themselves, who come up to make their salaam, and generally expect to receive a Christmas *backsheish*—in other words, Christmas *boxes*—a term which in olden times was probably derived from the East, in the same way as the slang of later days vulgarised the Hindoo word *cheese*, a thing, and "quite the thing" became "quite the cheese."

As a general rule, the recipient of the cakes and sweetmeats, having looked at them, bestows them at once upon his servants, who eat them with infinite delight, provided master has not touched them; but should they once have been laid on the plates in common use, none but the lowest caste will take them, or any other food that comes from our table. It is marvellous to see what piles of good things are at once handed over to these despised beings, while the other servants sit down, each by himself, to prepare their miserable dinner of rice and dahl (a vegetable something like pea-soup with a dash of curry in it), and great heavy chupatties, a species of bread like our scones, which every man must bake for himself, after divers washings and ceremonies. Should he be interrupted in the process, his flour is wasted, as no one else may take his place as baker. After all, the rice and dahl is not much worse than the potatoes mashed with mustard and milk which form the ordinary dinner of a vast number of our own sturdy Scots.

Hearing that there was to be a grand midnight Mass at the Roman Catholic Cathedral, we thought we could not better employ our Christmas Eve than by attending it. However, it proved a woful disappointment. Arriving very early, we had to watch the assembling of the congregation, who almost without exception were Portuguese and half-castes, dressed in those gaudy and most unbecoming colours which they generally affect, and as a rule, the older and uglier the women, the more brilliant and fashionable their European attire.

All the seats were locked, so the congregation stood crowding the aisles, till, at the last moment, a verger came, and, unlocking each pew, drove the people in like sheep, all chattering and laughing. At midnight the organ struck up rapid opera music, and the Mass which followed was but a few shades more solemn. We did not wait to hear whether, as in the Cathedral at Malaga, the organ would indulge in ludicrous imitations of the donkeys' bray, the low of the oxen, cock-crowing, the wailing cry of an infant, and other voices from the stable at Bethlehem, foı we were thankful to slip quietly away, and escape into the clear starlight, that it might whisper to us some message from the Syrian plains and the manger-cradle, and help us to forget the jarring incongruity of the scene we had just left.

We found a more congenial service in the early morning, at the English Cathedral, and though to a Briton it is always difficult to think of Christmas Day apart from glossy holly and crisp frost and snow, this had all the charm of an early Easter morning, with birds singing, and rooks cawing in the tall trees outside; while through the open windows the sweet cool breeze stole in, laden with the scent of flowers. The churches, too, were all decorated with flowers, and with the scarlet Poyntsetzia leaves. The cathedral was built by the late Bishop Wilson, and partakes of the ugliness of all our churches in India. It looks well in miniature, however, as you may judge from the alabaster model preserved in the Bodleian Library at Oxford.

Collecting the offertory in an Indian church is a curious and very lengthy proceeding. From a fiction that the coinage is too heavy to carry about (it is really precisely the same as our own, including every silver coin, from a threepenny-bit to a florin, *alias* rupee), hardly any one keeps money about him, so the plate is handed round, full of slips of paper and pencils, and every one writes down his name, address, and subscription, or, occasionally, that of his neighbour! These are collected with infinite trouble on the following day, when the effect of the stirring appeal having worn off, the generous fit has likewise subsided, and the collector is liable to be kept waiting so long, and the coin to be at length given so grudgingly, as to have sometimes called for strong remonstrance from the pulpit.

Speaking of the rapid variations of temperature in the inclination for almsgiving, I recollect the late Bishop of Oxford [1] relating, with infinite humour, a lady's account of the effect of one of his own sermons. She went to church determined to give a sovereign to a given object, but so eloquent and heartstirring was his appeal, that, instead of the sovereign, she produced a five-pound note. However, instead of an offertory, there was merely a collection at the door, and as the church was crowded, it took her some time to get so far—so long in fact, that her enthusiasm had quite cooled down; and though she did not, like a good many of her neighbours, look the other way when the plate was handed to her, she did replace the five-pound note in her purse, and once more produced the sovereign!

Another peculiarity of the churches in India is the punkah, which, as you know, is a framework of wood covered with cloth, and with a deep white frill. Rows of these hang from end to end of the church, suspended from the ceiling, and are swung by ropes which pass through holes in the wall, and are pulled by natives (in private houses there are relays of punkah coolies, who relieve guard night and day). Why some simple machine has never been devised to do this tedious work, is matter for wonder, but some one suggests that no machine would do it for sixpence a day, which is the wage of these men—certainly none would be so noiseless. And the gentle Hindoo has no objection to work that merely involves sitting still and pulling a rope. The effect of these rows of great white-frilled fans, chasing one another irregularly, up and down the church, is positively bewildering. Sometimes they seem to overtake those in front of them, then they are just left behind. After a while, as you watch them, the effect

[1] Samuel Wilberforce.

becomes soporific. To the parson it must be exceedingly irksome to preach to an invisible congregation, now revealed for a second, now again hidden in white moving clouds of cotton.

But at least he is spared the infliction to which his brethren in England must submit, of preaching to a sniffling, sneezing, coughing, Christmas congregation such as must sorely try the temper of one who has burnt the midnight oil in preparing close arguments, the thread of which is thus, in Britain, so often ruthlessly and hopelessly destroyed.

Here the natives seem to have a monopoly of "barking," and it is heartrending to hear the hollow consumptive coughs from which so many suffer. Even in these really chilly nights a great number sleep in the open air, merely wrapping their blanket cloak over their heads, perhaps taking what shelter they can find in the open verandahs. And yet they suffer far more from cold than we do, and their poor, frugal diet cannot add much to the internal heat. So, again and again through the night, when some extra severe fit of coughing in the street below rouses you to look out, you will see these lean, spare creatures, who minister so well to your luxuries, shivering over their little fire, or seeking what warmth and comfort they can extract from their hubble-bubble.

This last is a great institution, being the native pipe, and never very long out of sight and hearing. All night long you are sure to hear some one thus solacing himself. For the tobacco and fire being placed in a cup at one end of a tube, and the mouth-piece at the other, the middle of the tube, which is bent double, rests in a vase of water; thus the smoke is cooled; but every whiff causes a bubbling gurgling noise, like the boiling of a pot. This, and the incessant shrill cries of the kites, are the two sounds most thoroughly associated with every time and place in India.

The great bond of tobacco seems one of the few points of sympathy between dark skins and fair. The sahib's call is never responded to with such alacrity as when he shouts for fire, "Ag lau," and forthwith a burning coal or wood is brought, sometimes carried in small tongs, but more frequently *in the hand* of one of these salamanders! Even the good fellowship of the pipe is not, however, above all risk, and it is said that many instances have occurred in which travellers have been drugged by some treacherous companion, who has contrived to introduce detura into their tobacco; this being a powerful narcotic, stupefies the smokers, and leaves them an easy prey to robbers.

Nothing strikes a new-comer more curiously than the custom of driving for pleasure in the dark. For though instinct very quickly teaches you not to face the sun without a very thick sun-hat (a hat like a huge mushroom made of white pith), and a white cover for your umbrella, nevertheless the light is so beautiful and so pleasant that you long to be out all day; instead of which, the daily life-duty of the evening drive on the Esplanade or the Mall begins at sunset; and India has none of that twilight (the pleasantest hour of home life), that comes "'twixt the gloaming and the mirk."

The carriages come round at their appointed hour; good English carriages, driven by splendid natives in brilliant robes and large gay turbans, with attendant grooms (one of whom runs beside each horse), and if you start at once you may reach the Esplanade (the Rotten Row of Calcutta) just as the sun is sinking in a flood of golden light behind the forest of tall black masts. For the drive runs alongside the Hoogly, which is kept so deep by means of incessant dredging, that ships of very heavy tonnage find anchorage close to the shore, adding all the picturesque details of marine life to the endless variety of the scene. You will see no elephants, for these are not allowed in the streets, save at specified hours, for fear of frightening horses. But there are people of all sorts and colours, riding, driving, or walking.

Among the latter are innumerable young baboos[1] in white robes, and bareheaded. I know not how they came to adopt a custom so foreign to Hindoo fashion, which heaps endless yards of cloth upon the head, increasing the turban in proportion to the respect due to the day, or the presence in which they stand, so that

[1] Clerks.

it is no uncommon thing for a man to walk about with twenty yards of silk or muslin on his head, sometimes even thirty yards or more!

These white-robed clerks still abstain from stockings, but substitute patent-leather shoes of English manufacture for the usual native slipper, in consequence of a decree which allows such shoes to be kept on in any court, whereas all native shoes must be put off, in accordance with their own customs. But only a Europeanised Hindoo would think of wearing leather, which, being made from dead beasts, is impure, and the vast majority of Hindoos wear no shoes at all. Even the highest nobleman coming to call leaves his shoes outside the house in the verandah.

By the time you have completed one turn along the Esplanade it is so dark that you require lamps, which it is compulsory for every one to light. Then for perhaps an hour people drive up and down in the dark, going at a foot's pace, wearisome to a degree.

One thing which you cannot fail to notice is the multitude of grooms on foot, carrying yaks' tails, wherewith to flip away the flies. Not only has every horse his own syce (or groom), but the groom is supposed never to lose sight of his horse. However long a ride his master may go, or at whatever pace, the groom must run alongside—and a famous runner he almost invariably is. Occasionally he helps himself along by holding on by the horse's tail. In like manner with carriage-horses; the coachman is simply a driver, and while he sits in state on the box, the grooms must keep up with the carriage ready to be at the horses' heads the moment they stop. The amount of running thus entailed is something enormous, and certainly moves the compassion of a new-comer, though the old Indian considers it a matter of course.

(It is strange to think how recently it was the custom even in Britain to keep running footmen, who should be ready to accompany their master's carriage, lest it should stick in ruts or streams or otherwise come to grief. Sir Walter Scott mentions having seen these with his own eyes. They were also very generally employed in Germany and Austria in the beginning of the present century, but were said seldom to live more than three or four years, and then most frequently died of consumption. The distances which these men sometimes ran, in an amazingly short space of time, have been recorded among the strange feats of pedestrianism. Every runner bore a long light pole with a hollow knob at the top, in which he might carry a hard-boiled egg or some such light refreshment, and this is said to be the origin of the long silver-headed cane, still carried by footmen when hanging on in state behind a London carriage.)

When the ceremony of the drive is over, then comes dinner, with sundry agreeable peculiarities. Those delightful arm-chairs all round the table, and flowers in every finger-glass—probably a rose and a sprig of verbena in each—and the table itself so gracefully decorated—perhaps with leaves of the scarlet Poyntsetzia and delicate sprays and tendrils of the vine.[1] These Brownies do love flowers, and are very dainty in their use of them. They are for ever bringing you offerings thereof, and your rooms and table are always adorned as a matter of course. The plates, too, are a novelty; resembling a dinner-plate laid on a soup-plate, with a hole in the rim, to allow of filling the space between with boiling water. Thus the cold breeze from the punkah does not cool the gravy; nor are the dishes chilled when carried through the open air, from the kitchen, which is generally at some distance from the house. Of course a heap of such plates must be frightfully heavy to carry, but I rather think that a washing of dishes goes on close to the dining-room door, which diminishes the number in use.

Here as elsewhere, the value of everything depends on the difficulty of procuring it, therefore a *recherché* dessert generally includes grapes—not the beautiful well-grown bunches of our hot-houses, still covered with purple bloom and shaded by their own

[1] Such table-decoration was the rule in India long before this graceful custom was introduced into Britain—indeed, we are apt to forget that it is only about a dozen years since the civilised innovation of a "*Dîner-Russe*" was generally adopted in this country.

fresh leaves; but single grapes, generally, if not invariably, white, sold in circular boxes like French plums. They are cut from the bunch, and packed between layers of cotton-wool to exclude the air, and thus they are brought, with other stores of dried fruits, apples, and pomegranates, from the far-away mountains of Cabul seven hundred miles distant, by Cabulee or Afghan merchants. These are the wildest, weirdest-looking beings you can imagine; fine men, but the very strangest contrast to the smooth-shaven natives of the plains. They pitch their camp outside some city, where they find ready sale for their herds of strong, sure-footed ponies, as also for their Persian kittens—lovely, silky creatures of every colour, with great bushy tails. They have pure white kittens, and jet-black kittens, kittens grey or piebald, kittens brindled, kittens yellow or sand-coloured, in short, such kittens as would rejoice all cat-loving hearts. Some of the white kittens are blue-eyed,—large, beautiful, and of the brightest celestial blue, like lovely china. The law of compensation, however, makes them pay dear for this attraction, as the owners of such blue eyes are almost invariably deaf.

NOTE.

The recent Official Census of the trades and occupations of the people of India enables us to form a good general idea of the modes of existence of these our fellow-subjects.

OCCUPATIONS.	MALE.	FEMALE.
Officers of National Government	580,185	6,352
Officers of Municipal, Local, and Village Government	791,379	17,764
Officers of Independent Governments and States	133,285	865
Army	311,070	1,682
Navy	300	...
Clergymen, ministers, priests, church and temple officers	601,164	94,251
Lawyers, stationers, and law stamp dealers	31,628	10
Physicians, surgeons, and druggists	113,579	75,239
Authors and literary persons	32,177	3,464
Artists	10,347	584
Musicians	187,695	19,631
Actors	58,807	40,381
Teachers	166,356	4,345
Scientific persons	11,494	127
Wives of specified occupation	...	471,774
Other wives	...	3,321,366
Engaged on board and lodging	27,970	14,515
Attendants (domestic servants)	2,149,629	651,965
Mercantile persons	983,869	124,409
Other general dealers	686,149	286,464
Carriers on railways	61,031	1,157
Carriers on roads	635,482	13,770
Carriers on canals and rivers	322,688	2,877
Carriers on seas and rivers	104,237	574
Engaged in storage	64,667	2,157
Messengers and porters	174,598	15,063
Agriculturists	19,210	15,866
Horticulturists	166,355	54,448
Persons engaged about animals	754,512	235,830
Workers in books	19,384	127
,, ,, musical instruments	3,146	568
,, ,, prints and pictures	1,005	79
,, ,, carving and figures	15,338	4,463
,, ,, tackle for sports and games	4,101	1,283
,, ,, designs, medals, and dies	819	16
,, ,, watches and philosophical instruments	2,963	57

OCCUPATIONS.	MALE.	FEMALE.
Workers in surgical instruments	1	...
,, ,, arms	4,293	245
,, ,, machines and tools	52,095	9,979
,, ,, carriages	11,963	235
,, ,, harness	6,114	781
,, ,, ships	16,913	358
,, ,, houses and buildings	808,712	27,741
,, ,, furniture	9,343	797
,, ,, chemicals	61,220	19,813
,, ,, wool and worsted	178,519	69,670
,, ,, silk	51,085	34,355
,, ,, cotton and flax	2,607,579	2,877,876
,, ,, mixed materials	52,286	52,621
,, ,, dress	2,082,191	733,089
,, ,, hemp and other fibrous materials	108,729	164,367
,, ,, animal food	640,521	449,205
,, ,, vegetable food	1,445,916	1,719,513
,, ,, drinks and stimulants	708,699	204,331
,, ,, grease, gut, bones, horn, ivory, whalebone, and lac	37,107	70,889
,, ,, skins, feathers, and quills	263,056	48,559
,, ,, hair	943	344
,, ,, gums and resins	489,618	273,169
,, ,, wool	235,318	179,560
,, ,, bark and pith	3,092	68,550
,, ,, bamboo, cane, rush, straw, and leaves	403,375	277,375
,, ,, paper	7,670	1,410
Miners	3,428	549
Workers in coal	2,602	1,161
,, ,, stone clay	667,286	354,721
,, ,, earthenware	569,128	259,839
,, ,, glass	32,841	11,904
,, ,, salt	63,011	23,922
,, ,, water	227,673	198,758
,, ,, gold, silver, and precious stones	459,157	13,799
,, ,, copper	11,019	461
,, ,, tin and quicksilver	10,419	461
,, ,, zinc	139	32
,, ,, lead and antimony	992	155
,, ,, brass and other mixed metals	123,165	6,605
,, ,, iron and steel	454,555	18,806
Labourers and others (branch of labour undefined)	7,248,491	5,244,206
Other persons of indefinite occupation	426,109	33,873
Persons of rank and property not returned under any office or occupation	46,262	13,109
Persons of no stated occupation	48,794,195	86,135,617

CHAPTER II.

A RAILWAY JOURNEY.

Dust—A Tame Devil—Sleeping Carriages—Rural Bengal—Pigeon Flying—Night Watches—Pendant Nests—Moorshedabad—Ruined City of Gour.

BEFORE leaving Calcutta it is necessary for every one to lay in his own supply of bedding, as no house is supposed to keep more than the stock necessary for its own inmates. So whether you go as a guest to your friends, or as a lodger to an hotel, you will, in nineteen cases out of twenty, find that the sleeping accommodation provided in your bed-room consists only of a *charpoy*, which is a small bedstead of the rudest construction,—merely a wooden frame, with coarse tape laced across it. So it is necessary at once to invest in blankets, sheets, pillow, and a couple of *roseis*, *i.e.* wadded quilts, one of which will henceforth act as your mattrass. It is also very desirable to be provided with a strong waterproof case, in order to secure the said bedding from the chances of rain, and from the certainty of fine penetrating dust, which flies in clouds, finding its way in at every crevice.

In the matter of dress, one very quickly learns that this great dust question has to be considered, for you cannot brush against a wall, or sit down, or rise up, without being powdered over with pale grey dust, so that dark dresses are much to be eschewed, and light grey tweeds assert their superiority. For, in this stoneless country, the whole soil seems to float about at will, and the land is so entirely alluvial, that, within 400 miles of the sea, no stone the size of a pebble is to be found, save where the Ganges, after its inundations, forsakes its old channel, and chooses a new bed, leaving a stony watercourse to mark where once it flowed. Every building therefore is either of mud or brick, except in certain cases where stone has been brought from afar.

Crossing the river by steamboat one early morning, we made our first acquaintance with an Indian railway-station thronged with natives, some starting on pilgrimage, others on divers business. For the facilities of modern travel have developed a curiously locomotive tendency in the Hindoo. Their old proverb that "No one is so happy as he who never owed a debt, nor undertook a journey" is quite out of date, and now whole families start from one end of the country to the other, on the smallest pretext, carrying with them their poor stock of worldly goods, tied up in a little bundle, to which are added their cooking pots, and brazen drinking-cups, as no man could ever borrow the use of such articles from a neighbour, for fear of ceremonial defilement.

The incongruity between the appearance of these pilgrims to holy shrines (for such were most of my fellow passengers), and the solid business-like train, reminded me vividly of my brother's description of the sensation produced among the hill tribes of Bombay, when first a solitary engine came up the newly made railway, rushing madly onward, and yet stopping obediently at the bidding of the white man. The excitement was increased tenfold, when at night the terrible creature with red wrathful eyes flew over the ground, bellowing and snorting, in fire and fury.

What wonder was it that they believed it to be in truth a familiar spirit tamed by the white man; and that these worshippers of all evil powers came straightway crowding to "make pooja" and bring offerings to the tame devil? They brought garlands of fragrant flowers to hang around him, and pots of the red paint with which they smear their gods, and prayed to be allowed to daub the whole engine. They had to be content, however, with painting the buffers, which gratified them exceedingly, more especially as they declared they heard the familiar spirit roaring inside, and that (when the stokers stirred him up) they saw his great wheel-like limbs move. (The wheel, you know, is a sacred symbol wherever Sun-worship has prevailed.) So, as he undoubtedly was a devil, they sought to propitiate him with their accustomed offerings of little bowls of honey and ghee and sugar, and garlands of flowers; then stood by in reverential postures, while he went roaring on his resistless way.

Nor did their wonder lessen when trains commenced running, and they beheld this tamed and mighty demon rushing to and fro dragging along strings of enormous gharrys, which a hundred bullocks could not have moved.

Now the novelty is forgotten, the railroad and telegraph rank high among Britain's best gifts to India, and the crowd of travelling Hindoos equals that of a British excursion train.

So amazed are these easy-going Orientals by the punctuality of the trains, that, in dread of being late, they generally assemble at the station some hours before the time for starting—often overnight. Of course they carry their bedding with them, and as it consists merely of a wadded blanket-cloak of gaily coloured calico (or in the case of the very poor, only of a piece of coarse canvas) one realises how easy of fulfilment was the injunction once spoken in Judea, "Take up thy bed and walk!" So the early arrivals just lie down on the pavement, wrapping their cloak or canvas), tightly over head and body, and look like rows of corpses laid out in order. In due time these chrysalides begin to stir, and then shake themselves up, each revealing a long pair of lean black legs, surmounted by a bundle of raiment, out of which gleam two glittering black eyes. As long as their heads and shoulders are warm, they seem to care little for any chill about the lower extremities. Then they solace themselves, and try to counteract the chill of the night air by a few whiffs of tobacco, and the gurgling of many "hubble-bubbles" resounds on every side.

The carriages are ticketed off, for natives, native women, and Europeans. Some of the upper class natives still find themselves sorely perplexed how to combine railway travelling with the seclusion of women. Of this I had an amusing illustration, as we were no sooner comfortably ensconced in a carriage set apart for ladies, than a gorgeously apparelled merchant brought his wife and her ayah, both closely veiled, and shut them in with us. The former was richly dressed and loaded with jewels, and I hoped at last to get a glimpse of a real native lady. The jealous husband stood at the door, till the train was actually in motion, when he stepped in, chuckling at having got into a carriage where no other man dare follow. The officials were, however, on the watch, and, stopping the train, desired him to get out, as the carriage was reserved for ladies only. In vain he battled and raged, and finally, sooner than leave his wife in my dangerous society, he made her and her attendant get out with all their bundles, and go with him into another carriage.

As journeys to the far north may involve travelling without a break night and day for sixty hours or more, night travelling has of course to be provided for; so, long before American luxury devised Pullman's sleeping cars, these Indian carriages were built with a special view to the accommodation of sleepers, not being divided into seats, but left so that one person can lie down comfortably, while the padded back of each carriage is in fact the mattrass of an upper berth, which at night is raised, and fastened to the ceiling with strong straps, so that each carriage affords good sleeping quarters for four persons. Then the bundle of bedding comes into play, though not till the invariable basket of provisions has done its part.

All the windows have projecting shades to keep off the burning sun, and each carriage has a double roof of white for the same purpose. Some are provided with tanks of cold water, not merely for the comfort of washing (though that is very great, and it is well to secure a carriage with a dressing-room) but as a measure of safety in the fearful heat, when the constant application of wet cloths to the head is one of the best safeguards for such as are compelled to travel. Of the risk involved, one gains some impression by hearing of the number of persons, who, in the stifling summer months, are lifted from the train, stricken with heat apoplexy. In fact the possibility of death from this cause is such a well-recognised danger, that while we—

the pleasure-seekers—were revelling in the temperate climate on the great hills, we knew that the railway authorities found it necessary to keep coffins ready at every station, to receive such travellers as thus, too quickly, reached their journey's end.

For the first few hours after leaving Calcutta, our route lay through rich vegetation and fertile land, made more beautiful by the early lights and the clear golden sunrise, and the balmy morning air was still deliciously fresh and cool. New and full of interest to our eyes were the clumps of waving bamboos, the tamarind and neeme trees, the spreading banyans and slender palms with crown of feathery fronds, and even the hedges of aloes and tall sirkee grass which surround the little mud villages. These are almost invariably marked by the tall pyramidal dome, or the three low rounded domes which respectively denote the Hindoo or Mohammedan shrine. The cottages are half hidden by large-leaved gourds which trail all over them, heavy with golden fruit, and overshadowed by the gigantic glossy leaves of the plantain (the very ideal of tropic foliage), beneath which played groups of odd-looking little brown children, carrying babies as big as themselves.

So effectually are these cottage homes veiled by the rich foliage, that the casual traveller forms no notion of their multitude—still less does it occur to him that those brown babies form one of the most perplexing questions which harass Indian statesmen. For, thanks to the security of life under British rule (and the removal of many causes of death, which in past generations have checked a too rapid increase of the people), *the population of Bengal has actually trebled in the last century*, and the land which in A.D. 1780 amply sufficed to feed twenty-one million persons, now yields scant sustenance for sixty-three millions, and still (as very early marriage is a religious obligation, binding on every Hindoo, quite irrespective of means of supporting a family) the evil goes on progressively, and the population of India increases at the rate of two and a half millions per annum, so that ten years hence there will be considerably more than twenty-five million hungry extra mouths to feed.

Though much is now being done to relieve the pressure on land, by establishing in different parts of the country great manufactories which give employment to many thousands of the people, nevertheless about ninety per cent. of the rural population have to live almost entirely by tillage of the soil. In old days, when there was more land than there were people to work it, every farmer could select good soil, and the bad was left untilled. Now, every morsel, good and bad, is worked to the uttermost, and compelled to yield two crops annually, though, on the other hand, it is deprived of its needful nourishment; no longer do the jungles yield fire-wood for fuel, so there are no wood-ashes for manure—and the valuable produce of the cow byre is now too precious for the land, and must be converted into fuel. Consequently the land must go on deteriorating.[1]

Talk of our Highland crofters! Here in Bengal there are actually six million small tenant farmers (*i.e.*, two-thirds of the whole tenantry) who pay a rent of less than ten shillings a year, and whose whole existence is one prolonged struggle to extract a living from an unduly small portion of over-worked land.[2] So

[1] Within the last few years, necessity, backed by the persuasion of British officials, has induced the farmers to conquer their caste prejudices against the use of prepared town-sewage. Now the demand is far in excess of the supply.

[2] Dr. W. W. Hunter points out that whereas one acre of good soil is the minimum which can yield comfortable support for a human being, and that fertile France averages only 180 inhabitants to the square mile, and Ireland only 169 persons to the same acreage, here, in Lower Bengal, Behar, and the North-West Provinces, there is a vast tract of country as large as the whole of Ireland, which has to support an average of 680 persons to the square mile (a mile contains 640 acres) without any allowance for swamps, jungles, and other worthless land. Indeed in the province of Benares the population averages about 800 to the square mile, and in the delta of the Hoogly it rises to 1,045!

Throughout the whole of British India, exclusive of the more thinly peopled districts of Burmah and Assam, the population averages 243 persons to the square mile, which amounts to about three times the population of the native states.

From the very elaborate and interesting statistics collected by Dr. Hunter, he estimates that of the 63,000,000 of Bengal, forty millions are well fed, ten millions must suffer actual hunger whenever there is a deficient harvest, while

it is to be feared that there is a full share of human suffering and privation in many of the embowered homes, of which the traveller sees only the picturesque side. This, however, has its own interest.

Everywhere we see the inevitable Brahmin kite, and varieties of brown kites, and every mango tope is alive with thousands of chattering green parrots, exquisite creatures, with most unmusical voices. Bright russet birds sit on the telegraph wires, and blue jays, a thousand times more brilliant than our own, flash in the sunlight with strange metallic lustre. Golden-crested hoopoes also abound, golden orioles, blue king-fishers, black fly-catchers, doves, pigeons and crows, by turns attract our attention.

So too do certain frameworks, supported on tall single bamboos which are erected near many cottages. These are pigeon-roosts. The Hindoos are great pigeon-fanciers, and delight in flying their flocks against those of their neighbours; it is a favourite amusement in the evenings to sit on the flat house-tops, directing the flight of these tame doves, which ascend or descend, wheel or turn in the direction indicated by their owner, who points out their course with a long light bamboo, like a fishing-rod.

At the midwinter season the level rice, or as they are here called, paddy-fields, are all flooded, and multitudes of spirit-like white

thirteen millions are always half starved, and (except during the mango season) can never know the comfort of being fully satisfied. Taking the whole of British India, he estimates that two-fifths of the people enjoy a prosperity unknown under native rule—two-fifths earn a fair but diminishing substance—WHILE THE REMAINING ONE-FIFTH, EQUAL TO 40,000,000, GO THROUGH LIFE UNDERFED, IN A CONDITION OF CHRONIC HUNGER, and cannot possibly procure two full daily meals of any sort. And yet India annually exports as much food as would support five and a half million persons for a whole year!

The most hopeful temporary solution of this difficult problem seems to lie in the present unequal distribution of lands and people, and the hope that large colonies may be induced to migrate to Assam and other regions not yet fully peopled. In short, every question which has recently cropped up in Britain concerning over-crowded crofts in the Hebrides and Scottish Highlands, and the advantages and difficulties of emigration thence, is here re-echoed throughout immense tracts of British India.

cranes paddle about in those shallow waters. I believe the true name of these tall graceful birds is Aboo-gerdan, but they are invariably known as the paddy-birds, a nickname which to the uninitiated suggests the Emerald Isle, but really describes rice in the husk. A favourite feeding-ground of these pretty creatures is the back of the buffalo, and you rarely see a herd of these ungainly brutes without several of these ministering spirits in attendance, their delicate, snowy plumage contrasting strangely with the hideous, dirty creatures on which they perch. The buffalo's highest notion of bliss is to stand for hours in a muddy tank or stream, with only his nose and his back above water, so that all the small game seek refuge on that dry ridge, and well do the white cranes know what sure covert those little black islands afford.

The Indian farmer is dependent on his buffaloes and bullocks for all help in his work, as the cart-horse is an unknown animal in Hindostan. Camels and elephants lend efficient aid in transport work, but all agricultural operations are dependent on the strong, patient oxen.

It is only by noticing such details that we can fully realise the distinctive points of the country through which we are whirled by the swift train, for in truth, the general effect of the scenery bears a strong resemblance to that of England's midland counties, especially in some of the districts liable to be flooded in rainy seasons. The masses of foliage are especially English. At a very short distance a mango tope might pass for a group of sycamores, while the neeme, tamarind, peepul, &c., more or less resemble oak, ash, or elm. But the crops are richer and taller than those of Britain; fields of dahl or Indian corn, or of tall sugar-cane, and banana-gardens, and every field is guarded by several watchers, who sit, each in his solitary lodge—a thatched hut, either perched on a tree like some quaint nest, or raised on a skeleton platform of bamboos, that the occupant may be above the reach of the wild beasts, whom he is bound to scare from the crops.

Speaking of quaint nests, we passed many groups of date palms, with a dozen or more of the graceful pendant nests of the "baya," sparrow, sometimes fastened to the fronds by a finely woven grass cord nearly a yard long, and swinging in the breeze. The nest is in the shape of a chemist's glass retort, and hangs mouth downwards, to cheat the cunning monkeys, grey squirrels, tree-climbing snakes, and other foes, which might glide along the bough. Thus the wise old birds rear their brood in safety in this dainty cradle.

The weaver-birds and tailor-birds build similar pensile nests, with delicately interwoven fibres of grass, hanging from the light tip of a palm-leaf; but sometimes these cunning builders choose a leaf of the great elephant-creeper and fold and stitch it together with grassy thread, or downy cotton, which, with their long bill and slender feet, they twist till it becomes a fine cord. It is said that at night they stick a fire-fly in the wet clay at the mouth of the nest, to give them light!

Our first halting point was to be near the ancient city of Moorshedabad. We therefore left the main line of rail at Nulhattee, whence a branch line brought us to the river Bhāgirathi, the most sacred stream of the Ganges. Here a troop of natives quarrelled over our baggage, and finally landed us and it, in an open boat, and so we crossed the river. It was a brilliant moonlight, and the steep banks of the stream were lighted by many fires, round which squatted groups of wild-looking creatures, all attractive to the artistic eye.

One scene especially riveted our attention—the cremation of a Hindoo. It was the first time we had witnessed this strangely impressive ceremony, which, however, we soon learnt to look upon almost as a matter of course, and even with a very decided feeling of preference for its many advantages. To a Hindoo the special sanctity of this particular stream is such that no trouble is spared to bring the dying here, to end their days, and here commit their mortal bodies to the cleansing fire.

These funeral pyres are rarely kindled till after sunset, when they form a striking feature in the landscape. Wild, weird figures move about like shadows circling round the fires, sometimes tossing their arms aloft as if in wild grief; sometimes stirring up the fires till the merry sparks rush heavenward, crackling and sputtering, and the bright flames leap and blaze and vanish in heavy clouds of dark smoke; while red fires and black shadows and silvery moonlight are alike reflected on the dimpled stream.

On the further shore a friend's carriage awaited us, and then followed a two hours' drive through scenes to which the misty moonlight lent a rare fascination. We passed a succession of old temples, half hidden by rank vegetation, native houses and bazaars, red firelight and dark figures, white mosques and other great buildings appearing through the tall trees. Here and there we came to an open space, where great weird-looking elephants (magnified by the pale moonlight and the mist from the river) were quietly feeding under the dark trees. This was our first sight of the grizzly beasts, so it had all the charm of a new sensation.

We were in fact passing through the town of Moorshedabad, which Clive described as being a city as extensive, rich, and populous as London (the London of a hundred years ago). The fall of the Mohammedan Empire, however, shook its glory, and the fearful famine of 1770 tended further to its decay, so that there are now few remains of the grand old city. The chief lion is the immense new modern palace of the Nawaub Nazim of Bengal, who, with his sons, paid so long a visit to the murky shores of Britain, hoping to induce Parliament to secure to his descendants the same position as he himself still retains, *i.e.* a sort of monarchy under British supervision. Small as was his chance of success, he yet deemed it sufficient to compensate for years of voluntary exile from his luxurious home, his noble stud of horses, and elephants, and all his oriental splendours, and for the dreariness of several winters in London and Sussex, where wondering rustics followed his priest to the butcher's shop, to watch so strange a ceremony as that of blessing the animals about to be slain in the name of God, thus making them lawful food for the faithful.

Beneath the great dome of his marble-paved hall is a priceless ivory throne, for the carved ivory work of Moorshedabad is famous; and on the river float pleasure boats of fantastic forms, one of which is shaped like a gigantic peacock, gorgeously coloured and gilt. On gala days these are draped with rich and brilliant hangings, well in keeping with the gay dresses of the dusky beauties within.

Among the ruins of the ancient city, stand a few arches and pillars of a once magnificent palace of black marble, built by Sooraj-oo-Dowlah, who brought the materials thereof from the famous ancient Buddhist city of Gour, which is not far distant. It was once the capital of Bengal, but is now only a wondrous heap of ruins, wave after wave of change having swept over it First the Brahmins overwhelmed the Buddhists, and appropriated their temples. These were next used as quarries by the Mohammedans, under whose rule the city waxed great and stately, and of exceeding wealth. It was twenty miles in circumference and was surrounded by a wall sixty feet high. Here beautiful enamelled bricks were manufactured, and from the clumps of dark foliage rose stately domes, whose covering of highly-glazed green or bronze-coloured tiles, glittered in the sunlight. On every side were great fortifications and mosques, and fantastic towers and turrets, while on the sacred river—the Ganges—amid boats innumerable of every size and form, there were constructed floating gardens, bright with all that oriental imagination could devise of luxury and loveliness. On the great festivals these were illuminated with myriads of coloured lights, and must in truth have seemed as a dream of fairyland.

But three hundred years ago, an awful pestilence broke out. Thousands died daily, burial became impossible—Hindoo and Mohammedan, were alike thrown into the river, and the contagion spread far and near. Then the city was deserted—rank weed overspread the palaces—a thick forest has sprung up in the streets where the wars of conflicting faiths once raged. Now, you can scarcely force your way through this wilderness of deserted halls, by reason of the mass of tangled creepers and twisted roots of great trees—an uncared for jungle, wherein tigers and wild beasts roam unmolested. The brilliant river festivals are things of an almost unforgotten past; only at the feast of Beira, the Hindoo maidens still float their tiny lamps in cocoa-nut shells adorned with a few flowers, and watch the fortune of their love.

In almost those same words, I might describe many another once stately Indian city, to several of which we found our way, spending weeks of delight in exploring tombs, temples, and palaces, once centres of busy life, but now all over-grown with tropical forest, yet retaining the picturesque beauty of their exquisite marble carvings and richly coloured tiles, their sculptured columns and grotesque imagery, rendered all the more striking from contrast with the desolation which now reigns around them.

To the artist, the archæologist and the student of strange mythologies, these deserted cities, so fascinating in their ruin, offer an inexhaustible store of interest, while the sportsman and the naturalist find a rich field, wherein to follow their own bent. For many shy and beautiful creatures, birds, beasts and reptiles, now make their homes in forsaken palaces, or wander at large in the gardens, where veiled and jewelled ladies held their dazzling festivals, and life was one long dream of Oriental splendour and intrigue.

One of the perpetually recurring aggravations of travelling in India, is the impossibility of getting definite information as to what things and places are really best worth seeing. It is so very exceptional to find any one, who takes the smallest interest in anything native, unless it has reference to coining rupees. Consequently the majority of our countrymen generally assert that a city is, or is not, worth visiting, according to their recollections of its commissariat, or the weather, or something equally irrelevant. Thus I have constantly been assured, that there was literally nothing to see at such a place, and yet, have found there materials of beauty and of interest, that have afforded me a perfect feast of delight.

Some of the old native cities are, however, so very beautiful, both as regards their architecture and the surrounding scenery, that even the most casual observer cannot withhold his meed of praise. Such are the cities of Jeypore, Ajmeer, and Oodeypore. The fact, however, that these cities lie a short distance from the line of rail, adds so much to the difficulty of reaching them, that I was compelled to give up all thoughts of seeing these and many like them, and to be content on this northward journey with visiting such places of interest as lie within easy reach of the railway. Even from these, I very quickly gathered such a store of varied impressions, as few Anglo-Indians of the last generation had a chance of accumulating in a long life-time.

CHAPTER III.

MID-WINTER ON THE GANGES.

The Bhāgirathi—Tomb of Sooraj-oo-Dowlah—Sacred Jackals—Suicides in Wells—Camp in the Forest—Destruction of Wild Beasts—Pig-sticking—Allahabad—Station Life—The Old Fort—Asoka's Pillar—Ancient Hindoo Temple—Railway Bridges—Probyn's Horse—Truth-compelling Trees—Horseshoes.

IT was nearly midnight ere we reached the town of Berhampore, where kind friends welcomed us to their pleasant home in the English settlement, and we did such justice to our new quarters that the sun was up, and our host miles away, pursuing his morning work, before we awoke to share the charming *chota hâzeri*, the Indian "little breakfast," of coffee and fragrant fruits.

Then, looking out, we saw signs of military life, which reminded us that this station is said to have been the cradle of mischief, which resulted in the massacre of Meerut, and the terrible story of 1857. Here it was that the 19th Bengal Native Infantry, having been found guilty of mutinous conduct, was disarmed and disbanded. Strange to say, however, no further evil resulted in this place.

And very calm and peaceful it all seemed now as I sat in the pleasant verandah, sketching some fine old Indian-rubber trees in the garden. They have the same growth of stem as the banyan, *i.e.* very much divided into small stems round one parent mass; the leaves thick and glossy. Then we adjourned to an open summer-house, looking down on the broad, blue river, the Bhāgirathi (a stream held by millions of Hindoos to be the embodiment of all holiness), whereon floated boats of all shapes and sizes; some with huge square sails all tattered and torn, the boat itself square at bow and stern, with a bamboo framework projecting on either side, to allow more room for the cargo of cotton bales. Wild-looking brown men in the lightest of raiment were floating timber rafts from the up-country jungles, guiding their course with long bamboos; most of these rafts carry small red

CARGO BOATS ON THE GANGES.

flags to propitiate some spirit of wind or water. Each is escorted by a small canoe, formed of a rudely hollowed tree, to enable the men to land when they wish, but they sleep on their raft, beneath a small thatched shelter. The weather was perfect, like a calm English summer, scarcely a leaf quivering in the still, sunlit air.

After a while we started to explore some of the tombs and temples whose domes appeared at intervals along the wooded banks. We set out on foot, but meeting an elephant belonging to our host we thought it as well to secure a first experience of elephant-riding; clambering up by a ladder, then holding on during the terrific convulsion when the good old beast (who had knelt down to facilitate our ascent) suddenly struggled to his feet again. I am not sure that elephant-riding ever becomes altogether a pleasure, but its discomforts vary greatly with the individual animal, some trudging smoothly along, others jolting hatefully. The construction of seats also varies much in the amount of purchase they afford. In the present instance we captured our grizzly hahti[1] unawares, and rode him quite in the rough, with only a pad, on which we sat poised in fear and trembling.

Finding our position too precarious to be pleasant, our mahout (driver) bade his charge kneel, and so we clambered down again. The old man was, to our eyes, well-nigh as great a curiosity as his charge; his grey beard, and hair and eyelashes, contrasting so strangely with the dark brown of his loose wrinkled skin.

Having rowed across the river, a fatiguing walk through deep sand at last brought us to the tomb, where, shadowed by grand old trees and fair white flowers, lies the dust of Sooraj-oo-Dowlah, the amiable inventor of the Black Hole of Calcutta.

Superfluous though it may seem to recall that story, I need scarcely say how vividly we realised all its horrid details, here at the tomb of this miscreant, remembering how in the year 1756 this powerful Nawaub, at the head of a large army, attacked the English garrison of three hundred men, who alone defended the "English Factory," which, standing in a marshy jungle, then represented the Calcutta of the present day. After a gallant defence the Factory was captured, and a hundred and forty-six prisoners were immured in a dungeon eighteen feet square, with only one opening for air, and this, in the stifling heat of a burning Indian summer—a space too small for the confinement of even one European.

The horrors of that night may be imagined: the piteous cries for mercy; the vain struggles to burst open the door; the prayers

[1] *Hahti*, elephant.

for water; the mad despair in which at last the captives fought with and trampled on one another in the agonising effort to reach the window; entreating the guards to fire on them and end their torture. The fiends watched them from the window, and replied to their prayers with shouts of laughter. When the morning broke, and the Nawaub called for the prisoners, the soldiers had to pile up the dead to make way for the living to escape. Only twenty-three, more dead than alive, had survived those hours of indescribable horror, and were transferred to wretched sheds and fed with grain and water; some loaded with irons. As to the dead, their burial admitted of no delay, so a great pit was dug into which one hundred and twenty-three bodies were flung, and hidden out of sight.

Those deaths were swiftly avenged, when, in the battle of Plassy, Clive, with a force of three thousand men, utterly routed the Nawaub's army of sixty thousand, who fled, leaving guns, camp baggage, and a legion of cattle to the victors, who thus, in fact, became masters of the land, where, hitherto, they had only dwelt on sufferance.

The Nawaub fled to Rajmahal and sought refuge in a deserted garden, where he was discovered by a Fakeer whom he had deprived of nose and ears! Now was the hour of vengeance. The young tyrant—he was only twenty years of age—was captured and carried back to Moorshedabad, where he was murdered by order of his successor, and his mangled remains were placed on an elephant and exposed throughout the city, till they were finally interred at the spot where we now stood.

The Black Hole long continued in use as part of a warehouse, but was at length demolished. Many other horrible stories are current of Sooraj-oo-Dowlah's amiable propensities; one of these tells how he caused boats to be filled with men and then sank them in mid-stream, that he, sitting in the black marble palace which he had built at Moorshedabad, might watch their drowning agonies.

We returned home by boat, in the clear, beautiful moonlight. But some of the surroundings were by no means in keeping with its calm loveliness. Several dead Hindoos floated past us, bodies of men so abjectly poor that their relatives could not provide fuel for their funeral pyre. Our boatman ran foul of one, a ghastly object of horror. Vultures innumerable and tall adjutants were quarrelling over every such delicious morsel that drifted ashore, while countless frogs, foxes, jackals, and hyenas blended their voices in one sweet chorus, screaming, croaking, barking, baying, yelling. The piercing shrieks and yells of the latter are about the most unearthly sound imaginable, but one to which we soon got accustomed; a hungry pack of jackals often careering past our very door, or venturing almost into the verandah. Sometimes they do creep in, and hide in the houses, when they are detected by their fox-like smell. They rarely bite unless molested. There are, however, many stories of their carrying away children from the native huts, which indeed is only natural, as so many of the people worship the jackal as an incarnation of the goddess Doorga, who took this form when she carried the infant Krishna across the Jumna. So these worshippers lay food close to, or even within, their houses as an offering to the jackals, whose stone image is among the idols worshipped in Doorga's temple. A Hindoo meeting a jackal bows reverently, and should it pass him on the left hand he hails it as a good omen.

Nevertheless these poor animals are strangely utilised. I was sitting one day among the tall plantains in a garden at Allahabad sketching a picturesque old well, worked by bullocks, and could not think why men were continually coming past with dead pariah dogs and jackals, till I found they were being buried at the roots of the vines to enrich the grapes! That well, by the way, was very near becoming the scene of a little tragedy; for as I rose suddenly to watch a glorious red sunset I kept unconsciously stepping backward, till, literally, I almost *felt* my foot stayed on the brink, in the very act of stepping down into the horrible blackness—not "the way home" that one would choose! It made me shudder all the evening to think what news that mail might have taken home.

The method of working most of these wells is primitive to a degree. A long bamboo is poised on an upright stage. A leathern skin is attached to one end, and a heavy weight of earth to the other. A native, fully attired in a small pocket handkerchief and an enormous turban, stands on the stage, so as to weigh down the bamboo with his foot till the skin reaches the well and is filled, when he removes his foot, and the water bag rises and is emptied by another man. In some places a wicker basket lined with clay is used to raise water for irrigation.

These wells are a favourite means of suicide among Hindoo women, on the smallest pretext of any domestic quarrel. One magistrate told me that he had been tormented in his district by the multitude of such deaths, being convinced that deliberate murders were being committed at his very door, and yet baffling his powers of detection. At last he succeeded in fishing up one woman alive, and made sure of a full confession. So he promised her protection from all danger if she would betray her murderer, and was considerably taken aback when she indignantly denied having been thrown in, and said she had jumped in of her own free will. When questioned as to her reason for so doing, she replied that her husband had declared she could not bake his chupatties properly, "and did the sahib imagine that any woman would survive such an insult?" We have heard of certain Jewish rabbins who allow divorces on grounds so slight that they suffer an aggrieved husband to put away the wife who has only been so unfortunate as to let his soup be singed; but so deliberate a mode of "cutting off your nose to spite your face" as this Hindoo woman had devised to avenge herself on her lord is certainly rather startling.

New Year's Eve found us encamped in a beautiful jungle at Dewan Serai; the Nawaub Nazim having got up a great wild boar hunt, to which he invited all the ladies in the neighbourhood, providing elephants on which we should accompany the beaters. Only two ladies were able to go, and were rewarded by a most delightful expedition. A long drive through well-wooded country showed us some fine old banyan trees, and sundry temples. We found the camp pitched under a large group of splendid old mango trees, and had our first experience of those luxurious Indian tents with the invariable black and yellow lining. One large central tent made a first-rate dining-room, where we did ample justice to good fare. Several members of the Calcutta Tent Club were present, mustering, in all, seventeen spears. The Nawaub himself was detained by illness until the last morning; his son, however, arrived in time for the sport.

Nothing can well be conceived more picturesque than such a camp as this, at night; the dark trees on every side, their glossy leaves reflecting the blue moonlight, and their great boles lighted up by the red camp-fires, around which crouch all manner of native servants, in groups, according to their caste, with (or without flowing drapery and bright turbans. Beyond the white tents of the sahibs[1] are picketed their horses, and in the nullah below the bullocks are drinking; while tall camels and great dark elephants, and bullock-carts, and brilliantly-curtained native carriages (quaint little ekkas) stand about in all directions, guarded by a multitude of camp followers, and more fires. And all this lies in vivid light and shadow, clear as day, only softened and made beautiful by the dreamy moonlight.

We sat at the door of our tents, and watched the death of the old year, and the birth of the new one, in a style to us altogether novel—a foretaste of how we should spend very many of its nights. It was bitterly cold, however, and we were thankful to heap on all our warm clothes, and oh! so glad of thick worsted mittens. From the depths of the forest came the eerie cries of the jackals; and we tried to persuade ourselves that we could distinguish the bark of genuine *bonâ fide* wolves, which were said to be alarmingly on the increase in this province of Behar.

Next morning we were off betimes for a genuine day's "pig-sticking." It was a very pretty field. Fourteen elephants, each with several riders, formed in line to beat the long grass. Of course the gentlemen were mounted, ready to gallop in pursuit of any boars we started. All the morning we were on poor ground and found only three pigs, two of which were slain—not till one of them had shown fight, and severely cut one of the young Nawaub's horses. No one whose ideas of pigs are limited to the common domestic animal can have any notion of the amount of sport to be obtained from these wild boars of the jungles. Only

[1] Gentlemen.

rouse one of these gaunt, lean creatures from his lair in the tall grass, and he will dash through the thorniest hedges, spring broad ditches, tumble over, and scramble up again, and away he tears over the plain at a pace which will test the energies of the best horse in the field.[1]

[1] The official return of our war with wild beasts in British India are suggestive. Between the years 1875 with 1880 the numbers are as follows:—

NUMBER OF PERSONS KILLED.

	By Elephants.	By Tigers.	By Leopards.	By Bears.	By Wolves.	By Hyenas.	By other Wild Beasts.	By Snakes.
1875	61	828	204	84	1,061	68	2,015	17,070
1876	52	917	156	123	887	49	1,143	15,946
1877	46	819	200	85	564	24	1,180	16,777
1878	33	816	300	94	845	33	1,323	16,812
1879	38	698	277	121	492	28	1,270	17,388
1880	46	872	261	108	347	11	1,195	19,150

NUMBER OF CATTLE KILLED.

	By Elephants.	By Tigers.	By Leopards.	By Bears.	By Wolves.	By Hyenas.	By other Wild Beasts.	By Snakes.
1875	6	12,423	17,098	529	9,407	2,118	3,489	3,166
1876	3	13,116	15,373	410	12,848	2,039	4,573	6,468
1877	23	16,137	14,488	999	11,934	1,590	5,081	2,945
1878	13	13,129	15,101	590	10,497	3,229	4,317	1,825
1879	53	14,257	17,670	941	12,224	2,378	5,615	1,874
1880	—	15,339	19,732	482	13,507	2,279	4,511	2,536

NUMBER OF WILD BEASTS DESTROYED IN THE SAME PERIOD.

	Elephants.	Tigers.	Leopards	Bears.	Wolves.	Hyenas.	Other Wild Beasts.	Snakes.
1875	5	1,789	3,512	1,181	5,683	1,386	8,801	270,185
1876	4	1,693	3,786	1,362	6,976	1,585	8,053	212,371
1877	2	1,579	3,559	1,374	4,924	4,417	9,996	127,295
1878	1	1,493	3,237	1,283	5,067	1,202	10,204	117,958
1879	6	1,412	3,061	1,208	5,059	942	6,947	132,961
1880	3	1,680	3,047	1,100	4,243	1,215	3,589	212,776

The object of each pursuer is to get the first spear, in other words, to first draw blood. Sometimes a grim old tusker has pluck to turn and charge his pursuer, and then the luckless steed may chance to get some ghastly cuts before his grisly foe has yielded his life-blood to the rider's spear. When the brawny boar thus stands at bay he is no mean antagonist, as he stands champing in his rage and covered with foam, his savage little eye glittering and his sharp cutting tusks all ready for work; and very nasty work he can do if only he can get the chance, as divers men, even pukka shikarees[1] have ere now found to their cost. We heard of one officer in the Rifles, whose horse having been frightfully cut, threw his rider, leaving him at the mercy of the infuriated pig, which literally cut him from head to heel, inflicting upwards of fifty wounds ere his comrades came up to his rescue.

At midday we halted for tiffin beneath the cool broad shadow of a clump of mango trees, and a very pleasant picnic it was to all except the young Nawaub, who was keeping the rigid fast of Ramazan, and from sunrise till sunset could neither eat, drink, nor smoke. Even at sunset he only allowed himself a cup of tea and a bit of bread, content to wait till his return to Moorshedabad at midnight for a more solid repast.

After tiffin our road lay through most exquisite jungle, chiefly masses of tall feathering bamboos, and glossy plantains with their immense leaves. When we came to clumps so thick that we could not get through, the elephants deliberately broke off branch by branch till they had made an opening high enough to clear our heads.

The more open country is clothed with a fragrant species of feathery mimosa, commonly called the sweet babool, which at this season is covered with blossom—bunches of little balls of soft yellow fluffy down. To me it recalled a vision of home in long-ago years, when just such a tree grew in the dear old greenhouse, tended by our mother, and its yellow balls were the delight of our childhood. Long ago that fragrant tree outgrew its space and was doomed to perish—while the merry children who played

[1] First-class sportsmen.

beneath its shadow have either faded away with the flowers, or changed into weary men and women.

Thus it was that here in the Indian jungle the sweet yellow blossoms of the mimosa came as spirit messengers, when least expected, recalling a vision of home, and awakening memories of a sunny, flowery past, too radiant for this earth.

On reaching the grass again we started eight boars in rapid succession, of which seven were speared. The luckless pigs made wonderfully good running, and showed fight moreover, and more than one horse was terribly cut. The excitement was tremendous, but was soon changed to grief, for one fast and furious charge resulted in a list of casualties so serious as to bring the day's sport to a sudden close. Two men were down, with their horses, one rolling over with the pig, the poor brute already having two spears in him. Worse than all, one rider lay helpless in agony, his horse having rolled over him. He feared his hip was crushed. Mercifully it proved to be a broken rib and a dislocated ankle, but this was not known till next day, when a doctor arrived. Meanwhile, his friends improvised a litter, and carried him slowly back to camp. It was late before the torch-lit procession came in—a very different scene to the morning start, and an anxious night for the watchers. As our fagged elephants slowly trudged campwards, we drearily agreed that our hunting instincts were very imperfect, and (like our radicalisms) were mere theories that could not stand the test of practice!

So entirely upset were all our ideas that none even thought of saving the boar's tusks, so the camp followers divided the spoil, as they always do; for though the Hindoos have nearly as great an abhorrence as the Mohammedans of tame pigs, some of the lower castes have no objection to wild boar. They have a sacred hog, Baraha, under which form Vishnu was once incarnate, and raised the earth from the depths of ocean on his tusks, and I suppose that for his sake they make this honourable distinction. The English never seem to think of tasting wild pig, though it must be precisely the same as Westphalian hams, which are so highly prized.

Next morning the Nawaub arrived in person, but his son did not return. His highness is reported to have about forty children, and wives without number. It is said that his burial-ground contains a long border of infant Nawaubs, whose untimely deaths have been the occasion of much lamentation.

Thinking we had had enough of pig-sticking, the feminine element forsook the camp. Our route lay farther up-country, so we had to return to the railway, our next halt being at Allahabad, which involved about thirty-five hours of consecutive travelling. The dead level of the plains becomes very wearisome. We travelled on and on across an unvarying expanse of flat country, all rich alluvial soil—the deposit of the great rivers, in oft-repeated floods—and unvaried by one rock or crag. The only redeeming point in the general ugliness of the landscape lay in the multitudes of picturesque pilgrims on their way to various shrines, whole families travelling together, from the aged grandfather to the youngest child sitting astride on its mother's hip. Some of the men carried their children in a couple of baskets slung from a bamboo balanced on the parental shoulder—true devotion indeed—and many had travelled thus for hundreds of miles. Another interest lay in watching the exquisite birds, blue, green, and russet, that perched on the telegraph wires. Our thoughtful friends had provided us with all manner of creature comforts, so we did full justice to a champagne supper, and contrived to sleep tolerably, notwithstanding the exceeding cold. We were nevertheless very grateful to a Scotchman who brought hot coffee at daybreak to his unknown countrywomen.

We passed the great coal mines at Raneegunge, which extend right under the bed of the Domooder, a rapid, impetuous torrent, liable to wild floods; its stream is now bridged by a stately viaduct. The country seemed to become more and more dusty as we proceeded: all the green rice-fields lay behind us, and everything looked dry and parched. The air was intensely still, and the hot sunshine seemed to make even the birds heavy of wing. We noted that along the horizon lay a dull brassy red cloud, which was gradually rising. It was a dust-storm rapidly sweeping over the plain. As it approached, the trees were violently tossed and shaken, the ground strewn with the yellow blossoms of the sweet babool tree, branches were torn off—in fact it was a tremendous squall. In another moment we found ourselves in almost total darkness, by reason of the vast mass of floating sand, which was being blown along by the fury of the gale. We had quickly shut every window, yet in it came, so that we were half smothered. These storms are very destructive to houses; so rapidly does the eddying whirlwind approach, that there is hardly time for the precaution of shutting doors, windows, and shutters, and in some cases the very roofs have been torn off.

We reached Allahabad at midnight, and here another cordial Scotch welcome awaited me. How pleasant to find blazing fires and hot tea, to say nothing of the very unexpected luxury of a hot bottle in bed! Could this really be India? I had to send for a tailor next day to manufacture extra flannels! At the same time he had to make a white cover for my umbrella, as even my thick sun-hat was insufficient for safety when exposed to the sun's rays. Even in the daytime one step makes all the difference from extreme freshness of the shade into the pleasant but dangerous sunshine, and after nightfall the air is, in the winter months, decidedly chilly.

We were now for the first time living in a real Indian bungalow, with high thatched roof and pillared verandah. It had, however, a few special features of its own. Here my host held his magisterial cutchery, *i.e.* court, with his staff of moonshees (writers) and native police. Beneath the broad shade of the *neeme*, *i.e.* tamarind trees, waited the crowd of witnesses, those who came from afar having divers quaint carriages; there they sometimes sat for hours, smoking and devising how best to bamboozle the unfortunate magistrate, who, however, was happily gifted with perceptions too keen for the success of their little plots, and, guessing the truth by some intuition, would collect his mass of infinitesimal evidence with an acuteness which reminded me of those Australian trackers who, when searching for the body of a murdered man, suddenly, in the heart of the trackless bush, stopped, and picking up an ant, examined it minutely, and declared that it carried a minute atom of white man's flesh. They then watched, and saw other ants running in the contrary direction, and, judging that these were making for the feast, followed, and, sure enough, found the body of him they sought!

These Indian bungalows of the plains are always built only in one story. The rooms are large and high, but not so high as the roof. The ceiling is merely a sheet of tightly-stretched canvas, along which we can see little feet running, for the space between the ceiling and the thatch is the home of a multitude of lizards, grey squirrels, and divers other creatures. These Indian lizards are ugly little things, and the Mohammedans wage war against them, and call them "crab cheese"—evil things—and vow they bite. This, however, is a mere excuse for killing them, from some preposterous belief that the lizard hangs its head in mimicry of their attitudes in worship.

This, I think, is one of the few exceptions to the kindliness with which all living creatures are treated—the Hindoos of course protecting all life—from the ever-present belief in transmigration, and the consequent conviction that every bird or beast may be animated by some spirit once human. At the same time it must be confessed that the manner in which wretched post-horses and waggon-bullocks are maltreated is beyond measure brutal. Nevertheless, kindness to all living creatures is the general rule, so all manner of living things become tame, and scarcely move away at the approach of man. One family of pretty grey birds is known as the seven sisters; it is a species of minar which has adopted the number of perfection and always goes about in that company. These assemble outside the bath-rooms, along with the sparrows and the crows, well knowing the hour when the big wooden tubs will be emptied, and the water allowed to rush out, to freshen the roses. So the birds wait for their bath and drink.

Every bed-room has its own bath-room, with one corner built off by a little wall a foot high, to allow for the process of upsetting baths. Along this low wall stand a row of great round water-pots of red earthenware, and before daybreak a bheestie walks in with a skin of water just drawn from the well, and fills them all. They are literally round, like balls, so, to prevent their rolling over, there are either hollows in the clay wall on which they stand, or else rings of straw. To lift them you must hold them by the round mouth, and very heavy they are. Here a castor-oil lamp is kept burning all night, as darkness is supposed to be alike favourable to thieves and creeping things, snakes and centipedes. It is astonishing how quickly your instinct teaches you to be on the watch for these.

For my own part, I had such a morbid terror of finding some creature curled up inside my slippers, that I always took the precaution of keeping these under my pillow, and as to stepping on the floor barefooted, that would have involved an amount of courage to which I could lay no claim—more especially when the rooms are carpeted with that Indian grass matting of which sharp tiny points are for ever suggesting the presence of stinging creatures. The matting is sometimes made of grass, sometimes of bamboo, or a sort of papyrus which is split when green, and makes a smooth shiny flooring always cool and clean.

In some of the older bungalows, the bath-rooms and verandahs are coated with chunam, which looks like cream-coloured polished marble. It is a sort of fine lime, made of burnt sea-shells, and supposed to have been mixed with the white of eggs. The secret of its manufacture has however been lost, and no substitute has been found to compare with it.

Among the household pests especially dreaded, none entail more vigilant precautions than the destructive white ants, creatures no bigger than grains of living rice, whose armies work so swiftly and so silently, that, if left undisturbed for a day or two, they will completely destroy any woodwork to which they take a fancy; and although from their love of working in darkness they will not touch the outer surface, but leave a most respectable exterior, a touch will soon betray the hollow sham, and prove that nothing remains beneath so fair a show but crumbling dust. So strong is their aversion to light, that, as a general rule, it is sufficient safeguard merely to raise each box or article of furniture on such a stand as shall allow a free current of air beneath it. A couple of bricks or empty wine bottles laid like rollers are all that is needed; also, to avoid close contact with the wall. Wherever these busy workers make their way they form for their own safety, secure tunnels of hard mortar, as solid as stone; sometimes so entirely filling up the woodwork which they have hollowed that it becomes a more solid structure than before, though of a different material. Pictures and mirrors, when fastened to the walls, have sometimes been thus dealt with, all but the thinnest external crust of their wooden framework and back being entirely eaten away, while the glasses remain strongly cemented to the wall itself.

Countless are the annoyances consequent on books and papers being thus destroyed—indeed goods of all sorts. One tradesman told me he had received a large supply of English goods one day, and unpacked them in the evening. One single night they lay on the ground, and next morning were literally reduced to powder. He showed me his door, apparently of good strong timber, which, however, crumbled at a touch, utterly destroyed; and the worst of it is, that once they attack a house there is no limit to their devastations, nor any means of knowing which rafter or door-post will next give way. We happily escaped any serious damage from these tiny hidden foes, though sometimes a little ridge of hard earthy cement, running along a door or wall, would mark where they were beginning to tunnel a dark covered way for future operations, thus giving timely warning to experienced eyes. Another race of ants which sometimes proved troublesome are the little red fellows, which attack an ill-cured plume or any such pleasant article of ant-food, and reduce it to very small fragments indeed.

But the creatures that gave us the most trouble (chiefly in the hills) were the lovely little silvery fish-insects, never exceeding an inch in length, in form just like a little fairy fish, with several minute legs near the head. They chiefly delight in unwashed muslin and paper of all sorts, and their ravages were really without end. Any book left undisturbed on a shelf, any box left unopened for a few days, was sure to be detected by these beautiful innocent-looking silvery creatures, whom it seems so cruel to kill, but who, nevertheless, are so terribly destructive. One day, on unfolding a new piece of muslin, I found it absolutely riddled with holes bitten clean out by these sharp invisible teeth, and on inspecting the case where it had lain I captured fully a hundred of these mischievous little beauties, of every size, down to a mere pin's point.

Of larger creatures, not mischievous, none delighted me so much as the little grey squirrels, which make their home in every corner of the thatch and in every old tile on the roof of the gardeners' sheds. They are the loveliest little creatures, darting in and out in the sunshine. Sometimes I have seen one dart up to my side and carry off a scrap of biscuit or bread, and sit nibbling it in delight, till the great saucy crows with the grey necks came to snatch it from him. Their impudence knows no bounds. I have often seen them carry off bread from a child's hands, if she chanced to turn her head the other way, to the great amazement of the poor wee woman. And constantly twenty or thirty would come close round the verandah to see whether the large Angola cat could spare any of her breakfast. The cat, in her turn, would sit watching for the entrance of the kitmutgars (table servants), whose bare feet were a source of great delight to her ; so she would spring out suddenly and make a dive at them, to the great discomforture of the owners, who, however, have rather a weakness for cats, and are invariably kind to them.

The said bare feet do at first strike one as peculiar, but one soon learns to bless the noiseless step which makes these white-robed ministering spirits seem to float on air. The excellence of these men as waiters is astonishing. They are so very attentive, so quick and watchful. There is one thing, however, which the Eastern mind cannot master, namely, the propriety of helping ladies before gentlemen—a homage to the sex which they seem determined never to remember. (Of course their own women-folk would never presume to touch food till their lords have finished eating.) It is necessary for every one to have a servant to himself, as they have no notion of foraging for any but their own master, so that if you intend dining out you must merely mention the fact, and on reaching your friend's house you will find your servant there ready to attend to you. Possibly your host may not be provided with a sufficient quantity of plate, in which case his head-man will send word to yours that certain things are required. Should you recognise your own crest, you are not supposed to make any comment thereon, as probably *your* butler may have occasion to borrow in his turn. But after such joint entertainments the kitmutgars have a very solemn division of silver and counting of spoons. Though all alike are dressed in white, a variety of livery is marked by the pattern and colour of the waist-scarf, and of the peculiar flat hat which these men adopt in lieu of turban.

The only exception to the rule of having to be attended by your own servants is at the table of the Governor-General, where no outsiders are admitted. The servants at Government House are altogether clothed in scarlet, having a shield worked on the breast, bearing the royal arms in gold and colours, and a very gorgeous set of attendants they are—notwithstanding their bare brown feet. It must be confessed that an ordinary English dinner-table does look dull and colourless for lack of these varied ingredients, and the heavy tread of booted attendants sometimes awakens a regret for the silent footfall of our Eastern domestics.

Among the peculiarities of supply for Indian tables are the mutton clubs, when four families agree to have their mutton properly fed on *gram*, and killed and quartered, each family in turn getting the head and feet. This arrangement is due to the fact that no meat will keep in the hot weather. Being the sole means of supply, it is edifying to behold joints of the same animal alternately appearing with and without mint sauce, and diversified with the titles of mutton or lamb! Gram is the name of the dried chick-peas on which cows, horses, goats, and all domestic animals are fed, as are also the natives themselves; consequently the animals are supposed sometimes to be defrauded of their allowance. When such suspicion is afloat, the creatures are brought up to the sahib's house and made to feed in his presence.

To the new-comer it is somewhat startling at first to see this odd muster for meals in front of the verandah. The objection to "bazaar-fed mutton" *versus* "gram-fed," is that the former is always tough, and is supposed to have fed on all manner of rubbish. The same idea applies to the rich creamy milk of the buffalo, which certainly is an unclean feeder. It is in fact a mere scavenger, and will eat any offal it finds. There is certainly no reason why it should not be fed as carefully as a cow; however, the prejudice exists, and though the cream and butter are alike good (only very white in colour), no European will make use of them. It is one of the many proofs of the bliss of ignorance and the folly of prying into culinary antecedents!

Speaking of milk, the Indian cows have an intense antipathy to losing sight of their calves, which consequently are always brought into the maternal presence at milking hours; the gwalas (cowmen) declare that the cows will hold their milk if this is not done, so, should the real calf die, they stuff the skin with straw, and allow her to lick that; which she does with perfect satisfaction.[1]

This phase of maternal tenderness did not fail to attract the notice of the early Aryan poets. One of the hymns in the Rig Veda addressed to the Maruts or storm-gods begins by comparing two rivers rushing down from the Himalayas to the sea to two white cows longingly hastening to lick their calves.

Allahabad has acquired fresh importance to the general public since it has become the point of junction for the two great branches of the railway—Britain's great gift to India—namely, of the line from Calcutta, and that from Bombay.

But a far more important junction in the eyes of the Hindoos is that of the two holy rivers—the Ganges and the Jumna—which here unite their sacred waters.

Just at this point stands the old fort of Allahabad, a grand mass of red sandstone, built by the great Emperor Akbar. It now contains a very large English armoury—great guns and little guns, and cannon and mortars, and all manner of weapons. Here

[1] Just the same thing used to be always done in Scotland, and the sham calf was called a tulchan.

it was that the English found refuge during the Mutiny; and our friends showed us the balcony, overhanging the river, to which they thankfully hauled up any morsels of food or firewood brought to them by the faithful old servants, whom, however, they had been compelled to dismiss, with the rest of the native attendants, from within the walls of the fort.

The mutiny in this city was very quickly crushed by the timely arrival of General Neill with his "Madras Lambs;" not, however, till after one awful night, when, the doors of the jails having been broken open, three thousand miscreants were turned loose to lend their aid in burning and plundering the city. Upwards of fifty Europeans were massacred that night, including eight young cadets who had only just arrived from home.

In the centre of the fort stands a very remarkable monolith, surmounted by a lion. It bears an inscription in the ancient Pali character, and is known as the Lat or Stone of Asoka, a mighty emperor who reigned in Behar in Northern Bengal about 250 B.C., and who, (having zealously embraced the tenets of Buddha,) established Buddhism as the state religion.

So he convened a Council of one thousand yellow-robed elders to revise the Buddhist Scriptures, and sent forth missionaries into all lands, to preach its doctrines for the saving of mankind. He founded so many religious houses that his kingdom is said to have been hence called Behar from Vihára, *i.e.* the Land of Monasteries, and 64,000 priests are said to have been supported by the Imperial alms. In order that none might suffer through ignorance of the Way of Life, he published edicts proclaiming the principles of the faith, and these were deeply engraven upon rocks and caves and tall pillars, throughout the length and breadth of Hindoostan. He is said to have erected 84,000 such memorials, of which at least forty remain legible to this day.

One of these is at the Buddhist caves of Karli, and is called the Lion-pillar. It is a sixteen-sided monolith, surmounted by four lions. Another exists at Delhi, in the ruined fort of Togluck, though it is called after Feroze, a very modern emperor, whereas Asoka was, as we have seen, a mighty prince of pre-Christian ages. His pillars are sometimes surmounted by lions, sometimes by human figures, overshadowed by the seven-headed cobra, or some other emblems of power, such as the mystic umbrella—symbolical of Buddha—of which sufficient trace remains to be recognised, though time and weather have in the course of two thousand long years worn away the distinct form. Very similar pillars are at the present day erected in Nepaul, whereon are placed statues of kings, sometimes shaded by an umbrella made of metal—and in one instance by the serpent hood.

The pillar is not the sole representative of diversity of creed that exists within the huge Mohammedan fort, a fort now held by Christians, who have fitted up one of Akbar's buildings as a military chapel, wherein service is held daily. Half-way between this Christian church and the Buddhist pillar there still exists a Hindoo temple of exceeding sanctity, though how the Mohammedans came to tolerate its existence within their fort is a marvel quite beyond comprehension. It is a foul temple of darkness, extending far underground, and roofed with low arches. We descended by a flight of dark dirty steps, dimly revealed by a couple of tallow candles; and we followed the old soldier who acted as our guide, and who led us along dark passages, and did the honours of various disgusting idols, stuck in niches, some as large as life, others quite small, but all alike hideous, and all adorned with flowers, and wet with the libations of holy Ganges water, poured upon them by the faithful. The flowers are the invariable large African marigold and China roses.

Each image is generally smeared with scarlet paint, to symbolise the atonement of blood that should be offered daily, but which most of the worshippers are too poor to afford. This substitute for the sacrifice of blood is common all over India, where a daub of red paint administered to the village god is at all times an acceptable act of atonement. These village gods, however, are generally placed beneath some fine old tree, with the blue sky overhead; but this disgusting temple was one which you could not enter without a shuddering impression of earthly and sensual devil-worship.

Here we were also shown a budding tree, supposed to be of extraordinary antiquity; a fiction by no means shaken, though the Brahmans frequently substitute a new tree. So holy is this temple that when, at one time, all natives were excluded from the fort one rich Hindoo pilgrim arrived and offered twenty thousand rupees for permission to worship here. The commandant, however, had no authority to admit any one, so was compelled to refuse his prayer, in spite of so tempting a bait. It was with a feeling of thankful relief that we emerged from that noxious and oppressive darkness into the balmy air and blessed sunlight.

We spent some pleasant hours in one of the balconies overhanging the river, while in the cool room within fair women with musical voices accompanied themselves on the piano, in Akbar's old quarters; and so we idled away the heat of the day till the red sun sank into the water, behind the great dark railway bridge—a bridge which the Brahmans declared the gods would never tolerate on so sacred a river as the Jumna, but which nevertheless spans the stream in perfect security. It was a vast undertaking, as, owing to the great extent of country subject to inundation during the rains, it was necessary to construct a bridge well-nigh two miles in length. The Indian railway has certainly necessitated an amazing amount of work, on a scale so vast as to test engineering skill to the uttermost, and in no respect more strikingly than in the construction of these monster bridges, one of which, across the Soane, is about a mile and a quarter in length, while that on the Sutlej, between Jellunder and Loodiana, is about two miles and a half, being probably the longest bridge in the world.

On the sandbanks just below the fort, huge mud-turtles lay basking, and the gentlemen amused themselves by taking long shots at them from the balconies, whereupon the creatures arose and waddled into the water with a sudden flop. These sandbanks are favourite haunts of crocodiles—*muggers*, as they are called—which, however, declined to show on this occasion.

Perhaps the pleasantest of our afternoons at Allahabad was one spent in watching the evolutions of the native cavalry, Probyn's Horse, a beautiful regiment, whose graceful dress, and still more graceful riding, were always attractive. On this occasion they were playing the game of naza bazi, or the game of the spear, when, riding past us singly at full gallop, they with their long spear split a wooden tent-peg driven hard into the ground. Then they picked a series of rings off different poles; afterwards, with unerring sword, cleaving a succession of oranges, stuck on posts,

CROCODILES BASKING IN THE SUN.

as though they were foemen's skulls. Next followed some very pretty tilting with spear against sword. We had only one fault to find—their strokes were so unerring that they never allowed us the excitement of a doubt! Altogether, it was the prettiest riding imaginable, and a beautiful game.

The change from the fresh greenness of Lower Bengal, where the whole air seemed scented with the fragrant wild babool trees, to the dried-up country round Allahabad (and indeed all the North-west Provinces) was positively startling. Thick layers of white dust, inches deep, lay everywhere. The rains had proved a delusion, and it was said that in the previous twelvemonth there had literally been only two wet days. Consequently famine was imminent, and daily prayers for rain were offered, not only in the churches, but in all the temples, and still there was no sign of its coming, though every day as we looked at the grey, almost English sky, with soft fleecy clouds, some deluded being would say, "Why! I do believe it is going to rain!" Once or twice half a dozen drops did manage to fall, as though some angel had shaken a dewy wing above the parched city, and then the temples began to beat tomtoms and to rejoice aloud, but they soon found out their mistake, and renewed their prayers for the blessing so long withheld. Even then famine-stricken wretches were coming in from the country seeking food; and in truth it is difficult to imagine how life could be sustained on less than the regular allowance of these poor creatures—a little rice and pulse, nothing more.

For one of the many peculiarities of this strange Hindoo race is that they are practically vegetarians, so that animal food scarcely counts at all in the feeding of this great nation, whose unswerving obedience to rigid ecclesiastical law, would compel them to starve in presence of countless herds of sheep and oxen, even supposing that these could survive the drought. The highest feast of these, our brown brethren, is more meagre than a European fast, for since fowls are deemed unclean, eggs are of course prohibited, and although caste rules allow about 80 per cent. of the Hindoos to eat fish when they can get it, both the poverty of the consumer, and the scarcity of the supply, tend to make even this item less important than we might suppose. In fact, the very serious decrease of the fish supply in recent years furnishes a remarkable and distressing illustration of the manner in which the increase of the people acts on the commissariat generally.

The increased demand has caused the fisher castes to work harder and with finer nets. So close is the mesh that scarcely a stickleback could escape. Traps, nets, baskets—every sort of contrivance for fish capture has been worked to the uttermost; all means, fair and foul, even to draining off the water from ponds and streams. No close time is observed. The young fry are captured and sold by the thousand. Even the spawn is collected for food! No wonder that in some districts the waters are already utterly exhausted, and the fisher caste have had to take to agriculture. Now the frogs are eagerly collected, and classed as fish!

But in the present instance, the question was much more serious than the lack of what, to the Hindoo, is merely a luxury. Now the danger lay in the probable failure of all fruits of the earth, and the near approach of an appalling famine.

In addition to the compulsory hunger already being endured by multitudes of Hindoos, the Mohammedans were fulfilling a religious obligation in keeping their rigid fast of Ramazan, and were consequently growing daily leaner and more lean.

At length the fast was over, and the festival of the Buckra Eed followed, when goats are killed and eaten sacramentally in remembrance of the sacrifice of Ishmael on Mount Ararat by his father Abraham, which was duly averted by a Heaven-sent goat. Then the whole Mohammedan male population arrayed itself in fair linen, with gorgeously embroidered waist-scarfs and turbans and went forth to worship in the mosques (or musjids as they are called in India), and thence came to visit some grand old tombs in the Kooshroo Bagh, where we were sketching: so we surveyed them at our leisure. Bagh means garden, and here four tombs, each the size of a great church, mark the resting-place of the rajah of the glad face, and his wife, brother, and friend. The tombs are stately buildings, crowned with a great dome. They are still shadowed by some very fine old tamarind trees, though the finest specimens of these trees, unequalled for size and beauty, were cut down a very few years ago, by order of some tasteless and senseless magistrate. There were formerly beautiful avenues of these trees all round the towns, but these likewise have disappeared before the insatiable thirst for "improvements," and sorely their want is now felt along those broad dusty roads.

It is unfortunately not very often that the "improvements" take the form of planting with a view to creating shady boulevards, but even in this beneficent act a European is liable to find that he has unintentionally run against some native superstition, as was the case with a magistrate who thought he would confer a great benefit on the town by planting pipal trees (*Ficus religiosa*) in the market-place. To his astonishment the buniahs (tradesmen) came to tell him frankly that, as these trees are so sacred that no Hindoo dares utter a false word or do an unjust act beneath their shadow, their presence in the market-place would make it quite impossible to carry on business! So these beautifully picturesque trees are generally found apart from the business quarter, near to wells or temples, where their truth-compelling presence is less embarrassing. If no temple is near, a rude stone god placed beneath the sacred tree reminds all men of its sanctity.

Outside the Kooshroo Gardens is a large caravanserai, formerly a great halting-place for caravans, and crowded with camels, elephants, and bullocks; but the omnivorous railway has absorbed so much of the traffic that the travellers who now rest here are comparatively few. But there is still a picturesque bazaar beneath the trees, with great gates on either side, and a deep, cool well, where the women come to draw water and rest a while beneath the great pipal tree.

The principal gateway here is thickly studded with horse-shoes of every size and make. There are hundreds of them nailed all over the great gates, doubtless the offerings of many a wayfarer who has long since finished his earthly pilgrimage. We could not find out what was the exact idea connected with this custom—probably much the same notion of luck as we attach to finding a horse-shoe (especially one with the old nails still in their place!). We afterwards noticed that the sacred gates of Somnath, preserved in the fort at Agra, are similarly adorned. It reminded us of that curious old manorial right still kept up at Oakham in Rutlandshire, where every peer of the realm is bound, the first time he enters the town, to present a horse-shoe to be nailed on the old portal, which is well-nigh covered with these lordly tributes. It is said that in case any contumacious peer should refuse to pay this tax, the authorities have a right to stop his carriage and levy their black mail by unshoeing one of the horses. To avert so serious an annoyance the tribute-shoe is generally ready, some being of enormous size, and inscribed with the name of the donor. Whether these Eastern horse-shoes were taxes or offerings I cannot tell; but it certainly is very curious to observe how widespread is the superstitious reverence attached to this particular form.

It has been suggested, and apparently with some reason, that in ancient pagan times it may have been a recognised symbol in serpent-worship, and hence may have arisen its common use as a charm against all manner of evil. The resemblance is obvious, more especially to that species of harmless snake which, like our British blindworm, is rounded at both ends, so that head and tail are apparently just alike. The creature moves backwards or forwards at pleasure; hence the old belief that it actually had two heads and was indestructible, as even when cut into two parts it was supposed that the divided heads would seek one another, and re-unite. It stands to reason that in a snake-worshipping community, such a creature would be held in high reverence.

Even in Scotland various ancient snake-like bracelets and ornaments have been found which seem to favour this theory; and at a very early period both snakes and horse-shoes seem to have been engraven as symbols on sacred stones. We hear of the latter having been sculptured, not only on the threshold of old London houses, but even on that of ancient churches in various parts of Britain. And in the present day we all know the idea of luck connected with finding one, and how constantly they are nailed up on houses, stables, and ships, as a charm against witchcraft. In Scotland, and all parts of England and Wales, and especially in Cornwall (where not only on vans and omnibuses, but sometimes even on the grim gates of the old gaols), we may find this curious trace of ancient superstition. Whatever may have been its origin, it certainly is remarkable that it should survive both in Britain and in Hindoostan.

CHAPTER IV.

HINDOO PILGRIMS AND LIVING WATERS.

Water-supply—Three Holy Rivers—Death on the Ganges—Brahmans—The Holy Fair—Yogis — Barbers — Jewels — Suicides — Cholera Centres—Pilgrimages of brown men and white.

ONE of the first points which attracts the notice of a traveller in Hindoostan (naturally on the alert to mark peculiarities of social life) is the picturesque Oriental simplicity of the water-supply. There is no laying of pipes or taps, or even pumps. In some of the large towns a small rivulet of pure sparkling water is brought to the very doors of the people, by an open channel carried along the main street. This, however, is exceptional. As a general rule the people are dependent on their wells, and around these at all hours of the day, but more especially at the outgoings of morning and evening, they assemble in groups most fascinating to the artistic eye. The more crowded the city, the more abundant are the wells, yielding an unfailing supply to the thirsty throng who come to fill their great red earthenware jars, or brightly polished brazen lotas.

Many of the finest wells are presented to the city by some wealthy citizen for the use of the wayfarer and the poor, as an act of merit—a profitable investment in the treasury of a future life. Others, with the same end in view, erect temples, to which are attached tanks for ceremonial ablutions: for every Hindoo, man, woman and child, must worship before he dares break his morning fast, and he may not pray till he has washed himself and his raiment.

I was particularly struck by some very fine wells in Allahabad ("bowlies" is the correct word), to which the people descend by a broad flight of steps into a world of cool shadow, so pleasant after the glaring sunlight that one feels tempted to linger a while with those groups of water-carriers who are filling their buffalo skins from the deep well far below for the use of ordinary mortals. The higher castes, however, would be defiled by water that had been drawn in a leathern bucket, which being an animal substance is unclean; therefore each man and woman brings his or her own brightly polished brazen lota, which, by means of a long cord, is lowered to the well. The whole scene is fresh and clean and pleasant.

The tanks and wells are, however, by no means the chief attractions of Allahabad, "the city of God," to the water-loving Hindoos; for here the clear sacred waters of the deep-blue Jumna unite themselves with the still holier Ganges, or rather flow into one channel; for the pure waters seem loth to mix themselves with the foul yellow uncleanness of that muddy stream, and the two colours flow on side by side, yet never mingling, for some distance—just like the waters of the Arno and the Po. Devout Hindoos believe that a third river, the Sarasvati, here invisibly joins the other two, flowing underground, and this mysterious mingling of three holy waters fills these simple nature-worshippers with reverential awe. They recognise in the triple stream the presence of three goddess mothers, whom they worship as such; hence this sandy shore is accounted very near to Paradise, and death here is well-nigh as desirable as at Benares itself.

So the dying are brought here to receive extreme unction according to *their* creed. Once laid beside the holy stream, they must on no account venture to rally. They have been brought there to die, and die they must. A drink of Ganges water they may have — possibly Ganges mud shortens their dying agonies—but at sunset friends may, if they please, return home, in which case the crocodiles probably dispose of their relations.

Should a man thus left, obstinately survive and be rescued by any European, the poor wretch dares not return to his family, as he is considered to be wiped out of the book of the living. Instances have been known of men thus saved continuing for years in the service of their European deliverer! I am told that the village of Chagdah, about fifty miles from Calcutta, is inhabited solely by such unhappy outcasts as have thus presumed to recover, after having been prematurely consigned to the Ganges! But as a general rule the poor carcase becomes the prey of beasts and foul carrion birds, and as you walk along the shore your foot may stumble on a half-gnawed skull. Of course the relations ought to return in the morning to cremate their dead, but if the body should have disappeared there is no occasion for anxiety, as no animal would drag it away from the river, which sooner or later will rise and claim the bones, and so secure the salvation of the dead, for the touch of Ganges water purifies from all sin. Even in the case of a man so wicked that his spirit had become a malevolent demon, the fact that wild beasts found his body and dropped the gnawed bones, on the brink of the river, whence they were floated away, the magic of the waters availed, and the man was rescued and transferred to Paradise.

Along these sands stalk the tall adjutants (the six-foot-high grey cranes), seeking what fresh feast the stream has provided. Everything comes alike welcome to their voracious maw. Even tortoises have been found, shell and all, in their inside. In short, they are invaluable scavengers, and consume an incredible amount of pestilential filth. This, together with the Hindoo belief that the souls of Brahmans, of dubious holiness, pass into the adjutants, makes it a very evil act to destroy one; so they are rarely molested.

The Levites of Hindoostan show a wise forethought in thus protecting their possible asylum, for it is said that more crimes are committed by the Brahmans than by any other caste, inasmuch as they live in such comfortable certainty of ultimate safety, that they indulge in comparative recklessness as concerns this world's laws—little heeding the penalties which, after all, can but kill the body. It does not however follow that these sinners are priests, for the caste includes a multitude of laymen—there are lay Brahmans and clerical Brahmans—men of very mixed descent [1] or of pure Aryan blood. The latter are, in general, noble-looking men with clear-cut handsome features, possessing moreover, in a strong degree, the proud calm dignity of demeanour that we are wont to attribute to the conscious aristocracy of many generations; and that not of this world only, for so great is the power of the Brahmans that the gods themselves tremble at their wrath!

According to Indian mythology, even the great Indra, having been cursed by a Brahman, was hurled from his own heaven and turned into a cat! This being an article of the Hindoo creed, it follows that the reverence of the people for the members of this favoured caste is altogether boundless; no nation in the world is more thoroughly priest-ridden, and well do the Brahmans know how to keep the ignorant herd in subjection.

One of their grand opportunities occurs at Allahabad (or as the Hindoos would say, at Prayaga, *i.e.* "The Confluence," for Allahabad is the name given by the Mohammedans), in the middle of January, when the receding waters, having left a broad expanse of sand between the stream and the fort, a vast number of Hindoos assemble from every part of the Empire to celebrate the Magh Mela, or January fair—the new year festival of good cheer which marks that the sun has commenced its northward course.

This great festival commenced a few days after our arrival at Allahabad, so we had a full opportunity of studying its characteristics. Day after day, from every quarter, the pilgrim band came straggling in, men, women and children—weary and footsore, and heavy laden, pressing on to bathe in the dirty sacred river, and (simpler than children in holding the faith they have

[1] On the creation of non-Aryan Brahmans, refer to Chapter VII. and Chapter XXII.

been taught) here to seek calm of spirit, pardon, and relief, as the reward of their hard and weary pilgrimage. Some had come on foot from such far-away places that they had been months on the roads. Many who started with them had died by the way from the hardships they had undergone. But these had reached their bourne, and one dip in that sacred flood is a sure passport to heaven. So there was great gladness among these myriads, though many faces still looked sadly haggard, and anxious, and careworn.

Of course on such an occasion as this there are always vast numbers present to whom the scene is merely a merry fair—the Mohammedans, for instance, to whom the whole thing would be a farce but for the excellent opportunity afforded for selling their wares. However, whether for devotion or for gain, the people assemble in thousands, and it is a scene of noisy hubbub, and colour and motion, such as you can see nowhere but at these festivals.

Along the wide expanse of sand at the junction of the rivers a regular encampment is made, branching from one central main street of a mile or more in length, which is the extempore bazaar, where the Mohammedans drive a keen business, while their Hindoo brethren are intent on "making their sou*u*ls," as our friends from the Emerald Isle described it.

Everything you can possibly imagine is there displayed, both of native and belatee (foreign) goods, and there are booths exclusively for the sale of idols. Every hideous and horrible god that ever was devised is there for sale; and to make these more attractive, the loathliest Yogis (the Hindoo equivalent of the Mohammedan Fakir) sit with their disgusting children in groups, painted from head to foot so as to represent these interesting idol families in *tableaux vivants.* These horrible creatures lay sprawling about the sand in every direction, in revolting attitudes, to excite the public to almsgiving; and it stirred up one's indignation to see the real pilgrims so ready, out of their deep poverty, to bestow their poor alms on these foul idlers, generally giving to each one handful of grain from their own meagre store. This grain is thrown into a cloth which lies beside each Yogi, and on which all manner of dirt and dust also falls, so it is afterwards sifted.

The days of self-torture, when these dirty saints "sought to merit heaven by making earth a hell," are gone past. They are now merely mendicant friars, owning no brotherhood, nor superior. Sometimes, indeed, they are credited with the merit which attaches to perpetual fasting, but the irreverent foreigner suspects them of making a tolerable living off the offerings which they collect for the gods. They never work, and in general, instead of clothes, they merely paint bands and streaks of colour round their eyes, their cheeks, mouth, and nose, marking each rib with a line of white paint, and perhaps adding a few mystic signs and characters. Round their neck probably hang strings of heavy black beads, which are the rosaries on which they number certain oft-reiterated sacred texts, or attributes of the gods. Foully dirty, long elf locks matted with sacred cow-dung and ashes fall over the shoulders of these horrible gaunt figures.

Many of them travel from end to end of the Empire, carrying a framework covered with red cloth and adorned with tall peacocks' feathers and bells, to contain jars of sacred water from the Ganges or the still more holy Nerbudda.[1] Of this they sell a few drops at high prices to those who can afford to anoint their idols with an offering so exceedingly precious (though the profane Briton is apt to believe that the precious jars have often been filled at the nearest ditch!

Others wander about the country escorting some specially sacred animal—a monkey or a cow. I was much attracted by a beautifully sleek little dwarf cow, adorned with a head-dress of peacocks' feathers, and decorations of crimson cloth embroidered with the lucky cowrie shells; she wore ornamented anklets of

[1] The sanctity of the Nerbudda has recently become so great that the very sight of it cleanses from all sin. Its purifying power extends to all the waters within thirty miles of its course. To obtain the merit of the Ganges, the sinner must be sprinkled with its life-giving waters. Moreover, it is only the north bank of the Ganges that is specially advantageous for cremation.

brass, and a brass bell hanging from her neck. Another picturesque saint was leading a very handsome white bull, similarly adorned with brass bells, coloured cloth, and gay worsted tassels, but in addition to his crown of peacocks' feathers, a yak's tail was so arranged above the hump on his shoulders, as to form a waving plume; near him stood a wandering minstrel, not over-burdened with drapery, playing on an ektara, *i.e.* a violin formed of a split gourd with only one string, but enriched by a tuft of peacocks' feathers.

By the way, Allahabad owns a genuine Hindoo edition of St. Simeon Stylites—namely a Yogi who for upwards of half a century, has sat on a raised stone-pedestal, regardless of sun, wind, or rain, and receiving devout homage from the people who look upon him as exceedingly holy. In one point he is certainly superior to St. Simeon, in that he goes daily to the Ganges to bathe.

To turn to the real pilgrims, to whom this sacred bath is a matter of such intense earnestness. None may venture into the river till he has committed himself to the care of some of the innumerable pragwallahs or priests, whose three-cornered flags flutter all along the shore. One of these men kindly receives his offerings, and escorts him to the river bank. But first he must be completely shaven from head to foot, leaving only one celestial tuft at the back of the head. He has abstained from visiting his barber for some time previously, so the sand is literally strewn with fine silky black hair, of which, at the close of the day, we saw piles five or six feet in height!

This ought to be cast into the Ganges, but in these modern days when all things are utilised, we observed men going about with sacks, collecting raw materials for chignons and frisettes, for foreign women. Hindoo women are supposed to be superior to the use of such abominations. To wear false hair is deemed irreligious and defiling, therefore a woman of proper principles would sooner be bald than wear such a substitute for her magnificent raven locks. Mohammedan women however have no such scruples, and we were told by a lady whose own black hair had fallen freely during the hot weather, that her ayah told her afterwards that she had made for herself a beautiful plait of the hair she had daily saved!

A Hindoo woman glories in her glossy tresses, and being shorn of these is one of the bitter trials of widowhood. Only on such a great occasion as this sacred bathing does a woman ever voluntarily sacrifice one hair. Here at the junction of the holy rivers it is deemed the honourable privilege of a good wife, with her husband's sanction, to offer the tips of her long hair, which are most solemnly cut off by the priests with golden scissors, while reciting prayers and verses from the sacred books. The hair thus sacrificed is laid on a metal dish, with a gift of coin from the husband. The priest takes the coin, and the holy rivers receive the hair, the husband proving his consent by pouring water into the hand of the priest—a ceremony which might remind a Ross-shire Scot of the curious custom of thumb-licking, which in some districts is still the approved method of sealing a bargain![1]

As regards the men, this clean shave, followed by a plunge into the sacred living waters, is a most effectual means of obtaining remission of the direst sin. How vile soever they may have been, they emerge from this blessed bath as new regenerate creatures.

Men, women, and children all bathe together with the utmost solemnity, at the same time washing their clothes, so that they may come forth altogether pure; and very clean and fresh they certainly appear, in spite of the filthy condition to which they have reduced the water. It certainly is curious to see the Hindoo women thus composedly bathing in mixed company, clad only in a single fold of the very finest wet muslin, whereas, if you meet them on land, they will at once turn their backs and drag their cloth quite over their head. Certainly in so doing they display a great deal more than their ankles, but that is quite a trifle so long as the face is hidden!

Even among these earnest worshippers of the great goddess Gunga (the Ganges) evildoers find their gain, and a row of native police have to stand in the water all day watching for thieves, who

[1] See *In the Hebrides*, C. F. Gordon Cumming. Chatto & Windus.

with a long wire hook contrive to jerk off the heavy gold and silver bangles from the women's ankles, thus reaping a rich harvest and generally escaping in the crowd. These ankle-rings are fetters of exceeding weight, often richly chased and made of metal so pure as to bend in the hand. In form they are like a Celtic brooch, the ends not meeting. Each toe is adorned with rings, each finger also; sometimes the thumb is adorned with a small circular looking-glass. Heavy bracelets or bangles are worn on the wrist and below the shoulder; sometimes the whole arm is covered. Round the neck hang chains of gold and silver, and strings of gay beads or coral. The ears are adorned with rings innumerable, the whole rim being pierced with many holes. Married women have an immense nose-ring hanging from one nostril. It is very light, but generally three or four inches in diameter, sometimes nearly six! Often a flat gem, such as a star of turquoises, is let into the side of the nose like a patch.

You perceive that Hindoo women when got up for a festival are very magnificent indeed. But even in their own homes they rarely put off their ornaments, but pursue their household work glistening with jewels. Of course the very poor substitute baser metals. Widows are forbidden to wear any jewels, and are expected to do all the drudgery of the house. In short, though the days of suttee are past, their position is one of sorely unenviable humiliation.

The jewels of the bathers are not the sole temptation offered to thieves. Some of the wealthy rajahs throw in handful after handful of gold mohrs, just as an offering to the river—a sorry sight to men whose highest wages rarely exceed sixpence a day!

In bygone ages this lavish expenditure was carried to an inconceivable excess in the form of utterly irrational almsgiving. Mighty princes desirous of heaping up stores of merit, did so by bestowing uncounted gold on religious mendicants. A very curious account has been left by the Chinese traveller Hiouen Thsang, who in the year A.D. 629 started from China on a toilsome pilgrimage across Central Asia into India, to visit the cradle of the Buddhist faith.

Throughout Hindoostan he found the Buddhist and Brahman

faiths about equally in favour with the people, and when he reached the great plain of Allahabad he found that Siláditya, the mightiest monarch of Northern India, had invited all "the kings of the empire" and a great multitude of people to encamp at their self-same junction of the Ganges and the Jumna, where he held high festival for seventy-five days, at the end of which he made a general distribution of his property, which it seems he was in the habit of doing once in five years. Causing his treasury to be emptied, and the stores of his palace to be brought, he distributed all his goods to all comers, whether Buddhist or Brahmin, even stripping himself of his royal robes and jewels, all of which were promiscuously disposed of (surely there must have been faithful servants posted among the recipients to save *some* jewels !!). Then following the example of Buddha in his "great Renunciation" the king assumed the garb of a mendicant, and went forth to play at being a beggar.

Under the present rule, one of the serious duties of the police is to endeavour to prevent suicides — so sure an entry into Paradise offering to the sick and sad-hearted a tempting contrast with the ills of their hard lot here. So the lame and the halt, and many another "weary of light and life," try to slip into the river unperceived, having earthenware jars fastened to their bodies. These they fill with water, by means of a small cup, and so sink down into the broad bosom of the calm goddess, where no troubles can ever vex them more. And who in all that busy throng will ever miss them from their place?

Still fresh crowds pour in by every approach, a motley assemblage of many tribes merging all special differences in their one great purpose: all pressing along this grand high road to heaven, rich men and poor men, riding or on foot, but all so strangely picturesque—a kaleidoscope of ever-varying vivid colours. The enduring brilliancy of the native dyes would sorely puzzle our manufacturers: for the Indian style of washing, by thumping clothes on stones in the river and drying them in the burning sun, soon make English goods fade, whereas these native stuffs seem to grow more and more brilliant so long as the rags will hold together. And the invariable good taste of the people rejoices the eye. They seem to know by intuition what shades of vivid green, and lilac, crimson and white, scarlet and purple, blue and gold, will be both gorgeous and harmonious—and they themselves supply the rich browns which give tone to the whole. And on such a gala day as this, even those whose raiment is generally of the scantiest, contrive to be well dressed.

Happily the vagaries of changeful fashion are here unknown, and for at least three thousand years the same graceful simplicity has prevailed, the dress of men and women alike consisting of a bodice and a *sārī*, the latter being a long strip of cloth, probably a dozen yards in length, ingeniously arranged in folds and plaits so as to lie securely round the waist, one end being thrown over the shoulder so as to form a hood if desired. The Mohammedan women reveal very tight trousers which are particularly unbecoming by reason of the exceeding leanness of the wearers. Though tight they are apparently too long, for they invariably lie in wrinkles like a very ill-fitting ungartered stocking. These garments, however, are not always a distinguishing mark of creed, as a good many Hindoo women have adopted them.

All the children, too, are decked out like dolls. The boys, whose ordinary dress consists of a string and small coin, or key, worn round the waist; and the little girls who, *pour tout bien*, are adorned with a necklace and amulet, are to-day in holiday garb. Nor do the men despise ornaments. Through the fine muslin dress of the richer pilgrims you see gold bracelets, armlets, and necklaces. Even the poorer classes wear bracelets and amulets.

We devoted one day to going right into the heart of the holy fair, to get a full benefit of all its strange impressions. We were mounted on tall elephants, and so obtained a good general view of the scene, and moreover had the advantage of being raised a little above the clouds of dust and fine yellow sand which those myriads of pointed slippers were so vigorously stirring up. Nevertheless the incessant movement and the horrible concatenation of many noises soon became positively bewildering.

The deafening clamour for backsheish, the incessant beating of tomtoms and other discordant instruments, the cries of conjurors and jugglers, and of itinerant merchants of all sorts, the angry growling of many camels, the neighing of horses, lowing of bullocks, and occasionally the shrill trumpeting of an elephant mingling with the amazing roar of multitudinous human voices, all combining to produce one general hubbub, was overpowering, and at last we left the sands with a sense of thankful relief.

The one sound that lingered the longest on our wearied ears was the incessant howl for backsheish which rang on every side—those alms which the priestly crowd claim so proudly and so persistently as their right; while the throng of miserable, all but naked beggars, intensify their appeal to our sympathies, and explain their ravenous hunger in language not to be mistaken, by patting their unhappy stomach—a member to which an unvarying vegetable diet lends a most undue protuberance, more especially in contrast with the emaciation of the limbs. Even the tiny children are one and all distinguished by the same exaggeration of the centre of gravity, and can only be described as "pot bellied" to a most alarming degree.

In the midst of that noisy throng we saw one Christian teacher with a little knot of listeners, who, however, seemed merely to pause for a moment and pass on, little heeding his message. Close by was a rival Hindoo teacher, with *his* books. An American missionary had accompanied us to the shore, but we soon lost sight of him in the crowd—a man of countenance so winsome, as might well recommend his teaching, and who has laboured in this place for many years, gathering together a small but increasing congregation of native Christians. Strange, is it not, that this should be the state of things 1800 years after the Light has come to lighten the whole earth? Out of the vast multitude of eager worshippers who thronged the sands on this day we had good reason to believe that the Christians barely numbered half a dozen, and they were Europeans, as of course no native Christian would be present at such a scene. On the following Sunday the Padré gave us a very appropriate sermon on Naaman's bathing.

The establishment of this vast pilgrim camp outside the city walls was due to a recent and most wise sanatory regulation. Formerly the annual influx of pilgrims to any favourite holy place was the sure and certain signal for the outbreak of some form of horrible pestilence, bred of filth and overcrowded dwellings. Every wretched den that could possibly be converted into a lodging-house was crammed to suffocation, so that forty or fifty human beings were stowed away in houses smaller than the average labourers' cottages in England, and this, in an Indian midsummer heat. Thus year by year the advent of the pilgrims was looked upon as the inevitable harbinger of death and misery—a danger which is now vastly decreased by the very simple expedient of stationing police upon every road leading to the city, with orders to forbid all pilgrim bands to approach, and to point out to them the direction of the great camp on the dry sands, all trace of which will be, ere long, swept away by the cleansing flood.[1]

If only the same simple expedient could be adopted at all other great centres of pilgrimage, much might be done to avert the awful visitations of cholera—that fearful scourge which is said to be generated exclusively in Hindoostan, thence over-spreading the whole earth. It is positively stated by those most competent to treat of such matters that in every instance where the fell disease has slain its thousands in Europe, Asia, or America, its progress has been distinctly traced backward to a starting point in India, where it invariably appears first among the wretched half-starved pilgrims. Their miserable condition is therefore a matter which European selfishness cannot afford to look upon with indifference. An able writer on this subject has pointed out how at any moment "these overcrowded dens may become the centre from which the disease radiates to the great manufacturing towns of England and France. The squalid pilgrim army of Jugannáth,

[1] I am told that this year, A.D. 1884, has completed some period in Brahminical calculations, and that henceforth this great January holy fair will lose its virtue, and so be discontinued. It is also said that the Ganges itself will cease to be sacred in 1895, a prophecy which seems like foretelling that the sun will stand still.

with its rags, and hair, and skin freighted with vermin and impregnated with infection, may any year slay thousands of the most talented and beautiful of our age, in Vienna, London, or Washington." [1]

The writer refers especially to the great car festival of Jugannáth held at Puri, a sea-coast town a little to the south-west of Calcutta—a festival which in numerical importance is only exceeded by the monster fair at Hurdwar. The number of pilgrims who flock to Puri varies, of course, from year to year, and is estimated at from fifty to three hundred thousand. The chief festival of the year occurs at midsummer, when the journey of perhaps a thousand, or even fifteen hundred, miles, mostly performed on foot, is rendered more oppressive by the intolerable heat, in spite of which the weary pilgrim band, chiefly consisting of fragile-looking women, must push on, never falling short of their full day's march lest they should reach the hallowed spot too late, and fail to be present at the various ceremonies which are to secure their salvation. We should notice, by the way, that this thirst for pilgrimage and the persevering zeal which carries the wayfarers through all hardships of the journey are diligently fanned by priestly emissaries, who go forth into every corner of the land preaching the necessity of thus purchasing salvation, and of carrying suitable offerings to the gods, or rather to the cruel harpies who guard the shrines.

Ere the weary foot-sore creatures reach their desired haven, scarce able to crawl along on bleeding feet, the season of the rains arrives. Perhaps for a few days longer the sun may shine, and the wayfarers, refreshed by a bathe in some sacred tank, don the finery that was wrapped up in their dirty little bundles, and come forth like radiant butterflies to flutter in and out of every temple and drink of the elixir of holiness—a draught, however, which is by no means "without money and without price," for at every turn they are taxed by the wolfish priests, and compelled to give alms far beyond their ability.

[1] *Orissa*, by Dr. W. W. Hunter.

By the time they are shorn of every available coin, and have scarcely retained the sum necessary to purchase their daily meal of rice on their homeward journey, the rains set in in good earnest. Such of the multitude as have secured a right to lie down anywhere under cover are deemed fortunate, even though they be packed close as herrings in a barrel. Vast numbers have no option but to spend days and nights without shelter of any sort, exposed to the pitiless rain which pours down in sheets on the miserable multitude, who have no option but to lie still, helpless and hopeless —soaked to the skin, without the possibility of a change of raiment, and moreover half-starved. Meanwhile the rain is busy stirring up the foul accumulations of filth from every corner, and overflowing such substitutes for drainage as may exist, till the whole town becomes altogether abominable and pestiferous, and the lurking cholera and fever fiends start up on every hand, and hold high revel on a stage so admirably prepared for them. Of course multitudes perish, and their unburnt and unburied bodies are left a prey to foul birds and dogs.

The miserable survivors struggle homeward, while the ceaseless rain still pours down in floods, swelling every river to a raging flood, and making the roads well-nigh impassable. Sometimes they have to wait for days on the river bank ere any boat dares to ferry them across the furious torrent. They hurry on, however, for the demands of the rapacious priests have scarcely left them coin wherewith to support their wretched lives till they can reach their own villages. So, on the strength of one meal of rice they march from thirty to forty miles a day, and of course multitudes drop from sheer exhaustion, and are left to die where they fall, unless, indeed, they have the good luck to be within the boundaries of some British town, where Government servants are ready to carry them to hospital, and tend them with all possible care—a work of mercy which, however, the poor sufferers resist so long as they are capable of even crawling onward. It is rumoured that many of the younger women meet with a fate far more cruel than the death which they accept so calmly—for bands of ruffians haunt the roads whereby the pilgrims return, and watch their opportunity to kidnap such women as from weariness or pain cannot keep pace with the others and so get separated from their families; the helpless creatures thus captured are carried off to recruit Mohammedan zenanas.

Year by year this appalling sacrifice of human life continues (the annual death-rate among the pilgrims attending this one festival being computed at about twelve thousand, while in some years it is as high as fifty thousand) and all this is endured in the service of Vishnu the All-Preserver—most benevolent of the gods—to whom bloodshed is abomination, and whose temple would be defiled by the sacrifice of even a goat. Yet so deeply rooted in the national faith is a belief in the efficacy of these toilsome pilgrimages, that any attempt on the part of Government to prohibit, or even check them, would be considered the most cruel infringement of religious privileges, and would probably lead to a universal mutiny!

It appears that in this matter, as in some others, the superstitions of white men and brown run in a very regular parallel, else why year after year do French and English papers teem with accounts of Christian pilgrimages, no whit more sensible (though certainly more comfortable); and attended not only by the poor and unlettered, but by educated men of high position, including even English nobles? Such are the famous pilgrimages to Paray-le-Monial to commemorate the brain-sick vision of a foolish girl, and the annual average of sixty thousand pilgrims crowding to the shrine of Notre Dame de la Salette to buy water from the holy well which sprang from the Virgin's tears, or hurrying over the mountains of Auvergne to adore her precious belt! What are we to say of forty thousand pilgrims headed by seven bishops and other ecclesiastics of note, assembling to do homage to Notre Dame de Lourdes at the spot where, in 1858, a small peasant child is supposed to have been favoured with a special revelation concerning the immaculate conception of the Blessed Virgin? The Pyrenean rains do their utmost to damp the enthusiasm of these pilgrims, but certainly none have been called upon to prove their sincerity by tests as painful or as long-continued as invariably fall to the lot of their brown brethren. I doubt whether many of these white pilgrims would lay down their lives in this service with the unquestioning faith which inspires these earnest brown men.

CHAPTER V.

CAWNPORE AND LUCKNOW.

The Well—The Story of Cawnpore—Across the Ganges to Oude—Wolf Nurses—Sham Highlanders—Incongruous House Decorations—The Story of Lucknow.

DUST! dust! dust! Well, it really did seem as if Mother Earth had returned to dust prematurely! Dust overhead, dust under foot, on every side dust! Whatever we may have passed that was worthy of observation was all obscured by clouds of choking, blinding dust.

Brown skins and white skins, oriental robes and sombre European broadcloth—all were toned down by the all-pervading dust.

> "Black spirits and white spirits—brown spirits and gray,
> Mingle, mingle, mingle, on their dusty way."

There were crowds of natives pouring in to celebrate some great festival, and every shuffle of their pointed slippers stirred up the sea of dust more and more, till all their gay dresses, their glittering jewels, and brilliant colours, seemed as though flitting and disappearing like figures in some hot, hazy dream.

The roads are all made of kunkur, small nodules of limestone, which (true to her principle of saving unnecessary labour in tropical regions) Dame Nature has provided all over these alluvial plains as ready-made road metal lying very near the surface, merely requiring the top soil to be removed and the kunkur to be excavated. First class material for road-making is thus obtained, and the result is excellent, till, pounded by incessant traffic of heavily-laden bullock-gharries, and exposed to the action of much rain and much sun, the kunkur becomes reduced to fine powder, which fills the air, rising in suffocating clouds on the smallest provocation, forcing their way into every crevice, choking and stifling the luckless traveller, whose ears, nostrils, eyes, and mouth become so many dust-bins, and his clothing and everything in his carriage is overlaid with a thick coating of fine grey limestone.

Wherever the weary eyes turn it is the same thing. The country is brown and bare, every blade of grass burnt up and shrivelled, and the hot parched earth cracked in every direction; long chasms gaping like thirsty jaws, but receiving no comfort from the burning rays, which still pour down so ruthlessly. If this is the state of Cawnpore in mid-winter, what will it be before the blessed summer rains are due?

A comfortably-furnished bungalow having, with true Indian hospitality, been placed at our disposal, we ploughed our way thither from the railway through seas of white dust, literally up to the ankles. After early breakfast we sallied forth and again ploughed our dusty way to the Memorial Gardens, the scene of the awful massacre at the well, when the women and children and "a great company of Christian people" were brutally murdered by the arch-fiend, Nana Sahib, to prevent their rescue by their countrymen.

Here, as everywhere else in the city, every trace that could recall the horrors of 1857 has been utterly swept away, and where those blood-stained houses and the native bazaar then stood, a most beautiful garden has now sprung up. Only round the dread well is the funeral character kept up, and cypress alone planted. Just beyond are two other inclosures, where many soldiers were buried that same year—men who had given their lives willingly to avenge their countrywomen. These sepulchres of sad memory are now, as I said, the centres of a garden of such richness and beauty as to be exceeded by none in England—an expression which speaks volumes, as Indian gardens are generally laid out merely for shade, with scarcely a flower to be seen, the constant marvel being where the nosegays come from !

Into this sacred garden no dogs or natives are admitted, the latter at least, not without a permit; and perhaps it would be well if they might not go at all to see how trivial and flimsy a monument England has erected above her dead, in this land where the very barbers and servants of great men are honoured with tombs that will endure for centuries.

This pretty piece of ornamental work is built of stone so friable that even its delicate real carving is already cruelly chipped, while a considerable portion is merely fastened on with stucco, which of course cannot resist the alternations of intense heat and wet, and so is literally falling to pieces, the carved leaves scaling off wholesale. Several of the large stars round Marochetti's statue were actually lying on the ground, and it is commonly said that twenty years hence there will remain small trace of England's monument.

Moreover, it is unfortunate that the palms held by the angel should be precisely like the broom carried by all the sweepers—a very low caste, whose duty it is to sweep up all unclean things. The native's mind cannot rise above this idea, and (supposing the avenging angel to represent the bearer of the brooms wherewith that blood was swept up) continues to take a very material view of Britain's emblem.

But as to the garden, it is little short of a miracle to see such a triumph of art over nature—to pass from the world of dust outside to those smooth green lawns, with masses of such roses as might excite the envy of a Devonshire rose-gardener. Nor roses only, for all rare and beautiful flowers are here in the same luxuriance—walls of golden bignonia, and of a lilac creeper more exquisite still, the bougainvillia, whose long sprays of delicate lilac leaves festoon each shrub that comes within reach.

The gardener under whose care this Paradise has developed ought surely to look lovingly on all flowers; yet his answer was quaint when (after he had told me how many years he had lived in the Himalayas) I said, "Ah! then you can tell me in what month the rhododendrons blossom," he replied, "No, I cannot, I was a vegetable gardener then!"

Of course the soil of this fair garden is altogether artificial, and its luxuriance is due to an intricate system of irrigation, whereby the lawns can be flooded for hours at a time with water which flows in inexhaustible supply from the great Ganges Canal—a canal which starts from Hurdwar, nearly four hundred miles up country, and rejoins the Ganges at Cawnpore, bringing life and gladness to all the thirsty land.

Just outside the gardens our admiration was arrested by a number of lovely tall birds like cranes, with lavender body and soft pink neck—"sarus" they are called. In the trees above, innumerable monkeys were playing with their babies, and the green parrots chattering as usual.

From the Memorial Gardens we turned to the Christian church, erected on the site of the so-called intrenchments, that lamentable position, which only could have been selected under some influence of temporary insanity, a position exposed on all sides to the attacks, not only of an armed rabble, but of native regiments, thoroughly drilled by English officers, with an unlimited supply of large guns and ammunition, having moreover the advantage of tall houses from which to fire on the intrenchments

Against such a force as this, the weak mud walls so hastily thrown up could afford small protection to the handful of brave defenders, who nevertheless, with their gallant old chief, Sir Hugh Wheeler, and with only six guns, maintained their ground unflinchingly for twenty days. Including women, children, and civilians they numbered about 700 Europeans.

Some wretched single-story barracks alone sheltered these, not only from the burning midsummer sun, but from the fire of the foe, which, igniting the thatched roofs, burnt many houses and their inmates. Moreover there was but one available well within the intrenchments, and that was under fire. A second there was indeed, but it proved a well without water, mocking the sufferers in their hour of need. Into this were cast the bodies of all who died during those dreadful days—a hundred dead bodies, and in that summer heat! Think what it means as an addition to the stifling smoke of artillery!

At last even the one remaining well was dried up; and the only choice left was to die of thirst, or to surrender to the perfidious Rajah of Bithoor (the Nana, the courteous friend of the English, personally known to nearly all, and continually sharing their social pleasures). He was the adopted son of that Peishwa of Poonah, who for notorious misconduct had been deposed by the British from his high estate, but had been, nevertheless, magnificently pensioned. At his death his vast personal property descended to this adopted son; the Government however, while granting him sundry honours, refused to continue the pension.

Here was the secret of the mischief. A thirst for vengeance lay smouldering beneath the external courtesy which made his acquaintance to be so much sought after. The entertainments at his palace were so pleasant. He was so hospitable! so kind and civilised! Moreover he was very wealthy. His popularity was further enhanced by that of his secretary and prime minister, Azimoola Khan, whose striking beauty had caused him to be made much of in London, and who had also visited the Crimea during the Russian war in order to study our military tactics.

The Nana having undertaken to bring fifteen hundred men to our assistance, now swore by the sacred river Gunga that if the English would trust to him he would have boats ready and would warrant them a safe voyage to Allahabad. So the devoted little garrison believed in these perfidious promises, and, having no alternative, gave themselves to the care of this ruthless butcher. They were conducted safely enough to the banks of the Ganges, where at the Suttee Chowra Ghaut lay twenty house-boats—the common boats of the country thatched with straw or reeds.

The men were made to embark first, and not till then discovered that the boats were aground. Then the boatmen set the thatched roofs on fire. Masked guns posted along the bank now poured their volleys; and from within a temple where they lay concealed the Nana's sepoys, headed by Tantia Topee, rushed upon their victims. Then followed that wild scene of horror—flame, blood, drowning, massacre. Sir Hugh Wheeler was first cut down as he stepped from his palanquin. Only two officers escaped, Mowbray Thomson and Delaforce, who, with a couple of privates (all magnificent swimmers), managed to get across the river, and after incredible dangers, finally survived to tell the tale.

THE MASSACRE GHAUT, CAWNPORE.

The women and children were taken back to Cawnpore, where they were locked up with others who had been captured while flying from Futtyghur; in all, 206 European ladies and children were prisoned for a fortnight in two small rooms in the burning, suffocating heat of the Indian summer. Then just when the hour of their deliverance seemed at hand, the murderer's sword was steeped in their life-blood.

When our soldiers reached that house of death, they had to tread ankle-deep in the blood of our murdered women and children. They found locks of long hair torn from fair heads; and hats of little children and leaves of Bibles; and agonised last messages to their countrymen scrawled on the blood-stained walls, which were all scarred and scratched by sword-cuts. Just outside was the gaping well into which dead and dying had been thrown in one ghastly pile, all heaped up together—a sight from which brave, dauntless men, whom neither danger nor death could move, turned away in sickening anguish, to weep the bitterest tears of manhood.

As each detachment of our troops reached Cawnpore, they marched to the scene of horror, to steel their hearts for whatever stern work of vengeance might be before them; yet so marvellous was Havelock's influence with his men, that, although the city was wholly in their power, no blind massacre followed, nor was one British bayonet soiled with the blood of any of the inhabitants. Havelock marched to Bithoor, six miles from Cawnpore, but the Nana had fled, so the troops had to be satisfied with burning that palace at which the English had so often been welcomed to gay pleasure parties.

That ghaut beside the Ganges (known as the Massacre Ghaut, or bathing-place) is the only spot near the city that has remained untouched, and is therefore full of the deepest interest. Down the dry water-worn ravine we seemed to trace every step of that devoted band, the gleam of hope as they neared the river, and beheld the boats floating like arks of deliverance; then the awful scene of fire and blood, and dire confusion and terror; and last of all, the terrible retracing of that same path, the company of terrified widowed mothers and orphans driven back like sheep to the slaughter, struggling up that long hill in the burning heat of a summer sun, to the quarters assigned to them in the native bazaar.

We saw the bungalow whence the Nana watched the scene; we were standing on the bank where his chief men were hanged; though he, alas! escaped. Day after day we returned to this same spot, attracted by the intensity of its interest. We could not help thinking what good cover for the foe those tall crops must have been, reaching far overhead, so that the "budmashes"[1] (of whom we heard so much during the Mutiny) could lie there concealed by hundreds.

But now the scene was one of exceeding peace; and we were thankful to escape from the dust and burning sun of Cawnpore to wander up the banks of the broad calm Ganges, or rest a while upon the broken sandy cliff. All was still and peaceful. Already the shores of the river were one sea of waving greenery; and overhead, tremulous leaves quivered with every breath that floated down the stream. No sound broke the stillness save the voices, not unmusical, of a group of native girls, whose rich colouring, both of raiment and of person, was pleasant to behold; their dark eyes and hair, and warm copper-coloured skin, being all in harmony with the brazen and copper vessels which they were so diligently polishing.

Then, too, the heavy foliage reflected in the river's depths made these pale waters almost suggest the rich deep tones of some of our own woodland pools, though the silvery banks of tall aloes quickly dispelled that illusion. Sometimes we floated calmly down the stream or landed on the sandy shore opposite, where, so soon as the waters subside after the annual inundations, great melon-beds are made, and divers grain is planted, and only protected by tall fences of withered sirkee grass. It is said that otters love to bask on these sandbanks, watching for divers species of well-fattened fish. You sometimes see the native boats likewise fishing, and drawing their nets, which however is objectionable work, as they are very liable to dredge up some decomposed Hindoo!

One morning we were overtaken by a tremendous thunderstorm. The rain came down in earnest, forcing us to take refuge in the

[1] Scoundrels.

old temple where the sepoys had been concealed. As the storm cleared off, the dark cloud that hung over the city was edged with a brilliant rainbow, spanning earth and heaven—a very poetic picture, which we were fain to hail as a type of a hopeful future, in spite of such dark prognostications as sometimes meet our ear from those who look furthest beneath the smooth current of native life.

Certainly, as regards the mass of the people (the village agriculturists), that ruling power which oppresses them least must surely be the best loved, and they have small cause to desire either the return of a Hindoo or a Mogul rule.

Had these fully sympathised with the endeavour to drive us out of India, our position would assuredly have been almost untenable; but everything goes to show that the movement was almost entirely military, and more or less local—generally due to some malignant leader stirring up the soldiers from motives of private revenge, as in the case of the Nana. Such devilish scenes of murder and treachery as stained the name of Cawnpore were happily exceptional.

It is said, too, that multitudes of the stories which chilled the heart of England were utterly without foundation, as for instance those which told of awful mutilation of the living, of which not one single case has ever been proven. Government appointed special persons to go on board every homeward-bound vessel, in order to make provision for all such, but not one was ever found.

While we were at Cawnpore great crowds of pilgrims were assembling to bathe, by reason of an eclipse of the moon. Of course as the Ganges is the great highway to heaven, all native life and popular superstition cling to its shores, and every city along its course is liable to such incursions.

One large portion of the community live entirely on the river, having no other home but their boats. Some there are, whose work entails frequently crossing the river, which they do by lying on an inflated *mussuk* (the buffalo-skin used by water-carriers). Sometimes they prefer large earthenware jars, which are simply turned upside down so as to prevent the air from escaping; and lying across these a native will paddle himself across the widest river. Sometimes the milk-carriers fasten together a number of milk jars, or other marketable produce, and thus making a sort of raft, paddle it across, a man holding on and swimming at either side; thus they will sometimes bring their goods a long way down the stream. A more luxurious method of crossing, where boats are not forthcoming, is to fasten four mussuks to a common charpoy (bedstead), whereon you may sit in state while your men paddle you across.

A short distance below the Massacre Ghaut is a bank formerly crowned by a considerable number of temples. These however proved to be such convenient covers whence the foe could fire on Havelock's bridge of boats, that it was found necessary to blow them up. The priests and yogis pleaded for the mercy which the English Government had always shown to all places of worship; to which Sir Robert Napier replied that if one of them could prove that he had interceded for the life of a single Christian, then *his* temple should be spared. Not one voice replied, so the temples were blown up, and the hideous gods thrown into the river. Now, however, the Government is building a very handsome new ghaut at this spot, for the convenience and safety of bathers.

I do not know whether it is still Havelock's identical bridge, but by a bridge of boats we drove across the Ganges, large boats lying side by side right across the stream, with a broad tramway for carts and carriages, made of solid planks, overstrewn with earth and reeds. Each boat is strongly moored with a heavy anchor, and almost touches its neighbour. One or two of the boats in the centre are movable, and can be slipped out, and the planks lifted, to allow the river traffic to pass up and down. There was a heavy block of bullock carts, with creaking wheels, and drivers shrieking and groaning, also a great flock of goats, and our progress was so much impeded that we had close running to catch the train for Lucknow.

We were now in the kingdom of Oude, well called the garden

of India, and the change seemed almost miraculous, from the dusty plains of the North-west Provinces, to a land rich and fertile, such a land as might well "laugh and sing" because it stands so thick with corn. All the shrubs and trees seemed so fresh and green that the eye loved to rest upon them. None more beautiful than the castor-oil plant, which here grew to at least double the size we had seen on the other side of the river. It is said that its leaves when made very hot act as an excellent blister or plaister (I am not sure which !).

Here and there, under the broad cool shade of some wide-spreading banyan tree, we saw pleasant encampments with brown and white tents: green pigeons, paroquets, and all manner of birds chattering overhead, and dazzling blue jays flashing past. The sunlight gleaming through the large glossy leaves played upon the silvery-grey trunks and touched the busy camp life; sometimes the travellers were just preparing for a start, loading the camels and elephants and bullocks, and all astir.

As we whirled along, the talk turned on strange stories of jungle life in Oude, in those days when the king was reigning in magnificent state, and could collect more elephants to grace a gala-day than we need ever hope to see again.

One of my companions could speak of those days from long personal knowledge, and his life-like reminiscences lent keen interest to our daily expeditions. But there were stranger stories than these, which delighted me—true stories of wolf-nurses, proving the old tradition of Romulus and Remus to have been more probable than we generally suppose. We heard of two undoubted instances in which children, having been carried off by wolves, had been adopted and suckled by the she-wolf. One of these wolf-children was captured by hunters in the jungles of Oude. They had seen this curious animal running with the mother-wolf and several cubs, and tracked them to their den. They succeeded in taking this creature alive, though the wolves tried to rescue it, and followed the hunters for some distance. The child snarled and growled and tried to bite. It could not stand erect. It was exhibited in Lucknow, an English officer having charge of it, but it continued so savage that it had to be kept in an iron cage. It was covered with short hair, and when clothes were made for it, it tore them off with its teeth.

Many people came to see it, amongst others, a woman whose child, aged eighteen months, had been carried off by wolves seven years previously. By certain marks she recognised her lost little one, and gazed in horror on this monster. It lived for a year, eating voraciously, but only of raw flesh, and chewing bones like a dog. It never learnt to speak, but would give a hoarse growl when any one came near it.

The other instance, also a well-authenticated fact, was of a wretched child, taken by hunters at Mozuffernugger, and brought down to Meerut. It was a boy about five years old, running on all fours. Its hands and feet were quite hard, it was very savage, snarling and showing its teeth. It would only eat raw meat, and that only when left alone.

As we neared Lucknow, and caught our first glimpse of the "Indian city's crown of domes," we could not help regretting the magnificence of bygone days—the grandeur of the old kings of Oude, their countless elephants with gorgeous trappings and multitude of retainers. These are "a tale of the past"; and doubtless it is well, for there can be no doubt that those grand palaces were as an Augean stable that sorely needed cleansing.

My companion, who knew it so well in the days of the old king, was positively bewildered by the changes that had passed over it. Temples and palaces had been swept away, whole streets had vanished as though the plough had gone over them, there remained scarcely a trace of the spots where houses and gardens had stood. Only here and there a gatepost remained as a sort of landmark; the old mess was marked only by a taller clump of sirkee grass.

Enough however remains to make it a beautiful city—the mixture of rank vegetation with eastern buildings; the domes and cupolas and gilded spires of many palaces and mosques (or rather musjids), with their tall minarets rising above the mass of rich wood and varied foliage; the courts and gardens, the terraced roofs, temples and fertile country beyond, and the silvery river Goomtee glittering in the sun. One huge tower we saw, which, for lack of more accurate knowledge, we called the Tower of Babel.

When however, you come to a closer inspection, you find that the houses and many-coloured bazaars are poor and mean, and that these modern palaces are mere gingerbread. Their imposing gateways are showy enough, but though each gateway bears the two great fishes which mark a dwelling of the royal family of Oude, their grand façade is only of painted plaster, with stucco sham carving, a style of architecture which is emphatically described as "cutcha," a word most expressive to Indian ears and used to describe every species of rubbishy, unsound thing—in short, everything not permanent. The opposite word "pukka" is in equally common use, to express everything that is good and solid and enduring. Thus to speak of a pukka appointment, building, or road, expresses volumes.

This mean trashy style of modern building is doubly offensive by contrast with the magnificence of the past in this land of marble palaces, where decorations of such perfection are lavished everywhere in wasteful profusion, such noble archways and such massive pillars with richly carved capitals. But the modern Hindoos have no sense of congruities, and will place the utmost rubbish side by side with the most exquisitely refined work. In the courts and gardens of their finest palaces they will show you with great pride some hideous coloured statue of a sepoy, a grenadier, or a Highlander in full dress, alongside of casts from really good statues.

The Highlanders by the way are objects of intense admiration to the natives, who, in truest flattery, occasionally indulge in humble imitation. Thus the Gackwar of Baroda has a real Highland corps, correctly dressed in kilts and coats, brogues, and stockings, wearing feather bonnets and playing on native bagpipes. The garb of Old Gaul is very becoming to the brown faces, and brown knees would also look quite in keeping, but the Gackwar (little dreaming of the walnut juice with which fair-skinned men occasionally enrich the colouring of their too pale knees) here resolves on literal imitation, so pink cotton breeches are added, which cover the knee, and come down to meet the stocking on the calf!

The same incongruities are remarkable in the internal arrangements of a native house, of which the family rooms are furnished only with carpets and cushions, but the show room in which they receive Europeans is generally crammed with heterogeneous foreign articles—perhaps a dozen English clocks of divers pattern, all going; priceless vases and the most trumpery English toys; the cheapest framed prints of French damsels, and of sacred subjects (not cheap to their purchaser, you may be very sure!). Perhaps as a treasure beyond price, an old barrel organ, and some of the commonest statuettes side by side with exquisite jewelled cups.

I am not sure however that a Hindoo gentleman might not be equally astonished to find *our* rooms decorated with the brooches and anklets of the poorest Indian women, betel plates, brass ink-horns, and beautiful metal plates and bowls—nay, even funny little gods and goddesses surrounded by brazen lamps and bells, and sacrificial vessels intended for use in their temples; rosaries also and prayer-wheels, and hubble-bubble vases—no longer used for smoking, but filled with roses!—nay, even bathing-slippers of inlaid wood, and ridiculous Indian playthings.

We were taken to see the house of a wealthy merchant, the whole front of which is one mass of rich stone carving of most intricate design, utterly lacking in repose. The internal arrangements of such a house are interesting. The houses of the upper and middle classes are generally built of brick, and are two or three stories high. The entrance from the street leads into a court, round which on each story run galleries. On the ground floor are the well, the cow and goat stables, and the grain store; also the kitchen, which is well furnished with brightly polished brazen vessels. One room is reserved as the family chapel, for domestic worship. The kitchen, being scrupulously clean, is often the family dining-room. Its perfect purity is a ceremonial necessity, for though every action of life is performed by religious rule, eating is more especially so.

On the upper stories the airy front rooms are devoted to the men of the family, while the dull little rooms at the back, or looking into the courtyard, are the women's quarters, where they live their dreary lives, unenlivened by any interest in the outer world—no books or music, nothing but the care of their nurseries, their kitchen, and the idols.

We found very good quarters at an Anglo-Indian hotel, where however we realised to the full the aggravation of the mode of house-building which secures ventilation by making all rooms open into one another—an arrangement doubly distasteful in such buildings as these, where even the up-stairs bedrooms have windows looking down into the great public room. These are furnished only with venetian blinds, so that at night it is simply impossible for would-be sleepers to shut out either the conversation of the smokers in the central room, or the suffocating clouds which of course float upwards.

It cost us several days of pretty severe sight-seeing to go over most of the points of interest, all more or less connected with tales of the Mutiny. We drove to the dreary Alum Bagh, which Sir Henry Havelock held against such fearful odds, and where his honoured dust now lies. It is merely an inclosed field, with a very plain obelisk and long inscription.

We returned to the city by the Dilkoosha or Heart's Desire, the hunting-seat of the old kings of Oude, now used as officers' quarters. Here it was that Havelock died.

The grandest of the gingerbread palaces is that known as the Kaiser Bagh, which was the king's special abode. Its fame during his lifetime is evil beyond telling, and the court life here was one long scene of unutterable degradation, gilded however with all the magnificence that oriental splendour could devise. The old king is described as a mere crazy imbecile, steeped in vice more vile than a European mind could well realise.

The plunder of this palace at the time of the Mutiny sounded like some dream of the *Arabian Nights*. The marble floors were strewn to the depth of several inches with fragments of mirrors and crystal chandeliers, which had been smashed to obtain the jewelled setting: precious vases of china, alabaster, and priceless jade; jewelled caskets, gold and silver brocades, shawls—all manner of rich and costly treasures, for the most part lying in fragments, having been ruthlessly destroyed by our own troops in the heat of plunder. These courts and halls are now Government offices, and the garden with its shady walks and kiosks,[1] fountains and orange trees, is now open to all comers.

Crystal chandeliers are evidently among the most esteemed of foreign manufactures. We went to see a great Emambara or tomb specially dear to the Mohammedans, namely, that of Hossein Ali, a very holy saint, whose silver shrine is surrounded by a multitude of these, of every size and shape, hanging close together all over the building. Once a year they are illuminated with many thousand candles, and the blaze of light thus produced is almost unbearable. The Koran is then read from a fine pulpit of solid silver. In the court outside were sundry worshippers, some performing their ceremonial ablutions, others standing and prostrating themselves by turns with all possible formality.

Another of our expeditions was to visit a vast Mohammedan tomb, now used as an arsenal, where, among other objects of interest, are the guns of the *Shannon*, with which Sir William Peel's naval squadron did such good service at the Relief of Lucknow. Some of the party had been eye-witnesses of their valour, and spoke of their deeds as almost incredible. The dragging of those heavy ship guns under the burning summer sun, and the subsequent working of them, are among the deeds of our jolly tars that will not quickly be forgotten by the Hindoos. Peel was buried at Cawnpore, where we paid our homage to his brave memory. From the top of that great tomb we had a magnificent view of the city and of the country round for many miles.

We spent a pleasant afternoon at the Wingfield Gardens, which

[1] Summer-houses.

for their rare beauty vie with those at Cawnpore, being literally one blaze of roses.

The morning had been devoted to sketching at the Secundra Bagh, "the Garden of Alexander," a native garden inclosed by high walls, with but one entrance by a very picturesque gateway. This spot was the scene of a desperate fight, a great body of rebels having here taken refuge, and being thus shut into a trap from which there was no escape. Here they were attacked by the 93rd and 53rd under Sir Colin Campbell, and a desperate hand-to-hand conflict ensued, so that the garden was heaped with the slain, and upwards of two thousand of the foe were either captured or killed.

But to us, all the interest of the city centred in the Residency, whose battered ruins still bear the mark of the shot and shell which poured in such fierce tempests on those walls. Now the unsightly ruins are half veiled by heavy masses of the beautiful but treacherous elephant creeper, a plant like a giant convolvulus, which, spreading rapidly, too often overthrows the walls on which it climbs. The orange venusta, too, hangs like a golden curtain from the pillars that once formed the verandah, and in every corner grasses and creepers have niched themselves in the crevices of the warm brickwork.

The spots to which the deepest interest attaches are preserved with all possible care, but the intervening space has been levelled, and is now a rich and beautiful garden.

The entrance is beneath an arched gateway, literally battered by great cannon-balls (this is the Bailie Guard), by which the relief column forced its triumphant way—whence too, at last, the ransomed garrison sallied forth at dead of night, when the hour of their deliverance had come. Close by is Dr. Fayrer's house, where the brave and good Sir Henry Lawrence died, and where, later, the women and children assembled to welcome and bless their deliverers, and grasp the hands of the brave Highlanders who first fought their way within those beleaguered walls.

On the other side is the banqueting hall—the old mess room—whose mirth was silenced then, and the place given up to the sick and wounded. About the centre of the ground stands the house set apart for the ladies; a little farther, that where the women of

THE RESIDENCY, LUCKNOW.

the 32nd were lodged. Then comes the tower where England's flag floated throughout *those five awful months*, from June till

November, during which the little garrison held a post apparently so weak against such overwhelming odds.

Close to the tower is the room where Sir Henry was writing when the shell struck him. A little further lies the cemetery where sleeps his dust, mingling with that of many brave men and women, and many little children besides, who died of want and starvation during that terrible siege. The little church was altogether destroyed; no trace of it remains.

The covered well (whence alone drinking-water could be procured, and to which all went by turns, well knowing the fiery hail that would pour on them ere they could draw the priceless draughts) is now covered with a tangle of flowering creepers, which however do not hide the fatal bullet-marks. To this spot day by day we bent our steps, never weary of tracing out that ground, and trying to picture that heroic defence. It seemed impossible that so small a space should have been so well defended, when the native bazaar came up to the very walls, and every point of vantage was in the hands of the foe.

But Sir Henry's keen foresight had long been preparing the Residency for the chance of such a siege. He had laid in stores of food and ammunition—the latter in such abundance that it never ran short. For the last few weeks, as he scented the coming storm, he employed hundreds of men night and day in throwing up earthworks and such fortifications as could be most rapidly constructed. Then, at the first alarm, he gathered all the Europeans within his walls. These included about 1,600 fighting men, and 450 women and children. Of the fighting men nearly half were native troops, sepoys, who with marvellous fidelity stood firmly by the British throughout these long months of awful trial, resisting the most stirring appeals of the besiegers (their co-religionists and blood-relations), who were actually so close that they could call to their friends by name, imploring them to come out, and not remain to aid the infidel foreigners.

The majority of the native servants and workmen, however, at once decamped, taking with them all the tools on which they could lay hands—a very serious loss to the besieged. Those who know how helplessly Europeans rely on their servants, and how intolerable all exertion becomes during the hot weather, can imagine the position of ladies accustomed to all Indian luxury and comfort, suddenly left to their own resources, obliged to sweep their own rooms, wash clothes, and cook for themselves and their families, and for those working and fighting, besides nursing the sick in the crowded hospital garrison.

Sometimes several families were huddled into one room; those families who could secure an out-house or stable for their exclusive use were fortunate indeed; and this, in the burning heat of an Indian summer. Add to this, the noise of incessant firing of heavy guns close to them, and the consequent dense stifling smoke. The rains too were deluging the land. The officers, drenched to the skin, worked alternately with spade and musket.

Then cholera broke out, and small-pox and fever; food became scant, and the horrors of the siege thickened. On every side the besieged were surrounded by high houses, which sheltered thousands of experienced marksmen, well-trained by the English, and provided with abundant ammunition—a host computed at 50,000; while disease and wounds had reduced the garrison to 500, including sick and wounded!

Very early in the day their loved chief, the noble Lawrence, had gone to his rest. The shell that burst into his room had shattered his thigh. He was carried to Dr. Fayrer's house, as being more sheltered from the artillery of the foe. His leg was amputated, but the wound was fatal. He lingered two days, cheering the officers of his garrison with brave and Christian words, well in keeping with the tenor of his life. The storm and tumult and furious raging of the heathen all round that little sanctuary could not disturb the perfect calm and peace of that death-bed. Many of his officers knelt around him in the open verandah, exposed to a heavy fire of musketry, and together for the last time received the Holy Communion.

Then he bade each a loving farewell, and desired to be buried "without any fuss," in the same grave with any of his men who might die the same day. And so on the 4th of July at evening died a brave soldier, and a good and faithful servant of the Great Master. After sun-down his loved remains were buried beside the little garrison church.

So sharp was the raging of the foe that evening, that at this last hour his officers dared not be present, but rather did his bidding, by standing each at his post. But the soldiers who carried him to his burial raised the sheet which covered the face of their beloved chief, and each stooped down and reverently kissed him on the forehead before they laid him in the earth.

He was succeeded in the command by General Inglis, but his death was kept secret from most of the garrison for several days, in dread of the terrible depression it would cause. His grave is now marked by a plain broad stone, bearing the grand simple words whispered by himself with his last breath:

HERE LIES

HENRY LAWRENCE,

WHO TRIED TO DO HIS DUTY.

MAY THE LORD HAVE MERCY

UPON HIS SOUL.

✠

Born 28th June, 1806. *Died 4th July*, 1857.

—an inscription in striking contrast with sundry other epitaphs, written, not by great men themselves, but by loving survivors, who leave little to the imagination in the fulness of their praise.

One of the chief boons for which posterity will bless his name is the Lawrence Asylum, a great home among the healthy life-giving hills, to which the pale-faced, delicate children of European soldiers, and their orphans, may be sent from the burning plains (and from whatever evil attends the upbringing of little ones in barrack-life), to receive a careful education and wise training.

Tidings of the siege of Lucknow and the death of Lawrence reached Havelock on his return to Cawnpore after burning the palace of the Nana. With his little band of 1,500 men he at once started to their relief. First he made the bridge of boats, in spite of all difficulties, and brought his men across the Ganges. But the foes were legion, and the heat terrific—the country deluged by the rains, the supply of tents scant. Cholera broke out, and fighting was incessant. Eight successive victories reduced his force to 860, a number utterly inadequate to fight their way onward to the relief of Lucknow.

Moreover, tidings reached him that Cawnpore was again threatened on every side. He therefore returned thither and rejoined General Neill and his little garrison; and fought and won another battle against fearful odds, the mass of the foe being our own trained sepoys.

On the 16th September, General Outram arrived with reinforcements, and, though of superior rank, generously waived his privilege and left the command of that glorious column of relief in the hands that had done so nobly—*les braves des braves!*

Then came the toil of re-crossing the Ganges and the terrible march in the rains which fell in torrents. As he drew near Lucknow he found the foe drawn up in strong position at the Alum Bagh. His column was compelled to advance by a narrow road, with soft swampy marsh on either side, and all under fire. It was a splendid struggle, in which he was again victorious.

Another hot fight awaited him ere he could cross the canal bridge. Then followed a fearful march through streets apparently deserted, under a galling fire from the matchlocks of unseen foes; then a still more deadly fight at the Kaiser Bagh, the king's palace, whence a murderous fire poured on the troops an iron deluge of grape, cannister, and round shell.

At length this was silenced, and there followed a momentary respite. Faint and worn out by these terrible hours of deadly incessant fighting under a scorching sun, it was a question whether it would be possible to advance further that night. It was felt, however, to be positively necessary, so Havelock with the 78th Highlanders and Sikhs led the advance of that march through fire and death. Deep trenches had been cut along the road, and every species of obstruction placed in the way. From every window, loophole, and house-top, that "iron hurricane of destruction and death" rained upon them. There seemed no limit to the heavy artillery of the foe.

Still Havelock and his men marched steadfastly on, leaving the streets strewn with their dead and dying, including brave General Neill. In the darkness of night it seemed as if every wall literally streamed fire on the devoted band, till at length, with a British cheer, they reached the Bailie Guard; and the beleaguered garrison (nearly mad with joy from relief after the agonised tension of almost hopeless expectation) crowded round to bless their deliverers, to whom the triumph of that night seemed compensation enough for nearly a hundred days of such a struggle, and against such awful odds, as find few parallels in history.

Meanwhile the wounded and those in charge of them were having an appalling night—hunger and raging thirst, the incessant fire of a maddened foe, and,—more awful still, the agony of beholding the horrible tortures inflicted by the demons on such wounded as they could capture, many of whom were burnt alive as they lay helpless in their doolies. Not till daylight dawned were their comrades able to come up, bringing the heavy artillery, and, having rescued them, all advanced together to the shelter of the Residency.

At length Sir Colin Campbell drew near. He had reached Cawnpore just in time to save it a second time from the foe, and had now to face that terrible slaughter at the Secundra garden—a fight that was compared to the raging of a fiery furnace.

Then, at the Chutter Munzil Palace (which is now the Club), Havelock, Outram and Sir Colin met, while the din of battle raged around. They laid their plans for the exodus of the garrison—laid them wisely and well. In the dead of night—a dark November night—silently and rapidly the beleaguered garrison sallied forth from the Residency, and, passing through lines of pickets carefully posted to guard their pathway, men, women, children, wounded—every living soul, marched out; while the unconscious foe continued to pour their hail of fire, on the deserted building.

The fugitives carried with them what treasures they possessed, as well as the King of Oude's jewels; they reached the Alum Bagh in safety, whence they were sent to Cawnpore and Allahabad.

Worn out with fatigue of mind and body, the brave Havelock had finished his work. Attacked by dysentery—the scourge of India—he was removed to the Dilkoosha, where he died, and was buried close by, in the Alum Bagh.

This is the story which is whispered by every stone in Lucknow! Can you wonder that, early and late, we, who vividly remembered each detail of the story when first it reached us in England, found our way back to the Residency and the Bailie Guard?

THE TAJ MAHAL, AGRA.

CHAPTER VI.

AGRA.

> "A palace lifting to eternal summer
> Its marble halls from out a glossy bower
> Of coolest foliage, musical with birds."

History—An Ideal Tomb of pure White Marble—Oriental Kith-and-Kin Love—A Neglected Burial-ground—Beside the River—A Plea for Cremation—Indian Laundries—Akbar's Harem—His Fort at Agra—Sandal-wood Gates of Somnath—Horse-shoes—Destruction of the Temple of Somnath—Zenana Pavilions—Pearl Mosque—Ruined City of Futteypore Sicri.

WE were speaking some time ago of the relative joys of sight and hearing, and observing the curious fact that nine people out of ten say they would rather be deaf than blind. I think one half hour in Agra would convince them that no wealth of words falling on the most willing ear could ever convey the exceeding delight with which the eye, at one rapid glance, fills the whole mind in presence of any beautiful object whatsoever. And of all the lovely things in creation, whether of nature or of art, none has ever conveyed, to my mind at least, the exquisite delight of that fairylike, snowy, palace-among-tombs, the Taj Mahal; but as to conveying the faintest impression of it in words, or with black-and-white engravings, why the attempt is mere folly.

In olden days, the Eastern poet Sadi complained that his friends could not sympathise with his wearisome praises of his love; he said that could they but once behold her beauty they might understand his song, which must seem but as an idle tale to those whose minds had not been steeped in the same sweet influences.

So it is with the loveliness of this fairy architecture. A cluster of pearly, snow-white domes nestling round one grand central dome, like a gigantic pearl; these crowning a building all of purest, highly-polished marble, so perfect in its proportions, so lovely in its design, so simply restful to the eye, and withal so amazingly intricate in its simplicity, that it is in truth more like some strange dream in marble, than like a work of human hands. Its four sides being precisely similar, it follows that from whatever side you behold it, its perfect form never varies. Far from the city or from any other building, it stands alone in its transcendent loveliness, having its own rich Eastern garden on one side, while the warm red sandstone wall above which it is raised is washed by the blue waters of the sacred Jumna.

This noble deep red wall, which is sixty feet in height, surrounds the whole garden, a space of about forty acres, and the greater part of it, even those unseen parts down by the river, is all beautifully carved with great groups of flowers, as much like nature as any pious Mohammedan dares represent; part, too, is inlaid with white marble. The carved niches of that red stone seem to be all inlaid with some rare pattern of emeralds, which as you approach, prove to be living gems—myriads of green parrots, which dart forth with glittering sunshine on their wings.

Just above the river, as I said, stands a great quadrangle of pure white marble. It is 900 feet square and forty feet high—a meet foundation whereon to rest so fair a structure. On either side stands a small mosque of red sandstone, inlaid with black and white marble, and crowned with three white marble domes. A second marble terrace rises from the first, and from its four corners spring four tall and graceful minarets about 150 feet in height, also of pure marble, and capped with domes. They seem to gleam like pillars of steadfast light against the clear celestial blue. The great central dome rises to a height of 200 feet.

To stand in the fragrant rose garden beneath one of the great dark trees, over which the exquisite bougainvillea has crept, thence hanging in gorgeous masses of lilac leaves, like rich rhododendron blossoms, twining and intertwining all through the

THE TAJ, AGRA.

branches and falling again in heavy festoons—to see that fairest picture glimmering and glistening within so graceful a frame is a new sensation, which of itself is worth all the long miles of travel. It seems such a visible embodiment of that intensely loyal devotion to the dead, which all the dreamy metaphors of Oriental poets and all their flowery phraseology so vainly seek to express. There is a feeling of repose in its calm beauty, as though the builder had striven to symbolise that great peace into which his loved one had entered.

For this pearl among tombs was built by the Mohammedan Emperor Shah Jehan in memory of the love of his youth, his idolised Momtaz, known also as Arzumund Banoo, and as Taj Mahal, "the crown of the seraglio." She was the joy of his life, and had been his wife for fourteen years, and had borne him seven children. She died in 1629, in giving birth to a daughter. Then the great Emperor mourned with an exceeding bitter mourning; for the wife of his youth was dead, and, like another twin spirit so bereft—

"Of slaves he had many, of wives but one.
There is but one God for the soul, he said,
And but one moon for the sun."

So the Sun was inconsolable; but at length he bethought him to honour her memory by such a tomb as should fill the world with wonder. So he called together the skilful workers of all nations, and Italian architects lent their utmost refinement to work out the dreams of Oriental imagination.

Consequently the most exquisitely refined work is here lavished with unsparing profusion, the walls both within and without being enriched with inscriptions in Arabic, engraved and inlaid in marble, and with the loveliest decorative designs of floral arabesques. To Agra, as to the Temple of Solomon, were brought together all manner of precious stones, "onyx stones and stones to be set; glistering stones and of divers colours, and all manner of precious stones, and marble stones in abundance." The "marble stones" were brought all the way from Jeypore or Ajmere, but the red sandstone was found in the neighbouring Mewat hills. It is said that twenty thousand men were employed for upwards of seventeen years on the building, which cost somewhere about three millions, English money, to say nothing of materials supplied gratis by conquered foes and of compulsory work rewarded only by the daily supply of rice.

According to the original design, the Emperor was to have

had a similar tomb on the opposite bank of the river, and the two were to have been united by a bridge of fair white marble spanning the blue waters. Long ere this could be accomplished, however, he fell sick and was nigh unto death. Then his four dutiful sons commenced a violent contest as to the succession. Aurungzebe carried the day, and found means to dispose of his brothers and his own son, whom he imprisoned in the strong fort of Gwalior, a stronghold in which, as in the Bastile or the Tower of London, state prisoners whom it might not be desirable to kill at once, might find a dreary *oubliette*. There were few of the Mogul Emperors who did not assign to some of their relations apartments in this cheerful abode. Verily, kith-and-kin love must, in Eastern meaning, be unlovable indeed! As to his father, Aurungzebe was content with imprisoning him for the rest of his life (seven years), in the old fort at Agra (a majestic stronghold built of red sandstone), whence he might continually behold the beautiful tomb of his wife, and grieve over his unfinished work. From this durance vile, his people were never able to rescue him, though he was well loved in his empire. Perhaps in his sad hours of captivity he may have recognised a righteous retribution for the murder of his brother, whereby he himself had ascended the throne.

That, however, was quite in the natural way of Oriental succession, and his father, Jehanghir, the magnificent son of Akbar, "had deliberately *impaled* eight hundred of the race of Timour" who stood between him and the throne. The pleasant process of impaling was lightly to poise a man above a sharp stake, in such fashion that as he wriggled in the contortions of agony he should by slow degrees impale himself. By an exquisite refinement of brutality the unutterable torture of this lingering death was rendered still more protracted by withholding water from the writhing victim, that the cruel stake might work more slowly as it pierced the poor body, alike dried up by the burning fever of internal pain and the scorching rays of the sun that beat upon it. So no pitying passer-by, if such there were among the crowd of idle spectators, might dare to give the unhappy sufferer one cooling drop to allay the anguish of his burning thirst, lest by so doing he should expedite his death, and put an end to the horrors which, by judicious treatment, might be prolonged until the third day.

The amiable fiend who indulged so largely in this pleasant pastime was the husband of that Noor-Mahal, "the light of the harem," the fame of whose beauty gained her the name of Noor-Jehan, "the light of the world." She it was who took such delight in her gold fish that she spent hours daily in feeding them, and clothed them in fillets of gold.

The unfilial conduct of Aurungzebe having prevented Shah Jehan from completing his grand monumental dream, his body was laid beside that of his love in a chamber below the Taj, where, as in all these great tombs, the real sepulchre and the more ornamental sarcophagus stationed above ground, are totally distinct. Above the tomb lights are kept constantly burning, and fresh garlands of roses and marigolds are ever and anon laid thereon, and given to those who visit the Taj. Formerly attendants were for ever chanting verses from the Koran, and the sacred words were re-echoed by the great dome.

Entering the building from beneath an arch which seems to reach to heaven, you pass in by a low portal, and find that the whole interior is lined with a mosaic work more exquisite than even the most refined modern Florentine work, though the Mohammedan prohibition to copy natural forms, or the likeness of anything in heaven or upon earth, has somewhat cramped the artistic hand, and compelled the substitution of conventional arabesques for the graceful lines of nature. Certainly, however, the artist has made his flowers as life-like as he dared.

There is no doubt that many Italians were employed here, and the delicate beauty of their work can never be equalled by the coarser productions of modern Agra, which traffics largely in humble imitations thereof. Both here and in the palace, and also at Delhi, there are unmistakable hints of their nationality, more especially in the frequent recurrence of the exquisite virgin lily. Amongst the birds, too, has been noticed an admirable mosaic of a bullfinch, which is certainly not known in India; and above one of the doors of the palace there is said to be a mosaic copy of Raffaelle's Apollo playing on the violin.

So nearly akin to nature are some of the designs, that there are unmistakable wreaths of white jessamine, graceful tendrils of vine and clematis, red blossoms of the pomegranate, the white champac, the delicate pink oleander—every flower whereby an Eastern poet would seek to symbolise his thought, is there in *all but* life-like beauty, inlaid on slabs of polished white marble, not in the minute mosaic of the Florentines, but in fragments of such size as to leave the beauty of each stone discernible. Each leaf and petal is a separate gem, and sometimes a hundred different stones are required for a single spray of blossoms; and of these there are hundreds all over the interior, each a perfect gem. A lovely effect of dewy lustre is given to the more solid jasper, agate, and bloodstone, by the use of emeralds, aquamarines, and pearls; cat's-eyes, too, and amethysts glitter as the light touches them, while lapis lazuli, cornelian, and many another stone, each find their own place in this jewelled garden.

But the perfection of loveliness is the marble screen, which, in separate slabs, extends all round the marble tombs. These slabs are very large and several inches thick, but they are pierced and carved with the most elaborate open-work patterns, till they simply resemble a piece of exquisite lace, with border of chiselled flowers resembling fleur-de-lis. Just try to realise it—an immense circular screen of lovely lace, which on closer inspection proves to be all solid marble!

There is very beautiful inlaid-work on the outside also. Verses of the Koran in black marble (intricate Arabic characters) are inlaid round each giant archway, and delicate arabesques, also of black marble just pointed with red, carry the eye upward without distracting it. It is wonderfully perfect, in spite of those sudden and violent atmospheric changes which prove so trying to all buildings in this country. It is said, however, that the Mahrattas and other ruthless invaders could not refrain from damaging even this fair shrine to such an extent that when the East India

Company determined to restore it they actually expended a lac of rupees (somewhere about 12,000*l.* !), and now it is preserved by Government. Its huge silver gates were, however, irrevocably lost, the Mahrattas having carried them off and coined them into rupees. There was also an inner gate formed of a single piece of

PART OF THE SCREEN.

agate. Where it is no one knows. It was supposed to have been taken to Bhurtpore and there buried and forgotten, as is commonly enough the fate of valuables in India.

As you stand at the entrance of the tomb, your eye is carried beyond the marble terrace to a long canal, also of white marble, whose waters reflect the deep blue heavens, while innumerable fountains sprinkle the tall dark cypress trees with silvery showers.

The canal extends to the great gateway by which we entered, one of those immense buildings which guard the entrance to all these great Eastern gardens, the poorest and smallest of which would utterly dwarf our boasted gates of old York. This is a magnificent specimen, built of red sandstone and inlaid with white and black marble, having central arches of such a height as to make us feel pigmies indeed. This again is protected by an outer walled court, with great red sandstone gateways on either side.

In that beautiful shady garden, with its wealth of roses and all lovely flowers, we lingered for many hours, drinking deep draughts of delight. But it was not till we returned at night to see the Taj by the light of a full moon that we realised its ethereal, unearthly loveliness, softened and undefined like some fairy dream. In the warm sunlight it seems to cut clear and sharp against the blue, like a glittering iceberg. In the moonlight it is still dazzling, but seems as though newly buried beneath a deep fresh fall of snow, lying lightly on domes and pavement and minarets, and rising above the tall cypresses and dark rich mass of foliage like some strange vision of purity. You can scarcely believe that it is real—you hold your breath lest you should awaken and find that the beautiful picture was but a dream.

After a while we returned into that exquisite interior. Weird-looking figures were burning blue lights, showing every nook and cranny of the great dome. Awed by the scene, we spoke to one another in low, subdued tones; and, struck by the murmurous echoes of that wonderful tomb, we tested them by singing a few lines of "Brief life is here our portion." Straightway it seemed as though a chorus of unearthly voices took up the strain, and whispered the words again and again, and carried them away heavenward on the clouds of blue smoke that rose like incense.

Day after day during our week at Agra the same lodestar drew me back, morning, noon, and night. Other scenes of beauty, in truth, bade the needle sometimes waver, but never could shake its allegiance to that peerless loveliness whose perfection seemed only enhanced by every varying effect of sunlight or moonlight. Unfortunately our quarters were fully three miles distant, at an execrable and ruinous hotel. Had we but known in time, there are rooms to be had, as in a Dak bungalow, in one of the small mosques close to the Taj, where indeed one large room is, with most execrable taste, sometimes used as a ball-room. Imagine our feelings if the New Zealanders were to come and dance their war dances in our mausoleums, or rather our very unromantic cemetery chapels!

Notwithstanding the distance, however, there were few days when I did not reach the object of my devotion in time to see it transformed from its daylight character of a snowy pearl to that of a sapphire; in other words, the cluster of domes and minarets seemed transformed to vivid blue as they stood in bold relief against the clear sunrise, while the river gleamed below like molten gold.

Then the chief delight was to leave the beaten track, and find out all manner of delightful nooks almost unexplored, and for that very reason all the more enjoyable. One of my favourite haunts was a very old and neglected Mohammedan burial-place, shadowed by antediluvian trees, twisted and gnarled, and almost leafless from sheer old age. As a contrast, these quaintly picturesque, though humble, and often half-ruined, tombs of the poor, make a strikingly suggestive foreground to that of the imperial couple.

Another path, wholly untrodden by white feet, is outside the massive wall of red sandstone. Flocks of brilliant green parrots, startled by our approach, darted forth from each carved nook of the old wall like flashes of emerald light. Arrived at the Jumna, a coolie's boat ferried us to the other side, where we sat the live-long day on the yellow sands watching that calm white spirit with its dreamy reflections in the broad, still river, and strove with brush and colour to carry away some remembrance of so fair a scene. Sometimes the gleaming white was carried up into the blue by one soft fleecy cloud—

> "As if an angel in his upward flight
> Had left his mantle floating in mid-air."

I am bound, however, to confess that too often the clear image of the Taj is disturbed by a hideous object, round which foul birds of prey hover, and which probably sticks on the sandbanks till the wretched being whose caste assigns to him all such work from his birth to his grave, comes with a long pole to float it off again on its seaward journey. This is the worst contrast of all between rich and poor burial, for a Hindoo must be poor indeed if he cannot afford to burn his dead. At least he will buy as much wood as he can afford, and make a little pyre; but such is the dire poverty of many, that too often the remains that are committed to their last unrest in the sacred river, are anything but *ashes*.

My attendant in these sketching expeditions had a hunter's eye for all such loathly objects, and invariably called my attention to them, even when the nasal organ did not too quickly betray their approach; nor would the vultures, kites, and adjutants leave us long in ignorance of the feast they had found.

The river was so unusually low that I suppose the seaward journey was one of considerable difficulty. There seemed no limit to the number of little children, "babas," that floated past; at last we almost ceased to notice them. One day a group of mourners came close below the bank where I was sitting; they carried a little bier, on which, swathed in red linen, lay the body of a small brown baby. One man advanced into the stream, and with bitter wails threw the little body from him; and the whole party then followed him into the water to purify themselves and their clothes, after contact with death. Meanwhile foul birds of prey were gathering round the poor wee baby, threatening to make its journey short indeed.

I could not but think of the daisies and green turf of our own churchyards, and the peaceful rest of God's acre. I thought of little Florence Dombey's shudder at the thought of her mother being laid in the cold earth, and of that wise nurse who taught her that it was no cold earth, but the warm comforting earth, where the little brown seeds were laid and left a while, that they might turn to fair and lovely flowers meet for God's own garden.

Certainly, for the sake of old associations, our quiet green country churchyards may well be dear to us. Yet I am not sure that our Indian fellow-subjects are not wiser than we are in this matter. Certainly there is something very grand in the simplicity of an ordinary Hindoo funeral by cremation, which, instead of leaving the mortal body to undergo the slow and loathsome process of decay, resolves it in one little hour into simple gases and clean white ash. And assuredly no race in the world are more deeply imbued with reverence for their own souls and bodies than are these wise men of the East, who, from time immemorial, have adhered to the custom of their Aryan ancestors in thus disposing of the dead.

As regards the soul, we gather from the beautiful poems of the Rig Veda how intense was their conviction that death is but a heavenly birth, and that the righteous dead will hereafter meet in a land of blessedness. Hence the living force of such words as those chaunted round the funeral pyre, when, commending the fleshly limbs to the elements which gave them birth, Agni, the Lord of Fire, is besought, by his flame and brightness, to kindle the unborn part, and convey it to the world of the righteous; to bear and carry the dead, with all his faculties complete, so that "crossing the dark valley, which spreadeth boundless around him, the unborn soul may ascend to heaven; the feet of him who is stained with sin may be washed; that he may go upwards with cleansed feet; and that passing through the gloom, and gazing on every side in wonder, the unborn soul may rise to heaven, borne by the clouds (the water-shedding angels), who shall cool him with their swift motion, and sprinkle him with dew."

Then, when after an interval of a few days, during which the silvery ashes are temporarily buried, they are disinterred by the priest, who scatters them in the air that they may fall on the holy river, and, as he does so, he commends the dead to the four elements: to the earth, of which he was formed, and which sustained him; to fire, the emblem of purity, which has consumed his body, that his spirit may be purified on entering a new state of existence; to air, whereby he breathed; to water, which likewise tended to sustain him, and which at last receives his ashes.

Truly it seems strange to return from a land where this cleanly custom of cremation is *the only recognised legal mode of disposing of the soul's cast-off garment*, FOR nearly TWO HUNDRED MILLIONS OF HER MAJESTY'S SUBJECTS (and where the simplicity, cleanliness, and exceeding cheapness of this method of honourably consigning ashes to ashes must commend itself to every reflecting mind), to find folk in Britain so wholly wedded to earth, that, not content with maintaining their own right to earth-burial, they must needs try to prove illegality, in order to prevent less prejudiced men from so dealing with their dead that they may in truth be able to commit "dust to dust," and thus literally carry into practice these oft-repeated, but now utterly meaningless, words!

The mere suggestion is treated as though the touch of cleansing fire were destructive of all sentiment of reverence for the honoured body. Yet those who so speak are the first to shudder when the Hindoo, who is too poor to cremate his dead, commits him to the river (which so often means to the jackals on the shore), or when the wealthy Parsee deliberately exposes his dead to the ravening carrion birds. And yet, after all, is it any worse to be eaten quickly by a few large animals, than slowly, day after day, perhaps for years, to furnish feasts to hosts of small disgusting worms?[1]

[1] The subject is one of such intensely practical interest, that I will venture to quote two passages from the newspapers of the day. The first is an extract from Sir Lyon Playfair's speech in the House on April 30, 1884:—

"Both religion and science have now come to the belief that the disposal of the dead is a question of sentiment and convenience. Either burial or cremation produces exactly the same end, the resolution of the body, and differs only in regard to the time in which the resolution is effected. *Burial resolves the body into its simple gases and solids*, according to its efficiency, *in from three to twenty years.* BURNING PRODUCES EXACTLY THE SAME GASES

If we must force ourselves to look closely at horrible truths, there is something infinitely more repulsive in the thought of the ghastly details of decay and loathsome corruption, which we all know too well must of necessity follow an ordinary burial under any other condition save that of fire. Neither earth nor water can hinder the horrid process whereby the innocent dead so often endanger the health and safety of the living.

Only ethereal fire (the most sacred symbol in almost every varying faith of the world, as the universally accepted emblem of the

AND SOLIDS IN ONE HOUR. *The earth in its effective state is simply a slow, burning furnace; the crematory is a rapid one.* In the earth the body is slowly burned by the air within the pores of the soil. All the organic part of the body passes into gases, which escape into the air as carbonic acid, water, and ammonia.

"When everything is favourable to burial—*when there is no intervening coffin* to retard the decay, when the soil is sufficient in quantity and porosity—the decay or slow burning goes on as nature intended, innocuously to the living, and in fulfilment of an infinitely wise purpose of the great Creator.

"For these ultimate gases into which the body is resolved constitute the whole aërial food of plants, and are by them constantly moulded into new forms of organic life. And when we make our burials in this simple and complete way there is no violation of any natural law, but we help to fulfil the great cycle of the world, that death and life continually alternate, for death is a source of life, and the dissolution of one generation is necessary for the life of the succeeding one. . . . . This is the ideal burial suggested by the words earth to earth. . . . The actual condition of burial as commonly practised in this country both among rich and poor is too repulsive to quote. . . . . . It shows little respect to the dead, and is a continual menace to the living. It destroys the soil, it fouls the air, it contaminates the water, and is a fertile source of human disease. Are you, then, surprised, that a reaction against the abuses of burial has taken place, and that scientific men have proposed to re-establish burning as one means of remedying these abominable evils? The body is subject to the immutable law of resolution by decay, as the great provision of the Creator to nourish plants required as food by new generations. . . . . What this process of decay is, in even the best of our churchyards, I do not venture to describe. . . . . *Cremation yields to this law instant obedience. The body yields in the furnace the very same gases which it yields from the soil. The time only differs.* IN THE ONE CASE AN HOUR IS SUFFICIENT; IN THE OTHER CASE TWENTY YEARS MAY NOT SUFFICE. *The ultimate processes are not merely similar, they are absolutely identical.* Both fulfil the end—'ashes to ashes, dust to dust'—but in cremation that is a

visible presence of God) can avert all such noxious results; and yet, while for generation after generation no objection was raised against intramural burying-grounds (where thousands of bodies were crowded into a space where there was not room for hundreds, till the horrible ooze and damp of the bulging walls forced the authorities to interfere), the moment that the advantages of cremation are suggested, howls of indignation are raised, and it is asserted that at this point liberty of the subject ceases, and that the law of the land should be brought to bear against such persons as choose thus to dispose of their own dead!

reality; in burial only a postponed hope, which the survivor may never live to see realised."

One more extract shall speak for itself. It is from the Consular Report for 1883, by Mr. Corbett, of Rio de Janeiro, and embodies the investigations of Dr. Freire on the subject of yellow fever. Dr. Freire states:—

"I think it a duty to divulge as soon as possible a circumstance of much importance to the public health.

"Having gone to visit the Turnjuba cemetery, where those dying in the maritime hospital of Santa Isabel are interred, I gathered from a foot below the surface some of the earth from the grave of a person who died about a year ago of yellow fever. On examining a small quantity with the microscope, I found myriads of microbli exactly identical with those found in the excreta of persons sick with yellow fever.

"These observations, which were verified in all their details by my auxiliaries, show that the germs of yellow fever perpetuate themselves in the cemeteries, which are like so many nurseries for the propagation of new generations destined to devastate our city. A guinea-pig, whose blood examination showed that it was in a pure state, was shut up in a confined space in which was placed the earth taken from that grave. In five days the animal was dead, and its blood proved to be literally crammed with cryptoccccus in various stages of evolution." Could science speak more plainly, and is sentiment to get the better of its teachings? We have too great a faith in healthy public opinion ever to doubt its verdict in this matter.

There have also been cases in which an outbreak of the plague has been distinctly traced to the removal of earth in which plague-stricken corpses had been buried 300 years before. So, too, with the burial of diseased cattle. M. Pasteur, the great chemist, has obtained germs of disease as virulent as in the hour of death, from a pit wherein cattle (who, twelve years previously, had died of splenic fever) had been buried. Such germs may be brought to the surface by deep burrowing worms, and are thus the means of spreading contagion again, so that of the advantages of cremation in the case of diseased cattle there can certainly be no doubt.

The most remarkable feature in this opposition is the attempt to show that cremation is an unsuitable method of disposing of a Christian body. Men and women who devoutly believe that the noble army of martyrs has been largely recruited from the stake, and that multitudes of ransomed souls have been wafted to heaven on the smoke of their own burnt-sacrifice, nevertheless deem that it would be irreverent for us deliberately to deal thus with the dead. They dare not suggest that the martyrs will suffer in future because *their* ashes were sprinkled to the four winds, but they think it is by no means a precedent to be followed, as though He to Whom belongs "the fulness of the earth" was not also the true Lord of the Fire!

Nay, rather, if we come to such questions, the distinction is all in favour of fire, for whereas to be of the earth earthy, describes all that belongs only to our lower nature, light and fire are above all, the chosen symbols of the world's Creator. When the devout Aryan commended the spirit of his dead to Agni, the Lord of the Fire, he only followed the instinct apparently natural to mankind, which in all ages has accepted fire as the most meet symbol of the Almighty.

Without referring to ancient faiths, at the present day countless millions of Buddhists, Brahmins, and Parsees feed the holy fire in their temples as diligently as did the Levitical priesthood in obedience to the commandment delivered by God Himself to Moses, "The fire shall be ever burning upon the altar. It shall never go out."[1] In those days God sometimes revealed Himself as "a consuming fire,"[2] or, as on Mount Sinai, as "a devouring fire."[3] But at other times, as on Mount Horeb,[4] He appeared in the likeness of a flame of fire, a living glorious light, which shone around the bush without so much as scathing it.

Thus, during the wanderings in the wilderness, the Lord went by night before the Israelites in a guiding pillar of fire to give them light,[5] and when they had built them a city He promised to be a guardian wall of fire round about it.[6] Under the new

[1] Lev. vi. 18. [2] Num. xvi. 35. [3] Ex. xxiv. 17.
[4] Ex. iii. 2. [5] Ex. xiii. 21. [6] Zech. ii. 5.

dispensation the Holy Spirit revealed Himself to the waiting disciples at Jerusalem in the likeness of tongues of living fire. Therefore, in memory of that Pentecostal revelation of Himself do all branches of the Christian Church—Greek, Roman, Anglican —all, except only the strictly "Protestant," reverence the symbolic lights on the altar.

From first to last our sacred Scriptures continually recall this symbolism of the Most High, as when Elijah calls on the Israelites to choose between serving Baal and Jehovah, he says,[1] "The God that answereth by fire let him be God." Then came the direct answer to his appeal, and the fire of the Lord fell and consumed the burnt sacrifice, and all the people recognised that He alone was God.

Since, then, He Who maketh His angels spirits, also maketh the flaming fire his minister (or servant), why should we shrink from the funeral pyre, which may be to our beloved dead even as the chariot of fire, which of old bore the favoured prophet to the Master's presence? It seems to me that the question of religious sentiment is all in favour of cremation, and undoubtedly there is much to be said in favour of a process which secures incorruption by allowing no time for change. So I think there can be little doubt that ere long common sense will carry the day, and Britain will allow her children the option of reviving the custom of their ancestors—a custom which is said to have been kept up in Ireland long after the introduction of Christianity.

I can understand that many who have only witnessed cremation as practised in India, may shrink from the publicity of the scene, but no such pain can attach to the privacy and perfect simplicity of such a crematory as I have seen in a quiet corner of a beautiful burial-ground in Japan. Here at night the mourners deposit their dead, coffined in a chest of pine-wood, and at sunrise they return to receive the urn wherein are stored the pure white ashes, to which they then give honourable burial, erecting a picturesque monument, and returning from time to time with offerings of fresh flowers and incense. Everything in this place is clean and orderly,

[1] 1 Kings, xviii. 24—38.

and a poor Japanese has the comfort of knowing that there is absolutely no necessity for his funeral expenses exceeding the modest sum of five shillings. Indeed, the most exclusive rich man is only charged about twenty-eight shillings for a solitary first-class funeral. (Those who know how sorely funeral charges weigh on many an afflicted family in Britain will be able to realise the full meaning of this detail.)

As for ourselves, however we may revolt from the business-like mechanical nature of the scientific cremation furnace, it is but a choice of pain, and perhaps ere long we shall feel that it is best that the coffin should be allowed to sink from beneath its pall into a subterranean crematory beneath the chapel, there to be subjected for one little half-hour to the cleansing, consuming flames, and that ere the close of the accustomed religious service the ashes of the dead should take the place of the coffin beneath the funeral-pall, and be thence conveyed to their final resting-place, in family vault or beneath the daisied turf.

To return to the floating babies on their unrestful seaward journey. One other ingredient of annoyance mars the enjoyment of most Indian rivers; these are the *dhobies* or washermen—to my mind the worst evil of the two, for the dead glide by in silence, but there is no escape from the obtrusive noise of the living. Perhaps a dozen men, or more, stand in a row along the water's edge, armed with your linen and that of your neighbours, wherewith they scourge the water or some large stone—literally using your nice embroidered raiment as if it were a cat-o'-nine-tails, and as if their one idea of washing was to try how hard they could strike. And at every blow each man exclaims some pet sentence at the top of his voice, generally some one word of two syllables, and this he reiterates till it seems written on your brain; and when a whole troop of *dhobies* thus shout in chorus, the effect is deafening, and suggests some hideous war-whoop instead of being the peaceful song of these hard-working heroes of soapsuds, who, as a class, are about the best, and certainly the most diligent, servants in India.

Perhaps the most enjoyable of our evenings at the Taj were

those when, climbing those tall, white minarets just at sunset, we seemed to have risen into an atmosphere of purest light, whence, poised in mid-air, we could look down upon the glowing courts and domes and garden, and upon the vast circumference of the plains stretching away on every side, and upon the beautiful Jumna winding towards us from the fair city of Agra.

One other lovely spot we found, almost as rarely visited as the opposite shore. This is a certain flagstaff, from which you look right up the river, having the Taj and its reflections on your left hand, while beyond rises the magnificent old fort, built of massive red sandstone, yet all so exquisitely carved and so adorned with jewelled marble, that you feel Bishop's Heber's description to be still unsurpassable—"a fortress built by giants and finished by jewellers." It is in truth a marvel of strength and beauty, and as you look up at those mighty walls and grand red towers, you feel that the great Emperor, Akbar the Magnificent, might well deem his fortress impregnable, and, like another king of old, have looked in pride on the "great Babylon that he had made."

Among the natives, the city of Agra still bears his name, Akbarabad, the town of Akbar, and they remember his power, and his wisdom and goodness, as that of another Solomon, whom, in truth, he seems to have resembled in most respects. An amusing native account of his seraglio states that by a multitude of marriages with the daughters of neighbouring princes he made powerful alliances, and secured himself against invasion and insurrection. His harem contained five thousand women, each of whom had her separate apartment! They were divided into companies, like regiments, with a woman at the head of each, and one over all acted as generalissimo. Each woman had definite employment assigned to her, and the internal affairs of the zenana were conducted with as much order and regularity as those of any other department of the state. He was equally wise in his regulations for a standing army of 400,000 men, and in whatever affected the general prosperity of his kingdom—a kingdom whose annual revenue was forty million sterling.

Whatever these Mogul emperors took in hand, was done on a truly imperial scale; for instance, to supply the imperial wardrobe, skilled manufacturers were brought from China, Persia, and Europe, and established at Delhi, where also the most cunning craftsmen of all sorts were attached to the palace—makers of gold and silver lace, jewellers, engravers, workers in crystal, swordsmiths, and manufactures of beautiful inlaid weapons of all sorts. Though there was no "Royal Academy" for the encouragement of painting, Akbar had a private staff of artists, whose work he personally inspected every week, awarding premiums to such as excelled.

Akbar being directly descended from Mohammed, had a good right to the reverence of all Mohammedans. However, he seems to have been equally loved by all the creeds, inasmuch as being great and large-minded, yet thoroughly devout in his own faith, he was equally liberal to all other men. In fact he is described as having had a passion for the study of religion, and from north, south, east, and west, he summoned to his court all the learned divines of every faith, offering them all possible inducement to produce the older writings of their respective creeds. To the study of these matters he set apart the evening of every Friday (that is, the Mohammedan sabbath), and strove to gather the gems from every faith, and so to build up a system of truth, much as the members of the Brahm-Somaj are now striving to do.

The really old writings were then, however, still sealed books. The original Vedas of the Brahmins, the early Buddhist canonical books, the writings of Zoroaster, were still kept looked away among the treasures of old Time, as securely as the mammoths in the Siberian and North American ice-cliffs. The discovery of the ivory, and the key to the learning of the past, were both reserved for these later days, when from the Western world, such men as Max Müller have sent to the wise men of Hindoostan the true interpretation of the noble Sanskrit tongue of their own ancestors, with all its long-forgotten lore, and have thrown such new light on those sacred writings, as must inevitably compel them to retrace their steps to the old mono-theistic faith, when the use of images was forbidden, transmigration not invented, and caste of course, did not exist, as the vile native tribes had not been conquered and enslaved by the Aryan race.

So Akbar's study of the creeds was carried on at a heavy disadvantage. Altogether he was a very grand emperor. He died about the year 1600. For four generations his descendants kept up the credit of his name, and (making allowance for Oriental peculiarities) were all a fine race. In 1707 died Aurungzebe, and with him the glory of his dynasty.

Now all the grandeur of that mighty Mogul empire and of the imperial house of Timour is but a name—as wholly a vision of the past as the glory of Babylon or Nineveh. And these mighty forts and palaces of polished marble; these masses of red rock, carved with rich arabesques till they become marvels of art—all these costly and tasteful buildings, are the barracks or offices of white men from beyond the hated "black waters"; men whose paltry, hideous buildings of brick and mortar excited the derision of the people for many a day, till in these later years such things as railways and telegraphs, bridges and canals, suppression of armed robbers, security of life, schools for the million, the establishment of good hospitals, and of courts of justice, where bribery finds no entrance, an upright police, and many kindred advantages, have proved that Britain had gifts to bestow on India—gifts, not of beauty indeed, but of power.[1]

It is said that Akbar was not only an eminent statesman and a brave soldier, but also that he was skilled in darker mysteries

[1] Britain does not appeal to the eye in the matter of architecture (especially of Church architecture) as did these builders of stately tombs. But whereas these sought only their own pomp and glory, she certainly has the honour of having established a government for the good and security of the many. She found a nation of armed men, each compelled to be ready to defend his life with his weapon—a country full of banditti ravaging the land in immense gangs; upwards of a hundred predatory tribes of hill or forest, subsisting by plundering their neighbours; a seaboard and great estuaries of rivers infested by pirates—on all hands there were forays, raids and incendiarism. The land was full of blood; the hill-tribes offered human sacrifices to their gods, those

of magic art; and wondrous stories are told of his supernatural talents.

His majestic fort is nearly a mile and a-half in circumference; its great outer walls are of red sandstone somewhere about eighty feet high, and are guarded by a moat a hundred feet wide. But the frowning exterior, which might well awe besiegers unprovided with modern artillery, gives small clue to the fairy-like loveliness of the imperial palace within. Akbar's judgment-hall is worthy of the builder—the great hall where he gave audience to all who sought redress for any grievance whatsoever. One marvels how so mighty an emperor could find time for all these personal interviews with his people; but his wisdom and unceasing diligence in business have become almost proverbial, and the amount of work he got through seems positively amazing. Certainly he contrived to lengthen his days by stealing many hours from the night; for in sleep, as in food, his habits were abstemious as those of any fakeer, and his ministers had much ado to be always ready at their master's call.

of the plains endured self-inflicted torture; widows were burnt, children murdered.

Now the land is full of peaceful unarmed traders and agriculturists. The turbulent hill-tribes furnish us with loyal soldiers and police. The Thugs (professional stranglers) have ceased to exist. The Dacoits, or gang robbers, though at present giving some trouble in certain districts, are but an insignificant remnant of the powerful banditti who kept the land in terror in the early part of the century. The survivors of the pirates are now good seamen, and the Indian Navy having finished its work in clearing the sea-coast of this pest, is now a memory of the past, as are the various special branches of criminal administration which did all this good work on land.

A hundred years ago, the dead weight of caste slavery was unbroken. Now it is loosened in a thousand ways. Schools and railway carriages have taught men of all castes that they can sit together without contamination.

The very face of the country has changed—pestiferous swamps have been drained and are now fertile lands, with healthy cities. Wide tracts of jungle, the secure refuge of evil beasts, have been reclaimed. The great rivers are now brought under control; canals receive their surplus waters, and instead of causing desolation, supply irrigation. Railroads transport corn to famine-stricken districts. In short, the story of India's progress under British Rule is one of which she has no reason to be ashamed.

His throne still remains beneath its canopy of exquisitely carved white marble, inlaid with groups of flowers in cornelian, jasper, and all precious stones; much the same work as those at the Taj, but more graceful and natural, inasmuch as being a less rigid Mohammedan than his grandson he suffered his artists to adhere strictly to nature. There are also panels of flowers carved in white marble that are life-like in their beauty. Overhead the great hall extends in countless graceful arches.

Akbar's great hall is now used as a British armoury. Among its treasures are two beautifully carved and inlaid gates, twelve feet high, and adorned with shields of polished metal. They are said to be of sandal-wood, and to have once guarded the entrance to a great Hindoo temple at Somnath, but were carried off thence by the Affghan Sultan Mahmoud, who, in the year A.D. 877, ravaged the whole of Guzerat, with the double object of suppressing idolatry and enriching his own coffers with the spoils of the heathen.

The great sandal-wood gates, which were a marvel of elaborate Hindoo carving, were so beautiful and so immensely prized by the people, that Mahmoud caused them to be carried all the way to Ghuznee, where, after his death, they served as portals to his tomb, their presence there bearing constant witness to the supremacy of the Mohammedans, and to the humiliation of the Hindoos. When, eight hundred years later, an avenging British army marched to Ghuznee, it was deemed expedient by Lord Ellenborough to remove these celebrated gates, as a practical evidence to both Hindoos and Mussulmans that the supreme power was now vested in the hands of the English. Therefore they were with immense difficulty transported to Agra by our army, to the extreme disgust of the British officers who had charge of them, but much to the satisfaction of the Hindoos, who naturally triumphed in the discomfiture of their oppressors.

The Gates of Somnath were henceforth doubly historical; their capture holds a prominent place in Lord Ellenborough's celebrated proclamation at the end of the Cabool war; and thousands of Christians, Hindoos, and Moslems have flocked to gaze, nothing doubting, on so rare a specimen of the sandal-wood carving of Guzerat. It was not till a very few years ago that a well-known artist, Mr. Simpson, a canny Scot, and one much given to accurate investigation of all sorts, pointed out the curious fact that all the carving is purely Mohammedan, and that there is no trace of anything Hindoo in the design. Not an indication of any one of the three hundred and thirty millions of Hindoo gods. This led to further examination of the gates, which, on being inspected with a microscope, were proved not to be of sandal-wood, but only of Diodar pine. Hence it is evident that a fraud has at some time been perpetrated by some one, and the supposition is that the original gates were probably destroyed by accidental fire, during their stay at Ghuznee, and that when Mahmoud's tomb was repaired, new gates were made of the wood that could most readily be procured. They are old enough now, however, being battered and damaged, the carving injured, some panels broken, and rudely repaired with scraps of wood and iron. Moreover, as on the great gate we noticed at Allahabad, a number of old horse-shoes are nailed all over these curious portals, suggesting strange affinities between the superstitions of the eastern and western world.

That great temple of Somnath was one specially dear to the Hindoos, who loaded it with offerings. It was therefore an exceedingly tempting prize to the Mohammedan Sultan, whose cupidity could always veil itself beneath a holy zeal for the suppression of idolatry. Descending, therefore, from time to time, like an eagle from his eyrie amid the snows of the Caucasus, he pounced on what treasures he pleased, and carried them off to his mountain fastnesses.

Having thus descended on the province of Guzerat, on the shores of the Indian Ocean, he heard how two thousand villages were set apart for the exclusive support of this temple of Somnath, the judge of the dead, whose golden statue was washed every morning with sacred water brought from the far distant Ganges. The attendants of the temple numbered two thousand

Brahmans, five hundred dancing girls, three hundred musicians, and three hundred barbers. Mahmoud, determined forthwith to suppress an idol so wealthy, laid siege to his domains.

The temple was defended by a strong citadel, standing on a rocky peninsula jutting into the sea, and further strengthened by walls and battlements. These were guarded by men fighting for hearth and faith, who managed to hold their ground, till a large force had rallied to their assistance. Nevertheless Mahmoud carried the day, and entered the citadel and temple in triumph.

He found himself in a great hall supported by fifty-six pillars, and encircled with golden images of the gods, while the colossal statue of Somnath towered over all. To prove his abhorrence of idols, Mahmoud, with his own hand, struck off the nose of this great image, and bade his attendants reduce it to fragments. Then the Brahmins fell on their knees, and with tears and lamentations implored that their idol might be spared, offering for his ransom a sum so vast that the counsellors of the Sultan urged him to agree thereto. He, however, indignantly rejected the idea of becoming a seller of idols, and bade his people demolish it without delay; and well was he rewarded, for in the interior of the image he found a mine of treasure of all sorts, pearls, rubies, and diamonds, of almost incalculable value, and infinitely exceeding the sum offered him by the Brahmans. Thus, laden with booty, he returned to Ghuznee, carrying with him captives innumerable, and the great gates whose descendants have now, as we have seen, travelled yet further to find a resting-place in the British armoury at Agra.

From the Hall of Audience you pass into countless rooms and halls, courts and gardens, where cool fountains fling their spray over the clustering roses, and rare and lovely flowers cover the shady trellises.

Turning aside from the glare of hot sunlight into the deep, cool shadow, you find yourself in the bath-room of the zenana. Its whole walls and roof are encrusted with thousands of tiny convex mirrors, each one of which reflected the light of our torches, so that the whole place seemed to glitter like some wondrous mine of gems. The great marble baths where the nymphs disported themselves were supplied by streams of water which flowed in a multitude of little cascades, rippling over a crystal background, behind which were placed innumerable lamps, thus shedding a soft mellowed light into that pleasant bath-room.

But the palm of fairy architecture is reserved for the Zenana Pavilions—the loveliest buildings, perched like graceful turrets on the great wall of red sandstone overhanging the river, but of whose dreamy beauty no word-painting could give you the faintest shadow of an idea; roofs, pillars, balconies, all of the purest white marble, and all carved with the same marvellously-elaborate detail. Each panel is a study, and different from all its neighbours; each chamber seems as though a screen of rare lace had been drawn round it, and suddenly petrified, or as if some snow king had covered these shrines with fairy frost-work on a giant scale. You cannot realise that it is marble; rather it seems like the purest ivory carving. How insignificant our much-vaunted morsels of marble bas-relief do look after this lavish wealth of labour. Then there are more and more great panels of carved marble flowers, solid, and, to my taste, loveliest of all.

Each pavilion has an outer court. Delicate inlaid pillars support a widely projecting roof of great slabs—white marble, of course—and a similar balcony of rare carving rests on the red sandstone wall, whose base is washed by the blue Jumna. Myriads of green parrots nestle in every niche, or dart through the sunshine; and here you may sit and dream of all lovely things, as the cloud-shadows pass over the beautiful Taj, which lies reflected in the broad reach of the river.

Or, if it please you, you may moralise on the changes and chances of this mortal life, when you remember that he who built that fair monument to his love, was imprisoned in these very rooms by her son, just when he was about to prepare a similar tomb for himself on the opposite shore.

Here, in hopeless captivity, he pined away the seven years of life that still remained to him, during which he built that exquisite *Motee musjid*—" The Pearl Mosque," rightly so named—

ZENANA PAVILION.

since, like the true pearl, which owes its growth within the shell to the pain and suffering of its inmate, this fair gem owed its birth to the sore trials of the unfortunate father of Aurungzebe.

This pearl of architecture is a worthy companion to the Taj. From all parts of the country you descry its five domes of snow-white marble rising above the mighty walls of the fort, and gleaming in the sunlight. Nor are they less beautiful when cutting clear against a deep blue sky, which finds a quiet mirror in the tank of holy water in the court below; while the deep-red sandstone all around completes the fairy tricolour. Round three sides of the court runs an arcade of radiant white pillars; and clustering arches of the same pure marble form the temple itself—perfect in its symmetry, spotless in its purity—verily the pearl of mosques.

It is said that the idea of building this beautiful musjid was suggested by Shah Jehan's lovely daughter Jehanari, as being the best diversion for her father's sad thoughts. She had, by her own request, been permitted to share his captivity. She was a woman of the right sort—brave, benevolent, and of excellent wit. We saw her tomb at Delhi, a white marble sarcophagus, sculptured with flowers, and inlaid with gems; but in the centre, fresh green grass strikes the eye as strangely un-Eastern, and an inscription, written by herself, desires that only grass and flowers may mark the tomb of the perishable pilgrim Jehanari—these being the fittest adornments for the resting-place of a holy spirit.

Besides this beautiful Pearl Mosque there was one more gem-like still, for the exclusive use of the ladies of the zenana, showing a strangely liberal view of the requirements of the soul feminine, but to this we could not gain admittance. It has, I believe, been not only closed, but actually walled up, lest access to the armoury should be thence obtained.

Nor is this the only place walled up; for beneath these sunlit pavilions of beauty are long dark passages and gloomy recesses, which doubtless could tell many a dark tale, "of war and terror, tyranny and tears." Many a bloody crime is said to have been here enacted; many a helpless victim dragged along those narrow tortuous passages, and plunged into those dreary cells, there to await a tyrant's pleasure—perhaps to linger weary years—ere gentle death came to their release.

We groped our way along these dismal ways till we came to a place where some English engineers had pulled down a wall within which they found a chamber overlooking the river; and here lay three skeletons—one of a young man, and two of women, one old, one young, the latter richly dressed, and adorned with jewels. Here they had been left to perish by starvation; and though a deep well lay within the inclosure, there was no means of drawing water thence.

In one of the lower passages was found a horrible pit, above which was fixed a great beam, from which hung several female skeletons. How many more may have dropped into the darkness below, none can tell; but enough remained to prove that the zenana life was not altogether paradise, but that jealousy and hatred, and bitter misery and anguish, sometimes contrived to enter even there.

Nor had the Imperial Seraglio any monopoly of such sad hints. Various similar discoveries have been made in this and other cities. In Agra itself, not many years ago, some workmen who were deepening a drain in a beautiful garden came suddenly on traces of a great palace that had formerly stood there. As they advanced they found themselves in one of those underground rooms, or *tykhanas*, which secure a cool refuge from the heat. Here a double wall puzzled them so much that they broke it open, and found therein five ghastly skeletons, standing upright, clothed in their usual raiment. Three of them were evidently of very high rank—a young man, and on either side of him a young woman, with long dark hair. Their dresses and veils were of costly muslin, spangled with gold. On their wrists and ankles were gold bangles, and round their throats necklaces of pearls and amulets, whose charm had availed those poor ladies little in their hour of need. These jewels were said to be worth a thousand pounds. The other two skeletons were those of old grey-haired women, doubtless attendants, whose lives had thus been forfeited to the indiscretion of their young mistresses.

We devoted one long day to sight-seeing among the tombs

and gardens—tombs of poets and emperors—gardens, not of flowers, being purely native, but of cool, deep shade, where we might sit in marble pavilions overlooking the river, and rest in pleasant idleness.

A seven miles' drive brought us to Secundra, the tomb of the great Akbar, which is grand and massive like his fort—a huge red pile of the same dark-red sandstone. It stands in a great walled garden having four grand gateways, all of the same red stone. The tomb is built in four huge terraces narrowing as they ascend. At the four corners of each terrace is a pavilion with a dome, inlaid with marble and encaustic tiles, green, blue and gold, which seem wholly regardless of all variations of climate.

The upper story of this great mass of building is a court of white marble, in the centre of which lies the marble sarcophagus of the mighty emperor, with the broad blue sky for his canopy. On his tomb are inscribed in Persian characters the ninety-nine attributes of God, which were duly translated to us by a fine old priest. Good old man, he was not willing to deceive us as to our future prospects, so when he came to the title of Defender of the Faithful, he took good care to explain to us that we were beyond the pale!

All round this court are arches and pillars, which serve as an immortal page, inlaid with verses of the Koran, in black marble. In every niche of those long arcades is a window of the usual lace-work carving in marble. It begins to seem quite common. Yet if we could transport but one such window to some English church, how the people would flock to see it, and how the newspapers would laud the skill of the artist. But this is only the work of "those wretched niggers," so most resident Britons scarcely give it a thought—few go out of their daily course to look at anything "native."

Perhaps the place of all others where we were most amazed by the lavish profusion of such perfect work is at Futteypore Sicri, in the Bhurtpore hills. It lies twenty-four miles from Agra, a very beautiful drive.

As we left the city the sky was overcast, and the sultry calm of the morning seemed to threaten a storm. Nevertheless we thought it best to push on, and were rewarded by a clearer noon; only a few heavy drops of rain fell, just to cool the air. But the

RUINS OF FUTTEYPORE SICRI.

effect was infinitely grander than that of any blue sky, for, as we drew near the magnificent mass of red sandstone walls, palaces, and towers, which crown a high crag rising abruptly from the plain, the leaden clouds became positively inky, and the dark masses of foliage stood out in bold shadow, such as Salvator would have loved to paint. Only one ray of vivid sunlight gleamed on the mighty ruins of this stupendous, forsaken, summer palace of the great Akbar—a palace stately as our own Windsor, and incomparably richer in detail, yet deserted in obedience to the caprice of an anchorite, whose sanctity, in truth, had first attracted Akbar to settle on the hill where the holy man had made his cell.

And the way it came about was this. The emperor was great, and wise, and mighty, and all that gold or wisdom could give were his. Only the voices of children were wanting to gladden his home. Sons and daughters were indeed born to him, but all died in infancy. Then he determined that he would make a pilgrimage to the distant shrine of the holiest Mohammedan saint, Moinuddeen of Ajmeer, and that his favourite wife should accompany him. It was a journey of more than three hundred miles, and it was necessary to perform it on foot. Yet must the begum be shielded from the too curious gaze of chance passers-by. So long screens of cloth were stretched on either side of the carpeted road, which was made ready for the imperial pilgrims, in stages of six miles, at each of which they halted for the night, and these spots were thenceforward marked by the building of high towers.

When at length they reached Ajmeer the saint appeared to Akbar in a vision, and bade him retrace his steps to the hill of Sicri, where lived Sheik Salim, a holy fakeer, exceeding old and reverend, who would plead his cause with Allah. To his cell Akbar betook him, and the old man promised that an heir should shortly be given to his prayers. Accordingly the begum took up her abode in a humble dwelling, near to the fakeer's hermitage, and in due time she became the mother of the future Emperor Jehangeer.

The grateful Akbar determined to take up his abode permanently within reach of the counsels of this all-prevailing saint. So here he built his beautiful palace, and all his courtiers, his prime minister, and other great men likewise built themselves houses and palaces. They made gardens and wells, the hill was crowned with a lovely white marble mosque, and its rocky sides were laid out in terraces. In the plain below, a great artificial lake was formed, twenty miles in circumference, and the beautiful new city, which covered a circle of six miles in diameter, was fortified with strong ramparts and battlements.

But, alas! all the fuss and bustle attendant on this busy court life disturbed the devotions of the hermit of Sicri, who at last would bear it no longer, and sending for the emperor informed him that one of them must forthwith depart. Akbar was grieved for the fate of his fair new city, but his duty was clear. The aged saint must be left to pray in peace, so court and courtiers, great and small, departed straightway to the banks of the Jumna, and there built that glorious city of Akbarabad, the modern Agra.

When the churlish fakeer died, he was buried in the centre of a great cloistered quadrangle, and over his dust stands as lovely a tomb as ever eastern taste devised, a tomb of pure white marble, all inlaid with mother-of-pearl, gleaming with iridescent rainbow hues. Rich hangings are there, and holy books, and the whole is inclosed by screens of white marble, latticed and carved like the finest lace. Just beyond rises a cluster of three pure white marble domes, which crown the beautiful mosque.

All this is well preserved; but beyond, you wander on through endless courts, palaces, gateways, columns, tanks, which are left to old Time to deal with as he pleases. You only marvel to see with what gentle hand soft decay has crept on, only here and there leaving her trace. Outside the great gateway, ruin has sped faster, climate and rank vegetation having each done their part to dislodge great stones and loosen domes and pillars.

The Elephant's Gate was so called by reason of two great stone images, life size, which flanked the entrance; while a little further lies the Elephant's Tower, bristling all over with tusks, but whether these are genuine ivory or composition I cannot tell—I imagine the latter, as so rich a store of ivory would scarcely have escaped the hand of the spoiler. The chief gateway bears an Arabic inscription, which reads strangely in such a place—"Jesus has said, the world is but a bridge, over which you must pass, but must not linger to build your dwelling." Doubtless these words of wisdom were imparted to Akbar by his Christian wife Munee Begum, whose tomb is shown near his own at Secundra.

I wonder what she thought of some of his curious amusements, such as those games at *pacheesee*, where he and one of his ministers sat overlooking an open court paved with squares of black and white marble—a giant chess-board. Each player brought sixteen fair slaves to act as living pieces, and move at his bidding; four of these being draped in white, four in blue, four in red, four in yellow. When a player had won the game by manœuvring his four pieces into the centre, the thirty-two maidens became his lawful prize.

There were also labyrinthine passages where, in the intervals of state business, the emperor disported himself in merry games at Luka-Luki, hide-and-seek, with these fair damsels. The most remarkable feature of this riotous sport was the total absence of raiment, which seems to have been considered very amusing indeed.

By the way, although this peculiarly Oriental form of chess-playing has happily not found favour in Britain, it appears that we are probably indebted to an Indian queen for the invention of the very sedate game which is found so soothing by many of the wise and thoughtful men of Europe. Its invention is generally attributed to Wandodaree, the Ranee of Ravana, King of Ceylon, who is said to have reigned two thousand years before the Christian era. It was to beguile her lord, during the tedious siege of his capital by Rama (and although the sole object of that siege was the rescue of Rama's beautiful wife from the hands of Ravana,) that this pearl of wives devised this immortal game as a meet pastime for her warrior lord. Certain it is that for four thousand years chess has been common throughout Hindostan, whence it spread into Persia and Arabia. The Califs of the

East carried it thence into Spain, whence it rapidly spread over western Europe, and so found its way into Europe.

Its ancient Sanskrit name was Chaturanga, or Four Parts, and the game was played by four persons, two against two. The board was divided into sixty-four squares. Among the Persians the name was changed to Shatranj; *Shah* being, as we all know, the Persian for king. The Arabic *Sheik* seems to have been the word imported to Europe by the Moors, whence comes the term *check*, or its German equivalent *schach*. The word Rook is said to be derived from the Sanskrit *roka*, or the Persian *rukh*, meaning a check;[1] while Pawn is simply the word *Peon*, still in common use for certain attendants.

I fear, however, that the begum was not the sole claimant for the honour of this invention. It is said that the game was common among the Egyptians of old, and that records thereof have been found in hieroglyphic; their board consisted of thirty black and white squares; their pieces were twelve in number, made of ivory, glass, and china, carved in the forms of divers animals.

The game appears again among the sculptures in the caves of Beni Hassan, on the Nile, and also on the wall paintings of the palace of Rameses III., where the king is shown seated with a party of ladies, one of whom is his partner in the game, which is played with pieces formed like pegs on a chequered board. This seems to have amused some ancient Egyptian wag, for there is a papyrus in the British Museum wherein the King and Queen are audaciously caricatured, and represented as a lion and a unicorn playing the same game. It has also been found represented on divers tombs, on one of which it is shown to be the engrossing occupation of calm, meditative spirits in another world. Even Isis does not disdain to play it with the departed kings.

Whatever may have been the popular opinion of the imperial pastimes at Futteypore Sicri, there is no doubt that in working hours the people had good cause to bless the name of Akbar the

[1] Sh'ah m'at, or checkmate, means "the king is dead."

Just. We had already seen his great white marble Hall of Justice. Here is one as great and beautiful, built wholly of red sandstone, with clusters of pillars each marvellously carved. One pillar more curious than all stands in the centre of the hall, and on its broad capital was placed the great divan, where the Emperor sat daily, giving audience to all comers, the meanest of his subjects having free access to the Imperial Judge. From the top of this pillar four huge slabs of stone, pointing to the four "airts," typified his readiness to receive all who came to him, from north, south, east, or west. In the hours set apart to more private state business, he retired to a beautiful pavilion, with windows of marble tracery, to exclude light and heat. These walls are exquisitely carved or inlaid with precious stones; and figures of all manner of living creatures, flowers, and fruit, tell how lax a Mohammedan Akbar had become.

You know, the faith of Islam literally accepts the command to make no graven image, nor the likeness of anything in heaven or on earth; it was therefore a sore offence to Mohammedans of the straiter school to see that when Akbar appointed to each of his wives a separate house, he permitted each to decorate her home as she pleased, after the manner of her people. Consequently the house of the Hindoo Begum is one mass of carving in stone and marble, more exquisite than you can imagine, representing every conceivable variety of animal and plant. The flowers and fruit are so life-like that you could almost pluck them; only you perceive with dismay that each figure is mutilated. A head, a foot, a horn is always missing; and as you marvel what ruthless Goth has here left the trace of his barbarous hand, you learn that the son who succeeded to the throne of the great, wise Akbar worked this ravage, and, to prove his zeal for the law, went hammer in hand to deface all the carved imagery which too closely resembled the forms of nature.

The least ornate of all these buildings is the house of the Christian wife; I believe she was a Portuguese. Her taste in decoration was certainly not remarkable. As to the house of the prime minister, it is so covered with exquisite sculpture that from the ceiling to the floor not one inch of plain stone is visible. It is all worked out in the most refined patterns—diaper, and such fine, intricate work as we occasionally see in infinitesimal quantity about the east end of our churches.

And all this beauty is literally wasted on the desert air. Year after year the warm mellow sunlight pours its radiance on all this loveliness, but no human being is there to take delight in it. Wild creatures of all sorts—leopards, sometimes tigers—crouch in the rank jungle on the hill side, or make their lair in the cool, underground chambers. On the neglected terraces flocks of wild peacocks bask undisturbed; birds of plumage far more radiant than those which sweep so proudly over our English lawns; the Indian peacock, like the jay, gleams with a metallic lustre peculiar to itself, and flashes through the air like a living prism. So there these beautiful birds find a congenial home, and are well in keeping with those stately palaces. The inevitable green parrots are there in thousands, and many a strange and beautiful creature besides.

We collected a great bundle of porcupine quills from below Akbar's judgment-seat, and brought them away as suggestive memorials of the mighty emperor.

CHAPTER VII.

WAVES OF FAITH ON THE SEA OF TIME.

The Hindoo Cities of Muttra and Bindrabund—Once Buddhist—The Jains—Worship of Krishna—The Aboriginal Hill Tribes—The Rig Veda—A Sketch of the Successive Faiths which have prevailed in Hindoostan—Aboriginal—Pure Aryan—These together producing Brahmanism—Origin of Caste—The Holy Food—Ancestor Worship—Buddhism—The Stone Edicts of Asoka—Degenerate Brahmanism—Mohammedanism—Now toleration of all—Religious Census.

BEFORE passing on to Delhi, which like Agra, is one of the mighty strongholds of Mohammedanism, you must turn aside to see the twin cities of Muttra and Bindrabund—cities of about 20,000 inhabitants, and lying only six miles apart— both of which are crowded with fine specimens of native architecture, beautiful bathing-ghauts of red sandstone, and innumerable temples, both ancient and modern, of most intricate design, rising everywhere along the banks of the blue Jumna. Most of these are massive piles of red sandstone, but Bindrabund owns one, especially beautiful, of white marble, with noble monolithic pillars and many statues, which are the favourite seats of the monkeys. There is no evidence here of any falling away of Hindoo devotion, judging from the numbers of handsome new temples recently built by wealthy merchants and rajahs of neighbouring states. One of these is said to have cost a sum equal to about £200,000, while on another £500,000 was expended. Moreover the annual offerings made by pilgrims, and the sums expended on religious services at these two temples are said to be enormous. These cities gain interest from the fact that they have been the favourite battlefields of every successive faith that has arisen in this land. At the present moment they are purely Hindoo, or more properly speaking, Brahmanical.

Yet they were once centres of Buddhism, that strange dreamy faith, which (born in this land four hundred years before the Christian era) prevailed in India for twelve hundred years, then passed away into other lands, while every trace of its existence here was so diligently removed by the re-conquering Brahmans that we can now only guess where its great temples and convents once stood; feeling for its dim traces as in Britain we search wonderingly for hints of the old Druidic faith of our fathers.

It is known that at Muttra there were once twenty great Buddhist convents, where three thousand monks lived their strange contemplative lives.[1] There were temples innumerable, containing colossal statues of Buddha, in brass or stone. There

[1] Monasticism seems always to have found large favour with the Buddhists. In 250 B.C. we find the Emperor Asoka supporting 64,000 holy brothers, and six hundred years later, the Chinese pilgrim Hiouen Thsang found in Cashmere five thousand monks, scattered over five hundred monasteries. But when he reached the city of Kanauj, on the Ganges, he there found a hundred flourishing Buddhist monasteries, with ten thousand monks, side by side with two hundred Brahman temples.

At Nalanda, near the sacred city of Gaya, he found an immense monastery, which was practically a university, as it was the school of science, law, medicine, and philosophy, as well as the theological college where ten thousand monks and novices studied and worshipped.

Nalanda was one of the chief schools of the very advanced medical science of ancient Buddhist India; a science whose remarkable development calls forth the wonder and admiration of modern European physicians. Indeed these have adopted many remedies and drugs first discovered by celebrated Indian physicians, whose treatises in Old Sanskrit, were, in the eighth century, translated into Arabic by order of the Caliphs of Bagdad, and thence passed into Europe. Their boldness and dexterous skill in difficult surgical operations, is especially noted, and is attributed by modern surgeons to the facilities for continuous study afforded by the great public hospitals, established in every city by the merciful Buddhist emperors.

With the fall of Buddhism commenced the degeneracy of Indian medical science.

were seven great towers where lamps burnt day and night above the relics of Buddha and other saints—you know Buddha was not a god, only a saintly man, the ideal of what any man may become; and the veneration of his memory, kept up by treasuring his statues, his teeth, and the marks of his footsteps, is intended to be simply commemorative, and by no means savouring of worship, at least, not among the educated.

Such a faith was not one likely long to satisfy the cravings of the human heart, so after a while, the sect of Jains sprang up and seems to have become very powerful in these cities. Their faith seems to have first taken form in the worship of the twenty-four Jins, who are saints or spirits, whence developed a gradual reaction from Buddhism towards the old worship of Brahma. Their creeds seem very nearly akin, only the Jains bring the doctrine of transmigration more prominently forward; consequently their tenderness of animal life is proverbial. So fully are they persuaded that

> "He prayeth best who loveth best
> All things both great and small,"

that they refuse to crush the snake, scorpion, or other venomous creature which has bitten them, nay, more, will even remove vermin of the viler sorts from their raiment with reverent tenderness! In fact they herein rival that holy Christian St. Macaire, of whom it has been recorded that, having one day been guilty of crushing a louse, he condemned himself to seven years of penance, amid the thorns and briars of a dark and dismal forest.

It is said that the Jains even object to lighting a lamp during the rains, when insects abound, lest moths and beetles should thereby be attracted to their death. They found hospitals for mangy pariah dogs, diseased cattle, cats, goats, monkeys, and all manner of beasts and insects, no matter how foul and noxious. Such a one you may see at Bombay, in which presidency the Jain faith is most common.

A good Jain dares not sit down till he has swept the place with a brush, which he carries for this purpose, in order to warn off any tiny creature wherein is the breath of life. He wears a thin cloth over his mouth to prevent insects from flying into danger, he must strain water thrice ere he may drink, not for his own sake, but for that of the possible insects, and he must be careful to leave no liquid uncovered which might tempt them to suicide!

Just imagine the consternation caused among a people who hold the extinction of life to be a crime, when first they beheld the wonders of the microscope, and realised the inevitable consumption of insects and animalcules in their daily food! The first priest who saw one, offered all his fortune to buy it, and on receiving it as a present, he crushed it to atoms to prevent his friends being made as miserable in their perplexity as he himself had become. Then he besought the giver to import no more such instruments of knowledge and torment!

I believe all the Mahrattas are of this persuasion. Yet so far from extending their mercy to their fellow-men, their cruelty has always been such that, whenever they invaded the neighbouring states, it was said that the people would flee into the jungle to the more gentle companionship of tigers and hyænas!

The Jains have left a very distinctive mark in the form of many stupendous rock temples in various parts of India, rivalling if not excelling the florid rock sculptures of the Brahmans.[1] The marvellous rock caves of Ellora represent the successive supremacy of the three great faiths of India. First a group of Buddhist caves excavated about A.D. 800, then a series of Hindoo caves of the ninth and tenth centuries, and finally a group of Jain, dating as late as A.D. 1200.

After the Jains had had their little day, Brahmanism undiluted once more triumphed, and Muttra, from its position on the sacred Jumna came to be esteemed well-nigh as holy as Benares on the Ganges. But whereas the latter is especially sacred to Siva, these twin cities are wholly given over to the worship of Krishna, the

[1] Mr. Fergusson calculates that out of about 1,000 rock temples scattered all over India nine-tenths are Buddhist, while the remainder are partly Jain and partly Brahmanical.

darling of women (the eighth incarnation of Vishnu), to whom the bathing-ghauts and the magnificent red sandstone temples are all sacred. Their polished marble pillars, richly-carved capitals, and intricate sculptures, were doubtless of Buddhist origin, and simply adapted to the rival creed.

When the Brahmans, having regained the ascendency, destroyed the beautiful temples of their predecessors, they used them as quarries to supply materials for their own. Siva has but one temple here, but the fame of Krishna draws vast multitudes of pilgrims, more especially in November, when there is a great fair in honour of his birth. The temples are literally numberless. In olden times they were possessed of vast wealth. One had five golden idols whose eyes were of rubies. Another had a golden image of Krishna which weighed upwards of a thousand pounds, and was adorned with one sapphire which weighed three and a-half pounds. In the same temple there were upwards of a hundred large silver idols.

The majority of these temples were sacked by the Affghans under the Mohammedan Sultan Mahmoud of Ghuznee, who carried off one hundred camel-loads of their precious treasures. His intention had been to demolish all the idolatrous temples, as he had already done at Delhi, and the magnificent city of Kanouje; but he was so dazzled by their exceeding grandeur that he spared them, and their final destruction was reserved for the bigotry of Aurungzebe. He even took with him Hindoo masons who might build him temples as beautiful at Ghuznee, where accordingly, a mosque of red sandstone and marble was built, and adorned with rich ornaments, so that the fame of its beauty earned for it the title of "the Celestial Bride." Mosques and palaces were multiplied, and the Hindoo captives transformed Ghuznee from a mere village into a city noted for its beauty. So magnificent were Mahmoud's spoils from this and many another raid, that he was at a loss how to dispose of his treasures, though his hunting equipage alone was so gorgeous that each of his four hundred greyhounds and bloodhounds had a collar set with precious jewels, and their coats (such as are worn by all domestic animials in India) were edged with gold, pearls, and other gems torn from the throats and arms of his captives.

Amongst the Hindoo temples destroyed by him was one which had been built on the site of a famous Buddhist monastery. On the same site, the Mohammedans afterwards built a grand mosque which, though now disused, still holds its ground. The Affghans were not content with destroying the greater part of both cities, but also carried away the people as prisoners. In this one raid they are said to have taken fifty-three thousand captives; and so drugged the market, that the unhappy slaves were scarcely worth five shillings a head! They also slew cattle in all the temples, which, in the eyes of the Hindoos, was probably the worst evil of all. The town is now once more full of busy life, and is chiefly peopled by Brahmans of the highest caste, whose noble birth, however, does not make their clamour for backsheesh less maddening, especially as their importunity only increases with the supply.

As I before observed, these cities are especially sacred to Krishna, *alias* Vishnu, *alias* Hari, the Sun-god, the second person of the Trimurti, *i.e.* the Hindoo Trinity; Brahma the Supreme being worshipped in the three characters of Brahma the Creator, Vishnu the Preserver, and Siva the Destroyer. One of the finest sculptures in the great rock temple of Elephanta is a cyclopean image of this tri-une god.

Vishnu is essentially an object of personal love and devotion—a personal god who has ever taken the deepest interest in the welfare of mankind, having in two principal incarnations assumed human nature, first as Rama, then as Krishna. Both of these were princely heroes, of the highest earthly birth, but Krishna deigned to spend his infancy and youth among peasants. The nature of Vishnu being both male and female, his feminine half—Lakshmi, the beautiful goddess of good fortune—also became incarnate, as Sita the goddess-bride of Rama, and as Rādha the wife of Krishna.

Vishnu is worshipped under names and forms innumerable, representing his various incarnations. Of these, the principal arc those ten avatars, or births, when he has appeared on earth. 1. as a Fish; 2. as a Tortoise; 3. as a Boar; 4. as a Lion; (in these four characters the upper half of the body is human, though endowed with an extra pair of arms.) 5. as a Dwarf; 6. as Parasurāma, a Brahman who put down the arrogant Kshatriya or military caste; 7. as Rama who belonged to the said caste, being a son of the King of Oude; 8. as Krishna, whose special mission was to destroy the tyrant Kansa, who represented the Incarnation of evil; 9. as Budh; 10. as Kalkee, the Deliverer in human form, seated on a white horse. His ninth appearance as Budh is probably a judicious adaptation by the Brahmans of the wisdom of Gautama Buddha, though his followers have found small mercy at their hands.

As to the tenth avatar, it has not yet been accomplished, so the faithful await the return of Vishnu at the end of the Kali-yug, that is, the end of the present cycle of time wherein the powers of darkness have so entirely gained the ascendant, that all creation is said to be groaning in pain under the burden of iniquity. Vishnu on his reappearance is to sweep away all evil by the destruction of the visible world. He is to descend from heaven carrying a flaming sword, and attended by a comet, and will be mounted on a great white horse which will stamp with its right fore-foot as the sign that the end of the world is at hand.

Meanwhile the worshippers of Vishnu chiefly adore him as Krishna, the joyous and beautiful, who in one of these twin cities was miraculously born as the son of a cowherd; an incarnation which the Vedas date 1,300 years before the story of the manger of Bethlehem, though there are points of similarity which might lead us to think that Krishna's historian had borrowed some hints from Judæa, such as the story of how the life of the baby-god was vainly threatened by the tyrant Kansa, but preserved by his loyal foster-father, the herdsman.

Of course the neighbourhood is full of legends of this wonderful infant. How, at the sound of his flute, stones and trees became animated; how he sang to the milkmaids and wood-nymphs; how he cursed a patch of ground which has remained barren to this day; and how he was wont to stand on a certain hill to heal the people who thronged round him, and made them whole, whether their disease was bodily or mental. He taught the people that he himself was at once their creator, their refuge and their friend; their sacrifice, and the road of the good; their counsellor and their teacher; and that they who knew and trusted in him also knew and trusted in Brahma the Supreme.

But mixed up with words that sound like a foreshadowing of the Messiah's message are grotesque mythological stories, such as the Oriental mind rejoices in. Many a romantic tale is told of Krishna's adventures, more especially of his merry games with the pretty milkmaids of those pastoral districts, who tended their flocks beside the river. One of their favourite amusements was a circular sun-wise dance called the Ras Mandala, in which the dancers twisted and turned and wheeled round about, in supposed imitation of the course of the sun, moon, and planets, a very pretty homage to the true character of Krishna as the Sun-god.

The chief delight of this cheery god was to watch when the girls came to bathe, and stealing their clothes, hang them all over the branches of a great tree; then climbing to a convenient position he would sit calmly waiting till the damsels (with no other drapery than their own raven tresses) came to supplicate for their garments! The identical tree is still pointed out, and pilgrims hang linen rags on its branches, as votive offerings, in memory of this god-like action.

Sometimes, however, Krishna was more helpful to these maidens, and one bathing-ghaut at Bindrabund marks the spot where after a terrible conflict, he strangled the huge black water-serpent Kaliya, which had poisoned the sacred river, so that the kine which drank thereof died. Hence Krishna is constantly represented as a young, handsome lad, glad and triumphant, holding up the great serpent whose head he crushes beneath his foot, not, however, till the reptile had bitten his heel. In the similarity of this legend to those of Egypt and Greece, which told how Horus and Apollo slew the mighty serpents which had terrified their respective mothers, as well as various other mythological stories both of east and west, which tell how some great deliverer has arisen to bruise the serpent's head, there must surely be some lingering tradition of the curse on that old serpent who haunted the beautiful garden in earth's early days. Certainly many such legends are mixed up in these ancient Indian creeds.

The heaven promised to his followers is a vast golden city. Of the multitude of halls, mansions, and palaces contained therein there is no end. The arches, the pillars, the ornaments, are all built up of most precious stones, and radiant gems glitter in the emerald streets. Rivers of crystal flow through the city, and broad beautiful lakes are overshadowed by fair fruit-bearing trees. These lakes are covered with water-lilies, red, blue, and white, each blossom having a thousand petals; and on the most beautiful of all these calm lakes floats a throne, glorious as the sun, whereon Krishna the beautiful reposes.

These lovely water-lilies hold a conspicuous place in all Oriental dreams of heaven. As Buddha sits enthroned on the Lotus, so Great Brahma himself was revealed at the creation of the world cradled in a lotus blossom. So too was the goddess Lakshmi, the wife of Vishnu, though some say she rose from ocean with a lotus blossom in her hand.

Bindrabund has passed through the same changes as the sister city, and is now one picturesque mass of red sandstone temples and ghauts, rising from the banks of the Jumna, and shaded by the overhanging foliage of banyan and neeme trees. On every side, rich carving, costly shrines, images, flowers; all the strangely picturesque ingredients of such a scene; life, motion, form, colour, all thoroughly Oriental, scarcely a day passing without some festival which attracts multitudes, decked out in their best, and no matter how poor the material their colouring is always in good taste. In short, these cities are to the Jumna what Benares and Hurdwar are to the Ganges.

Moreover they are equally infested by monkeys, which are literally the pest of the city. In the shady, luxurious gardens fifty or more will take possession of one tree, and hold a monkey parliament; thence descending on the fruit trees, will help themselves to the ripest and best fruits. Each window has a latticed framework, which has to be kept constantly closed to prevent their entering the houses and pilfering. Nevertheless they constantly do get in, and carry off whatever they fancy.

In this city of Krishna one eyesore to his worshippers still remains, namely, a magnificent Jain temple of red sandstone, with a huge pyramidal gateway. Its courts, cloisters, and pillars are literally without number, and the richness of its sculptures beyond telling. On some of the great festivals all this is illuminated, and the effect is described as most imposing. And yet, so repeatedly has northern India been ravaged by successive conquerors of diverse creeds, each of whom has ruthlessly destroyed the finest ancient temples, that absolutely none remains in the north which can compare in grandeur with those still to be seen in southern India, where they escaped the shocks of war.

There are perhaps few places in India, save Benares and Sarmath, where all these successive waves of diverse faiths have swept so mightily over the land as the spot where we now stand.

In very remote times the whole of Hindoostan seems to have been peopled by innumerable tribes, very dark in colour, and in the lowest scale of civilisation, each having its own especial mythology—if indeed the worship of snakes, apes, and devils can be so called. Somewhere about 1700 B.C. (while the Patriarchs still fed their flocks on the Syrian plains, and when Joseph was saving the land of Egypt from famine) the mighty Aryans, with the fair skin and the rich musical speech, are supposed to have swept down from central Asia and taken possession of the land, wholly subduing these feebler tribes, and reducing them at once to the rank of slaves, hewers of wood, and drawers of water. Only such as fled to the deep forests and inaccessible hills escaped this fate, and there remain unto this day as lawless, independent hill-tribes, noted as hardy warriors and keen sportsmen.

I think we, in England, scarcely realise the multitude of

these hill-tribes; and the consequent diversity of their languages. We have a sort of impression that the country is peopled with Hindoos, and imagine that one language with slight variations is current amongst them all. Or perhaps we may know that there are several great divisions of the people. But of the multitude of non-Aryan tongues we certainly have a very small conception. How many of us realise that there are fully *two hundred* aboriginal tongues in India, each unintelligible to all the others? In one single district near Assam twenty-eight distinct dialects have been counted, not one of which is understood by its neighbours.

Sometimes the course of a river is a boundary sufficient to separate these, a fact which will scarcely seem strange to a Scotchman, who recollects the strongly-marked line of demarcation between the Gaelic and English population of some of our own villages and towns—Nairn for instance, which still verifies an old joke of James VI., namely, that he owned one town so great, that the inhabitants of one end could not understand the language that was spoken at the other end!

As to the variety of speech among these aboriginal tribes, it may more easily be realised when we recollect that they still number upwards of six million souls.

It has been no easy task for the ruling power to modify and adapt the details of Government so as to suit the special need of all these primitive races, each wedded to its own distinctive customs, which include every conceivable variety of social, domestic, and religious life. There are tribes, such as the Nairs of south-western India, and others in the far north, whose social framework is all based on the practice of polyandry, while others rival the Koolin Brahmins in the multiplicity of their wives. There are tribes who live in grasshuts in the depths of the forest, clothed only with tufts of leaves, and have no weapons save bows and arrows, the latter being till very recently pointed with flint. Some file the front teeth of their women as a marriage ceremony (some degrees more unpleasant than the Japanese tooth-blackening)! Others have interesting funeral customs, such as those of the Goands in central India, who, believing that they were created at the foot of Dewalagiri peak in the Himalayas, worship "the great mountain" as their chief god, and have for ages buried their dead with their feet towards the north, ready to arise and return to the land of their forefathers.

Of course the prevalent ideas of worship are chiefly forms of propitiating demons, but the strange creeds of these wild men are just as diverse as their tongues, and amongst them still linger traces of those cruel old superstitions which the British have striven so hard to put down, and which have well-nigh vanished from all districts accessible to ordinary mortals. Only in the depths of these wild hill jungles do we still occasionally hear of some of the old practices of dark cruelty. One of these tribes, the Kookes (inhabiting the forests near Chittagong, about a hundred and fifty miles from Calcutta, and dwelling chiefly like monkeys, in huts erected in the uppermost branches of trees), were, till late years, notorious cannibals, catching and eating whoever they could lay hands on; while the Goands, in the hill country near Nagpore, had solemn religious feasts when they ate the flesh of such human victims as they sacrificed to their demons.

But the most horrible of all human sacrifices were those offered by the Khonds in Orissa, a tribe whose women are much tattooed on the face and who wear no clothes above the waist. The offering was made to their earth-goddess to secure a favourable harvest. In order that the sacrifice should be acceptable, it was necessary that the victim should have been purchased, so that the tribe should thus offer their own property and be free from the guilt of murder. So they bought their "meriahs," as they called their victims, from a race of professional kidnappers, who captured them wherever they could; they were generally Hindoos from the plains. A well-to-do village kept a stock of meriahs always on hand, ready for any sudden requirement of sacrifice. They were kindly treated and well fed, till the fatal hour arrived, when he or she was pitilessly put to death, while the tribe shouted "We have bought you with a price, we are guiltless of your death."

In the month of January each village held its great annual

festival when the people assembled, some clad in bear skins, some adorned with peacock's feathers, and several days were devoted to wild revelry. During this period the wretched victim was fed with milk and ghee, and reverenced as being in a manner sacred. But on the awful day of sacrifice, he was bound to an upright post, and the savage crowd, armed with sharp knives, pressed forward to cut off small strips of his flesh, with which they rushed off, every man to his own field, where they squeezed the warm blood upon the soil, and burying the fragment of flesh secured the fertility of the land. Thus the miserable victim endured the unutterable torture of being hacked into small pieces, and the height of devilish ingenuity was to prolong this dreadful anguish by never touching a vital part, for should death occur before the blood was dropped on the field the virtue of the charm would be annulled.

When all available parts had thus been used, the remainder was burnt, and the ashes mixed with the grain ere it was sown. This, till very recent years, was the only approved method of fertilising the land.

When the district of Khondistan came under British rule, and human sacrifice was declared to be a capital offence, and the chiefs were admonished to offer only buffaloes and goats; having no alternative but obedience, they formally apologised to the goddess, entreating her not to be angry with them for bringing her blood of beasts instead of human blood, but to wreak her vengeance on the white chief, *who was well able to bear it.*

But, of course, they continued to endeavour to evade the law, so an agency for suppressing human sacrifices in Orissa was established, and in the course of about twenty years no less than *seventeen hundred meriahs were rescued from sacrifice.* Of these, about 250 were placed in the asylums of the Orissa mission, where some embraced Christianity, and one of those who was earliest rescued has for upwards of five-and-twenty years been working as a devoted missionary among his people.

These Khonds, like the Santals, have now become a peaceful and orderly tribe, but some have necessarily died out before the advance of civilised law. Such were the Thugs, whose ruling principle of life and worship was strangling inoffensive travellers, an aimiable propensity which it was necessary to check; so the great organised robber-gangs known as the Dacoits and Thugs were broken up with a strong hand, and the last batch of Thugs have died out one by one in a sort of honourable captivity, regarded as interesting survivals of a vanished era.

Whereas debasing superstitions such as these, seem to have been the indigenous growth of Hindoostan, the Aryans brought with them a noble faith, probably much the same as their Druidical brethren taught in Britain; and, just as these deemed it impious to commit their creed to writing (so that Ossian's dreamy Gaelic legends are now our oldest link to the forgotten past), so did these Aryans of the east bring with them grand poems, psalms of victory, and prayers for deliverance, which for many centuries were orally transmitted from generation to generation; but as they were numerous, and all men are not endowed with good memories, it followed almost naturally that some men became the special repositories of ancient lore, and of the sacred poems and sacrificial hymns and liturgies. It became customary to call these in, to officiate at the great tribal sacrifices, and as the all-prevailing prayer was known as "*bráhma*" the man who offered it naturally came to be called BRAHMAN.

Gradually the profession became hereditary, and hence sprang the tender sapling which has developed into such a mighty tree, overshadowing the whole land. Very soon the men of intellect asserted their sway, and became the great ruling power of the empire, and well have they retained their position through all outward changes of faith and of dynasty.

In course of time they committed to writing, in the ancient Sanskrit tongue, a collection of 1017 short poems, containing 10,580 verses, which they and their descendants at the present day declare to be directly inspired by the Almighty. These form the celebrated Rig-Veda, each line of which is now interpreted as bearing deep and complex meaning; while its strong, nervous words and subtle thought afford food for much study to our most learned men.

The date and authorship of the Rig-Veda are questions as utterly vague and unanswerable as are those of the Book of Job. Though generally estimated at from 3,000 to 4,000 years back, both are lost in the mists of bygone ages. Only by a retrogressive process can we arrive at any sort of conclusion concerning the antiquity of these strange, beautiful poems; by recollecting that about four hundred years before Christ, the great Buddhist reaction against Brahmanism commenced; and that the degenerate form of faith, against which Buddha protested, had been established in India from time immemorial; being embodied in the Brâhmanas, whose authority and antiquity were alike unquestionable. These Brâhmanas are full of allusions to the Rig-Veda, as to a well-known authority, from whose pure and beautiful teaching they had, however, already departed so widely as would seem to have involved centuries of slow estrangement.

For instance, so far from authorising any species of idolatry, these sacred writings declare in the clearest terms that there is but one Supreme God, of whom Brahma, Vishnu, and Siva, in their several capacities, are but divers manifestations, co-eternal and co-equal. In some verses indeed, Vishnu appears merely as one of the Adityas, which were twelve characters of the Sun, answering to the twelve signs of the Zodiac.

Moreover in these grand old hymns, that intense belief in immortality, which has always so strongly marked the Aryan races, was never blended with those childish theories of transmigration which form so marked a feature in the teaching of the Brâhmanas. That these must have crept in early, that is to say, before the great Aryan wave parted eastward and westward, is evident from the traces thereof which we find in the old Celtic faith. (I have elsewhere noticed the curious fact that the Celts would even lend money, on the promise of repayment in the next phase of terrestrial existence!)[1]

Yet while the earlier Vedas contain no allusion whatever to the doctrine of transmigration, they are full of the promise of a future life. They tell how Yama, The Lord of Death, was monarch of

[1] *In the Hebrides*, p. 267. Chatto & Windus.

this world till sin entered, and then came sorrow, disease, and death; but Yama, passing through "the grave and gate of death" into the land of immortality, obtained a kingdom for himself, and is now continually seeking to guide men thither. He is worshipped as "the assembler of men, who departed to the mighty waters; who *spied out a road for many.*"

Hence the dead is adjured to clothe himself in "a shining form, a new and glorious body, that he may meet the Lord of Death with the ancient ones, who, through meditation, through laying down their lives for others, and bestowing their goods on the poor, have obtained the victory, and gone to heaven." "Go to thy home; may thy soul go to its own, and hasten to the fathers." "Do thou, O Lord, conduct us to heaven; let us be with our wives and children." "In heaven, where our friends dwell in bliss, free from all infirmity, there let us behold our parents and children." "Place me, O Pure One, in the everlasting and unchanging world where light and glory are found. Make me immortal in the world in which joys, delights, and happiness abide; where the desires are obtained."

The life described in those old hymns was hearty, earnest, and practical; not the melancholy, listless state of existence engendered by unreasoning faith in childish fables, and a continual straining after a life of unnatural contemplation and dreamy mysticism.

The most strongly-marked superiority of the Rig-Veda lies in its monotheistic teaching. Certainly it personifies all the powers of nature, earth, sea, and sky; stormy wind and tempest, mists and vapours, sun, moon, and stars; fire and frost, light and darkness, and speaks of them as of Spirits and Shining Ones.

Thus the sun is addressed as Surya, Savitri, Mitra, and Aryaman, in his various phases of rising and setting, just as the early Greeks bestowed divers poetical names on the same natural phenomena; while their descendants, losing the clue to the old poems, recognised Daphne, the dawn, and Endymion, the setting sun, as beings wholly distinct from Cephalus and Phœbus, and evolved strange fables from names which, in the mouths of their fathers, were probably merely graceful phraseology.

Just as in the old Gaelic poems of Ossian, so in these Sanskrit hymns (the phraseology of each being as strangely akin as are the tongues in which they are recorded), there is the same blending of the mysterious powers of the beautiful material world, with aspirations after things spiritual and imaginative. Beautiful as are the songs of the wild storm-gods, of the raving tempests, or the dreamy spirits of the mist, yet to One Supreme Creator do all these bow and obey. "Mountains and all hills, fruitful trees and all cedars, dragons and all deeps, fire and hail, snow and vapour, stormy winds," are all shown to be alike fulfilling His word.

But inasmuch as no one title could describe the infinite attributes of God (even the Mohammedans invoking Him by ninety-nine divers titles), these old hymns devised different names for His different characters. Hence He is addressed as Indra, the Giver of Rain and Lord of the Firmament, who has the winds for His messengers, and is said to smite the rain-cloud Vitra, and to send down freshening showers upon the earth. "Slayer of Vitra, ascend thy chariot, for thy horses have been yoked by prayer."

As Lord of Fire, He is adored as Agni, under which title He watches over the hearth. Hence the Aryans held the presence of fire indispensable at their marriage ceremonies; indeed, the presence of fire as a divine witness was in some cases deemed a sufficient ceremony!

Under the title Varuna, God is worshipped as Lord of the Ocean, of the Sun, of the Day. "Whatever two persons sitting together devise, Varuna, the king, knows it as the third. This earth, too, is Varuna, the king's, and that vast sky whose ends are far off. King Varuna sees all—what is within and beyond heaven and earth; the winkings of men's eyes are all numbered by Him." "He who knows the place of the birds that fly through the sky, who perceives what has been, and what will be done: He who knows the track of the wind . . . . may He make our paths straight all our days; may He prolong our lives."

"Yearning for Him, the far-seeing, my thoughts move onwards as kine to their pastures. O hear this, my calling, Varuna; be gracious now. Longing for help, I have called upon Thee. Hear my calling, O Varuna, and bless me now. Without Thee, O Varuna, I am not the master even of the twinkling of an eye. Do not deliver us unto death, though we have offended against Thy commandment day by day. Accept our sacrifice, forgive our offences. *Let us speak together again like old friends.*"

Strangely similar (is this not?) to what our own Scriptures have taught us of a Christian's "fellowship" with his God; communing with his Lord "as a man talketh with his friend." Such was the beautiful faith of these ancient races, who, so far from acknowledging caste and Brahmanical priesthood, "held that God had made all men equal, and that He was to be worshipped by no priestly formulas;" who, consequently, had no temples for public worship, but built altars under the open heaven, or beneath some stately tree, and offered sacrifices, every man for his own family.

It may well seem strange that a faith so simple could ever have developed into such a tissue of complex absurdity as the modern system of Hindooism. The solution lies in the fact that the nation itself is composed of a multitude of amalgamated races, and as with the people, so with their creeds, Hindooism has gradually absorbed the distinctive features of each.

Departing from the purity of their old faith, the conquerors tolerated every species of grossly idolatrous practice of the nations whose lands they conquered. Thus the flood-gates were opened to the wild orgies of devil-worship, snake-worship, adoration of the planets, trees, rocks and streams, and all grosser forms of nature-worship, with every species of aboriginal fetishism. While these were sanctioned for the vulgar herd, intellectual dreamers devoted their lives to meditation on the sacred writings of their ancestors, seeking to elicit hidden meanings in every line, and so, little by little, they contrived to evolve a whole mythology, concerning which they wrangled and quarrelled, and split into countless sects with elaborate rituals.

Thus it is that every conceivable absurdity is found mingling with the pure lofty thought of Aryan sages, and that the monstrous fabric of Hindooism with its 339,000,000 of gods has been reared on the grand foundation of the ancient monotheistic creed.

The Rig-Veda says little or nothing that can possibly be twisted into an allusion to the vexed question of the origin of caste, but the aboriginal tribes are always spoken of in the old Sanskrit writings with the utmost loathing. They are called the Dasyans, *i.e.* the "enemy," or "demon," and their imperfect, savage-language was constant matter for ridicule in the eyes of the conquerors, whose rich, clear tongue seemed formed for the expression of all ideal mysteries. Hence their prayers for victory over "the men of the inarticulate utterance and of the uncouth talk;" men, whose language had no terms whatever for the expression of any abstract idea, such as time, space, number; past, present, or future; earth, heaven, or hell.

Then, as now, the fair skin despised the dark. "The vile Dasyan colour" is perpetually alluded to with repugnance, and the gods are repeatedly thanked for having "scattered the slave bands of black descent, having destroyed the black skin," while they protected the Aryan colour. "The Thunderer" is said to bestow on his white friends the fields, while the stormy gods scatter the black skin.

The supreme contempt with which the magnificent Brahman, however poor he may be, treats all other castes, as having been created only for his service, is precisely the feeling with which his fair-skinned ancestors with the clear complexion, finely-chiselled features and intellectual form of head, treated the conquered children of the soil; that is to say, all the non-Aryan tribes, whom they reduced to serfdom and whose descendants are those miserable oppressed castes known as the Sudras, and those still more wretched outcasts, or Pariahs, rejected even by these, and often distinguished by flattened features and thick lips, peculiarities duly noted by the Aryan poets, who speak of the snub noses and squat features of the aborigines, while praising the "beautiful nose" of some of their own ideal gods.

The gross use of all manner of animal food was, above all, repulsive to the more refined habits of the Aryan; the use of raw meat, of horse flesh, even of human flesh, and the savage and bloody sacrifices offered to propitiate malignant demons, as well as to supply the voracious worshippers with an abundant store of food—all these habits of the Dasyan were as revolting to the strict refinement of the Aryan as those of the modern Sudra are to the Brahman. Hence the title, "the Raw-Eaters," by which the Vedas describe these inferior animals—these "snake" and "monkey" tribes.

This demonology seems to have been the sole idea of worship among these people, the lowest form of servile fear. As to any knowledge of a future life, they have not even a word to express it. Like a poor African Bushman, to whom we once vainly hoped to convey some notion of immortality by speaking to him of his dead mother, but who could realise no more exalted view of the case than to repeat, with a grin of amusement, "Ah, massa's sister! my mother is rotten!—she is rotten!" so these strangely ignoble tribes could conceive no possibility of a resurrection; nor had they any funeral rites save quickly burying the corpse, and adjuring the dead, who could no longer eat with them, never again to come near them.

No wonder that such people as these should have quickly accepted their position as the natural slaves and bondmen of the more enlightened races. "*L'occasion fait le larron;*" and it is worthy of note that those Aryan tribes who settled in Cashmere and beyond the Indus, and who apparently did not find such good raw material for serfdom, have continued to believe in the equality of all men, and utterly ignore all distinctions of caste.

It is very curious to note the gradual development of this system from those early days, when the Aryan faith, beginning to degenerate, embodied itself in those later Vedas which teach how from the body of Brahma sprang four great castes—the Brahmans, Kshatriyas or soldiers, Vaisyas or agriculturists, and Sudras or servants, who respectively came from his mouth, shoulders, thighs and feet; while the miserable aborigines of the land were classed as Pariahs, or outcasts, who claim no descent from Brahma, and consequently are despised to an extent not to be told.

Gradually these four castes came to be subdivided into the incalculable varieties we now find in such endless complication.

Thus THE BRAHMANS ALONE COUNT TWO THOUSAND DISTINCT FAMILIES OF THEIR ORDER, those of Northern India being esteemed the most holy, having kept their old blood more pure than those who pushed southward, and who in some measure blended with the people of the land. There are, however, several distinct classes of Brahmans dwelling in the great northern mountains (the Himalayas), who are held in the utmost contempt by their namesakes in the plains, and who return this feeling with interest.[1] *The Brahmans of Bengal alone number one hundred and sixty-eight subdivisions, who may neither eat, drink, nor intermarry one with another;* though the holiest of all —the Coolin Brahmans—may marry wives by the score from all the other families, their sanctity being an inexhaustible store, which, like a flame of fire, may be imparted to others, but never loses aught of its own pure light.

There is one caste of Brahmans, called Poorbeea, who carry their niceties to such a pitch that they may not even take fire from one another. Hence the saying, "Twelve Poorbeeas and thirteen fires," because, supposing twelve brothers about to dine, they must first kindle one fire for general use; then each (having made his own little mud-oven, smeared with cow-dung) takes fire thence and proceeds to cook for himself.

Perhaps the most remarkable instance of the subdivision of castes is that of the oil-makers in Telingana, whose only distinction is that one-half work their oil-mills with one bullock, while the others use two; yet they cannot intermarry, nor even eat together!

Among the most curious of caste statistics is the contempt in which astrologers are held. Dr. Hunter states that they are reckoned so impure that, although wearing the sacred thread of the Brahmans, they dare not sit down in any house they chance to enter till all the mats have been taken up. A strange penalty for seeking to extort the secrets of the stars, and one which seems to suggest the contempt wherewith the Aryan conquerors were wont to regard the aboriginal planet-worshippers!

[1] On the creation of non-Aryan Brahmans, see Chapter XXII. on Benares.

All laws and enactments of course go to secure the exaltation of the Brahmans, who alone are allowed to read the sacred books, and who claim universal obedience from their neighbours. The most barbarous decrees are still unrepealed against a man of low caste who would presume to take the smallest liberty, such as to sit down on the carpet of a priest; and though the Brahman may be ever so poor, he can exact any amount of deference from others. Thus the Brahman school-boy will make his companion carry him through the muddy stream, or otherwise make himself useful. Rather an awkward power in the case of two men enlisting in the same regiment, when it may chance that the lowest Sudra may be of higher standing than the Brahman to whom he owes reverence. One disadvantage to the Brahman is, that he must in every case cook his own food. He may also cook for all his neighbours, who cannot be defiled by eating that which he has touched, but they can never render him the same service.

The low-caste Sudras are often possessed of vast power and wealth, being considerable land-owners. As a general rule, most mercantile and agricultural castes rank as honourable, but any trade involving death of animals, or the use of any animal substance, is considered low. Such are fishermen, hunters, laundrymen, snake-charmers, curriers, shoemakers, butchers. Distillers and palm-wine drawers are impure, from the fact that all intoxicating liquors are forbidden. Sweepers, washers, burners or buriers of the dead, are sheer outcasts. In this, as in every other phase of Hindoo life, endless anomalies exist—barbers, for instance, rank higher than bankers. There seems, however, no insuperable barrier between one profession and another, and certainly men do occasionally pass from one position to another. The son of a goldsmith may become a carver, a potter may turn his hand to the loom, nevertheless caste distinctions are as plain as the caste mark painted on their forehead—not a dead letter, but a living fact enforced by the whole community. Thus for a damsel of one caste to marry into a lower, would shock the nerves of society almost as much as if an English girl were to marry her groom.

In the matter of food the Brahman is supposed to abstain from all animal food and all intoxicating liquors; but the average castes will eat goat, sheep, and such like, as well as all manner of game—not poultry however, that being impure. But if possible, they will always eat in secret from a dread of the evil eye of any passer-by, and cooking must also be done in private for fear of ceremonial defilement, as even a glance from a man of lower caste, or a foreigner, renders food unfit for use. Its uncleanliness would contaminate both soul and body, and entail long penance, so it must be thrown away, even if the family have to fast for the whole day.

They are especially strict in the drawing of water, every man for himself, in his own brass lota: and this it is which makes it impossible for a Hindoo to visit England without losing caste, as in crossing the "black water," as they call the sea, the difficulties of maintaining ceremonial purity in cooking are insuperable, and only a man of the lower castes could eat food cooked by another person, or with water of uncertain purity. There are castes so low that they will eat whatever comes to hand—carrion, rats, and river tortoises, or *even food from the table of a Christian!* they will also drink all fermented liquors.

To us free Britons, it seems scarcely possible to understand the existence of a system so rigid and so real, or which can possess such crushing power against those who trangress its regulations, affecting even the details of a man's most private domestic life. Expulsion from caste is in fact a civil excommunication as far-reaching as ever was fulminated from Rome. It cuts a man off from all intercourse with his fellows. No one will do business with him; the houses of his old companions are closed to him; he is cast out of the temple where he was wont to worship; his children cannot be given in marriage, for no one would venture to become connected with him. He becomes an isolated being, dead as it were to the world, and bereft of friends and relations, who prefer disowning him to sharing his miserable fate. None dare eat with him or give him so much as water to drink. No lower caste would receive him. He becomes a Pariah, and sinks to the lowest depth of degradation, and should he die unshriven, none will, in his last hour, carry him to the sacred river, or after death, to the burning ghaut.

There are, however, certain ceremonies whereby a man may make atonement for small sins and be restored to his own caste. He must pay a certain fine, and must swallow a foul compound of the various produce of the sacred cow, and observe other religious ceremonies, and may thus in time regain his social position; but should he have been guilty of tasting beef, *that* crime is beyond redemption, and he is eternally lost.

This is the more curious, because the prohibition of beef is a thing of even more recent date than the growth of caste itself. The most ancient Sanskrit books describe solemn sacrifices of bulls and heifers of divers colours, and dilate on the jovial feasts of beef and ale which ensued—a comfortable phase of living, which seems to have continued till the seventh century of the Christian era, when the prohibition is first heard of. Moreover the sacrifice of a cow was one of the ancient funeral rites specially ordained by the Vedic ritual.

It seems that from time to time efforts have been made with more or less success to break through the caste system.

Thus, in the worship of Vishnu as Jagannáth, we find that the teaching of equality lies at the root of his amazing hold on the Hindoo race. It is because the "Lord of the World" is also the god of the people, that they continue year by year to flock to his shrines in such countless multitudes, and in defiance of such cruel hardships, that thousands and tens of thousands annually perish by the way; not beneath the wheels of his car in voluntary self-immolation, as has been so often falsely asserted, and so entirely disproved, but from weariness and exhaustion, in striving to press onward to the shrine where the lowest outcast is as welcome as the proudest Brahman, and where both together may partake of that sacrament of the holy food which is the pledge of common brotherhood among the worshippers of one lord. I cannot resist quoting a passage on this subject from Dr. Hunter's *Orissa*. Speaking of the worship of Jagannáth, he says:—

"As long as his towers rise upon the Puri Sands, so long will there be in India a perpetual and visible protest of the equality of man before God. His apostles penetrate to every hamlet of Hindoostan, preaching the sacrament of the holy food. The poor outcast learns that there is a city on the far eastern shore in which high and low eat together. In his own village if he accidentally touches the clothes of a man of good caste he has committed a crime, and his outraged superior has to wash away the pollution before he can partake of food or approach his god. In some parts of the country the lowest castes are not permitted to build within the towns, and their miserable hovels cluster amid heaps of broken potsherds and dunghills on the outskirts.

"Throughout the southern part of the continent it used to be a law that no man of these degraded castes might enter the village before nine in the morning, or after four in the evening, lest the slanting rays of the sun should cast his shadow across the path of a Brahman. But in the presence of the Lord of the World priest and peasant are equal. The rice that has once been placed before the god can never cease to be pure, or lose its reflected sanctity. In the courts of Jagannáth, and outside the Lion Gate, 100,000 pilgrims every year are joined in the sacrament of eating the holy food. The lowest may demand it from or give it to the highest. Its sanctity overleaps all barriers, not only of caste, but of race and hostile faiths; and I have seen a Puri priest put to the test of receiving the food from a Christian's hand."

This holy food, of "the great offering,"[1] is believed to be endowed with a power of working miracles more marvellous even than those which have been attributed to the consecrated wafer of Christendom. Dr. Hunter quotes a legend concerning a proud pilgrim, who swore that though he purposed looking upon the Lord of the World, he would assuredly eat no leavings of any mortal or immortal being. But lo! ere he set foot within the sacred city, he was stricken by the angry god, and his arms and legs fell off, and there remained of him only a miserable body,

[1] Maháprasád.

which lay by the roadside for two months, dependent on the charity of passers-by. But at length it chanced that a dog came by that way, with a mouthful of the holy food, and as it passed the place where the pilgrim lay, some grains of rice fell on the ground. Then the poor humbled wretch managed to roll himself forward, so that with his lips he might gather up the precious grains, the leavings of a dog, whose mere shadow falling on ordinary food would defile it. Nevertheless, as he gathered them reverently, albeit mingled with the saliva of the unclean creature, lo! the mercy of the good lord Jagannáth was extended to him—new limbs were given him, and he was suffered, in lowliest penitence, to approach the shrine.

But beautiful as is the theory of brotherhood, symbolised by this sacramental feast, it seems to be in a great measure ignored by the degenerate Brahmans of the present day, and many a weary pilgrim of the lower castes is in danger of finding himself excluded from the immediate presence of the Lord of the World, for no other reason than that he inherits the social position of his father, and follows his trade. Although in direct violation of the spirit of the feast, and of the laws of the founder, admission to the temple is now generally refused to all castes who have to do with handling unclean substances, such as corpses, or skins of beasts; all who have to do with the destruction of animals, birds, or fishes; all Christians, Mohammedans, or aboriginal tribes.

Criminals are also excluded till they have expiated their crimes by costly penance; while for a woman, who has once fallen, there is no possibility of remission. However deep her repentance, she may never again set foot within the sacred precincts—a rule which seems strangely arbitrary, considering the character borne by the dancing girls belonging to the temple! Thus a very large proportion of the pilgrims are by priestly intolerance declared to be outcast, notwithstanding the direct declaration to the contrary by the early apostles of Jagannáth, who taught that "God's pity knows neither family nor tribe." "Not the learned in the four holy scriptures, but the lowly man who believes, is dear to Him."

But rigidly as the Brahmans guard their inner sanctuary from the intrusion of the despised low castes, they dare not refuse them their share of the holy food—more especially as the sale thereof is a source of revenue to the temple. They therefore go through the solemn ceremony of presenting it to Jagannáth in the outer court of the temple, and then sell it to the vast hungering multitude outside, in red earthenware pots, which may not be used a second time. Therefore every evening thousands of these are thrown aside, and the thrifty husbandmen of the district make use of them in building up frail boundary walls around their fields.

It appears that even the holy food itself becomes an additional cause of suffering to the wretched pilgrims, for not only is it often ill-cooked, but it is served out by the priests in such large quantities that the pilgrims cannot consume it in a day, and as they dare not waste the least fragment of the sacred food, they are constantly compelled to consume it on the second day, in a condition of fermentation or putrefaction; a fruitful source of illness to the dense multitude of half starved and exhausted wretches, enfeebled by long travel, and perhaps already cholera-stricken. But whatever failure there may be in the practical working of this great festival, its theory remains unchanged, and forms one of the mightiest holds of Vishnu on the affections of the people.

Even the miserable leper (most wretched of all outcasts) cannot be denied the privilege of worshipping at this holy shrine, so that numerous bands of leper pilgrims drag their weary limbs thither, in the vain hope of here finding pardon and healing. These of all men are surely the most miserable, being deemed so horribly unclean that even a man of the highest caste, thus afflicted, loses all caste and all privileges. In life he is an outcast even from his own family, and after death his body is consigned to the care of the lowest scavengers. It is estimated that upwards of a hundred thousand of our Indian fellow subjects are thus afflicted. Human mercy does something for their aid in the way of leper hospitals, but these are wholly inadequate to their requirements. So to the all-embracing mercy of the pitying Lord of the World they turn as to their only refuge—sustained during their lone and toilsome journey on the alms of their fellow pilgrims, only to learn at last how hopeless is their sad case.

Among these very varied developments of all manner of worship, I need scarcely say that that most widespread of all religious acts—the offering of gifts and homage to deceased ancestors—is not neglected, though it is not so obvious to the casual observer as in other countries, such as China. Here, however, are two hundred million people who believe that no matter how good a man has been, if his funeral rites are not properly conducted, and his cremation is neglected, he becomes a bhuta, that is, a malignant demon (unless, indeed, his remains find their way to the holy river Ganges, which cleanses from all sin). It is therefore of the utmost importance to recover the body of any man who has died in any out-of-the-way place, and if this cannot be done, his son ought to make an image of sacred kusa grass and cremate that as his representative.

As only sons can officiate in the funeral rites, it follows that these are ever more welcome than daughters, and the man who dies son-less not only becomes a demon-spirit himself, but inflicts a grievous wrong on the two previous generations. Hence the religious obligation of early marriage. To avert such a catastrophe, special services of most intricate ritual (requiring the presence of sixteen orders of priests—and of extraordinary length, inasmuch as they generally continued for weeks, and sometimes for years) were prescribed in ancient Vedic days, in order to obtain from the gods an unbroken line of descendants for three generations. For, as all the dead relations in the three last generations are dependent on the living for their supplies, and deliverance from Put, *i.e.* purgatory, so are these, in their turn, dependent on the three generations which succeed them. Thus are seven generations of every Hindoo family closely knit together by ties of most active self-interest.

That the modern sanctity of cattle had not been invented in the early Vedic days (500 B.C.) is plain from the ancient ritual, which prescribes, as one of the funereal rites, the sacrifice of a cow, in order that the dead might feast on the aroma (while doubtless the survivors enjoyed the substantial reality, though the luxury of salt was denied them for three days). Three funeral pyres were then erected, and the dead having been laid on the central one, small pieces of beef were placed in his hands and on various other parts of the corpse, which was then cremated, and the spirit was wafted upward by the smoke.

But as yet it was only a poor restless disembodied ghost, alike incapable of enjoying the bliss of heaven, or of suffering the anguish of such hells as only oriental ingenuity could devise. Its spiritual body was as yet a small undeveloped germ, dependent for its growth on the daily offerings of rice balls, presented by the living at the place of cremation. By about the tenth day this little body had expanded, and the spirit entered into it, and passed to its appointed place in heaven or hell, whereupon the cremated ashes and bits of bone were collected in an urn and reverently buried.

Nowadays the ashes are collected on the fourth day, and after lying buried for a few days in an earthen vessel, are cast into some sacred river—if possible the Ganges. Of course the sacrifice of the cow is now dispensed with, and in lieu thereof sacred cow-dung is spread in the centre of the collected ashes. On this charming centre-piece are spread green plantain leaves, on which is laid an elaborate offering of little earthenware saucers containing rice balls, wheaten cakes, flowers, honey, sesamum-seeds, betel-leaves, areca-nut, sandal-wood, lighted wicks, milk, and water. These last are poured over the rice cakes as a libation.

The nearest relation then walks five times round this curious offering, on which he pours water from an earthenware vessel which he afterwards breaks. Strange to say, he makes these turns against the course of the sun, keeping his left shoulder to the centre. The relations add to the offerings threads drawn out of their own garments, to symbolise the clothes which they would willingly give to their dead kinsman. All the earthenware saucers must be broken at the end of this service, for they can never be used a second time, and the rice cakes and balls are either left for the birds, or thrown into the nearest river.

Periodical services on behalf of the dead are held from time to time either in a temple or an equally sacred cow-stable. The number of ceremonies required, and the number of days to which they are prolonged, are only limited by the capacity of endurance of the poor survivors—for the great feature of these ancestral services is the feasting of the Brahmans, who are loaded with gifts, in the belief that whatever is given to these darlings of heaven is as acceptable to the dead as if given to themselves. Moreover, only the Brahmans have power to deliver from hell, and they are certain to exact the uttermost farthing in payment of their services. The sums said to be thus expended by wealthy families are almost incredible, and have in some cases been estimated at upwards of 100,000*l.*!

Besides these occasional great ceremonials, the pious Hindoo (they are ALL pious) performs acts of filial reverence before his domestic altar every morning of his life, by offering homage to his ancestors, and repeating his own genealogy, thereby enumerating them all. Should he be a Brahman, he arranges his mystic threefold cord over his right shoulder and under his left arm, and then, pouring out a libation of water, he prays that the water consecrated by the merit of his sacred thread may be accepted by such of his deceased relations as have died without sons to offer for them.

As regards the spirit worlds, into one or other of which the spirit has passed in its newly-developed body, it may happily be arrested in one of the seven lower worlds, which are all beautiful paradises, though inhabited by demons and nagas; the latter are half men and half serpents, and are governed by three great snakes which reign over all the snakes on earth.

Beneath these worlds lie the twenty-one hells. These and the road thither are indescribably appalling; imagination and the power of word-painting are exhausted in the effort to describe them. One is a dark forest where every leaf is a sharp sword;

another is paved with iron spikes which pierce the naked victims; a third is a sea of foulest mud; a fourth is inclosed by living walls of poisonous serpents intertwined in horrible contortions—and so the list runs on, in ever-deepening horror.

On the other hand there are seven upper worlds, of which ours is one. These are the dwellings of the three hundred and thirty million of gods, and the inhabitants of these happy lands have bodies which never perspire and cast no shadow, eyes that never shrink from the sun's brightest glare, and gorgeous fragrant flowers which never fade.

It is worthy of note that with all the ingenious varieties of horror which are accumulated around the hells of Hindooism, there is no hint of an eternity of evil. Temporal sin receives temporary punishment, and after the sins of earthly life have been expiated in one of these purgatories, a new life begins—a transmigration into some animal, insect, or plant. Hence every living creature, wherein is the breath of life, is entitled to reverence, as possibly sheltering the soul of some ancestor!

To return, however, to those early days, when the first germ of the now mighty caste system sprang from the contemptuous pride with which the Aryan conquerors treated the inferior races. Despised as were these, they nevertheless seem to have had their full share in modifying the religion of their conquerors. A mixed race soon led to a mixed faith, and the demon-worship, once so abhorrent in their eyes, rapidly gained ground, growing up, together with the new faith, like rank tares among good seed. Thus it came to pass that Mahadeo (the great god) was no longer worshipped simply as the lord and giver of life. He became identified with Siva, in which character he became the destroyer of his own work. In course of time these opposite principles were reconciled by the doctrine of transmigration, according to which, destruction in one form implies only a new material birth. In his character of destroyer he is ably assisted by his wife, in her most maligant character as Kali or Doorga, who appears as the most terrible of those insatiable fiends who can only be pacified by an oblation of warm human blood.

Although under the English rule these demons are forced to be satisfied with the blood of sheep and goats, there have been instances so late as the famine of 1866, when the more precious offering has been procured, and a ghastly human head has glared from among the flowers which decked the altars of these monstrous gods.

Dr. Hunter remarks that in Northern India, where the aborigines at once succumbed to the Aryans, this demon-worship hardly appears, whereas in Lower Bengal, where they in some measure held their ground, its presence is far more decided; while in those hill and forest districts where the Aryans never settled, and where the aboriginal black races of Bengal still hold their ground, the very lowest form of unmitigated devil-worship still prevails.

It is so firmly rooted in the affections of the people that neither Buddhism, in the days when its influence swept in a resistless tide over the length and breadth of the land, nor Christianity of any sort, have been able to wean even their nominal converts from their adherence to these rites; more especially the daily offerings of flour, water, red paint, and rice, to an unknown god, supposed to dwell in some sacred tree, and to be the guardian-spirit of each village. Several times a year all the people of a village assemble to sacrifice goats, chickens, and red cocks, which they then cook at great fires, and after dancing in a large circle round each tree in the sacred grove, so as to make sure of doing homage to every possible god or devil, they have a grand feast and jovial merry-making.

Within the last few years, however, an extraordinary religious awakening has taken place among the Santals and the kindred tribe of Kols, many thousands of whom have been converted to Christianity through the influence of two German missionaries, who, having first observed some of them working in Calcutta, bethought them of seeking them out in their mountain homes. There they were ill received, and pelted from village to village. Yet for five years they persevered in the effort that seemed so hopeless. At the end of that time two men came to them to inquire further, especially desiring to *see* Him of whom they taught. When they found they could not see Him literally, they went away again. Yet after a while they returned, and eventually requested to be baptised.

This beginning was as the opening of a mighty floodgate. Others crowded to hear and learn. By the end of the twelfth year the Christians of this Chota Nagpore Mission numbered many thousands: of whom eight hundred were communicants. These men, you see, are not trammelled by those social difficulties which beset the Hindoo of the plains; they neither have the subtle intellectual refinement of the Brahman in defending their own creed, nor the dread of losing caste, so that when once convinced of the truth they have fewer obstacles in accepting it. They are described by one, whose official work lay amongst them for many years, as being a very noble race, honest, and honourable; exceedingly truthful and chivalrous; brave to infatuation; true and just in all their dealings.

Among such tribes as these, Christian teachers go to work hopefully, as the Culdees of old came to these Isles of Britain to teach our pagan forefathers. It may be that as our own most rude heathenism has so utterly melted away, that Britain now ranks high among the Christian nations; so these wild tribes may prove as a focus of that Light which may yet spread over the length and breadth of the land in a wave so mighty and resistless as to sweep away all vestige of the faiths of Brahma and Mohammed, as utterly as they, in their turn, extinguished that of Buddha. Perchance the Hindoo antiquarian of some future generation may speculate and theorise over each trace of these forgotten mysteries, just as our own learned men now do over such meagre hints as they can gather from Stonehenge and other speechless stones.

Once more to return to that long period during which the Aryans carried all before them in India.

They held sway till the birth of Buddha, 623 B.C., whose strange career was chiefly run in these provinces. It was in the kingdom of Oude that, upwards of two thousand years ago, this young prince (Siddhartha, *alias* Gautama, *alias* Sakya-muni, *i.e.*

the solitary or monk, *alias* Buddha, the wise, the enlightened one, he to whom truth is known) found himself surrounded by all the splendour of a luxurious court, of which he himself was the centre. Nevertheless he quickly learned old Solomon's lesson of vanity and vexation of spirit. Vainly did he seek counsel of the most learned Brahmans, hoping from them to receive that key of a spiritual world that might unlock the mysteries and perplexities of the present. But the Brahmans had already lost the purity of their own grand old faith. Even in those early days the simplicity of the Vedas had given place to a mass of traditions and puerile fables.

Such husks as these could never satisfy the cravings of Gautama's hungry soul. At length, escaping from his grandeur in the garb of a religious mendicant, he devoted himself to an ascetic life of contemplation, seeking with unutterable longing for peace of spirit. Though exposed to sore temptation from vile demons, he still persevered; sitting for weeks in abstracted thought; striving to think out many of the problems that have in all ages given food for deepest speculation. At length he came to the satisfactory conclusion that ignorance is the cause of all evil and misery, and that by a rigid course of well-doing every man may at length (probably after various transmigrations) be freed from the burden of existence, and delivered from the necessity of ever being born again to any new form of being. In other words, he may attain Nirvana, a condition of dreamless rest; some say, annihilation.

Having thus discovered the root of perfect wisdom, he rose from his lengthy contemplations, and assuming the title of the Buddha, the enlightened one, he determined to impart that light to all his fellow-creatures. Commencing at Benares, he wandered over the Northern Provinces, teaching and preaching a doctrine of human brotherhood, which, without abolishing caste, made it null and void. The new system breathed universal charity and sympathy with all men. To the lowest outcast, the blessedness of Nirvana was as freely open as to the highest. Woman was henceforward, in her own sphere, to rank equal with man.

Thousands flocked to listen to this new doctrine of kindliness, brotherhood, and humanity. A mighty reaction set in against the narrow bigotry of Brahmanism, and the exclusiveness of its caste system.

It has commonly been stated that Buddha himself was descended from the royal Aryan race of Sakyas, who reigned in Oude, and that the exalted rank thus voluntarily abjured, tended greatly to attract the people to hear him. It is curious, however, that all his statues invariably represent him with the heavy features common among the lower castes; the thick lips and flat nose of the aborigines, and curly hair like that of a negro, whereas all castes alike in India have straight silky hair. Just as the calm features of the Sphinx are simply a reproduction of the sullen Coptic type, so these contemplative Buddhas would plainly seem to represent a cast of countenance in nowise related to the intellectual Aryan Brahman, and by him utterly despised.

It was no marvel then that multitudes of the enslaved aboriginal tribes should eagerly gather round their great champion, hoping to throw off the Aryan yoke which had so long weighed heavily on soul as well as body. But not only among the poor and oppressed classes did Gautama number his converts—kings, princes, nobles, rallied round him, to listen to his words of persuasive eloquence.

At the age of eighty he died, in calmest serenity, in the kingdom of Oude, and his body was burned with all honour. From that funeral pyre, his disciples in later times, pretend that all those worshipful relics were preserved which now receive a homage that would doubtless have vexed poor Buddha's soul. After his death his devoted missionaries zealously preached the new faith, so that about B.C. 300 it had spread all over Asia. In every place, his followers erected colossal statues in his honour. We hear of the Chinese capturing one of these in their raids to the north of the great desert of Gobi, B.C. 120. It was said to be made of solid gold, but was probably gilt, like those we find in the great Buddhist temples in China. The ensuing bronze-casters of Japan produced stupendous brazen images of the

Great Reformer, while gigantic stone images of Buddha still remain in the wilds of the Southern Jungles of India; and hundreds of rock-hewn temples, miracles of stupendous stone carving, are found in all parts of the country, to tell of the faith which once reigned supreme throughout Hindoostan, though it has long since passed away hence.

Among these speaking stone memorials must be ranked such buildings as the great tope at Sanchi, that mighty relic-shrine, whose huge stone portals are to this day a marvel of mythological sculptures, representing the primeval worship of sacred serpents and holy trees, and displaying wheels, umbrellas, and other symbols more particularly suggestive of the new faith—which the Emperor Asoka established as the religion of the state. This mighty despot having determined that the new maxims which had become binding on his own conscience should henceforth be law to his subjects, proceeded to inscribe them on stone in every corner of his dominions, that the wayfarer might read them for himself.

Thus it is that, besides finding his edicts engraven on his buildings and pillars,[1] they are also found inscribed—as on imperishable tablets—on great rocks scattered over the country from Orissa to Peshawur. One of these huge boulders, twenty feet in height and twenty-three in circumference, lies in the lonely jungle in the district of Kathiawad in Western India. Here the Emperor states, that being convinced of the iniquity of slaying living creatures, he will henceforth desist from the pleasures of the chase. Henceforth, no animal must be put to death either for meat or sacrifice; and this law which the Emperor appoints for himself, is to apply to all his subjects, who are in future to feed only on vegetables.

His protection of the brute creation applies not only to their lives; medical care is to be provided for all living creatures, man and beast, throughout the whole empire, as far south as Ceylon. Wells are to be dug, and trees planted, that men and beasts may have shade and drink. The Emperor forbids all convivial

[1] See Chapter III., Allahabad.

meetings, as displeasing to the gods or injurious to the reveller. He declares that he will himself set the example of abstaining from all, save religious festivals. On this huge "Junagadh Rock," as it is called, allusion is also made to four contemporary Greek kings. The date thus obtained is proved to be about 250 B.C., which just corresponds with that of Asoka himself.

The edicts go into various other matters. They inculcate the practice of a moral law of exceeding purity; they enjoin universal charity; and bid all men strive to propagate the true creed. To this end, special missionaries were to be sent forth to the uttermost parts of the earth, to preach to rich and poor, learned and ignorant, that they might bring those "which were bound in the fetters of sin, to a righteousness passing knowledge." Nevertheless, a liberal margin was to be allowed for diversity of opinion, and nothing savouring of religious persecution was to be tolerated.

For one striking feature in the rapid spread of Buddhism is that (unlike the faith of Islam, whose gentlest persuasive reasoning lay in fire and sword,) it has never employed violence, but, like the mightiest powers in the physical world, has diffused its influence calmly and silently, and at the present moment its disciples number upwards of five-hundred millions of the human race!—in other words, about one-third of the earth's population.[1]

Nay, more; its influence seems to have extended to many an undreamt-of quarter, and to have even given something of its own tone and colour to the Christian Church, many of whose most cherished institutions—such as the veneration for relics, the canonisation of saints, the use of rosaries, the divers orders of monastic life, the rigid vows of poverty and asceticism, celibacy of the clergy, priestly robes and shaven crowns, processions carrying banners, chaunted litanies, the use of incense and of holy water, the ringing of a small bell during service, midnight masses for the delivery of souls in purgatory, and very

[1] It is estimated that the nominal Buddhists throughout the world number 500,000,000 and the Christians number 360,000,000.

many other ecclesiastical details—can hardly be accounted for, save on the supposition (which indeed is well-nigh a certainty) that they were adopted by the Christians of Egypt from the practice of Oriental Buddhists, by whom all these things were as religiously observed before the Christian era, as they are at the present day.

Except in the modified sect of the Jains, the faith of Buddha now owns comparatively few adherents in Hindoostan, the land of its birth, save at least in the mountains on the frontiers of Thibet and Chinese Tartary; and since the Mikado has abjured the creed of his fathers in favour of Shinto-ism, it can no longer claim to be the national religion of Japan, though its temples there are still storehouses of art-treasures. But in Ceylon, Burmah, Siam, and the adjacent countries, this dreamy faith still holds undisputed sway, while it extends north through China, Thibet, Nepaul, Mongolia and all Central Asia, right up to Siberia and Lapland.

It is said that in Thibet the Buddhist monks actually number one-third of the population! It is probable that the monastic system similarly overdid itself in India, and that, while the cleverest and best men were thus flying from their fellows, or seeking to attain to still higher sanctity by a living burial in caves and deep forest solitudes, the masses found the new faith too spiritual and negative to suit their daily need, and quickly relapsed into the grossest devil-worship.

Then Brahmanism crept out again, and seems to have given up the attempt to teach its sublimer dogmas, and, while its learned men adhered to the spiritual worship of the Vedas, they encouraged the people to offer bloody sacrifices to such malignant demons as Kali and Siva, and built up the present system of ultra-idolatrous modern Hindooism. Then they devised new sacred books for the people, the Puranas, popular religious works, for the especial benefit of women and Sudras, or low castes. There were mythologies of the grossest sort, to which by degrees they have added all manner of secular matter, till they are said rather to resemble curious encyclopædias than theological works.

Thus the Brahmans artfully regained their ascendency, and the Buddhist monks found that out of sight is not always out of mind, for so soon as homage ceased, persecution began, and they were driven forth from every corner of the land. Only in the mountain glens and rocky defiles of the Himalayas could they find a refuge: for the soft sons of the plains cared not to scale those mighty ramparts for the mere pleasure of hunting down their fallen rivals. So in Burmah, Nepaul, and Thibet, the persecuted monks found sanctuary, and there remained unmolested. In after ages, when the sword of Mohammedan persecution ravaged the land, the Brahmans in their turn found refuge and liberty of conscience, in the same free mountain air.

Last of all these successive waves comes one which we trust will in due time overflow the whole as a flood of living waters, but which as yet is but a wavelet, scarcely more than a ripple, on this vast ocean. Out of a population of upwards of two hundred and fifty millions, less than one million and a-half are professedly Christian, and even this small number is divided into two widely distinct sections, inasmuch as two-thirds are Roman Catholics, and the remainder Protestants of all denominations. This does not appear a large result as the fruit of a century of contact with Europeans; but this would be a very unfair test of mission work, considering how very few, even now, are the Christian teachers compared with the vast multitude of keenly intellectual men whom they must seek to convince of the fallacy of creeds in which they and their forefathers have had such intense belief.

Think of the mass of positive heathenism which still prevails in Britain, notwithstanding the combined labours of multitudinous clergy and Christian workers of all sorts,[1] and then

[1] Recent statistics give some startling revelations of the number of persons in our great cities who never enter any place of worship. In one district of St. George's in the East, only 39 out of 4,235 persons are found ever to do so, and the majority of these only on the occasions of certain annual distributions of charity. Multitudes, upwards of fifty years of age, are found to have never crossed the threshold of a church. In one street off Leicester Square, only 12 persons out of 246 families attend any religious service, and similar statistics might be multiplied.

consider, that *throughout Hindoostan the missionaries average* ONE TO EVERY HALF MILLION OF THE POPULATION, and even of these, the majority have charge of English congregations, and many are engaged most of their time in teaching in Government schools and colleges, where the education given is purely secular. They are obliged to teach only the prescribed subjects, and the natural result is that the scholars may become members of the Theistic Brahmo Church, but are not likely to become Christians. An exceedingly small number of these clergy are engaged in preaching in the vernacular.

Nevertheless, notwithstanding all these drawbacks, such a man as Lord Lawrence (Governor-General) has publicly declared his conviction that, "much as the English have done to benefit India, the missionaries have done more than all other agencies combined." The same testimony is borne by such men as Sir Donald McLeod, Sir Bartle Frere, Lord Napier, and many others well acquainted with the undercurrents of Indian life. The marvel seems to be that so much has been accomplished by a body so numerically weak. Now that so large a number of natives of intellectual mark and culture are being trained for the ministry, there seems some prospect that the prophecy made by a Brahman may be fulfilled, namely, that *the mighty tree of Hindooism will at length be felled, when the Christian axes are supplied with handles cut from its own boughs.*

It may be that some of these native preachers will find means to set forth the truth in such a simple yet forcible manner as may best appeal to Oriental thought, and, adopting something of the method of St. John the Baptist (who represents the type of preacher who best appeals to the mind of India), may so arouse their countrymen, that the Great Awakening may begin, which shall stir the whole land.

And although the British Government places all religions on precisely the same footing, there can be no doubt that the mere fact of two million boys and girls receiving an enlightened education wherein their caste is utterly ignored, must go far towards freeing them from the bondage in which they have hitherto been held by their Brahman teachers, and justifies Dr. Hunter's description of Indian Government schools as "those pestles and mortars for the superstition and priestcraft of India."

One very remarkable point connected with these schools (in which young India learns that under the rule of India's Empress *all* professions are open to all competitors, of whatever caste) is, that the proud Mohammedans stand aloof, refusing to attend schools which are open to all men, irrespective of birth or creed. Consequently they fail to qualify for Government examinations and employment. The practical result of this is, that although they number one-third of the whole population of Lower Bengal, they only hold one-tenth of the whole Government patronage. Out of 504 Government appointments in Bengal, only fifty-three are held by Mohammedans. Thus the race, who, in the last century, were the mighty rulers of Hindoostan, are now falling out of power simply because of their own exclusiveness.

Having thus glanced over the principal great changes of faith which by turns have held supreme sway in this land—Aboriginal, Pure Aryan, these blending to produce Brahmanism; next Buddhist, Jain, very degenerate Brahman, Mohammedan; and now once more Brahman, or Hindoo—we will leave the twin cities of Muttra and Bindrabund to their many memories, and travel northward to the great Mohammedan city of Delhi.

NOTE.—Here is the result of the census giving the number of Her Majesty's subjects in Hindoostan in A.D. 1881, according to their creed—

Hindoos	187,937,450
Mohammedans	50,121,585
Aboriginal Hill Tribes (Nature worshippers)	6,426,511
Buddhists	3,418,884
Christians	1,862,634
Sikhs	1,853,426
Jains	1,221,896
Parsees	250,000

CHAPTER VIII.

DELHI.

The Punjab—Modern Delhi—A luxurious Camp—The Cashmere Gate—The Mutiny—Capture of the Great Mogul—Past history—Skinner's Church—A Novel Studio—The Great Mosque—The Ancient City—Successive Emperors—Magnificent Tombs—Deep Wells—Homes of the Poor—Broken Earthenware—Fakirs—No Old Dwellings—Stone Observatory—At the base of the Kootub—A Paradise for Artists—The Giant Minaret—Hindoo Columns—The Iron Pillar—"Dhilli, the Unstable."

If Agra held us spell-bound as in a dream of all that is pure and lovely in architecture, Delhi remains stamped on our memories as the very embodiment of power and strength, a dwelling-place of giants. Nowhere will you find more marvellous proofs of the might of the Mohammedan empire, or be more impressed with reverence for the master minds which designed such wondrous structures, than in these two cities of the Moguls.

Fain would I linger in telling you of the marvels of Delhi, of the great walled city wherein the wicked king so recently held his vile but gorgeous court, of the solemn beauty of the mighty mosques wherein the white-robed worshippers assemble in throngs so vast; and, above all, of the wild, silent desolation of the great plain beyond, thickly strewn with stupendous ruins of Cyclopean forts, huge tombs with gigantic gateways—the smallest of which would make the finest of our old English bars seem utterly puny and contemptible—and marble mosques, whose glittering white, contrasts with the world of carved red sandstone on every side. Here each successive Emperor of the mighty Pathan dynasty has left his mark, and you may wander in every direction over an expanse of four-and-twenty miles, exploring the wonders of this marvellous world of ruins.

We had bidden adieu to the North West Provinces (which include Agra, Cawnpore, and Allahabad), and were now in the Punjab, or land of five rivers; a name which, like the Doab, two rivers, is a compound of Hindoo and Persian; *ab*, meaning water in the latter tongue. The five rivers are, I believe, the Beeas, the Thelum, the Ravee, the Sutlej, and the Chenab.

The modern city of Delhi (Dhilli, the Unstable), is called by the natives Shah-Jehan-abad, or the city of that great Mohammedan Emperor whose work we have already seen at Agra. He founded this city in 1631. Its streets, palaces, mosques, and mighty fort of red sandstone, (which even now are marvels of strength and beauty,) covered a space seven miles in circumference, which he inclosed by immense walls of the same dark red stone, pierced by seven great gates. On the third side, the city is washed by the blue waters of the Jumna, from whose brink rise the domes of stately mosques with their tall graceful minarets, like fingers pointing heavenwards.

Strangely in contrast with these memorials of Mohammedan conquerors, is the one great work of the present rulers, a work still so new, that the native mind has not yet ceased to marvel at it; I mean the railway, by which we had already travelled a thousand miles from Calcutta, and which, had we been disposed to continue our journey, would have carried us right up to Lahore without a pause. Now it brought us into the city of Shah-Jehan, actually passing through his palace wall, and the picturesque old five-arched bridge; and almost touching the grand state-prison of Selim Ghur.

Our first days in Delhi were spent just outside the walls of the present city, in the luxurious camp of an old friend, whose work involved such perpetual locomotion that his camp was literally his home; and a very cosy home it was, with large double-roofed drawing-room tent and dining-room tent, and capital tents for friends. These formed one group, while our hostess's sleeping tent and nurseries were inclosed by a high canvas wall, within which the merriest and rosiest little ones might play to their heart's content, and certainly they proved that their patriarchal life agreed with them. The servants and cooking were established somewhere in the background; while, under shadow of the trees, a flock of forty camels browsed, or grunted or roared, as they felt inclined.

The camp was pitched near the Cashmere Gate, a name recalling brave deeds of daring in the terrible days of 1857. Our host had himself served throughout that campaign, and beneath these very walls had received such a wound, as had helped to stamp those scenes indelibly on his memory. So, as we wandered together, step by step over all that hard-fought ground, our thoughts could not but revert to the terrible scenes of fighting and bloodshed that had been here enacted, and in which we knew that he had borne so gallant a part.

Here was the spot where a breach was effected in the walls; here a garden, now one tangle of roses and jessamine, where blood then flowed like water. Behind us lay the great rocky ridge, a sort of back-bone to the country, where on a commanding height the British army lay encamped, like an avenging legion, ready to sweep down upon the polluted city, and wash it free from the stain of English blood, and from the un-utterable wickedness that had so long lurked in its high places.

On that ridge of glorious memory we lingered in the cool of the evening, looking down upon the beautiful city, whose clustering domes and minarets, rising from the mass of rich green foliage, seemed as though embosomed in coolest gardens; though in truth it all looked hot and dry enough, as we drew nearer.

A tall monolith bearing date B.C. 300, was brought here from Meerut, and marks the boundary of the British entrenchments; where, through those long burning summer months, while the foe raged without, and cholera within the camp, the Standard of England still floated securely, in the sight of her foes, never to be lowered, till it was transferred to the walls of the Great Mogul.

In the wonderful calm and stillness of the short twilight, we tried to picture the scenes that were here enacted, when from the city at our feet, shells sometimes reached the very spot where we stood; and when treachery and death lurked on every side. Now scarcely a sound stirred the silent air, though here and there we could distinguish groups of women and little children, going on their way in perfect security.

It was easier to recall that awful time, when we stood on the drawbridge before the Cashmere Gate, one of the great gates in the fortified wall by which the British troops had resolved to enter the city. Lieutenants Salkeld and Home, R.E., led the forlorn hope, whose work it was to blow up the gates. They advanced calmly to almost certain death, bearing heavy powder-bags on their heads.

The foe seem to have been paralysed by the audacity of the proceeding, and eight or ten powder-bags had been safely laid ere they recovered themselves sufficiently to fire. Salkeld fell wounded on the drawbridge, and was laid in the ditch: two of his sergeants fell back mortally wounded. Salkeld lingered a few days, then died of his wounds. Home survived to fight and fall at the blowing up of another fort, at Malaghur. But they had done their work here, and done it well. A few seconds later, a terrific explosion shook the mighty walls, and the massive gateway lay shattered. Then the bugler sounded the advance, and, with a loud cheer, the storming party marched in.

But a terrible day of hand-to-hand fighting still awaited the troops; every house and every housetop was crowded with thousands of desperate men. The heat from sun and fire was so terrific that the troops were well-nigh overpowered. Their wary foes had laid open tempting cellars, well stored with arrack and the most intoxicating kinds of spirit. By command of General Nicholson vast quantities of these were destroyed; but it was impossible to prevent the soldiers from, in some instances, transgressing, and there is reason to fear that a terrible number of those who touched and tasted the accursed thing fell easy victims to the foe.

All day long, every street and lane of the city resounded with cries of conflict and of death, and the fearful din waxed louder and louder. Ere nightfall the city was fairly conquered, and the Great Mogul had fled with a handful of followers to seek refuge in the tomb of one of his ancestors, leaving his palace in the hands of the conquerors. But that day's fighting cost England upwards of a thousand men killed and wounded, and sixty-six officers, amongst whom was the brave General Nicholson, who was shot while leading his troops through a narrow lane near the Lahore Gate.

Of the few followers who had accompanied the wretched old King of Delhi in his flight, one proved a traitor and revealed his hiding-place to Hodson and his Sikhs (the Guides, as they were called). To him the miserable old man surrendered, and he was taken back to his own palace, where he was formally tried, and whence in due time he was sent to Rangoon and there died.

It has been noted as curious that almost the last act of the last representative of the East India Company, should have been thus to sentence the last Great Mogul, and heir of the House of Timour, to be transported across the seas; and that the trial should have taken place in that very palace where, little more than two hundred years previously, its first representatives stood awed in the presence of his gorgeous ancestors, humbly craving an audience from the magnificent being, whose Peacock Throne, glittering with priceless gems, was among the marvels of the East.

That throne was valued at upwards of 1,200,000*l.* (according to one authority 6,000,000*l.*). It was made by order of the great Shah-Jehan, whose jewellers wrought upon it for seven years. It was a golden throne incrusted with precious stones, and overshadowed by a golden canopy fringed with pearls. At the back of the throne were two jewelled peacocks with expanded tails, the natural colours being produced by the lavish use of rubies and sapphires, pearls and emeralds. In that palace jewels were so abundant that they must have been of small account. Even the Imperial umbrellas of gold-embroidered crimson velvet were fringed with pearls, and the golden handles, which were eight feet high, were studded with diamonds. But then the Oriental umbrella has a right to be gorgeous, inasmuch as it is a recognised emblem of Royalty. For this reason in the early days of "The Company," British ladies and gentlemen were forbidden the use of an umbrella to shield them from the blazing sun, when in presence of any mighty potentate.

The wonderful Peacock Throne disappeared after the Mutiny and no one has ever found out what became of it. The miracle was, that it should have escaped the wholesale plundering which Delhi and the greater part of Hindoostan received in 1738 when invaded by Nadir Shah with a vast army of Persians and Georgians. A place is still shown in the main street of Delhi, as the spot where for two whole days he sat holding his drawn sword as a signal that his cruel hordes should slay, without mercy, all whom they could find. The number thus murdered was beyond calculation.

After this frightful massacre of the inhabitants, the cruel conqueror, having plundered the city, set it on fire, and is said to have climbed to the top of one of the highest minarets to watch the scene. At the end of five months, he retired, carrying with him, plunder to the value of twenty-four million sterling; besides camels, horses, and elephants, without number. He also carried away captive vast numbers of the most skilful workers in wood and stone.

Before the country had rallied from this wholesale spoliation, the Mahrattas, and then the Afghans, came to vex and plunder the people, and to glean such ears as had escaped the rich harvest of the Persians.

We stood in Shah-Jehan's beautiful Hall of Audience, with its colonnades and countless pillars of pure white marble, and courts open to the deep blue sky. On the entrance are the words which Moore has rendered famous—"If there be an Elysium on earth, it is here."

Like most other fair things of earth, this paradise was all too quickly polluted, till it became a very den of foulest wickedness, where the world, the flesh, and the devil, ran riot undisturbed.

At the time of the Mutiny, besides troops and attendants of every class, there were actually three thousand persons of the blood royal living within the palace; who, for once, merged their mutual hatred and plots one against the other, in one common determination to wrest back from the English their lost power and wealth, and utterly to exterminate the white race.

Now all that princely mob has passed away, with its luxury and its crime, and as we entered the Great Hall the deep silence of those beautiful halls was only broken by the voices of workmen, who in the coarsest fashion, were restoring with coloured plaster the vacant spaces in the exquisitely inlaid marbles, whence ruthless bayonets had contrived to dig out precious stones, as from a mine. So firmly however were they embedded that almost every gem seems to have been broken in the attempt.

Here one most lovely little marble mosque (whose carved pillars, arches, and roof, are alike dazzling by their spotless purity,) recalls the beauty of Agra, as do also the baths, and the delicate marble tracery in the Zenana.

Turning away from the palace, we loitered a while among the tempting shops in the Chandnee Chouk, or Silver Street, which is the main thoroughfare of the city, and the especial quarter of the rich buniahs (merchants). It is a broad thoroughfare, nearly a mile in length. Down the middle of the street there is a raised canal of the clearest water, overshadowed by large trees, whose grateful shade is to the people a boon well-nigh as precious as the water itself.

The greater part of the canal is covered, and is only open here and there, that the inhabitants may draw unlimited supplies. The same priceless stream fertilises the city gardens and the neighbouring fields.

Delhi is one of the few towns we saw which boasts of rather a handsome English church, the white dome of which, appearing over the Cashmere Gate, might be mistaken for a mosque, but for the Cross on the cupola, on which the natives look with some awe, inasmuch as when, in the terrible days of 1857, shot and shell flew round it like hail, and greatly damaged the roof, it escaped all injury. The church was built by Colonel Skinner, who having for forty years made India his home, had become so liberal in his views that he simultaneously erected a very fine mosque for the Mohammedans and a temple for the Hindoos, not knowing on which to bestow his preference. However, a small tablet in the church records that in his later hours he decided in favour of Christianity.

He it was who raised the body of irregular horse bearing his name. He was a brave officer, and much distinguished in the wars of Lord Lake and Lord Hastings. He also seems to have brought his arms to the assistance of divers native princes, and altogether passed through a strangely chequered course of service. He was a good type of a race of British officers which has died out with the facilities of return to England; men who in course of thirty or forty years forgot all difference of colour and of faith, and took to themselves wives of the daughters of the land, assimilating in their manners and customs to the people amongst whom they lived, themselves becoming half Hindoo and half Mohammedan. Hence in several idol temples we were shown beautifully-wrought bells and other things, which the priests affirmed had been presented by Europeans as thankofferings for recovery from illness ! !

One pleasant morning we started, as usual, at daybreak, the air crisp and fresh on this January morning as on an English May-day. We drove to the old palace, and through the grand gateway, perhaps the strongest we had yet seen—arch beyond arch of solid red sandstone, more like a huge tunnel than a mass of building. We walked all along the great walls in search of the best point from which to sketch the Jumma Musjid, a magnificent mosque. That point we ascertained to be the flat roof of a *baboo's* house, so an intimation was sent to him that a great "mem-sahib" desired to honour him with her presence.

The baboo, however, had gone into the city, but a bystander

offered me the use of his roof, if I could only get on to it. He was a poor farrier, but a thorough gentleman, and did the honours of his house admirably. He took me up his crazy stairs to an upper court open to the sky, off which opened various small rooms. Then he placed his poor rickety *charpoy* (bedstead) on end against the wall, that I might use it as a ladder. I managed to scramble up, and there sat all the morning without intrusion, my feminine presence being considered sacred. The good man declined going to his work all that day, having had so great a charge committed to him. We ventured to suggest that he might depute that responsibility to his wife, but he scouted the idea as preposterous—to think that *she* could look after any article so important! So he sat patiently at the foot of the ladder, hour after hour, till the *sahib-logu* (gentlefolk) came to reclaim their hostage, when he helped me to scramble down again, and vowed that his roof had acquired a new interest!

Apart from the novelty of the studio, it always astonishes the natives to see any one drawing or painting from nature. They themselves paint exquisite architectural miniatures, but they invariably say that the white men only photograph. Certainly the intricacy of arches, domes, minarets, and cupolas involves an amount of patience and care that few might be disposed to give.

This grand mosque, and another very similar one (which, rising from the brink of the river, has the additional charm of being therein mirrored), are fluted with divers marbles. It stands on a foundation of rock, and all the space around it having been cleared for military purposes during the mutiny, it has the advantage of being well seen.

An immense outer wall of red sandstone arches forms a quadrangle, at the four corners of which are towers, whose marble domes rest on slim red pillars. At the three sides, immensely wide flights of marble stairs lead up to three great gateways: the central one, which faces the east, is so holy that only on great feasts is it used. By these gateways you enter the usual great open court surrounded on three sides by long colonnades of red sandstone. On the fourth side rise the arches of the mosque itself, which also of course faces the east, so that the worshipper as he enters may find himself looking towards the west, that is, towards Mecca.

All is of the same deep-red stone inlaid with white marble, and verses from the Koran in huge letters in black marble. The three great domes of white marble are fluted with black, and carry the eye up to the glittering pinnacles; the tall minarets are fluted with red and white alternately, while every little turret is crowned with a marble dome supported by red pillars. Add to this a few green trees, a clear blue sky with fleecy white clouds, and an atmosphere of balmy sunshine, and you have before you a temple worthy of the name.

Strange (is it not?) to think for how short a time the Mohammedans held their sway in this land, and yet how quickly they multiplied these grand buildings in every corner of the country. It is said that this one alone cost Shah Jehan a sum equal to 120,000*l.*, and *that* was two hundred years ago, and in India, where labour is a very cheap commodity even now. Certainly, if the Christians were driven out of India to-morrow, their successors would find little to admire in their puny chapels of brick and mortar, few and far between. The mosques are open at all hours and seasons, that every passer-by may enter and worship. So all day long you see a constant succession of men going up to the temple to pray. They lay down their shoes and their bundles beside them, and go through the ceremonial washings at the great marble fountain. Then, having prayed, they go on with their day's work.

Every good Mohammedan is bound to pray five times a day, at dawn, at noon, in the afternoon, at sunset, and at night. Before he ventures to pray, however, he must at least cleanse his hands, his feet, and his face, for the Prophet has declared that "Ablution is the half of prayer." If he cannot get water, especially running water, wherewith to wash, he may rub himself with a little earth or sand, which is also purifying. Then, bowing down with his face to the ground, he lays his forehead in the dust. His prayer is accompanied with perpetual changes of posture; perhaps if he is in a great hurry, they occur eight or ten times in a minute. Sometimes he stands with hands extended, repeating the ninety-nine attributes of God; then falling prone on the earth, covers his mouth with his hands; then kneels with hands laid palm to palm; then raised heavenward, while his body is bowed to earth, or curved backward, but always facing Mecca. The bystander is very apt to look on all this as mere formalism. Doubtless in many instances it is so, for our dark brothers do not monopolise the virtues any more than the vices.

But if you enter such a mosque as this on a Friday—the Mohammedan Sabbath—at one o'clock, the hour of prayer, and look down on that vast congregation of white-robed worshippers, going through the moves with a precision that would reduce a rigid Ritualist to despair, you will be forced to acknowledge that you have never beheld a scene more solemn. There is room in that great court for twelve thousand persons, and the whole of this assemblage kneel, pray, prostrate themselves, rise again, stand up with uplifted hands and heaven-turned faces, as though touched by an electric spring. The great quadrangle is paved like a chessboard in black and white marble, that every man may stand on his own square, and that all may be equal. And overhead, the broad, calm, blue sky is spread as the sole canopy.

Just before the service began, a kind old man took us up to a small alcove in the great Mecca gateway, whence we might peep into the mosque at the further side, and look down on the sea of turbaned heads below. A few women knelt apart near the doorway. The fact of their being there at all was of dubious propriety; moreover the teaching of Mahomet seems to have left it very uncertain whether the prayer of a woman has any chance of reaching heaven. However, the poor things would not lose that chance, and, as they passed out, they gave alms of such things as they had, to the miserable beggars who are always ready to be made use of as stepping-stones heavenward.

Intensely interesting as was the comparatively modern city, there was to us an irresistible fascination in the great desolate plain, where beyond the walls of modern Delhi lie the stupendous ruins of the past. A space of fully twenty-four square miles is thickly strewn with colossal tombs, forts, public buildings, and other remains of the once mighty city, where one proud dynasty after another has left its little mark upon the earth, only to add one feature more to that widespread desolation.

The ancient Hindoo name of the city was Indraprasth, but each successive emperor bequeathed his own name to some great portion of it. Thus on one rocky cliff stands the old Fort of Togluck-abad (the city of Togluck), a mighty fortress built by the emperor of that name; now silent and deserted, not even a sign of life round the beautiful white marble mosque so pure and spotless that it positively gleams amongst the surrounding mountains of red stone-work, which stretch away on every side, in walls and towers so vast that they seem as though built by giant hands of old.

The great walls which inclosed the palace of Togluck are still traceable in places. They were once defended by seven mighty forts, and fifty-two strong gateways gave access to the city. The houses of the living have long since crumbled away, but thousands of tombs still cover the dust of these turbulent princes and their favourites.

One is pointed out as that of the son of Togluck, who caused his own father to be crushed to death, and who devised sundry merry sports of the same class. It is recorded that his chief delight was to go out with his warriors hunting his own peaceful people, and bringing home their heads to mark his day's sport! The gates of his city are said to have been adorned with thousands of these ghastly trophies!!

On the other hand, when in a generous mood, he would go forth in state, followed by elephants loaded with precious coin, which was showered among the people as he passed: a backsheish so liberal atoned for a good many heads, and so, his selection of happy hunting fields was considered merely an imperial eccentricity.

So likewise was the pomp and solemnity with which, attended by his whole court, he gave burial to one of his own teeth, over which he erected a magnificent tomb!

Another giant fort and mosque bear the name of Shere Shah, an emperor of the Pathan or Afghan dynasty, and worthy of honourable mention, as having done much to open up the country and establish the security of all travellers and merchandise. His reign was a short one. Five years after he had driven the Emperor Humaioon from the throne he was himself deposed by the great Akbar, son of Humaioon. Yet in those five years he made roads of great extent, bordering them with trees that might give a grateful shadow from the heat. At every stage he established rest-houses—caravanserais wherein all travellers should be entertained at the public expense. He built mosques for their benefit, lest in travelling they should forget their devotions. He also established relays of horses at short distances, so as to keep up communication with every corner of his empire.

Feroze Shah is another of the emperors who has left many memorials of his reign: fifty great sluices for irrigation, thirty schools, twenty caravanserais, 100 palaces, five hospitals, forty mosques, 100 bridges, 150 wells, and gardens without number, are among the improvements ascribed to him. We turned aside from the desolate plain and clambered up a rocky height to see a great stone monolith which bears his name, though learned men who have puzzled out its long inscriptions refer it to a far more ancient date, namely, that of Asoka (B.C. 250), whose tall monolith supporting a lion we noticed at Allahabad.

Our first expedition into the ancient city was to see the tomb of the Emperor Humaioon, grandson of Mahomet, and father of the great Akbar. These huge tombs are very much like the mosques, minus the minarets, and instead of the invariable three domes, they have generally one great central dome, and a cluster of lesser ones. To realise the tomb of any Mohammedan of note you must picture to yourself London's great St. Paul's converted into marble, and set down in a great garden, with all the bars of York piled into one, to act as gateway. Climb to the top of one of these, and as far as your eye can reach, for a circle of twenty miles, the whole plain is dotted with similar buildings, only varying in size, material, and curve of the dome. Round each great man are smaller domes, to his doctor, his ministers, and other favourites.

That of Humaioon is of white marble, and that of his barber is of exquisite green enamel. It is too ponderous to make a good picture by itself, so I wandered among the ruins in search of a foreground, and found another tomb to another emperor, of the Pathan dynasty, a cluster of tall pillars and arches, supporting a nest of domes, all inlaid with encaustic tiles of every brilliant, metallic colour—green, blue, gold—fresh as if they had been the work of yesterday. A few native huts beneath the dark trees supplied the precious blue smoke, which is to an Indian picture what the mist is to a Scotch one—invaluable. I found a perch on the top of a neighbouring tomb, and there sat undisturbed for hours overlooking that desolate plain, with its colossal ruins, and specially noting one giant on the horizon—a mighty minaret towering far above its fellows. This was the famous Kootub.

The chief interest of Humaioon's tomb dates from the mutiny, when, as I before said, the miserable old king sought refuge here, and finally gave himself up to Hodson.

But the wicked princes still remained in their hiding place, surrounded by about 7,000 followers, the very scum of the earth. Hodson returned with 100 of his Sikhs, and only one other officer, Captain Macdonald. Riding in advance of his men, he coolly commanded the rebels to pile their arms. The extraordinary audacity of such an assumption of power must have strangely over-awed these men, for without a word they obeyed, and the arms were straightway carried to the city in cart-loads. It is said that to assume more perfect composure, Hodson never took his cigar from his lips.

Then commanding the princes to come forth, in the presence of these 7,000 followers, he carried them prisoners towards the city. But ere he reached it he seems to have feared a rescue, and then and there shot them with his own hand—an action for which he has been sorely blamed. But it is hard for men in times of peace and safety to judge their fellows in such circumstances as these. Suffice it to say that the dead bodies were laid, in the great thoroughfare of the main street, on the very spot where their hands are said to have been dyed in the blood of Englishwomen, and their own followers, beholding the dishonoured corpses, acknowledged the righteous retribution of Allah.

Not far from Humaioon's tomb, and in the midst of desolate ruins, and rubbish, and forsaken gardens, we came on the tomb of Nizam-ud-deen, a very holy saint. I think of all the exquisitely refined carving we had yet seen, this excelled. The pure white marble screen round the sarcophagus with its fairy lattice-work, and the delicate arches and pillars, are all covered with graceful birds and butterflies, in spite of the Mohammedan prohibition contained in the Koran which lies at the head of the grave. The dome has a copper roofing with gilt pattern of flowers on a deep-blue ground.

White-robed priests, whose life-work it is to keep the lamps burning, have charge of this lovely tomb, and pray and read the Koran aloud, that the dust of the saint may be refreshed by the sound of holy words. The tomb is covered with rich stuffs spangled with gold, and surmounted by a canopy of gorgeous drapery, whence hangs a string of ostrich eggs. Fresh flowers are continually scattered over this and the neighbouring tombs, several of which lie near together, each in its own little court, inclosed in a screen of marble lace-work, and overshadowed by cool foliage.

In one court lies the dust of the poet Chusero; in the next, beneath the green turf, sleeps Jehanari, the beautiful daughter of Shah Jehan, who voluntarily shared his captivity, and after a life of such purity and holiness as earned her a place among the Mohammedan saints, desired on her death-bed that she might be buried without pomp or splendour, as grass and flowers were the only covering meet for the poor in spirit.

A little further is the beautiful marble tomb of one of her kinsmen, who died in the attempt daily to increase his capacity for drinking cherry-brandy, in defiance of the Prophet!

Close by is a large tank, one of those sacred *bowliės* or deep wells, into which the natives are always anxious to make suicidal leaps from frightful heights, for the smallest possible backsheish. Some of those near the Kootub are of incalculable depth; and it is decidedly alarming as you stand in the dim twilight peering down to the water far below you, suddenly to see a dark, naked figure rush past, and, leaping feet foremost into the yawning abyss below, disappear in the darkness, falling with dull splash into the fathomless waters. Eventually he will regain the upper world by a subterranean passage, and long flight of steps. These creatures are regularly trained to their work, beginning as mere children to leap from low stages, and gradually increasing in audacity.

Here and there, in the midst of this great desert of colossal ruins, we came to a little cluster of huts, which, like all the houses of the poor, consisted only of mud walls and straw thatch on a framework of bamboo. The contrast between the perishable dwellings of the living, and the massive tombs of the mighty dead seemed strange indeed; yet how poor soever a native may be, his hut is invariably clean, being constantly plastered with fresh coatings of mud which dries quickly, leaving a shining surface. His clay fire-place and clay settle are alike clean, so are his bright copper or brass vessels, which are always brillantly polished. He who is so poor that he cannot afford such metal-ware substitutes the coarsest earthenware, which, however, he must break after every meal, as he cannot clean it properly. In fact, he carries into daily life that Levitical law of the sin offering which[1] commanded the breaking of the earthen vessels and the scouring of brazen pots—hence the heaps of broken crockery near the very poorest huts. You see here, as elsewhere, he who lacks capital pays dearest in the long run.

Some, however, are content to use a green leaf for a plate, and make lamps and drinking cups of gourds; a couple of stones as pestle and mortar, and a coarse mat and rickety charpoy, complete the furniture of a Hindoo hut.

This enormous consumption of crockery entailed by perpetual breakages of course keeps many a potter's wheel at work, and I

[1] Lev. vi. 28.

always found a certain attraction in watching the manufacture. The lump of clay in the hands of the potter, moulding so obediently to his will, recalled so many old Scriptural illustrations. And then too, we were told, that "the potter's field, to bury strangers in" is a fact of the present day, for that, whenever a clay field has been used up, it becomes a convenient burial-ground for Mohammedans and others who prefer committing their dead to mother earth, rather than to the flames.

Interesting, though very unpleasant objects, were certain miserable fakirs (Mohammedans), whom we met prowling among the tombs, like grim and ghastly ghouls—starved, shrivelled skeletons, doing life-long penance in atonement for their sins, or striving to heap up stores of merit, and craving alms from all passers-by for the building of some temple, or the digging of some well, or other pious work.

Like the Hindoo yogis, they have made a vow of the strictest poverty; they must eat only once a day of rice and vegetables, and that sparingly; no "early" breakfast, and "heavy" breakfast for them, no tiffin, no five o'clock tea, no late dinner, no evening tea and coffee! They are bound to be indifferent alike to cold, heat, and hunger; to the praise of men, and to their reproach. And if, after all, they find it impossible thus to master their natural being, they become more criminal than ever by having embraced a life of holiness, of which they have fallen short!

What *can* be the reason that in all ages and in all faiths, the odour of sanctity seems to have been thus identified with unspeakable filth? If it were only among savages, one could understand it, but how Christians first came to set their cleanliness and their godliness at opposite poles is a perpetual mystery. Really, to read the lives of the old Christian saints, and see what stress is laid on their unwashen clothes, and personal filth, their matted hair, never even combed, their nails like talons, their garments a sort of menagerie for all manner of creeping things, does make one marvel at such strange developments of the religious life.

As to these Indian saints, whether yogis or fakirs, Hindoos or Mohammedans, you cannot imagine a more living picture of squalid wretchedness than these poor creatures, whose sole raiment (save an almost invisible rag) is their own filthy mass of tangled hair, while their sole possessions are a hollow gourd with which to draw water, and a miserable charpoy, *i.e.* the light framework on which every one sleeps for fear of serpents, and on which they squat under shadow of the sacred peepul and banian trees.

Such picturesque old trees ! like great wide-spreading old oaks with gnarled snake-like roots twisting in strange contortions, here and there breaking through the carved stone-work of some old temple on which the sunlight just glances, but the ruins are half veiled by the brown fringe of beard-like filaments and trailing fibres. The leaf of the sacred peepul somewhat resembles that of our own poplar, both in form and in its tremulous habit. It quivers ceaselessly like our aspen. Green pigeons and parroquets by thousands hide among the foliage, and sometimes a company of flying foxes hang head downwards from the upper branches, or flap away on heavy wing, uttering querulous cries as if complaining of our approach.

From time to time we noticed curious twin trees ; a date palm growing out of the heart of a banian, or a peepul from an Indian-rubber tree. These are sometimes of natural growth, sometimes grafted by devotees, but in every case such tree-wedlock is held by the Hindoo in deepest veneration.

On and on we drove over the wild desolate plain, and through the sea of ruins—ruins on every side of us. Tombs and domes literally without number, mighty walls and fortresses and innumerable mosques, gateways, wells and old gardens with shady trees.

But what can have become of the habitations of the builders is a continual source of wonder, for human dwellings are the one thing conspicuous by their absence, and we can scarcely suppose that these princes and nobles built their palaces of such very perishable materials as to account for their total disappearance.

We wandered from one to another of the Cyclopean forts till we were fairly exhausted, finding so much to admire, and to wonder at. We especially marvelled at the giant observatory built by Rajah Tey Sing, of Teypore, where every instrument is a massive pile of masonry; instruments of which we neither knew the name nor the use, but could only gaze in amazement at such strange inventions of science. We saw a similar observatory at Benares, and heard of three others, all attributed to the same builder.

As the day drew on, we passed many picturesque groups of veiled women and their brown children going to the wells to draw water, or else to make their evening pooja (sacrifice) to some favourite god—probably a hideous monster smeared with red paint to represent the offering of blood—set up under the nearest peepul tree, each woman carrying a brass plate whereon are laid her simple offerings, a brass cup with clear water to be poured over the sacred image, a handful of rice, a little bright-coloured powder, and a few flowers. The colour of the flowers and of the powder depends on the object of worship. The monkey god and the elephant-headed Ganesa, and Siva and his wife, prefer red, but Vishnu and Krishna and their wives are honoured with yellow, as is the case also in all western legends of sun-mythology.

Then, as the lengthening shadows of the great ruins vanished with the setting sun, we returned to the hospitable camp, to a tent home, scarcely more transitory than those vanished halls of the emperors, over the total disappearance of which (the dwelling-houses, I mean) we marvelled more and more.

There was a fascination about the wild silent desolation of the great plain that attracted us irresistibly. So we resolved to take up our quarters in the very heart of it, at the base of the mighty Kootub, which is a stupendous minaret of red sandstone towering like a giant above every other ruin near it; here we found a very comfortable dak-bungalow, a travellers' rest-house, kept by a shrivelled-up, little old man, who looked as though all life's energy had been fairly baked out of him. Nevertheless, he cooked for us and made himself generally useful.

The place is not altogether one of spotless repute, inasmuch as there is a village somewhere in the neighbourhood whose inhabitants bear a very bad character, and are said to be consummate thieves, as my sister and her husband had on a previous occasion found to their cost; their horses' coats and those of the grooms having been carried off in the night, while the latter slumbered peacefully. However we got off scot free, and enjoyed ourselves beyond measure.

Here, as at Futteypore-Sikri, every species of wild beast and bird find refuge among the ruins, especially flocks of gorgeous wild peacocks, green parrots and doves; deer and black partridge are also abundant. So it is a Paradise for sportsmen as well as artists. Only think! game of all sorts and sizes, and no taking out a gun licence, or fear of trespassing. You may wander about alone the livelong day, perhaps flushing some peafowl which glance like a flash of rainbow light as they vanish among the dark trees; or you may startle an irate porcupine from his mid-day siesta, or some sleepy owl which sits blinking in the gloom of the ruins; but the chances are that you will never see a human being, except, it may be, a poor goatherd trying to collect green branches to keep his flock alive during the long drought; or else some wild-looking camel driver, whose hungry charge are foraging for themselves, cropping the foliage of the sweet babool trees.

The grand old city is now literally "a couching place for camels." They are stabled in some of the old tombs, as are also flocks of quaint Indian goats, and sheep with long drooping ears. The goats are wonderfully sensible creatures, almost as wise as dogs. I saw one tumble into a large tank, a drop of eight or ten feet. The water was very shallow, and the poor creature was on his hind legs in a moment, crying for help. The goatherd vainly tried to reach him, and at last went to fetch a rope with a noose. The goat seemed perfectly to understand his share of the business, and, placing his fore-feet as high as he could reach, against the wall, stood immovable while the noose was dropped over his head, after which he allowed himself to be drawn up without one struggle.

Among minor details of animal life we noted great flights of white butterflies, which seemed specially attracted by the euphorbia bushes, which, however, were also haunted by pretty pale green spiders, whose webs were apparently set as butterfly-traps. But, though some fell victims, most of the white-winged darlings floated away in tremulous clouds like snow flakes.

As we wandered on, every turn revealed some new ruin, tempting us to explore further some tomb whose enamelled tiles appeared more brilliant than all we had yet seen—bronze tiles and violet tiles, some silvery, some like burnished gold, others the most brilliant azure, or glittering green, crimson or salmon colour. They are generally used in external decoration, being set in regular patterns round many of the domes. But here and there in the old gardens we came on open halls or kiosks, the interior of which was all thus adorned, well-nigh as perfect as the day it was finished.

And far overhead, its top reaching up to heaven, towers the stupendous Kootub-Minar, probably the most gigantic minaret in the world. If the Taj is the embodiment of purity and loveliness, this surely is the very type of power and grandeur. I never before felt oppressed by any human work, but this ponderous giant seems to awe one.

I suppose the feeling is only due to its huge size, for so far from possessing any beauty of form, it resembles a Cyclopean red telescope, divided into five sections by four great projecting balconies. There was a sixth section, which was taken down, as being unsafe. Its height is now 240 feet; it was then 250. Its diameter at the top is thirteen feet; at the base forty-nine feet. The three lower sections of the pillar are fluted. One section has angular flutings, another round flutings, a third angular and round alternately. The topmost sections are smooth, and inlaid with white marble.

From the base to the summit broad bands of writing, several feet in depth, run round the pillar. These inscriptions, which are in high relief and edged with delicate carving, are in the Kufic, that is, the ancient Arabic character, setting forth the praises of divers emperors, together with quotations from the Koran, and the ninety-nine attributes of God. The inscriptions on the base are to Mohammed Ghori and to his successor, Kootub-ud-deen; that on the top to a later sovereign, Altamah. One sentence sets forth that "In the name of God the most merciful, the Lord invites to Paradise, and brings into the way of righteousness, whosoever is willing to enter." Another sentence declares that

"Kootub-ud-deen, on whom be the mercy of God, constructed this mosque."

Now Kootub-ud-deen, "the Pole-star of religion" was originally a slave, brought from Turkestan, and purchased by Mohammed Ghori, who was the first of the Pathan or Afghan emperors. In his service Kootub rose to the rank of a general, and succeeded his master on the throne. In the year A.D. 1193 he conquered Meerut and Delhi, and here established his seat of government. After the manner of the Mohammedans, he converted all Hindoo temples into quarries for the building of mosques, and the native tradition declares that this great pillar was among the ancient work so transformed.

The Hindoos believe it to have been built by a king in remote ages to gratify his favourite daughter, who, by ascending to its summit, might, while she worshipped the rising sun, behold its first gleam glittering on the sacred waters of the Jumna. They say that round the column were carved figures in bas-relief, illustrative of Hindoo mythology, and that these were artfully transformed into Arabic characters, and thus appropriated by Kootub. They point out that the rich carving below the balconies consists of clusters of bells and other symbols, essentially Brahminical, and never used by the Islamites.

Moreover the door faces north like those of the Hindoo temples, while the Mohammedans of India always face the east, that the worshipper on entering may look westward to Mecca. The Mohammedans invariably build their minarets close to a mosque and on a platform. This, like the Hindoo towers, has no platform, nor any trace of a mosque (though that, of course, may have vanished, as well as the palaces of the emperors). It is known that when Tamerlane invaded Hindoostan, some building stood here which struck him as so perfect that he carried a model of it to Samarcand, and took with him Delhi masons to build one similar for his capital.

Now all worshippers, Mohammedan and Brahmin, have alike passed away; the glorious ruins are deserted, and the peerless pillar stands majestic in its grand solitude. One magnificent fragment of some ruin is a wall eight feet thick, covered with graceful flowered tracery and pierced by tall pointed arches. Just beyond stands one great domed building which above all others fascinated us by the rare beauty of its exquisite carving.

It was built by Akbar as a college where his wise men might meet for discussions. Being open on all sides, it acts as a great gateway, and from its position, so near the giant minaret and the old Hindoo pillars, it seems as if purposely built as a magnificent portal to that court of rare art-work. Its four sides are alike—deep-red sandstone inlaid with white marble, and covered from the base to the summit with rich tracery standing out in bold relief. From each side you enter by a flight of steps beneath a tall Gothic arch, edged with beautifully-chiselled dog-tooth pattern, which I did not observe on any other building. Your eye passes from the intensely warm depth of maroon and claret-coloured shadow of the interior to the dazzling blue of the sky seen through the dog-tooth arch opposite. Over every inch of the interior the same wealth of carving is lavished in endless variety of geometrical patterns, standing out in bold relief, and in utmost refinement of execution. Nothing but photography could convey an idea of its richness of detail, and *it* would lack the charm of warm delicious colour.

A few steps further we came to long colonnades with endless rows of beautifully-carved Hindoo pillars, chiefly ornamented with bells, but of infinite variety. Though all these columns bear precisely the same character, every one is different in design, showing an amazing fertility of invention. Of these there still remain several hundred, but the people say there were originally upwards of a thousand, the spoil of divers Hindoo temples, the materials of which were thus appropriated by the Islamites.

This theory of amalgamation would sufficiently account for the utter lack of repose in these strangely grotesque pillars, among which the eye wanders, but can never rest, or shake off a feeling of confusion as though perplexed by some troubled dream. But the same thing is true of every Hindoo building I have ever seen, and forms a notable contrast with the grand simplicity and harmony of Mohammedan architecture. It seems as though the monotheistic faith of the latter must needs declare itself in the unity of design which gives such sublimity to all their great mosques; whereas the intricate and grotesque confusion of the Hindoo temples seems but a reflex of the labyrinthine mysteries of their mythology.

One thing worthy of note in these long colonnades is that they are surmounted here and there by small domes; ugly enough compared with the thousand beautiful domes dotted over the plain, but full of interest when you remember that to these Hindoos the arch was unknown, so the domes were formed by nicely posed layers of stone, laid horizontally.

I greatly fear that to any one, not having the beautiful reality before their mind's eye, all these descriptions of mosques, tombs, and gateways must become very wearisome. I keep continually thinking of a Scotchman's comment on a very lengthy sermon descriptive of the broad and narrow gates: "Eh! he was fully stawsome about the yetts!"[1] but really I do not know how else to convey to your mind any notion of these wonderful cities.

But before passing on, I must first tell you about an extraordinary iron pillar, which stands near the base of the Kootub; and *to which the city owes its modern name.* It is a solid shaft of metal, sixteen inches in diameter; it stands twenty-two feet above ground, but there seems to be a difference of opinion among engineers as to the depth to which the shaft is buried. One declares its base to be twenty-six feet below ground, while another maintains that it only extends a few feet, and terminates in a bulb like a turnip. In either case, it will ever be a marvel how such a massive column could have been produced at a single forging, and that so early as the third century of our era. It certainly would puzzle our own ironmasters to rival such work without the aid of their modern steam-machinery—a power which we can scarcely imagine to have lent its might to these Vulcans of old.

It is wrought like our finest metal, and shows no symptom of rust, though it has stood here for many centuries. It bears an inscription in Sanscrit, describing it as the "triumphal pillar of Rajah Dhava, A.D. 310, who wrote his immortal fame with his

[1] Eh! but he was wearisome about the gates!

sword." This however, is the only record extant of his deeds. There are several other inscriptions on the pillar, but of more modern date.

The Brahman tradition is, that this pillar was erected in the sixth century, after the stars had pointed out the auspicious moment. It went so deep that it pierced the head of the serpent god Schesnag, who supports the earth. The priests told the Rajah that thus his kingdom should endure for ever. But, like a child gardening, he could not be satisfied till he dug it up again, just to see if it were so, and sure enough the end was covered with blood. Then the priests told him that his dynasty would soon pass away. He planted the pillar again, but the serpent eluded his touch, and the pillar was thenceforth unsteady. So the priests called the name of the place Dhilli (unstable) and prophesied all manner of evil concerning the Rajah, who shortly afterwards was killed, and his kingdom seized by the Mohammedans, and since then, no Hindoo has ever reigned in Delhi.

Nevertheless, the pillar is now firm as a rock, and has even resisted the cannon of Nadir Shah, who purposely fired against it. The marks of the balls, are, however, clear enough. The Hindoos believe that so long as this column stands, the kingdom has not finally departed from them.

Now I have given you enough and to spare of dry detail, but you must picture for yourself the delight of our gipsy life among the ruins. How the long days slipped by; sometimes exploring, sometimes drawing; wandering from one deserted garden to another, sometimes among rocks, sometimes on arid plains, but almost always in utter solitude and silence, only broken by the tinkling bells of some long string of camels, whose great flat feet fell so noiselessly on the earth, that, but for the bells, we should scarcely have noticed their approach. Occasionally, a noisier chime reached us from the neighbouring village, where one of the temples has a peal of eighty-four bells, all rung by one single rope.

But the crown of delight was when at early dawn we gazed up at the mighty pillar of fire, towering to the very clouds; its summit glowing in the sun's first rays, long before the purple shadows of night had faded from the base. Then we sometimes climbed that long spiral flight of well-nigh four hundred steps,

THE KOOTUB MINAR, DELHI.

that, like the Hindoo princess, we might catch the first gleaming light on the Jumna, and gaze far away over the vast, silent plain.

And when the evening drew on, we took up a position within hail of the bungalow, lest any stragglers from the village should molest us; sometimes we sat on a curious old ruined pyramid, near the base of a second huge pillar, which, had it ever been completed, would have been far more gigantic than its brother, but was very early given up and left unfinished. Thence we could watch the red gold of sunset flood the plain, and once more transform the red stone column into a glowing pillar of orange fire. And as "the serpents of night" crept upward, the fire fled heavenward, till at last it vanished, and a solemn hush and silence told that the day was done.

The only sound that broke that great stillness was a faint chaunt from a Hindoo temple, so mellowed by distance, that it sounded something between a Latin litany and a Gaelic hymn. It came as a dreamy suggestion of some evening service at home, and we listened and lingered, till the mighty giant before us towered solemn and black against a deep-blue sky, lighted only by a young crescent moon with her train of glittering stars. Then in the waste wilderness around, the voices of the night began to awaken; weird cries of jackals; plaintive wails and unearthly laughing. We bethought us of the leopards which might be lurking at our very feet, and with all due speed, retreated to safer quarters.

CHAPTER IX.

MEERUT.

Life in a Military Station—The Old Church-yard—A Steadfast Elephant—The Bazaar—Itinerant Tradesmen—Jugglers—Snakes—Native Servants—War of Words, not Blows—Hindoo and Mohammedan Festivals—Monkeys—Sketching in Public—The Roast Beef of Old India—Cathedral at Sirdhana—The Begum Somroo.

We found our gipsy life in Old Delhi so thoroughly enjoyable that we sorely regretted when the time came to settle down to civilised life at Meerut. Nevertheless it was very pleasant, after some experience of Indian hotels and rest-houses, to find ourselves again *at home*—in an unknown country certainly, but with an unmistakably home-like feeling about the pretty drawing-room, with its comfortable sofas and arm-chairs, and fresh, bright chintz curtains, and crimson and white *purdahs*[1] draping all the unsightly doors, which form such a conspicuous feature of every Indian room.

In the cool shade stand quaint Indian vases of some silvery metal, with delicious nosegays of roses and orange-blossoms and all manner of sweet flowers, which the *máli* (gardener) brings in fresh each morning. If you have any doubts of their being the produce of your own garden, you need ask no questions; nobody does so. So long as your table is duly supplied with vegetables, and your vases with flowers, you may rest satisfied. The *mális* are supposed to have a system of exchange or black-mail, and the

[1] Portières.

best servant is he who best forages for his master. Indeed some maintain that the best system of all is to keep a gardener and no garden!

Meerut is a purely military station, and has therefore little of an essentially native character to mark it. It is far from any river, and its situation is altogether hideous. It was selected in olden days as an advantageous spot to concentrate a strong European force wherewith to overawe Delhi, only forty miles distant; for it had been stipulated in one of our treaties with the Moguls, that no British infantry or cavalry or European troops whatsoever should ever be quartered in the imperial city or its immediate neighbourhood. Consequently, the whole town is modern, having no buildings of any especial interest. The cantonments are divided into four sections, namely the infantry, native cavalry, hussar, and artillery lines. The European quarters consist of innumerable bungalows, each standing quite apart from its neighbours in its own compound, which may be field or garden, shady or bare, according to the taste of some previous inhabitant.

Happily that taste has generally inclined to shade, so that all the pointed thatch roofs, and white or green verandahs (the houses are only one story high), are veiled by abundant greenery, and a fair show of flowering creepers, and the general effect of the town is pretty enough. Of course where each house and shop has so large a compound, the town straggles over a very large space, and a call at the other end of the station is quite a morning's work. The social mechanism of India has one peculiarity in this matter of visiting, namely, that the new comer must call first. Hence the remark of an Anglo-Indian lady—"country-bred" as the phrase goes—about to visit Britain for the first time, that as soon as ever she reached London she "intended to invite all the station to dinner!" The story reminded me of a certain dear old lady—one of my earliest friends—who drove her own carriage and horses all the way from Forres to London, and as she neared the city bade her coachman drive into town the back way, as she did not wish to meet people that evening!

In so fluctuating a society as that of India, this arrangement of first calls is really a very kindly institution, supposed to admit the stranger at once to the full swing of social life, or else, should he prefer solitude, to the full enjoyment thereof. It also allows people time to shake into their new houses before being molested by visitors, and this, in a country where a change of home is of such frequent occurrence, is a decided advantage.

On the other hand it is very overwhelming to receive a list of the inhabitants, all utter strangers, and, without any knowledge of their various peculiarities and endless "cliques," to go the round of the station, knowing that should any one be accidentally omitted, it would be a cause of most dire offence. Of course, once this grand round has been accomplished, you are at liberty to select as limited a circle of friends as you please out of the mass of acquaintances.

The most absurd thing is, that the hours of calling are from twelve till two, the only time of the day, during the cool season, when it is unpleasant to leave the shade of your own verandah; and very few ladies have as yet found strength of mind to break through this custom, and institute undisturbed forenoons and social afternoons. Consequently the old definition of morning callers as "the pestilence that wasteth at noonday" is rigidly true.

After these ceremonious visits, some of your more intimate friends will probably drop in to tiffin, and remain chatting till the hour for the evening drive; and as another batch of friends probably looked in after the early morning ride, it follows that the whole day is more or less cut up by perpetual small-talk; and some churlish spirits there are who, wearying of this pleasant, easy society, are sometimes tempted to wish that people would inflict less of their idleness on one another. The real grievance, you see, lies in the mid-day calls, a grievance kept up by the genuine old Anglo-Indian, who adheres so inflexibly to the old custom, that after 2 P.M. he considers your visit quite a matter of ignorance or incivility—if, indeed, he admits you at all. More frequently the white-robed attendants have orders to dismiss all comers with the curt announcement of "darwaza band"—"closed door."

The expenditure of pasteboard on these occasions is very great, as, owing to the native mispronunciation of names, it is always considered necessary to herald your entrance to the house even of intimate friends by sending in your card, which, having been duly inspected by the lady of the house, results in her either sending you her salaam, which is equivalent to a welcome, or else, by that metaphorical closing of the door, you are dismissed, after waiting some minutes in an open carriage under a grilling sun.

The only persons who are exempt from the law of making the first call, and indeed from the necessity of returning any, are the governors of provinces and their families. But as we passed through the various large towns we found a curious social war raging here and there. It had occurred to the wives of a few men holding high offices that, as their husbands are mentioned in the public services of the Church in the same clause as the governors, they were of course entitled to the same social homage. This being by no means the opinion of the other ladies of the community, a ludicrous schism ensued, which, in the lack of more worthy matter, proved a fertile subject for conversation and dispute.

In the mother country, we had so often heard many disparaging remarks upon Indian society that it was like a glimpse of a world not realised to find, wherever we halted, so large and so very pleasant a colony of kind and agreeable Britons, bearing the well-known names of every good family in the United Kingdom, in fact, the younger sons and brothers of all who constitute good society at home; the chief perceptible difference between the two being that in the one case both bread and position have invariably been earned by hard labour, while in the other they have generally been inherited; and I am not sure that the advantage lies wholly in the scale of inheritance.

As a matter of course, honour and precedence are likewise things to be earned, so that the rank which a man holds as his birthright is set aside as a mere accident, social position being determined by office or length of service, and consequent wealth. Everybody knows to a fraction how many rupees per month every one else draws, and both breadwinner and family take rank accordingly, not only among their equals, but in the estimation of the natives, who, aided by the rulers of the household and house-keeping, do all that in them lies to make a man's expenditure advance with his income.

Foremost among the oft-repeated charges brought against social life in India are those which tell of incessant broils and bickerings as the inevitable result of the fiery climate. I doubt, however, whether the sunny East has any monopoly of these amusements, or whether the Western "pot" has any right to revile the Eastern "kettle" on that score. "Fulness of bread, abundance of idleness, and neglect of the poor," do their work pretty much alike everywhere; and there are few country towns or small social cliques in Britain that could not tell the same tale of how (not only in the case of mistresses, and servants, but even of gushing friends) the angels of one year are the devils of the next, and the whitest swans are proved to be the greyest geese. I suppose it is a natural result of the exceedingly intimate social life which some one has so well described as "living under a microscope."

During our stay at Meerut we were very fortunate in the position of our bungalow, being on the edge of the Maidân, or common—a wide open space where all the troops exercise, and where field-days and large reviews are held, generally in the early morning, when batteries of artillery pour their volleys, and skirmishing parties gallop about the Hindoo villages, to the extreme disgust and awe of the natives. The Native Cavalry and our own Horse Artillery are very picturesque ingredients; the former of course have British officers, whose rich puggarees (turbans) are the only exceptions to the thick helmet of white linen worn by all our English troops. The Highlanders seem to be the only men proof against sunstroke, adhering steadfastly throughout the winter months to their feather bonnets, though the heavy mass of black must draw heat frightfully, and of course gives no shelter to neck or face. In summer, however, even they are driven to wear the invariable white helmet. Except during the few winter months all the troops come out in white uniform, and very clean they look, not to say glaring.

There is a very large church, always crowded, and the first thing that arrests the eye fresh from England is the enormous preponderance of men, the women being a mere handful. The services are very short—litany and sermon, or morning prayer and sermon, on alternate Sundays, being the general allowance for which the mass of the congregation assembles. This is in consequence of a pleasant fiction about heat, although these winter months are really only like our own summer, and the wide-open windows keep the interior of all buildings so cool that punkahs are not required, nor do we suffer from the stuffiness and bad air too common in European churches.

When the real summer heat begins, the troops march to church on Sunday or to drill on week-days at 5 A.M., and before 7 A.M. must all be shut up for the day in their several quarters, with native servants to do all needful work. Very tedious these long days must be, in darkened rooms, under the incessant monotonous swing of the punkah; every breath of the scorching air from the furnace outside jealously excluded, except such as enters through screens of fragrant cuscas grass, on which water is incessantly thrown, and the rapid evaporation produces some coolness.

The "Therm-antidote," which consists of great fans of the same grass, set like a wheel, so as to revolve rapidly, is another means to the same end, and woe be to the careless attendant whose weary hand slackens at his work. There are not lacking instances in which half a dozen men have been found dead in one morning in barracks from heat apoplexy, owing to the *punkah-wallah* yielding to the soporific monotony of his work. Not that he is himself exempt from danger. One gentleman told me that the previous summer, turning suddenly round to revile the idle hand that had ceased its work, he perceived that the man lay dead, with the rope in his hand.

These being the conditions under which the English in the plains must gasp through the weary summer, with friends and acquaintances on every side sun-smitten, or fever-stricken, it is little wonder that the crowded church-yards tell so dire a tale of quick mortality.

As I now write, there pass before my mind visions of a multitude of kindly faces of those who were so recently my companions in those pleasant days; those who have shared our wanderings and our mirth, young brides and young soldiers, sailors and civilians, bright young girls or careworn mothers, and children without number, all passed away; and the stream of life has flowed on, and their absence has scarcely been noticed even in the little circle of changing Indian society.

Nothing strikes a new comer with such amazement as the apparent apathy with which these tidings of sudden deaths are received. You inquire for the friend of last week, the belle of that ball, the winner of the last race, and the answer commonly enough is, "Buried this morning. Taken ill yesterday afternoon, and only lived a few hours." Most probably unconscious all the time. One instance I know of a man who attended his commanding officer's funeral in the morning, and was himself buried at noon. Another day, two young officers started together for a morning in the jungle. They were to meet at breakfast time. One duly returned, but becoming anxious about his comrade, started in search of him. He found him lying in a nullah, dead. One ray of "the Life-giving Sun" had been the swift messenger to call him home. Again and again the orderly in going from barracks to the officers' quarters has been stricken down in a moment, and all the Bheesties in the neighbourhood have been at work hour after hour pouring mussocks of cold water over him, to restore him to consciousness, or allay the agony of a brain on fire; a fire which Death in very pity so often cools by laying his own chill hand on the throbbing brow.

Should the victim be an officer, or the holder of any appointment worth having, the prospect of promotion—a step gained—or the speedy applications for the vacant post, generally seem to be the uppermost thought. And all this time the gay life of the place goes on with as little interruption as though we were in the great whirl of London itself, where nobody expects to be missed, even for a day.

Close by the church at Meerut is the great uncared-for church-yard, where many an exile in this Indian land has found his last rest. It is scarcely seventy years since the first was laid there, and now it covers nearly five acres of ground; a wilderness of forgotten dead, whose tombs, old or new, are already half in ruins. They are mostly built of brick and mortar, and covered with white plaster, which soon yields to time and climate. Here in regular rank and file, sleeps an army of several thousands of England's sons, slain by no visible foe; victims of a climate created for another race—a race who love the sun, and delight in lying down to sleep with its full rays pouring on their unturbaned heads.

In one corner a line of several hundred tombs lying in file three deep, marks the graves of the Cameronians, decimated by fever. Then a vast number of the Buffs who died of cholera. The men of each regiment lie together. The infantry in one body, the cavalry in another, the artillery beyond. Civilians keep aloof in death as in life. Farther off, in the children's corner, sleep countless little ones. Here, in one tomb, sleep two hot-headed boys, who fought a duel to decide a dancing question, and both fell mortally wounded. Beyond lies the once beautiful cause of their quarrel, she having fevered and died of grief.

Long ago, an old soldier used to have charge of many of these tombs, and had touching stories to tell of those whom he had seen buried there. One of the first laid in the new church-yard was a fair young wife, to whose grave, through forty long years, her faithful husband returned at intervals; twice he came all the way from England to spend a day or two alone beside the love of his youth. There were other tombs that told no such tale of constancy. One was a ruined heap of red sandstone and marble, the unfinished monument to a lady so sorely mourned that her husband had to be carried by force from the church-yard. He brought materials from Delhi and Agra to do her honour, but before the costly tomb was half finished, the noisy grief had expended itself. A new queen reigned, so the memorial to the dead was left half finished!

The old soldier had a strange companion in the church-yard, namely, a huge cobra capella, with which he had lived on terms of intimate friendship for thirteen years. He gave as his reason for never molesting him, that on one occasion, when a native came by night to steal the iron railing placed round a newly-made grave, this snake bit and killed the thief. But when the old man worked at his tombs, and sang his low songs the while, the snake would crawl out of his hole and bask in the sun, lying coiled up and quite still, charmed by "Kathleen Mavourneen," and various old English ballads. Old Mortality was murdered in the Mutiny, and the further history of his cobra is not on record.

One thing which strikes a new comer as somewhat singular, is the extremely simple law of chaperonage. It seems to be quite the thing for the prettiest young girls to accept horses and escort from any gentleman, and ride or drive with them wheresoever and whensoever they please; and though Mrs. Grundy is bitter enough on most occasions, she is pleased to sanction this convenient arrangement to any extent.

Among the anomalies of Indian life in the stations is the hour of daily driving. After having devoted the two most dangerous hours (twelve to two) to the great business of making calls, it is considered unsafe to venture out for mere pleasure till just at sunset, when all beauty, animate and inanimate, is alike invisible, and people drive up and down in the dusk like owls, hardly able to distinguish their dearest friends, still less to profit by the elaborate toilets that are considered essential for an appearance on the Mall. Then comes the drive to dinner, and this also seems curious at first. Evening dress and wreath in an open carriage, in the months which *we* call winter; returning home in the clear moonlight, or by the flashing sheets of lightning, while the air is fragrant with Eastern blossoms.

As concerns the out-of-door varieties of so-called amusements in the various stations, they struck me, as an outsider, as being more wofully dull than any phase of sad pleasure I ever witnessed in the mother country. The man who said that life would be endurable but for its amusements must certainly have had a good spell of India! The daily drive along the Mall, and the bi-weekly halt around the band-stand, when all the people sit still in their carriages without an attempt at amalgamating, looking unutterably bored; or the archery meetings, when each carriage-load marches with business-like precision direct to the spot assigned to it, never to move thence till the game is over; and worst of all, the deadly-dull races, at which no one seems to get up any enthusiasm, except in the rare instance where the rider is so popular personally as to compel some interest! The chief excitement always seemed to be among the native spectators, who dearly love anything in the shape of horse-racing.

To me there was infinitely more satisfaction in going to see the wise commissariat elephants at work or at dinner. It was a never-ending surprise to see the matter-of-fact way in which each huge beast accepted its portion of enormous chupatties[1] and a small mountain of sugar-cane and other trifles, and how soon the whole disappeared.

One day a native gentleman, who had made acquaintance with some of our party on the hunting field, invited us to his stables, to see a young elephant just brought in from the jungle, and about to begin its education. The poor little thing was dreadfully frightened, though the presence of sundry elephantine patriarchs awed it into good behaviour, to which it was further encouraged by being tethered with a strong rope of straw, illustrating the old Hindoo proverb that "Little things must not be despised, since many straws united will bind an elephant." I believe that every working elephant in the empire has been thus free-born and enslaved, as it seems that few, if any, are ever reared in captivity.

Some of the tales of loyal obedience on the part of these strong, gentle creatures to the master whom they have once accepted, really surpass even stories of the faith of dogs. Such, for instance, is the historical record of how the rocklike steadfast-

[1] Flour cakes.

ness of a standard-bearing elephant turned the tide of victory in favour of his master, the Peishwa of Poona, the conquering Mahratta chief.

The troops were drawn up in line of battle, and the elephant bearing the royal standard had just taken up his position and received command to halt, when his mahout, conspicuous by his post of honour, fell mortally wounded. All day long the battle raged, but (like the immortal Casabianca on the burning deck) the heroic elephant stood his ground, in brave obedience to the last command of his master.

Again and again, the Mahratta host rallied around their steadfast standard-bearer, but when at last victory was theirs, and they swept onward in pursuit of the routed foe, the poor elephant was left alone on the deserted battle-field, alone with the dead and dying, who lay heaped around him, marking where the battle had been hottest, in defence of the ensign which he had borne so immovably.

When, weary of slaughter, the victors retraced their ground, they sought to lead their hero home with all honour, but he utterly refused to move. For three long days and nights he stood his ground, eagerly listening for the word of command from the master whose voice he might never hear again.

At last a messenger was despatched to a village on the Nerbudda river, distant about a hundred miles, to fetch the mahout's little son, a mere child, to whom the father had sometimes deputed the honour of directing his charge. The majestic beast instantly recognised the child, and as a valiant soldier swears allegiance to his infant sovereign, so did this gentle giant do homage to this little one, accepting from him the order of release, consented to abandon his post, and meekly followed the child back to his home.

Here, as in all Indian stations, the Native town is quite apart from the European, and very few English ever set foot in it, though to all lovers of the picturesque it offers the usual attractions of a native bazaar. The narrow street of small open shops, with all goods exposed to the passers-by; the white-robed, turbaned shopkeeper, folded up within; the groups of idlers around in every variety of dress; sellers of fruit, of gleaming brass vessels; stalls of the favourite native sweetmeats; stalls of money-changers, with heaps of divers coins and shells; sellers of caged birds, doves, parrots, hill minas; shops of every species of cloth, others whose whole trade is in embroidered skull-caps of brilliant silk and gold. These are worn as demi-toilette instead of a turban, or by young children who have not yet been shaven.

Then there are stalls for gold and silver lace—some for jewellery—many for all things connected with the joys of smoking, especially the pretty vases of silvery metal to hold water through which the smoke must pass. These, and a thousand more, all in brilliant light and shadow, are among the items which make native life so wonderfully picturesque, though to the Anglo-Indians they have so utterly lost their novelty that you can hardly induce them to drive you through a bazaar.

But if such a drive is interesting, a stroll is infinitely more so, when you can linger as long as you please, to watch these skilful workmen producing their exquisitely-refined artistic work with the rudest, simplest tools, such as no British workman would deign to touch, but which, in those delicate, flexible hands, produce such admirable results. Then too in every department we are watching true manufacturers—hand work—so that each object has a certain individuality; there is none of the wholesale multiplication of articles by the gross. Two points which conduce to the perfection and careful finish of all work are, first, the natural patience of the whole race, and further, the fact that all work is done as a religious duty; the worker realises that he is fulfilling his appointed mission, and must do it to the best of his power, so he will not be hurried, neither will he scamp his work.

One great secret of his skill lies in the fact that in all things Indian, fashions remain unchanged. He has not to expend time and thought in devising novelties and how to produce them, but has only to perfect the work of his own ancestors, for all trades are transmitted from generation to generation. Moreover all the workers in one trade live clustered together in one special corner of the bazaar, rarely blending with other trades.

This individual perfection is however just one of the things which is in danger of being lost by the introduction of wholesale British manufactures. Very useful as giving employment to many of India's superfluous thousands, but certainly tending to dull uniformity. Already vast factories have been erected, and steam power introduced, and multitudes who hitherto have worked individually, each in his own home, now crowd in gangs to attend to the mechanical work of the 1,250,000 spindles already employed in the cotton factories, or the 40,000 which are preparing jute.

One of the regular Indian institutions is the race of pedlars and itinerant merchants of all sorts, who wander from house to house, followed by two or three coolies bearing enormous bundles, and, unless summarily dismissed, the contents of these are in a few minutes, spread all over your verandah. Sometimes they are precious cloths, shawls, and jewels from Delhi, or beautifully embroidered woollen things from Cashmere—gorgeous kincob woven of gold, silver, and many coloured silks, or muslins from Dacca, so marvellously fine as to merit such names as "web of the wind" or "woven air," so wondrously fine is their texture. Sometimes we have the verandah strewn with every variety of carved wood and toys, or skins of birds of radiant plumage. Some bring stores of fruit and jams; then comes the *roti-wallah*, or bread-fellow, with tempting biscuits wherewith to bribe the children, and so mollify the mothers.

The itinerant jewellers would astonish Storr and Mortimer by the glittering treasures which they produce from a heap of dirty old rags. Each jewel, which in London would be deemed worthy of a satin-lined velvet case, is here wrapped up in a bit of old linen, and by the time the elaborate process of opening each little parcel is finished, your verandah becomes a sort of rag fair, with a little heap of really valuable brooches, bracelets, and earrings, and a wider circle of trash. It is quite in vain to protest that you have no intention of investing in any of these treasures, the snares must be duly set, and the very smallest purchase seems to repay these patient traders.

The *sonar*, or goldsmith, is another variety of jeweller, the tinker of the trade. His simple apparatus consists of a blowpipe, a few seeds which act as weights for miniature scales, and a tiny pannikin. Should you have any mending to do, or your servants possess any morsels of gold and silver which they want fashioned into rings for their noses, or ankles, or toes, the *sonar* will quickly prepare his furnace. He scoops a small hole in the earth, fills it with charcoal and dry cowdung, and with his iron blowpipe produces such a blast of air that the little furnace soon glows hot and red; then the little pellets of precious metal are weighed in the tiny scales, and the servants keep close watch for any sleight-of-hand that might suggest dishonesty. Then in due time the new adornments are fashioned, and the proud owner goes off to the bazaar to display his finery.

A very numerous class are the *Chicken wallahs*, or sellers of white embroidery; admirable work, like our best Irish needlework, though too often the labour has been spent on muslin too fine for lasting wear.

But the most useful of all are the *Kapra wallahs*, or cloth-fellows, who carry a whole draper's shop with them; and the *Box wallahs*, whose store is much the same as that of a general merchant in a country village. (I remember one, in the Highlands. who advertised "Tea, tar, and treacle, godly books and gimlets"!) Well, his Hindoo counterpart carries everything you can devise, from Parisian jewellery and Sheffield cutlery to the last new novel or patent medicine; and knowing that the value of a thing is precisely what it will fetch, he finds out its market value by asking double its worth, but generally ends by taking a very fair price, which is more than can be said for the English shops, where double and quadruple prices are unblushingly asked, and no reduction is made.

The most curious specimen, however, of itinerant salesmen is he who brings an anonymous box from some lady who is just leaving the station, and selling off her old clothes and other rubbish —*such* rubbish! Old bonnets, half-worn; white shoes, cracked fans, sham jewellery, books, trash without end. Having dismissed him with ignominy, tempered by gratitude for the amusement his box has given us, we turn to welcome a solemn Wizard of the East, who is sure to be worth some moments' attention.

There are a certain set of tricks which most jugglers can practise with considerable skill, such as swallowing knives, or even a sword, and blowing fire from the mouth.

The sword swallowing is no sham; eighteen inches of bright cold steel do actually find their way down the man's gullet, he taking no other precaution than to oil the blade, which of course is blunt. His throat has gradually been hardened by astringent gargles, and in his early days has cost him many a sharp pain, and restricted his food to spoon-diet. By the time he has got well used to swallowing steel, he is ready to do likewise with snakes, which he holds by the tip of the tail and lets them crawl down, while he draws in his breath. As soon as he breathes again they shrink back from the heat!

Another curious feat is to throw a cocoa-nut into the air and catch it on the head, when the nut shivers to atoms instead of breaking the head, as might be expected. Of course this is all knack, just like breaking a poker across your arm, and has been capped by an Englishman, who substitutes nodules of flint for the cocoa-nuts, and produces the same result!

Among the most common, yet most striking proofs of sleight-of-hand is the mango trick. The juggler, whose drapery consists of half a yard of cotton; his theatre, your own verandah, his stock-in-trade, a mere handful of toys, proceeds to bury a mango-stone in a little mud and covers it with a jar. A few minutes later the jar is raised, and lo! a tender green seed-leaf has sprouted. When next we peep into that magic hot-bed, the tiny leaf has long since withered, and a flourishing young tree has developed with a rapidity the secret of which would be a boon indeed to our patient foresters. The same trick is shown with the pineapple plant, whose ripe fruit, presented to the spectators, gives a charming flavour of reality to the deception.

There were, however, some of these tricks for which I looked in vain. One, in particular, which I cannot refrain from quoting from the words of an eye-witness.

He describes how a stout, ferocious-looking fellow stepped forward, and made him examine a light wicker basket, which he then placed over a pretty little girl about eight years old, utterly guiltless of raiment. The ruffian then asked the child some question, and the little voice answered from the basket. Question and answer grew loud and rapid, till the man, in violent passion, threatened to kill the child, who vainly prayed for mercy.

There was a stern reality in the scene which was terrible to witness. The man set his foot on the frail basket, beneath which cowered the terrified child, and seizing a sword plunged it into the basket again and again, with the blind ferocity of an excited demon, his face frantic with rage. The shrieks of the child were so real and distracting that the spectators stood pale and paralysed with terror. Blood ran in streams from the basket; the child was heard to struggle under it; her groans gradually sank to a faint moan, fainter and fainter, then all was still. So vivid was the scene that the impulse of the spectators was to rush on the monster and fell him to the earth, when, to their inexpressible relief and astonishment, the juggler muttered a few cabalistic words, took up his basket, and there exhibited—no mangled corpse—only a little blood-stained earth; and the little child, with a graceful salaam, advanced from among the crowd to claim a backsheesh, which was readily bestowed. What made the deception more remarkable was that the man stood quite aloof from the crowd, not a creature within several feet of him.

After this he took a large earthen vessel with wide mouth, filled it with water, and turned it upside down, when all the water, of course, ran out. He then reversed the jar, which, all present perceived to be quite full, and all the earth around was perfectly dry. He then emptied the jar, and handed it round for general inspection. He bade one of the company fill it to the brim; after which he upset it, but not a drop of water flowed;

nevertheless, to the astonishment of all, it was quite empty. This trick was shown repeatedly, and at last he broke the jar to prove that it really was nothing but the ordinary earthenware that it appeared.

Next a large basket was produced, and on lifting it a pariah dog lay crouching on the ground. The basket cover was replaced, and the second peep showed a litter of seven puppies with their interesting mother. A goat, a pig, and other animals successively appeared from this magic receptacle, although, as before, the exhibitor stood quite alone, and in full view of all spectators.

Though we had not the luck to come in for any exhibitions so striking as these, we, being novices, found a store of interest in the curious beings who did find their way to us. Snake-charmers came continually. They play on a sort of squeaking bagpipe, which is supposed to have wondrous charms for all manner of serpents, and it must be a deaf adder indeed which will not come forth to listen to the voice of the charmer. There have been undoubted instances in which really wild snakes have been thus attracted, probably those which had a fine ear for music. We heard of one instance in which a young Englishman, much addicted to playing the flute, had been compelled to give up that harmless pursuit because his house was in a snaky district, and his gentle melodies attracted such a multitude of serpents that even the natives objected!

But of course, as a general rule, those so triumphantly produced from the garden hedge have been very well trained by their dancing master. It is a horrible thing, however, to see a shrinking child adorned with serpents of every size as bracelets and anklets, with a great boa constrictor or a cobra curling about his feet or round his body,—especially when we know for a fact that there have been instances in which the poison fangs have not been removed.

Mr. Forbes mentions a dancing cobra which lay on his table for an hour while he painted it. He frequently handled it to observe the beauty of the spots and the marks on the hood like a pair of spectacles, all the time fully believing that the venomous fangs had been extracted. A few hours later the same vicious reptile sprang at a young woman, bit her in the throat, and in half an hour she was dead. Nor are even the most experienced snake-charmers always proof against accidents. Many horrible cases have occurred where a cobra has caused his master's death.

But the strangest thing of all is to hear of a serpent causing its own death, as in a case mentioned by Dr. Dearing, where a snake having been much irritated, turned suddenly round, open-mouthed, and caught its fang in its own flesh. Very soon after it rolled over and died, poisoned by its own virus.

Bruce, the Abyssinian traveller, mentions having seen a snake-charmer at Cairo plunge his hand into a tubful of serpents; thence take a cerastes (a most venomous snake), and putting it on his bare head, cover it with his red cap. After a while he put it in his bosom, then twined it round his neck like a necklace. Shortly afterwards it sprang at a hen and bit it, and the bird died a few moments later. In order to prove that the snake was no precious favourite, the man finally took it up by the neck, and beginning at the tail, ate it up, as you would eat a piece of celery, without the smallest repugnance!

I have myself seen a refractory snake give his keeper a bite so severe as to cause him very great pain. However the wound bled freely, and after the man had sucked out as much of the venom as he could, he produced something of the shape and colour of a bean, very hard and polished. This he laid on the sore finger. It seemed to draw out the venom, and then fell off of itself. He called it snake-stone, and said it was made of stag's horn. So you see we are not the only people who know that hartshorn, or ammonia in some form, is a cure for such venomous bites.

Every one travelling in the East should have spirits of ammonia in his medicine-chest, or still better, eau de luce, which is a preparation of hartshorn, oil of amber, and spirits of wine, as the servants' bare feet are terribly liable to be found out by snakes and scorpions; and although in cases of a severe bite the only safety lies in *instantly* burning or cutting out the portion of flesh bitten (having previously stayed the flow of blood by the tightest possible ligature, for which purpose a supply of whipcord should be kept ready besides the ammonia), it is always well at once to administer stimulants freely, the best being half a teaspoonful of eau de luce, or forty drops of strong spirits of ammonia, in a little water; a dose which should be repeated frequently, till the pain gradually passes down the suffering limb, and seems to be drawn out at the finger-tips or toes.

This is precisely the result produced by applying the snake-stone, or horn. A piece of this was analysed by Professor Faraday, who believed it to be "a piece of charred bone, which had been filled with blood several times, and then carefully charred again. It consisted almost entirely of phosphate of lime, and if broken, showed an organic structure with cells and tubes." I have been told of various cases of very severe bites, even those of the cobra, in which immediate application of this snake-stone has effected a cure.

The natives also have a kind of wood which they call the root of the snake plant. They wave it close above the reptile, which seems to shrink down, cowed. This plant is the Aristolochia, which is much used in the West Indies as an antidote to the bite of serpents. It is said also to be fatal to all manner of snakes, and serpent-charmers stupefy their playthings with its juice. The difficulty must be to insert it into their mouths! It is like the simple operation of removing the poison sacs, which is easily performed "by making an incision beneath and behind each eye." But the question to ordinary mortals would be how to set about it!!

Certainly these snake-charmers are a race by themselves. Their power is undoubtedly hereditary; and there can be no doubt that (like the Psylli of ancient Egypt) they have some mysterious influence over the most deadly and venomous foes of our species. There are most clearly proved instances in which enraged snakes have first been lulled by the music of these men; then allowed themselves to be played with; have shrunk back in dismay if they were spat at; have lain for days curled up in their charmer's turban; and then, perhaps, broken loose, to try their fatal fangs on some less masterful spirit.

It is said that in some cases the snake-charmers have anointed their whole body with some decotion of herbs, hateful to the serpent, so that the very smell of their skin is repellent to them; and that men not pretending to be professional, who had been thus prepared for action, have been seen deliberately taking up snakes and handling them, without receiving injury.

Many medical authorities assert that, when once the venom has been thoroughly and intentionally injected, its career through the whole system is so rapid that no antidote can be of much avail. Nevertheless, I have been assured by one, through whose hands hundreds of cases of snake-bite had passed, that he scarcely knew of one instance in which the spirits of ammonia had failed to work a complete cure, though the bites were often of the worst possible character.

You can fancy how much this element of possible danger adds to the fascination which the snake-charmers, with their baskets of dread playthings, always possess. The reptiles are, in truth, so beautiful, with their varied colouring, some grey, some brown, some yellow, some beautifully marked with bands of black and gold, and divers patterns; all gliding so silently in the sunlight, now raising their heads to watch with glittering eye the movements of their master, or, with sudden dart, springing at some unwary fly, as you might fancy their springing at and striking some nobler foe.

How strange it did seem to us, while, with an irrepressible shudder, we watched these creatures wriggling along in their horrid coils, to remember that we were looking on the creature above all others whose worship has been most universal, and which held a place of honour even among our own forefathers![1]

Although the living serpent has ceased to hold a prominent place in public worship, it is still recognised in all villages

[1] See *In the Hebrides*, p. 51, C. F. Gordon Cumming. Chatto & Windus.

throughout Hindostan as the principal corn-god, to whom sacrifice is offered at seed-time and in harvest, and at all other times when rain or fair weather is unseasonably delayed. Even the Brahmans (!) join in these snake festivals and receive their share of the offerings. Some carry a snake-skin in their holy books. The chief festival is held just after the season when the snake, having cast its skin, comes forth in renewed beauty.

In the mythology of Hindostan, as in that of many other lands, the serpent maintains his two-fold character—sometimes as a power of good, sometimes of evil. Even where he is not ostensibly worshipped, he appears in connection with the gods, either as a symbol of Siva, as Mahadeo, the Lord of Life, or twined round the neck or arms of Vishnu, Juggernaut, Parvati, and others; sometimes he is coiled up as a couch whereon the god slumbers, the head of the cobra (sometimes single, sometimes five-fold, sometimes seven-fold) forming a protecting canopy. Thus Vishnu sleeps on the thousand-headed serpent Sesha, which symbolises Infinity. Yet his attendant, the man-eagle Garunda, slays a great serpent.

We know, too, that the chief feat of Krishna was to slay the wicked serpent Kaliya, which, nevertheless, continues to receive a certain share of worship, just as the Pythian snake was adored at Delphi, even by the worshippers of Apollo, its destroyer, on the principle that powers of evil must be conciliated; and in truth this is a necessary precaution, for in the Hindoo hell, as in that of Scandinavia, there are living walls of poisonous serpents, intertwined in horrible contortions.

The open and avowed worship of the serpent was so strenuously prohibited by the Aryan conquerors that comparatively few shrines of any note are to be found in Northern India. But in the neighbourhood of Nagpore ('the city of the Naga or snake,') and Kanara, and Southern India generally, the old worship is still prevalent. Thus a richly jewelled image of the seven-headed Naga is one of the three principal gods in the great temple of Madura.

The presence of living serpents is encouraged, and earth taken from their holes is believed to cure leprosy, if it be rubbed on the leprous spot. It also finds favour with women who have no children. Persons suffering from leprosy or from ophthalmia, or who are childless, believe those curses to be the penalty for having killed a cobra or other snake, in some former state of being. So they make pilgrimage to the serpent shrine, and laying themselves prostrate on the ground, they wriggle round it a given number of times, in sunwise course, imitating the movement of a serpent. They then present as their offering a stone symbol of Siva or of Krishna, with a five-headed snake upreared as a canopy. This they deposit beneath the sacred Peepul tree, anointing it with water, if possible from the Ganges.

In the native almanacs the fifth day of Srawan is noted as the birthday of the Naga king, and the day whereon serpents must be worshipped. So the people draw a serpentine figure on their houses, and do homage thereto. Then they adjourn to the nearest rocks or trees where serpents are known to live, and which are marked by small cairns smeared with red or black paint. They plant sticks near the hole, and, winding white cotton thread round them, hang up festoons of fragrant flowers; then they lay offerings of fruit, sugar, ghee, and flour round the hole, into which they pour milk, or lay it in saucers. Then the women, joining hands, circle five times round the snake's dwelling, after which they prostrate themselves, and anxiously await his appearing to know whether their gift is graciously accepted. Should the serpent prove sulky, the omen is dire indeed. He receives similar bribes in all times of sickness. Moreover, when a child is first shaved, after teething or other infantile ailments, the hair is generally offered to some serpent, the Brahmans being present to sanction proceedings which they cannot prevent, and to accept small offerings.

The Buddhists have equally displayed the wisdom of the serpent in this matter, and finding they were unable to prevent the veneration of the serpent, they judiciously incorporated it in their own teaching. Hence the seven-headed Naga which forms Buddha's canopy.

This being the case, it is natural that the natives should strongly object to killing a snake if they can by any possibility drive him away. They infinitely prefer to catch him alive, and carry him by night to the lands of the next village, where they turn him adrift. If, however, compelled to kill him, they put a copper pice in his mouth and give him a funeral-pyre, and, while burning his body, assure him that they are guiltless of his blood; that they slew him by command of their masters, or because they could not otherwise prevent his biting their chickens or their children.

These serpent funerals must latterly have given a good deal of trouble to the natives of certain districts, where the destruction of these reptiles amounts to quite a large item in government expenses, so it is to be hoped that the desire of gain may induce the natives to overcome their superstitions and attack their foe in real earnest.

It has been suggested that a graduated scale of reward should be offered for different species of snakes, varying with the deadliness of their bite, the highest sum being of course given for the cobra—at once the most sacred and the most dangerous—to whose fang are attributed one-fourth of the annual deaths from snake-bite. These, as a total, are annually estimated at from 15,000 to 19,000, in a population of 250,000,000.[1] It is hoped that a judicious addition of strychnine and carbolic acid to the offerings of milk and sugar placed at the entrance to the nest of the reptile, may prove among the most efficacious means of ridding the country of this pest.

By the way, this offering of milk to snakes and to symbolic stones, is worthy of notice. In our own Highlands and Western Isles the same libation was poured over sacred stones till very recent times.[2] I have seen bowls of good milk poured into the

[1] *Vide* Census tables—Snakes, Chapter III., p. 63; Inhabitants, Chapter VII., p. 200.

[2] *In the Hebrides*, pp. 71, 192.

sea from a sacred rock in Ceylon, and if a Hindoo is so unfortunate as to be compelled to make a sea voyage (thereby endangering his caste) he likewise pours an oblation of milk into the waves. Then, too, a man who is suffering from a form of witchcraft, produced by the utterance of an evil mantra or charm, can annul it if only he can find out which mantra was said by repeating it while bending over a bowl of milk, which he must then drink. The difficulty is to find out which charm was uttered, as the professional mantra-wizards reckon 70,000,000 of these formulas, which are supposed to render them omnipotent in working spells of love and hate.

To return to the verandah of our bungalow, whence the snakes have tempted me to wander.

Owing to the absurd manner in which caste rules limit the work which may be done by any one servant, the most moderate household necessarily possesses quite a retinue of these, and as they are perpetually flitting about, they naturally become objects of considerable personal interest.

They certainly are a curious race. So strange a mixture of childishness and cunning, delighted by the simplest pleasures, children with children, unwearied in their devotion to the delicate, white-faced little ones whom the climate renders so terribly fractious; great solemn men walking up and down for hours with unruffled patience, trying to soothe shrieking babies, and probably getting a good dose of the same sort at night in their own little hovels—hovels, by the way, from which I doubt whether any European could come in such spotless white robes.

As attendants they are wonderfully good. Quick, noiseless, detecting in a moment what is wanted, patient and "answering not again" to an extent that might sometimes shame their masters, who certainly have no more claim to faultlessness than "the niggers" of whom they think so lightly; for to see an Englishman fly into a passion with a native, and strike a man who dares not hit him back, is humiliating indeed. If not cowardly, it certainly is horribly derogatory to British dignity, and quite the most painful sight you are likely to witness.

Happily the present state of the law enables the aggrieved servant to summon his master before a magistrate, when a tolerably heavy fine may be exacted. On the other hand, the master will then probably refuse to give the man a chit, or note of character, without which he may wait long enough for a re-engagement.

These chits, however, are often of little value, as they may have been just forged in the bazaar by some unprincipled baboo,[1] or, if genuine, may have been given to some very different man by a master either dead, or returned to England. I used to wonder at the way in which servants would come to me in any house where I might be staying for a few days, to ask for some chits (which of course I could not give), till I discovered that they were saleable, which cleared up the mystery. A native will do anything for pice; he even seems to consider a timely backsheesh abundant compensation for any amount of abuse or even maltreatment—like the old sexton who used to rejoice in his vicar's petulance, for to provoke him into saying "D——l take you!" was worth a shilling any day, whereas so mild an expletive as "the deuce!" was a shabby sixpenny speech, only fit for a curate!

The most curious thing in the way of compensation is, on the occasion of any accident which has proved fatal to life or limb, to note how readily the mourning relatives are solaced by such a backsheesh as shall supply a funeral feast; a gift of fifty rupees to the widow and children seems positively to turn sorrow into joy. Economical masters avail themselves largely of the habit of fining their servants on every occasion, and for every breakage or every misdeed you hear "I cut you a rupee," or "I cut you eight annas"—fines which, if always exacted, would leave little due to the luckless servant, whose wages are at all times small, and are invariably kept a month or two in arrear, as otherwise the master has no hold to prevent a man from going off suddenly, at the moment when he is most needed.

I do not know whether the habit of mistrusting native servants

[1] Clerk.

may not of itself make them dishonest. Some masters say so, and certainly he is a very exceptional man who will be better than his character. But certainly, as a rule, the amount of cheatery that goes on is desperately annoying. The most curious thing is the composure with which it is done. A native is not in the least ashamed of being found out in the most flagrant lie or dishonesty. A European master and servant under such circumstances would feel a mutual distrust and disgust that would probably result in immediate separation. With these curious beings this is not at all the case. It seems as if the masters became more amiable towards the poor fellows whose little game they have foiled, while the miscreants themselves have quite a feeling of reverence to the superior intellect that saw through them; so that for a few days after a little scene of this sort, domestic life seems extra smooth and pleasant.

I remember one day in particular, when the culprit was a very superior baboo—a sort of private secretary to his master. He talked perfect English, and had for days been marching with us, and discussing every subject, terrestrial and celestial; pointing out the meaning of his name, which was "Born in the light of God," and otherwise edifying us. When he, in the presence of us all, was proved to have invented a tissue of lies to throw some slight blame on another man, why, we commiserated the poor crushed worm, and thought he would be overwhelmed with shame, especially as his master lost no opportunity of playfully chaffing him on his discomfiture; but he seemed to take it as a matter of course, and comforted himself with his usual dignified grace. Of course we have to bear in mind, that some of the gods whom they so deeply reverence, so far from discouraging cheatery and theft, are actually its patrons!

One unpleasant point in the Hindoo servants is their readiness to brawl among themselves. Of course I do not mean that they would so far forget themselves and their abject submission to their master as to quarrel in his bungalow, but once seated on their own flat roofs, the most trivial dispute generally ends in a noisy quarrel, in which there is no limit to the execrations heaped on one another, more especially on their feminine relations to the third and fourth generations. Then the women's voices chime in, loud and shrill (painfully discordant when thus high-pitched), and aid the general din with scolding and shrieks. They are as prodigal of choice expletives as the men, and it is said that no race on the face of the earth has so large a vocabulary of oaths as the Hindoo. Their swords are bitter words, but as a general rule no other weapon of offence comes into play. Such cases of stabbing as we hear of in England are unknown, and a good honest trial of fisticuffs equally so. The loudest, angriest tones rarely result in a blow; generally each man stands on his own roof and throws handfuls of harmless dust at his neighbour, or, if they are in closer quarters, the knocking off of a turban, or a blow from a slipper creates a confusion perfectly appalling.

These quarrels often result in an action at law, when the patient magistrate has to sit in broiling *kutchery*,[1] weighing evidence and striving to get at the rights of some question involving lucre to the value of twopence farthing. And the difficulty of separating true evidence from false must in itself be oppressive, for falsehood and equivocation seem to come so naturally to native lips that those who know their character best avoid ever asking a direct question.

This amiable peculiarity of our Aryan brother leads to most extraordinary cases of perjury in our courts of law. I have heard one instance after another when an acute magistrate has unravelled the most complicated cases, in which all the witnesses had apparently rehearsed the trial beforehand to insure success in acting their false parts; and perhaps all this would be for a matter of a few rupees. Certainly the old motto, "Straightforward makes the best runner," is by no means appreciated here; and a life without artifice and all above board would seem to have small attraction for the average Hindoo whatever bright exceptions we may find.

Among the milder terms of reproach which you will frequently hear, such qualities as we describe by "owlish" and "chicken-

[1] The court.

hearted" are almost literally rendered "*ooloo ka butcha,*" or "*moorghie ka butcha,*" meaning "child of an owl," or "of a fowl." Why the Grecian emblem of wisdom should in these later days bear so different a character in both the eastern and western world, I know not. "*Toom gudha,*" "you donkey," is another playful observation common to both. After seeing the high honour with which this most willing and energetic animal is treated in Egypt, it is curious to land in India and find that its touch is defilement, and that none but the lowest castes will have anything to do with it.

We had a curious proof of this when it was proposed that the children should have a donkey instead of being carried by men. The servants came in a body to my sister to represent the horrors of the case. Surely she could not be in earnest in wishing to subject the children to such an indignity; but if indeed it were so, they must with one voice protest that not one of them would touch it. So great was the excitement, that as she passed through the public bazaar strangers came up to her in a most respectful manner to express their hope that the mem-sahib would not think of such a thing, for indeed Charlie-sahib was worthy of more honour—surely he might have a pony. Charlie-sahib, however, resolutely refused to ride his pony, so a goat carriage was substituted, to the satisfaction of all concerned; whence you may infer that the Indian goat is not afflicted with the fragrance of his British brother, whom indeed he in no way resembles, being a smooth, short-haired creature with short horns, with none of the beauty of our silky-haired, long-horned old Billy-goat.

The Hindoo abhorrence of the luckless donkey is so great that the very acme of revenge would be to slay an ass on the threshold of a foe, whereby the house would be for ever defiled. In such a case, all the inmates must for ever quit their home before the blood has had time to cool, else their caste would be destroyed, and the usual disgusting ceremonies required for its restoration, the chief of which consists in swallowing *each* of the six products of the sacred cow! Of those in ordinary use, only milk, curds, butter, and ghee are here recognised. Cheese is apparently an unknown article, whether on any religious ground I cannot say.[1]

It is certainly wonderful to see the extent to which this veneration for cattle triumphs over the usual habits of exceeding cleanliness. If it is startling to see cow-dung applied to the floor of a room, as the most purifying of substances, and the best preventive of vermin, it is still more so, at first, to see a stately woman, bearing her water-jug on her head, kneel (not daring to bend her neck), and with her pretty, well-formed hands gather up fresh material for fuel, which she will carry home triumphantly, and thereof make cakes, which she will plaster over the walls of her house to dry in the sun. This, however, is as much a matter of economy as of reverence.[2]

. On one great festival in the month of March, we saw thousands of women and children, gaily dressed in bright-coloured jackets and very tight trousers of brilliant blue or crimson silk, the common muslin shroud being replaced by a great veil of the finest tissue, sometimes wrought in gold; and every woman and child in that vast procession carried in their hands one of these objectionable fuel-cakes, to be offered at some idol shrine.[3]

From a purely artistic point of view, I must confess that all these native festivals are wonderfully fascinating. One of the most celebrated festivals, which occupies several days at the time of the full moon in February, is known as the Holi. It is the spring festival which celebrates the awakening of nature to renewed life after her winter sleep. It is a sort of carnival in which the

[1] Strange to say this filthy reverence for the products of cattle even extends to the Parsees, by whom it is practically exemplified in the ceremony of initiation for every young Parsee.

[2] I am told that this is done nearer home, namely in some parts of Cornwall and the Orkneys, where fuel is as scarce as it is here, there being no firewood; and coal, and peat even, are luxuries too expensive for the very poor. The sweepings of the byre are therefore so precious as fuel that the land is obliged to accept sea-ware as a substitute for ordinary manure.

[3] It is satisfactory to learn that in several parts of India coal mines have been discovered, so there is no fear of a real failure of fuel. Moreover, employment, however uncongenial, is thus afforded for thousands as miners.

Roman showers of sugar-plums and plaster-of-Paris are replaced by red and yellow powder, which is thrown by every one over his neighbours. The effect of this on the white linen robes is particularly obnoxious. This is one of the few occasions on which the natives indulge in fermented liquors, and as they are very easily affected, much drunkenness results. Practical jokes of every sort are indulged in, and the festival degenerates into a most unseemly saturnalia. Consequently the whole population is more or less "agee" during the continuance of this festival, which forces itself on the unwilling attention of foreign householders from the determination of all the native servants to spend these days in the bazaar with their friends.

Fortunately for foreigners, the Hindoo and Mohammedan festivals are generally quite separate concerns, though some days are equally observed by both. One peculiar to the latter is that of "Buckrah Eade," or Goat Festival, observed in memory of Abraham having offered up his son—not Isaac, on Mount Moriah, but Ishmael on Mount Ararat—and it is from Ishmael they trace their descent. Many prayers are devoutly offered, and either a goat or a camel is slain and its liver fried, small portions thereof being eaten with bread as a sort of sacramental remembrance of that sacrifice.

A very remarkable religious ceremony, strangely suggestive of the scape-goat of Levitical law, was practised at Meerut at a time when cholera had been raging and had carried off hundreds of the people. Of course the visitation was attributed to the wrath of Kali, who could no longer be appeased by the customary offering of a goat. The people left their dwellings and took up temporary quarters in open spaces and by the roadsides. They then selected a buffalo for sacrifice, and drove it in procession round the town, preceded by a company of musicians, and followed by attendants who from time to time poured out offerings of milk, water, or wine. After these came a company of Brahmans repeating passages from the sacred books. When they had completed the circuit of the city, one ear of the poor beast was cut off and offered to Kali as a propitiation, but the creature, instead of being sacrificed, was driven out by "a fit man"[1] into the wilderness (which here means jungle, *i.e.* a land not inhabited), and there abandoned. Should it approach any other town or village, the people recognising the mark of Kali would drive it away, lest it should bring upon them the punishment due to other men's sins.

One great festival is especially held in honour of Hanuman, the monkey-god, to commemorate the day when with his army of monkeys he rescued from Ceylon a beautiful goddess, wife of Rama, and slew the wicked giant Ravan. On the feast a gigantic figure of Ravan is made on a frame of wicker-work, robed in inflammable cotton and covered with fireworks and gunpowder.

Vast crowds assemble in their white holiday robes and gay turbans, the wealthier coming on their camels and elephants or in picturesque vehicles. A great procession represents the triumph of the monkey-god and his friend Rama. The latter, amid a brilliant display of fireworks, smites the giant with his spear, and forthwith the whole framework bursts into flames, while the people dance and shout with delight at so brave a bonfire! Most of their processions seem to end with some such infantile fun.

This reverence for Hanuman extends itself to all the monkey tribes, which are considered very sacred indeed, and roam at their own sweet will from end to end of every Hindoo city, careering over the roofs, leaping from tree to tree, making a sudden descent on garden or bazaar to help themselves to whatever dainty they may fancy. Round the temples they may muster in exceeding force, as the Brahmans feed them regularly. At one temple in Benares we saw fully five hundred of all sorts and kinds, sizes and ages, from the hoary grandfather down to the tiniest little baby in arms.

We heard of one gentleman who had brought a pet monkey of a rare species from the hills to the plains. A deputation from Hanuman's temple forthwith waited on him, craving permission to conduct this stranger to the temple with all honour, as it was incumbent on them to worship it! So the monkey had a night of it, and was restored to its owner on the following morning, none

[1] Leviticus xvi. 21, 22.

the worse for this curious episode. Just imagine what a treasure Landseer's great monkey picture would be to a devout Hindoo! What a magnificent altar-piece it would make!

We generally observe a temple of Hanuman at the entrance of almost every village, and although his hideous image, smeared with a fresh coat of scarlet paint, is by no means attractive, he is deemed a most beneficent being, so his worshippers adorn his lovely brow with chaplets of fresh flowers, and hang long strings of tiny lamps or of alternate leaves and marigolds all about the temple; lamps are kept ever burning in his presence. Saturday is specially sacred to Hanuman, and all night long the clouds of incense rise, amid beating of tomtoms, shrill pipes, monotonous songs, and wild dancing. But every evening the women bring him offerings of lighted lamps (an oil cup with burning wick), and jars of water whereon float yellow marigolds. If on their way they meet any one whom they wish to honour, they wave before him the brass dish whereon stands the lighted lamp, with intent to avert all evil from him and give him welcome. Sometimes they will even pour out the water and the marigolds at his feet!

The favourite drive in Meerut is round a very large artificial tank, vulgarly called "the Monkey Tank," by reason of the sacred apes and monkeys which come for their daily food to the temples by the water side. The native name is more poetical: they call it Sooraj Koond (the Fountain of the Sun), and it is held alike sacred by heathen and Mohammedan.

You may see the latter drive up at sunset in his smart "buggy," whence his servant will take a brilliant carpet and spread it near the tank, and the stately worshipper will thereon kneel and worship with his face turned westwards towards Mecca, little heeding the poor Hindoo who kneels at the shrine close by, making *pooja*[1] so fervently, and presenting his humble offering of cakes and flowers, thereby trusting to avert the wrath of the dread Goddess of Small Pox, whose ruthless hand threatens to leave his home desolate.

[1] Worship.

Some of the most picturesque festivals are held at this spot, where thousands assemble under the dark trees, on foot or in every variety of native carriage. The aristocrats are mounted on elephants, with rich trappings of velvet embroidered with gold and silver. Here and there are raised platforms, where nautch girls, in brilliant dresses and glittering jewels, dance and sing; and as the hours pass by unheeded, thousands of torches light up the scene, dancers whirl round with enormous fans of peacocks' feathers and banners, while blue lights in the background throw a wild glare over wood and water, temples and people. These gatherings generally unite business with pleasure, and long rows of booths for the sale of every species of native and foreign wares to tempt purchasers.

Of course all the children are laden with grotesque toys, but even these cannot raise more than a passing smile on those grave little faces. There is something in the subdued mirth of Eastern children which is singularly oppressive. You never hear a clear, ringing laugh, or see an honest, hearty, romping game, such as our little ones love. They are all grave and silent. Curious small brown creatures, in long dresses of brilliant flowery calico, with gold-embroidered silk skull-caps, and long silk shawls, the small girls in tiny, tight trousers and veils, like diminutive women. Long ago, Charles Lamb, speaking of the children of the poor, described them as being adults from their cradle—little old men and women in all the cares and anxieties of life. So it is with the grave children of India.

There are noble faces amongst these people. Clear-cut features and large eyes—soft, speaking eyes—and clear olive or copper complexion, with the finest, glossiest black hair. The amount of hair they may retain depends upon their caste; some submit to a complete tonsure, no matter at what sacrifice of beauty. Among my sister's servants there was a beautiful boy whom we used to think like the picture of "The Cenci," with the great white turban, and large dark eyes. One day he came back from the bazaar, and lo! all his beauty was gone. He had been shaven with all due ceremony, and his glory was departed.

Meerut has little to show in the way of architectural beauty. One very large tomb, known as the Tomb of Aboo, is the only striking thing, and though it lies only a hundred yards off the daily drive, few of the oldest inhabitants know of its existence; still fewer take the trouble to go and look at it.

It consists of a great raised platform of fine red sandstone, in the centre of which lie white marble tombs. Above them, many clusters of tall red sandstone pillars and arches support a group of domes, of various sizes, all inlaid with bright green and blue encaustic tiles. Smaller pillars and domes stand at the corners of the platform, and others are raised in the neighbourhood over humbler members of the same family.

This was the only place where I found drawing was really a matter of difficulty, owing to the crowd of inquisitive natives, of whom fully a hundred gave me the benefit of their society for the whole day. As usual, they were perfectly civil and obliging, except in utterly refusing to go away. All Hindoos delight in pictures, and like to stand by the hour watching the progress of any painting, their remarks thereon being always intelligent and to the point, which is more than can be said for those of a good many pale-faced art-critics.

No Mohammedan ought to look at anything so wicked, as he is commanded by the Koran to abhor all likeness of everything in heaven or on earth. Nevertheless, I suspect that my pupils often included the followers of the Prophet, who had no objection to *my* infringing the law, provided *they* were sinless. It seems that Mohammed has declared that at the Day of Judgment all pictures and graven images will be set before the makers thereof, and they will be commanded to breathe life into them, failing which the unfortunate artists and sculptors will be cast into hell for a season!

I fancy the native interest in watching the sketching is very much due to its rarity. They invariably told me that though they often see the Sahibs making photographs, handwork is quite a novelty. Doubtless also it is startling to the Eastern mind, to see a high-caste white woman sit with unveiled face, quietly pursuing her avocations in presence of all comers. Our habits, however, are a riddle which they never hope to solve. I think the native mind was considerably impressed by my invariably sitting Hindoo-wise on a large waterproof with gorgeous lining, so much resembling the Mohammedan prayer-carpet, that they doubtless considered the whole proceeding to be some new form of making *pooja* (*i.e.* worship)!

I was much amused at the way in which my guardian spirit made the best of the crowd which he could not disperse. He awarded reserved seats in the dress circle to those whose drapery entitled them to such honour. Those whose whole raiment consisted of a string and a coin were ignominiously expelled; but the smallest strip of linen was considered quite respectable. Certainly it is curious how rarely this native "undress uniform" strikes any Englishwoman as being indelicate; for the beautiful silky brown colour of these living bronzes, and the total unconsciousness of any lack of raiment, prevents any impression of the sort.

When luncheon time arrived, a happy idea struck them, and they asked my attendant whether my sandwiches were made of beef, which he assured them was the case; whereupon they all retired to a discreet distance, lest any chance crumbs should be blown towards them, and they should thereby be polluted.

This curious phase of reverence is one of the many wholly unauthorised modern additions to the early faith of Brahma. The ancient Sanskrit books make frequent allusions to feasts of beef and ale, when solemn sacrifices of oxen were offered to divers gods, each of whom had a well-known weakness for some special colour or sex. One coveted the sacrifice of a bull, the next of a heifer. Some preferred red, some grey, some black, and others piebald. When duly offered, the animal was divided into thirty-six portions; the priest, of course, reserving the daintiest parts for the god. The flesh roasted, with ghee, was then feasted on, and washed down with jovial draughts of ale and soma-juice. It is supposed that these comfortable sacrifices were only forbidden in order to counterbalance Buddhist teaching of tenderness for animal life; a reason which, however, would equally apply to the sacrifice of goats and buffaloes, which still continues. But of the actual beef-eating festivals, there is no doubt, as has been recently pointed out to the astonished Brahmans, by an intelligent Hindoo, who has given several lectures in Calcutta on the subject of the Beef and Ale of Old India, to lean rice-fed hearers, who consider the sacrifice of a bullock, or the touch of beef, as sacrilege and defilement unutterable.

The only place of much interest in the neighbourhood of Meerut is the Roman Catholic Cathedral at Sirdhana, containing marble groups by Tadolini, which you certainly would not expect to come upon, after sixteen miles drive into this (so-called) jungle. The cathedral was built and endowed by the Begum Somroo, who began life as a Nautch girl; and, having succeeded in captivating the Nawaub, worried her own husband till he committed suicide. She was equally successful in disposing of female rivals, and having been duly established Queen of the Harem, she, at the death of the Nawaub, succeeded to supreme power, and like our martial Queen Bess, commanded her own troops, and rode at their head.

She was a tiny woman but wonderfully clever. Foreseeing that the English would be better friends than foes, she became our most staunch ally; and, having embraced the Christian faith, and compelled a number of her subjects to do likewise, she built this large cathedral, and endowed it so handsomely, that about 300 native Catholics continue faithful to it, and have the privilege of eating all manner of meats, which they consider to be the distinguishing feature of our faith. It is said that she also contributed handsomely to the Protestant Church at Meerut, which accounts for its being somewhat less shabby than our churches at most other stations.

The Begum showed great kindness to a son of the Nawaub, by name Dyce Sombre, formerly well known in England. Being greatly attached to his stepmother, he paid large sums to the Church of Rome to procure her canonization, which honour was accordingly conferred upon her. The ceremony on that occasion was described to us by a lady who was living in Rome at the time, and on whom, knowing the Begum's history, it had made a vivid impression. Dyce Sombre also caused the Italian sculptor, above named, to execute a very elaborate monument to her memory, in which his own ungainly statue in full uniform contrasts strangely with beautiful Italian groups of veiled figures, weeping round the statue of the little Begum; an anomaly which the aggrieved sculptor seems to have revenged by infusing a touch of the ludicrous in some of his other statues.

Our stay at Meerut was happily curtailed by a sudden order that the cavalry should march to Umballa, to grace the state reception of the Ameer of Afghanistán. For the first few days their march lay along the line of railway, and the daily "play" of all disconsolate wives was to make amusing expeditions to the camp and see the marvellous rapidity with which the direst confusion gave place to most perfect order; more especially in the great mess-tent, where snowy linen, and plate and glass, and an elaborate bill of fare, would scarcely allow you to remember that the good "Brownies" who had produced it all had just come off a weary march, and that their cooking-range consisted of a row of stones and mud ovens in the open air! Weather never discomposed their equanimity, and in drenching rain everything was as well served as in the sunshine; a proceeding which would puzzle European *chefs* and footmen, more especially if clad in white linen drapery and turbans.

There were, just at this time, a good many days of soaking rains, with heavy thunderstorms, which must have made a camp life unutterably disgusting; but it was considered greatly to the advantage of the troops, as tending to cool the atmosphere; and though there were some delays, to allow the heavy wet canvas to dry, before the camels could resume their loads, there is little doubt that to this cause they were greatly indebted for so clean a bill of health at Umballa.

CHAPTER X.

A GRAND DURBAR.

Seharanpore—First sight of the Himalayas—Umballa—Gorgeous Rajahs—Elephants—Camels—Reception of the Ameer—A Durbar—Travelling to the Hills—Indian Post Horses—The Foot-hills—Detention at a Rest-house—The Mountain Battery—A Storm—An Art Critic—Scarlet Rhododendrons—Simla.

THE journey from Meerut to Umballa which cost the cavalry and artillery ten days under canvas, and ten morning marches before sunrise, was accomplished by the rest of the world in an afternoon by rail. The line was still so new as to be liable to considerable irregularity. On the present occasion we waited three hours before our train appeared. Happily, being a cheery set, we cared little; and the railway officials had the more time to master the intricacies of our baggage. I listened with much amusement to my sister's explanation: "You see I have tickets for four horses and two dogs. Two of the horses are cows, and one of the dogs is a goat, and the other is a cat!" I bethought me of *Punch's* picture of an old lady whose menagerie had been thus classified—all, save her pet tortoise, which, "being an insect," did not require a ticket. She looked as much disgusted as did one of my friends on being told that her lovely green frogs and pet salamander were "vermin!"

Late in the afternoon we passed Seharanpore, where we had already spent some pleasant days. It is one of the headquarters of the Government Stud Department, which has immense stables here; whence, at the periodical sales of rejected horses, wide-awake individuals recruit their private stables greatly to their own advantage. Seharanpore is famed for its gardens, whence all India is supplied with plants and seeds. Here an old well, of the sort called Persian Wheel, struck me as extremely picturesque. The water is drawn from an immense depth by an endless chain of great red earthen jars, fastened between two ropes, and passing over a wheel, which is in connection with another wheel, turned by bullocks, and driven by brown men in white turbans, the whole overshadowed by fine old trees. One of the ropes, being new, was adorned with a large bunch of flowers as a votive offering to the Spirit of the Well.

Before us stretched a wide hill-range, bounding the intervening plain. It did not seem to us very grand; very much like the Ochils from some points near Stirling. Only we knew that these were indeed the low spurs of that mighty range we had come so far to see, and that those little patches and peaks of glittering white were our first glimpse of the eternal snows of the Himalayas.[1] One mountain in particular, the Chor, we were afterwards taught to look up to with reverence, but I cannot say that was our first impulse.

It was late and dark when we reached Umballa. Our luggage-ticket was mislaid in the confusion, and there was no end of tantalising trouble, and going to and fro, before we were allowed to rescue one atom of our property, which lay piled before our eyes. We forcibly carried off one box of nursery goods, and the authorities, after wearisome delays, allowed the rest to follow us. Tired and hungry, we at last found ourselves safe in a large empty bungalow, of which a friend had kindly allowed us the use. The house was literally empty, so we had commissioned a furniture agent to supply such things as were actually necessary. The sudden influx of strangers made all such supplies meagre in the extreme; and you can imagine nothing more dreary than a large, empty Indian bungalow, where the uncarpeted floors and bare whitewashed walls make every voice and footstep resound; every

[1] Himalaya, "the abode of perpetual snow"—from the Sanskrit *hima*, "snow," and *alaya*, "an abode." *Himmavat* means the "snow-covered."

room acting as a passage to its neighbours, and no curtains to veil the ill-fitting doors.

However, when morning returned, with its flood of warm sunshine, we no longer thought it dreary, but turning plaids into table-cloths, and filling every native bowl and hubble-bubble vase, on which we could lay hands, with loads of roses and jessamine, we soon made our quarters cosy enough. Afterwards, when we saw how every nook and cranny of the town was crowded with strangers, we felt thankful indeed for our large cool rooms and shady garden, where orange and pomegranate-shrubs (those "busy plants," as old George Herbert calls them) mingled their white or scarlet blossoms with their own ripening fruit, and where, more beautiful than all, the tall beauhinia or camel's foot (so called from the shape of its leaf) showered down exquisite blossoms like large white geraniums, with lilac markings.

Here we often lingered in the cool evening watching the vivid sheets of lightning, while crashing peals of thunder made the night solemn, and harmonised the various camp-sounds on every side, bands playing, bugles calling, voices of men and of camels. One native regiment quartered near us seemed to be for ever marching to the sound of a very musical little French horn. In short, we soon made *aural* acquaintance with our many neighbours.

On one side stretched the great Maidan, a fine, wide plain, affording scope for all manner of military evolutions. The troops were camped all round the edge of this plain; and the mass of white canvas cutting against the background of dark foliage, the Himalayas lying blue in the distance, and the brilliant foreground of native figures gorgeously attired, combined to make a very fine picture. At the farther end of the great plain lay the Governor-General's camp, a white city of tents, all ready for his reception; and a little farther was that of the Commander-in-Chief, both overshadowed by the Union Jack.

Such a plain would on most occasions have been veiled by its own dust, stirred up by the ever-moving crowds and galloping troops. Fortunately, however, the nights of heavy rain, which conduced so much to the discomfort of those under canvas proved not merely a safeguard of health, but a great addition to the enjoyment of the days.

Besides, we were indebted to those kindly showers for a glimpse, often repeated, of a genuine, unmistakable mirage. For the sun's hot rays drew from the moist earth a tremulous haze of misty dew, which hung quivering over the plain; and the dark, distant trees and white tents not only seemed raised, so as to float above the mist, but their inverted images lay clearly reflected thereon, as on the bosom of some quiet lake.

We had arrived on a Saturday, and our Afghan allies were not expected till Wednesday, nor was Lord Mayo to arrive from Calcutta till the following Saturday; so we had time enough to explore the neighbourhood, and to admire all the magnificent natives and their gorgeous suites. Sixteen "burra" Rajahs, very great men, had assembled, besides innumerable lesser potentates, each bringing his military escort; his elephants with magnificent howdahs; his camels and gorgeously caparisoned horses, covered with a network of silk and jewels, in addition to their jewelled trappings and long sweeping yak's tails. Some of the horses were partly dyed pink, others stained russet with henna, a few were adorned with anklets of gold and gems.

But a good deal of this splendour was reserved for the show days, and it must be confessed that many of these great men cut but a poor figure on first arriving, as most of them chose to drive into Umballa in their English carriages, which, as a rule, were of the shabbiest. Their followers too, were, naturally enough, travel-stained and weary, and trudged along, in anything but orderly style, to the intense dismay of our servants, who had striven hard to impress upon us the overpowering magnificence that was to dazzle our bewildered sight. These men have a good deal of the old Highland pride in the greatness of their chiefs, and never lose a chance of extolling their wealth, and apparently with good reason.

The greatest man of all was the Rajah of Putialah, whose camp was said far to outshine that of the Governor-General. The whole place seemed to swarm with his retainers. He brought so many regiments that they amounted to a small army. The excellence of his artillery corps drew forth much praise, while their band played "Begone dull care," "Cherry ripe," "The Bailiff's daughter of Islington," and many such popular airs, admirably. His elephants were apparently without number, and the magnificence of their trappings was suggestive of the old Arabian nights. Some had howdahs of silver; others of silver inlaid with gold. One huge elephant was accompanied by a very small one, bearing a great ladder of solid silver, whereby his master might climb down from his tall perch. Sometimes his rider preferred a gallop on horseback; then the stately old elephant knelt, and salaaming with his trunk, remained immovable during his master's descent, which was by no means the graceful action of "vaulting from the saddle," then rising, he salaamed again, and marched on with majestic solemnity.

Some of the howdahs are quite too gorgeous; divans of gleaming metal, apparently silver or burnished gold, and with a canopy of the same to represent the honorific umbrella, the whole lined with richest velvet and most luxurious cushions. This splendid couch rests on a thickly-wadded velvet quilt, while a gorgeous gold-embroidered velvet cloth hangs to the ground on either side, so that the elephant is almost hidden with crimson and gold housings. The attendants are well in keeping with all this splendour, some bearing great fans of peacock's feathers, others waving yak's tails as fly flaps, while some are privileged to hold the regal oriental umbrellas. This was my first sight of elephants in full dress, and I own I was rather startled to see those wise faces painted with lines, stars, stripes, and curling patterns in brilliant colours, more elaborate than the caste-marks of their masters. Their great flapping ears, too, are pierced like a woman's, and adorned with jewels. Their huge ankles are circled by heavy bracelets and bangles of silver and precious stones. Their crupper and necklace consist of many large plates of gold or silver, suspended from a great chain. On their forehead they wear some costly jewel, and the tips of their tusks are sheathed in richly embossed gold or silver. Sometimes they wear a golden crown as well, and a jewelled network on their head and neck. Others simply have the head stained of a saffron colour, with ears shaded off to green, all elaborate decoration in arabesque being lavished on the proboscis, while very large tusks are added on to those bestowed by nature, a piece of cunning dentistry which is deftly concealed by golden bands. The legs are also painted, and adorned with massive bracelets of gold and silver. The finest elephant is none the worse for being thus got up, for when in undress it is a wondrously untidy-looking beast, in its loose, flappy, wrinkled skin, which seems much too large for it. It does look so shabby, and no one, looking at its ugly little eyes, would ever give it credit for so much sagacity as we know it possesses.

The natives seemed much gratified at our admiration of their barbaric splendour. One *mahout* (driver) (himself gorgeously apparelled) showed me the heavy prod of solid gold, incrusted with large turquoises, wherewith he encourages his charge, often striking the poor brute on the skull till he bleeds horribly.

Whatever sameness there must necessarily be in describing such a scene, there is considerable variety in the reality, one star differing from another in radiance, but each individually splendid. Only one thing is alike in all—the strange uneasy swaying of the proboscis, which is never for a moment at rest.

Within each fantastic howdah sits some dark chief, glittering with jewels, and robed in some brilliant material; silk or velvet or cashmere, stiff with gold and silver; dress, turban, and waist-cloth, each more rich than the other, yet always harmonious in colouring. I confess our admiration was fairly riveted by some of these beautiful beings. We had never yet seen such gorgeous embroidery as this raiment of needlework, wrought with divers colours—such cloth of gold, and priceless *kincob* from the looms of Benares; such jewels, worn all over head and body; large emeralds, often destroyed, in our eyes, by being elaborately carved; pearls, diamonds, and rubies of immense value, set in silver; even the yak's tails, wherewith the servants flick away the flies from their lord's presence, often have beautifully jewelled handles.

The odd thing is, that with all this splendour there is invariably some tawdry ingredient, very often something positively dirty—in short, just such a lack of cleanliness as I have too often noticed in certain churches, where fair white linen has been superseded by richer, but non-washing, materials. As to these natives, one of the commonest additions to their magnificent oriental robes is a pair of common woollen or white cotton gloves, which certainly do look out of place!

Moreover in some cases both the Rajahs and their troops assume English uniform, believing imitation to be truest flattery! But oh, Ichabod! their glory vanishes straightway. The dress and the wearer are utterly incongruous, and the combination is one of hideous vulgarity.

Of all the native troops none were so picturesque as an artillery camel corps belonging to the Rajah of Putialah. The camels and their riders are draped in scarlet and yellow, and each carries a long gun, which revolves on a swivel fixed to the pommel of the saddle. They are said to be a capital and very efficient corps. An officer who has seen them on service describes how the bombardier, sitting astride behind the gun, loads and fires with wonderful rapidity, apparently placing the poor camel's head in imminent jeopardy. "The animals move along at a swinging trot, following each other, with long outstretched necks, like a flock of wild geese. At a word they halt, fire a broadside, and jog off again at the rate of fifteen miles an hour."

Our acquaintance with camels had hitherto been limited to the Arabian camel or dromedary, with a single hump, which is the only variety now in use in the plains, being by far swifter than the Bactrian camel, to which it bears much the same relation that a hunter does to a cart-horse. Moreover, the foot of the dromedary, which is only fitted for walking on sand or dry earth, naturally points to its use on the parched and arid plains; whereas, its Bactrian brother has no objection to any amount of hill work. Not that the dromedaries refuse a moderate amount of climbing (as we saw at Cairo, where the patient creatures toiled up the steep Mokattem crag, bearing water for the guard at the powder magazine); the only walking which is positive misery to them being over wet or slippery ground, when their feet slide in every direction, and their long legs are in such constant danger of dislocation that it is sometimes necessary to strap them together, compelling the creature to advance with the shortest possible steps.

The Bactrian camel is preferred for the artillery corps, for the double reason that its foot is better adapted to variety of ground, and also that it can carry nearly double weight. It is, however, far worse-tempered, and in one sense is less enduring than the dromedary, as it cannot go for more than three days without a fresh supply of water; whereas the latter can carry nearly a week's store in its wonderful cistern stomach, thence drawing at need. On the other hand, the Bactrian camel has a great advantage in the double hump, whose cells of fat do undoubtedly act as a larder in cases of starvation. Both humps will actually shrivel almost up to nothing before the rest of the body wastes from hunger. They are merely excrescences, nowise affecting the structure of the animal, so that it is only a skilful anatomist who can discern between the skeletons of the two species.

It is said that the most serviceable of all camels are those of mixed breed; that is to say, of Bactrian parentage by Arabian mothers. A corps of two thousand of these was employed by General Harlan in a winter campaign on the snowy Indian Caucasus, and more hardy beasts of burden were never known; in fact, during seven months only one was lost, and that was killed by an accident. It is a curious fact that the original home of the camel is not known. Apparently no wild species now exist; even those untamed herds which roam on the frontiers of China being all private property.

Like the elephant, the camel and dromedary move both legs on the same side at once, thus swinging the whole body with an awkward motion, which, like some other novelties, is very unpleasant till you are accustomed to it. Nevertheless, the fact of their being able to travel upwards of seventy miles daily for many consecutive days would make them precious in other lands besides the plains of Asia; but the attempt to transplant them to Europe or America has invariably failed. They seem to pine for home, and very quickly droop and die. The camel express messengers are very striking features in oriental life. The camels are adorned with trappings of gay cloth and tassels, ornamented with blue beads and cowrie shells, and small brass bells round the neck, to give notice of their swift approach. They are guided by a thin cord attached to a bit of wood piercing the nostril. It is said that their rough and rapid trotting, sometimes at the rate of eighty miles a day, is so trying to the riders as to shorten their lives.

Perhaps the most curious of all the quaint varieties of equipage in the great gathering at Umballa was an English open phaeton drawn by a pair of dromedaries; and I heard of a similar carriage and four! Anything more utterly incongruous you cannot imagine. Of course, it was an object of special aversion to all other carriages, as no horse can endure meeting either camels or elephants, for which reason both are generally prohibited from appearing on the Mall.

But as to the native vehicles, they are always picturesque. Scores of queer little *ekkas*, with their curtained hoods, and high shafts, balancing two wheels, were for ever tearing along as fast as one fat pony could gallop; while the more stately family coach, with its double pyramidal hood (a small hood in front and a large one at the back), all closely draped with scarlet and gold, is drawn by beautiful white oxen very richly caparisoned, and stepping as proudly as though they knew how precious a burden of "lights of the harem," "coral lips," "heart's desires," "delight of the eyes," "morning stars," and other dainty dames, were hidden from the vulgar gaze by that envious drapery. Sometimes a little jewelled hand would cautiously draw back a corner of the curtain, and a pair of beautiful bright eyes would peep forth, and even favour us with a smile; then all too quickly retreat again, and leave us to the contemplation of the casket only, wherein were concealed so many dazzling gems.

As to the turbaned crowd on foot, each ingredient was a picture in itself, and there were thousands upon thousands of such picturesque mortals, each gaily attired, and all turbaned, and perpetually forming new combinations of bright colour in the clear sunlight. There were much the same figures as we had already seen at various holy fairs. Women attired in jackets and in the very tightest of silk trousers, worn on the leanest of legs; their veils of finest muslin, gold-spangled or plain, as the case may be. Others were more draped. All alike were adorned with every jewel they could muster, including small looking-glasses set in silver and worn as thumb-rings. For the most part they carried a child astride on the hip. Sometimes on the other shoulder sat a still younger child, its head resting on its mother's. Perhaps the whole family were present, in which case the father probably carried a bamboo across his shoulder from which two large baskets were suspended by long cords. Probably one basket contained a little brown boy, in robes of rich satin or silk, really valuable jewels, and a gay silken cap embroidered with gold; the other represented the luggage of all the party, food and cooking-pot included.

Even the varied methods of driving divers animals was not without interest. The bullocks being driven by a rope through the nose, and by a twist of the tail; drawing, as I before said, only by pressure of a wooden yoke against the hump. The camel's bridle is attached to a piece of wood with small bits of cork, also passing through the nostril. The elephant is generally obedient to his driver's voice; but if obstinate, a little gentle suasion is applied with a spiked iron prod, horrible to behold.

Wednesday morning came, and with it should have arrived our Afghan guests. Every one was waiting at the station, at dawn of day, anxiously expecting the train. Crowds of Europeans and brilliantly dressed natives, and a large cavalry escort, waited till they were weary, when tidings were brought that His Highness Shere Ali Khan, Ameer of Afghanistan, had unfortunately eaten a whole bottle of pickles and drunk the vinegar, and would certainly be unable to come till the afternoon. So in the afternoon we returned. Again there was a great gathering of Europeans, as well as of gorgeous natives; the road was lined with native cavalry and other troops; an escort of Hussars awaited our guests, and altogether the scene was as brilliant as heart could wish.

The poor Ameer looked decidedly ill, and it must be confessed that he seemed as horribly frightened as you or I might have done, when twenty-one fog-signals successively exploded under the engine as it came in, preparatory to a grand artillery salute! You must recollect that the railway was in itself a startling novelty to him, and to one trained from his cradle in the villanous treacheries sanctioned in all Asiatic policy, such a step as venturing unarmed, and with but a handful of followers, into the heart of the British Empire, might well be accompanied by some qualms, which, however well concealed in general, were likely to be fairly roused by the first fog-signal! Of the treacheries so freely sanctioned in the politics of Asia, few better examples can be offered than the career of Shere Ali's father, Dost Mohammed, who may be said to have founded the Afghan kingdom by the assassination of one after another of the leading chiefs, till all power was vested in his own hands. He appointed Shere Ali, his third son, as his successor, a decision naturally objected to by his elder brothers, and one which led to five years' civil war ere his position was established, and he himself recognised by the British Government and accepted as an ally.

Next morning all the troops turned out at daybreak for a grand review, but His Highness, not having quite got over the pickles, deferred it till the afternoon—rather to the disgust of all concerned, as the morning was exquisite. Happily the evening proved just as fine, so we magnanimously forgave him. It was a beautiful field. The mixture of native troops in turbans, the 79th Highlanders, with their tall feather bonnets defying the sun; the European cavalry and artillery with white helmets; the picturesque corps of native horse; and the brilliant native foreground, with camels, bullocks, elephants, and horses, without number, each with trappings and housing more brilliant than its neighbour. In the background lay the city of white tents and dark trees; and far beyond all, bathed in the soft evening light, lay the snow-capped Himalayas, aim and end of our wanderings.

The next morning dawned with a strange feeling of incongruity. It was Good Friday. How it came to pass that the Holy Week should have been the season of all others selected for this Grand Durbar I do not know, but the utter lack of harmony between scene and season jarred at every turn. Umballa has the advantage of an unusually fine church—quite the best I saw in India—with a full complement of well-ordered services. These would, I believe, have carried the day if balanced against commonplace pomps and vanities; but when it became a question of such irresistible barbaric pageants, why, we argued like that worthy Scot, a keen fisherman, who (looking from his windows one lovely Sabbath morning on the quiet trout stream gliding beneath the birch-trees) determined that "he wadna bide to be tempted, he wad just gang!" So the week slipped by, in the difficult attempt to combine things incompatible, and with the usual result; for too often the loud clear tones of the bells that sounded athwart the plain to call all Christian people to matins or evensong rang vainly in our ears; too wholly engrossed by the strange new sights and sounds that surrounded us.

But on this one great day the Ameer was informed that there could be no reviews, for it was the Christian's holiest day, and from morning till night there was a succession of services, when the great church was crowded to overflowing. But as we crossed the plain in the afternoon we found a greater gathering than we had yet seen, for all the Rajahs and their retainers were rehearsing their part in the great pageant of the morrow, being therein instructed by the English authorities.

Again the church was crowded, and "a great company of Christian people" knelt in its solemn twilight, but strove in vain to shut out the jarring sounds of the outer world; for just as the service commenced the distant roar of voices drew nearer and nearer, and the whole array of Heathendom slowly marched back to its own camp, passing right in front of the great western door; every strange fantastic form, of camels with long guns, elephants with their howdahs, men on horseback, men on foot, all seeming weird and unearthly as they cut black against the flood of golden sunset-light. It was vain alike for the organ to pour forth its most solemn tones, or for the full clear voice of the preacher to attempt to make itself heard above that maddening din—the voices of native officers shouting to their men, the beating of tomtoms, the jingling bells of all the elephants, the creaking of wheels, the march of that vast mass of human beings, while each regiment had its own band playing every conceivable tune simultaneously—operas, valses, polkas, every horrible discord you can possibly imagine.

It was a strange accompaniment to that grand service.

I doubt whether Mohammedan authorities in a Mohammedan city would have thus suffered a Christian procession to silence the worship of their Mosque; but, you see, they are not troubled with false shame in these matters, and do not try to hide their faith in any corner, so it be out of sight.

By daybreak the following morning all the world was astir, to receive the Governor-General. The English and native cavalry were drawn up at the station as his escort. A broad green road right across the Maïdan led direct from the station to the Vice-regal camp, a distance of two miles, the whole of which was lined, on either side, with a living wall of Rajahs, and all their belongings—their troops, their camels, their elephants. The effect was somewhat spoilt by the width of the road, whereby all effect of rich detail was lost. As the viceregal carriages and their Hussar escort came slowly down the middle, each band in turn struck up "God save the Queen," and as all played in different keys, and began in succession, the effect was truly astonishing, yea, electrifying! There was an attempt at a cheer, but the Hindoo lungs, however willing, seem quite incapable of making themselves heard in that form.

This procession having reached the white tent where floated

England's flag, with the Himalayan background, we next drove to a corner of the plain, where we knew the whole of that vast array must march past us; and this, I think, was the prettiest sight of all. It was the first time we fully realised the mass of human beings present, and they all passed so close to us that we had full leisure to inspect every detail of physiognomy, armour, dress, and jewellery, both of men and animals.

In the afternoon we returned to the Viceregal camp, to be present at that embodiment of all our dreams of Oriental splendour—a Grand Durbar—of which, as of most kindred enjoyments, one taste proved sufficient. We would not have missed it on any account, but henceforth we can sympathise with the Frenchman's summary of the joys of hunting, and say with infinite satisfaction, "*J'y ai été!*" or, we may say, as Horace Walpole did of the coronation of George III., "Well, it was all delightful, but not half so charming as its being over!"

The 79th Highlanders were on duty, as were also the 4th Hussars. On one side of the great tent were seated all the English ladies; on the other sat all the gorgeous Rajahs, and between them stood the unoccupied throne. In due time the Governor-General arrived, and walked up to the throne. Then followed a most awkward pause. The Ameer had somehow been delayed; and as it seemed against etiquette for the Viceroy to speak to any lesser potentate on such an occasion, every one stood waiting in a silence which became more and more oppressive. At length he came, accompanied by his nice little son, a pretty child with large dark eyes, the pet of the harem, and his father's special darling. He and all his followers were dressed as usual, in a sort of dirty old brown dressing-gown, with a tall black Astrakan cap; his retainers being a few shades dingier than himself, and presenting a striking contrast to the array of magnificently dressed native chiefs, who had assembled to grace the reception of the ally whom England delighted to honour.

On these occasions the number of steps which a great man must advance to meet his guest are all matters of rigid etiquette; Lord Mayo, being desirous to do great honour to the Ameer, advanced to receive him as far as the door of the tent, and they returned, I think, hand in hand. As they passed up to the throne, and there sat for some time conversing, I think all present felt proud of England's representative, and glad that the dignity of our Queen and of our race should be so well upheld before these native princes, as they assuredly were, by one so calm and stately, and withal so thoroughly courteous and genial, as was he whose untimely death India and Britain were so soon to mourn.

In striking contrast with his dignified mien and commanding presence was the appearance of the dark dingy man, with the subtle, cunning eyes, and arrayed in the dirty brown robe, and tall woollen hat, who certainly did not impress us favourably at the time. Yet I think that when two years later tidings reached England of that dastardly murder at which the whole world stood aghast, there were few who were not touched by the genuine sympathy and personal sorrow shown in the letter of the Ameer to the Acting Viceroy, in which, after speaking of the universal love and esteem in which Lord Mayo was held for his many high and excellent qualities, and of his own personal loss in the death of his friend, he added, that the unvarying kindness and friendship shown him by Lord Mayo had been such as to induce him to determine (should the affairs of Afghanistan permit of such a step) to accompany his Excellency on his return to England, that he might have the gratification of a personal interview with Her Majesty, as well as the pleasure of travelling in Europe. Such trust spoke volumes for the confidence inspired by the Viceroy's wise policy, and for the influence he had acquired with these half-civilised sons of the mountains. How far the loss of that wise strong counsellor may account for subsequent events it is of course impossible to say.

The conversation at the Durbar was all carried on through an interpreter, and in a low voice, and while we, the spectators, all sat round in dead silence, gazing at the two great men, we could perceive that Lord Mayo sometimes had hard work to suppress a smile. For, as we afterwards learnt, Afghan phraseology is peculiar, as you may judge from the Ameer's reply to a courteous inquiry whether all arrangements had been made for his comfort, that since entering the British territory his stomach had been full! Some other replies were equally remarkable.

The Queen's presents to the Ameer were next produced; trays without number were carried in and laid at his feet, and removed again. Silver hubble-bubbles, clocks, trays full of gold and silver ornaments, musical boxes, field-glasses, vases, guns and pistols innumerable, gold-embroidered shoes, dresses of richest brocaded silk of every colour of the rainbow, stiff with gold embroidery, rich Cashmere raiment for his favourite wife, and jewels for her and for the child. Of course it would be unseemly that he should even glance at these things, far less seem pleased. Yet at the sight of the fire-arms his eyes sparkled, for he was an out-and-out soldier, who cared for nothing so much as weapons, and the pleasure of using them. In addition to the trifles above named, which were valued at £5,000, England presented her ally with a whole battery of artillery (nine-pounders), also with many elephants and horses, and a sum of £12,000 in money.

The interview lasted about half an hour, after which the two great men departed, and the Viceroy having escorted Shere Ali Khan to the door, had the satisfaction of himself escaping for a gallop on the Maïdan, leaving all the gorgeous Rajahs and Europeans still sitting in solemn silence round the tent, and the Durbar was over.

Ere we dispersed, however, we took another lesson in Eastern courtesies, and learnt by what small distinctions our degrees of homage may be varied. So soon as the Ameer had driven off, having received his full salute, two aides-de-camp returned, and silently taking the great Rajah of Putialah by each hand, led him out. Then one of them returned, and handed out each lesser Rajah by one hand, each being on his departure saluted by one or two guns fewer than his predecessor, till the turn came for the very small ones, who got no hand, and no salute at all! It is scarcely possible for an Englishman to realise what immense importance the natives attach to these minute distinctions, or how immeasurable is the distance between the man who ranks as a five-gun Rajah and he who is entitled to fifteen!

Easter morning dawned fresh and home-like, with a light breeze, cool and balmy. It was still early when we reached the crowded church, whence a very large military congregation had already dispersed. The building, as I before remarked, is so good as to be quite exceptional, with very fine stained glass. The Easter decorations were lovely. Masses of roses and jessamine, and all green things of the earth, not reduced to the exceeding refinement of modern English decorations, but a good old-fashioned wealth of flowers, in great bunches and garlands, and twining in festoons round every pillar and arch. I suppose this was the work of some of the soldiers, and there was a well-trained military choir.

A vast number of natives assembled near the door to see the congregation "scale," as we say in the north. Not a very entertaining process, I fear! I think after that, they must all have gone to sleep, for the town seemed empty, and the quiet of that evening's service was in very marked contrast with the pandemonium during that of Good Friday. As we wended our homeward way, there was no sound to disturb the "soft stillness of the Indian night," save an occasional bugle-call, or the silent footsteps of some peaceful pedestrian like ourselves.

One more day was devoted to the Afghans. By sunrise all were astir to see a grand review and sham fight—a scene so picturesque as to make everything of the sort in Britain seem utterly commonplace, not even excepting the great Volunteer Reviews at Holyrood, with Arthur's Seat and its living throng for a background. The ground itself was admirable, the great plain affording ample room for the movement of troops, and the surrounding trees, fields, and bridges serving as an enemy's country, where they might skirmish to their hearts' content, appearing and disappearing through the clouds of their own smoke. But to me the endless centre of delight lay in the native spectators. I might tell you, till you were weary, of groups of twenty or thirty elephants here, a score of camels there, and all the other ingredients of that enchanting kaleidoscope, but I could not give you the faintest idea of the life, colour, and movement that surrounded us on that sunny fresh morning as we rapidly drove from point to point.

The Ameer scanned the field with the keen eye of an old soldier, and in Oriental phrase, compared it to a fair garden with many blossoms, those on which his eye rested with most pleasure being the Highlanders and the artillery. He showed his appreciation of the former by bestowing large backsheesh on the fifteen pipers, whose wild music doubtless pleased his ear far better than the more polished strains to which in the Viceroy's tent he listened so politely. Probably they carried him back to his own wild hills, and his own regiments of sturdy hill men.

Do you remember how much Sir Walter Scott was interested in noticing the similarities of these Afghan Highlanders with our own ancestors? The intense love of both for a wild untrammelled life, the same curious superstitions, the same quaint method of divination by reading marks on a sheep-bone whereon knife had never come, the same frugal adherence to one meal a day, the same curious form of submission, when resistance had proved utterly hopeless, by delivering up their sword held by the point, then laying their head on a block as if to await death. This last acme of humiliation is one which, we may hope, did not often occur in the north!

The admiration of many of the hill tribes for the Scotch bag-pipes has often attracted attention. During Sir John Lawrence's Durbar at Lahore, the Maharajah of Cashmere was so enchanted by the pipers of the 93rd Highlanders that he sent an embassy to Sealcote requesting that some of his own men might be taught the use of the pipes; and another chief sent to Scotland direct for divers stands of pipes, to ensure his getting the genuine article. It is said, too, that in Nepaul, where a variety of the same instrument is now considered national music, it was first introduced by a Scotch officer of the name of Macræ, a Highlander from Kintail, who beguiled his leisure by playing the old pipes, and teaching the natives to do likewise.

But, however much the Ameer admired the Highlanders, his keenest interest was reserved for the cavalry and artillery; more especially the Mountain Mule Battery, which consists of small guns, each of which can at a moment's notice be separated from its carriage and its wheels, and, together with its ammunition, may be carried almost anywhere by sturdy mules, and at once be made ready for action. These were to the Mountain Chief a source of intense interest, and England's gift of a similar battery was to him a matter of unfeigned delight.

Having thus seen His Highness in his own element, it only remained for us to meet him once more at the Viceroy's evening reception, or, as the natives would say, at the Lord Sahib's and the Lady Sahib's great feast. There he appeared with all his attendants, in the identical brown dressing-gowns and tall black caps of curly sheep-skin, looking dingier and dirtier than ever, in contrast with the magnificent evening raiment of the bejewelled Rajahs; to say nothing of the multitude of English ladies present. What may have been the Ameer's private opinion of the latter I know not, for he had learnt wisdom in his travels, and kept his own counsel. He had been less cautious, a few days previously, when all the beauty and fashion of Peshawur had turned out to receive him; when, after coolly surveying them all, he remarked to the gentlemen beside him, that he perceived that the English, just like their neighbours, kept all the pretty women safe at home!

This reception was held in great tents opening one into another, and it was curious to see the Ameer and the Rajahs being formally led about by the hand whenever it pleased them to pass from one tent to the next. As to the Rajahs, they looked like a body of magnificent dowagers; you almost expected to see white satin shoes, instead of brown bare feet, appearing from beneath their splendid brocades. One magnificent old chief attracted my special admiration. He was robed in green velvet, and his show of diamonds was moderate yet priceless. Some of the other Rajahs were like locomotive diamond mines. One, whose head-dress blazed with gems was dressed in dark green and brown velvets richly embroidered, and even his attendants were draped in priceless raiment of needlework in the form of costly shawls.

The admiration of the ladies was divided between these heavy butterflies and the Ameer's pretty son with the large dark eyes. This child, Abdoolla, seemed at that time destined to play some part in Afghan history, Shere Ali having determined to repeat his father's political blunder, and (passing over his two elder sons) had appointed Abdoolla his successor, thus threatening once more to plunge his country in civil war; a war which would have been the more certain, inasmuch as the second son, Yakoob Khan, was a man of rare ability and bravery, and one who, as governor of Herat, had gained vast popularity with his subjects.

It is said that Shere Ali's success in securing the throne was greatly due to Yakoob's wise tactics and firm support. Yet so small a part does gratitude play in Eastern politics, that when, in 1874, Shere Ali formally declared Abdoolla his successor, he did not scruple to induce Yakoob to pay him a friendly visit in Cabul, under pretext of reconsidering the question, and treacherously detained him prisoner. On that occasion British influence succeeded in averting the ordinary Asiatic catastrophe, and induced the Ameer to recognise Yakoob Khan as his heir.

Britain's influence however, was not of long duration. We all know how quickly the promise of peace melted away, to be followed by the prolonged Afghan war. In 1878 Shere Ali abandoned Cabul, leaving Yakoob Khan to carry on the war with Britain, while he himself found a refuge on the northern frontier, where he died a few months later.

Peace was signed in May 1879 by Yakoob Khan and Major Cavagnari. The British army then returned to India. Cavagnari was appointed Resident, and arrived at Cabul in July. In the beginning of September he and his companions, Mr. Jenkyns, Lieutenant Hamilton, V.C., and Dr. Kelly, were treacherously murdered. Then followed the second part of the Afghan war. The British forces under General Roberts returned to Cabul. Yakoob Khan resigned early in October, and was sent to India, and new blood was introduced in the person of Abdul Rahman Khan, who was appointed Ameer, and appears to hold his position satisfactorily.

These circumstances add interest to the recollection of the little child at the Durbar, who greatly excited our commiseration, because, being trained up in the way he should go, he was only allowed two meals a day, and having breakfasted at daybreak had tasted nothing since then. How he must have longed for his supper! Nevertheless he looked quite happy, and stood by the piano, watching the motion of the inner leathers with a child's usual delight. There was some excellent singing, but I believe all oriental races consider that music is the one thing of which we are incapable, infinitely preferring their own wearisome, monotonous chants.

The following morning we bade adieu to Umballa, which continued in a state of ferment for some days longer, ere the British and native camps broke up, and the multitude of visitors once more scattered to their divers quarters. We were, however, anxious to reach Simla, and so started without further delay, travelling as far as Kalka at the foot of the hills by dak or post gharry—a mode of travelling the joys of which have been pretty often described, but never amended. The gharry itself is comfortable enough. It is in fact a small travelling van, a long box on wheels, hung high on account of the streams which may have to be forded. A sliding door on each side acts as a window; there is no glass, of course, so though you may shut out the sun in some measure, there is no chance of excluding dust, which pours in in stifling clouds. Level with the door is a long cushion whereon you lie at full length; generally your bedding is unrolled and outspread, so as to be less in your way. To sit up you must either squat like a Hindoo, or send your toes out of the door. There is a well beneath the carriage in which your smaller luggage is stowed, but this has to be removed to the top if the rivers are swollen. Inside the gharry are all manner of pockets and shelves for your books, sketching-blocks, dressing materials, food, and so forth. In short it is a house on wheels. As a general rule each person has a gharry to himself, as it is rather close quarters for two, especially on a long journey and in hot weather and choking dust. So far, nothing could be more suitable to the work.

But the crown of sorrows lies in the unhappy team; miserable brutes, whose happier days, if they ever had any, have been long forgotten, and to whom the knacker's yard would be a blessed release from the torture of daily life. At each stage they seem to grow worse and worse, so that to start them on a fresh run is work for a dozen men, and never done under half an hour. On a tolerably good road you are only allowed one horse; should a second be necessary, he is harnessed outside the shafts, as an outrigger, and simply runs alongside. At every halt you are sure of some trouble before you are again under way; constantly the poor beasts that await you are galled, and exhausted by their last run.

Should they chance to be fresh they are brought out biting, screaming, plunging, kicking, rearing; held by main force of a dozen coolies and syces. Once harnessed, nothing will induce them to move. Vainly all their attendants seize the wheels, and turn them so as to force on the gharry. The stubborn brutes either turn right round, or throw themselves down. Then some burning straw is produced, which probably brings them to their feet again. A rope is now tied to their forelegs, another to their heads, the wheels are turned by strong arms, and thus they are dragged along for perhaps a mile, accompanied by an ant-like black swarm of all but naked coolies, screaming, howling, yelling, shoving, beating; alternately pouring forth maledictions and persuasions, terms of endearment and of opprobrium, with amazing volubility.

After half an hour has thus been wasted, the steeds probably go off at a tearing gallop, when you fully expect to land in the ditch. Perhaps after a while you fall asleep. You awake to find everything at a standstill. The coachwanee and syce are quietly hubble-bubbling (*i.e.* smoking) together by the roadside; the wheels are sunk up to the axle in a bed of sand and shingle, or wet kunker (which becomes a sort of heavy clay), for the roads have been cut up with heavy traffic, and long trains of bullock-waggons are working their way to Simla, with the heavy baggage of the whole English community.

There is nothing for it but to wait patiently till a squad of men can be collected; all passers-by are impressed, and lend their aid to extricate the wheels from the deep ruts. Sometimes even this fails; then you must wait till bullocks can be procured to drag you through the mire; and then comes all the trouble of another harnessing and another start.

About nine hours of this work brought us to Kalka; at the foot of the Himalayas, which cast their grand cool shadows far over the weary land. Here we still have the rich vegetation of the plains. Sugar-cane, maize, plantains, all manner of flowering shrubs, the sweet babool tree, with its silky yellow blossoms, and tall date-palms (we have seen no cocoa palms since we left Calcutta and the sea breezes).

Kalka is a pretty village, wonderfully like Dunkeld without the river. These low spurs of the Himalayas are just like average bits of Scotland, only rather more abrupt, with red sand cliffs. The resemblance is further increased by our having to decide between the rival claims of Bain's Inn or MacBarnet's Hotel. In either case, however, the landlady proves a talkative half-caste. We selected the former—with a jovial, bustling old landlady, who evidently ruled her natives with a rod of iron.

From Kalka to Simla, you have your choice of two routes, the old and the new; the former the more picturesque, the latter the better road; so much better, that on our return from Simla we drove back all the way to Kalka. Once you reach Simla no wheeled vehicle of any sort is allowed, for fear of accidents; indeed I believe that the driving to Simla was a short-lived experiment, very soon prohibited on account of its danger.

But no carriages had been started at this time. There were only the bullock-carts in which vast quantities of luggage and stores were being conveyed to Simla. Human beings had either to ride, or to be carried by coolies in a *jampan*, a *doolie*, or a *dandie*. The first is a sort of uncomfortable armchair, with four poles and curtains, in which you are carried on a level with the shoulders of your bearers. The second is a narrow bed, in a long curtained box. In this you are carried almost on a level with the ground, and get all the dust from the men's feet. Moreover you are so low that you can never see over the parapet, which protects the outer edge of the road, all the way to Simla. Both jampan and doolie are carried by relays of four men at a time, and the motion is just like continuous trotting without a stirrup.

These vehicles are first cousins to the old English sedan-chairs of our grandmothers—grandfathers too, according to Thackeray's description of the time of George III., when a day of fashionable life invariably ended "by making two wretches carry you home in a sedan-chair, with three pints of claret in you; three miles for one shilling." Of the three vehicles aforesaid, I infinitely preferred the dandie, of which there are two varieties. In one of these you sit up as in a chair, looking straight before you—this is called a canoe. In the other you sit sideways in a bit of carpet slung on a bamboo; and feel much less motion, especially when only carried by two men at a time.

We had already despatched all our heavy baggage by bullock train; nevertheless we found that fifty coolies were necessary to carry ourselves and our small goods—a regiment which assembled beneath our windows long before daybreak, talking and hubble-bubbling in a style that insured our not over-sleeping ourselves.

From Kalka to Simla is generally considered a four days' march, at the rate of about fourteen miles a day. Of course a rider can get over the ground faster, but if it is a question of being jolted along by coolies, fourteen miles involves sufficient fatigue for one day, even for the person carried, as the motion much resembles rough trotting without a stirrup!

There is, however, nothing in the way of beauty to tempt one to linger. These low spurs of the Himalayas are singularly uninviting to the artistic eye, especially in this early spring time (I speak of the beginning of April), when the great swelling mountains seem altogether arid and barren—vast shapeless masses of dry red earth, without so much as a wreath of kindly vapour to lend mystery to their ugliness. There is something intensely wearisome in this endless succession of long unbroken lines, extending from far overhead to the deep valleys below. Every hill-side or khad, as these braes are called, is so exceedingly steep that it becomes a most difficult (I might say dangerous) scramble to keep your footing, the moment you step off the road.

Yet it has none of the beauty that you might expect from such precipitous ground; in fact, till you go two or three marches above Simla, you need never expect to see a natural precipice. The only suggestion of such a thing is caused by the cutting of the road, which, as it winds along the face of the hill, certainly has a considerable rock wall on the inner side.

The timber, too, is of very average size and interest; small pine trees, immense quantities of wild barberry, and great cacti (I had almost said cactus trees, they are so large) stretch out their bare jointed arms like huge candelabra, with invisible yellow blossoms; not the handsome palmated cactus of the plains, but a much more ghostly plant. I am quite aware that these our first impressions of these hills were unfavourable. When we returned over the same ground after the rains, those steep red khads [1] were clothed in a verdure so brilliant that they seemed to us like richly-shaded velvet draperies, over which the light mists floated in soft gauze-like clouds. But now there was no such illusion, and when we reached our first night's destination, at a little roadside bungalow, near the Military Hill Station of Dagshai, we agreed that we had rarely seen anything more truly hideous than these great bleak hills.

Of course they were not without some redeeming features. Here and there the great red khads were gemmed with patches of vivid green, marking where diligent hands had been at work, cultivating tiny fields in long narrow terraces, only a few feet wide, wherever a morsel of ground could be levelled. These very crops were among the beautiful things that delighted us later in the year,

[1] Steep hill-side.

when they had turned to scarlet and gold, matted with brilliant white and blue convolvuli, and attracting clouds of lustrous butterflies. Even now, there was a wealth of wild flowers, and my coolies, true highland lads, were for ever darting up and down the steep khad to bring me some new treasure; so that very soon my jampan (the funereal armchair with the black curtains) was all wreathed with wild roses and long trails of delicate white clematis and sweet jessamine.

Our halt each night was at a dâk bungalow; in other words a Government rest-house, where on payment of one rupee, every traveller has a right to remain four-and-twenty hours, at the end of which he may be required by any new comer to move on. The larger bungalows have accommodation for six or eight sets of travellers; that is to say six or eight rooms, each containing a table, two or three chairs, and a charpoy or bedstead. Each room opens on to the public verandah, where all the servants sleep, and as the door is generally open for air, it is provided with a chick, or thin blind made of grass. This room also opens into an inner bath-room, and that again to the outer air, so that each room has its own front and back door, thereby securing thorough ventilation.

Every bungalow is supplied with a regular staff of Government servants, and the khansamah, or head man, will supply you with food on his own terms. Not that he has much variety. The inevitable moorghie (chicken) alternates with mutton with unerring regularity. The moment you arrive and call out for food, you are certain to hear a scuffle among the poultry, and should you be rash enough to look out at the back door, you would certainly see an unlucky hen having her throat cut according to the injunctions of the Prophet. (Of course these men must be Mohammedans, as no Hindoo would touch an unclean hen, sacred beef, or many other good things dear to the gluttonous English.) The moment the hen is dead she is plunged in boiling water, which saves all trouble in plucking, as her feathers then come off with a rub, and half an hour later she appears at your table, either as a "grilled moorghie," or disguised in an excellent curry. Bread you are not likely to find, but chupatties, which are very thick flour scones, are the order of the day.

A most unexpected addition to our little nursery party occasioned a considerable detention at Kyrie Ghat, about sixteen miles from Simla, and gave us ample opportunities of studying the manners and customs of dâk bungalows, and of the very varied travellers who halt there—the loud and self-asserting, who try to impress the public with a vague idea that they must be "somebody in particular," the courteous and unassuming, and all the intermediate species. It was certainly not a spot conducive to the ideal quiet of a sick room! And besides, we were painfully aware that the new comers must necessarily be over-crowded in consequence of our compulsory detention, though all were most kind in making the best of the situation.

Every one was now pressing up to Simla, to escape from the heat, which was already beginning to be oppressive in the plains, whereas here the air was balmy and delicious, and a cool, sweet breeze came to us from the far-away snow peaks, which we could just discern on the horizon. But of "mountain stillness" we experienced little, for though, happily, the majority of travellers selected the old road, there was a continual influx of new comers, each accompanied by thirty or forty chattering coolies, who, together with the unhappy servants, vainly attempted to keep themselves warm in the chilly night by continual smoking—and a hubble-bubble is *such* a noisy, gurgling pipe. Then with the earliest glimmer of the dawn, they were all astir, and such a clatter ensued of breakfast and packing, and getting away again!

And all night long the jackals were careering about, and uttering unearthly yells close to the house; sometimes rushing on to the verandah in their mad scampers. Sometimes they even come into the empty rooms, and curl themselves up in a corner.

And worse than the jackals is the Chokidar, or policeman, who guards each house all night, and is bound to yell from time to time to prove that he is awake. An admirable method of improving the sleep of the neighbours, and of showing thieves whereabouts he is!

And day and night alike there was the incessant grinding of never-ending strings of heavy bullock-waggons, with their creaking wooden wheels, making almost as much noise as the "kites"—which to Indian ears speaks volumes. These bullock-trains were perpetually passing up and down the steep hill road, either taking baggage to Simla, or returning heavily laden with wood.

One poor bullock sank exhausted near our windows, and was of course left to die. We would fain have had it shot, but no one dared touch the poor sacred creature. All we could do was to carry water to it in a brass basin, but it was too ill to drink. Next morning it died, and the first passers-by threw its carcase down the khad. Meanwhile eagles, kites, and vultures had assembled in a great body on the hill above us. We watched them perched in a row, expectant, till apparently one gave a signal—their dinner-bell, I suppose, whereupon they all swooped down simultaneously, and started fair. In ten minutes, only the carcase remained, picked quite clean, and the bones were finally polished by swarms of ants.

Another day a large troop of monkeys came over the mountains to have a look at us; but our favourite playfellows were two lovely little black and white silky Indian kids, "Kidlings blithe and merry"—the veriest darlings—which were for ever running away from their natural companions, the cook's black babies, and coming to skip about our room, and dance attendance on the new white baby.

Besides the travellers who actually put up at the bungalow there were sundry others who brought their own tents, and who would gladly have camped elsewhere, could they have found a morsel of level ground. But such a thing literally does not exist in any part of the Himalayas that I have seen. Even the tiny spots on which all the bungalows are perched have invariably been artificially levelled. And so at Kyrie Ghat, the only level ground within many miles is a small bit in front of the house.

Here one day we had a most picturesque arrival, namely, that new Artillery Corps, the Mountain Battery, which had attracted so much admiration from the Afghans at Umballa. It was now going for the first time to the hills, to be quartered at Jatog, near

Simla. They were marching in detachments. The first day all the married men, women, children, and sick came up. They had covered carts, in which to live night and day, but as a terrific thunderstorm came on as usual, at night we shared our quarters with some of the women.

They had scarcely departed the following morning, when the whole battery came up. Such a "natty" corps, with their beautiful little guns all taken to pieces; wheels, carriage, gun, and ninety rounds of ammunition for each gun; all packed so neatly on many mules. I think there were a hundred and seventy mules to six guns. Also a considerable number of bullock-carts with baggage, and a long string of camels bringing up the tents. The camels came and knelt beside our verandah, with their noses almost in at the windows. Then they retired, as did also the mules, which were picketed on a narrow ridge below us. In less than no time the guns were put up in front of the verandah, and the white tents beyond, while the bullock-carts were drawn up for the night all along the road, and the blue smoke from all their fires made up a very picturesque scene. Of human beings, there were about ninety artillerymen in white uniform, with white helmets, and a great number of native mule-drivers in dark-blue uniform with scarlet turbans.

I can never forget the kindness of those men when they heard that a lady was ill in the house, and their hearty good wishes for the tiny little one, whose young life had commenced in so strange a home. Literally, there was scarcely a sound to be heard. Certainly not a tithe of the noise made by many private parties; though I must say that these, one and all, had done their utmost to hush their servants and their coolies. Next morning at daybreak we saw the last of the gunners. For as the sun rose

> "They folded their tents like the Arabs,
> And as silently stole away."

That is to say, their departure would have been silent (and so, perhaps, would that of Longfellow's Arabs), but, unfortunately, where camels are to be loaded there never can be silence; if they are not grunting, and roaring angrily, and showing their wicked teeth, they are groaning so plaintively that it is heartbreaking to hear them. And I think, perhaps, we should groan too, if we had a bit of wood passed through our nostrils, and jerked, to make us kneel down. All the time a camel's load is being adjusted, some one holds a rope passed round the neck and under the leg, to prevent his rising. When he is loaded, one vigorous shake and struggle brings him to his legs, and he stalks off, still grunting and groaning as he goes.

On the crest of the hill, high above the house, we could just discern a small hill temple, whence from time to time some solitary worshipper descended by a steep craggy path to our lower world. This temple we determined to explore. It was late in the afternoon before we started, and of course the distance doubled as we advanced. Still we were determined to push on, though it was not till sunset that we reached the little "chalet," which, after all, contained only a few of the very roughest specimens of idols.

From the temple, however, we had a very fine view of Simla, but had scarcely time even to glance at it, for that strange, brooding stillness that comes before a storm warned us that mischief was brewing; and sure enough, as the sun sank, a wild thunderstorm rapidly blew up from the west, and lurid red quickly turned to total blackness. We commenced hurriedly to retrace our steps—no easy matter; for in the excitement of clambering up, we had scarcely noticed how very rude a path we trod among scattered rocks, with small broken stones, and the most slippery of dry grass. It was very nasty walking, and we knew that a false step would land us a good deal farther down the khad than we had any wish to go.

Meanwhile the storm had burst around us in full violence. Sharp tongues of fire seemed to cleave the heavens; and then again the pale lightning quivered as though encircling all earth and heaven in broad sheets of flame; while, from the blackness around, the great cactus arms were outstretched like grey spirits, such as Gustave Doré would love to draw. So vivid and incessant were the flashes of fire that we literally scrambled down the hill by the light of those celestial lamps, and not daring to take one step at random, we waited for each flash to show us where next to set our feet.

Meanwhile the deep echoes of the storm reverberated among the rocky gorges of the surrounding hills, while the thunder crashed overhead in awful tumult. Presently great drops of rain began to fall, and in a very few minutes there came such a downpour as was positively bewildering, and made us indulge in many futile resolutions against being caught in future in Himalayan thunderstorms. It was not our last, however, by a good many. We did get down in course of time, and having indulged in a precautionary pinch of quinine, for fear of possible fever, had the satisfaction of finding ourselves none the worse for our ducking.

I was much amused at this place by receiving a message from the big man of the neighbouring village, that if only I would show him pictures of the plains he would supply us with vegetables as long as we remained at Kyrie Ghat. Evidently the subject had been discussed in the bazaar. Of course I signified my willingness to show him my portfolio; so presently he arrived. He was an unpleasant-looking man, whom I had frequently noticed, as one who would be dangerous in times of mutiny. However, he proved a gentle savage, and the servants gave him an elaborate description of each drawing as I turned it over, so I have no doubt his mind was greatly enlarged. The supplies of flowers and vegetables duly arrived, and their somewhat withered condition proved how far the poor fellow must have sent for them.

A few days later we accomplished the last stage of our journey to Simla. As the road gradually ascended we left the great, many-armed cactuses, and the wild barberries, the heavy scent of which was most oppressive. Then we came into a belt of lovely wild flowers. For about two miles we passed through tangles of the most exquisite large white clematis, each blossom being about three inches in diameter. Of course we gathered long, graceful trails of this, till our hideous jampans were transformed into fairy bowers, and we confessed that no flower had ever been more appropriately named, than this "Traveller's Joy."

Then, when we had passed this clematis line, we found ourselves entering the region of scarlet rhododendron *trees*. Real, bonâ-fide trees, all flaming with gorgeous blossom, more beautiful than any words can tell when seen in the immediate foreground, cutting against deep-blue ranges of distant hills, with glittering snows beyond, and the bluest of skies overhead. But as a general feature in the landscape, they have actually less value, as a bit of colour, than the good Scotch rowan-tree, by reason of the richness of their glossy green leaves, which actually neutralise the scarlet blossoms. How many of these we added to our starry garlands of the great white clematis I need hardly say. Even our flower-loving coolies laughed at our delight over our new treasures, and as to the exceedingly grave and well-dressed inhabitants of Simla, who were just setting out to perform their daily round of duty on the Mall, I have no doubt they mistook our procession for some Arkite festival of the Paharis, *i.e.* the hill-men—a conclusion which would certainly have prevented the majority from ever giving us a second thought.

And so at length we were all safely landed in Simla.

CHAPTER XI.

SIMLA.

View of the Snowy Range—Life at Simla—Annandale—How to Soothe Babies—Wood-carvers—Thunderstorms—Luminous Plants and Insects—Monkeys—Rhododendrons—Itinerant Tradesmen—Cuckoos—Wild Thyme—May-Day—Difficulties of Water-supply.

Now that we *had* reached this much-desired spot I fear we were rather disappointed. Certainly it has much the same kind of beauty as many of our Scotch "hill stations." In fact, as I have already said of Kalka, it for ever suggested Dunkeld, greatly magnified, only minus the Tay, for there is not a drop of water visible anywhere.

But I believe we had expected to find ourselves close to the snows, and to see wonderful pinnacles running up into heaven; whereas what we did see, was a group of somewhat uninteresting hills all clad alike with small deodars which, when young, are precisely like spruce fir, in general effect, and, farther, ranges of interminable hills, where red earth supplies the place of heather, and myriads of tiny fields suggest toilsome cultivation.

Then, on the far horizon, distant fully a hundred miles, and not higher, apparently, than the level on which you yourself stand, lies a long, narrow white line, stretching right across the landscape, and indented like the teeth of a saw. And *this* is the snowy range! After a while we learned to know and love each line of that picture, and to recognise the infinite variety of shapely peaks; but now I am giving you our first impressions. There is no denying the fact that the first *coup d'œil* was disappointing, partly, I suppose, because everything is on so vast a scale, yet all is so perfectly in proportion that it needs a perpetual intellectual effort to realise its size. You have to say to yourself again and again, like a child trying to understand its lesson, here is a mountain range fifteen hundred miles long, and so broad that you must travel for weeks before you get to the other side. And those peaks of glittering snow, which seem only like crested waves on the sea-line, are for the most part seven times as high as those great Skye hills which a few months ago seemed to us to tower up to heaven. In fact, one peak, Mount Everest, is very nearly ten times as high as the Cuchullins, and fully 5,000 feet higher than the crowning peak of the Andes.[1] I believe its height has now been fixed at 29,002 feet, while that of Kinchinjunga is 28,176, and Dwalagiri, the white mountain, is not far behind. But then you have to remember that instead of standing on the sea-level, you have unconsciously risen to a height of 7,400 feet, which is the height of the Mall at Simla, an ascent so very gradual that, as you wind upward from one valley to the next, you never see any very great depth or height either below or above you.

I believe that Simla owes its fame as a hill station to Lord William Bentinck, who selected it as his summer quarters. Then Lord Combermere made the Mall, that is, the broad riding road right round the hill of Jakko, and now, as we all know, it is the regular summer quarters of Government, and of as many white faces as can follow in the train of so luminous a comet.

[1] It is, however, thought probable that in that vast mountain range, of which we really know next to nothing, there is probably a still higher range beyond Mount Everest, and that this is the true water-shed. When Mr. Graham and his companions recently succeeded in reaching a point on Mount Kabru 24,015 feet above the sea (*i.e.* 1,700 feet higher than any other Alpine climber has yet attained), he beheld over the slope of Mount Everest a further range, beyond which towered two high peaks, which appeared to them considerably higher than Mount Everest. They record that on their various ascents to great heights they had no headache, no bleeding at the nose, no nausea. Only the violent beating of their hearts was *audible* in the stillness at that great altitude.

The majority of the houses are so placed that they do not get even a glimpse of the snows, though a few of their inhabitants find a compensating fact in having a far-away peep of the plains where their friends are still grilling; plains which stretch away in the immeasurable distance, right down to Calcutta, like a boundless blue ocean, and lose themselves in a hot mist on the horizon.

Many of the houses, however, are placed too low to get any distant view at all, being dotted about, all over the fir-clad hills, and right down into the cup at their base. There are upwards of 300 of these bungalows, all bearing the strongest family likeness to one another. They are a good deal like Swiss châlets, having verandahs up stairs and down. Moreover, they are generally two stories high; a style of building which, as we had hardly seen a staircase since leaving Calcutta, astonished the servants considerably. Moreover, they have fire-places and blazing fires, which are a great centre of attraction.

Each bungalow—I might say "villa"—stands by itself on a morsel of artificially-levelled ground, only just large enough for the actual house. The tiniest garden is a luxury almost unheard of. It is the most difficult thing you can imagine ever to find your way to any house in particular, as the hills, which are all alike, are intersected by hundreds of paths—also all alike—and all running through precisely the same fir wood.

The paths leading up to each bungalow are frightfully steep, zigzags cut into the hill-side, and generally built up on the outer edge. It would be no joke to have such a clamber for nothing, so the name of each proprietor is generally painted on a wooden board, and nailed up on some conspicuous tree at the point where his steep and narrow approach diverges from the public path.

You can fancy that a round of morning calls on such hills as these is a very severe exertion. At first we rather despised the white men and women, who, in this invigorating climate, which is just like Scotland at its best, adhered to their habits of the plains and would never walk a step. But we were soon driven to confess that, if conventionalities and the drudgery of morning calls were to be the order of the day, there was nothing for it but to resign ourselves, like our neighbours, to being carried about by a small regiment of strong highland lads, a detachment of whom form as necessary an item of your establishment in these hills as your ponies do in Scotland. They also act the part of grass-cutters, and forage all over the hills for your horse's fodder.

These lads are known as jampanees or dandie-wallahs, according to the variety of carriage you prefer. The dandie, as I before said, is the lightest, being merely a carpet slung on a bamboo : and we considered it the more comfortable vehicle. Most people, however, preferred jampans or armchairs, which, with their shining leather canopies and black curtains, are suggestive only of coffins ; and when accompanied by eight (I have even seen twelve) bearers, dressed in black and dark blue or green livery, are funereal to a degree.

These men are under command of a superior, known at Simla as the mate, and at Mussourie as the tyndal. He never lends a hand to carry you himself, and merely walks alongside of the others ; and, so far, is more ornamental than useful. Moreover, he levies blackmail from each of his men, who, nevertheless, will not enter your service unless you engage through him. So you see there are trades' unions even in the Himalayas. A good mate is, however, really a very important servant. He not only keeps his men in order, engaging or dismissing them at his own good pleasure, but he also trims the lamps, carries notes, those incessant chits, as they are called, and makes himself generally useful in a thousand ways; sometimes even carrying a child.

Children, by the way, have a special variety of doolie—namely, a bed with wicker walls, in which they sleep at night, and which in the day-time can be slung from a bamboo, and carried by two men. The multitude of attendants required for these small creatures verges on the ludicrous. I remember one baby in particular, provided, of course, with two ayahs, a high-caste and a low-caste, nurse and nurserymaid in fact, as also with a bearer. These three individuals being insufficient to take the little innocent for its airing on the Mall, had called out the whole retinue of jampanees—eight in number—who gravely shouldered their burden; and so these eleven human beings marched along with their microscopic charge. Its mother, who happened to be on foot, met the ludicrous procession, and was so struck by its absurdity that she confessed afterwards to having disowned her own baby.

The dress of the jampanees is a fertile subject for invention, as every lady devises her own livery, and a very difficult matter it is to produce sufficient variety. The men come to you as coolies with a minimum of raiment, and must straightway be clothed in a thick woollen blouse, trousers, and head gear. That of the mate is of a pattern peculiar to itself. The great question is how to vary the combinations of black, blue, green, yellow, scarlet, and so forth. Commonplace mortals, who only look for use and wear, generally adopt black, with scarlet or yellow facings; but some tasteful ladies invent all sorts of varieties. The Lady Sahib (that is, the wife of the Governor-General) has an exclusive right to pure scarlet. In fact, all the Government servants don this royal colour; those who wait at table having the royal arms wrought on their breasts in gold and colours—and a very fine race of "buffetiers" they are—as gorgeous as the so-called beef-eaters of old England.

You cannot imagine what a curious sight it is, at any place of public resort, to see the enormous multitude of these human ponies squatting in long rows, in charge of their respective coffins, and waiting for their masters. It always amused us to come quickly out of church to see this motley army rushing to the door, and trying to get the foremost place in this desperate charge: pounce on their master or mistress, and rush away again. Suppose that of the 1,200 Europeans said to be in Simla, 300 were present (not that I ever saw so many), and that of these, 100 were riders, there would remain about 200 vehicles of all sorts, averaging six bearers each. Thus you would have about 1,200 natives scrambling for the congregation as it "scaled," even without including the 100 grooms (*syces*), who run off after their masters, holding on by the horse's tail. The confusion, hubbub, and hustling which ensue are beyond description. Even the inhabitants of the nearest houses seem to think it would be quite *infra dig.* to walk half or a quarter of a mile to church, and evidently thought it extraordinary of us to prefer doing so.

The worst of this multitude of bearers is not only the amount of dust which they raise, and the annoyance of their very presence, but also that, suppose three girls meet on the Mall, or in the narrow streets of the actual town, and want a few minutes' chat, their attendants make a mob of about twenty men, literally blocking up the road. It is curious how very rarely any one seems to dream of varying the route from the daily routine row. It seems as if every man, woman, and child has but one attraction—always the same thing—up and down the Mall. Should you diverge into any of the by-paths, you may be pretty certain not to meet a soul, unless, indeed, some picnic to the waterfalls or to Annandale has drawn them from their usual round.

The former are the most miserable apologies for waterfalls that were ever seen; but the rarity of the article lends them value. The coolies look on this expedition with extreme aversion, as well they may, for the little streamlet flows in the depths of a ravine down which you scramble by a path of interminable length and steepness. But the favourite gathering point is at Annandale, likewise a deep valley; but one which, instead of being merely a narrow gorge like most of its neighbours, allows considerable space for locomotion. Here, too, is a marvellous rarity, a very good garden, where, if you happen to be on the alert, you may buy a tolerable supply of fruit.

Here you may notice one curious custom of the Pahari women. Soothing syrup and such infantile narcotics have not yet been introduced in their nurseries, but the mother, who has a good day's work before her, carries her little one to the edge of the rippling streamlet, and there lays it down on the green bank; then, making a hollow reed or bit of bark act as a conduit, she diverts a tiny rill, which drips from a height of six or eight inches on the head of the chota Baba, and soothes it into the calmest sleep. Thus you may see a row of these little sleeping innocents near the "Falls" at Annandale. One might fancy that the babies rocked by so strange a water-nurse would surely grow up idiotic, but all the people declare that it is very good for the little ones, and makes them hardy.

Here, in a corner of the old forest, stands one of those little rough stone temples, roofed with cedar-wood, and having a certain amount of rough carving; such temples as the hill-men love to build to some forest-god, wherever they find a group of trees of somewhat larger growth than those around: a graceful creed, which reverences these silent forest sanctuaries, as places consecrated by nature herself to the mighty unknown Spirit, and so seems constrained to build some tabernacle in His honour.

> "A temple, 'neath the pine and chestnut shade,
> A green, and dim, and ancient solitude, where hidden streams
> Went moaning through the grass in sounds like dreams,
> Music for weary hearts!"

The most attractive native manufacture at Simla is wood-carving; good work and very effective. There is no end to the variety of tables, chairs, and frames in which you are for ever tempted to invest. But the homeward carriage of such goods is an objection which prevents your storing many things that would be treasures in England. In fact, every change of residence in India involves a complete selling off of your household goods at a most frightful loss; while the new kit is never to be purchased under its full value. Some one must profit on the arrangement, but I fancy Europeans rarely do so. Really the exorbitant prices charged for all manner of goods in Simla, and the merely nominal sums which they fetch when sold off a few months later, would suggest the possibility of furnishing a house for nothing, should you choose to arrive there when Government leaves in October, and spend a regular British winter among the beautiful snows and fir-trees, a time which various residents described as most delightful.

Speaking of fir-trees, by which I mean the deodar cedar, it is very curious to notice to how small a growth it attains on these low spurs of the Himalayas. Go a hundred miles into the interior, and explore those glorious forests which no woodman's axe has yet profaned, and you will wander on and on beneath mighty monarchs, the very sight of which fills you with awe and reverence. Trees of from twenty-five to thirty feet in girth, and perhaps two hundred feet in height, and growing in flat layers precisely like the Cedar of Lebanon. It is difficult to realise that these are merely the elder brethren of the little graceful deodar, as we know it in Britain. At Simla it never exceeds the size of an average spruce fir. On our return from the interior we noticed this fact to some of our friends, who replied, "Oh, but you have not seen the big trees at Annandale." Thither we accordingly went, and looked in vain for the big trees. We found that the timber alluded to was a group about the size of well-grown silver firs. But as most English men, and almost all ladies, who once reach Simla, seem quite content never to go any farther, the glories of the primeval forests must to them remain sealed books.

It seems as if the mere fact of a refuge from the heat of the plains was all that could be desired from these beautiful hills; in fact, social life here bears much the same relation to that of Calcutta, that Brighton does to London; it is an atmosphere too silky and perfumed to be in keeping with wild mountain scenery. Fancy coming to these uttermost ends of the earth to be pursued by latest Parisian fashions; satins, velvets, "the newest thing" in bonnets, which have just been sent direct to the wearer by pattern post—to say nothing of the last thing in white satin boots!

Not that I wish to deny the charms of Simla society; nothing could possibly be pleasanter than many of its social gatherings, its amateur concerts, its admirable private theatricals, its burra nautches, as the natives call our balls, where to their amazement they see ladies and gentlemen dancing *for themselves*, instead of hiring dancing girls to do it for them. All these things in fine weather are very charming, and have the additional advantage of very early hours.

But when violent thunderstorms come on, as they are very apt to do at night, it is not altogether pleasant to be carried along in evening toilette in a downpour of rain, with the leathern curtains of your jampan flapping about, and utterly refusing to button; while the flashing lightning reminds you of a dozen fearful accidents that have occurred hereabouts. There was one house very near ours which actually would not let, by reason of the attraction which it seemed to have for heaven's fire; the last instance of which was, that as a mother stood on its verandah, with her baby in her arms, watching the storm, a sudden flash struck her dead, leaving the little one untouched.

One evening I especially remember, when there was to be a great ball at Government House; but so appalling a storm came on that even the enterprise of Simla ladies was defeated, so that a mere handful of the nearest neighbours were all who managed to be present. Some who actually started, were fairly blown home again, having had their curtains torn away; while one lady beheld the whole canopy of her jampan whirled into mid-air and tossed over the khad, while she herself was left in her ball-dress, exposed to the pitiless rain.

This I call society under difficulties; nor is it pleasant, when you have reached your destination, to know that your unlucky bearers are sitting shivering outside, coughing their very hearts away. Even if the mate has the wisdom to curl himself up in your rugs, and keep himself dry in your jampan after the manner of the London "cabby" (woe betide him if he is caught there!), there is no such refuge for his underlings; nothing for them but to grin and bear it.

But in fine weather these evening expeditions in our uncovered dandies were quite delightful. The air is so cool and pleasant, the vivid glow of sunset, and the fleeting twilight as you go forth, and the brilliant starlight in which you return, are all so beautiful that we could not wish the distances shorter, though in some cases they were a matter of four or five miles, as we followed the windings of the paths. The mate generally led the way, bearing a lantern to guide his men, and the light flashed sometimes on masses of dark Indian oak, wreathed with virginia creeper, or on the glossy rhododendrons, whose scarlet blossoms faded all too quickly. Then through the depths of the dark fir wood floated little dancing, gleaming lights, which at first we believed to be fire-flies, but a closer examination proved them to be beetles, with transparent tails, within which, just as in a real lamp, glows the palest green light.

More wonderful than these fairy fire-bearers, because so much less widely known, are some of the luminous grasses and other plants found in parts of the Himalayas. Some years ago a report reached Simla that the grassy hills round Syree, on the old road, were every night illuminated with a strange, pallid fire, which gleamed with a tremulous spirit-light. On inquiry, this was found to emanate from a grass, called by the Brahmans *jyotismati*,[1] and common at Almorah and various other places in the hills. It was only observed during the rains; nor was it the property of every root, only perhaps of one in a hundred. Nevertheless it was sufficiently powerful to make the whole grass seem to glow here and there with a blaze of phosphoric light. Another plant[2] is also found in these mountains, which is reverenced by the fire-worshipping people, as "a bush burning yet not consumed." Its light has been proved to proceed from a volatile oil, which at times evaporates to such an extent that on bringing a lighted match close to it the plant will be enveloped in a transient flame, and yet will be in nowise injured.

There are various other instances known of these luminous plants. I have been told of a beautiful phosphorescent fungus which grows abundantly on the dwarf palms of Brazil, as also in Australia, and which emits a pale-green light, so vivid that a few specimens brought into a dark room will give sufficient light to read by. Australia also produces a luminous moss,

[1] *Anthistiria ananthera.* [2] *Dictamnus Fraxinella.*

which gleams like a nest of glow-worms from the dark recesses of the rocks. I was also told that some of the timber, floated down from Thibet by the Cashmere rivers, has the same property, which, however, it loses when dry. The root of certain orchids likewise shines while moist, and though quite lustreless when dry, renews its light as often as it is thoroughly saturated. These are a few of the lamps dear to the fairies, which mortal eyes are sometimes privileged to behold.

The church of Simla is the central point at which all diverging lines seem to meet. Here for once mosques and temples have retired into the background. Christianity holds a prominent place, being represented by a rather large, ugly church, overlooking the native town and the bazaars. These are perched on terraces down the face of the hill. The backs of these native houses are decidedly picturesque, being several storys high, and having verandahs and balconies of coloured wood, and a certain amount of window gardening, with tall Indian corn and similar grain. This is a place where no Europeans ever dream of going, but my sketching propensities drew me thither, and the flat roof of a cottage made a capital studio. The novelty of the proceeding proved too much for the curiosity of the inmates of the upper windows, who, after peeping cautiously forth for some time, and making quite sure that there were no dangerous white men in the neighbourhood, crept down to my side. Such courage proved infectious, and I had on that occasion more glimpses of bright eyes and rich jewels than have often fallen to my lot.[1]

The hill on which the church stands rejoices in the name of Jakko. One might imagine it has been so named in honour of the monkeys; for certainly they are legion, both the common

[1] I have been told that the only way in which a foreigner can ever obtain a glimpse of Hindoo domestic life is by frequenting the native theatres. These, strange to say, do not seem to possess the same interest for foreigners that they do in China and Japan, and none of our friends ever suggested that "we should go to a play" in India. And yet, that theatrical entertainments hold high favour with the people is evident, as the official lists of native publications show a large annual return of dramas printed in the vernacular. Some years give birth to upwards of a hundred such compositions.

brown ones, which come careering all over the houses, and the great big grey ones, with black face and paws, and fringe of white hair round the forehead. I am told they are sometimes five feet high, but I should imagine four feet was nearer the average.

They also come close to the houses in troops, and scamper about all over the tall trees, swinging themselves from branch to branch, leaping from tree to tree, and playing all manner of antics; sometimes springing suddenly across the road, to the great alarm of the horses, and no small danger of the riders, considering the nature of the roads. It was too ridiculous sometimes to see the exceeding gravity with which they would sit among the great scarlet blossoms of the rhododendrons, and stare at us. Sometimes an old grandmother would come with a wee baby in her arms, and play all sorts of games with it, giving it a swing on her tail, and playing hide-and-seek among the glossy green leaves, in contrast with which these monkeys look almost pure white.

One day a great, big, brown fellow came so close to the house, and behaved so boldly, that the servants surrounded and captured him; a proceeding to which he showed so little objection that we suspected him of having escaped from some previous master. We detained him for some days, in case his owner should claim him, but as no one came forward, he was eventually presented to the artillery at Jittog, where he quickly signalised himself by treacherously pulling out handfuls of hair from the head of an unwary gunner.

From the extreme steepness of the densely-wooded banks, it follows that in many of the bungalows the tree tops are literally on a level with the balconies, and their branches actually sweep the windows, thus affording famous cover for the monkeys, should it please them to enter and help themselves to any tempting food, or other object. They did not favour us with any such visits, but some of our neighbours were less fortunate.

None, however, suffered so seriously as Lady Barker, who has so charmingly described the fate of her first dinner-party at Simla. Being anxious to have an unusually pretty table, she had herself expended much care and trouble in its adornment *à la Russe;* and having just received from Europe certain dainty china figures and ornamental dishes, she had arranged such a show of sweetmeats, flowers, and fruit as should have filled all beholders with admiration. When dressing-time came, she charged her servants on no account to leave the room till her return; but hardly was her back turned, when the temptation of hubble-bubble prevailed, and they slipped out for a quiet smoke, quite forgetting the open window and the great tree just outside, where sat certain watchful monkeys vastly interested in the proceedings. Judge of the feelings of the hostess when, coming down to receive her guests, she just looked into the dining-room to make sure that her work was perfect, and there found a busy company of monkeys hard at work, grinning and jabbering, their cheeks and arms crammed with expensive sweetmeats, while the table presented a scene of frightful devastation—broken glass and china, fair linen soiled—everything tossed about in hopeless confusion! From this wreck she had to turn aside, and try to look pleasant and quite at ease while entertaining the hungry guests, who had to wait patiently till something like order could be restored, and a dinner served, shorn of all frivolous adornments.

Nor was this her only quarrel with her troublesome neighbours. She tells us how her favourite little terrier had conceived a violent antipathy to the whole race, and never lost a chance of barking at them, and frightening them off the premises. The monkeys waited their time, and at last had their revenge. One day, as little Fury was accompanying his mistress through a dark thicket of rhododendrons, she saw a skinny arm suddenly dart out from amid the scarlet blossoms, and quick as thought the poor little terrier was seized by his long, silky hair, and in a second had disappeared in the thicket. Vain were all attempts at rescue; vainly and piteously the poor doggie yelped and howled, while a shaking of the branches, and a sound of scuffling, were all that betrayed his unwilling ascent to the top of a high tree, where a monkey jury had assembled to try the criminal. Once there, his unhappy mistress beheld her little favourite passed from one to another, that each in turn might have the satisfaction of pinching and tweaking, and pulling out his hair, till his particular grudge was revenged. Then, when all were tired of this amusement, they took him to the extreme end of a branch, and dropped him far down the precipitous khad. And so ended poor Fury's feud with the monkeys!

We were sufficiently unsociable to consider ourselves very fortunate in the situation of our house, "Raby Lodge," which stands on Jakko, just above the Mall, and about one mile on the unfashionable side of the church—a sort of "back of beyond," where we could reach "the world" on the shortest notice, but were virtually beyond its pale, and, to all intents and purposes, sole monarchs of the beautifully-wooded hill that rose some five hundred feet above the house, with lovely paths in every direction, where we might wander all day in the cool delicious shade, and never meet a living soul. Partly because, as I before said, every one is wedded to the Mall, and partly because the custom of the plains is kept up—except to make full-dress morning calls between twelve and two—no one goes out for pleasure till dusk.

This to a new comer is incomprehensible, the climate being in every way suggestive only of the most heavenly summer weather at home. There is, however, no doubt that experience has taught her own lessons, and that there is too good reason to beware of lurking treachery even with these sweet breezes.

For the delicious freshness of the atmosphere at these high levels is no warrant for forgetting that you are still beneath a tropical sun, and by no means beyond the danger of its vertical rays. Apt as we are to think precaution no longer necessary in these cool hills, the fact remains the same, and the risk of sunstroke is not less here than in the plains. Even when the sky is veiled by soft grey clouds, the natives warn you that the danger is just as great, in fact they say greater; and they have some curious proverbs which compare the sun unveiled to a mosquito, and the clouded sun to a scorpion.

One remarkable health statistic is the number of cases of liver complaint developed in people of average sickly Indian health on first arriving in the hills, where every breath of keen exhilarating air would seem to be laden with new life. That blessed air is itself the cause of the mischief, for the languid frame feels suddenly invigorated, and a delightful, almost forgotten sensation of hunger entices the new comer to eat so voraciously that the enfeebled internal machinery is unable to cope with such unwonted labour, and too often gives way just when its luckless owner imagines he has found an atmospheric elixir.

The house next to our pleasant home is known as the Priory, and is that wherein Dr. Russell, of *The Times*, wiled away the weary hours of convalescence with all his pets—his menagerie, I might say—his young hill bears, monkeys, mountain rams, costurah (or hill thrush), green parrots, chickore (hill partridge), ninety-six aberdavats, &c., &c., besides sundry hill minas or blackbirds, which are the favourite cage-birds in these parts, though not always agreeable companions, inasmuch as they can at their own sweet will vary their notes from a sound like the most musical bells to the very harshest croak.

This hill of Jakko, on which we were now perched, is, I think, a perfect Paradise for a home. It is clothed from base to summit with the richest mixed timber, chiefly the Indian oak, with a holly-like leaf, and the dark glossy green of the rhododendron trees, with their gorgeous masses of blossom, the most vivid scarlet, shaded with deep crimson. The only thing to be regretted is that their glory is so short-lived. Early in May they are on the wane, and by the end of the month a few withered blossoms are all that remain to tell of their bright, short lives.

But when first they begin to flutter down in the breeze, they fall like a shower of fire, and alight on the richest carpet of maiden-hair fern, and blue dog-violets, which everywhere clothe these hanging woods, so that you can scarcely set your foot on the earth without crushing a tuft of such treasures as would enchant the heart of an English gardener.

And now just imagine the loveliness of such glimpses of the snows as you from time to time catch when you look down some

THE SNOWY RANGE, FROM RABY LODGE, SIMLA.

deep ravine, clothed on either side with these dark trees and flaming blossoms; down, down, down, over wave after wave of billowy foliage, till all form is lost in the depths of blue haze far below. Then as your eye once more rises from the gloom, it rests on a group of dazzling snow-peaks, no longer dwarfed by their own multitude, inasmuch as what you now see is a mere fragment of that unbroken line which stretches right across the horizon, and which seems to lose itself in the wonderful blue of the heavens.

Anything more dazzling than that marvellous scarlet, blue, and white, with the intensely dark foliage to give tone to the whole, you cannot imagine. And sometimes Dame Nature seems to crave more and more colour, and needs but the faintest pretext of mist or shower to bridge the deep valley with vivid rainbow lights (constantly a double arch), which seem like a softened dreamy reflection of that more lasting prism which she has set here for our enchantment, and which will remain unchanged for weeks together.

This was the vision of loveliness that met us at every turn from that beautiful hill-side; and from our own verandah we looked down over the rich masses of foliage into what seemed unmeasurable depth, and past the endless ranges of hills to the long, unbroken line of eternal snow. If we had had our pick of all Simla we could not have selected a more perfect spot than that on which the house was placed; nor a more delicious sitting room than the broad upper balcony, which extending round three sides of the house, commanded the view from every corner, including such glimpses of the Mall just below, as gave human interest to the whole. A lounge so delightful, tempted us to linger there for many a pleasant hour rather than explore more distant scenes, good opera-glasses making us familiar with many a ravine and peak which our feet might never tread.

Long before daybreak I was generally at my post, for then each pinnacle of the distant hills stood out in clear, pale blue against the welling light that foreruns the day. But when the first kiss of the rising sun had transformed that steely blue into a sea of glittering ice-peaks, then soft grey clouds rose up to meet the dawn, and all the distance was veiled for a while.

With daybreak came the invariable tap at the nursery window, and there stood the old gwala (cow-man) with a great bowl of sweet new milk for the little ones; and then came chota haziri, the little breakfast on the balcony, and afterwards a delightful scramble, knee-deep in maiden-hair fern, beneath the scarlet rhododendrons, where the white monkeys were playing their antics, and sometimes pelted us with blossoms.

Of course in the evening light the colouring was all reversed. As the sun sank, it made the great hills fling their broad cool shadows athwart the deep valley, and the pure white snows were flushed with delicate rose light and tender lilac shadows, while the sky beyond was tinted with faint sea-green. Ten minutes later, it was the sky that was flushed rosy red, and the snow-peaks had changed to a ghastly grey.

This was the colouring that we saw again and again without any very remarkable effect of sky; nothing, at least, that differed much from the loveliness of our own mornings and evenings in Scotland, and I am more and more convinced that the people who speak so enthusiastically of Eastern atmospheric effects, are those who habitually oversleep themselves when in Britain, and prefer their book or their dinner to watching a sunset! Even in "the rains," in the month of September, we only saw about four sunsets which, I could honestly say, exceeded many of those on our northern shores.

One indeed there was, the glory of which did surpass my wildest dreams of possibility. The rain had been pouring all day; pouring as it only can pour in the tropics and in Skye. In the evening, however, it cleared, and we were sitting in our beloved balcony watching the black tree-tops appearing like spirits from among the clouds of white mist which floated in the valley far below. As the sun set, it seemed as though the mist had suddenly taken fire; it rolled towards us rapidly like a sea of flame. Every white vapour seemed changed to a thousand tongues of liquid fire. You could hardly think it possible that it was not in truth the dread consumer. We watched its progress breathlessly. Literally we could not stir; for it seemed as though indeed the "Brath" of the old Highlanders had come, and that the earth was now in truth to be purified by fire from Heaven. Still it rolled on and on. The whole valley was full of fire, for ever floating and curling upward, and writhing with unquiet motion. The wooded banks on every side of us, and the great, dark trees, glowed like a sheet of molten iron. You felt convinced that had you touched them they must have burnt your hand. Even the brown faces of the awestruck natives shone ruddy-red. Where the fire could not reach the mists because of the broad shadow of the hills, they seemed all illuminated with weird blue lights, and these were reflected on the deep grassy khads that lay in the same shadow, so that they shone like intensely emerald velvet. And in the far, far distance, the same spectral light gleamed on the eternal snows. A few moments later the fiery glory faded away, and was succeeded by a wan and pallid light which shed an ashen hue on the cold grey hills, and a death-like repose overspread the land.

Can you wonder that we loved to linger in a balcony from which such sights were possible?

Sometimes colour came to us in a more tangible form, for our friends the Delhi shawl-merchants, followed the stream of trade, and brought vast stores of their beautiful goods to tempt the English at Simla. So, often we would look up suddenly, conscious of some human presence, which had approached unheard, for the natives all leave their slippers outside the verandah, and their bare feet glide silently up the stairs. There perhaps stood a figure in spotless white, making his lowly salaam, and followed by two or three coolies with huge bundles on their heads. In a few moments the balcony from end to end was strewn with the most exquisite raiment of needlework that human hands ever wrought, all the work of hands masculine—just imagine their patience! There were piled the most gorgeous hangings, shawls, cloaks, cushions, materials of dazzling hue, half hidden by the richness of gold and silver, and silken embroidery of every colour, and in every pattern that art could devise; such hangings and such drapery as might carry a dream of Oriental grace and harmony of rich colours into the pale greys of our murky, western mists.

Sometimes our tempters were traders from Cashmere, whose goods were all of softest wool materials, and quiet Quaker greys and browns, embroidered with darker shades of the same. The wool of which they are made is a silky hair peculiar to the goats of Cashmere, each of which yields about three ounces at a time. It requires ten fleeces to make one average shawl. We were told that sixteen thousand looms were employed in Cashmere, each giving employment to about four men, whose joint work produces two shawls a year. I fancy that must refer to the shawls of many colours, as these delicious browns and greys are not suggestive of so much labour, even though they *are* all richly embroidered. It is a strange example of the manner in which nation acts upon nation, to hear that the first effect of the blockade of Paris should have been to throw forty thousand of the shawl-weavers in far Cashmere out of work.

With regard to Indian silks we were told that all the best raw silk is brought from Bokhara; the finest quality of all being described by the natives as "Hathee Singal," "strong enough to bind an elephant," and consequently ultra-durable. It is chiefly manufactured at Lahore, not in one great factory, but in private houses, where all the men of a family work together in small, confined rooms, labouring in dark, dingy, stuffy holes, to produce these delicate tissues. No women are employed, as with the hand-loom workers of Britain, but a vast multitude of men find work as weavers, twisters, dyers, and winders.

The shawl and silk merchants were by no means the only tradesmen who created a locomotive market for their wares. Here, as in the plains, sellers of fruit, toys, biscuits, cloth, haberdashery, jewellery, skins of birds, screens of peacocks' feathers, and nondescript articles of every conceivable sort, were for ever wandering over the hills in search of customers at the most remote bungalows, perhaps walking miles before effecting the smallest sale, and waiting with inconceivable patience till it might suit the inmates to look over their wares, all of which must be carefully packed and unpacked a dozen times a day. One who was generally sure of a welcome carried a great basket of jams of every sort, from strawberry and apricot, down to rhododendron and grass, these being supposed to have a strong local flavour!

I need scarcely say that only a select few of these itinerant tradesmen presumed to invade the sanctity of the upper balcony —which was in fact our family sitting-room—and one which certainly found more favour than the comfortable English drawing-room down stairs. The mere fact of being up stairs again was such a novelty!

In every niche of that verandah was a nest of the loveliest young swallows. All the morning they were skimming about in every direction, just as happily as our own dear little summer guests in the old country, and many a pleasant vision they recalled. Only when the young birds began to try their wings, and sometimes fluttered to the balcony, they became to us a source of most painful anxiety, as our educational efforts all failed utterly to teach our little jungle kitten that young swallows were not fair game. Indeed, she watched the nests day and night with a true hunter's eye, which never quite closed, even when she pretended to be asleep, and many a dainty morsel she contrived to secure.

But of all reminders of home none gave me such a thrill of pleasure as a fragrant breath which one day reached me in a far corner of the hills; and soon I scented out a purple bank of wild thyme, with patches of white clover. There was a ruined bungalow near, and at first I thought some exile had sown these seeds for love of the old home beyond the great waters. But afterwards I found other patches of the same sweet flowers, and many more besides. Indeed, the multitude of such reminders of old days struck me even more than the novelties of India.

This was especially true of human beings, for, from the first day we reached the Indian land, it seemed as if some old friend cropped up at every turn, generally the very last person we should have dreamt of meeting. Every one we had ever known and lost sight of, seemed to have drifted to some part of India, in *some* capacity, high or low, rich or poor. At Meerut, for instance, the first amazed voice that greeted me on arriving was that of our own station-master from the far north. Another was a soldier's wife, from our own home, and from my sister's Sunday school. Then came a dozen callers, of whom one half were north-country friends, the other half proved to have been schoolfellows or "chums" of our brothers and nephews. On entering the church we recognised, both in pulpit and reading-desk, faces long ago familiar to Inverness, and others seemed to multiply as we looked round. And this is merely an average sample of Scotch links in most colonies, and of the consequent cheery welcome which we found wherever we halted.

Next to the wild thyme, the most startling suggestion of spring-time and olden days was the first song of the cuckoo, whose clear ringing note was answered by a perfect chorus of his brethren; no shy, timid warblers shunning "the passing hoof," but bold birds, who sing out bravely in defiance of all comers, though the high road just below the house might be crowded with human beings, equestrians, and ladies "eating the air," as the natives say, when they see them carried out "for an airing." More often there are long strings of wild-looking Paharis—hill men and women, alike staggering under tremendous burdens of timber, great wooden planks, such as no Englishmen would dream of carrying half a mile, but which these comparatively small highlanders have probably carried ten miles at least, from the dark pine forest of Mahasso, or even farther.

May-day came, all too quickly, and with it came the hill black-birds and hill thrushes—bluish birds about the size of our own. Long before daybreak we were astir, to greet "the morning gale of spring," and, in obedience to old habits, to wash our faces in May dew. But for once Beltane had no morning dew to give us. We sought in vain, but solaced ourselves by bringing home ferns and wild flowers innumerable, and by filling every corner of the house with gay scarlet blossoms.

I think, perhaps, the most wonderful thing about this fair earth's loveliness is the way in which its balance is preserved, so that no beauty of any one spot can in anywise detract from the enjoyment of the next, each new scene in the panorama of travel bringing its own fresh delight with it, filling with calm and gladness the heart that allows itself stillness to drink in these sweet influences. Enchanting as was this May-day among the mountains, I think the following one lost little by comparison. It found us revelling in Kentish cherry, and pear, and apple orchards, the whole air fragrant with their gummy perfume, and the country looking as though a shower of white and pink snow had fallen, indeed was still falling, for every gentle breeze shook down soft showers of blossom into the rich meadow-grass, to the intense delight of multitudes of white frisking lambs, and of a few toddling cottage bairns in large white sun-bonnets, who were wearing daisy-chains, or pelting one another with fragrant cowslip balls.

If we turned aside from the orchards it was only to linger by the clear purling brook, with its fringe of forget-me-nots, and its golden kingcups and marsh-marigolds, overshadowed by silvery beech-trees still in the first flush of their delicate spring green. In the wood beyond, sweet melick grass and young ferns crept up through banks of creamy primroses, and deep blue hyacinths and orchids. And from every bush and tree came the voice of many birds; a chorus of song, always in time and tune, and with a constant undertone of wood-doves cooing to their mates from their hiding-places in the dreamy depths of the dark yews—the most soothing sound in all sweet nature's harmonies.

No such soothing note fell on my ear on this May morning in the Himalayas, although in truth it seemed as if the summer music of the woods had all awakened. Not only were the cuckoos calling with the energy born of a winter's silence, till every wooded hill echoed back that dear old song of home, but the cicada, whose voice had been unheard since we had fled from it at Point de Galle, began this morning that sharp metallic note which, rising simultaneously from under every leaf, and every crevice of bark, produces a deafening chorus of whirring sound, like the hum of countless spinning-wheels.

To some ears this sound is said to be musical; the Greeks described it as "the nightingale of the nymphs." To me it was a perpetual annoyance, jarring on the ear throughout the day. Each morning for one precious hour I might revel in stillness while peering into that wonderful range of clear cold peaks cutting so sharp against the sky. Then, as the arc of lemon-coloured light rose higher and higher in the blue heaven, I knew my hours of torment were drawing nigh, for the moment the sun could overlook those snows, and gild the wooded mass on every side of me, the whole army of noisy insects awoke with one accord, and continued their ceaseless monotonous din without one moment's intermission, till he sank again below the horizon. Then these true courtiers of the great day-star were suddenly silenced, and the effect on the ear was very much like that of suddenly stopping a roomful of sewing machines.

I was told that these creatures are a sort of grasshopper, but I could never succeed in catching one. One species has been described as something like a moth with the most delicate gauzy wings, just tinged with green, and body striped green and yellow. Their musical apparatus is said to consist of "two membranes tightly stretched, and acted on by powerful muscles; the sound issues from two holes near the articulations of the hind-legs." The minstrels when caught were by no means silenced, but "rattled away as merrily as ever," even when prisoners in the human hand.

The one great drawback to most of these hill stations is the terrible deficiency of water. To us, who consider it a remnant of barbarism to build any house without having water laid on, even to the topmost story, it is bad enough to know that even on the plains every drop required for all household purposes must be brought from the well by water-carriers; this inconvenience, however, is common to all India, I suppose to all the East. But in these hills the distances which these poor fellows have to go in search of their supplies is something startling, and the bheestie has hard work indeed, especially in a country where bathing is a luxury indulged in, perhaps several times a day. Ours was considered fortunate in having, at first, to go *only* about half a mile down the khad to fill his water-skin. But as the season drew on, the water retired lower and lower, so that he and all the other bheesties of the neighbourhood had to go far down a deep, rocky ravine, and sometimes wait long enough for their turn at the well. It was no joke to have to climb that rugged footpath a dozen times a day, especially with a burden so heavy as a water-skin. Some bheesties living far above us on the hill kept a strong pony to help them. But these little beasts have an awkward habit of tumbling over the edge of the khad, and divers horrible accidents occurred while we were there. In the plains you sometimes see bullocks used for this same work.

Certainly the bheesties and dhobies (laundry-men) have no easy work in these hills; and you can scarcely marvel at the change in the habits of the people, from the wonderful religious cleanliness of the dwellers in the plain, with their incessant ceremonial washings both of themselves and of their clothes, to the exceeding filth of the Paharis or hill-men, who only wash once a year on one of their holiest festivals; and who wear the same thick woollen blouse, plaid, and trousers till they have spun themselves a new suit, that is, till the first is worn out.

A month at Simla brought us to the end of May, by which time the glory of the scarlet rhododendrons was departed, and the delight of being grinned at by white langours and brown monkeys had lost its novelty. Moreover the longing for a nearer view of those distant hills grew more and more intense.

It was therefore with infinite delight that I arranged to join our friends, Captain and Mrs Graves of the Buffs, in order to see as much of the great mountains as we could accomplish during their three months' leave.

CHAPTER XII.

CAMP LIFE.

Start for the Valley of the Sutlej—The Fair in Mahasso Forest—Dress and Jewels of the Paharis—Wilderness of Wild Roses—Sweet Jessamine—Hatto Forest—Divers Altitudes marked by Diversity of Vegetation—Bears—Varieties of Pheasants—Narkunda—An Allegory.

THE preparations for our delightful expedition were soon made. Stores were laid in, sketching materials sorted, tents and baggage overhauled, and having loyally celebrated the Queen's birthday by a grand evening reception at the Viceroy's, we celebrated mine on the following morning (26th May) by a start towards the Snowy Range.

We had determined to follow the Thibet road as far as the frontier. Our daily march would, we knew, vary from six to twelve miles, according to the supply of water. A halt at any intermediate point involves sundry difficulties; chiefly in the supply of next day's coolies, and of the servants' food which they calculate on buying daily in the little native bazaars.

We were each provided with the smallest of tents, about six feet square, and often could scarcely have found sufficient level ground to pitch even these, except at the regular camping spots, where previous travellers had levelled a space for themselves. A light native charpoy (*i.e.* a bedstead consisting of a network of strong fibre on a frame six feet by three, and raised a foot from the ground, a contrivance for safety, not for luxury), a bundle of bedding (with waterproof cover), a strong carpet, a large flat tin box for drawing materials, a second for raiment and nondescript treasures, and a large native brass basin, completed the furniture of my fascinating little gipsy home. Our provisions were packed as for a monster picnic, in long native baskets, called kilters; they are covered with leather so as to be tolerably waterproof. In these were stores of all sorts—preserved meats, flour, tea, sugar, chocolate, lanterns, candles, oil, everything, in short, that a wise housekeeper judged necessary.

A train of about thirty coolies shouldered all these treasures. They are for the most part lithe, lissome men, whose spare, lanky frames can get over the ground apace. They shouldered me into the bargain, in my dandie, which is simply a strip of stout canvas scientifically adjusted and fastened to the two ends of a bamboo forming a sort of bag in which the person carried sits sideways. The bamboo rests on the shoulders of two or four coolies walking in line; not side by side, consequently this is by far the safest mode of being carried on these narrow precipitous paths.

Mrs. Graves, being a first-rate walker, steadfastly refused to be carried, and actually walked every step of the way, occasionally diverging down some frightful native path, or over some tremendous hill-top, whence she returned a few hours later to make me envious by descriptions of spots to me unattainable.

The method of locomotion must always be an important question for every one starting on such an expedition. Personally I much preferred human ponies to quadrupeds, as the latter are very apt to take fright when on the worst bits of a narrow track on the verge of a precipice. Then they refuse to stir, and neither coaxing nor whipping avail—they back, and slip, and sometimes occasion frightful accidents. Moreover, most horses naturally object to letting a rider carry a large open white umbrella, which is an essential safeguard against sunstroke. Many of the paths to be traversed are just tracks of loose shale, and often pieces are dislodged by the heavy step of a horse, and fall so as to startle him. Some of the steepest hill-sides are cut into regular stairs, with very deep steps, which make ascent or descent alike difficult and dangerous. There is also the probability of an occasional landslip, where bits of the road have entirely disappeared.

Then too the horses are very apt to lose their shoes on these terrible paths and there is no possibility of getting them re-shod except at certain points, few and far between. Sometimes local blacksmiths are sent for from distant villages, and on arrival prove quite unable to perform the simple job. So the traveller must then get on as best he can, his groom being fully occupied in leading the horse and occasionally struggling by main force to prevent his falling over the cliff.

Naturally I much preferred being carried by men whose bare feet or flexible sandal enables them to grip the ground as if they were endowed with extra hands.

The pay of each coolie is sixpence per diem; in other words eight men will work all day to earn the same sum as an Englishman pays for one great bottle of beer—for the bottle which at Calcutta costs you one rupee, has just doubled in price ere it reaches Simla—not that the consumption of Bass or Allsopp is thereby one whit diminished! The notion of paying a man sixpence for his day's labour strikes the new-comer as being decidedly mean, as, of course, he has to feed himself and his family. It is, however, the regular wage of the country, and the poor creatures not only contrive to exist on it, but even lay aside a fraction as an offering for their gods. The only objection of the hill-men to act as coolies is that they are often obliged to neglect their own fields just when their presence is most required. Their attendance is, however, compulsory; that is to say, the headman of each village is obliged to furnish any reasonable number required by travellers. Our regiment of thirty was about the minimum with which it is possible for a party to travel.

We had also half a dozen servants, namely, *khansamah*, *khitmatgar*, *dhobie*, *bheestie*, *bearer*, *shikaree*, and *syce*, which being interpreted, are cook, waiter, laundry-man, water-carrier, valet, gamekeeper, and groom. The latter proved a most useless article, and was left half way in charge of his horse, riding being very undesirable on these dangerous paths, and being the cause of almost every accident that occurs.

After leaving the Routine Road of Simla, our way lay along

narrow paths, winding up and down along the steep hill-sides, sometimes through thickets of rhododendron (now only brightened by a few lingering blossoms) and sometimes skirting wearisome hills of bare brown earth, so ugly as to give double value to the bright lilac acacia which clothes the sheltered nooks.

At last we reached a belt of finer timber and of luxuriant wild roses, and soon were fairly entranced with the forest glories of Mahasso, where we made our first halt.

Diverging from the regular path, a long very steep scramble down a deep ravine, landed us in a gloomy gorge, with dark hills on every side, and darker deodars and pine-trees overhead. Here a most picturesque fair was being held. It was a great annual gathering of all the wild hill tribes: uncouth-looking men from every part of the country, with very handsome women. Some of them were quite fair; one had blue eyes.

They are not shy like the women of the plains, and never dream of veiling their faces; on the contrary, they look at you with a bright pleasant smile, and would be quite ready for a chat, if only you could understand them. But for the very exceptional blue eyes, all, as a rule, have the same large, soft, beautiful brown eyes, with long, silky lashes, and the soft, rich colouring of the Spanish brunette, rather inclining to olive. Their expression, when in repose, often inclines to melancholy, but brightens into the utmost animation when speaking.

Their walk, too, is singularly graceful, being full of that natural ease which strikes us so forcibly among our own Highlanders. Only, curiously enough, whereas, in our Scotch Highlands, it is the men who own the light foot and distinguished bearing; here it is all absorbed by the women, who look almost like creatures of some other race from their husbands and brothers. I noticed such a pretty woman, balancing on her head a great basket full of bright brass lotas, and her baby perched on the top of all! She was accompanied by another who carried her child astride her hip, and while with one arm she encircled the little one, the other was occupied in leading a somewhat unwilling goat, by its long soft ears. It was a charming group, with a background of noble fir-trees.

On such a gala-day as this all the women are loaded with every jewel they can command. Very rich silver ornaments are worn so as to fall all round the face, besides the usual large ear and nose rings; to say nothing of an occasional large turquoise set in one side of the nose. Sometimes the hair is plaited in a multitude of little braids, in which are twisted silver chains, and these are twined into one thick tress at the back. Then, on arms and ankles, are worn such a profusion of armlets and bangles as are oppressive even to behold.

The weight of these ornaments would literally weigh down any European woman. Ears and nose, though decked with multitudes of rings of all sizes, certainly carry little weight; but the necklaces of glass or stone which are worn, together with heavy brass chains, the large brass brooch, the heavy anklets of solid bell-metal elaborately wrought, and six or eight bracelets on each arm, as well as those worn on the wrist, make up a serious amount of metal. The average weight thus carried by the women of the hill tribes is fully twelve pounds; while the ornaments of a damsel in full-dress sometimes weigh upwards of thirty pounds. Nevertheless she carries them gracefully, in addition to the weight of her heavy woollen skirt and plaid, and is ready for an extra burden if necessary. Thus equipped, she will walk for miles over hill tracks that would make you shudder; and on reaching the rendezvous at some hill temple, is ready to dance all night by moonlight and torchlight, and return to her field-work next day.

At this fair we still saw a sprinkling of the dress of the plains. Otherwise I might say that at Simla we had bidden adieu to turbans and white drapery, and to veiled women clad in "breeks." The dress of the Paharis,[1] though varying somewhat in different districts, is very similar to that of the Lowland Scot. All the men are dressed alike in a warm blouse and trousers of grey home-spun, with a similar plaid over the shoulders. They carry a rope round the waist ready for emergencies, to tie up bundles, or whatever else may be required. They also carry a hatchet, a small skin pouch for tobacco, a net bag, containing two or three coarse

[1] *i.e.* Hill-people, or Highlanders.

chupatties, their day's food, and an amulet worn round the neck. Their cap is of thick woollen material, not very unlike a Scotch bonnet. All the hill-women wear a round woollen cap just like that of the men, but sometimes with a scarlet top. At the back of the head they have a great chignon of scarlet wool, with long plaits of black wool. Both men and women almost invariably wear a bunch of natural flowers in their hats, generally a tuft of sweet yellow roses.

The women are dressed in bright, striped, woollen material; a long petticoat and plaid, sometimes in one piece, like the old Scotch dress. This is caught in a heavy fold at the back (*en panier*), and, leaving one shoulder bare, displays a very shapely arm, with quaint bracelets. These ornaments are sometimes of great value; but the very poorest girl fastens her plaid with a large brass brooch of precisely the Old Celtic pattern, though with an Oriental addition of a curly pattern forming two outer circles.

These fairs are generally held in some spot where the forest is held sacred, and where a small cedar temple contains an image of some hill-god who presides at the festivities. There were many little booths for the sale of divers treasures, and we looked about for something characteristic in which we might invest as a remembrance of the Mahasso fair, but we found that the viceroy's party had already ridden out from Simla and had bought up everything that was in the least curious. One of the chief amusements was highly suggestive of Greenwich—namely, the presence of a number of "merry-go-rounds," in which these wild-looking Paharis whirled round and round with infinite delight. The whole scene reminded us forcibly of the pictures of Norwegian festivals.

The various pine-trees here are all more or less like gigantic spruce firs; upright as masts, and festooned to the topmost boughs with graceful virginia creeper or clematis, which now was starry with beautiful large white blossoms. We felt that at last we had reached something worthy of the name of forest. Not that Mahasso can show any of the magnificent twisted and gnarled deodars which we find farther up the country, but finer specimens of the morinda and rye pine could hardly be found, some of them towering a hundred and fifty or two hundred feet without a bend.

Leaving the dark valley, and the picturesque groups of natives camped round their great wood fires, we wearily re-ascended to the upper level, and resumed our journey till we reached the spot where our little white tents were already pitched, and all creature comforts duly awaiting us.

On the following morning we resumed our march to Theog, only a distance of six miles, but we were not anxious to hurry on, preferring to travel leisurely and allow me time for sketching.

On this, however, and on the following day's march to Muttiana —there is little to tempt an artist's pencil. On every side lie somewhat shapeless hills, which in this spring-time are all of one dull, red earth, though a little later they will be clothed with vivid green, like velvet drapery. Here, too, as we noticed below Simla, although the depth of the khads is very great, and the slope so rapid that you can scarcely find footing when once off the beaten path, they have none of the beauty of rock or precipice, and the long interminable lines in continuous sweep, nowhere relieved by streamlet or lake, become very wearisome to the eye.

Moreover every hill facing the south is utterly barren, and when our route lay along these, the dreary expanse of red earth was truly hideous. On the other hand, as we turned to face the north and west, we found ourselves surrounded with a wealth of vegetation that made amends for the bleaker side; a stunted, lilac acacia clothing the whole khad so thickly as to give the appearance of heather, while masses of very sweet roses—red, pink, white, and yellow—covered every tree with their long, graceful clusters, growing in such profusion as you can hardly imagine. They clamber to the topmost boughs of the tall trees, and thence droop in long, graceful sprays, every spray bearing perhaps thirty branches, each laden with bloom. Sometimes the supporting tree is so wholly veiled by these luxuriant blossoms as to suggest a pillar of rosy flame, or newly sprinkled snow. The yellow rose is especially fragrant, and the hill-lads, who love wild flowers, will climb far down the steepest bank to secure a bunch of them. As I before said, almost every hill-man you meet wears a bunch of flowers in his cap.

All these grow in the densest luxuriance, actually struggling for space, though, the moment you turn the hill, facing southward, you find the same dreary, barren, red earth, which at best will only contrive, after the rains, to clothe itself with short grass. Besides the roses, there is a perfect wealth of the large white clematis, and sweet white jessamine, which scents the whole air. I can never forget the delight with which for the first time I recognised the scent of that dear white jessamine, which in one second carried me far away from Himalayan crags, back to the old porch at home, and conjured up one pleasant picture after another of the merry groups that have gathered there in bygone days, twining wreaths of its fragrant stars. In another moment I had found the beautiful shrub, and robbed it of some of its wealth of blossoms, as much for the sake of "auld lang syne" as for present enjoyment.

One spot was pointed out to us as the scene of one of those fearful accidents which bring the dangers of these hills so vividly before us. It was the usual story of a startled horse, growing restive, and backing over the khad; backing the more resolutely as the terrified groom strove to lead him forward, till with one frightful backward plunge, the horse and his rider, a lady, disappeared over the precipice.

Our fourth day's march, from Muttiana to Narkunda, was very beautiful, lying partly through a rocky gorge, and through picturesque wood. At this point I think the real beauty centres. Hence we had perhaps the very grandest general view of the snows, still stretching right across the horizon, but apparently immeasurably higher than when seen from Simla, in fact, floating sometimes far above the clouds. On one side of us lay the dark forest of Hatto, running right up to the sky, and in the cultivated valley, far below us, lay the Christian Mission Station of Kotghur.

We would fain have encamped in the forest itself, but the usual thing, lack of water, prevented us. The only spring had been dried up by the long drought, and when we wanted a drink we found only hard, dry mud. We had therefore to be content with spending a long day there. We clambered up through beautiful forest scenery, grand old silver firs and all manner of pines clothing the steepest hill sides. On reaching a very high point, in the heart of the forest, we suddenly came on what I have seen nowhere else in the Himalayas, a long green glade, like an English meadow, embosomed in grand timber, and commanding an exquisite view of the snows for hundreds of miles. The grass was enamelled with blue and white anemones like those in our gardens, and carpeted with the usual wealth of maiden-hair fern, while beautiful creepers festooned the trees.

It is heartrending, however, to see how this splendid forest suffers from the carelessness of the Paharis, who are for ever kindling fires to cook their food or light their pipes, and the fire smoulders on till one after another of these grand old giants is a victim, and at last the blackened remains fall with a crash, and then kindly creepers twine green wreaths above the poor charred remains of the forest kings. I confess we followed the vile ways of other men, and let our coolies light a fire in a great hollow tree—not that they asked our leave, for after all, we were only visitors, while they were doing the honours of their home. So they lighted their fire as they had been accustomed to do all their lives, and in a few minutes the flames rushed up to the very top of the tree in a fiery, red pillar. The old trunk seemed, however, to be so well accustomed to acting chimney, that it was flourishing in full leaf, notwithstanding many previous experiences, so we hope it was none the worse for our misdeeds. Then we cooked our potatoes in the wood-ashes, and enjoyed them vastly.

Nevertheless, we entered our protest against such vandalism, as we came on one magnificent tree after another, such as in

THE SNOWY RANGE, FROM NARKUNDA.
Looking down to Kotghur Mission Station.

England would be accounted beyond all price, even as timber, now reduced to scorched, ghostly skeletons, standing up ghastly against the sky, with outstretched arms like Gustave Doré's spirit trees. The mighty monarchs had stood their ground bravely, and would not yield even in death, though their leafy crowns had fallen, and wintry storms and summer suns had bleached their upper branches, and though the soil around their burnt and blackened stems was but a heap of wood-ashes and charcoal, relics of their own departed glory.

Others there were (like that wherein the coolies had kindled our gipsy fire), whose huge stems had been gradually hollowed by fire till they were merely shells, and you marvelled how they could uphold the lofty branches—these, in their turn, sustaining the weight of green creepers, which seemed as though they would lovingly strive to veil the unsightly ruin wrought by the fire-spirits. In truth they grew all the more luxuriantly on account of the thick layers of charcoal and wood-ash.

Here and there some poor old tree had been fairly worsted in the unequal fray. Fire, storm, and tempest had done their worst, and at last it had succumbed after many a hard-fought battle, and now the scarred timbers lay rotting on the ground, which was strewn in every direction with half-burnt logs, in all stages of decay.

I need scarcely add that this is not a British state, but belongs to a small Rajah. It is under British protection, however, and the damage would be prevented if possible, but the careless Paharis are many, and the white men few. In any case they are slow to learn the value of timber, and even in cutting up grand cedar-trees for their own use, they make such clumsy work from the fact of having no saws, only hatchets, that they can hardly get half a dozen good planks, where an English carpenter would get fifty. Luckily the wood splits very readily, or they would have harder work still. From its fragments they extract an "oil of cedar," which they consider a specific for various skin diseases. I fancy it is something of the same sort as the fir-tree oil, the value of which is now so fully recognised in Europe as a preventive of gout and rheumatism, or that spirit which in Scotland is extracted from birch-wood, and considered so excellent a remedy for rheumatism.

You must not run away with an impression that Hatto is all a burnt forest. On the contrary it is even richer and more beautiful than Mahasso, as you would admit, could you once look down a vista of dark firs, and over the waves of the sea of foliage, extending for miles, while here and there some splendid group of pines sends up its tall tapering spires in dark clusters, like spectral fingers pointing to the gleaming snow-pinnacles, which, rising from the misty valley, seem to cleave the blue sky.

The general effect of the forest is a dark evergreen; yet here and there you find yourself beneath high twining arches of transparent golden green, where the light falls through glittering emerald leaves and radiant blossoms—true bowers of roses—as if through the rainbow windows of some old cathedral. From that calm solitude comes the soft, murmurous cooing of mother wood-doves, and frisky little grey squirrels dart along with their young ones, peeping in and out among the blossoms, one moment in the clear golden light, the next in the green shadow.

And on every side you hear a low subdued humming of all the buzzing, busy creatures, whose home and life-work lies between those rough scales of bark and the smooth solid bole of the old trees; while grasshoppers are chirping and leaping among the leaves, and doubtless enjoying the warm, mellow sunshine, just as much as those strange human creatures who have presumed to invade their sanctuary, and to steal one glimpse of all that loveliness—such beauty as you know to be lavished in every untrodden corner of the wide world—the device of One Who "rejoiceth in His work," and for Whose good pleasure such fair things are, and were created.

Of the infinite variety of foliage through which we passed day by day, the greater part is very much akin to that of Britain. The different species grow in clearly-defined belts at given altitudes, so that when we had in the course of a long march ascended so many hills, and descended so many khads as to have fairly lost all notion of our height, we could generally form a pretty good estimate thereof from the character of the shrubs around us.

Thus, on the very high levels, at about 13,000 feet, are found common birch, gooseberries, and strawberries—real strawberries, —not the dusty, tasteless species which grow lower down. Below this grows the neoza, or edible pine (*Pinus Gerardianus*), a pine with silvery bark, and whose cones are full of long-shaped nuts, good to eat, which fall out when the cone is half-baked. At about 9,000 feet you find magnificent deodars, which love a dry rocky soil, and flourish best where they can take root in the crevices of the granite rock, and there hold their ground for centuries, for they are slow of growth—slow and sure—for their timber is imperishable. They decrease in size on lower levels. At the same height you find wild apricot, on which the mistletoe grows abundantly, also mulberry-trees, and walnuts of two species—the common sort, like our own, and another variety, in which the nut is so incased in an inner coating of wood that it is almost impossible to extract it. The Paharis bring quantities of the good nuts to Simla, where they sell them at absurdly low prices, in spite of the distance they have had to carry them. At about 8,000 feet you find sycamore, rhododendron, holly, ilex or evergreen oak, of which there are three varieties here, horse-chestnut, yew, and various pines. At about 5,000 feet are large cactuses, acacias, oleanders, plantains, and other vegetation purely tropical.

Among the commonest varieties of pine is the morinda, which resembles a fine spruce fir with very short branches. It grows to a height of 120 feet, straight as an arrow, and is sometimes upwards of twenty feet in circumference at the base. Its foliage is very dark.

Next comes the rye, which bears much the same general character, only its branches and needles are longer, and more pensile —a weeping pine. Its wood is far more perishable than that of the cedar, and therefore has comparatively little value. The tall dark spiral forms of the morinda and rye, constantly combine in most effective groups, all interlaced with the brilliant virginia creeper. The cheel-pine greatly resembles our common Scotch fir, and makes excellent, resinous torches.

The kolin is another common pine, growing on the lower spurs. Of the Himalayan oak there are three varieties, all evergreen. One of these, the kharso, abounds on the higher levels. It has the great merit of taking kindly to the neglected eastern and southern slopes of the hills, so that you often see one side of a hill clothed entirely with this oak, and the other side with divers pines.

On some of the very high levels the white variety of tree rhododendron is found, as also the crimson species; while the bush rhododendron, which rarely exceeds eight feet in height, is found, both white and lilac, at the same level as birch, that is, just below the snow.

We had been weak enough to imagine that the abundance of game in these forests would give large variety to our commissariat—a notion, the fallacy of which we very soon realised. In fact, the idea of shooting for the pot soon became a standing joke, the extraordinary lack of all animal life being among the most remarkable features of these hills. It was quite an event to see even a hill blackbird; and as to a covey of chickore, or hill partridges, it was a thing to be chronicled.

The fact is that these wild creatures have such boundless feeding-grounds that of course they shun the path that is ever trodden by human foot, albeit only the foot of the goat-like native. He, however, is just as likely to carry a gun as the white man, and is, moreover, a wary shot, for, as he cannot afford to waste his powder, he generally contrives to shoot his game sitting. One way and another, these native shikarees do bag a considerable amount of game, which they bring to Simla for sale. Sometimes, however, they fall into the clutches of the bears, and get frightfully mutilated. We saw several men whose faces had been literally torn off, and what remained was without feature of any sort—horrible to behold. When I bethought me of my own brother clasped in that awful embrace, I felt thankful indeed that the grisly mother-bear had been content with crunching his arm, and had spared his face.[1]

[1] *Wild Men and Wild Beasts.* By Colonel W. Gordon Cumming.

As to bears, we met various gentlemen—several of whom were experienced old sportsmen—who had been vainly toiling in pursuit of the creatures, seeking them among the ripe apricots in the valleys, and on the strawberry beds close to the snows, and the more they sought the more they declared that the thing was a snare and a delusion—that there was no game in the country; and indeed it seemed as if they were right, for not one of the men we met had had any sport worth mentioning, only a great deal of very hard work.

For you can imagine that toiling up and down these dreadful khads is not exactly like a walk on a Highland moor. Perhaps, as you pick your steps over the slippery short grass and fir needles, your foot may give one little slide, then woe betide you. The whole bank seems one polished surface, glittering with fir needles, and away you glide over the steepest, driest, most slippery grass-slope that ever was created, at an angle all but precipitous, happy indeed, if you do not go helplessly on, till you crash down over the crags into darkness and annihilation.

But, apart from so horrible a contingency, sport on such ground is at best a toilsome pleasure—emphatically pleasure under difficulties. If you have the luck to shoot a bird, it will certainly fall at some incredible distance below you, where the chances are you never find it; or, if it is a wounded creature, it may crawl up the other side, where you are bound to follow it. Sometimes the ravine is so narrow that you can shoot game on the opposite bank, but it may cost an hour's scramble to reach the place where it lies.

How, under such circumstances, you would envy the great eagles and kites that float so easily about, sailing across the valley with such smooth, gliding motion. Great lammergeyers, and bearded vultures which sometimes measure nine feet from tip to tip, and keen-eyed falcons, are among the birds of prey that contrive to pick up a living. So we infer that some food must exist.

Dr. Russell, in travelling hereabouts, says that in the month of September his party killed an immense number of chickore, kallidge pheasants, and minaul, and that in November, when the cover is not so thick, they might have had far better sport. They were on their way to Rampore by the old road, which is now impassable. So perhaps the birds take refuge there still. Certainly in the months of June, July, and August they were invisible.

The only exception we heard of, in the general chorus of exasperated sportsmen, was in the case of Mr. Buck, a very keen ornithologist, who is so perfectly skilled in imitating the calls of different rare birds that the deluded victims respond, and, coming close to the beguiling voice, pay the penalty of their curiosity. This chiefly applies to the argus, or horned pheasant, wary as his namesake of old, but withal so jealous that he can brook no rival, and at once responding to the far-away call, flies to give battle to the intruder, but finds the odds are hopelessly to his disadvantage. Besides the argus, there are the kallidge, or black pheasant, the cheer, or snow pheasant, and the minaul pheasant.

The latter is a magnificent bird. When you do have the luck to see him on the wing, he flashes past you like a ray of prismatic light, a dazzling mass of iridescent metallic green, blue, bronze, gold, purple, and crimson, changing in every light, and glossy as satin, with a beautiful crest of drooping feathers. The argus is more quaker-like, but beautiful in his neatness. His plumage is brown with black and pearly-white spots. The snow pheasant is rather a dirty-grey bird. There ought also to be sundry varieties of partridges, snipe, and woodcock, but we had little chance of making acquaintance with them, either on the wing or in the larder.

Having spent a delightful day in Hatto forest, we returned to our tents, which had been pitched near the travellers' bungalow at Narkunda, 8,676 feet above the sea. We had by this time become thoroughly enamoured of our gipsy life, and were daily more and more enchanted with its freedom. The escape from every phase of civilised formality, from all fixed laws of action, from regular hours, each meal being henceforth a movable feast, no wearisome seven or eight o'clock dinner to waste two precious hours, but a merry supper by our camp-fire whenever we were ready for it; and then "early to bed and early to rise"—in short, it was an escape from the old stereotyped existence whose comfortable, commonplace round we had run, till it had become altogether monotonous and humdrum; and we rejoiced exceedingly to think that for three whole months we could know nothing of the well-appointed British social life, and its wearisome sameness; but that day after day, and week after week, must slip by in ever-changing scenes, while we wandered from one beautiful spot to another, snail-like, carrying about our locomotive homes, or rather not snail-like, making others fag for us.

So here on this lovely starlit night we found our tent-homes pitched on a grassy bank; a blazing camp-fire, both for warmth and safety, as the leopards are apt to be troublesome in the dark, and the most comfortable of suppers all ready for us.

And then, an hour later, looking out from the little tent, an oft-recurring allegory of "the near and the heavenly horizons" seemed to paint itself on earth and sky, an allegory of enduring light, veiled by the nearer trifles of the moment. A very common parable, but one which suggests itself as often as you sit at night working beside an open window. Your work is engrossing, everything within the rays of your little camp is so distinct, while without all is thick night.

One breath extinguishes that earth light, and within your home all is dark. But suddenly the great heaven is lighted by 10,000 gleaming worlds; and to-night as I looked up, not the stars only were there, for on the far horizon a pale, cold line of glittering peaks towered above the mist like white spirits at rest.

And one little glimmering taper close at hand had hidden all this peaceful loveliness!

CHAPTER XIII.

UNDER CANVAS.

Opium Fields — Kotghur Mission Station — Native Christians — Devil Worshippers—Ascent to Thandarh—A Tea Plantation—A Sociable Pariah—Descent from the Temperate Zone to the Tropics—Gorge of the Sutlej—A March under Difficulties—Rampore—A Spoilt Rajah—Rest-house *versus* Tent—A Plague of Flies—Camp at Gowrah.

ON leaving Narkunda we likewise lost the general view of the snowy range. Henceforth our path was to wind in and out of valleys, and up and down steep hills, whence we could rarely see more than a few peaks at a time. Of these we often caught such glimpses on reaching our night's camping-ground, as promised good subjects for the morrow's sketch. Too often, however, the morning revealed only a sheet of grey vapour, so blending with the sky that we could scarcely believe it possible that hills lay hidden behind that filmy veil. There was nothing for it but to finish a careful drawing of rocks and trees and nearer hills, in the faith, rarely disappointed, that sooner or later a light breeze would stir the clouds. Then, like some spectral vision, a great shoulder would reveal itself here, and a tall peak there, looming fitfully through the mist like phantoms from the spirit world.

Our route lay through Hatto forest, far below the green glade where we had spent the previous day. The path lay along a khad so steep that it sometimes rose and fell almost precipitously above and below us, and we had to look far down for the bases of the grand old pines whose tops seemed to reach up to heaven. The hill was here clothed with magnificent silver fir, also with the morinda and rye pine. The latter occasioned an irresistible confusion in our natural history, *rye* meaning mustard; and certainly these tall "mustard" trees were the "greatest of all herbs." I fear, however, they would scarcely have supplied our cruet-stand!

Here, as usual, we noticed that the trees half burnt away were always the most richly festooned with virginia creepers and wild roses. In the sheltered hollows were clumps of fine horse-chestnut in full blossom, also a large kind of bird-cherry, and a few scarlet blossoms still lingered on the rhododendrons. The ground in places was blue with larkspur and covered with primrose plants; I also found one delicate lilac auricula, which carried my heart straight home to the old garden where these fragrant blossoms used to bloom so luxuriantly long ago.

On emerging from the forest we passed by a multitude of tiny, terraced fields; some were full of white poppies, shortly to be converted into opium, that curse of many lands. I had heard of the poppy fields as being rainbow fields, purple, yellow, white, and pink, and those of China are blood-red. Those we saw were all pure white, which I believe is the case generally throughout India. So fair a crop gave no hint of the evil which those fair blossoms might be made to work, when transformed to that malignant poison which has done so much to degrade and enervate myriads. The opium is drawn from the seed vessels; as soon as these are fully formed, an incision is made in each every evening, and by morning a drop of milky juice has exuded. This is scraped off carefully and boiled, and is thus prepared for market.

Happily this evil crop does not seem to be extensively cultivated hereabouts, but it monopolises a terribly large proportion of the richest land in the fertile valley of the Ganges, especially in the province of Behar, and in the neighbourhood of Benares—the most thickly-peopled districts, where it would scarcely be possible for the land to support so dense a population, even were it all devoted to growing grain and cotton, instead of the most fertile tracts being given up to these wretched poppies.

It is known that the produce of an acre of fair soil will keep a human being in comfort, but the same extent of the very richest irrigated land will only produce fourteen pounds' weight of opium, and yet India's annual export of poison is something considerably over sixty-thousand chests of 140 lbs each.[1]

Is it not pitiful that notwithstanding the indescribable misery resulting, on the one hand from the use of opium, and on the other, from oft-recurring years of famine (which might at least be mitigated, were good food grown on all the land now devoted to raising deadly poison), Christian Britain actually continues for filthy lucre's sake to promote the still further increase of this devil's traffic, merely raising the price paid to its cultivators, to enable it to maintain its ground against such crops as wheat, rice and potatoes (which, of late years have doubled in price !).

[1] I have heard it asserted that the Supreme Government of India has no monopoly of opium. This may be true as regards Bombay, which derives its Opium Revenue from the Transit Duty of £70 per chest of 140 lbs., paid by inland native states, for the privilege of transporting their produce through British territory to the shipping ports.

But the opium shipped from Calcutta is purely the property of the Government, which does not allow one acre of British India to be devoted to the cultivation of poppies without license, and which encourages the poppy farms, by granting advances of money without interest. All the opium produced must be given to the official agent at Government price ; not an ounce may be retained by the cultivator under heavy penalties, and any dispute concerning weight or quality can only be determined by the opium agents, no reference to ordinary courts being allowed.

The opium thus produced costs the Government about £40 per chest of 140 lbs., and brings in from £120 to £130. In the year 1878-79, fifty-five thousand chests were sold by auction for six million, seven hundred thousand pounds.[1] In the following year the Indian revenue derived from opium had increased to about eight millions sterling, and now has risen to about nine millions sterling !

The openly avowed intention of the Government is "to push the cultivation by every possible means, and obtain as much revenue as possible out of opium," avowing itself "perfectly indifferent to the deleterious effect which opium may produce on the people to whom it is sold." This was the official statement of a recent Lieutenant-Governor of Bengal, and Sir William Muir remarks that

[1] 55,500 chests realised £6,798,639.

It is bad enough, that *one-third of all the barley grown in Scotland should be converted into whisky*, for the destruction, body and soul, of so many of our own countrymen, but here it is a question of preparing poison of an infinitely worse type.

As a general rule there was so little possibility of making any mistake as to our day's destination that our little party constantly divided in the morning, sure of meeting again through the day, or at least of finding the tents at night.. Thus I was free to halt four hours at any good sketching point, while my companions went in search of game or explored the forests. Very often I started with my dandie-bearers long before the others were awake; a watchful brownie having brought me bread and chocolate for breakfast, together with a bottle of milk and a supply of cold meat and bread for the day. So it was very often evening before we met at our next camping-ground to talk over the adventures of the day as we gathered round the red wood-fire.

All we knew at starting was that we were to halt at a distance of so many *coss;* a delightfully vague expression. A *coss* is supposed to be about a mile and a-half, but this, like the Scotch mile and a bittock, is capable of indefinite expansion.

On this particular morning we were bound for Kotghur, and my companions started first, hoping for a chance of game in the forest, before the coolies had disturbed the ground. In due time I followed, and my dandie-wallahs very naturally took the road to the Mission Station at Kotghur, whither the whole procession of coolies followed with tents and baggage. The path wound down an interminable hill, till we reached the level of the river

"the Government has strained every nerve to carry out the policy it has adopted, endeavouring to secure a wider area of poppy cultivation by the bait of large advances among an unwilling peasantry, at the risk of inoculating them with a taste for the drug."

This reads strangely when compared with the despatch of the East India Directors in 1817, when they state that if it were possible to prevent the use of the drug altogether, except as medicine, they would gladly do it, in compassion to mankind.

Sutlej, and came to a dâk bungalow. Nothing was, however, to be heard of the others. It was evident they had taken some other road, and, as several other bungalows were dotted about the hills, it was very uncertain where they might be found. At the dâk bungalow I found an Englishman who had just returned from the wilds of Kulu. He of course could give no information.

In this emergency I bethought me of consulting the "Padre," and so made for the Mission Station. I was welcomed by Herr Rebsch and his family to a pretty home with a wide verandah full of flowers, and covered with trellis-work and vines; a home with all the comforts of civilised life—piano, harmonium, pictures. The very sight of mine host's kind, benevolent face seemed a haven of rest from perplexities. In a very few minutes messengers were despatched to the various spots where the wanderers might have gone, and while we waited their return I accepted a cordial invitation to breakfast, and did full justice to the unwonted luxury of excellent, home-made bread, for it must be confessed that the never varying chapatties very quickly became exceeding distasteful to us, especially when, as in the early morning, we had to eat them cold, and our souls loathed the heavy, round cakes, and recalled the remark once made to us by a Highland lassie, that it was "so *dull* eating bad bread!"

On our return two months later, we made a long halt near Kotghur, and had further opportunities of proving the kindness of these good friends. Here they had lived seven years, and have a fair handful of native Christians, whom we saw assembled for daily morning prayer, and were struck by their very superior look to the low castes, whence our converts are usually drawn. It is, however, a very small proportion of the children trained in the schools who show the slightest tendency to become Christians in after years; the most that can be hoped is that gradually prejudice may melt away, and that the people may lose faith in their own superstitions.

Already very many are ashamed openly to call themselves Devil-worshippers, as in fact they are, but the more unsophisticated still point out their temples as "Sheitan ka Bungalow."[1] Their faith differs greatly from that of the Hindoo of the plains, in more ways than merely in abstaining from ablutions, which is the most palpable difference. They say that, as it is quite impossible to worship all the thirty-three millions of gods, they must omit the good spirits who will not harm them, and devote all their energies to propitiate the evil spirits, who are always on the alert to do mischief.

So every here and there along the road you see a sacred bush covered with strips of rag, as votive offerings to the spirit of stream or forest, and here every passer-by halts to do obeisance, or "make *pooja*" as they say.

In a couple of hours tidings were brought of the runaways, who had been found at a road bungalow at Thandarh, fully three miles farther, where they were impatiently awaiting our arrival. They had kept to an upper path, and had never lost level at all. The tired coolies looked ruefully at their burdens, as they thought of that weary three miles up a steep hill, and it needed all the hope of backsheesh to brace them to their work. However they "set a stout heart to a stey brae" with the usual happy result.

My poor dandie-bearers groaned audibly, but, being utterly unable to walk myself, I had to abstain from all commiseration, remembering another good proverb which tells that "pity without relief, is like mustard without beef," a stimulant which it was as well to withhold. I confess I often did feel sorry for these poor fellows, and would fain have lightened their burden, but I found that the more I walked myself, the more they grunted when they resumed work; so, knowing that the fatigue would only involve an extra sleep for them, while it would certainly mean exhaustion and fever for me, I found it best generally to practise a judicious selfishness, and to sit still, knowing that when they were really tired they would deposit me, dandie and all, and go off for a smoke.

They are stout, sturdy little chaps, much the same build as our strongest Highlanders, and it takes a good deal really to fatigue

[1] House of Devils.

them, though they would rarely miss their laugh, at the weight of the "chota Missi Baba" (little Miss Baby), as they derisively called their heavy burden. They are merry enough as a rule, with a bright, independent manner, very different from that of the subdued, obsequious Hindoo of the plains. It has often been noticed of these latter that, like the Scotch Highlanders, they cannot endure "chaff." These hill-men, however, seem to give and take any amount of it, and are for ever laughing and joking, and ready to make the best of everything. I invariably heard gentlemen speak in the highest terms of those who accompanied them on their shooting expeditions; no matter what hardships they encountered, they were always sure of their men.

At last we reached the brow of the hill, where our hungry companions were waiting, having found shelter from the sun in a small bungalow, alive with flies. You would imagine that all the flies that had ever been created assembled in these road bungalows for the special annoyance of travellers; every nook and cranny, every shelf, every chair, literally swarms with them. It was a glad moment when our tents were pitched and we were "at home" once more. There were dark clouds threatening on every side, as indeed they had been doing for some days; but we had learnt to think nothing of a passing thunderstorm, which only added grandeur to the hills. A few extra tent-pegs, and a little wall of earth round the tent, leaving a tiny ditch to carry off rain, made all snug for the night, whatever might happen, and we knew that at this season we were not likely to be washed away.

How the servants managed to keep themselves alive was a continual mystery. Even when we camped near a house, the best they could hope for was a corner of the open verandah, and often they had not even the shelter of a big stone, but just lay round the fire all through the chilly night. And yet they were always ready and willing. No matter how long and weary a march they might have had, the fires were kindled and dinner cooked in less than no time; and when I wanted to make an unusually early start, at whatever hour of the night I might order breakfast, it was certain to be brought to my tent as punctually as clockwork. Just imagine how British servants would grumble should such service and such irregular hours be required of them ! !

Our camp to-day was pitched on the edge of a tea-garden; perhaps it would be better to say a tea-plantation. The young trees were planted in rows, several feet apart, and at this season resembled well-grown cabbages. On our return we found them about three feet high, pruned down to little dumpy shrubs, like dwarf orange-trees. The young leaves are picked off, and carried every evening to a factory near, where they are rubbed by hands till most of their juice is squeezed out; they are then baked in large metal cauldrons, after which they are dried in the sun, and sorted. It is said that the finer sorts of tea grow best on the higher levels, but that lower down the leaves are more abundant, and the crop consequently heavier.

The jungly ground beyond the tea-fields was crimson and white with the profusion of wild roses, and we also found a quantity of most delicious, yellow raspberries, the berry somewhat resembling the avron or cloud-berry of our Scotch mountains. From this point we looked right up the gorge of the Sutlej, of which we could catch an occasional glimpse in the valley far below. Its deep roar reached us only as a distant, subdued murmur, as it floated upon the breeze. On every side of us lay richly-wooded hills, fragrant with the resinous scent of pine-needles baking in the hot sun ; and beyond the river rose tier above tier of great reddish mountains, snow-capped.

At Kotghur we were supposed to have reached the Ultima Thule of civilisation. Beyond this point there is no regular post, and whatever is required must be sent for by coolies, to whom you entrust a chit, *alias* letter, which they carry at the end of a split stick, just in the way that English village children bring you bunches of sweet violets. Thus your letter is carried for days, and is at last delivered as clean as when it started. We found, however, that two or three gentlemen, having work farther up the country, had established a runner of their own. Consequently we were never beyond reach of letters. Moreover, the baboo in charge of the post-office proved a most invaluable traveller's right-hand. Whatever we might require—from live minaul pheasants to bring home, down to sacks of potatoes, flour or sugar, for present consumption—we had only to send word to our most intelligent friend, who forthwith supplied all our need.

So we went on our way rejoicing, still followed by a huge pariah dog, who had offered us the nose of friendship on the morning we left Simla, and had utterly refused to leave us ever since, a mark of affection which gratified us vastly, though, as we discovered two days later, the curious creature had merely availed himself of our escort for safety as far as Rampore, where, for reasons of his own, he wished to go. At Rampore, therefore, he bade us farewell, and refused to go another step!

Our next march was to carry us down to Neritt in the gorge of the Sutlej. It was a frightfully steep descent of five thousand feet, which brought us back to the tropical vegetation of the plains, to large-leaved plantains and great cactuses in every crevice of the rocks, while wild caper (suggestive of boiled mutton) draped the cliff with its graceful tendrils and silky blossom, which resembles a white and lilac passion-flower. Imagine the suddenness of this change from the English temperature and vegetation which we had quitted in the afternoon. We tried to shorten the march by a short cut, which as usual proved the longest way, inasmuch as the track was intolerably steep. Of course my dandie was useless, and the scramble was one much to be avoided.

The heat in the gorge of the river was so great that it was not considered safe to halt there for many hours. We did not, therefore, descend till the evening, so that ere we reached the valley the sun had set, and it was quite dark when we reached our destination. We found our tents pitched near the stream, which roared with deafening noise, and we could just discern a picturesque village, and houses roofed with great slabs of stone.

By 3 A.M. we were again astir, drinking our chocolate by the pale starlight, which lent mystery to a curious old temple just below us, overshadowed by plantains, whose broad crinkled leaves glistened with dewy jewels, and by pink oleanders, and other flowers too lovely for a *Sheitan ka Bungalow.*

To me it was irresistible, and not having yet learnt a wholesome dread of Indian heat, I could not but linger long enough to get a slight sketch of the place. The others pushed on; the baggage followed. Only the blue-eyed shikaree stayed to watch over me, and a very faithful watch-dog he proved on this occasion, for, owing to some mistake about the coolies, our number was deficient, and only two could by any means be procured for my dandie, a bad look-out, as we had fully fourteen miles' march before us, in really oppressive heat.

At last, when things began to look serious, Nanko (for so he of the blue eyes was called, and, by the way, he was the only blue-eyed native *man* I ever saw) contrived to capture two more, and with promises and threats succeeded in getting them under weigh. I believe the poor wretches were really anxious about their fields; certain it is that when we had gone two or three miles they bolted. This was a pretty fix, for my scramble of the previous evening had not improved my limited walking powers, and the men generally relieve guard every few minutes. However, sometimes walking, sometimes carried, we got on some distance.

Here I encountered the famous "Briton of the Desert," one whom I knew well by sight, and knew his word was law with all these natives, so I concluded my troubles were over. By no means. We had never been formally introduced, so although there was perhaps not another white woman within a hundred miles, except Mrs. Graves, who by this time was near Rampore, this knight-errant of the Sutlej, although a Scotchman, quickened his pace to a trot, just as I tried to screw up the necessary courage to ask his aid, and so we passed in solemn silence. So there was nothing for it but to struggle on.

At length we reached a village, and then halted by a spring overshadowed by a great banyan tree, and after wearisome delays two other men were captured—a very insufficient number for so long a march; but there was no alternative. We learnt afterwards that the difficulty of obtaining coolies in this district is greatly due to the fact that there are in this district several purely Brahman villages, and as these fair-skinned aristocrats will not cultivate their own terraced rice-fields, they compel the dark-skinned race to work for them. Foreigners are therefore obliged to procure coolies from villages further up the mountains.

For fourteen miles our route lay close to the Sutlej, a most uninviting stream at this season, when, swollen with melted snow and full of white mica and sand, it rushes along in a vast mass of dirty, turbid water, great tossing waves of dirty yellow and white foam, very rapid and horribly noisy. O dear! how weary we did become of the roaring of that stream, when sometimes we could not get away from it all day long, being hemmed in on either side by great precipitous cliffs.

But to-day it was all quite new—and this march was certainly most beautiful—here and there we crossed small streams clear as crystal, coming, not from the snows, but from their source in the hard rocky mountains, far up the lovely little valleys which opened from this main gorge, sometimes bare, sometimes richly wooded, while here and there a waterfall came tumbling over the rocks, boiling and hissing, adding its note to the deafening din, as it fell into the deep dark pool below.

We met one or two men suffering from goître—most hideous deformity—the penalty of drinking ice-water. Undoubtedly in the exceeding heat of these low-lying valleys it must be a sore temptation both to bathe and drink of the cool streams, even though they do come direct from the glacier and are fraught with such danger. Certainly wherever we came to any little reach of the river where a quiet back-water made such a thing possible, there were sure to be a few bathers, and my little body-guard went in and out of the river like a troop of seals.

At one place we came on a group of black tents of coarse goats' hair or camels' hair canvas, round which were lying a vast number of goats. It was the camp of some Thibetan traders from far up the valley, essentially Chinese in countenance, having narrow oblique eyes and flattened features. They wear jackets of coarse fur or leather; men and women seem to dress much alike, but the

RAMPORE, "THE CITY OF RAMA."

latter have sometimes coloured petticoats. Their fine black hair is plaited in countless braids, and apparently never brushed; but the common head-gear consists of a broad band of cloth, on which are fastened large turquoises, coins, and lumps of agate; beads of common English glass and the most precious gems are stuck on quite promiscuously. These are generally heirlooms, from which the owners never part.

At another place, as we toiled along through deep, dry sand close to the river, we glanced up at the face of the cliff, and there perceived some grass wattling high up. It was a regular home in the rock, and a large family had here found shelter. Even the smallest children clambered up and down the most dangerous-looking ledge as if it were the smoothest pavement. Imagine what a strange place to call home—among barren, naked, almost inaccessible crags, with the roaring, rushing river for ever raging just below. Fancy the utter loneliness of such a place when wild storms come sweeping down the gorge, bringing great masses of slaty rock crashing from the cliffs; and never a living thing comes near save the stately eagle, soaring against the tempest! There is something strange, stern, and solemn in the very thought of such a cradle, where every influence of mountain gloom and mountain glory must by turns exert its might on the spirits of these wild children of nature.

That our course must lie along the Sutlej valley was a matter not left to our choice, as the only practicable road is that which has recently been made by the English Government, and which is still slowly progressing towards Thibet *viâ* Rampore, which is the capital of Bussahir and stands on the brink of the river. The name of this town conveys to the Hindoo mind precisely the same idea as Allahabad does to the Mohammedan; it is emphatically "the city of God." Rampore is the city of Rama, whose name is the Hindoo's bond of brotherhood over the length and breadth of the land; for just as two Mohammedans invariably greet one another in the name of Allah, so the invariable salutation of two Hindoos is simply the cry of Ram, Ram.

One of the largest fairs of the Himalayas is annually held here, and all the treasures of Thibet, Yarkand, and all those far-away districts are brought here to be exchanged by the merchants from the plains for such simple products of civilisation as may find use among men whose requirements are so few.

It was therefore necessary that whatever road was made to the frontier districts should pass through the city; and as the old native path was merely a track, winding among difficult and dangerous cliffs—sometimes by natural ledges, sometimes over a bit of plank, bridging some frightful chasm, and often so steep that no beast of burden larger than a goat could clamber up—it became a question of very difficult engineering to make such a road as that now in use—one at any point of which two laden mules should be able to pass one another in safety. It was also necessary that the road should be constructed below the ordinary limit of snow, which is estimated at 12,000 feet above the sea level; and so it was found that by generally following the course of the river, some of the most overwhelming difficulties would be avoided.

There was formerly, however, another road of English construction, with certain advantages of its own, for which we, travelling only in search of the beautiful, did long exceedingly. It commanded distant views of far-away snows, and led away into a region of silence; whereas by this new road one hardly ever escapes from the noise of the waters, or from the steep precipitous cliffs which hem one in. The old road formerly ran from Narkunda to Serahan, which is two marches beyond Rampore, keeping a high level the whole way, and altogether avoiding this dangerous hot valley. There were good dâk bungalows at intervals all along the road. Now there are no travellers' bungalows beyond Kotghur; and although, by the courtesy of the road commissioners travellers are allowed to halt at the road bungalows, these are for the most part rough and ready, and have, of course, no staff of servants. Moreover, you are always liable to find them occupied, so you must necessarily carry your own tent. Since this new road has been made to Rampore, the old one has been allowed to fall into disrepair, and is now impassable; so whether you like heat or not, you must travel up the gorge.

As I before said, this march is very beautiful, and quite unlike any other, from the purely tropical character of its vegetation, the enormous cactuses which everywhere clothe the rocks, and the silky blossoms of the wild capers. Nevertheless we were right glad when at length we caught sight of the town of Rampore, with its *jula*, or rope bridge, its temples, and all its quaint hill houses, with their overhanging upper storys and balconies of carved cedar-wood. The foreground was peculiar, having a great gallows beside the river, where the Rajah of Bussahir hangs malefactors.

The Rajah (though of very noble ancestry, and priding himself on a pedigree which carries him back through a hundred and twenty generations to some legendary hero) is himself a very contemptible mortal, being a youth of semi-English up-bringing. His education seems to have been entrusted to a baboo, who taught him good English and the abuse of strong liquor, which he at once demands from all travellers whom he honours with a call, occasionally prolonging his visit for so many hours that his forcible removal becomes necessary. One of his great topics is the subject of English guns and gun-makers; and every gentleman whom he visits is invariably requested to sell his favourite rifle or his travelling clock, a negotiation which is generally closed by the fumes of brandy obscuring the princely intellect.

His picturesque palace is perched on a rock overhanging the river, and just opposite is his zenana, the balconies of which are entirely closed in with carved wood. He generally, however, prefers living in his summer palace at Serahan, much farther up the hill.

All the houses in this part of the country are more or less alike. A square base of stone acts as granary and stable for cattle. A staircase outside leads up to an overhanging balcony which surrounds the wooden dwelling-house. Perhaps a second still wider story is above this. The roof is peaked, and slated with large slabs of grey shingle or slate, or even of cedar-wood. All the gables are elaborately carved with hanging ornaments of wood—arabesques, or curious heads.

I was very anxious to buy some of the brightly-striped woollen material which most of the women hereabouts wear, and for which this town is noted. It seemed, however, to be only forthcoming at the time of the great fair, when all manner of treasures are to be had. One or two pieces were offered to me, but as the pretty damsels who brought them had obviously had considerable wear out of them, our trading came to nought.

All this time the hot air was blowing down the valley like the blast from a furnace, scorching our faces, which was the more curious as it seemed to blow right down from the snows. I suppose, however, that in passing over the burning crags it caught heat on its way. We hurried through the town, having decided to spend the night at a road bungalow about two miles farther—on considerably higher ground, and consequently somewhat cooler. We were still close to the river, surrounded by dark rocks, from every cleft of which the great cactuses thrust forth their pale, many-handed arms. They are such uncanny-looking plants that I am sure they must hold some place in the ghost stories of the land!

We agreed to sleep in the bungalow, so that we might get away sharp in the morning, and not have to waste time in packing the tents. We paid the penalty, however, for so doing, having been nearly consumed by sand flies, most aggravating little pests. It is bad enough to be bitten by some creature that you can pursue, but nothing can exceed the annoyance of these painful bites from invisible foes. Moreover, the house was literally swarming with flies, which clustered in black, disgusting masses on every crumb of bread, and every grain of sugar. Knowing that the next march was likely to be very hot after sunrise, we deemed it well to get as far as possible while the hill lay in shadow, as our route lay straight up its side. We were therefore astir at 3 A.M. in the cold grey morning. Somehow in this clear atmosphere less sleep seems necessary, and we wake feeling buoyant and up to anything. We are glad of all our extra wraps too, for even the invariable cup of hot chocolate cannot keep out the chill light breeze—that chill that always sets in before the dawn, 'twixt night and morning.

But for the noise of the river, from which we are now rising rapidly, there would be no sound to break the spell of silence which hangs around, save the calls and cries of wild birds welcoming the returning light. As we look upward from the deep shadow, we see the hill above us glowing like burnished gold against the bluest of blue skies, where delicate vapour-wreaths float like angel wings; and as the ruddy light of sunrise kisses the golden lichen on the rocks, they seem as though gleaming with living fire.

A few minutes later the sun clears the horizon, the light breeze falls, but we are still glad of our thick woollen raiment, to protect us from his burning rays. Such are the perpetual variations in this climate—so cold in the shade—so hot in the sun. One day in the depths of a tropical valley—the next in the heart of the snows. No wonder that many people find such variations sorely trying.

To-day our march was from Rampore to Gowrah, about eleven miles, up and down very steep hills, the track being partly cut into steps forming almost perpendicular stairs, very fatiguing to climb. We crossed sundry very pretty streams, and, as usual, passed through different belts of vegetation, varying with our altitude. Sometimes in the gloom of dark, pine-scented forests—then at some very low level, overshadowed by rich hard-wood. One variety of fragrant acacia especially delighted us, with its large blossoms like great bunches of floss silk.

On reaching the brow of the hill a glorious view opened before us, a foreground of rich foliage whence we looked down through deep masses of forest, far into the valley, where we caught glimpses of the river, beyond which rose tier above tier of great hills; and above all, a whole line of snow-peaks and rock pinnacles.

Oh! the delight of choosing the very spot, overlooking such a scene, where you may pitch your own dear little tent—knowing that in three minutes your home will be homelike. No bare walls of a ghoulish bungalow, perhaps still reeking with the tobacco of the last occupants, or full of buzzing flies attracted by their good cheer, but all your own cosy arrangements of rugs and boxes; and above all, the delight of having chosen your own pet nook, and the very best angle for your tent door, so as to see least of your own species, and most of the glorious scenery around you. Verily there is no such music as the hammering of your tent-pegs—the earnest of having secured a pleasant resting-place on totally new ground, where you may halt for exactly so long as you please, and then strike once more, to seek "Fresh woods and pastures new."

Of all pleasant camping-grounds I enjoyed none better than Gowrah; camped on the farthest angle of a little promontory, projecting into the valley, so as to look down on three sides into the deep gorge, or up a dark solitary chasm between bold, precipitous rocks, and there to sit alone,

> "Gazing on pathless glen and mountain high,
> Listing where from the cliffs the torrents thrown
> Mingle their echoes with the eagle's cry."

It only needs the shadow of murky vapours, and of dark thunder-clouds, such as are sure to rise ere long, and you get a touch of awe which gives the finishing stroke of delight. Then the sun will set, lurid and gloomy, throwing a warning, blood-red glow over the mountain-tops, and lighting up the dark, troubled sky, while the low rumbling of stormy voices suggests the awakening of all weird spirits.

CHAPTER XIV.

THE SACRED ARK.

Wild Apricots—"So Near and yet so Far"—Frugal Highlanders—Spoilt Milk!—Spinning—Sunwise Turns—The Ark of the Mountain Goddess—Sacrifices—Links to Judea—And to Abyssinia—Other Cars—Willows and Water-cresses—A Hateful Forced March—Sir Alexander Lawrence—Cholera—Able-bodied Women—Forest of Poindah.

At about this point we entered the region of wild apricot trees, which are scattered all over the steep hill-sides, and which were now laden with fruit, the golden crop attracting flocks of green pigeons. In the absence of more exciting game, these offered an irresistible target, and moreover proved excellent eating, as did also some *chickore*, the red-legged partridge; so with apricot tart, and wild apricots and raspberries for dessert, we dined as kings. The apricots, however, proved too much for poor blue-eyed Nanko the shikaree, who suffered so frightfully from unrequited attachment to unripe "plums," as he called them, that he utterly lost heart, and literally never smiled again. He, who had been the most zealous and energetic of the party, became so utterly wretched that he was allowed to return alone to the bosom of his family, beyond Simla, where he found consolation, and in due time rallied in health and spirits. I fear the poor fellow had been subjected to a good deal of "chaff," and chaff under such circumstances is apt to go against the grain!

At this place we came in for the only instance of dishonesty we ever heard of amongst these Paharis, whose general character in these matters is irreproachable, "Honest as a Pahari" being a proverbial expression.[1] In fact, theft is almost unknown, and these men carry treasures, which to them would be priceless, for days and days, along wild mountain tracks, whence at any moment they might diverge, and never be traced. Even money is safely entrusted to them, and is invariably delivered into the right hands, though they are as ready as their neighbours to haggle for a few pence in all their bargains.

The temptation which on this day proved too much for even Pahari honesty, was a wretched sheep in which we had invested, and on which our dinners for a couple of days depended. The sheep was duly tethered in a place of safety, whence, however, it shortly disappeared. Great was the hue and cry; great was the righteous indignation of the *chokedar*, who nevertheless was proved to be himself either the thief or the instigator of the theft. From his house was our unlucky mutton rescued, and the crestfallen expression of the whole man when thus detected was pitiful to behold. It was a dear sheep to him, as he was of course dismissed from a position of such trust.

For a chokedar is a sort of policeman who has charge of these bungalows, and is bound to provide coolies and any provisions that travellers may require, the general demand being for sheep, which the people are most unwilling to sell, though the full value is always given. But the people hate selling anything, however high the price offered.

A new feature of the hills here is that little shelves of table-land occur every here and there, on each of which is perched a village surrounded with terraced fields. Sometimes six or eight such villages are in sight at once, clustering all down the face of the hill; and the natives, when they want the men from some other village, instead of toiling up one *khad* and down another in search of them, stand at their own doors, and call their friends,

[1] This was somewhat dubiously expressed by a native, whose English was not altogether faultless, when called upon to give evidence in favour of a man accused of dishonesty. "Sir," said he, "I have known the accused for years, and am prepared to swear that his character is *unbleachable!*"

with a shrill intonation that seems to travel for miles, and you hear the voices echoing among the distant hills. Then the owner of the curious name, the Himalayan Donald or Ronald, responds in a shout which reaches you, mellowed by distance, and explains why he cannot come. So then Hugh or Ian are summoned, and these, having put a couple of large bannocks into their string bag, that they may be ready for all emergencies, start from the home, from which they may perhaps be absent for many days.

Perhaps, in addition to the bannocks, they will take with them an extra plaid and an extra supply of tobacco, and then they are ready for whatever may happen. This is all the provision they make for the longest march, for they are wonderfully frugal and abstemious—just like those old Highlanders who scorned the degenerate rising generation, when first it introduced the custom of taking a light breakfast of oatmeal before starting for the chase, and so necessitated the invention of new terms for the great and little meal, instead of the old word *Lon*, which was the only genuine Highland word for the daily meal. These men are almost invariably short and well knit; they are strong and hardy, game for any amount of work and fatigue, on what would seem to us starvation diet.

It has been noticed that this good qualification for a soldier is utterly wasted when hill regiments are raised from these tribes, as they are at once provided with the same luxuries as other troops, consequently there is the same necessity for a baggage train when on active service, a soldier's bedding and other gear being a fair load for a coolie. Think how astonished an agricultural Pahari must be to see his military brother thus equipped!

These Highlanders are sometimes very slack in keeping up distinctions of caste. They will constantly, as a matter of expediency, and for the good of trade, eat with the merchants from Tartary and Thibet. They will even sometimes accept a biscuit offered them by Englishmen, and are generally willing to share their meals one with another, provided they are *not cooked with water*. Hence each man must make his own bread; but should game be killed, they will roast it, and have no objection to sharing that, or fruit or dried grain. I fancy this distinction must exist also in the plains, as I have seen a high caste Brahman accept fruit from my hand, though I dared not offer a child a sugar-plum or a biscuit.

The Paharis are, however, by no means wholly free from the shackles of caste. One day a whole regiment of wretched-looking coolies came to us in great turmoil, declaring that they had proved Ratna, our head servant, to be the son of a cobbler, which is a very low caste, and that as he stood between them and the sun his shadow had fallen on their milk, and so they had been compelled to throw it away. Poor Ratna could not deny the foul impeachment, but meekly declared his willingness to pay for more milk and to remove his noxious shadow, and so the matter ended. In other matters the coolies fully recognized his authority as bear-leader, and were quite willing to honour him with the title of Gee.

These cobblers, or shoemakers, are treated almost as slaves by the villagers; they, and still lower castes, called Domes and Mehters, being compelled to do all the work, even to cultivating the land; and as they may have no land of their own, they only receive food in return for service done. Much of the farm work is done by women, while the men look after the cattle and spin. Every man you meet is invariably spinning. They work very slowly, but incessantly, carrying a bundle of loose, short wool in the breast of their blouse; a bit of stick does the work of a distaff, and so they prepare endless supplies of yarn, which they will afterwards weave into sonsy "home-spun" raiment.

I cannot say that this sort of spinning has the charm of our own old wheel, which, whether in cottage or in hall, in the hands of a grey-haired granny or of a beautiful and high-bred dame, certainly lends its aid in composing the most attractive of all home scenes, with its low humming murmur, winding on and on like some continuous old crooning song; soothing you into a delicious, dreamy, idleness, while you watch the play of the red firelight among its pleasant lines and curves.

This, however, is locomotive spinning, which allows of no idle hands. The coolie who waits for hours at your door, draws his distaff from his bosom, and lies in the sunshine at his work, and he who plods along the well-known road will, if not overburdened, spin half a hank before reaching the next village. Sheep-shearing occurs thrice a year, so the spinners must be diligent to keep pace with the supply.

One very curious custom prevails among these shepherds, which reminded us of the strange old Highland ceremony of the turn Deisul, or Sunwise, round all manner of objects, partly for luck, partly as a lingering trace of the sun-worship of our ancestors.[1] Here the villagers occasionally collect all their flocks into one great herd, and, walking at its head, lead it slowly round the village, following the course of the sun. They gradually quicken the pace to a run, and so go thrice or oftener right round the village.

The same turn sunwise occurs in various other instances. Thus in case of sickness or accident, sheep and goats are solemnly led twice or thrice round the sufferer, and then have their heads cut off. In the case of a rich man, many are thus sacrificed to divers demons, who are suspected of having enviously caused the mischief. Should the man recover, it is supposed that the demon has been propitiated; but should he die, it is said that doubtless the Almighty, who over-rules all lesser powers, has so willed it. To them this Great Spirit is a Being of infinite terror, to be served with exceeding fear; a mighty power that will send all manner of famine and disease, unless they are for ever striving to appease Him. As to anything in their faith that can gladden life—anything like love, or companionship, or daily help, *that* is utterly unknown, and quite incomprehensible.

Nevertheless they say the God of gods requires no sacrifice—only worship. Their sacrifices, therefore, are offered to the lesser gods and demons; sometimes merely offerings of sweetmeats and such delicacies, or even flowers. This notion of propitiating evil spirits, is, however, by no means peculiar to the hill tribes, for the

[1] See *In the Hebrides*, C. F. Gordon Cumming, pages 241-245. Chatto and Windus.

whole Hindoo race are from their cradles to their graves haunted by the fear of demons—malignant beings who ever find pleasure in doing them harm, causing illness and trouble—loss and disaster.

These demons are assorted in numerous classes, concerning whom stories innumerable are told. Some are dwarfish monsters —some are tall as palm-trees. A horrid kind are the man-eating Rakshasas, who keep their souls in parrots, and who are so bold that they even dare to disturb holy rites and harass saints.

Then there are the Bhūtas, the spirits of men who have been eaten by tigers, or have died a violent death from any cause, and have not received proper funeral rites. There are also Pisāća demons, who are embodied ghosts of very wicked men, and Pretas, who are restless spirits of cripples or deformed persons, sufferers during life and after death; no wonder that such spirits should be malignant, ever on the watch to do evil, and woe betide the man who yawns and neglects to cover his mouth, or snap his fingers—a watchful spirit may dart down his throat, and thenceforth establish himself within, feeding on the food swallowed by the man. A demon specially dreaded by women is the spirit of a woman who has died within fifteen days after childbirth, for her special joy is to attack all young mothers.

There are, however, some points of especial interest in the worship of these mountain tribes. Some of their sacrifices are most solemn, and suggestive of old patriarchal days. The people assemble in the dark cedar forest, and set up an altar of unhewn stones, whereon fire is kindled, and sheep and goats are offered for a burnt-offering.

In spite of their belief in the thirty-three millions of good and evil spirits, their worship seems to be not so much directed to general deities as to the special god of each village, to whom is dedicated a picturesque temple of cedar-wood, somewhat resembling a Swiss châlet, and enriched with a good deal of ornamental wood-carving. Within this temple there is a draped shrine, forming a sort of ark, wherein dwells a veiled image of the Devi, or goddess. This ark is, fastened to long poles and is carried out in state for a daily airing. In front of the temple there is a circular platform, in the centre of which stands a sort of summer-house (simply a cedar-wood roof, supported by pillars of the same). Beneath this shelter, which is called a Dharmsalah, the ark is deposited, while the worshippers circle around, dancing or making music.

Once a year, about the middle of July, this mysterious veiled goddess is carried in most solemn procession, when all the people of the village assemble, and dance before the ark, from the greatest man to the least. Above this tabernacle, which is draped with hangings of some bright material, is generally set a brazen head, having four or more faces, above which nod huge plumes of dark or scarlet wool; they are yaks' tails, such as are used on the plains to brush away flies from the presence of great men. Sometimes other faces of polished metal are set all round the tabernacle, and glance in the sun as the procession moves on. Generally a deep fringe of silky, white yaks' tails hangs all round, reaching almost to the ground, effectually concealing the bodies of the men who carry the goddess, so that she seems to be stalking along, like some hideous centipede, with black legs; (an effect, by the way, which constantly occurs to you as a string of grass-cutters comes along a road, each presenting the curious appearance of an immense load of grass moving on two lean black legs).

The ark is escorted by attendants waving chowries, to keep off the flies, and musicians who produce a hideous din by the aid of very large trumpets, four or five feet in length, some straight and some curved, but all alike torturing to the ear! Though there is no Brahmanical priesthood here, each village has a set of people devoted to the service of the temple. The men must beat a *reveillé* at dawn in honour of the gods, and to waken the villagers, and in the evening the same sound of unmusical shells, bells, and cymbals, acts as a combination of curfew and evensong. Although these people only think it necessary to wash themselves and their clothes twice a year in honour of their principal festivals, the goddess must be washed and dressed daily in water scented with leaves of wild mint, which grows near the well, and is gathered as a daily offering; incense also is burnt before the Devi.

Some of the more solemn festivals are made the occasion of immense gatherings of all the tribes. Each village sends forth its ark, accompanied by all the women and most of the men, dressed in their gayest holiday suit, and covered with all their jewels, so it is a very bright and festive gathering. They sing and dance as they go, and play all manner of antics. The ark is carried by specially appointed men, the leader walking backwards to avoid

DEVI AT CHEENEE, SUTLEJ VALLEY.

turning his back to the goddess. I do not think any of the other worshippers ever touch it; certainly they would on no account have allowed us to do so, or to obtain even a glimpse of the veiled presence within the curtains, though these, being sometimes blown aside by the breeze, might otherwise have revealed some hint of the beauties of Durgâ Pârvati, she being the pet goddess in these hills.

They call this tabernacle of their god a Khuda. As they carry it along up the hills and through the forests, all present must dance and sing. Probably the forest sanctuary whither they are bound is one of those temples of rudely carved cedar-wood, which we so constantly see, beneath any remarkably fine group of trees; for

> "The simple savage, whose untutored mind
> Sees God in cloud, and hears Him in the wind,"

believes that such fair trees are His chosen dwelling-place; so they are spoken of as "the trees of God," and wherever a little temple shows that the spot is held sacred by the Paharis, the Government officers who have charge of the forests are bound to respect that place, and the stately timbers are spared from the ruthless axe, which else would have turned them all into railway sleepers. So all we, who love these glorious monarchs of the forest, have good cause to rejoice over the reverence which protects these choice cedar trees, "the trees of the Lord, even the cedars which He hath planted."

Near this little temple there is generally a space artificially levelled, perhaps paved. Here the Khuda is laid down. Perhaps other villagers have assembled, bringing their Khudas, and all the people rejoice greatly, and for, perhaps, three days, they keep up their sacred mirth; and the sellers of grain make rather a good thing of it, for they set up their little white tents and booths and provide divers refreshments for the hungry dancers. Every now and then the Khuda is lifted from the ground, and carried in a little circle, sunwise, while the huge plumes wave and shake, keeping time to the rude music; and an outer circle of men, joining hands, dance a wild dance, all keeping step. Then the idol is once more deposited, and all the people make obeisance, while the dance continues; and the women, linked in one long undulating chain, go on circling round the Khuda, strange to say, moving with their left hand toward the centre, consequently making a contra-sunwise turn.

They are linked together with one arm; each woman, clasping her neighbour by the waist, keeps the other arm free, and therewith, as she bows to the Khuda, she waves a plume-like chowrie or yak's tail; not all waving together, but in rapid succession, so that the wave of motion never ceases, but rolls for ever and for ever with singularly graceful action. When one woman is tired, another slips into her place; sometimes the men form the circle, then both men and women join, and keep up the same winding and turning, circling round and round. And when night comes, great fires are lighted and torches of pine wood, and still the wild dance goes on, and the incessant monotonous music of tom-toms and great trumpet shells (*sankhs*) and other discordant instruments never ceases, as you will have good cause to know, should your camp be pitched too near these sacred revels.

At length, when their energies are exhausted, the meeting breaks up, the annual festival is over, and each group of villagers carries their patron goddess back to her own temple, while the rest of the congregation disperses in little groups along every path, up hill and down dale.

A ceremony so strange, naturally sets one wondering what it all means, and how it all originated; various suggestions have been made as to the possibility that some tradition may have reached even these remote hills of that Sacred Ark whereby the Hebrews were taught to realize the actual Presence of the Most High.

That some legends of a remote past still linger in these mountains is well known, as for instance that tradition of the Deluge which tells how Manu and the Seven Sages built them a mighty ship, wherein were stored seed of all living things, and how Brahma, taking the form of a great fish (in whose honour, it may be, that so many fish are still held sacred, and preserved in all the tanks), rescued this ship, when the Great Deluge came and overwhelmed the earth. And Brahma drew the ship for many days, till at length it rested on one high peak of the Himalayas, to which he bound the vessel. And the mountain has ever since borne the name of *Naubandhana*, which means the fastening of the boat. Which peak bears this name, the people themselves do not know, but this is their legend; it is, however, one which they hold in common with many other nations, and need prove no connection with Judea.

It would certainly be deeply interesting to know if any such connection had at any time existed. Some have even fancied that they might here find traces of the lost tribes of Israel, and have pointed out various other resemblances between the simple, primitive religious ceremonies of these people and those of the old patriarchs.

I believe the first person who called attention to these remarkable Arkite ceremonies was my friend Mr. William Simpson, who spent a couple of months at the village of Cheenee, in this

KHUDA OF A POOR VILLAGE.

valley, closely observing the manners and customs of his neighbours, and reproducing all these striking scenes in admirable water-colour sketches. To him I am indebted for the accompanying illustrations of the Khuda and prayer-wheels (I may remark, that when I visited Cheenee the Khuda had been enriched by offerings of so many yaks' tails as to form a fringe sweeping the ground).

He was vividly impressed by the strongly defined Jewish type of countenance, so common among these people. Still more was he struck by the strange similarity of their heathen worship with certain parts of the old Jewish ceremonial. "Here," he says, "are a people, scarcely one of whom had ever been a dozen miles from their own village. It was almost impossible for a single idea from the outer world to reach them. Yet they had been practising the most ancient rites of worship, which must have remained shut up and unaltered in that wild valley for ages."

He goes on to tell how the people, having indulged in the rare luxury of a good (ceremonial) washing a few days previously, had assembled at the village of Coatî to do homage to the strange mysterious Khuda; that many-headed goddess whose faces only appear above the covered box, or ark, or tabernacle, the veil from which is never withdrawn, and which no stranger is allowed to touch. Only, as we have already observed, her devout worshippers are honoured by being allowed to carry this ark by turns, by means of long poles attached to it, and one must walk backward so that both may face her holiness.

Thus borne, and escorted by all the great men of the village, dancing before this their goddess, to the tune of drums, trumpets, cymbals, and horns, her procession came winding through the primeval forest, and through deep, dark glens, till they reached a temple, standing alone near some grand old cedars. In front of this was a roughly paved court, precisely similar to the threshing-floors in common use. Here they deposited their ark in front of the temple of carved cedar wood. A village patriarch with strikingly Jewish features, who officiated as priest, and wore a red robe like those of the Lamas in this district, washed all the faces of the goddess with mint leaves and water, then he offered incense, flowers, fruit, and bread.

As my personal acquaintance with the Khuda was limited to its ordinary processions, and I was never present at one of these sacrifices, I must give you Mr. Simpson's most interesting description of this in his own words. He says: "A number of playful young kids were now brought forward, and Dilloo, the patriarch, sprinkled them with water. A large flat brazen dish was placed on the ground, and one of the villagers stood ready with an ornamental sacred hatchet belonging to the temple. With one blow he struck off the head of the kid; then the priest's assistant raised the head, and advancing to the Khuda presented it, muttering certain words. *He put his finger into the blood, and then by a jerk flicked it upon the idol. Thus the blood was 'sprinkled.'* After doing this once or twice, *he dipped his fore-finger into the blood and touched the Khuda with it.* The head was then deposited with the other offerings. Meanwhile the body of the kid had been so placed that all the blood ran into the brazen vessel, and when two or three animals had been sacrificed and the dish was full, one of the men lifted it up, and, first

DILLOO, A MOUNTAIN PATRIARCH.

presenting it to the Khuda, turned round, and giving a great swing of his body, *emptied the blood against the whitewashed wall of the temple.* This ceremony was thrice repeated."[1]

A curious sort of game was now played, whence the festival takes its name, the *Akrot-ka-pooja*, or Walnut Festival. The priest and a few companions having ascended to a balcony in the temple, all the young men present assailed them with volleys of walnuts and green pine-cones ; these the men on the balcony gathered up, and threw back at their assailants. This quaint

[1] Compare Exodus xxix. 12, 16.

fight lasted half an hour, when the besieged descended, and once more mixed with the throng. Mr. Simpson failed to ascertain the meaning of this ceremony, but alludes to the frequent occurrence of the pine-cone as a religious emblem in the Assyrian sculptures, and to its ornamental use in Cashmere and throughout India and Central Asia.

It is doubtless due to this symbolic sanctity of the cone, wherein lie cradled the germs of life, that some special idea of reverence seems attached to so many of the coniferous tribe, as we may gather from many of the native names for divers kinds of fir trees.

Thus, the Abies Morinda, that weeping fir, whose long pensile branches are laden with narrow cones, sometimes six inches in length, is here called the Khudrow, a name signifying, in the native dialect, "sacred tears," in reference to the resinous drops which exude from the cones and bark, and which are made into cakes as offerings for the gods. The name is of course derived from the same source as Khuda.

Of the Indian Silver Fir, known to botanists as Picea Webbiana, both wood and cones are, or were, used by preference in the offering of burnt-sacrifice. Its cones are long and narrow varying from four to six inches in length, and are of a purply-green colour.

As to the Sacred Cedar, the Deodar (or, as it is called by the natives, and in the sacred Shâstras—Devadara or Devadaru), its name, whether derived from the Sanskrit *Deva* or the Latin *Deus*, alike describes the stately cedars as emphatically the Trees of God. The second syllable, variously rendered as Da or Do—Dara—Daru, may be translated, the gift—the spouse—the wood, but all alike denote the sanctity of the tree.

While the young men and priests were engaged in pelting one another with these sacred cones and walnuts, the slaughtered kids were being cooked, ready for the solemn feast which followed. Then "the people having seated themselves all round upon the space before the Khuda, the cakes and flesh were dealt out to them and eaten. *The women were helped before the men*, which is altogether foreign to Eastern custom."

Just as the people were preparing to return home, the Khuda commenced shaking violently, and in some mysterious manner, and so intimated its intention of visiting the neighbouring village of Cheenee. It was at once obeyed. The people recommenced singing and dancing with all their might, and were in a state of wild excitement. The trumpets sounded, the tomtoms were beaten, and the strange procession went on its way through the dark forest. Some of the men ran on before to give warning to the authorities of the honour in store for them. So at the confines of the village of Cheenee, the rival goddess was waiting with her trumpets and drums to receive her guest with all due honour. The two Khudas spent a night together, after which the lady of Coati returned to take care of her own dominions.

Now turn to the description of a very different scene; a scene nevertheless which has points of resemblance so strange as surely to imply some traditional link in far bygone times. It is a story of Judea, of the return of that "Ark of God which dwelleth within curtains," that Holy Place within the vail, into which even the high priest might enter but once a year, with the offering of sweet incense, and the blood of atonement, wherewith to sprinkle the mercy seat.

The king and thirty thousand of his men had gone to fetch the ark, to bring it to the city of David, and they set the Ark of God upon a new cart. And David and all the house of Israel accompanied the ark. And they played before God with all their might, on all manner of instruments, made of fir-wood; even on harps, and on psalteries, and on timbrels, and on cornets, and on cymbals, and with singing, and with trumpets. But, ere long, the oxen stumbled, and Uzzah put forth his hand to hold the ark. And the anger of the Lord was kindled against Uzzah, and God smote him there for his error, because he put his hand to the ark, and there he died before God. Then David was afraid to bring the terrible ark to his city.

But after three months he took courage, and remembered that "none ought to carry the Ark of God but the Levites, for them hath the Lord chosen to carry it," so he called the priests and told them, that because they had not sought GOD after due order, therefore He had made this breach upon them. So they sanctified themselves, and carried the ark upon their shoulders, *with the staves thereon.* And with them were a great company singing, and playing on instruments of music. And David danced before the LORD with all his might. So he and all the house of Israel brought up the Ark of the LORD with shouting and with the voice of the trumpet. "And they brought in the Ark of the LORD, and set it in his place, in the midst of the tabernacle that David had pitched for it, and David offered burnt-offerings and peace-offerings before the LORD. . . . And he dealt among all the people, even among the whole multitude of Israel, *as well to the women as men*, to every one a cake of bread and a good piece of flesh." Then all the people returned, every man to his own house.[1]

I think we must admit that the trumpery, tawdry ark, wherein the poor Pahari reverences a presence, which he desires to honour, has, to say the least of it, some curious affinities to that glorious Tabernacle of the Israelites. Even the coincidence in size is very remarkable, the measurement of the holy ark being generally reckoned at two and a-half feet in width and height, while the length was something under four feet. The proportions of the Khuda are slightly variable, being probably decided by rule of thumb, still they approximate roughly to the above.

The name of this Himalayan ark and some of the ceremonies connected with it are also singularly suggestive of certain customs in that strange Abyssinian Church which still continues to blend some trace of Jewish tradition with its Christian ritual. The priests have a legend which tells that when Menelik, son of the Queen of Sheba, was sent to Palestine for his education, he was on his return accompanied thence by many Jews, in compliance with the advice of King Solomon, a fact which fully accounts for all the Jewish colonies in Abyssinia. Amongst these emigrants were many of the chief priests, who, however, were greatly averse to deprive themselves of the guiding presence of the holy ark. They therefore made one exactly similar, which they contrived to

[1] 2 Sam. vi. 17-19.

substitute for the original, and thus were able to carry the real ark to Abyssinia, where it is now concealed in the Church of Axum, none save the primate, or high priest, being allowed to enter that Tabernacle or look on that most holy thing. The Governor of Axum is known by a title signifying "Keeper of the Ark." But although this city alone claims possession of the true Ark, each church, like the modern Jewish synagogue, has, within its inner sanctuary, a representation thereof, supported by wooden posts, which have been fashioned without the use of any instrument of steel or iron.[1] Here the priests consecrate the sacred sacramental elements, and at each division of the service they march three times, sunwise, round the ark, carrying the cross, the book, and the incense.

This Holy of Holies is hidden from the congregation by a heavy curtain or veil. The part of the church which surrounds this most holy place is called the Kudist, answering to Kodesh, the name by which the Hebrews describe the sanctuary, while the title Kudosh, or holy, is uttered before the name of any Christian saint. Moreover in the Mohammedan catalogue of the ninety-nine titles of the Almighty we find Kuddūs, the Holy One. So the Himalayan Khuda shows its origin pretty plainly by its title and its affinities.

Its existence, however, is not confined to these regions. When Mr. Simpson, who first called attention to these Abyssinian arks, pursued his travels into Japan, he there also found small *arks carried on staves*, in religious processions, and I have myself seen them used in Ceylon both by Buddhists and Tamils. The former thus carried a small ark containing only a golden lotus blossom. The latter, at Ratnapoora, and probably elsewhere, have a full-sized ark, wherein, on great festivals, are deposited the sacred arrows of Rama, which are brought forth from an inner sanctuary, and closely veiled from the curious gaze by heavy curtains, while,

[1] In all Celtic superstitions it was believed that the touch of steel or iron deprived sacred plants of all mystic virtue. In Rome also a statute of the Twelve Tables commanded that the funeral pyre should be built of wood *untouched by the axe*.

mid music and dancing, the ark is borne on staves, and the car of Jagannáth is dragged round the precincts of the Temple, as it is in many an Indian village.

Having made the most of a day's halt at Gowrah we again pushed on, up and down the steepest of braes, sometimes crossing streams clear as crystal, overshadowed by the exquisite acacia with blossoms like pink and white floss silk. The wild apricot-trees were loaded with fruit, and mulberry, walnut, and pear-trees all gave promise of an abundant crop. The people were busy harvesting in the tiny, narrow ridges, sometimes not four feet wide, which act as fields, even these being artificially levelled all down the hill-side. The reapers cut the heads off the grain and burn the straw as it stands, to enrich the land; straw, remember, which stands six or eight feet, the size of the ear being in proportion. The heads they carry home, and throwing them on the flat roofs of their houses, or on a threshing-floor, they beat out the grain, and shaking it against the wind, winnow the grain from the chaff. (Just so did our Anglo-Saxon forefathers nearly two thousand years ago, according to an old Sicilian historian,[1] who, writing a hundred years before Christ, described the mode of gathering the harvest in Britain, when the reapers cut off the ears of corn and carried them home, to be stored in underground granaries.) I generally saw women at this work, sometimes very handsome girls, whose well-shaped bare arms were clasped by large silver armlets, and their wrists covered with bracelets, their ankles and their toes being likewise adorned.

This night our halt was at Serahan, where we found a house so large and so comfortable that we had no excuse for putting up the tents. An excellent garden supplied us with abundant vegetables of all sorts, even to artichokes. Close to the house rises the brightest of crystal springs, overshadowed by weeping-willows, and the clear stream which flows thence is full of the most delicious watercresses. These were found in divers streams along the route. The natives did not seem to know their excellence, and looked rather astonished at our gathering them,

[1] Diodorus Siculus.

but they soon tried the experiment for themselves with evident satisfaction.

With unspeakable pleasure we rested beneath the shade of those beautiful drooping willows, nibbling the fresh green cresses, or drinking from the clear bubbling spring just for love of its beauty. Some months later, on a dull grey day in Edinburgh, I alluded to this Himalayan paradise, and a lady,[1] then unknown to me, replied that she knew it well, for she had lived in that bungalow for months while her husband was employed in engineering the road, and that she herself had planted both the willows and the watercresses. I think her name ought to be inscribed in letters of gold beside the fountain, that all future travellers in these wilds may bless it!

Just above this bungalow stands the summer palace of the Rajah of Bassahir, whose winter quarters we had seen on the cliff at Rampore. He intimated his intention of honouring us with a visit, but fortunately for us, was too drunk to do so. The situation of his palace is beautiful, as is that of all the grounds hereabouts. A beautiful mixture of grey rock, terraced fields, and dark foliage (horse-chestnuts, I think) extending far down the steep hill-side to the brink of the river, while right overhead the grand snow line towers far above the clouds, its gleaming white broken by quaint pinnacles of black rock. The tiny villages on the hill-side seem numberless and very picturesque; the houses are a good deal like Swiss châlets.

Groups of lads and lassies in holiday attire, were assembling from all these, and making for one point on the hill-side, where some festivity was going on, which was kept up all night long, for the music and dancing never ceased. One very handsome woman, whose dress was of unusually rich colours, and the weight of her jewels startling, came and fraternised with us, showing us her finery with a very pretty half-bashful manner. From her nose to her toes she was covered with ornaments. I regret to say that her toes were not adorned with bells, only with rings. As to her ears, she must have had fully a dozen rings in each. Her dress and

[1] Mrs. Houchin.

plaid were, as usual, of striped wool, very heavy, and of brilliant colours. The heavy fold at the back was precisely the pannier then in fashion in London, and the large chignon differed only from that of our dames in that, instead of being made of some convict's hair, it was of scarlet wool—a foil to the silkiest black hair and clear olive complexion. Of course she wore the invariable plaits of black worsted hanging down her back like false plaits attached to the scarlet chignon, and on her head the usual round woollen hat, with scarlet top, and a bunch of sweet yellow roses stuck in coquettishly in front.

No one was more delighted with beautiful Serahan than our excellent dhobie, who here found such facilities for his laundry work as rarely fell to his lot. Imagine the feelings of a British laundry-maid at being turned adrift on these hills with a large washing to do, when and how she could, in any stream she came to. Then having to bundle up her wet heavy linen and get it dried and ironed as best she might, marching twelve or fourteen miles between each process!

So the dhobie, like ourselves, rejoiced in being at rest in pleasant quarters, and would fain have lingered for many days. Imagine, therefore, his dismay and ours, when a detestable baboo, who was himself hurrying on to a farther point, and who had received orders to make himself generally useful to us, came up, and in most fluent English poured forth a stream of eloquence, to prove what frightful danger we should incur by halting many hours at the next point, namely Tranda, where cholera was raging, and the people were dying "like rotten sheep," as the saying is; that, therefore, we must arrive there late one evening, and leave again at daybreak. This might have been excellent advice for a future day; but he pointed out such difficulties that would attend our attempt to get coolies there without his valuable assistance—in fact, the impossibility of our doing so—and he was altogether so determined that we should push on at once, that in a weak moment (oh, how weak!) we gave in.

Again the poor dhobie bundled up his half-washed goods; again we packed our books, our bedding, our divers treasures, and with very heavy hearts turned away from the willows by the water-courses—to say nothing of the watercresses—where we had purposed spending so peaceful a Sunday, or rather a Sabbath, of welcome rest.[1] Already the sun was high in the heavens, and of course all the coolies were scattered all over the fields at their work. However, the baboo would have his way; so he despatched messengers to all the villages, and they were gradually collected. By midday a small detachment of unwilling men had arrived, and were got under weigh, together with half the servants. Then Mrs. Graves and I started; she, with her unflagging energy on foot, I, as usual in the dandie. The march was unusually long, ostensibly fourteen miles, but certainly a good deal more; with perpetual ascents and descents of very steep khads. Certainly it was wonderfully lovely, both for mountain views and beauty of foreground.

We passed the Drali Cliff, where a stone cross marks the scene of a terrible accident. It is the place where Sir Alexander Lawrence was killed. The path, which is now blasted on the face of the precipice, was then in places carried over wooden

[1] It doubtless sounds strange to ears unaccustomed to Indian manners to hear Sunday spoken of by Christians as a suitable day for laundry and other household work, and certain old words relative to "thy man-servant, and thy maid-servant, and the stranger that is within thy gates," very naturally suggest themselves. Probably the extreme laxity of Sunday observance among white men and women may in great measure account for its total disregard by their household. In point of fact, the gardeners and the tailors are the only members of an Indian establishment who, as a matter of course, take their Sunday holiday; and it certainly is a dubious question whether there is much advantage in enforcing an institution which, of course, is nowise binding on the conscience of men who have their own innumerable fasts and festivals to attend to. For instance, while the Mohammedan servants are required to observe Friday, the Hindoos must on Saturday make their offerings to Hanuman, the Monkey-god, while Monday is sacred to Maha-deva, "the Great Lord," *i.e.* Siva, whose wife Durga claims the eighth day in every lunar fortnight, when all study is prohibited.

Moreover, in the matter of day-labourers, such as coolies, whether working for Government or for private individuals, no work means no pay—a very serious consequence of a compulsory (and to them) unmeaning holiday, which is no *holyday*.

bridges, which lay across frightful chasms. Sir Alexander was

THE DRALI CLIFF.

riding a heavy horse, at rather a quick pace, along this dangerous ground, when one of the bridges gave way, and he was hurled down an appalling distance—sheer down to one of the clear streams which flow into the Sutlej. His horse was stopped half-way by a projecting rock. It is said that his dog, unable to follow his master, turned back to meet Sir John Lawrence, and so conveyed the first dread that some mischief had befallen his nephew.

It was late in the afternoon before Captain Graves, having got all the baggage started, was able to overtake us, happily accompanied by one coolie with a kilta of provisions; so at sunset we halted beside a delicious stream, in the greenest ferny dell, with overarching trees, and did most thoroughly enjoy our dinner, as did also a sheep which was marching with us, ready for future use, but which in the meantime proved itself a genuine cannibal, and ate up every scrap of mutton that we could spare. Then on we went again.

My dandie-bearers had proved a weak lot from the beginning, and I had walked fully half way. A good deal of the path lay along the edge of a precipice, where a false step of either coolie would have sent us down thousands of feet. As the darkness closed in, the men stumbled so that I had to give up the attempt to use the dandie, and we all struggled along on foot in the starlight. Presently the men lighted blazing torches, which are made of bundles of long resinous splinters bound together. Each torch is about three feet long, and burns for nearly half an hour, so that one man can carry such a supply as will last for hours. We passed sundry encampments of wild-looking Paharis and Thibet merchants, whose tents and blazing fires were most picturesque, especially one lot, who were camped beside a clear, beautiful stream.

The last two miles, up a very steep hill, seemed interminable; and it was ten o'clock before we reached Tarandah road bungalow. Oh! but we were weary, weary, and oh! how glad to be at rest! Most of the servants and coolies never appeared till ten o'clock the next morning, having yielded to the attractions of the comfortable fires by the way. Happily the cook was not among the defaulters, and with the usual amazing power these men have of girding themselves to serve their masters, after the longest march, he rapidly gave us hot tea and other good things. Happily, too, one bundle of bedding had arrived, which we divided, and soon slept the sleep of utter exhaustion.

As usual I woke with the dawn to see the snow peaks far overhead, glowing in the red morning light; and to revel in the fragrant scent of pines that came wafted from the dark cedar forest close by. Everything felt strangely solemn and still. Hardly a breath stirred in the valley, and never a sound, save the deep, hoarse roar of the Sutlej, hidden in the chasm far below. It was a most unusual silence, for generally the voices of the villagers calling to one another from hill to hill make anything but mountain stillness. This strange hush would therefore generally have been most welcome. To-day, however, it spoke only of pestilence and death, of a valley decimated by cholera—mysterious and terrible scourge—from which the affrighted villagers had fled, no one knew whither; they and their wives, and their little ones, their flocks and their herds, to seek a refuge in some remote corner of their mountain fastnesses, until the evil hour was past, and the Angel of Death had passed on, weary of lingering where there were none to smite.

The cholera had been capricious as usual in its selection of victims. Not those homes only which lay low in the valley, in the hot steaming miasma, had yielded their dead, but those in the clear pure air, perched on the edge of such cliffs as ensured their own good drainage, had likewise suffered. And even at this very house, the servant of an Englishman who had but passed through the valley had died within a few hours. It was hard to realise that such danger lurked in so fair a spot, where the bright sunlight glanced so pleasantly on the slopes of vivid green turf, and chequered the cedar shade with such sparkling gleams. Nevertheless, it was the part of wisdom to hurry on, so we watched anxiously for the arrival of the truants.

Meanwhile a party of merchants from Ladawk came up, terribly dirty, but the women loaded with quaint jewels. They brought with them a poor fellow who had just fallen from a high tree, and was considerably damaged. They wanted *dawai* (medicine), but were well satisfied with a supply of rum, which was all we had to give. It was with some satisfaction that we saw him some days afterwards decidedly on the mend, and knew our treatment had not fevered our patient. Few of these men are above the vanities of dress, and they generally wear some quaint jewel or charm. This poor fellow had a large tuft of peacock's feathers in his cap, which were all broken and draggled by his fall, giving a most comic-pathetic look to the group as they came up.

Most of these people have no knowledge whatever of medicine, not even of the medicinal properties of their own herbs. Their one idea is the use of fresh turpentine from the pines as a poultice, or of cedar oil for skin complaints. Firing, as an Englishman would fire a horse, is a favourite remedy for all manner of pains. Nevertheless they have a perfect passion for physic of all sorts, and were continually asking for dawai, and putting unlimited faith in our prescriptions. The most popular medicine is quinine, especially with the servants from the plains, who are very liable to get a touch of fever.

The demand for quinine is apt to become so heavy that it is sometimes well to substitute *chiretta*, a tonic and intensely bitter febrifuge, which is by no means so popular or so expensive, and which is a fair test whether they really need it or not. *Chiretta* can be purchased in most villages, whereas, to run short of quinine would be serious indeed. As a general rule, however, a *petit verre* of spirits is the best medicine to administer at random. This *shrab*, as they call it, is a forbidden luxury, but so long as we call it medicine their consciences are at rest—much on the same principle as the lax Mohammedans evade the sumptuary laws of the Koran, and declare that one drop of vinegar poured into a cask of wine changes the prohibited beverage into one worthy of an Islamite.

Our friend, the baboo, had kept faith with us, and in due time fresh coolies arrived. I must do him the justice to confess that without his aid we probably could not have captured any in this cholera-smitten district, but the summons of a great man's head clerk was one which none dared to disobey. Henceforward fully half our daily supply of coolies were women—women of wonderful strength, though often fragile in appearance, with pleasant refined faces. Others were great strapping wenches, who shouldered loads from which I have often seen a railway porter shrink, while these girls carried them for a whole weary march up and down these dreadful hills with never a murmur—and that for the beggarly sixpence a day! Not only did the women never murmur, but they constantly laughed and chattered all the way, chaffing the men, who worked twice as well in consequence.

I suppose this is common work for women in other parts of India, as we were told that when the Madras cavalry were on active service in Bengal, a number of wild-looking women followed their lords, often doing the work of syces in grooming the horses, and always acting as grass-cutters; a sort of foraging that sometimes involved long, wearisome expeditions in addition to their day's march. Perhaps we might see something of the same sort nearer home, for some of our Highland lassies can carry a very fair burden for many a long mile. I remember seeing one delicate-looking little woman in Skye shoulder a heavy chest that had arrived by the steamer, and march across the steep hills up and down for fully twelve miles to her home. So our maidens are not altogether *fusionless*,[1] even compared with these Himalayan damsels!

As soon as the truant servants and coolies arrived, we at once made a fresh start for Poindah, a very short and beautiful march along the face of a steep hill with long slopes of greenest grass. The higher ridges and crests hereabouts are generally of gneiss intersected by granite veins. Masses of limestone and sandstone, however, crop up in various places, giving varied character both of form and colour. We halted by a cool waterfall in a deep, wooded valley, where all the coolies, men and women,

[1] Without strength.

bathed in the clear stream which comes rushing and tumbling down through Poindah forest; above which rise a succession of dark solemn hills clothed with divers varieties of pine, and topped with snowy crests.

Poindah itself is a beautiful spot with a foreground of great boulders of grey rock and fine foliage, and with three distinct views, each more beautiful than the other. On the one hand we looked up to the Babee snows, while right in front of us lay a long reach of the river, with precipitous cliffs, and a distant vision of yet more snows. Then when the eye wearied with gazing on those glittering peaks and the dazzling blue of heaven, it turned with a sense of relief to rest on the sombre hues of the changeless cedar forest which clothed the deep gorge on our right. A night of heavy rain gave us soft fleecy mists in the morning's sunshine. A scene more peaceful and beautiful could hardly be devised, and we drank greedily of its loveliness, dreading the summons that should once more bid us hurry on and forsake that happy valley.

CHAPTER XV.

THE CEDAR SHADE.

Mirage—Sungri Forest—Smokers—Cholera—New Arrivals—After the Storm—Himalayan Bridges and Roads—Stupendous Cliffs.

A SUCCESSION of soft grey days were pleasantly in keeping with the dark forest scenery now around us, where every hill wore that sombre hue which marks a forest wholly composed of resinous trees, albeit of many species. On every side were dark ravines clothed with the same everlasting pine, where in the brightest midday the gloomy shadows of night still lingered. Sometimes a gust of wild wind came moaning down the gorge, tossing the dark plumes of the morinda and rye pines, as though the shadowy spirits of the forest were wailing dirges for all their dead. And far above this broad cedar shade the snowy peaks stood out, pure, cold, and majestic in the unbroken stillness of a solitude where no foot of man or goat could rest, the ice-mountains and realms of eternal snow, in whose dark and dreary caverns dwell only the awful giants of the frost.

Some travellers in these regions have told us that sometimes, when the deep valley is filled with level mist so as to give the impression of a quiet lake lying in deep repose, the illusion has been infinitely heightened by its actually reflecting inverted grey rocks and trees with all their trembling shadows ; a very lovely species of mirage, which we had not the good fortune to see.

About two miles from Poindah lies Sungri forest; the first place where we really saw something of the glory of old deodars. Here, thanks, I believe, to the especial request of Lady Canning, a little corner of the forest has been left untouched, and groups of magnificent old cedars, some well-nigh thirty feet in girth, still hold their ground as they have probably done for a thousand years or more.

We were told that on the more inaccessible spots scores of such trees of even larger growth, perhaps twelve feet in diameter at six feet from the ground, are still common enough; but alas! for this age of utilitarianism, wherever it has been possible to bring this precious timber to market, the monarchs of the forest have been ruthlessly felled, and their poor scarred logs, tossed from khad to khad, floated down torrents, and finally committed to the foaming rivers to be for weeks the sport of mocking waters, at length to be drawn ashore on the burning plains, hundreds of miles from their birthplace, and consigned to some timber-merchant's yard. The value of this timber is such as to make it worth any amount of labour; as when well seasoned it is almost imperishable; those bridges for instance which are built of deodar logs are considered a *fait accompli* once and for ever.

Here, however, for once, a morsel of primeval forest remains intact, and very grand it is. These cedars rarely exceed a hundred and twenty or at most a hundred and fifty feet in height, but their flat branches reach out laterally on every side, forming a great pyramid of dark green with a sunlit edge, and dozens of large pale-green cones resting on each flat layer. So when your eyes are dazzled with gazing on snows, you turn with double delight to look down into the cool depths of this delicious darkness. Only here and there a solitary sun-ray falls on the silvery grey rocks with their golden-brown lichens, or on the carpets of delicate ferns and mosses which flourish in the deep, rich leaf-mould. But the ferns and mosses find no welcome on the great grey and red stems and mighty branches of the old trees. When after the rains they cover every bough of the oak and other hard wood, I do not think you will find one green frond so venturesome as to take root on the cedars.

In this old forest I lingered alone for many pleasant hours of the sleepy midday, listening to every harmonious whisper of wind and stream and corrie; all nature's voiceless melodies for ever murmuring low "songs without words" in dreamy delicious cadences—such music as Mother Nature sits crooning in the deep stillness of noon. And beyond this forest sanctuary, the hot, bright sunshine bathed the snows in subtle light; while in the immeasurable space above, soft vapoury clouds, like angels' wings, floated on the dreamy blue.

I said I was alone. Such luck as that, however, was rarely in store for so indifferent a walker as myself. But my brown brothers generally retreated to some quiet corner, where they might smoke to their hearts' content, and then lie down and sleep till they were wanted. Sometimes, during the mysterious process of sketching, they would sit for hours, like patient bronzes, watching with the utmost interest. Occasionally if they were very anxious to get to their journey's end, they would pretend to have forgotten to bring their dinners, and to be half starving. As I generally knew this to be humbug, I would offer them half of mine; and then so excellent a joke as my supposed ignorance of the laws of caste would keep them laughing for an hour or two.

Sometimes when they struggled to explain something about the country, I did sorely regret my ignorance of their language, which prevented the possibility of learning anything from themselves of their legends and customs; and the more intelligent men often looked much disgusted at finding they had charge of a speechless log. However, I daresay the peace and quietness thus secured fully counterbalanced my loss.

The worst of their smoking was generally the exceeding badness of their tobacco, which sometimes was anything but fragrant. The method of smoking here is quite different from that in the plains, or rather the pipe is of simpler construction. The commonest thing is to make two holes in the earth, some inches apart, meeting underground. Into one hole they place dried grass lighted, and over that drop their tobacco. Then covering the other hole with their hand, they inhale through the fingers, or insert a bit of bamboo grass as mouth-piece. Every man carries flint and steel, and a bit of inflammable cloth or fungus. Some curl up a leaf as a pipe, and smoke it as they go along. Others carry a very rude sort of hubble-bubble, with an oval leaden bowl for water, and the smoke which has been cooled, by thus passing through water, is greatly preferred.

But whatever be the form of pipe used, these frugal beings will not waste their tobacco by lighting more than one pipe for a whole party, so each patiently waits his turn while his brethren take their three whiffs, the last so long and so deep that the smoke is taken in and held, for about a quarter of an hour, at the end of which it is ejected from mouth and nostrils like a cloud. Sometimes they manage to inhale a breath so deep that they turn stupid and giddy, to the great disgust of their fellows, who consider this sheer gluttony.[1]

[1] The sight of these human chimneys giving forth their clouds of tobacco reminded me of the story of poor Sir Walter Raleigh (who had learnt the soothing art from the North American Indians) sitting down by his own fireside to smoke his first cigar in England. To him entered an old servant—a regular family "piece"—who, seeing smoke issuing from his master's mouth, immediately suspected spontaneous combustion, and without one word, rushed for a bucket of cold water, wherewith he douched the luckless smoker without allowing time for remonstrance!

Those were strange days in Britain when tobacco sold for its weight in silver—one shilling being weighed against so much tobacco, the heaviest shillings being "waled out" to act as weights—days when, at the tables of English gentlemen, as now among the Paharis, one pipe was handed round, and passed from mouth to mouth; wealthy folk having devised a silver pipe, while ordinary mortals used a walnut-shell, with a straw or a small reed. On one occasion Sir Walter was guilty of lighting his pipe in presence of ladies, at Acton Park, whereupon they one and all retired, till the noxious weed was burnt out and the tainted atmosphere purified.

However, the delights of the aromatic weed seem to have been very quickly discovered, as fifteen years later we find King James publishing his curious *Counterblast to Tobacco*, wherein he states that some gentlemen bestow £300 and £400 a year on smoke, and although the duty thereon was the greatest custom that came to the royal treasury, the king would fain check a practice so detrimental to his subjects, and gravely asserts that certain great tobacco-takers had been examined after death, when it was found that their insides were coated with an unctuous and oily kind of soot!

Four miles beyond Sungri forest lay our next camping-ground, at Nachar, another bit of grand cedar forest where splendid old trees overshadow a glade of greenest grass, chequered with vivid lights and deepest shadows. At this lovely spot an officer of the Forest Department has wisely made his home, a cheery Briton, commonly known as "the Laird of Nachar," who gave us a cordial welcome to his domain, and pointed out a quiet, delightful nook for our tents, beyond his rough-and-ready little bungalow—a nook whence we could overlook the beautiful cedar glade, where, in the sacred grove, stand two very picturesque hill temples. One of these is a regular temple, built, like all the native houses here, and farther up the country, principally of wood, with overhanging roof, and a wide, elaborately carved balcony round the upper story. The other is merely a wooden roof above a paved terrace, whereon to rest the Khuda (the idol tabernacle) on the occasion of the great festivals.

It would have been a pretty sight to see the hill tribes all dancing their twining circles in this grassy glade, beneath the grand cedars; but there were no festivals now, only lamentation, and mourning, and woe, by reason of the cry of those stricken with cholera; for on every side, on hill and in valley, the people were dying wholesale. Of course these poor creatures, whose diet always is what to us would seem starvation, have terribly little stamina to resist any attack of illness; and though they have immense powers of endurance in the way of bodily fatigue, they at once succumb to sickness of any sort; and so, when cholera or kindred scourges come, their ravages are frightful.

One of the upper men who was attacked, told me in excellent English (he was a baboo, or clerk) that having been very busy the two previous days, he had neglected to cook his own food, and had eaten nothing but a large bag of sour apples and sourer grapes. As soon as he was taken ill, his amiable servants, instead of coming to get medicines for him, fled, and left him to die alone, though he had himself nursed those very men in previous illnesses. Illness seems a test that few uncivilised tribes can stand, and the Paharis are much like others in this respect, neglecting

OUR CAMPING-GROUND AT NACHAR.

their sick very cruelly. One poor woman who was seized with cholera, sent to ask us for medicine. We desired her husband to give her certain cholera pills, which he administered on the point of a long stick, to avoid nearer contact. In fact, it seems as if most wild men, like wild beasts, leave their sick to die alone—fortunate for the sufferers, that they do not, like these, also peck them and goad them to death!

Close to the *deotas* (god-houses) is another building, a rest-house provided by the gods for their worshippers. Of this our servants took immediate possession, and soon were most comfortably established. Altogether we found this place so fascinating that we halted here for a week both going and returning. For my own part, I believe I was very near having a long sleep under those glorious old cedars. Not from the workings of imagination, for it had never occurred to any of us that the cholera could possibly affect ourselves, but from the most vulgar physical causes. Chiefly, I believe, from very bad potatoes, which were all we could get, but which we had nevertheless eaten, on the principle that travellers must not be squeamish; and also from the insanity of sleeping in sheets which had become damp from the heavy rain and mists, though the tents were perfectly water-proof.

Whatever was the cause, I certainly thought my summons had come, and felt infinite satisfaction in the certainty of so beautiful a resting-place—the one in all the world which I should have selected. Moreover, it was pleasant to think that I had just finished a most careful drawing of the green glade, which would give every one at home a capital notion of the place where these poor bones were laid, and that they would never look at it without remembering the dear old song that tells how

> "The Indian knows her place of rest,
> Far in the cedar shade."

It really was quite a throwing away of romance to get well again. But the truth is, that in one of those tin boxes was stowed a precious store of all manner of useful remedies for possible evils —vulgar but most precious castor-oil, sulphuric acid and quinine, brandy and chlorodyne, to say nothing of Brand's essence of beef as consolation for the convalescent—so, thanks to a series of experiments with these, the foul cholera-fiend was routed ignominiously.

Then there came a day of most wonderful excitement. Three tents were pitched one evening beneath the great cedars, and straightway their unknown owners became objects of intense interest. Now such meetings in the wilderness have a charm of their own. People must be very churlish indeed who cannot find a few pleasant words for one another under such circumstances, and, generally speaking, they are only too glad to make themselves agreeable. Sometimes, too, the arrival of the baggage and the little white tent heralds the most unexpected meeting of old friends, whose kindred love of wandering has led them from opposite ends of the earth to the same spot.

On the present occasion there was good cause for excitement, for among the servants who had arrived with the tents we detected an ayah,[1] and sure enough there presently arrived a lady, the only one whom we met in our wanderings in the character of sister gipsy, though we afterwards found two ladies *resident* in the far wilds. We did indeed hear of another lady who had accompanied her husband on a shooting excursion right into Thibet. She had last been seen vanishing into space on the back of a yak, like Una and her lion, and whether they have ever been heard of since, deponent knoweth not.

One marked peculiarity of the new comers proved to be a passion for bézique. (Imagine cards in these forests!!) They seemed to live in a chronic state of bézique, and if they happened to be in the middle of a game when the hour for marching arrived, they carefully noted their cards, and renewed their battle the moment they reached the next halt. Notwithstanding which, however, the two gentlemen of that party had done more in the way of sport than any others whom we met.

Meanwhile we were having a fair foretaste of the rains, thunder, lightning, and tempests; and though our social instincts drew us

[1] Native lady's maid.

together for the pleasantest of merry meetings in the Robinson Crusoe bungalow of the Laird, we had sometimes to keep on our waterproofs, and hoist our umbrellas in the house, and so sat, during the most elaborate of amalgamated dinners, each cook supplying what he could. How they managed to cook at all was a standing mystery.

Robinson Crusoe's *ménage* was a matter of much interest; it included live-stock of various sorts, but especially poultry, which were in a state of perpetual antagonism with his garden. Poultry, by the way, was a luxury which we had well-nigh forgotten, being as unattainable as beef in this purely Hindoo region, the former being as unclean as the latter is sacred.

But the chief luxury of this home in the wilds, was the excellent white bread, manufactured by Pier Bux the king of the household, who strove hard to rule his master with the same rod of iron with which he guided other men, failing in which laudable effort, master and servant were in perpetual phases of loggerheads and reconciliation. Not least in that household was a gigantic leopard-dog, so large, and so fierce and rough, as to be a terror to all beholders, while his iron-spiked collar rendered him proof against sudden assault from nocturnal marauders.

When our evening party broke up, we sallied forth, bearing lanterns, and picked our way through the wet moss and mire to the little white tents, which had kept out every drop of rain; moreover the carpets had been lifted, and charcoal fires lighted all day in a hole in the earth, so that our nests were warm and snug. The rain had ceased, and the clear stars gave promise of a glorious morrow. Nor were we disappointed. So lovely was the dawn that we determined to march straightway, and get to higher regions beyond the influence of the rains.

It was a morning much to be remembered. No trace remained of the dark thunderstorm of yesterday, save that on every side countless streamlets, clear as crystal, were rushing down every cleft in the mountains, and dashing over the precipitous rocks in headlong fall, filling the air with a murmurous sound as of the voice of many waters, which floated upward on the breeze, as it "soughed" through the topmost branches of the dark dreamy pines; and, save where the delicate cloud-shadows rested for a moment, the whole valley lay bathed in that clear shining after rain, in which the eastern mind so readily perceives the glad rejoicing of what we call inanimate nature—the trees of the forest, the laughing harvest fields, the mountains and hills, the winds of GOD, and all green things of the earth, yea, *all* the deep-toned harmonies of nature, taking up the chorus of praise, which lightning and cloud had proclaimed through all the tumult of the tempest.

At a very short distance from Nachar we first caught a glimpse of that group of snow peaks, towards which we were specially directing our steps; as also of the deep wide valley into which we were about to descend; thence, crossing the Sutlej and the Wanga rivers, which here meet, but which must nevertheless be crossed by separate bridges, our route lay along the precipitous cliffs on the other side of the Sutlej, which at this point narrows into a very confined gorge.

The river here comes down with a frightful rush—its velocity in the rains being frequently over twenty miles an hour, and masses of snow are occasionally washed down, which endanger the existence of all bridges.

One of these was carried away one beautiful night, when neither storm nor tempest seemed to threaten evil. But when morning broke, the bridge was gone, and there remained only a well-defined water line, which left it to be inferred that a large avalanche must have passed down in the night, having probably lain wedged in by cliffs, till the pressure of a great body of water accumulating behind it had caused it to burst down with overwhelming violence, sweeping all before it.

The bridge built by Capt. Lang, R.E., which we were to cross this day, had a narrow escape of being destroyed in its infancy, a great mass of rock having fallen from a perpendicular cliff about 1,500 feet above the bridge, and a large fragment lighted on the bridge itself, which was partially destroyed.

Just above this point the lovely Wanga river mingles its

crystalline waters with those of the turbid, yellow Sutlej, which, swollen by a vast body of melted snow, rushes impetuously along, carrying with it whole beds of mica and sand, and by no means improving its own beauty by the addition. The Wanga itself is a clear and beautiful stream, rushing down with tremendous violence over huge boulders of water-worn granite. One of the loveliest expeditions possible lies up this valley, to the Spiti Pass. It offers no great difficulty, and no one who is master of his own time should miss going at all events as far as the head of the valley, which is three days' march.

This bridge at Wangtu is a very fine specimen of the Himalayan construction, wherever a solid roadway is required. It is built entirely on the principle of leverage. Several large trees are felled on each side of the river, and their trunks are laid on either shore, with the narrow ends projecting over the river, and heavy stones laid over the thick ends to increase their counter-weight. Cross-bars of wood are then laid over the projecting ends. Thus the first layer is complete. The process is repeated again and again, each layer of trees projecting some feet beyond the last, till the two sets of timber almost meet in mid-air; and one more layer crowns both. Then planks laid crosswise form the roadway. The base of the timbers on either side is imbedded in solid masonry. Strong railings guard against accidents, and an excellent substantial bridge is thus formed. The timber generally used is the deodar, which seems almost imperishable, proof alike against heat and wet, and all other influences tending to decay. The same principle of bridge-making, but in rough-and-ready style, is to be seen on a small scale on many little streams, such bridges being occasionally rapidly made just when required! Rough logs are laid on either bank, weighted by stones. On these are laid others, tied together with coarse ropes of goat's hair, and of course overlapping the first layer, then a final layer unites both. Still narrower torrents are bridged by a couple of tall trees felled so as to fall across the stream side by side; on these are laid flat slabs of stone, and the bridge is complete. There is no sort of rail, and often the spray from the foaming waters dashes right over these slippery logs.

Such solid bridges as these are, however, generally confined to the lesser streams. The broader rivers are more frequently crossed by different varieties of rope bridges. In some cases ropes are slung across from rock to rock; from these hangs a kind of seat fastened to a triangle, which slips along the main ropes as the traveller works it with his hands. Sometimes he sits in a coil of rope and is drawn over from the opposite side—a very giddy operation, as I can testify. The more experienced Paharis disdain any extraneous aid, and I have watched them crawl along a single rope like monkeys, just holding on by arms and legs, with the boiling torrent thundering along far below them, and the knowledge that one moment's giddiness or hesitation would plunge them beyond all reach of human aid.

These ropes are made of grass, and in an old neglected bridge they occasionally slacken so much as to dip right down in the middle, and as the great snow-waves rise and heap themselves up in mid-stream they sometimes reach the rope, and dash over the luckless traveller till he is actually drowned. Such an accident had occurred at the Jula[1] of Chargaon a few days before we had to cross by it,—a sad story which the natives took good care to impress on us, by way of encouragement. Sometimes, too, an old rope breaks and leaves the passenger short time for shrift, as the angry waters whirl him playfully along.

We heard of an instance in which a party of foreigners had to cross a raging torrent by a single rope, over which was slung a bamboo, bent into the form of a horse-shoe; below this each was slung in turn, and having been allowed to slip rapidly down the steep incline to the middle, they were pulled up the other side by a draw-rope. Just before the last man crossed, one strand of the solitary rope broke; it was however supposed that it would still bear his weight, but on reaching the obstacle thus formed, the bamboo could slide no further! The man on the bank he had just left, strove in vain to draw him back. There he was stuck fast, —no effort could draw him backwards or forwards, and for hours the luckless traveller hung suspended in mid-air, with the raging

[1] Rope bridge.

waters leaping and roaring below. At length, by an almost superhuman effort he contrived with his own hands to hoist the bamboo over the broken strand which had caused the hitch, and at long last reached the further bank in safety.

Another variety of rope bridge is a very dangerous species of ladder; two ropes slung across the river being connected by steps of wood fastened at short intervals. Two other ropes act as supports for the hand, generally attached to the former by an occasional bamboo. As you pick your steps along the frail ladder, you see the turbid waters rushing below you, and many a stout heart has turned sick and giddy before reaching the opposite shore. Not even a goat can be induced to cross a path of such open-work construction, so when a flock has been led to the one shore, the shepherd must carry each creature over, on his own shoulders. When acting as beasts of burden, they must of course be unladen, and their little saddle-bags carried over separately. You can imagine that this is rather serious work, with a flock of perhaps one thousand goats![1]

Sometimes, as we wound securely along the dizzy height, so comfortably profiting by other men's labours, the thought would flash across us of what it must have been for the first workers, and the awful danger of beginning such a road, winding round sheer precipices where one false step would hurl the bold cragsman into an almost fathomless abyss.

Along perpendicular cliffs of the very worst description, where natural ledges are few and far between, galleries have to be constructed. The most able climber in the district will creep along, where hardly a goat would venture, and will contrive to bore holes at intervals of about fifteen feet, and therein fix strong iron bars, from which to suspend ropes and planks, to enable his fellows to begin work.

Suppose, however, the leader comes to a part of the cliff so smooth that even he can find no footing, he must scale the cliff, and either scramble down a little farther on, or else, fixing an iron bar at a higher point, must be let down by a rope thence

[1] Himalayan Bridges. See chap. xvii.

suspended, till he finds himself once more on his original level. Then he must repeat the old operation of boring the rock, and fixing a jumper; after which, a rope bridge must be suspended between this and the last point gained, and men can then set to work to bore, and let in bars at the intermediate points.

Thus, foot by foot, the work progresses, and every characteristic of a keen cragsman is called into play—a cool, clear head, a steady foot and hand, and great power of endurance.

We met Mr. Cregeen, the "Road Sahib" as the people call him, on some of his surveying expeditions, and I think I cannot do better than quote his words, and those of Captain Lang, his predecessor, to describe this portion of our route.

"Below Serahan we find very precipitous cliffs rising several thousand feet above the Sutlej. Of these, the Taranda, Wangtu, Neoza, Maizong, and Rogi cliffs, are fine examples, and more grand and dangerous than anything that has been before attacked in the construction of the Hindostan and Thibet road.

"The first passage of the smooth, water-worn, granite face of the Wangtu cliff, rising like a wall from the foaming waves of the Sutlej as it rushes through the narrow Wangtu gorge, a feat possible to but few men in the world, was unhesitatingly executed by Bhulku, celebrated as the keenest cragsman in Bussahir, who fixed in the crevices of the cliff all the first irons for the attachment of the rope and planking, on which, suspended above the river, worked the coolies, who constructed the viaducts.

"Near Rogi are precipices of stupendous height, scarcely to be surpassed in grandeur by any in the Himalayas; and, to carry a road across their apparently inaccessible faces required bold and active hill-men, careless of being perched on dizzy pinnacles, boring for blasts, of being suspended on narrow planks over infinite space, or of crawling or creeping where there seemed no place for hand or foot to advance the work."

The Rogi and Maizong cliffs are at an elevation of several thousand feet above the Sutlej. They have doubtless been caused by immense landslips, and are very precipitous. The cliffs are rugged, many parts overhanging, and there are in many

THE ROGI CLIFF—GREAT KHYLAS PEAKS.

places drops of 500 feet before touching another projection, whence, rebounding, the hapless climber whose foot has failed him, must be hurled down and down, till his shattered fragments find anything but a *resting* place, in the tossing, raging river.

The Rogi cliff is of very compact gneiss, and, from its continual tendency to scale, very great additional difficulties arose, as ordinary methods of blasting generally brought down any rock but that which was intended. For instance, after boring upwards of eight hundred mines in one cliff, it was hoped that by simultaneously firing them a continuous line of fracture would be produced. Instead of this, all the result was that immense quantities of overhanging rock were brought down from above, while the rock over which the road should have lain scaled off entirely; the cradles were smashed, the stanchion bars twisted—serious losses, where every tool and nail has to be carried up by coolies from the plains, a march of many days. The weather-worn rock face, being thus impracticable, it was found necessary to cut it back considerably, and thus reach a mass less liable to scale.

In the Wangtu cliff, on the other hand, the chief difficulty lay in the smooth water-worn granite face, along which, at about 100 feet above the water, the road must be led—scarcely one crevice, projection, or ledge marks the slippery face along which men must crawl. "If a man had the misfortune to slip or make a false step, the chances were very considerably against his ever having another chance. There is really and literally nothing which a man could hope to clutch; nor could assistance be rendered him if he fell. In an instant, the waters of the Sutlej would hurl him along, and he would either be dashed to pieces against a rock or large boulder, or be jammed between a couple of them."

These, then, were some of the dangers and difficulties which had attended the making of that path along which we now wound so safely, though in truth it still looked somewhat "kittle work"[1] as we say in the north, to see the path projecting from the smooth granite face, and carried over wooden supports overhanging the river.

[1] Kittle, uncertain, anxious. Scotch, unreliable.

The opposite cliff has its own sad tale to tell. Another of those terrible accidents when a restive pony backed over the khad, and the strong right arm that strove to hold it up by main force could avail nothing, for in the agony of the moment the rider had fainted, and fallen from her saddle, unconscious of all the misery that in that moment fell on two sunny homes which, by her "going away," were left desolate.

For a considerable distance after crossing the bridge at Wangtu, our rocky path lay so close above the river that its noise was almost deafening. The vast body of melted snows, which at this season come rushing down the gorge, swell the stream to such a size that it goes tearing along in huge, yellow waves, foul and turbid. It was, therefore, with positive delight that we turned up a steep zigzag path which at last brought us to Urni.

Our recollections of this place are, I fancy, considerably tinged by the small discomforts of the moment. The fir-clad hills were round us, and snowy peaks as usual, but my chief impression is of a night spent in the dirty mess of a half-finished bungalow, for as we could find no convenient place to pitch our tents, we put up in half-built rooms, with a fair view of the sky through all the chinks. While we sat at supper by a blazing fire, a silvery hill-fox crept up to have a look at us. We only caught sight of two of these pretty creatures, and both were wary enough to escape, and preserve their valuable fur for their own benefit.

CHAPTER XVI.

VILLAGES ON THE CLIFFS.

Scale of Size—Vegetation of divers Altitudes—A Great Dinner!—Three Mighty Pinnacles—The Mountain Heaven—Villages on Cliffs—Pahari Customs—Polyandry—Goat Caravans—The Snow-line in Europe and Asia—Snow-blindness—Stone capped Ice Pillars—Cheenee—Pangi—Celtic Brooches—A Study for Murillo—Scarcity of Animal Life—The Yak.

NEXT day a beautiful march of twelve miles up the Kunawur valley brought us along the face of tremendous cliffs, with the river far below, and dark masses of wood, running like broad shadows right up to the snows. While looking at such a scene without any especial sense of its vastness, it was curious suddenly to catch some landmark that acted as a scale of measurement. Here, for instance, where at an immeasurable distance below us flowed the troubled yellow waters of the Sutlej, I noticed that they were just edged with a line of cliff. That cliff I knew to be far higher than the highest cliff along our Moray sea-coast of which we think so much.

And I knew too that in every crevice of that rock there grew tropical plants, such as belong to the plains of India, while as the eye slowly travelled upward, it noted one belt after another of changing vegetation; and I knew that though I could distinguish nothing save a general mass of greenery, each changing shade of colour marked the plants of divers altitudes, passing from the cactuses and acacias of the tropics, to the oak and rhododendrons of cooler levels, thence to the cedar forest, higher still to the neoza pine, and finally to a fringe of birch, of juniper, and green pasture land, reaching to the very verge of the snows, where the smooth sheets of dazzling whiteness are only broken by the green shadows of glaciers, lying between huge masses of bare, black rock. On those grassy slopes above the birch grow cowslips and polyanthus, sweet as those of our own green meadows, and with them beds of strawberries, and other well-known favourites. Thus at one glance the eye ranged from the torrid to the arctic zone, but it was only by some such mental effort that it seemed possible to realise the colossal scale of all around. Sometimes too we noticed some little atoms of dark foliage, dotting the face of the precipice, like flies on a castle wall. On nearer approach, these generally proved to be fine old cedars, whose gnarled and twisted roots had taken a mighty hold of some crevice, though their great weather-beaten trunks, and bare, contorted arms, told what awful battles they had fought with storm and tempest.

Thus, sometimes winding along the face of stupendous precipices, (where one false step would have hurled us from the safe path into the immeasurable depths of an almost fathomless ravine,) and sometimes through the cedar forest, we reached the road bungalow at Rogi. On its balcony, to our dismay, we detected two topee-wallahs, or wearers of hats, as white men are called. A very few minutes, however, sufficed to prove them both Scots, and nearly akin to friends whom we had just left in the far north ; so it did not take us long to fraternise. To these were presently added two others, officers of the Rifles, and as we all agreed to make common cause, this halt in the wilds proved a very pleasant gathering.

We did our best to make our meeting suggestive of home, by producing all the Scotch dishes at our command. At dinner a famous bowl of hotch-potch (thanks to the admirable preserved tins), and at breakfast Findon haddies and genuine porridge. There was always some amusement at these amalgamated dinners, in seeing what each housekeeper had produced. One would provide Liebig's soup, cod's roe, and minaul pheasant; another a dish of white-bait and roast mutton; a third a genuine lobster salad (the lettuce sent perhaps for miles by a coolie, from some oasis in the mountain desert), and a chicore stew; perhaps some bear-steaks also, and a *pâté de foie gras*, also potatoes, perhaps curry—rice inevitably—or the young curly tops of common bracken stewed with butter, which we then considered fully equal to asparagus. I cannot say that on repeating the experiment in Scotland, they seemed quite as good! We also found that young nettles made capital spinach; watercresses we gathered in the brooks, and green peas we had imported from England! Several other vegetables grow wild, including gooseberries and rhubarb; but these make too heavy a demand on limited stores of sugar. We were especially charmed at finding loads of excellent mushrooms on some of the grassy slopes, and when our gathering exceeded our daily consumption, we had a grand brew of ketchup—the real unadulterated article, with no fear of fried liver, and blacking, or other foreign ingredients!

As I before said, the supply of game is most uncertain, and the only meat that can be purchased from the natives is the wearisome *toujours* mutton; even that being sometimes difficult to procure, while, as I have already observed, the absence of Mohammedanism makes itself quickly felt in the commissariat, inasmuch as the Hindoos consider poultry too unclean, and beef too holy, for human food.

Therefore for all variety of diet, travellers chiefly depend on the inestimable tins of preserved meats of all sorts, the value of which is so well understood by all Anglo-Indians, that one lady was heard to remark, that doubtless nothing else was ever used at Her Majesty's table! Just imagine the luxury of opening a tin of fresh lobster, or perhaps salmon—possibly a little "tender" as the cockneys say,—and with the addition of excellent lettuce and cucumbers from the Road Sahib's garden, making a salad that would rejoice the veriest gourmet in the kingdom! I dwell at some length on all this good fare, for I am telling you of a great social gathering—a sort of Lord Mayor's feast. Our daily bread was of course very much simpler, having for its main feature a *pot au feu* wherein divers meats generally found themselves reduced to a savoury hash, always ready on the shortest notice.

Our feast was spread in the open verandah, whence looking upward beyond the awful desolation of that chaotic waste of rocks, "the tumbled fragments of the hills," towered three mighty pinnacles of whitest snow, with blackest peaks—peaks of hard black rock, so steep that even the light snow could there find no resting-place, only here and there a ledge where it might cling, marking the barren precipice with veins of silver. The great central mass, known as the Raal Dhang, rises to 21,000 feet; while on either side the greater and lesser Kylas follow closely, being upwards of 19,000. All day long we watched the ever-varying lights and shadows playing over these untrodden ice fields, as they glowed fiery red at morning and evening, or changed to deepest purple as storms swept over them. But oftener than all, the cold white snow glistened with strange, spirit light against a pale, green sky, while strange, fair vapours drifted restlessly to and fro, half shrouding those phantom peaks.

Then, as our glance turned downward, we looked beyond a waving sea of foliage, the tops of apricot and other forest trees, to another vast precipice of yellowish stone, dotted with old gnarled cedars, each one a study for an artist. Beyond that again, rose hundreds of tiny terraced fields; then a great cedar forest, shelving downward for thousands of feet, till it reached the waters of the Sutlej, which lay hidden in the black chasm far below, only betraying its presence by the hoarse, hollow murmur of its sullen waters, as they boiled and foamed and thundered on their way. On the opposite cliff, the waters, rushing down from the melting snow had formed a torrent which leapt from height to height in its headlong career till it dashed over the precipice in a cloud of silvery spray, seeming to lose itself in rainbow light.

We had risen considerably since we camped at Rampore, which is only 3,000 feet above the sea. Now we were looking up to the source of the Sutlej which issues from a sacred lake famous in Sanskrit mythology, which lies on the slope of great Kylas at about 15,000 feet above the sea.

As there was no convenient level spot close to the bungalow where we could pitch our tents, the previous occupants resigned half the house to us. A tiny wooden room fell to my share, in which I found a strange reminder of England, for some previous tenant had papered it all over with the *Illustrated London News* of 1864; so when I awoke in these distant regions, I found myself surrounded with pictures of St. George's Chapel, Windsor, and the Prince of Wales's marriage; Edinburgh illuminated; quiet reaches of the Thames, and all the principal pictures that we remembered in that year's Royal Academy.

It was a pleasant vision of home, but soon forgotten in the entrancing beauty of the reality before me; the early dawn throwing its flood of pearly light on the peaks right in front of us, and revealing cliffs, crevasses, and glaciers vast and wonderful; while all the valley below lay bathed in silver mist. Looking up to that mysterious world of whiteness, we could not but share the awe with which the Paharis gaze on those pathless snows, where human foot may never hope to tread. For they believe the mighty Kylas to be the chosen dwelling-place of the Great Spirit, chief of all the gods; and heaven, they say, lies high among those inaccessible peaks. (I wonder if there can be any connection between this word Kylas and the Latin Cœlus, or between Himalaya and the German Himmel?) The word Kylas would seem to be applied to any especially heavenly spot, as we find the Kylas temples at Ellora, hewn in the solid rocks.

We also find the same faith which invests the hill tops with a sense of religious awe, in Southern India, where the Todas point out Makarty Peak in the Neilgherries as the portal of heaven, whence not only the souls of their dead, but also those of the spirits of the buffaloes slain at their funerals, pass into the dreamy unknown world.

Such of the Paharis as care to find a name for the Great and Awful Spirit, say that on the Kylas, Siva sits enthroned, together with his wife, Durgâ or Pârvatî, who is the favourite goddess of the hills. She has another name, which describes her as the lady of the fishy eye. At her temples there are frequently tanks full of sacred fish. What connection may exist between these and her eyes, I cannot say!

Looking up the valley, we could discern two villages—one clinging to the face of the cliff among the cedars; another perched on a little plateau far below, jutting out from the precipice, so that on three sides this village on the cliff literally overhung the stream. How any children survived so dangerous a nursery was a standing miracle. Some one suggested that they were tethered, which possibly might be of some use. Literally, I have scrambled through such villages as would have turned most heads giddy. Luckily for me, however, my early training in scrambling along the steep cliffs of the Findhorn has made me proof against such weakness.

In the tiny, terraced fields the people were working busily. Some had already gathered in their little crop, and were ploughing the land with just as rude a plough as the *caschrom* of Skye; merely a crooked piece of stick, of which one end acts as a handle, while the other is shod with iron, and tears up the ground. The crops were of many sorts—chiefly Indian corn, and a deep crimson grain with scarlet leaves, which produces a field red as blood, and of which a red pottage is made; in colour, at least, like poor Esau's pottage of lentils. They grow lucerne, grass, and green stuff for forage; also buckwheat, and a very tall corn, a sort of millet which hangs in a bunch of loose grain like giant oats—a very pretty crop as the breeze ripples over it.

We were told that the people sometimes have much ado to protect their fields from the bears, when these come down in search of wild apricots. We should have been uncommonly glad if they had come while we were there, as a supply of fresh bear's grease would have been particularly useful. But the gentlemen toiled in vain; and as a general result of two or three days of stiff walking right up among the snows, would bring us back a few snow-balls, and tantalise us with accounts of the delicious strawberries on which they had feasted. They only shot one bear all the time we were out; and so far from his supplying us with bear's grease, the natives forthwith ate him up to the uttermost fragment, and left us only his skin as a trophy.

Meanwhile the apricot crop was safely gathered in, and the golden fruit was spread in masses on the flat roofs of the houses, and there left to dry in the sun. They are then pounded into flour, and form the staple food of the Paharis, to whom attah, or grain flour, is far too expensive a luxury for ordinary use. From the habit, which I suppose is necessary, of gathering the fruit before it is fully ripened, the flour is very sour, and when made into gruel, tastes much like tomato sauce—a good accompaniment to more solid food, but very poor diet. No wonder that the men to whom this sour porridge is daily food should so quickly succumb to the cholera. The apricot kernels are carefully collected and subjected to pressure, when they yield an oil which is burnt in the rude lamps.

The village on the cliff of which I spoke just now is a fair sample of many others. It seems as though they were invariably perched on the very verge of the steepest precipices, and in the most inaccessible places. Each house is built of wood, and several stories high, with widely projecting roofs and balconies, where all manner of scenes in domestic life reveal themselves to the passers-by. The roofs are often high and peaked, composed of heavy slates of irregular form, and very thick. Sometimes they are made of great cedar planks: occasionally they are made flat, supporting a wooden cistern to catch the rain-water.

On many houses you see a luxuriant crop of cucumbers, vines, and gourds, climbing all over the roof and carved wood-work, twining round arches and pillars, the large fruit covering even the roof.

Formerly it was common to build houses of five or even six storeys high: now they rarely exceed three; though some of the old sort are still standing. One sportsman mentioned having seen three such, near the source of the Ganges, that were six storeys high; he had also taken the trouble to measure a house door which was made of a single plank of cedar-wood, one foot thick and six feet wide. The lower storey is almost invariably of rough stone-work, being the cattle stable; an outer staircase leads to the dwelling-house, the door of which is generally so low that you must stoop to enter. The women have no separate quarters, as in the plains, but the family live together, much as they do elsewhere. Occasionally the houses are whitewashed externally, which, however, does not denote any special cleanliness of the interior, as there is no sort of drainage, and dirt of all sorts is allowed to accumulate. I do not think, however, that these villages are as foul as many of our own.

One thing which tends greatly to their dirt (may I say their richness of colour?) is the amount of pine and cedar wood which is burnt in the chimneyless houses; and no fuel could be more smoky and sooty in its deposits, though at the time, it burns with a clear, ruddy blaze, which cheers the inmates through the long winter evenings, while they wile away the hours with stories and wild legends of old adventure on hill or in forest; stories of the chase, or traditions of demi-gods and weird spirits. Like our own old Highlanders, they delight to sing or recite (as they sit round the red wood fire) such stories as find favour with a race superstitious and imaginative; peopling the dark forest, and the blue ice-caverns, with a spirit-world such as that recognised by our forefathers, to whom the soughing of the wind before a gathering tempest seemed the sigh of the mountain spirit, and the voice of the rushing storm whispered of terrible, dark demons of the night, flying on the wild wind, bearing to some devoted wretch the dread doom of death—while every mountain and valley was the home of some mysterious creature, and Echo, "the Son of the Rock," was as truly a living being as any of those now reverenced by these Paharis.

Like all dwellers among the mountains, these men have a passionate love of home, and of their dear native valleys. Of their extraordinary honesty I have already spoken, and of that we had good cause to speak well, having never missed the value of a farthing at their hands. Their character for truthfulness does not stand so high. Those who have most to do with them say they cannot rely on their word, and that they not only lie without scruple, but are scarcely annoyed at being detected. Moreover to prove how truly "evil-doers are evil-deemers," they are always ready to accuse one another of falsehood, and are said to be vindictive and envious among themselves.

Of that we can say nothing—to us they seemed a cheery race, generally ready to make the best of things; but then the white skin always secures more or less ready service from the dark, it being part of the native character to submit at once to proven superiority, whether of intellect or brute force—to refuse things to a man weak and helpless, and obey with alacrity in obedience to sharp words. So that sometimes the supplies of goods and of coolies that had been refused to courteous demands have been brought quite pleasantly in obedience to threats.

Still the hill-men are undoubtedly very independent, and dearly like to show off occasionally. Thus in some of the more remote districts, where English influence has less authority, sportsmen have sometimes been compelled to give up their choicest hunting-grounds, because the village *mates* have point-blank refused to provide coolies; and not one would volunteer, though offered any wages they liked to ask—a state of things not suggestive of deep poverty. These villages also utterly refused to supply sheep and flour at any price.

One curious thing that we were told was, that from some odd superstition, akin perhaps to the feeling which makes a Highland wife speak of her husband as "Himsel" without mentioning any name, these Pahari women have the strongest objection to utter their husband's name, and that he, likewise, will always call his wife by that of the village from which she came, but never by her own.

There is a curious distinction in the social customs of the people in the upper and lower part of this valley. Below Wangtu it is said that polygamy prevails, as elsewhere; every man buying his wives from their parents for a given number of rupees. When he is tired of one of these, he sells her to his neighbour for something under cost price, and purchases a new inmate for the zenana!

Farther up the valley, however, where the people are very poor, and the tiny ridges of cultivation will not support large families, polyandry is common, as among the Todas in the Neilgherries, and certain of the Cingalese tribes. The elder brother of a family chooses one wife for himself and all his brothers. The children are common property, and seem equally beloved by all the family, so *they*, at least, do not suffer by the arrangement. Possibly this curious state of domestic life may account for the fact, so often commented on, of the intense love of the Paharis for their children, for whose sakes they are content to make any sacrifice, whereas this sentiment is by no means reciprocated by the rising generation, who, as a rule, are cruelly neglectful of their parents, even of the mothers, who, it is said, generally nurse their offspring for two or three years!

The sisters of the wife, being considered "detrimentals," are placed in Buddhist convents, whence they come forth to work in the fields, or as coolies. Many men also find homes in these convents, though this seems rather a matter of social convenience than of religious feeling.

This extraordinary, and, to our feeling, revolting system of fraternal polyandry, combined with that of nunneries as a home for the superfluous women, is common throughout Thibet, and all regions where its language is spoken; in other words, it is legally recognised by many millions of the Turanian race, who find it expedient, both on account of the deep poverty of the sterile land, which makes increase of population so undesirable, and also because of the dangers and difficulties which would inevitably surround any woman left alone in her remote home, during the prolonged absences of her lord, whether he be engaged in traffic or in the chase; whereas, in the case of two or more brothers, owning but one fireside, it must be a rare occurrence when both or all are compelled to be absent at once. So it seems that something may be said in defence of even so startling a social arrangement as this, at least among races of so phelgmatic a temperament as the Thibetans.

In this valley we saw goats employed as beasts of burden,

bringing the products of Thibet for barter in the lower lands. These consist chiefly of wool and salt, the latter brought from the "salt-licks," where it seems to ooze from the rocks on the high steppes.

The goats go in large flocks, each being laden with a small pack like two saddle-bags; each goat carrying eight seers (sixteen pounds). A small child generally walks at the head of each flock, its little dark shaven head being a curiosity in itself. Several goatherds are of course in charge, but so great is the trouble of catching and loading a flock of perhaps a thousand goats, that they are often not unloaded for two or three days and nights. The long string winds its dangerous way among the crags, for many a weary *coss*, and when at last they reach some quiet nook where they may halt in safety—something as near akin to "green pastures beside still waters," as Himalayan valleys can yield—then the flocks are turned adrift, the little black tents of camels' hair are pitched, the goods are stored under canvas, and the Tartar encampment is complete.

The goats are generally the property of Ladakh merchants, a curious-looking race with the jolliest good-tempered faces, always ready for a laugh; a character borne out by their invariable kindliness to whoever they have to do with. They have the oblique eyes and flat features of China, with the most placid countenances; and are robust and muscular. They are dirty beyond description, with heads of rough hair never combed since they were born. Some, however, remedy this by cropping their hair like convicts, and wearing it about an inch long. The women have, at some remote period, dressed theirs elaborately in countless small plaits, generally all caught back together and twisted into a thick pigtail, tipped with a woollen tassel. Across the head from the forehead they invariably wear a strip of dark cloth, incrusted with every jewel they can command, chiefly very large, coarse turquoises two or three inches in diameter, and stuck on about an inch apart. This hangs right down the back, the principal woman of the party having invariably the largest gems. They sometimes wear good strings of amber, together with the commonest English beads.

We were told that their houses in Ladakh are generally whitewashed, and coloured with broad bands of red, yellow, or blue. It is curious that people caring thus to colour their homes should dress so dingily. Men and women dress just alike, in blouse and trousers of coarse woollen stuff; and jackets of divers skins. The blouse, like that of the Paharis, is tied in at the waist, and made to bag, so that the bosom becomes a convenient receptacle for all manner of treasures; little balls of dough, made of coarse flour; little packets of tea; a little wooden saucer, tobacco, knives, string, bundles of wood, and small tobacco-pipes, in form much like a common "cutty pipe." A wooden spoon is generally stuck in the girdle. The men, like the women, wear necklaces, bracelets, and amulets; chains of bright metal, and ornamental boxes for flint and steel. Their shoes are of coarse grey yarn, and soled with the same material, which gives the foot a grip as though walking in stockings: (I noticed that our servants from the plains, generally went barefoot on any difficult ground, their smooth-soled slippers being ill-adapted for rough walking.)

Many of these merchants had come across immensely high passes; sometimes through storm and snow. Even the Paharis themselves suffer much from sickness and headache owing to the rarified atmosphere of these high levels; also from languor and difficulty of breathing. They have great faith in certain apricot cakes, which are supposed to be a good remedy. It seems to be only men who suffer, as dogs and loaded sheep are apparently happiest when nearest heaven. It seems, however, that this oppression is not felt at so low an altitude as on European mountains. In the Alps, for instance, men say that they can hardly breathe at 15,000 feet, while on these passes there rarely seems any great difficulty even at 18,000. One gentleman returning from Thibet told us he had felt no inconvenience whatever at that height.

A similar difference seems to exist as to the limit of eternal snow, which certainly is very much higher here than on the

Alps, where 8,885 feet is stated to be the average snow-line.[1] This is said to be subject to modifying influences, such as the neighbourhood of much water, which should warm the atmosphere. Yet here, where the vast mass of land with hardly any water (certainly no lakes) would seem to demand a lower snow-line, it is certainly very much higher. The level varies with climate. Yet on the Himalayas the snow-line is calculated at an average of 16,000 feet on the southern slopes, and 17,400 on the northern, the south being invariably, as we have seen, the bleaker aspect, while the more sheltered north absorbs all richness of vegetation.

As an example I may cite the wheat crops and other grains which flourish in the neighbourhood of Dankar, the capital of Spiti, which is situated 12,774 feet above the sea-level. Here small willows and other stunted trees are the only foliage.

Among the chief inconveniences of which men complained on these high passes were the excessive alternations of heat and cold. Of course an atmosphere so rarified can hold but little moisture, and the clear air allows the sun's rays to strike with very great heat during the day. This is succeeded by intensely cold nights, and dew, of course, is almost unknown. Few travellers start on such a journey without providing shelter for their servants; but these, in any case, suffer very severely from cold,

[1] The Alps in some places extend from the 44th to the 48th parallel of North latitude, and the mass of the Himalayas from about the 27th to the 40th, a difference in latitude which accounts for the higher snow-line. To any general statement, however, concerning snow-lines, those of the Himálayas form a striking exception. *The line is about* 4,000 *feet higher on the north* than on the *south* side, owing to the greater depth of snow which falls on the *south* side, and to the greater dryness of the climate of Thibet on the *north*, which increases the evaporation and the heating power of the solar rays, and to the bare rocks and soil of the north absorbing more heat than the southern surfaces, which are densely covered with vegetation. The immense range of the Himalayas, which extends over more than 22 degrees of East longitude, forms a screen which intercepts and condenses most of the moisture which the winds carry up from the Indian Ocean and deposit on the *southern* face of the mountains either in rain or snow, the quantity of rain measured at a considerable altitude having been known to amount to 600 inches in a year.

in spite of hunting out the warmest nooks under the lee of big stones, and building up earth-walls round their little tents. The coolies lie curled up in their plaids, or croon over the big fire which must be kept up for fear of stray bears.

White men and dark are alike subject to agonizing attacks of snow-blindness, from the terrible glare and wind. It is said to be positive torture; though there is nothing like inflammation of the eye: only a convulsive spasm causing the eyelid to close involuntarily with such force as to press upon the pupil, which seems to burn as though on fire, and the only relief is incessant bathing in ice-water. This may continue for two or three days, during which, if it is necessary to continue the march, the sufferer has to be led by the hand, and goes tottering along in blind agony. After a while the pain rapidly subsides, and the eye generally seems none the worse.

I am told that the most efficacious of all preventives is simply to take a burnt stick and blacken a large circle all round each eye. How it acts, I cannot imagine, but it is said to be even more efficacious than wearing spectacles of smoked glass. I should incline to try both!

Some of the gentlemen who returned from these high levels gave us most tantalizing descriptions of their wild magnificence. Their camping-ground had been, perhaps on some great moraine on the verge of some mighty glacier, which, they said, seemed to glimmer in the darkness with something like phosphoric light; its edges of clearest green, and its depths of an intensely deep cobalt blue. All round them were piled stupendous masses of black rock, heaped together in wild confusion, with pinnacles of ice, and seas of mixed ice and snow, which, however, was too often dirty and soiled with muddy earth, in fact rather a hideous object. But there were deep fissures in the ice-cliffs, and dark rocky ravines, half choked with great boulders of rock and fragments of far-away hills, brought thither by the ever-moving glaciers, in their slow, sure wanderings.

Of the distant views their praise was not so warm. Generally they could see only the next ridge, or at best a sea of wavy

DEODARS AT PANGI.

mountain ranges, just crested with billowy snows and glaciers, so they comforted us by declaring the views we saw at our lower levels were in reality far lovelier; an unction so flattering to the soul of a bad walker that I tried hard to believe it: and to be satisfied with our nine thousand feet, which was the average height of our camping grounds.

There is one phase of that upper world which we would fain have seen; when the ice-field is dotted all over with ice-pillars, six or eight feet in height, about the thickness of a man's body; each supporting a great block of stone, much larger than itself, as a capital; something like a huge mushroom-bed, or like some marvellous Druids' temple, with a thousand pillars. It is supposed that these blocks have fallen on the ice-field when at a much higher level, and that it has gradually melted down, save where these, acting as a sun-shade, have sheltered the ice, and so preserved these slender columns, which, however, are always gradually melting, giving way at the base, where the sun's rays can strike soonest. Then new blocks fall, and repeat the process. Sometimes a fresh avalanche sweeps down from above, and then it may be long years before the ice-pillars are again formed, so that the traveller who has climbed these heights on purpose to behold the scene, described by others, may chance to find it all buried deep beneath the snows.[1]

Well, as we could not reach this wonderful ice-world, we contrived to be uncommonly happy at our humbler level, exploring all manner of lovely nooks in cliff and forest. Nowhere did we find more beautiful groups of gnarled old cedars than those clinging to the face of the precipice at Rogi;—the extraordinary richness of colouring of those red stems and grey rocks, with many-coloured lichens; the great, twisted roots, and weird, dead arms, are alike

[1] Akin to these Himalayan ice columns are the stone-capped mud-columns in the valley of Botzen in the Tyrol; where hundreds of such pillars, some twenty, some fifty, and some a hundred feet high, are now standing. The stone capitals brought there in bygone ages by the great ice-rivers, have protected the earth beneath them from the perpetual, perpendicular action of the rains, which have washed away the soil from the rest of the valley.

bleached pure white; while here and there the storm has torn off some great limb, revealing an intensity of orange that painter's brush can hardly imitate. Cadmium and burnt sienna are pale before such cedar-wood in sunlight. And then the intense shadows from that dark foliage! And beyond all, the hills and deep valley in purple shadows and grey mist.

Our next march lay along the face of a stupendous precipice —the Maizong cliff; a sheer fall of several thousand feet, declared by the engineers to be probably the mightiest precipice in all the Himalayas. After a couple of miles, the angle of the ground allows cedars to find a hold, so our path lay in deep forest gloom. Far below, we could catch glimpses of a whitish line, that was in truth the boiling torrent whose voice mellowed as it rose through the still air.

Suddenly, as we rounded a corner, we seemed to have entered some other world. Before us lay the sweetest, greenest valley, watered by sparkling brooks half hidden by tall bracken. Meadows of rich grass were golden with large yellow buttercups, and quiet, well-cultivated fields lay beyond. It was more like a bit in Berkshire than anything else I know, with the addition of a background of low Scotch hills. This is the Happy Valley of Cheenee or Chini, as it is variously spelt.

Here, near a group of tall dark pines, stands a bungalow built by Lord Dalhousie, who delighted in this place. Since he left India it has been a refuge for all travellers, but has now been allowed to fall to pieces for want of the simplest repairs, and is used by the villagers as a stable for their cattle! It really is incomprehensible that this pleasant house should have been allowed to go to ruin; one would rather have expected it to become the nucleus of a European settlement, being one of the very few places in these hills where nature offers room for house building. Here is level land, good water, beautiful trees, a fine fall of ground down to the Sutlej, allowing perfect drainage, and a climate almost beyond the reach of the rains.

When I say these green meadows were suggestive only of England, I speak of course of one half of the picture. The other side remained unchanged; there were the same huge terraces of dark granite, the same ridges of crags and ice-cliffs, the same wild barren expanse of desolate grandeur, and the same three mountain-tops—" three silent pinnacles of aged snow"—reaching up to heaven.

I found a lovely halting-ground beneath a clump of apricot and larger trees, and let my brown brothers go and amuse themselves in the village. It was so delightful to wander by those tiny rippling burns, gathering large marsh buttercups and fresh water-cresses; or in the hot noon to rest on some cool bank of fern and moss looking up through the tremulous pale-green cloud to the tender blue overhead; or watch the dancing light reflected from glossy leaves on to the white stems, which else were hidden in shade. And ever and anon came a sound of flapping wings, an undertone of murmurous hidden waters;

> "The song of bird and bee,
> The chorus of the breezes, streams, and groves,
> All the great music to which nature moves."

Presently there came past me groups of laughing girls with the musical voice so common among the Pahari women. They were got up in their best, with sweet flowers in their hair; one of them wore a vest of pure white linen, which was very unusual. Her hair had just been done in countless fresh plaits, and twisted with silver chains. Both she and her companions wore an unusual number of silver ornaments, and all looked bright and pleasant. I cannot imagine why these girls are so much better-looking than the men. Some of them walk quite beautifully, with light, graceful carriage.

These, I believe, were bound for some wedding festivities. We were told that one dish at a Pahari wedding feast is roast goat; the goat having been sacrificed to the gods, has had his head cut off at one blow. He is merely "gralloched,"[1] and is then roasted without even being skinned. This nice dish is eaten with ghee and sweetmeats.

[1] Had the entrails removed.

Three miles beyond Chini we came to Pangi, one of the most picturesque of the very striking Himalayan villages; it seems as if the people purposely selected the steepest precipices and the most inaccessible cliffs, there to perch their eyrie. Here the highest available point is crowned with a temple like a very large *châlet;* thence all down the face of the hill the houses nestle among apricot-trees and other foliage. Right above the river one group of houses occupies the top of a projecting crag, with the river boiling below. Surely these hill babies must need double care from their guardian angels!

This, I think, was quite the most beautiful spot where we had yet been. The valley was more open, the expanse of snow wider, the foreground more striking. One magnificent group of old gnarled cedars overhung the path, and carried the palm over all we had yet seen. Half a dozen stems each from fifteen to twenty-five feet in circumference all started from one twisted mass of roots which turned themselves snake-like in every crevice of the rock face. A second great cedar close by, met the first overhead and their branches interlaced, framing a beautiful mountain torrent that rushed down through dark pine forest from a new mass of snows that had just opened to our view. For we were now in the heart of the snows, and white crests rose on every side of us.

That cedar group gave me pleasant work for several days; though sometimes it was rather awkward to "dodge" the little stones that rolled down the crag, and were uncomfortably suggestive of larger ones in store, such as occasionally come crashing down from far up the mountain side, leaving the unhappy traveller whose path they may cross short time for shrift. One such grievous accident occurred at Simla, where four men of the Governor-General's band were crushed in a moment. Four brothers were sitting together in a bullock-cart, which slowly toiled up the hill, while the father and another brother walked on in front. Suddenly, without a moment's warning, an immense mass of earth fell from the cliff right upon the cart, crushing the unlucky inmates and breaking the leg of the driver. The bullocks escaped unhurt. It

SNOWY RANGE FROM PANGI, THE VILLAGE ON THE CLIFF.

so happened that Lord Mayo and one of his staff were passing within sound of the crash, and hastened up in time to help the wretched father in extricating the bodies of his sons.

So you can imagine that on the whole I felt a good deal safer when sitting under a large apricot-tree, drawing the village, to the immense amusement of the inhabitants, whose acquaintance with white women was very limited. My water-colours, paint-box, and the growth of a sketch, were subjects of much interest; moreover our watches delighted them exceedingly. They would listen with astonishment, then as they moved off we could hear them repeat "tick-tick" to one another.

But the unfailing source of delight was my opera-glass, with which they could explore some of the marvels of that icy world to which no human foot might penetrate. And many a long hour's solace did this afford to the patient brownies, while they sat waiting during the mysterious process of making pictures. In general these were my sole companions from early dawn till they carried me back to camp at night, and leal, kindly Highlanders they proved. Sometimes they were of a musical turn, and their weird, monotonous songs with abrupt endings reminded me strangely of those which but a few months before were sung to us by the boatmen of the Hebrides. This resemblance often struck me forcibly, when in the evening a wild, wailing song rose from some of the temples, recalling some old Gaelic psalm, till I almost fancied myself once more on a brae-side in the bonnie north, instead of being in the cool shadows of these spectral hills.

I use the word "cool shadows" with good reason, for n where are you more vividly conscious of the sun's presence; so long as you are in the shade you feel almost chilly, as the cold breath from those white snows blows upon you. Yet you could not move one step into the sun without your thick sun-hat and white umbrella. In sketching I always had a great umbrella pitched above that. Then in good, thick, woollen clothes you might sit or walk just as you would do in Scotland, and I must add that woollen under-raiment is a matter of much more serious importance here than on our own hills. I told you that all these women wear thick woollen materials with bright stripes. It so happened that my last investment in Skye had been in a fishwife's petticoat of many colours. This greatly took the fancy of these people, and I constantly noticed them quietly take up a corner and feel it, and then discuss it among themselves, so perhaps the Pahari weavers have adopted a new thing in stripes *a l'Ecossaise.*

COOLIE'S TINDER-BOX, FULL SIZE.

After the cringing manner of the natives of the plain there is something very pleasant in the frank, cheery way these people come up to you; not caring to conceal their wonder and interest at the curious and almost unknown variety of the species that has come among them: they show you their ornaments and inspect yours with such endless amusement.

We tried to persuade some of them to sell us their amulets and curiously wrought knives, but without success. They had no objection, however, to sell us tinder-boxes of curious patterns, and a considerable variety of the brass brooches with which every girl, however poor, fastens her plaid. These vary from three to eight inches in diameter. The actual brooch, and very peculiar pin, are of precisely the old Celtic pattern as worn in Scotland and Algeria, and as dug up in Irish turf-bogs. But the simple old form has been adapted to Oriental taste by the addition of two elaborate circular wings, so that the form of the ornament is

HIMALAYAN BROOCH.

now a trefoil. To the brooch is attached a brass chain with sharp hook, which catches the plaid on the shoulder for additional security, and I am told that some of the old Scotch brooches have the very same. These brooches fasten the heavy plaid of striped colours, very much like those worn in our own Highlands, and caught in precisely similar folds. It certainly is curious that the Celts of Scotland, the Khabyles of Algeria, and these Paharis of the far East, should fasten their striped woollen raiment with the same very peculiar brooch. But here, the belted plaid leaves one shoulder and arm bare, showing heavy metal bracelets.

The writers' inkhorns are also curious. They are made of wrought silver or brass, and have a bottle fastened alongside of a case to hold pens or reeds. They are worn in the belt like a dagger, just like those alluded to by Ezekiel[1] when addressing the children of Israel in the Babylonian captivity—that captivity whence they never returned. So possibly if there be any truth in the theory that some of the lost tribes did find a refuge in the mountains of India, they may have brought these inkhorns with them, as well as those more curious eastern customs we have already noticed.

We had now got fairly beyond the influence of the rains, and if only "leave" had permitted us to linger, we might have remained in this paradise with the blissful consciousness that not one drop of rain could come near us. As we looked down the valley whence we had come, the dark lowering clouds told very plainly what a wet world lay there, while we were revelling in unchanging sunshine. Just imagine the artistic delight of returning day after day to your sketching-ground with the certainty of seeing just the same light you saw yesterday and the day before that!

If I had not far to go and so could dispense with bearers, a nice, venerable-looking old man was always on the look-out to carry my goods; then he would ensconce himself as watchdog under some fine old tree. One day I was conscious that a third person had joined us. Struck by the unwonted silence I looked up to see a study worthy of Murillo. A strikingly handsome girl, with clear, olive complexion just flushed with pink, and large, pensive, brown eyes with silken fringe, sat under a great apricot tree. The venerable old head rested on her knee while she pursued most successful entomological researches in the elf locks, just as in the old ballads, the unkempt warriors, returned from their forays, laid their heads on the lap of some fair princess, who doubtless performed the same kind office, while the knight

[1] Ez. ix. 2, 3, 11.

recounted his adventures! In the present instance the old patriarch was too happy for words, but lay still in the cool shade, lazily cracking apricot-stones with an expression of serene enjoyment. Just imagine my feelings! But there was no use in being disgusted, it was as natural a part of village toilette as the work of the barber in the plains; and one which we constantly saw being quietly performed on the open balconies for the edification of all passers by—girls thus tended their lovers, and mothers their children, and as Paddy observed on the subject of picking up wee beasties, "indeed there was no question of picking—he just took them as they came!"

Sometimes where a tame monkey forms part of the establishment it is considered immensely amusing to let him sit on the shoulder of one of the family diligently seeking for hidden treasures. The creature beats his preserves with the same neatness and regularity that you may observe any day in the zoological gardens, but I must say he keeps his own hair a good deal neater than the tangled unkempt jungle provided for him by his human descendants.

We were now in the grape country; and from about this point, and up the valley, vines are extensively cultivated, chiefly, I believe, near the river banks, for we did not see very many vineyards, though some of the houses were half covered with the graceful trailer. About a month later when the fruit is ripe, you may buy a whole kilter full, that is, a basket like a gigantic strawberry pottle, two feet high, for sixpence. This, you must allow was an additional reason to regret being compelled to turn away from this laughing valley. We were also struck by the quantity of mistletoe growing on the wild apricot-trees. Just the common English plant reverenced by our ancestors.

As to animal life, I have already stated that our attention was not distracted by its abundance. One bear and a few pheasants and partridges of divers sorts were all that rewarded the gentlemen for many and toilsome expeditions. And for my own part I saw only two silvery hill-foxes, a number of black ants fully three-quarters of an inch long, and a couple of snakes.

Amongst the domestic animals, however, you may here see the yak, which is a most precious addition to the herds of the hill people. There was much joking going on, about an Englishman who had recently stalked and shot one of these tame cows to his own immense satisfaction, which, however, was sorely damped on finding himself compelled to pay heavy damages for his sport!

This little Ox of Thibet is a very precious possession in such a country as this. He is short and thickset, like our Highland cattle, and covered all over from his nostril to his tail with long shaggy hair,[1] perhaps I should rather call it wool, which all but touches the ground, and which when cleaned is soft and silky, and spins remarkably well. It is familiar to us in Europe in its manufactured form as yak lace. The hair becomes thicker and longer, and the creature larger, that is, as tall as fourteen hands, on the high table-lands of Thibet. Its natural home being in a climate so severe, and where pasture is so scanty, it seems to be altogether indifferent to both, and is therefore an invaluable beast of burden; as it will carry the heaviest loads across the most inaccessible passes quite regardless of paths, content to pick up the scantiest and foulest fare.

Nevertheless the little yak cows yield an abundant supply of the very richest milk, thick and creamy, and producing just twice as much butter as the common cow of our dairies, also excellent cheese. The butter is rather hard, but if the milk of the yak is mixed with that of the common cow in equal parts, the result is highly satisfactory. Various experiments of this sort have been tried at the dairy farms in the Vosges, where the little yak has been successively acclimatised. In India it does not seem to thrive at a lower level than 9,000 feet. Here, as in the plains, the cowherds declare that the cows will not yield their milk unless the calf be present. So that if the calf be dead, they either give the

[1] It is somewhat remarkable that both the appearance and the name of this shaggy Bull-horse should bear so strong a resemblance to the common description of the mysterious water-bulls and water-horses of the Celts, the dread Yak-Urisk.

mother its little foot to lick, or else have its skin stuffed with straw; in short, it is precisely the "Tulchan" in which our Scotch dairymaids used to place such implicit faith. The yak is of divers colours, but generally black and white; the length of its wool increases so much on the higher levels as sometimes to trail on the ground.

As a beast of burden it is slow, but wonderfully sure of foot, picking its way in perfect safety over the very roughest ground. Sometimes when a difficulty arises about getting coolies, a traveller is supplied with quite a little herd of these, which carry his tents, his goods, and even himself if he so wills it. The only objection to riding one of a herd is that his social instincts draw him so close to his fellows that he may bring you into undesirable proximity to tent-poles and cooking-pots. The shaggy little creature has the broad hump peculiar to Indian cattle, and which doubtless, like that of the camel, is nature's provision for times of scarcity, affording a storehouse of fat on which to draw, when other food fails. Instead of lowing like other cattle, its conversational powers are limited to an almost inaudible grunt, which to a creature so gregarious must really be very trying. Perhaps this accounts for his anxiety to walk close to his companions. Hence his scientific name, *Bos grunniens.*

It is the tail of this creature which is so common on the plains of India, as the chowrie, wherewith to drive away flies, and ornament horses and elephants. Its horns are short and massive, beautifully curved and pointing forward.

So this curious little cow, with a horse's tail and sheep's wool, combines the properties of all three animals. It finds its own scanty food, yet yields the richest milk. To the plough it brings the strength of an ox. It clothes its master in silky and abundant wool, while to a beef-eating people it would also supply meat and leather. So it may well be prized by these poor highlanders.

More surefooted than the surest pony, it carries its load or its rider along pathless mountains, and is most at home on the highest passes. The only point where it fails is in climbing very steep broken ground, where climbing from rock to rock is necessary.

Here its very short legs are a serious obstacle, and riders find it necessary to dismount.

At Pangi we lingered for a happy fortnight. Arriving as total strangers, we received a cordial welcome from the "Road Sahib," Mr. Leupolt, whose wife and child had made their summer home in this paradise. Instead of pitching our tents, therefore, they made us share their house. Other little white tents, however, soon appeared on the morsel of artificially levelled ground close by, occasionally without even going through the courteous form of asking leave, or making the smallest acknowledgment to the inhabitants of the bungalow, who, however, were invariably ready to show their hospitality to all comers. Several parties of gentlemen arrived on their way to or from various mountain passes, such as the Rupin Pass, the Buspa and Sangla Valleys, Thibet, and other places. So we got tidings from the wilds: and tidings too from the civilised world, for even here the daily post came in with as much regularity as in Simla itself.

A PEEP INTO CHINESE TARTARY.

CHAPTER XVII.

A PEEP INTO CHINESE TARTARY.

Prayer-Wheels of all Sizes—Water-wheels—Village Wheels—Thibetan Genealogy—Tartar Funerals—Edible Pine—Crossing the Sutlej by a Rope Bridge—A Pleasant Home in the Wilderness—A Deserted Village—Flying Squirrel—A Glorious Forest—Felling Timber under Difficulties.

ONE march more brought us to our farthest point, at Rarung. Beyond this there was no road, and though I believe a dandie can be carried wherever a man can walk, there was no particular object in pressing on farther; at least so we were told, and so, at the moment, being entranced with the loveliness of the spot where our tents were pitched, we were content to believe. Of course, as soon as you get home again you begin crying over your "spilt milk," and feel convinced that if only your last grain of energy had not failed you, you might have seen something more beautiful than all else. It is vain to say that "what the eye sees not the heart rues not." In your secret heart you believe that *that* gorge in the far-away forest, *that* crystal stream which you might so easily have traced to its parent glacier, *that* ruined city, which at the moment you assumed must be just like all the others, and so passed by, would in truth have eclipsed all that you *did* see, and have become to you a joy for ever. So the wanderer is never satisfied. At all events, we had the childish joy of having got "the best for the last," for indeed the loveliness of this place exceeded even that of Pangi. Whichever way we looked the beauty was the same. In every direction snows, huge hills, mixed foliage, and rushing water. Close behind us a grand expanse of cedar forest, and far up the valley a shapely group of snow-peaks, which we were told were to be our only glimpse of Chinese Tartary.

A very few miles more would have taken us right into that land of Huc and Gabet, but we should no longer have been travelling under British protection, and might have met with divers difficulties. So although we were now fairly in the country of the

POCKET PRAYER-WHEEL.

Lamas, that is to say, the Buddhists, we never even saw one of the great Buddhist monasteries of which we heard so much, but what did strike us as very strange was, every now and again to meet respectable-looking hill-men, twirling little brass cylinders, only about eight inches long, which they were incessantly spinning round and round as they walked along the road. What these toys were, we could not at first make out, till it was explained to us that they were prayer-wheels, and that turning them was just about equivalent to the telling of beads, which in Christian lands we have sometimes seen devout Catholic workmen counting as they go forth to their morning's toil, or wend their homeward way at eventide.

But if we think the telling of beads a somewhat mechanical piece of formalism, just imagine finding all the adoration of a whole village being ground by machinery like so much corn! These ascriptions of praise to Buddha (they are not supposed to be prayers, those being unnecessary) are all closely written on strips of cloth or paper, the same sentence repeated many thousands of times. These are closely rolled round a spindle of which one end forms the handle. The upper end is inclosed in a metal cylinder on which also the sacred words appear in embossed characters. From the middle of the cylinder hangs a small lump of metal, which whirls round, and gives the necessary impetus to the little machine, so that it twirls with the slightest exertion, and goes on grinding any given number of meritorious acts of worship, while the owner, carrying this pretty little plaything in his hand, goes about his daily work.

Of course his mind *ought* to be absorbed all the time in quiet meditation on the perfections of Buddha, but that would be too much to expect from a busy, working man, so he says the sentences aloud at the beginning and end of his devotions, and in the meantime twirls slowly, while a tiny bell marks each revolution and reminds him if he is unconsciously going too fast.

There is one who speaks of prayer, as that whereby

> . . . . "the whole round world is every way
> Bound by gold chains around the feet of God."

But such material metallic links as these gold, brass, or copper cylinders are indeed strange ties to bind earth to heaven!

Some of these little pocket cylinders are very beautifully wrought; some are even inlaid with precious stones. I saw one great beauty which I coveted exceedingly. The owner would on no account sell it. I returned to the temple next morning, wishing at least to make a drawing of it, but I think he mistrusted me, for he and his plaything had both vanished, and I had to be content with a much simpler one of bronze, inlaid with copper.

The people have the greatest reluctance to sell even the ugliest old mills. They cling to them as lovingly as you might do to your dear old Bible; not merely from the charm of association, but from a dread lest a careless hand should turn them against the sun, and so change their past acts of merit into positive sin. So there was a great deal of talk, and many irons in the fire, before I was allowed to purchase two of these, at a price which would have supplied half the village with new ones.

One of these was procured for me, and sent, together with a copy of St. John's gospel in Thibetan, by Mr. Pagell, the Moravian Missionary at Poo, far in the interior—a green oasis surrounded by bare rocky hills—a wild desolate region, where he and his wife have for many years devoted their lives to the almost vain attempt to Christianise their neighbours; their labours being attended with the usual discouragement, and their earnest endeavours to teach others resulting in a very small handful of converts. Nevertheless, they are content, for their work's sake, to remain in exile, very rarely seeing even one white face; and that only when some stray sportsman wanders so far into the wilds.

During their twenty years' residence, *i.e.* till 1881, only three white ladies have found their way to this remote station. Once in two years Mr. Pagell travels to Simla, there to lay in needful stores, and exchange ideas with his fellows. Imagine, in so solitary a life, the trial of having to part with their son, their only child, when it became necessary to send him to Europe for education!

Mr. Pagell told me that the mill he had procured for me contained a strip of paper, on which was written a short, but very comprehensive prayer in Thibetan; a prayer for the six classes of living creatures, namely, the souls in heaven, the evil spirits in the air, men, animals, souls in purgatory, and souls in hell.

But as a general rule, all worship begins, continues, and ends, with one unvarying sentence, OM MANI PADME HOUM. These words are known as *the six-syllabled charm.* As I have just said, they are raised in embossed letters outside the cylinder, and are closely written, perhaps many thousand times, on strips of paper inside. They are engraved all over sacred places—on the face of the rocks—on the walls of the temple—in one great monastery in Ladakh the wall is literally covered with these words of sacred mystic import, ascribing perpetual adoration to Buddha, as the Jewel on the Lotus, in reference to his lotus-throne;[1] that is to say, the pattern symbolical of the lotus or water-lily with which his throne is always adorned, and which is supposed to convey the same idea as that suggested by the words, "The LORD sitteth upon the flood, yea, the LORD sitteth King for ever."

The literal meaning of the sentence is as follows: A.U.M. or OM equivalent to the Hebrew JAH, the holiest and most glorious title of the Almighty; MANI, the Jewel, one of Buddha's titles; PADME, the Lotus; HOUM, equivalent to Amen. This "six-syllabled charm," is the sovereign balm for every conceivable evil.

Some Buddhist sects vary this magic sentence. Those of China and Japan substituted the reiteration of the Sanskrit name of the Buddha for whose coming they now look, *Amitabha Buddha.* But somehow the original form of the invocation has been lost by priests and people to whom Sanskrit is an unknown dead language, so the unvarying refrain of all Buddhist worship in Japan is *Namu Amida Butzu*, which is rendered, "Save us, O Buddha!"

In China where the name of Buddha becomes transformed into

[1] As an instance of how literally Brahmanism has adopted the symbols of Buddhism I may cite a sample of Benares brass-work, a small but most comprehensive compendium of symbolism. The sacred bull of Siva bears on its back a lotus blossom, whose petals opening reveal, enthroned within it, a small oviform pebble.* The sacred blossom is overshadowed by a hooded cobra, holding a minute brass water-vessel, so perforated as to allow one drop to fall from time to time on "the jewel in the lotus." Here Hindooism has appropriated not only the lotus-throne, but also the cobra canopy, which generally overshadows the images of Buddha.

* For reference to sacred symbolic pebbles; see chapter xxi.

Fu or Fo, the millions of Fo-ists repeat the name *Ommi-to-fu* in endless chorus. Every devout Fo-ist desires to utter these charmed

PRAYER-WHEEL.

words at least three hundred thousand times [1] in the course of his life. To this end, many of their priests shut themselves up in the

[1] Buddhism does not monopolise vain repetitions. We find them in all faiths. In India, the worshippers both of Siva and Vishnu accumulate merits and secure admission to heaven by merely reiterating their sacred names. One votary of Krishna devoted his life to the *daily utterance* 300,000 *times* of the name of Hari, the Sun-god. Another was promised a vision of Vishnu when he should have repeated one text 800,000 times. After three months' hard labour he completed his task, but with no result, whereupon the Brahman teacher told him that he must have made some slip in one repetition, which would invalidate the whole, and advised him to begin again!

temples for months together, with no other occupation than that of repeating these words over and over again, day and night. Sometimes ten or twelve devotees will thus voluntarily imprison themselves, and continue all day shouting the holy name in chorus, while at night they take it by turns, and one party keeps up the weary, monotonous chaunt while the others sleep. Those who have undertaken this means of heaping up merit must never leave their cell for any purpose whatever, till the appointed period is ended, but sit immovably, incessantly jabbering their idiotic song, with vacant faces.

Nor are the laity slow to practise this simple method of laying up treasure for eternity. As they go about their daily business, the same words are for ever on their lips. The devout and the aged carry strings of beads, whereon they instinctively count their reiterations of the life-insuring spells, and while they speak to you, or to one another, on all manner of secular subjects, between each sentence comes a low murmur *Om-mi-to-fuh!* Then as they pass away down the street, still you see their lips moving, and you know that they are still whispering the unvarying ascription of praise to Buddha, *Om-mi-to-fuh! Om-mi-to-fuh!*

That first word OM is said to have been the holy and mystical name of GOD amongst the ancient Celts. Here in the East, it is precious alike to all sects, for while the Buddhists reiterate it as their one infallible charm, and sculpture it on all holy places, the Brahmans esteem it so holy that they will not utter it aloud; while the Jains, laying the hand upon the mouth, whisper it in deepest reverence.

Thus finding the same sacred word in use at the opposite ends of the world, suggests a link which carries us far back, from the ceremonies of the Buddhist, working his little charm, to some remote age when these dead customs were all instinct with life, and were to the worshippers merely symbols of some grand reality, well known to them all. That reality was once probably embodied in the worship of the revolving sun; accepted by so many nations either as GOD, or as the representative of the Almighty Creator.

Hence the intensely strong feeling in favour of always following the course of the sun;—that term *Deisul* of which we find so many traces still lingering in our own Highlands,[1] and which here, in India, crops up at every turn. As we there noticed the old custom of walking sunwise round people, cattle, houses, or chapels, so here we find the people making *Deisul* processions round their temples, leading their flocks sunwise round their villages, dancing sunwise round their idols, and turning the *mani* (prayer-mill) in the same course.

Very early in the world's history, a revolving wheel of light came to be reverenced as the symbol of the Sun-god. Such an one was turned as an act of worship in the temples of the Greeks, who derived the custom from the still more ancient Egyptians. The Scandinavians represent their god of time, "the Seater," as holding a wheel in one hand, and flowers in the other. And the image of the Saxon Sun-god has also a wheel of fire.

The same idea is said to attach to the wheels of the car of Jagannáth, and similar idol cars, common throughout India, which once a year are drawn forth, and perform a solemn circuit, supposed to be symbolical of the course of the sun.[2]

[1] See *In the Hebrides*, C. F. Gordon Cumming. Chatto and Windus.

[2] That this really was the original meaning attached to this ceremony is plainly proved by the season at which the great car festival occurs, namely, Midsummer, the very worst period which could possibly be imagined for a pilgrimage, and one which even Hindoo obstinacy would surely alter were it not acting in obedience to the sun's fixed laws. It is the season when its most burning rays alternate with such floods of rain as make the land wholly unfit for prolonged travel, and yet these devoted worshippers start year after year on the journey that must occupy many weeks, and on which at least ten thousand of their number, and sometimes a very much larger proportion, perish miserably from exhaustion and exposure to the inclement weather. This, remember, is in a land where every variation of weather can be foretold with the utmost certainty, and consequently nothing but a steadfast determination to do honour to Midsummer could account for the selection of such a season.

We all know the picture of those three huge towers, the principal of which is forty-five feet high and thirty-five feet square, and *rolls on sixteen great wheels, each measuring thirteen feet in diameter*, which form the cars whereon "The Lord of the World" and his fellow idols sit enthroned, as they are dragged over the bodies of prostrate worshippers,—a form of self-immolation

You must bear in mind that Jagannáth is only another name for Vishnu, the All-Preserver, who, in another incarnation, is worshipped as Krishna, the Sun-god. The temples of Vishnu are almost invariably marked by a mystic wheel, generally crowning the spire, just as the temples of Siva are marked by the trident. Moreover, Vishnu is represented holding a wheel in one of his four hands. And the same sacred symbol is stamped on the breast and arms of his worshippers, with a golden brand.

ANCIENT SCULPTURE SHOWING THE WHEEL AS THE OBJECT OF WORSHIP.

The wheel being thus recognised as the symbol of supreme good, it was natural that it should be adopted by the early disciples of Buddha as the emblem of their master, who is accordingly

which, by the way, is now proved to be of the very rarest occurrence, and indeed is wholly unauthorised, as this beneficent god protects all living creatures and rejects all animal sacrifices. Though his vast temple at Orissa is that best known to us from its superior sanctity, there is scarcely a village in Bengal without its car of Jagannáth. Dr. Duff says that in Calcutta and its neighbourhood there are scores of them, varying in size from a few feet up to thirty or forty feet in height, and on the day of the great car festival—that is to say, at Midsummer—all these are brought forth, in the most remote districts and cities and villages, that the myriads who cannot have the privilege of a pilgrimage to Cuttack may nevertheless behold *the same mystic circuit* performed.

reverenced as the Tchakravarta Rajah, or King of the Wheel. Thus it is, that in some of the most ancient Buddhist sculptures at the Bilsah and Sanchi topes in central India, Buddha is represented simply by a wheel, overshadowed by a golden umbrella, which is a common emblem of his power. His worshippers are represented as making their offerings to this symbolic wheel. The same sacred emblem is found again and again among the Jain and Buddhist sculptures in the Caves of Ellora and Ajunta, in most cases projecting in front of Buddha's lotus-throne. In one instance an astronomical table is carved above the wheel. In another it is supported on either side by a stag, supposed to represent the fleetness wherewith the sun runs his daily circuit. Others again show the wheel supported by kneeling elephants.

When, therefore, it came to be accounted an act of merit merely to turn over the pages whereon holy words were inscribed, the adaptation of the already sacred wheel to this purpose might very naturally present itself, and the necessity of invariably turning it sunwise would follow as a matter of course.

The Buddhists trace back the use of these wheels, or rather barrels, for at least 1,400 years, and believe them to have originated from the notion that it is an act of merit, and an efficacious cure of sin to be for ever reading or reciting portions of the sacred writings of Buddha. But as many of the people could not read, it came to be considered sufficient to turn over the rolled manuscripts containing the precious precepts. This convenient substitute was found to save so much time and trouble, that the custom rapidly spread, and the action was further simplified by the invention of wheels known as *Tchu-Chor*—great egg-shaped barrels full of prayers; a cord being attached to the base of the barrel, which on being pulled, sets the cylinder twirling like a child's whirligig.

These are set up in all public places in Thibet, so that the poor, who do not possess such luxuries as little pocket Wheels of Devotion, may not lose their chance of thus heaping up merit; or, as our friends in the Emerald Isle express it, "making their souls." They are erected at the doors of dwelling-houses, that every man going in or out may set them spinning for his own benefit and that of the inmates, and in some of the Lama monasteries there are many rows of such cylinders, about one foot in height, so conveniently arranged, and so lightly poised, that the most casual passer-by could scarcely abstain from running his hand along them, and so set them all spinning diligently, weaving "a garment of praise" for the behoof of him who set them to work.

Only think what a benefit it would be to the annoying little boys in London, who *will* rattle sticks all along the area rails, as they run along the street, if only the said rails responded by jotting down in their favour a score of acts of merit!

In the case of the great terraces on which devout persons have laid innumerable stone slabs, each inscribed with the charmed words, merit must be acquired by walking round them in sunwise circuit. Some of these *Muttis*, as they are called, are half a mile in length, one near the town of Leh is a mile long. They are generally about ten feet in width and the same in height. They are erected at intervals of from two to eight miles, along the principal thoroughfares in Thibet, and the road is invariably led on each side of them, so that the traveller may pass them on one side in going and on the other in returning on his way.

In this case, however, as also in turning the Barrels of Praise, I believe that the direction to be followed has reference to the sacred words written and engraven on barrel or terrace, as it is necessary that the characters forming the holy phrase should pass in proper order before the eyes of the person turning. So as all oriental books are read from the right hand of the last page, towards the left, this direction must be followed in walking round the great terraces and other buildings on which the holy words are inscribed, thus keeping his left hand towards the object round which he is walking. Happily a doubly satisfactory result is thus produced, as the merits of the sunwise turn are thus combined with the reverential homage due to the six-syllabled charm.[1]

[1] I am told that Buddhism has now made its way farther down the Kunawar valley, and that a small terrace covered with the six-syllabled charm is to be seen in a ravine between Nachar and Tarunda.

It is not only on these terraces that the mystic words are engraven. Near the town of Ladakh there are in every direction great cairns of slates and slabs, all bearing the same inscription, and in every village, and by every road-side it meets the wayfarer, sometimes roughly hewn on the rock, sometimes elaborately carved, sometimes coloured, in characters varying from a couple of inches

WATER PRAISE-WHEELS.

to half a yard in height. The cylinders likewise vary in size, from the little hand-barrels the size of a policeman's rattle, to huge vats perhaps fifteen feet in height by ten in diameter, co-operative casks wherein is stored the mead of praise, which (at the touch of a heavy iron crank) flows forth for the benefit of a whole district! I have been told that in some of the monasteries at Ladakh a mechanical arrangement like a clock is so contrived as to make a number of these cylinders revolve, by means of a system of heavy weights which are wound up at sunrise and sunset.

But far more ingenious, and I may say poetic, is the device which has enlisted the breeze and the mountain streams in multiplying a never-ceasing silent *benedicite*, ceaseless ascriptions of praise whereby the villagers acquire unlimited stores of merit without any trouble save the preliminary labour of erecting wind or water-wheels. In the latter, the cylinders containing the mystic words are placed upright in a shed, built over running water. A spindle passing through each terminates in a horizontal wheel, having the cogs turned diagonally to the water. These wheels rotate with the action of the running stream, and so turn the cylinder. Sometimes several of these are placed abreast across the stream, the rudest form of cedar-wood temple being built to support and shelter them.

The wind-wheels are so constructed as to rotate obedient to the action of fan-like wings, these also being inscribed with the sacred words.

Another form in which the winds do duty may be seen at Darjeeling, where there is an important Lama temple and a large prayer-wheel. Here ceaseless ascriptions of praise are offered on behalf of the dead, whose names, together with the mystic words, are inscribed on flags of great length, and only about four feet in width. These streamers are affixed to lofty poles, and as they flutter in the breeze they are accounted to be offering praise in the name of the dead. Similarly inscribed flags flutter from many a cairn on the lonely mountain passes.

Close below the little green spot where we had pitched our tents stood a Lama temple, and beyond that, on a crag overhanging the river, was perched the village, in the middle of which stood the Hindoo temple, for even this little spot in the depths of these glorious hills had its religious dissensions, and its divers paths in search of the unknown. So the earliest stillness of dawn, and the hush of evening were alike disturbed by bells, horns, and trumpets calling the people to worship in one temple or the other, or else to do homage to the Khuda, that is, the tabernacle in which the veiled image of Durgâ is daily carried out for an airing in her curious, closely-curtained ark, similar to those of which I have already told you—an ark set on long poles or staves, and carried by two priests, one of whom always walks backwards, and into which no one save the priest is allowed to look.

Whenever the Khuda was carried past it was always surrounded by a large number of the villagers, playing on divers instruments, and leaping and dancing. I suppose this temple is wealthy, for the metal faces which are always set round the box seemed to me to be of silver, instead of the usual brass, as was also the large head

DEVI AT BALAH ON THE GANGES.

surmounted with a tuft of yak's tails on the top, while lower down hung the usual fringe of long silky yak's tails, almost sweeping the ground as the ark was carried along.

What with Buddhist prayer-wheel and Hindoo ark, we found ample interest in the religious peculiarities of our neighbours, but the Lama temple was the height of attraction, as being the greatest novelty, and the old Bonze (priest) always gave us a cordial welcome, and doubtless looked at us with equal curiosity, we being the first British women who had found our way so far by this route. Of course we were equally objects of inquisitive interest to all the villagers, and as it is the custom for them to testify their surprise or admiration of any object whatsoever, by constantly putting out their tongues, the frequent appearance of these was at first startling to the uninitiated, and of course struck us as barely civil, which, however, was by no means the case. The same curious custom is expressive of most joyous greeting when two friends meet!

Unlike the lightly-draped yellow-robed Buddhist priests of Ceylon, these in the valley of Kunawar are dressed in scarlet, with a scarlet or orange-coloured cap like a biretta. Further in the interior, the Lamas of Spiti wear an orange-coloured under-garment reaching to the ankles, and over this a loose jacket of dark red, with long wide sleeves. They are closely shaved and go bareheaded. I am told that a much more curious difference exists in the regulations of these two orders, in that the priests of Kunawar are celibates, but are allowed the solace of tobacco, whereas the Spiti monks are allowed to marry, but are denied their 'baccy! In Spiti the majority of the brothers in each family are Lamas, and even small boys wear the ecclesiastical yellow robe, but without the red jacket. The Lamas all wear rosaries, but the lay brothers indulge in necklaces and earrings of coral and turquoise beads strung on wool—a primitive adornment which is passed through the ear, and fastened with a knot at either end.

The relations of these Buddhist priests and people seemed very kindly. You may see one going along the road twirling his little prayer-mill, and the people meeting him bow lowly, and crave a blessing, which he bestows, laying both hands on the head of the suppliant. A bunch of specially attractive flowers is sometimes carried for miles, as an acceptable offering.

The general arrangement of this little hill temple is curiously like that of an ordinary Roman Catholic Church; there are divers small altars, with images of saints and vases of flowers, and incense burning before each image. All round the walls are admirably drawn mythological pictures, especially one fair saint riding a tiger, which recurs frequently. On one side of the temple sits a grand gilt image of Buddha, calm and contemplative, his throne, as usual, edged with lotus leaves. Before him is set a low table, whereon are placed many small cups of water, tea, flour, milk, and butter. These, and the aforesaid wild flowers, are the offerings brought by worshippers, to whom animal sacrifices are forbidden. Those are reserved for the neighbouring Hindoo temple, and to a creed which appeals more to the superstitious fears of the people.

Beside Buddha stands a second image almost as tall (eight or ten feet), representing an exceedingly hideous being, quite unlike any Hindoo image. A creature with enormous eyes painted on its stomach, and wings of the orthodox demon type. Who was thus represented we could not make out for certain, but we were afterwards told it was a thunder-devil, a personage wholly unknown to Buddha. At his feet lay the Thibetan holy books, written on strips of parchment about eighteen inches long by four broad, bound with wooden boards and wrapped up in curiously embroidered silk; a large Sunkh shell on which was carved the sacred lotus; a very precious trumpet, made of the thigh-bone of some deceased Lama, elaborately carved; some medallions made of the ashes of another holy Lama; a row of little vases containing flowers and peacocks' feathers; seven brass cups filled with water; cymbals, and an incense burner. All manner of gaudy drapery was hung on every side, by no means clean. Indeed, I must confess the whole place was very dirty, and smelt so very filthy, that my companions beat a precipitate retreat, and I could hardly even sit at the door long enough to get a rough sketch.

It was curious to see what trash some of the offerings were, but the people are very like children in some things, and like to hang up any queer thing they find. Mr. Simpson told me of one temple in which a *great* treasure was found hanging up. This was an English tailor's book of patterns, with all the prices for coats and trousers marked thereon! He also mentioned the delight with which they had received an old gin-bottle, marked with a large cat, symbolical of Old Tom. This and some empty brandy-bottles found honoured place on the altar as vases to hold flowers and peacocks' feathers, while some crystal stoppers of old decanters were held more precious than diamonds!

But the really striking feature of this temple is a colossal Prayer-wheel, like a very large barrel-organ, turned by a great iron crank, which acts as handle. It is a great cylinder, about twelve feet

LARGE PRAISE-WHEEL IN THE LAMA TEMPLE AT KARUNG.

high and six or eight in diameter. It is painted in circular bands of gold and bright colour, and on every band is inscribed the one, oft-recurring Buddhist ascription, which usurps the place of all prayer—the ascription of praise "To the most glorious Jewel, the

Lotus." The cylinder is said to be full of similar sentences, and as it slowly revolves on its axis, a most musical bell marks each revolution, and the worshipper is accredited with having uttered that short compendium of devotion just so many times as it is repeated within the cylinder. This great barrel is the devotion-store for the neighbourhood, and men from distant villages which are not provided with such time-saving wheels of devotion, take advantage of a visit to Rarung, to work off a few thousand acts of praise on their own behalf and that of their relations. It is rather hard work, as a stiff handle works the great iron crank which causes the cylinder to revolve on its axis.

Each would-be worshipper, too poor to possess a little hand-mill of his own, comes to the temple, *kotows* to the head Lama, who, laying his hand on his head, blesses him; then squatting in front of the great wheel, he turns the crank for himself and those dear to him. If many worshippers arrive simultancously, the priest works the crank, that all may share alike in this unspeakable benefit. It seems really hard work, but when first I went to the temple I found my poor coolies, already weary with carrying their human burden so far, grinding away, as though in very truth their hearts' desire depended on their diligence, the mechanical striking of the musical bell marking how rapidly their store of celestial credit was accumulating. You see there was no prayer-wheel at Pangi, where they lived, so they were making the most of their opportunities.

Is it not strange to think that for at least fourteen centuries, successive generations should thus have continued grinding their acts of devotion to the saintly philosopher whose words of wondrous wisdom even now afford food for deep study to the wise men of Europe—and that this dreary formalism should have emanated from a faith so subtle and metaphysical as Buddhism?

I am told that these Wheels of Praise are now to be found only in these wild Himalayan regions—in Mongolia, Thibet, Chinese Tartary, and other dominions of the Grand Lama, the teacher of the way of life (*lam* being the Thibetan for *path*), who still turns the wheel of Buddha for the benefit of upwards of four hundred millions of the human race in all solemnity and earnestness.[1]

The flippancy and the enlightenment of this nineteenth century, its progress or its scoffing, are to him alike matters of supreme indifference. He knows that during his earthly life none can gainsay him, for he is at once high priest and king; and he knows that after death his soul will be re-absorbed into the Divine essence, so if there is anything more for him to learn he will know it all then.

Finding that it was impossible for us to penetrate into Thibet, our friends comforted us by very uninviting pictures of the bleak plains that lay beyond the beautiful peaks that bounded our horizon. They told us how after climbing on and on, from one high pass to another, they had at length reached a high cool tableland. There they saw no more picturesque beauty, no more beautiful timber, in fact no timber at all, not even sticks for firewood. But they found dirty tribes living in dirtier tents, leading a wild pastoral life; their flocks of goats, sheep, camels, and oxen supplying them with all the necessaries of life—raiment and tent-canvas, food and fuel. Add to these a bowl of Tartar tea, thickened with oatmeal, and an inch of melted butter floating on its surface, and the happiness of these frugal folk is complete. The fuel is called *argols;* that of sheep and goats is said to burn with a heat so intense as to bring a bar of iron to a white heat. So you see Mother Nature has provided for the lack of firewood. As to the suffocating smoke produced by this noxious fuel as well as by the clouds of tobacco, which blind unaccustomed eyes, and blend with the fragrance of garlic and rancid oil, the people seem rather to enjoy these things, and are moreover wholly indifferent to the swarms of vermin of every species which here congregate.

All this sounded by no means inviting, so we were quite content to limit our circle of Thibetan acquaintance to such

[1] I subsequently found many large Scripture-wheels in the Buddhist temples in Japan—revolving libraries containing the Sacred Books. I also discovered kindred wheels or barrels containing images of Buddhist saints at the Lama temple at Pekin; also among the ruins of the Summer Palace.

wandering merchants as we met on the narrow high-roads, those quaint dirty creatures, women whose frowzy hair had been guiltless of brushing since the day they were born, though it was plaited in such an incalculable number of small tails, and ornamented with such large turquoises and lumps of amber. And, you must know, we accounted ourselves highly honoured in adding these ladies to our visiting list. Talk of old blue blood! why, here are a race who pride themselves on their direct lineal descent from the King of the Monkeys! They tell how he came to dwell in the mountains, and made his home in a cave, there striving to live a life of holy contemplation, undisturbed by the outer world. A beautiful demon, however, sought him out, and prayed the monkey king to marry her. The apish St. Anthony resisted her blandishments for a while, but finally yielded. So the beautiful demon became the mother of children more cunning and imitative than any mere human beings, though they were content to wear the human form, and the descendants of these ape demons peopled Thibet, and their posterity hold their memory in loving reverence!

Nor were these the only people of whom we heard strange stories, as we gathered round the bright cedar-wood fire beneath the clear starry heaven. We tried to exercise strong faith, while recalling Huc's curious accounts of Tartar funerals, telling how, when a great chief dies, several of the finest young men and women of the tribe are made to swallow mercury [1] till they suffocate; the supposition being that those who thus die continue to look fresh after death! Their corpses are placed as a solemn body-guard round the bier of the dead chief; one holding his fan, another his pipe, a third his snuff-box. Thus they are left within a great tomb, covered with frescoes of Buddhist saints, the entrance to which is curiously guarded by a cluster

[1] Quicksilver is believed to endow the body with power to resist death and avoid further transmigration. So Hindoo wizards prepare elixirs of mercury and powdered mica, which are supposed to contain the very essence of the god Siva and one of his wives. By a long course of swallowing this decoction the devotee believes that he becomes actually one with Siva.

of bows ready strung, with arrows poised; ready to fly at any rash intruder!

While great men are said to be thus honoured after death, the bodies of the middle classes are burned in furnaces, and their powdered bones are mixed with a little earth and water from the sacred Indus, and of this clay small images of Buddha are modelled and deposited in tombs. The very poor are either carried up the mountains or cast into ravines, a prey to wolves and birds of prey.

Sometimes while we were thus gleaning whatever travellers more adventurous than ourselves thought fit to tell us, a flourish of bells, trumpets, and horns, from the neighbouring Hindoo and Lama temples, would summon the people to their evening worship; and at each rotation of the great Praise-wheel the soft, musical bell chimed with a pleasant tone, which, together with the subdued hum of human voices, seemed borne away by the breeze, through the solemn cedar forest, till it floated higher and higher, and died away among the glittering snows.

But other notes there were, by no means so musical,—horrible, discordant sounds produced by a large shell, or by that trumpet which we have noticed, made of an elaborately carved human thigh-bone, the thigh-bone of a Lama. The longer the bone, the more valuable the trumpet. These are generally brought from Thibet, procured from such bodies as have simply been exposed to kites, and other birds of prey, instead of being burnt. Sometimes figures of Buddha are very beautifully carved on these thigh-bones, and become household gods. One such was sold to me by a woman, who, with her family, had done it homage for many years, but had latterly come to the conclusion that it was not good for much, and that rupees in the hand were preferable. The sun-bleached skulls of such Lamas are also sought for, and the upper portion is highly esteemed as a medicine-cup. They are of course endowed with special properties. Such a cup is mounted in gold, silver, or copper, and is treasured as an heirloom.

Here, and at Pangi, we made a new acquaintance in the great family of pine-trees, namely with the *neozo* or edible pine (*Pinus*

Gerardii). Its stem is of the most silvery white, like that of a very smooth birch, and its cones are full of oblong seeds which are obtained by half roasting the cone. They are very nice and nutty, though generally rather charred in the process of extraction. This tree abounds here, and runs up as high as the birch and juniper level. Then come the slopes of short green grass, which some one has compared to the twilight, gleaming softly between the broad expanse of dark forest gloom, and the dazzling dome of snow, which glitters in the eternal sunshine; not a bad threefold description of the great, grand mountain, from the very base of which we looked up, feeling ourselves such insignificant pigmies as our glance travelled upward, past great walls of black rock, and green glaciers, and sharp pinnacles of dark crag, right up to the summit of the great mountain mass, which towers to a height of 21,000 feet; a mountain—

> "Whose head in wintry grandeur towers
> And whitens with eternal sleet,
> While Summer in a veil of flowers
> Is sleeping rosy at his feet."

Pigmies though we were mid scenes of such stupendous grandeur, we were very happy in the little white tents on those glorious moonlight nights of never-to-be-forgotten beauty. And all night long, great fires blazed to scare away the leopards, which we knew abounded, and though unluckily we never had the luck of seeing them, we knew that they were none the less prowling silently round the camp, ready to make short work of the dogs should they venture only a few yards into the darkness, and so give their watchful foe a chance of making a sudden spring, and taking them unawares. The servants revelled in the warmth of the great cheery bonfires, and lay close round the fire curled up in their blankets, and all was very peaceful and still.

When our eyes could spare time to gaze earthward, they had the joy of resting on many lovely wild flowers—specially abundant were the deep blue gentians. I am told that about one march further, we might have seen handsome wild hollyhocks, crimson and deep mauve. Moreover, had we gone on to Spiti beyond the Kansum pass, we should have found the edelweiss growing so abundantly, that in places it literally covers the ground, and travellers sometimes select camping-grounds where their tents are furnished with a thick carpet of these much-lauded woolly blossoms.

It was with unutterable regret and many a lingering backward look towards all the unexplored beauty we were about to leave (more especially that lovely group of peaks up the valley), that we were forced to bid adieu to beautiful Rarung, and turn once more towards civilisation. Happily, however, we had not got there yet; and still allowed ourselves some pleasant days in the happy valley. Even here, however, some rain contrived to come, making it a great matter of exultation occasionally to find that some huge stone had so poised itself above the roots of some great cedar-tree as to form a natural sketching tent just in the right place!

We had now added considerably to our anxieties by having adopted a large family of young chicor, little baby partridges; which we hoped to be able to rear and take home. I need scarcely say, that one after another died, and our little nursery was sadly reduced ere we reached Simla. However, they amused us considerably, being beautiful little creatures.

To avoid too closely retracing our steps, we determined to cross the Sutlej at Urni, and explore some of the grand primeval forests which are all too quickly disappearing before the ruthless British axe. We had been promised a welcome from Mr. Paul and his sister, who had made their pleasant home in this wilderness, and who had undertaken to have the jula or rope-bridge put in good order for our benefit. We were therefore considerably dismayed when the mate, that is, the head man of the village, assured us that there was certainly no jula at Urni, and the nearest was three miles down the river at Chergaon, and utterly unsafe; the last person who had attempted to cross by it, the previous week, having been drowned. Of course the servants were terrified, and the coolies vowed they would not risk their lives.

However, we had too much faith in our friends to believe in the unsoundness of the bridge, and (tantalizing as it was to look down on their bungalow at Kilba [1] just opposite to us) we started on a very rough three miles' scramble to Chergaon, where, sure enough, we found a most horribly unsafe jula—four ropes, quite decayed, stretching from rock to rock, while far below raged the turbid river, swollen by the mass of melted snow, and tossing up angry waves, whose spray, blending with the heavy morning mist, made the farther bank almost invisible. It was evidently impossible for us all to cross, and the question was how to get a message sent to Kilba for new ropes.

While we were anxiously discussing the knotty point, one of our party, an officer of the 60th Rifles,[2] having made up his mind that the ropes would bear his weight, and that in any case it was fairer to risk his own life than that of a servant, had quietly taken his place in the coil of rope, which was the only seat provided, and gave the signal to the men on the other side to draw him over. We could not hear their voices for the raging of the flood, but they wrung their hands, and evidently implored not to be compelled to obey, while the coolies round us added their protestations as to the imminent danger of the proceeding. However, British *sangfroid* had made its calculations, and in another minute the little coil of rope, containing the plucky atom of humanity, was trembling in mid-air, the mad river boiling and foaming below, and any accident involving certain death. It was a moment of breathless anxiety when a hitch in the rope kept the coil poised in mid-air for some seconds before it could be dragged up to the rock, and with thankful relief we could just discern through the mist a dozen strong arms out-stretched to draw it in.

We knew it would be several hours before the new ropes could arrive, so made up our minds for a quiet picnic, and having now time to look around us, we were much struck by the

[1] The Sutlej at Kilba is 6,000 feet above the sea-level. It descends 1,000 feet ere reaching Wangtu, where its elevation is about 5,000 feet.

[2] Lieut. O'Brien.

CROSSING THE SUTLEJ BY A JULA OR ROPE BRIDGE.

beauty of the spot. Before us lay a very fine fir-clad ravine, down which tumbled a hill-torrent into the raging river, and looking up the valley, one snowy peak, 21,000 feet in height, towered above the mist. In the foreground were grouped the native servants, cooking our breakfast; and all the picturesque coolies, in their bright, striped, woollen raiment. Some of them had attempted to follow the Sahib's example, and cross the river with some luggage, but the fact of two of the ropes having given way, though happily without serious accident, had been a warning not to be disobeyed. So they all sat patiently about the bank, chatting and laughing. Just at this spot, Chergaon, a bloody battle had once been fought, in which the brave little Ghoorkas distinguished themselves, but who their opponents were I am not certain.

Any one who is very anxious to try the effect of crossing such a jula as this, on a small, safe scale, can get a capital notion of it without coming so far, as there has from time immemorial been a rope-bridge wherein people are drawn across the Dee at Ballater in a basket.[1]

On these Indian streams (and I suppose elsewhere, for we hear of precisely similar rope-bridges being suspended by the natives of Upper Peru in the Cordillera mountains) the method of beginning a bridge is that a party of natives post themselves on either side of a river, each carrying a coil of thin string with a small stone attached to the end of it as a weight. Each flings his string as far as ever he can, and after an immense number of failures, and perhaps several hours' time, they succeed in entangling their strings. Then one thin string after another is twisted on till it can support a rope. And to this is added another and another—loosely twisted ropes of wool or of grass. At last half a dozen or more strong ropes are laid side by side and fastened to a stout wooden beam on each side of the stream. This is weighted

[1] Till recently an outlying crag in the Shetland Isles was thus connected with the mainland, and "The Cradle of Noss" was a very fair specimen of the *jula*. It became so dangerous, however, that it was deemed prudent to remove it, and I am not aware of its having been replaced.

with heavy stones. The ropes are drawn as tight as possible. Then it is ready for use.

Some of the natives swing themselves along just like monkeys, holding on by hands and legs; but this is horrible to see, knowing that one moment's dizziness would involve certain death. Sometimes you sit in a rope coil, like that in which we crossed; at other places a wooden triangle is slung on the rope pointing upwards, and you sit in the base of the triangle; if you are sensible, you will be lashed in for fear of accidents. Then halyards are fastened to this locomotive seat, and so you are pulled across in due time.

In some of the rough and ready julas across mountain torrents, far from any village, and where you might wait long enough before any one appeared on the other side to draw you over, there is no second rope for that purpose, but sitting within a hoop slung on the main rope, the traveller must work his own way across—a matter requiring no small strength and steadiness of nerve, especially when giddy with the mighty rush and roar of the torrent dashing with fearful force down the steep mountain side, and the certainty of being himself dashed to pieces among the cruel rocks should he slip or fall.

Another variety of native suspension-bridge has a wattling of wicker-work laid on strong ropes, and *sometimes* has side ropes with the same wicker trellis-work; even with this such a bridge is horrible to cross, as the foot is apt to slip through the open wicker-work, through which you see the water rushing below. The natives too are apt to be careless in renewing the ropes, which are very liable to decay.[1]

A still more dangerous form of jula gives no flat roadway at all for the foot. Only a stout rope of twisted osier or bamboo, while two similar ropes give some support to the hand, the sides being slightly interlaced to connect them with the foot rope. Such a bridge quivers at every step, and sways with every breath of wind. No goat even will cross it, and the shepherds who bring their laden flocks from Thibet must carry each goat and

[1] Himalayan bridges. See Chapter XV.

its burden over separately in their arms. Such work requires the head of a Blondin, while the ropes are anything but "tight ropes." And yet bridges such as these are the sole means of crossing many streams perhaps a hundred yards wide, from rock to rock.

In smoother rivers, where such a thing is possible, a traveller sometimes floats his own charpoy[1] on four inflated massaks,[2] and four natives then swim the stream and draw after them this floating couch, whereon he sits in royal state.

After a delay of some hours, a welcome shout announced the arrival of the strong new ropes. These were quickly slung across and made fast, and in a very few minutes more we each in turn took our seat in the coil of rope, taking the precaution of being tied in. I should imagine the sensation was akin to that of travelling in a balloon. It was supremely unpleasant.

Though our rope hung about a hundred feet above the seething, foaming torrent, it seemed as though we must touch the waters, also it seemed as if the waters were at rest and we were dashing up the stream. The noise was deafening, and the time of crossing seemed interminable. It was like a horrible nightmare, in which there was no escape from the surging, tossing mass of yellow waves below, and from the inaccessible black rock that rose perpendicularly far above. The hitch of the ropes seems an invariable part of the programme, allowing ample time to realise the situation, and the frailness of the barrier which alone separates the two worlds. At last you feel your rope coil once more in motion, and by a succession of short jerks you are hauled upward to the rocky ledge, where you still hang poised for a few moments, till a dozen strong brown arms can catch the coil and draw its helpless inmate safely to the shore with some pleasant words of cheery welcome. Then you can sit perched on the rock and watch your friends, your coolies, and the baggage being drawn over piecemeal, and very thankful you are when the last human being has come safely to land.

A long, steep scramble eventually brought us to Kilba, where

[1] Bedstead. [2] Water-skins.

we received a warm and hospitable welcome. It was strange to find ourselves surrounded by all the luxuries of a London home, except indeed a piano—nevertheless we had the pleasure of hearing the very newest and most difficult songs warbled without accompaniment, by an Anglo-Himalayan nightingale, who possesses the rare gift of accurately singing at sight all the treasures of music brought her by the European post. This was a strange life for an English lady, often left quite alone for weeks among these wild mountaineers, while her brother was looking after his workmen in distant forests, leaving her in charge of money and of stores for the supply of hundreds of men. Doubtless the knowledge that she was fully prepared in case of need to make good use of her dagger and life-preserver in guarding the treasure-chest, may have done much to deter midnight robbers. But in truth, such a life involved an amount of energy and pluck rarely met with.

Among her more practical accomplishments was a sufficient knowledge of medicine to enable her to comfort and aid many sick and wounded, while her equally precious skill as a baker supplied her brother and her guests with the rare luxury of delicious bread—a delightful change after a prolonged course of chupatties.

Nor was it only while under this hospitable roof that her countrymen shared in its comforts. Scarcely a day passed without some coolie being despatched with a load of excellent newly-baked bread to some little tent, pitched perhaps thirty miles off on some wild pass, whose inmate had well-nigh forgotten the taste of such dainties. In truth, no travellers whose far up-country wanderings have been cheered, and his commissariat again and again replenished by Miss Paul's thoughtful care, can abstain from adding his tribute to her praise.

Speaking of medicines, I forget whether I have already told you that the Paharis extract from the deodar an oil which is found to be highly efficacious in the treatment of rheumatism, just as we in Europe are now learning the value of fir-tree oil, and of garments made of fir-wool fibre, for the same painful malady.

Now came the explanation of all our morning's adventures. It seems the jula at Urni had been thoroughly repaired for our benefit, in fact, twelve new ropes had been put on the previous day. But the villagers of Kilba, being determined, if possible, to keep away all mutton and flour-consuming sahibs, had sent to the mate at Urni desiring him at all costs to prevent our crossing the river; in compliance with this request he had denied the existence of the Urni jula, thinking that we would probably be deterred by his report of the other from even giving it a thought, and so would return by the same road as we had come. He little knew what it was to have to do with "the dominant race." Some one suggested that a little personal chastisement would be the only form in which our righteous retribution was likely to be felt, and I think we all agreed that it was well merited. However, the administering thereof would have been illegal and perhaps somewhat derogatory; so the lords of the creation practised a "masterly inactivity," and I fear the rascal escaped scot-free.

The villagers, finding that their little stratagem had failed, tried a new plan, and when we reached the village we found it deserted; every soul had vanished with their flocks and their herds, nor did they return for some days after the departure of their unwelcome visitors. We wandered in and out of their vineyards, among their fields and picturesque carved houses, overgrown with rich tangles of gourds and divers fruits, in every corner of their sacred inclosures and temples. We might even, had we been so inclined, have taken Durgâ's sacred fish from their tanks—for there remained literally no one to say us nay.

Meanwhile we could get no milk, and even firewood was difficult to obtain, while the servants found no bazaar at which to replenish their stores, and of course, would not touch our food. Happily our kind hosts were able to supply this last deficiency from the godowns or storehouses, whence Mr. Paul supplies his army of woodcutters with their daily flour.

But for this inconvenience, there was something rather pleasant in the unwonted stillness of the village, and while the gentlemen were exploring the forest, and the other ladies were crooning in a *real* drawing-room, I spent a long, pleasant day sketching a very picturesque cedar temple, richly carved, perched above terraced vineyards, with the river sweeping almost calmly below, in a broad, smooth reach, and white snow-peaks far above. That temple was adorned with many trophies of the chase, chiefly ibex-horns, the offerings of Pahari sportsmen.

Sometimes travellers in crossing the higher passes of these mountains come to some great cairn of huge stones, which have been heaped up to the honour of the Spirit of the Pass, and here the skulls and horns of all manner of wild creatures have been fastened as to a shrine. The skulls of the barral, the ooriyal, the ovis ammon, and the ibex are among those which have thus been offered. I fancy that the sight of a good specimen thus abandoned to the winds and snows must be rather a temptation to most sportsmen, but the reverence and honesty of the Paharis would certainly prevent the sacrilegious appropriation of such treasure-trove. No coolie would care to shoulder such a burden.

Among the various charms of Miss Paul's mountain home were all manner of tame creatures, the greatest pet of all being a flying squirrel, a most delightful little animal. It is just the size of a common squirrel, but the fore-paws are united to the hind ones by a membrane, covered with soft thick fur, and these outstretched act the part of wings. Even the tail assists its flight, as each hair seems to set itself, as a bird would set its feathers, and so acts as a rudder to guide the little creature in its flight. It is the gentlest of pets, with very large soft eyes, and the richest warm brown fur, and never seemed so happy as when curled round his mistress's neck, or eating bread and milk from her hand.

A less pleasant reminiscence of this place was finding a large snake in Captain Graves' tent. It was, however, detected and slain. But though we never lost the conscious dread of possible serpents lurking in every corner, they certainly are not so common as our fears would suggest—in fact this was only the second snake we have seen since leaving Simla.

When the gentlemen returned from their expedition in the

forest of Kunai, they one and all burst into such unwonted rapture over the glory of one especial group of magnificent old cedars that I determined to find my way there next morning. I think if I had realised beforehand how difficult a scramble it would entail, I might have added it to the list of unattainable beauties. Happily I did not quite believe the general account of the road, and though even our hostess had never found her way there, I accepted the version of her brother, whose seven-league boots make light of all difficulties. So next morning, when all the gentlemen had gone off in search of bears, I started alone with six sturdy Paharis, who quite entered into my wish to reach this almost inaccessible spot, and carried my dandie bravely in such places as was possible.

Very soon, however, this became literally an impossibility, the path being so frightfully steep that each had enough to do to look out for himself. So fastening a rope round my waist, for fear of a false step, which they seemed to think inevitable, they helped me in the dizzy climb. Sometimes we clambered up the steepest banks of shingle and large stones, clambering from one to another, while our feet sank in loose earth and pebbles which slipped from under us, so that we lost ground almost as fast as we climbed. These long slides seemed almost interminable. At other times the path was merely a ledge along the face of the precipice, where even a wild goat might find its footing difficult; wherever this slight support failed, a bit of rude scaffolding was built out from the rock-face, whereon were laid narrow bits of plank and shingle, so as to make a giddy roadway actually projecting from the cliff; and as the loose stones or planks were rather apt to tilt beneath the foot, it was always a satisfactory moment when we had crossed the abyss, and reached the farther rock in safety, steadying ourselves with one hand against the face of the precipice, while at every touch loose stones would fall, and go rumbling and tumbling down thousands of feet into the valley. Meanwhile the path wound higher and higher, and at length with intense delight we reached the cedar shades of Kunai.

As we strayed farther and farther into the pathless depths of that glorious primeval forest, or glanced far above the dark cedar tops, to where the glittering ice-peaks flashed against the deep-blue of heaven, I thought of Longfellow's song, telling how Nature, the dear old nurse, taught her child day by day to read her precious book. She says to the little one:—

" 'Here is a story book
Thy father hath written for thee.

" 'Come wander with me,' she said,
Into regions yet untrod,
And read what is still unread
In the manuscript of God.'

" And he wandered away and away
With Nature, the dear old nurse,
Who sang to him day by day
The rhymes of the Universe.

" And whenever the way seemed long,
Or his heart began to fail,
She would sing a more wonderful song
Or tell a more wonderful tale."

—and in truth she had never yet shown this child so grand a picture as the forest sanctuary which we at last reached in the depths of that dark shade.

It was only a little cedar-temple, a mere pigmy beneath the magnificent clump of deodars that seemed to reach up to heaven. But the fact of its being there had shown that the natives considered those trees "God's trees," so they were sacred and safe from the cruel axe which was making such sore havoc on every side. It really must be dreadful to a lover of nature to be sent to explore a splendid forest such as this, while yet untouched by workmen's tools; and to know that henceforth the aim and end of his life must be to devise means of conveying those beautiful trees to the burning plains to be converted into railway sleepers and bridges, and all manner of commonplace useful things.

Certainly it is a wonderful thing to see the various contrivances by which their transit is effected. In most cases the trees grow out from the precipice at such an angle as to make the mere work of cutting them a matter of danger and difficulty. When at last the cloven giant has fallen thundering down the khad, the chances are, that in its fall it has been smashed into two or three pieces; in any case it must be sawn into suitable lengths of about twenty feet. Even then the weight of these ponderous beams is enormous, as they are frequently of immense girth. When the huge logs have thus been felled, they must be stamped with the brand of the contractor or Government, as the case may be. A system of leverage brings them to the next descent, probably an artificially constructed slide down the face of the khad, at a very steep incline, and down this, when wet and slippery, or when newly frozen, the great timbers glide, and lie heaped together in piles, all tossed at random and exceedingly dangerous to handle. No wonder that serious accidents sometimes occur.

Several of these slides in succession, assisted by occasional leverage, carry the logs from khad to khad, probably landing them at last in the bed of a mountain torrent; and when the next flood comes, roaring and thundering, foaming and dashing down over the rocks in a mighty cataract, it will bring the great beams crashing down the abyss, and will at last hurl them into the raging snow-flood far below, where the Sutlej will toss them to and fro in its seething waves, and at last float them down to the plains hundreds of miles away (the river itself being upwards of a thousand miles in length), where only poor, mutilated, scored logs (massive indeed, but oh! so battered), are all that will survive to tell of the peaceful, green solitude in which the first thousand years of their calm, restful life glided so gently by.

The unaided force of the current only suffices to carry them to a certain point where the Forest Department has a station, and where the timber is collected and formed into rafts, and so is floated to a place near Loodiana, where the railway crosses the Sutlej, and carries the poor remains of the forest to the cities.

The forests themselves tell a mournful tale of wholesale destruction, and though enough of beauty remains to fill one with delight, the joy is sadly tempered by the sight of countless stumps of far more mighty monarchs than any now remaining. And cut, as we should think, so wastefully; always several feet above the ground, leaving great blocks such as might veneer half the tables in London.[1]

Can you not almost hear the "sad daughter of the River-god" making her low, heartbroken moan for the devastation of her dear solitudes by ruthless men?—

> "They came. They cut away my tallest pines
> My dark tall pines, that plumed the craggy ledge
> High over the blue gorge; and all between
> The snowy peak and snow-white cataract
> Fostered the callow eaglet. From beneath
> Whose thick mysterious boughs in the dark morn
> The panther's roar came muffled.
> . . . . Never, never more,
> Shall lone Œnone see the morning mist
> Sweep through them—never see them overlaid
> With narrow moonlit slips of silver cloud
> Between the loud stream and the trembling stars."

Now poor Œnone must take refuge in still more remote solitudes, if perchance some spots may prove inaccessible to her foes —some sanctuary where silence yet reigns, and where the presence of mankind has not yet insulted her lonely majesty.

Imagine how glorious these forest depths must be in winter, when the light snow falls in dazzling layers on each flat surface of those mighty pyramids of green which tower aloft so still and so solemn; half revealed through the silent, drifting showers, with here and there a tree half burnt and blackened, standing alone, monstrous and spectral. Sometimes when each weird and awful form is

[1] Just think what a prize such massive lumps of cedar-wood would have been to those old Roman connoisseurs who were willing to give such fabulous prices for furniture made of it, that we hear of Cicero having paid a sum equal to four thousand pounds for one table, while others sold for the price of a fine estate; those most prized being carved from a single block of cedar, mounted on an ivory pillar, and surrounded with a circular band of gold. Pliny has recorded how the charms of this ivory and cedar-wood had caused all the forests of Libya to be stripped. Imagine his feelings if he had seen them converted into railway sleepers, or used for firewood, while the green forest glades are strewn knee-deep with torn and ragged branches—all that now remains of the beautiful and lost!

magnified by the cold grey mist, they must seem transformed into an army of mysterious spirits—so pale and dreamy, appearing and disappearing amid the vapours like gigantic blue phantoms.

But to-day the forest was all bathed in sunshine, and the glowing light shone on great red stems and glossy layers of green, studded with paler cones, and the air was scented with the breath of wild flowers, and resinous fir-needles. Presently the hill-women assembled from far and near, with their little ones, to inspect the first *white* woman—so still called from courtesy, though in truth retaining small claim to such a distinction!—who had penetrated to their fastnesses. Some of them were strikingly handsome, with very fair complexions, and masses of beautiful dark hair; having moreover calm, thoughtful faces, that agreed well with the deep, dreamy eyes of these children of the forests.

As usual, we could fraternise only by signs, for I hardly knew a dozen words of Hindustani, and not one of the semi-Thibet patois spoken in the hills. But though we could not exchange ideas, the human courtesies are always easily understood, and the novelty of watching a sketch being made, and the pleasurable alarm of looking through my opera-glasses, was sufficient attraction to keep them happy for some hours. As to my watch, it had unfortunately ceased to tick, a matter however of very small importance, where the position of the sun and its lengthening shadows were an all-sufficient guide for such vague laws of time as those we owned.

These lassies, thus assembled in picturesque groups around the little temple, afforded a good standard of size, whereby to judge of the real magnitude of the stately giants which overshadowed them. At first the mind could hardly take in the possibility of anything much grander!

Yet I suppose that scarcely one tree in that group could have much exceeded thirty feet in girth; so that, in the wonderful scale of Creation these are, after all, mere pigmies compared with some of the mammoths of the New World—the stupendous cedars of California.[1]

[1] For notes on the glorious Californian forests, see *Granite Crags*, by C. F. Gordon Cumming. Blackwood and Son.

Yet while I am driven to confess that my dear cedars of Kunai cannot claim a foremost rank among the giants of the tree world as regards actual size, I do maintain that no group more stately and majestic ever ruled in the broad greenwood, in any corner of the globe, and many a time they rise before my memory as a vision of beauty that sadly dwarfs the smaller growth of other lands.

It was quite distressing to have to turn away again, but the afternoon was drawing on, and the long steep descent proved fully more difficult than even the morning's climb, so that the snows were sunset-flushed, and the valley bathed in purple evening light, long ere we reached the pleasant bungalow, where an evening of rest, and of music, proved even more acceptable than usual.

From Kilba we were sorely tempted to diverge, and explore the lovely Baspa Valley, at least as far as the village of Sangla, where the climate in summer is said to be quite delightful. It is beyond the influence of the rains; and for months together we might there have found the bliss of one long summer's day, feasting on the grapes which abound throughout the Koonawar district, and which are fine and of excellent flavour. They are of many varieties, some of which are made into wine; others dried and exported to Thibet.

The Baspa Valley is about sixty miles long, and mostly is richly cultivated, or else is green pasture land, with rivulets, flowers, and fruit trees. The valley is sometimes wide, sometimes narrow, dotted with most picturesque villages. The hills are clothed with cedar, walnut, pine, and birch, above which rise the glittering snow-peaks. A rise of 8,000 feet brings you to the source of the river, near which there is no wood, only a wide grassy valley, with grassy hills on either side, and the snow-ridge appearing just above.

Many pleasant plans were discussed for exploring this paradise. Could we have lingered for one blissful month, our homeward march would have been quite delightful, as we should have altogether missed the rains. However, having already obtained a short extension of leave, there was no possibility of extracting more; so with sore reluctance we turned from all this unattainable beauty to face the wet world which we knew awaited us within a couple of marches.

CHAPTER XVIII.

CHILDREN OF THE MIST.

"Unprotected Females" in Ramnee Forest—Fleas!—Noise—Himalayan Collie Dogs—A Dear Dog—Life in the Forests—Thunder-storm—Mists—Locusts—Scarlet and Crimson Grain-fields—Rough Night Quarters—Kotghur Mission Station—Orchard—Wild Flowers—In Hatto Forest—Simla in the Rains—Leeches—Start to Spend a Month at Massourie—Journey to Umballa.

> "To roam at large among unpeopled glens
> And mountainous retirements, only trod
> By devious footsteps: regions consecrate
> To oldest Time! and while the mists
> Flying, and rainy vapours, call out shapes
> And phantoms from the crags and solid earth,
> . . . . And while the streams
> Descending from the region of the clouds
> And starting from the hollow of the earth
> More multitudinous every moment, rend
> Their way before them—what a joy to roam
> An equal among mightiest energies!"

OUR next camping-ground was in the dark forest of Ramnee. Thither the would-be sportsmen had preceded us, in search, as usual, of those mythical bears. We two ladies preferred remaining a few days longer at Kilba. When, however, we judged that it was time to follow, we started one afternoon for Ramnee. On arriving, we received a message that the gentlemen had prolonged their hunting expedition, and had gone for some days to higher ground.

I believe that in our innermost hearts we were both very much delighted at the novelty of finding ourselves thus literally "unprotected females" in this wild place; so on the morrow we pitched our tiny tent (we had but one) on an open space in the heart of the great forest. On the night of our arrival we and our coolies were so weary that we dispensed with even the exertion of unpacking the tent, and made the best of a room in a wretched old bungalow. Luckily the night was dry, as we could see a foot of star-lit sky at intervals through the shingle roof! But oh!! the fleas! the starving host of fleas! "No sleep till morn, when flesh and hunger meet!" We reminded one another of the gentleman who complained to his landlord of the bugs in his lodgings. The host indignantly asserted that there was not a single bug in his house. "Right you are," was the reply, "for they are all very much married, and have large families!"

Assuredly the fleas of Ramnee had multiplied as miraculously as those other nice insects in the Egyptian plagues. Like them, they invaded all our property, and though on the morrow we rose up in haste and pitched our tent as far off as we dared, hoping to shake off all memory of our miserable night, our tormentors migrated in our baggage, and formed a flourishing colony in our new abode! We dared not move our tent farther from the servants' fire, for fear of the leopards, which abound.

Another crook in our lot was the incessant noise. We had imagined that here at least we should surely be allowed to revel undisturbed in the blessed stillness of the mountains, but, as usual, we were doomed to disappointment. Hundreds of wild Paharis were at work in the forests all round us; while others were hammering away early and late at a new bungalow, which was to be the home of the Officer of the Forests, who was one of the shooting party. In truth, all our visions of the grand stillness of these ancient forests had long ago been dispelled. Wherever we went, Sunday and week-day alike—from early dawn till deepening twilight—the unvarying noise of the axe, the crash of trees smashing over rocks far down the khad, and the incessant monotonous chant and refrain of the coolies as they work, greeted our wearied ears, varied by the barking of dogs at night, or the Hindoo chatter and hubble-bubble, which seem never to cease. So we were fain to spend much of each day in a nook close by the stream, whose ceaseless noise, in some measure, drowned the human voice.

The forest in which we now were, much resembled that of Poindah, the tall tapering spires of morinda, rye, and kindred pines greatly predominating over the deodar. One dark hill towered behind another, all pine-clad, and beyond lay the Shatool Pass, where the sportsmen were encamped; a pass just the height of Mont Blanc, but overlooked by one great peak towering five thousand feet higher.

> "A peak of dread
> That to the evening sun uplifts
> The griesly gulfs and slaty rifts
> Which seam its shivered head."

A magnificent crown to this savage forest scenery, a crest where oft-times the eternal sunshine rests steadfastly, while dark clouds gather round its base, and the voice of rolling thunder whispers of the raging storms that have shattered so many of the grand old trees, and of the wild winds that have uprooted others, leaving the depths of the forest strewn with priceless timber, rotting where it fell.

The rocks hereabouts include granites of divers colours; also mica schist, which we were told is full of garnets. We did not care, however, to add our hammering to the various distracting noises; but rather loved to sit in idleness beneath green leaves, sometimes watching the great logs gliding down long grassy slopes from the crags above, right down to the river, sometimes content with merely watching the light drapery of mist, the silvery cloud that sometimes

> "Lost its way between the piney sides of this long glen;"

and that curled and twined in and out among the dark trees, as though it could not escape.

On the third evening our Nimrods returned. As soon as we espied their torches glimmering on a far hill-side, we lighted blazing wood fires to guide them to our camp. Their foray had, as usual, been unsuccessful; they had found literally no trace of animal life, though enough of beautiful scenery to make some amends. They brought with them, however, a very great prize, namely two "Pahari Koote," hill dogs. The only sort that will face leopards, therefore the only dog of any use in guarding the flocks. In size and form they are like very large Scotch collie dogs. As soon as the dog is old enough to bear it, he is adorned with a wide metal collar, armed with strong spikes. Thus protected, he will face and often kill a leopard.

Nevertheless, these, by cunning craftiness, sometimes take him unawares, and contrive to spring on him, so that sooner or later almost every hill dog falls a victim, for although the leopards are very rarely seen (as they only prowl about at night, and hide shyly and warily in the daylight), they are nevertheless very numerous. Nor are they the only foes of the flocks, for although the bears are properly speaking vegetarians, they are not proof against an occasional feast of mutton. Generally they feed on grass and roots, fruits and berries, often attacking the corn-fields, or sitting on the branches of some big oak or apricot-tree, eating their acorns and fruit, their animal food being confined to beetles, scorpions, and such insects, but once they have tasted sheep their preference for blood is incurable. They become worse enemies than sheep-worrying dogs. Then, too, they become fearless, and will attack men, generally making for the face; several times we saw their victims, whose countenances, horribly mutilated, told a hideous tale. When the flocks are thus endangered, traps are set and baited with flesh; and the bears, having now learnt to eat unscrupulously of any meat they can find, are thus snared.

The pluck of the hill dogs of course makes them priceless treasures to the shepherds, who greatly object to allowing one to leave the country, especially as they are morbidly jealous of allowing the breed to pass into other hands. We were indebted to a Forest Officer for procuring us these two black puppies, which already were about the size of an average sheep-dog. They were only three months old, yet the poor infants were already orphans, father and mother and various other relations having been eaten by the leopards. Henceforth it was our anxious charge every evening to tie them up in camp at sunset, lest they should share the same fate. Mrs. Graves called her dog Kilba; mine was named Ramnee, in memory of our two last halts. A more beautiful pair of dogs never were seen than these silky creatures, of the glossiest blank and tan. They were the admiration of all beholders. All the natives of the lower valleys would gather round to look at them; and amongst white men too they proved a fertile subject of conversation, as every one declared that, beautiful as they were, the whole breed was horribly treacherous, and that sooner or later we would find good cause to repent having adopted such playfellows.

I overheard many such pleasant prophecies when we returned to Simla—stories of such dogs having become household pets, and then turning savage. In one instance, when a huge dog had thus made himself the terror of the whole family, more especially of the natives, he continued perfectly obedient to his little master, a child of about six years, whose commands he would at once obey implicitly. All I can say for our beautiful puppies, is that as they grew up, they became more and more gentle. In character they proved as unlike as most other brothers. As to Kilba, his intellect and his affections were alike concentrated in his stomach, and he transferred his allegiance so entirely to the mess, that his mistress shortly resigned all claim to him.

But Ramnee proved a perfect darling, and became the pet of the household. He would lie for hours on the balcony, beside the nursery window, and would allow the children to pull his ears and his tail and his great brown feet, and sometimes would take a little hand quite gently in his great mouth; or else lie sleepily wagging his tail, just to show how pleased he was with things in general. Another of our household pets was a jungle kitten, who had adopted my brother-in-law for its master, and coming shyly to the house, used to ask him for daily milk, till at last it became a natural inmate of the house. At first we were rather nervous as to how our canine and feline pets would agree; and with good reason, for the kitten would sometimes make most unprovoked attacks on the puppy, who could not always resist giving an indignant snap in return. But very soon they became sworn friends: and it was the prettiest sight imaginable to see the huge, black puppy playing great, heavy antics with the neat, active little kitten, springing about and attitudinising in the most affected way.

As to the brown monkeys and the white langours who came to inspect him, they were to him a source of endless astonishment. He would fly at them the moment they approached, and very quickly banished such intruders from the premises; whereupon they would take up safe quarters in some tree close by, and chatter derisively at him. We did not think, however, that he might have equal influence with the leopards who had occasionally carried off dogs from the neighbouring verandahs, and would doubtless have thought him a delicious morsel. So he always slept in my room, and had his morning cup of tea like the other members of the family, while Miss Kitten had her bread and butter.

We determined that kitten and puppy must never be separated, so when the time came for our return to England the kitten was provided with a travelling basket, to which, however, it showed so unconquerable an aversion that after reaching Meerut, it was handed over to a family *en route* to Peshawur, and was last seen perched on the back of an elephant on its way thither. As to the dear black dog, his journey was a time of exceeding misery. The railway officials could give him no cooler carriage than a dog-compartment, next the engine, and all we could do was to give him a great brass basinful of water to freshen him a little. His antipathy to the sacred monkey-tribe came near to causing me trouble on our return to the plains, for as we neared the sacred Nerbudda river he suddenly espied a great encampment of devout yogis accompanied by a regiment of revered monkeys. He was sitting beside me in an open dak-gharry, and ere I could possibly check him, he sprang out and made for them. To their usual caste horror of being defiled by a dog, was added the terror which even in the plains attaches to a "Pahari Koote," so in an instant the whole camp was routed, and men and monkeys put to flight by this cleanest of unclean animals. The general confusion produced was too ludicrous, but I was heartily glad when, tardily obedient to my recall, the great big gentle puppy returned, like a gentleman, to his seat in the carriage.

Then the obnoxious-looking company plucked up courage to approach and claim backsheesh for their insulted monkeys, when happily it occurred to me to turn the tables, and claim backsheesh for my beautiful dog who was sitting gravely at my side. Whether they were dumfoundered by the exquisite absurdity of the demand, or simply considered that a white woman who would sit beside a dog was altogether impracticable, I cannot say; but they grinned and departed. This was poor Ramnee's last scamper in India.

By the time we reached Bombay he was seriously ill, and the heat there being very great, although it was December, he lay for a week panting breathlessly, though our balcony, at the top of the Byculla Hotel, caught every faint sea-breeze.

On the homeward voyage he suffered still more. A halt at Cairo, however, quite set him up, and when he reached England and had the delight of once more rolling in deep snow-drifts, Ramnee was himself again. He wandered about the park, making friends with all the bucks; and fraternised with all the Sussex farmers, amongst whom he established a regular visiting-list; trotting off to any house he fancied, condescending to accept a drink of milk, and presently trotting home again.

But alas! evil days were at hand. A summer, well-nigh approaching Indian heat, proved too much for this child of the snows. One Sunday, like a respectable Christian, he accompanied the family to a church so unenlightened as to make no provision for dogs. So he had to wait outside. Next day he was seriously ill, and for a whole week he lingered in great suffering without any apparent cause. It has been suggested that he was maliciously poisoned by some miscreant, but we tried to believe it was a case of sun-stroke.

The following Sunday he died, and though he was "only a dog," few human beings have been more truly missed and mourned. He was buried beneath a fine old beech-tree beside the water where he used to sit and contemplate things in general. And this is all I have to tell you about the dear hill dog. He was the first dog I had ever cared to call my own, and he has had no successor, for herein I hold with that faithful dog-lover who said, "*On n'a dans la vie qu'un chien, comme on n'a qu'un amour!*"

We remained one day more in Ramnee forest, then started again. At first our route lay through greenwood—filbert, elm, ash, walnut, horse-chestnut, and so on. Then along very precipitous cliffs above the Sutlej, on the opposite side to those we had traversed on our way up the valley. The river seemed fuller, and its yellow waves more noisy and boisterous than ever. We could scarcely believe those who assured us that a month or two later, when the snows had ceased to melt, a calm clear river reflecting the blue sky would here run its peaceful course. We had now reached Wangtu, whence we merely retraced our former steps. Three miles more brought us back to Nachar, where we again camped so as to overlook the green glade beneath the great deodars.

The rains were now setting in in good earnest; yet such sunny hours as came between the storms seemed all the more brilliant in contrast with the sullen grandeur that had gone before, when the dark clouds had rolled away, and the distant thunder still muttered among the black crags, giving a voice to every mountain, so that wooded valleys and icy peaks seemed to call one another in some strange language of their own. We halted here another week, partly detained by lack of coolies, for the cholera had not stayed its ravages, and many more victims had died while we were up the valley. To us it was no hardship to be detained in such beautiful quarters.

We explored different forests—for the most part, however, sorely devastated by the hand of man; while here and there the shattered pieces mark the ravaging storms that sweep down from the mountains with such overwhelming force—grim, weather-beaten veterans, stately mourners that will not bend though often the tall stems are stripped of their limbs, and remain torn, battered, and desolate.

Sometimes we lingered in the forest under shelter of some great rock, to watch the gathering storm, when the low "soughing" of the wind in the tree-tops and the hush of every twittering bird told what was coming. Then over earth and sky would spread a lurid, leaden colour, stern, cold, and desolate. Grey clouds, grey rocks, grey stems. Soon the distant trees begin to rustle and bend, heralding the approach of the tempest, and the wind sweeps down in hollow intermittent gusts and then loses itself in the forest, howling and moaning on its way. The gusts come quicker and quicker, till the wind is incessant. The tall pine-trees bend and sway and writhe, as though wrestling with some invisible foe, raging in fury. Sometimes they disappear in the cloud wreath. Then comes a crash, and some great stem has snapped and fallen, mortally wounded by the spirit of the storm. The hills are all shrouded in grey drift, and heavy blackness rests on the mountain-tops, but every now and again, the whole earth and heavens are lighted by the crimson fires that play round the summits,

> "Flashing through lurid night infernal day."

Then a rumbling, rolling sound tells that some riven rock has been shaken down by the thunder, and leaping from height to height is dashing downward in headlong career.

Presently the lightning's glare is followed by an awful darkness, and a perfect deluge of rain. It is more than rain—it is a water spout. Then comes a sudden change. The tempest is past, the rain ceases, the storm-spirits flee, and capricious lights and shadows begin to play hide-and-seek in every corner where you least expect them. First comes one vivid gleam falling on moss-gnarled stems, and revealing delicate ferns in the sheltered crevices of the rock. Soon the sun bursts forth in his glory, and shows every hill-side streaked with silvery streamlets, while in the valley float white wreaths of mist, noiseless as spirits, which glide ghostlike through those dark glades, shrouding the ghastly, burnt trees with softest, fleeciest drapery, and lending a strange veil of mystery to the primeval forest, where every bough of the gaunt old timber is bearded with pale grey lichens, falling in long filaments from beneath the dark foliage of the pines. There is nothing so deathlike as this silence of the mist, when your own footfall sounds dull and muffled, and even the insects cease to chirp; awed by that still spiritual presence of

"Ancient silence, robed in thistledown."

There was one crag not far from our tents that was my especial delight on a misty evening such as this. A patch of the forest had accidentally been burnt years previously; but still the ghostly white stems pointed heavenward, like weird fingers, and the place had such an eerie feeling of desolation and solitude that the dullest imagination could not fail to people it with spirits such as the Paharis recognise. I found my way back to the same spot night after night.

Looking from here, one day, we saw a curious effect of what seemed to be quivering light in the valley. At first we thought it was the tremulous haze of steam rising; then it seemed almost like a snow shower, with the bright sun glittering on each dazzling flake. We could scarcely believe those who assured us that it was "only a locust cloud": yet so it was, the valley was full of them. They had come, tempted doubtless by the lovely pale green fields, of which they would soon make sore havoc, and meanwhile, as the light glanced on their gauzy wings, the whole air seemed quivering.

Once more we started on our homeward route, still retracing our former steps, yet often almost wondering whether the scenes so altered by rapid growth of vegetation could really be the same. The change of our own valleys from the barren ploughed lands of March to the laughing harvest-fields of August could not be more complete. Each mossy stem was now clothed to the topmost bough with every species of graceful fern, growing in wild luxuriance. Each crevice of the rocks, each stem of fallen tree, was alike veiled with the same delicate tracery; the light, feathery fronds of what we call hothouse ferns: some powdered with gold, some with silver, some smooth and glossy, some like finest lace-work. And the ground below was one bed of dewy moss brilliant with large white anemones, scarlet or crimson potentilla, and masses of forget-me-not of a blue more vivid than any paint can render. Whole fields of the plant we call "Prince's Feather" are here cultivated as grain, and a beautiful crop it is; the grain being of the deepest crimson, hanging like a plume, while the leaves are vivid scarlet. These lie like patches of deep red, among the rich ripening corn-fields, and light green pasture lands, which here and there nestle amid the dark forest.

The hills we had left so dreary and brown, were now one vivid green, with deep blue shadows running right up to the snows, and showing red and purply cliffs, the whole half-veiled by soft mysterious "clouds of dewy steam," which one of our men pointed out, unconsciously reminding us of our unscientific translation of King David's words. "See," he said, "how the mountains do smoke!"

Beautiful as were the curling vapours, revealing wonderful glimpses of mountains magnified even beyond reality, and vivid the glorious outgoings of morning and evening, we bitterly regretted the fate which was bringing us more and more into the rains, the ground in many places being so complete a swamp that camping was impossible, and we were generally compelled to halt at the road bungalows. Several of these were in process of rebuilding, so that on one night a couple of sheds, with a fine view of the sky through the open rafters, and on another, one unfinished room with neither door nor window to keep out the drifting storm, was the only refuge for all our party—human and animal, young hill partridges and Pahari puppies included. The servants found refuge under a big rock, in a cactus-grove hard by (the cactuses were as large as well-grown elder-trees), and there turned out a dinner which to us, blessed with keen mountain hunger, seemed all that could be desired.

At Kotghur our friends at the Mission Station lent us a charming bungalow on the hill at Thandarh for as long as we liked to remain. Right glad we were when we had accomplished the last steep ascent of five thousand feet, and once more reached the pleasant rest-house, overlooking the tea-plantations. It was with positive joy that we heard the wearisome roar of the Sutlej growing fainter and fainter, till at last it became merely a low, distant murmur that from time to time floated upward in whispering echoes on the pine-scented breeze.

It was with great regret that we at length bade adieu to our kind friends Herr Rebsch and his family, who had proved such good friends in time of need. On my last morning, when I was to start alone for Narkunda, I went down the hill at break of day, and spent a pleasant hour sketching their vine-covered home. After a cheery breakfast, I went on my way rejoicing, escorted for same distance by these kind genii of the wilds. As we passed through their orchard (where European fruits grow well—peaches as standard trees, and apples and pears in abundance) they shook a laden tree for my special benefit, and filled my dandie with golden apples, a share of which won the hearts of many brown bairns.

My companions remained at Thandarh two days longer, but I was anxious to halt at Narkunda to finish a drawing. On arriving there I was greeted by dear little Ramnee, the hill puppy, whom I had left at Thandarh with his brother, but who came in search of me on his own account. So he and I went off drawing together; and two lovely brown children, all eyes and eyelashes, who had seen me gathering flowers, devoted the whole afternoon to collecting armfuls of scarlet, and white, and blue, till they had heaped up a flower-wall round us.

Next morning was glorious. Just the day to paint in Hatto forest; so thither we went, Ramnee and I, with the usual lot of brown Highlanders. Far overhead the tall tree-tops were still wreathed with clustering masses of red and white roses clambering in endless profusion to the very topmost boughs, and thence hanging in rich festoons, while every breath that stirred sprinkled

HATTO FOREST.

the earth with showers of rosy petals. And the ruddy sunlight shone warm on roses and trees, and played in broken gleams on the feathery undergrowth of ferns and reeds, glancing on the velvety black and gold mosses till they, too, sparkled like jewels. And far above all, the glittering ice-peaks seemed to reach up into heaven, and their brightness so dazzled our sight that as we gazed they seemed to lose themselves in the glowing light.

But our path lay down the hill, and from the valley far beneath us, quiet grey mists were silently stealing upwards. Soon we had left the sunlight, and the shadow of the great pine-forest encompassed us. Still we descended, and slowly the mists were creeping upwards, and a chill breath seemed to go before them, as though giving warning of their approach, and hushing all nature to silence. Even my brownies shivered as we entered that cloud. As they carried me down, it felt as though they were bearing me on into the Valley of the Shadow of Death. On every side white spirits seemed to float, impalpable, and grave, and solemn. As I stretched out my hands it seemed as though I could well-nigh grasp some tangible form, but the pale shrouded ghosts passed on unheeding, with slow, measured, noiseless pace.

Even the trees seemed floating by, as if I were at rest and they in motion. The rugged half-burnt stems seemed transformed to earth-dwarfs and frost-demons—those strange shadowy beings who dwell in these dark forests. On every side the tall cedars reached out giant arms. They seemed doubly giants now—pale diaphanous blue ghosts, like the shadowy, moonlit heroes of weird German or Gaelic legends; mighty sentinels, keeping watch in solemn silence—an oppressive silence; a stillness so intense that you could not but feel it. Fain would I have broken the spell by speaking some human words, but I could find none, for the language of the hill-men was to me an unknown tongue; and the brownies, too, were hushed, like every living thing.

Soon the chill mist gave place to heavy drops of rain, and ere we had time to seek a sheltering rock a very deluge was upon us. No English rain, gentle and summery—not even an English storm—but a rain pouring as though the floodgates of heaven were opened wide and their work must be done quickly. Soon from every crag the waters were rushing down, leaping in sudden torrents; and the path seemed gliding from beneath our feet, while streams rushed past us, as though along their natural channel. Then overhead the heavens gathered blackness. The red lightning streamed and flashed on every side, till to our blinded eyes it seemed to glance down the black tree-stems at our very feet.

When the storm had in some measure abated, we returned to Narkunda soaked and crestfallen. It was mortifying to see the calm sunshine in the afternoon, as if the morning's work had been all a dream. As usual, however, it was only a case of *reculer pour mieux sauter*, and at night again the whirling tempest raved and shook the house, and the tall pines rocked in the howling blast, while all manner of plaintive night-voices mingled with the roaring of mountain torrents, swollen by the rains.

> "The thousand sparkling rills
> That from a thousand fountains burst
> And fill with music all the hills."

Henceforth each day's march was just the same story with variations. Nowhere were we more struck by the grandeur of storm effects than in the black pine-forests of Hatto and Mahasso. Beautiful as these had been in sunlight, the intense, misty darkness now overhanging them gave a weird solemnity to the scene, which lent to it an inexpressible charm. Every day we were overtaken by terrific thunderstorms, which crashed around us with deafening grandeur; then lingering echoes reverberated from one dark mountain to another, and ere they died away the next vivid flash of lightning seemed playing all around us. In truth it was very glorious, and we felt only exhilaration at the majesty of the scene.

Still there is no denying that our perceptions of the sublime were apt to be somewhat damped by the drenching rains that invariably followed, and that, when at length on a day of calmest sunshine, we once more found ourselves at Simla—

> "a wondrous token
> Of Heaven's kind care, with necks unbroken"

—we were forced to admit that its luxuries were very charming, and that a cheery welcome home was no bad termination to our delightful three months in the wilds.

I fear we must have bored our friends a good deal with the attempt to make them realise the scenes in which we had found such enjoyment, for of course all verbal descriptions must be full of sameness, while nature is always varied; and we may use up all the superlatives expressive of beauty without conveying the ghost of an idea of what the reality was. At best our bored hearer can but evolve some fancy picture from out his "inner consciousness." In the present instance, however, there was as much to hear as to tell. Simla small-talk for three months—births, marriages, and oh! how many deaths!

Then we got our map of the Himalayas to trace our route, and felt what pigmies we were when we found that the whole ground of our three months' wanderings lay between the H and the I of

H I M A L A Y A   M O U N T A I N S

and that the mountain region covered a tract well-nigh as wide as it was long!

For a whole month longer the rains continued, sometimes pouring and clattering, till you would have fancied the house must be washed away—a perfect deluge. There was no whole day, however, of which some hours, or at least some small portion, was not beautiful, all the more so by contrast; but even then the whole world seemed shrouded in dense grey mist, veiling the hills, and trees, and sky.

We were, indeed, true children of the mist, for often from dawn till night it encompassed us on every side, sweeping into the house in dull leaden clouds, so thick that often we could scarcely see the other end of the verandah, or even the tall Indian oaks close round the house, or the tops of those growing on the khad below, whose masses of dark foliage appeared one moment only to vanish the next, like spectres in a dream. Even the ferns, which fringed the dripping branches, looked black, as the light mist played in and out amongst them.

Perhaps after several consecutive days of this dull, grey cloud-world, some invisible hand seemed to draw aside the thick curtain for a moment, and show you a glimpse of what might well seem a spirit-land—a few glittering peaks of snow, distant upwards of a hundred miles. You never saw the whole range; only a little mysterious peep, perhaps just flushed with rosy light. No foreground—no middle-distance—nothing but one little rift in the grey cloud-curtain. Before you had half drunk in this vision of delight, it was gone. Perhaps a few moments later you might catch a glimpse of the valley far below you,—of deep khads richly wooded, or terraced fields of many colours, dotted with tiny villages, or perhaps only a sweeping drapery of emerald green pasture, like smoothest velvet, or it might be a group of dark oaks and rhododendrons, with blackest foliage. But only one thing at a time, and all else utterly blotted out in cold grey mist, as if a great picture had all been sponged clean out, save some little pet bit in the middle. There was, however, almost always an hour before sunrise when the whole snowy range stood clear from end to end—in clear cold outline. Then soon after dawn, the mist rose.

With the rains came an increase of insect life; nothing very serious however. A considerable number of those lovely little silver fish-insects, which riddle muslin and destroy paper with their sharp invisible teeth. And a vast number of flying creatures, a sort of ant, I believe, which dropped countless wings all over the table every night. In fact, but for their wings, we should hardly have noticed their presence.

But our bath-rooms were the favourite haunts of horrible creatures. Some people found scorpions, and occasionally the mother scorpion carried several babies on her back! when the whole family were exterminated at one fell swoop. Our discoveries were limited to creatures with lean bodies, and a hundred long, hair-like legs; not the true centipede, but doubtless some near relation. And as to spiders!!! There is a picture by Gustave Doré showing "The spare attic" in some fairy tale, where every corner of the room is haunted by huge, hairy, horrible black spiders with long thick legs. That spare attic is the counterpart of every Indian bath-room in the rains.

Occasionally, to complete your entomological studies, you may find a young leech in your tub. These abound in the warm damp valleys, and sometimes find their way even here. They are of two species—the land and the water leech; and prove intensely annoying both to human beings and other creatures, as they lie hidden in rank vegetation or in deep stagnant pools, and fasten on the animals that come to drink, getting into their nostrils or throat, or adhering to the legs of human beings. The natives rub the bites with tobacco and lemon-juice, with some effect. But once a leech has taken up its abode in the nostrils of a dog, it is very difficult to extract it again. The poor creature's head swells. Everything is tried by turns. It it tied up far from water, and its nostrils filled with salt. Then after some hours it is brought close to water, yet not allowed to drink. A cup of Tantalus, it is thought, will induce the leech to crawl out. Even this rarely answers, and the only remedy is for some native to sit watching for hours with pinchers, ready to seize the little black head the moment it appears.

The "rains" made wonderfully little difference in the gregarious propensities of the Simla world. There was just the same continuous round of balls, theatricals, concerts, parties of all sorts, by day and by night, and a very pleasant social life it was, whenever the weather happened to be fine—and somehow it had rather a kindly habit of clearing up towards evening—so that on the whole, a wetting was not quite so common as might have been expected, and we learnt to look on waterproof cloaks as the natural finish of our evening toilets.

As the rains began to cease, the country became beautiful, the hills so clear, the people so pleasant, that it became a matter of positive regret when the last day of September came, on which I was again to leave my own people and go to other old friends at the hill station of Massourie, *alias* Landour: the former being the Civil, the latter the Military division of the same station on the great mountains, of which I thus obtained another glimpse far away from the scene of our previous wanderings.

My start was delayed a few days, owing to a landslip which carried away part of the new road, and there was no possibility of getting away by it, and not a coolie could be obtained to go by the other road. The Dâk Gharry (*alias* little travelling van) Company had now for the first time discovered that it was possible for a carriage with real horses to go up and down moderate hills with a good road; and that instead of the journey from Simla to Kalka involving a three days' march, it might very easily be done in one. So startling a discovery had hardly yet explained itself to the Indian mind, and in fact, the only time the experiment had been tried had, I think, been the day before the landslip, when the carriage had unfortunately rolled over the khad with all its inmates.[1]

However, I had every intention of repeating the experiment, so waited patiently till the road was repaired. I confess I had some qualms as to how my six words of execrable Hindustani would carry me over so long a journey. However, in India these matters are made very simple to the verdant traveller. Some one "lays your Dâk" from Simla to Umballa. Thence the railway to Seharanpore is of course plain sailing. And there you find that your friends at Massourie have again "laid your Dâk" right up to their door. In fact you are merely a bundle of goods, consigned to a series of intelligent natives, who will not fleece you more than they can be sure of doing with impunity.

As no carriage is allowed to enter Simla, this enterprising company had established itself beside the new road, about a mile below the town, fully two miles from our house. Thither I went by agreement, early in the forenoon, preceded by all my worldly goods. But owing to one delay after another, and conflicting reports as to the condition of the road, it was 4 P.M. when my gharry started at a tearing canter downhill. That of course was too good to last. The road all along was frightfully cut up; and when we got a few miles from Simla the parapets had all been washed away, and were replaced by piles of small rocks, which

[1] I believe the attempt to run carriages on this road was very soon given up, owing to several serious accidents having occurred.

had rolled down from the hills into the road, and had thus come in useful in building a temporary dyke, the road itself being just sufficiently cleared to enable us to pass, and still very much resembling the bed of a mountain torrent, in which, indeed, the waters were still flowing.

The owner of the carriage, or gharry, or caravan, had requested me to spend the night at Kyrie Ghat, to avoid the danger of travelling in the dark. There we were due in a couple of hours. However, it took us more than that time to get half way. As we neared the landslip, which it was very desirable to pass in good daylight, we found a whole bullock-train, extending over nearly half a mile, encamped for the night, in double row along the road, blocking it so effectually that the bullocks had to be yoked, and heavy waggons drawn aside, ere the carriage could pass. Long ere this was accomplished the sun had set; and we had still seven miles before us.

The horses at the next stage were such miserable brutes that they could not move the carriage at all. A whole hour was wasted in vainly battling with them. One of them fell three separate times, and then apparently went through all the agonies of death. It was sickening to witness. At last the vain attempt was given up. The coachman and *syce* went off leading the one available horse, and as soon as they were gone the other staggered to his feet again—poor brute! There I sat alone in the dark for a whole hour, as no lantern was to be obtained. I had made so sure of having no further use for one, that I had left mine in Simla.

At last two great, comfortable-looking white bullocks were procured, and slowly drew the carrrage to Kyrie Ghat. It was midnight when we reached the Dâk Bungalow, and found every room full of sleepers. The old Khansamah brought me out hot tea in the verandah, for which he utterly refused payment; a fact which, together with that of a sweeper having refused all *backsheesh* when we halted here for so long on our way to Simla, is worthy to be recorded in letters of gold, being quite without parallel. I tried to sleep in the *gharry* for the next three hours, by which time, there was clear moonlight; then, calculating that there was no time to spare, we again started, and except when the horses took to jibbing, which they occasionally did for half an hour at a time, found no further difficulty.

When daylight broke it was pleasant to see how here also the brown hills, which in the early spring had seemed to us so hideous, now on this first day of October were all covered with greenest pasture, and softened with a light drapery of mist. And in the little fields grew tall corn of divers sorts—green and gold; handsome crops, eight or ten feet in height. Especially lovely were the blood-red fields of Prince's Feather—I think the natives call it *Bâtou*—they eat the young leaves and the grain which hangs in great tossing plumes of deepest crimson; each spike was about seven feet high, with scarlet and gold leaves. There was also a pale pink variety; and another yellow, with leaves of rich olive.

The whole fields were sometimes interlaced with large beautiful convolvuli, fully four inches in diameter; some purest white, others the most vivid blue, pink, or purple; some white with blue edge and pink heart, in fact all varieties; but the pure bright blue predominated, like great bright stars against the scarlet grain. And floating amongst these the loveliest butterflies, of every hue—some like burnished gold; others, metallic crimson; some of bronze and delicate violet; some of emerald powdered with golden dust; others, opal or salmon colour; and some that flashed in the sunlight like gleams of silvery azure—all of surpassing loveliness. But I never again saw a pure scarlet dragon-fly like one which tantalized me near Pangi and then fluttered down the rocks far out of reach.

At midday we reached Kalka, which in the spring had seemed so dry and arid, like an ugly bit of Scotland; now it looked simply lovely, for softest showers had capped the hills with mist, and the fresh greenness of semi-tropical vegetation was quite enchanting. It was also pleasant once more to see a picturesque bazaar, and a fine old banyan tree twisting itself all round an old temple. Here, however, I had short time to pause; for the jolly old half-caste landlady, Mrs. Bain, not only "welcomed the coming" but certainly also "speeded the parting guest," for she would only allow me five minutes to wash and to swallow hot tea; then started me again, threatening the driver with condign punishment, bamboo backsheesh, and all sorts of dreadful things, if he did not catch the train at Umballa; which he accordingly did, starting as usual at a hard canter down the hill!

CHAPTER XIX.

FROM UMBALLA TO MASSOURIE.

Up the Mohan Pass—Dehra Doon—Night March to Massourie—Grand View of the Snowy Range—also of the Plains—Gorgeous Wild Dahlias—The Convent—Romance Shattered—Military Station at Landour—Customs of the Hill Tribes—Usury and Slavery—Views of the Plains and of the Snowy Range—The Siwalik Range and Giant Fossils—Game.

EXACTLY six months had elapsed from the day when we had first set foot on the low spurs of the Himalayas, till I now found myself retracing the same road. On the 1st April we had commenced the ascent from Kalka to Simla, and now on the 1st October the same cheery landlady was speeding me thence to Umballa—across the belt where the Mighty Range so abruptly blends with the Plains.

It was a very striking contrast to find oneself one half-hour still toiling up and down among the mountains, where for the last six months I had never seen half an acre of level ground; and the following half-hour to be driving over a dead level, as though we were heading straight for a boundless blue sea—but in truth we were only passing to the immeasurable plains. It was the suddenness of the transition that was so strange—and the effect of looking back to the mountains across this wonderfully rich green level foreground was one of most unwonted repose to the eye.

Each field seemed more beautiful than the last; heavy crops of tall rich grain of every sort, growing to a height of six or eight feet

—Indian corn, and sugar-cane, the haunt of all manner of birds; golden-crested hoopoes, and bright blue jays, and flocks of tame pigeons, purple, and green, and white; and then large fields of lucerne and other sweet succulent grasses, of which diligent grass-cutters were binding up huge bundles for their masters' horses. It was so charming to be once more among palm-trees and sweet yellow-tufted acacias, and surrounded by all the picturesque life of the plains—camels, elephants, ekkas, bullock-carriages, natives in

CROSSING THE GOGGRA.

fair linen and turbans, even to the darling little grey squirrels that scampered about in every direction.

We reached Umballa about 10 P.M., just catching the train, and four hours (in a comfortable railway carriage, built on purpose for the convenience of sleepers on long journeys) brought me to Seharanpore, where another gharry or van was in readiness. We started all fair, and I soon fell asleep, and awoke towards day-break to a sense of unwonted repose, to find the coachman and syce comfortably hubble-bubbling, as they had apparently been doing for the last hour. We had reached the banks of the Goggra, a wide expanse of sand with a river of moderate size. This, however, when full, is a very different matter, as Lord Clyde found to his cost, when, hoping to have surprised a body of rebels on the bank, he found they had succeeded in crossing just a few hours before, carrying every boat to the other side. The river was in flood, and proved an effectual barrier to his further progress.

To-day, however, it was moderate; and a whole regiment of half-naked coolies had assembled to drag the carriage across. It really was rather alarming to be thus forcibly carried off, but it was all in the day's work, and evidently part of the programme.

After this it was all plain sailing till we reached the Siwalik hills, which separate the plains from the beautiful valley of Dehra. The road lies through the Mohan Pass, when a gradual ascent of six miles brings you to a level two thousand feet above that which you have just left. There can be no reason why horses should not run here, quite as well as along the new road to Simla; but the Indian mind had not then mastered this possibility, so every carriage must either be dragged up the weary six miles by coolies, or else the inmate must be carried in a jampan, while the luggage is divided among coolies just as on a march, another carriage being in readiness at the top of the hill.

The latter is by far the more rapid method; but a stupid clerk having misunderstood his orders, insisted on the carriage being dragged up the weary road, to the intense disgust of a whole army of coolies, who gathered round the carriage in vehement expostulation, and made me plainly understand that they wanted to carry me and my luggage separately. This hubbub had continued for about a quarter of an hour, when to my great satisfaction I espied, as I thought, a fair-haired Englishman sitting under a tree. Thinking he would be able to interpret the rights of the case, I went up to him; but imagine my disgust on perceiving that the russet locks which I had mistaken for the sure sign of a countryman belonged only to a fair native, who, like certain dark-haired maidens in our own land, had dyed his glossy black hair a golden auburn![1]

His imitation of Western fashions had not imparted any knowledge of the English language; so I returned unsuccessfully to the malcontents, and grimly bade them obey the sahib's hookam, in other words, the orders they had received; never of course imagining that the clerk could have made so stupid a mistake. All I could do was to soften the unpopular decision by a promise of backsheesh, whereupon a team of fourteen wretched coolies yoked themselves to the heavy carriage, and slowly dragged it up the long ascent of about seven miles. This transaction occupied four hours, during which I walked on, following the course of a brawling mountain-stream, which rushed down the valley over great rocks and boulders. Here and there a patch of dense jungle, and everywhere endless varieties of tall rank grass, each beautiful.

All this time I found myself provided with an honorary escort, namely, a white-robed moonshee[2] who had taken a lift on the top of the carriage, and who, in return, was continually bringing me fruit, and insisted on teaching me to chew betel-nut as the greatest delicacy he had to offer. It was unspeakably nasty, and I was thankful next day to find that my teeth were not permanently stained red.

At the head of the Mohan Pass we first caught sight of the fertile valley of Dehra, or, as it is called, the Dehra Doon, a rich plain, with wealth of tropical vegetation, large clumps of graceful bamboo, and large-leaved plantains; rich crops of all sorts, and here and there picturesque villages. The valley is about sixty miles long and fourteen wide. On its farther side rise the Himalayas, where, at an elevation of 5,000 feet, lie the scattered bungalows of Massourie; and 1,000 feet higher is perched the military sanatorium of Landour, where soldiers from Calcutta and elsewhere are sent on sick leave.

[1] So, at least, I supposed at the time. I am, however, informed that such *lusus naturæ* are not unknown, being a phase of albinoism which chiefly affects the hair.

[2] Scribe, or teacher.

In the middle of this plain is the town of Dehra, like a lovely English village, each house surrounded with rose hedges, and bowery, billowy greenness. There is scarcely a house that has not its own group of beautiful bamboos, growing with a richness such as I have never seen elsewhere. These form a long avenue as you drive through the town, the general appearance of which is most attractive. No wonder that many old Indians never wish to return to Britain, but make their winter home in this fàir semi-tropical spot, and in the warm summer days merely move their camp to Massourie, whence they can look down on the blue, ocean-like plains, while the eternal snows tower above them.

Driving rapidly through this pretty town, I caught a glimpse of several native temples half hidden in the rich foliage. One in particular was so striking that I resolved to halt here on my return, on purpose to see it. Meanwhile we hurried over the next six miles, and reached the town of Rajpore at the foot of the hills so late in the afternoon that the friends who had come thus far to meet me, had given me up in despair, and I found them just starting for a long evening's ramble, to which my arrival put a stop. The part of wisdom would have been to remain at the hotel, but it was Saturday night, and I preferred a quiet Sunday at Massourie to spending it on the march; besides, the thought of a cheery welcome to a sunny home was very pleasant; so the order was given to have coolies ready at once for my dandie and lighter luggage, my companions trusting to their own walking powers.

It was with some trouble that these were procured, owing to the immense demand occasioned by the crowds of English flocking to the Dehra races; moreover the supply of men at Massourie is always rather deficient, and doubly so now, owing to the high wages given at Sacrata, a new hill-station in this district. Of course the number of men required is immense, as not only must every household have its own regiment of human ponies, but all supplies of every species of goods must be carried up from the plains on men's shoulders. You can scarcely conceive anything more awkward than to meet a dozen men, or more, carrying heavy furniture, such, for instance, as a great piano, up these narrow footpaths.

To a population thus dependent on the multitude of human workers, any cause that diminishes the supply is a serious matter. Imagine, then, the effect of a story having, some years ago, been circulated among the hill tribes that the Europeans required a vast supply of "Pahari oil," and intended to take every hill man, woman, or child, whom they could catch, and hang them up by the heels before a big fire in order to extract their oil! This story was so universally believed that all the coolies ran away from Massourie, and were only persuaded by slow degrees to return; and for months they continued to work tremblingly, still believing in danger. Indeed it was some years before they were altogether satisfied about the matter.

To-night there was considerable difficulty in procuring even six men to carry my dandie, bedding, and bag, and we found out, too late, that they had only been bribed to go at all by receipt of double pay *in advance*, and the promise of backsheesh at their journey's end.

How we came to start without a lantern I cannot imagine. Generally the natives are in such terror of leopards that they will not stir from one house to the next without either torch or lantern. To-night, however, we started on this twelve miles' march without one. Our path was a narrow zigzag, cut in the face of the hill, and running up pretty steeply. Very soon the sun set, and thick darkness with heavy mist rolled down upon us. The thick foliage of the oaks which overshadowed the path added so much to the obscurity of the night that we could scarcely distinguish anything.

Thus we plodded on for the first four miles, when with a sudden *bump* I found myself sitting on the ground, on the very verge of the khad, over which my leader had walked, vanishing in the darkness. The others raised a shout of "Killed, killed!" which was truly horrible to hear. Happily the poor fellow had stuck half way, and before long managed to scramble up again, having mercifully escaped with some bad cuts and bruises. Had we been a few steps farther, he would have had a frightful fall. What possessed the other wretches I cannot imagine, but they maintained that another man had fallen over, and as several other coolies had by this time overtaken us, we could not possibly distinguish whether one of ours was missing. We vainly shouted down the khad, but there came no answer—and they all declared the man must be dead. There was nothing for it but to despatch one of them to the nearest village, about a mile farther, for ropes and lanterns. I need scarcely say he never returned!

After some delay another traveller came down the hill, and by the light of his lantern we had the pleasure of just distinguishing all our rascals taking to their heels, leaving us alone with the wounded man, who proved a very good fellow. As soon as he had recovered sufficiently to walk, we pushed on to the village, leaving the dandie at a corner of the road. Here we found the two baggage coolies quietly waiting with their bundles to see what would happen next. They declared the others had fled for fear of being beaten for letting me fall! a dread which, I must say, was by no means justified, as these men are generally treated with great kindness by the English. In the present instance, the three who remained were treated to an extra supper by way of encouragement, immediately after which, one of them bolted. But the poor wounded man shouldered the bundle of the runaway and marched cheerily on.

We had still six miles to walk, up hill, about two miles being generally my utmost limit, and to-day I had already trebled my average in walking up the Mohan Pass. However there was nothing for it but a grim determination as usual to set a stout heart to the *stey brae.* It was now pitch dark, and although we had succeeded in borrowing a lantern from the merchant, not a bit of candle could be obtained. Luckily, oh joy! I recollected a small piece in the depths of my bag; a treasure which was forthwith fished out. Then we started cheerily. By this time the rain was pouring in a perfect deluge, literally like a waterspout, and rushing down the path, till it felt as if we were walking in a river against the current. A violent gust blew out the feeble lamp, leaving us in total darkness, feeling our way with one hand along the side of the khad.

THE PLAINS FROM MASSOWRIE.
Looking across Dehra Doon to the Siwalik Range.

At last we espied a hut, where we again got a light, and so struggled on till we reached Massourie, and found ourselves on the Mall, an excellent broad road. We had still a long and very steep ascent before we reached the top of Vincent's Hill, where we arrived at midnight, to receive such a welcome as made amends for all the dangers and perils of the night: only one sad memorial of that midnight expedition still haunts me, in the shape of a beloved old manuscript music-book, whose blurred and blotted pages show too plainly how grievously its constitution suffered on that occasion!

Sunday, as you may imagine, was a genuine day of rest. We could see the pretty church in the heart of Massourie, but the thought of the long descent and the weary climb up again was quite too much. It was enough for to-day, that sky, plains, and snows were all steeped in rest and in sunshine, and that every voice of nature seemed to blend in one joyous hymn of praise.

From the house itself we looked right down, past wooded hills, to the Dehra Doon, six thousand feet below. Beyond, as on a map, lay the low range of the Siwalik hills, intersecting the picture, and beyond that again, two thousand feet below, stretched the plains—a wide expanse of blue, vanishing in a boundless horizon in soft atmospheric blending of earth and sky. Here and there fine threads of glittering silver marked the course of divers rivers. On the one hand the Jumna, on the other the Ganges, and far in the distance a little straight line, like a scratch of a pin, represented the great Ganges Canal.

All round us were grassy hills, studded with grey rocks and Indian oak, of which not the mossy stem alone, but literally every branch, was covered with rare ferns of every species. And now, in the beginning of October, every bank was literally carpeted with wild flowers in richest luxuriance.

Above all, every here and there you came on a perfect jungle of brilliant dahlias, possibly once tame, as I do not hear of them elsewhere in these hills; and so it has been suggested that they must have been brought here by the first settlers. In any case, they are wild enough now, and grow in patches of half an acre together, in such dense luxuriance that you can hardly distinguish one green leaf. They are almost all single[1] and very large, and of every brilliant colour that you could possibly imagine—white, yellow, orange, scarlet, lilac, purple, deepest maroon—literally one dazzling blaze of colour. To lie on a grassy bank, looking up past such a sea of colour as this, to the grey rocks and intense blue of the sky, is a sense of bliss rarely equalled! It seems as though the sun's rays fell through crystal prisms, scattering rainbow lights in every direction.

It certainly is quite a new sensation in dahlias to see these lovely blossoms which have never been subjected to the rigid educational theories of gardeners growing up, as Nature intended them to do, with all the freedom of gigantic anemones. They are as different in charm from the highly cultivated dahlias of our flower-shows, as a judge's tightly curled wig differs from the glossy ringlets of a joyous child!

In the afternoon we crept up to a hillock just above the house, where the grey rocks were fringed with scarlet virginia creeper and other graceful plants. We still looked down on the boundless earth-ocean below us, and across the scattered town of Massourie, which is the abode of civilians, to Landour, the military station; far beyond which—faint and spiritual—gleamed the mighty fields of everlasting snow; not a mere line, as at Simla, but apparently twice as high; for Gangoutri, where the Ganges finds its source, is nearer to Massourie than are any snow-peaks to Simla.

There, far away in the distance, beyond the intervening abyss of deep, blue shadow, lay piled the mighty mountain ridges, rising tier above tier, their shapeless summits lost in soft fleecy clouds, from which, as phantoms in a dream, rose a long line of snowy peaks, stretching right across the horizon; each form distinct in its own beauty, yet all so soft and shadowy that they almost blended with the sea of billowy grey clouds, above which they seemed to float.

[1] What a curious instance of fashion in garden flowers is the recent discovery of the beauty of single dahlias, as though gardeners had invented some new wonder in suffering a flower to bloom naturally!

SNOWY RANGE AND LANDOUR FROM MASSOWRIE.

The rosy evening light just flushed the summits with a delicate pink, marking deep clefts and crevices with a touch of lilac, and melting away into that tender ethereal green, paler than a thrush's egg, which we know so well in our northern skies. Not a sound broke the intense stillness save the occasional cry of a great brown eagle, soaring in the valley far below, where the deep, calm shadows of night had already hushed the noisy whirr of insect life.

Never elsewhere have I experienced the same sensation of vastness as when in presence of these two boundless semicircles. One half of that wide horizon was marked only by the faint, hot haze that told of the burning heat of those plains which seemed to stretch away into immeasurable space. And then, you had but to turn your head to behold ridge beyond ridge of huge mountains, heaped together in endless confusion: while from right to left of *that* horizon the snow-peaks glimmered and melted away into the light.

I spent a very happy month at Massourie, or rather, I should say, a fortnight there, and a fortnight on Vincent's Hill, which is incomparably the finer situation, being very much higher, and commanding a more extensive view, including the whole of Massourie and Landour, both of which come in as a foreground to the snowy range.

The finest position in Massourie is occupied by a great Roman Catholic convent, the sisters of which undertake the education of a very large proportion of the Protestant girls in the station. The convent is perched on the brow of a hill, whence the view on every side is magnificent; in fact, no view to be compared with it is obtainable without a weary scramble to the top of Vincent's Hill. The bungalow in which we were living is situated at the farther end of this hill, and just above it, at a considerable distance from the convent, lies the little lonely burial-ground where sleep such of the sisters as have died in this far-away land—a peaceful and calm resting-place, with the great solemn hills outspread on every side. To me there was a charm in this quiet nook, associated as it was with the thought of the meek lives that had here spent themselves in patient well-doing. And often at sunset and at dawn

I found myself tracing the little woodland path that led from our domicile up to the nuns' graves, till I had acquired almost a romantic interest in the sisterhood, and a sincere desire to cultivate their acquaintance.

Judge of the sudden collapse of these kindly feelings, when, one evening, as I was returning alone by the brow of the hill from a distant sketching expedition, and laden with a heavy sketching block and other paraphernalia, lo! I encountered a grave and silent band of solemn sisters, the foremost of whom accosted me with the utmost acerbity, and informed me that the whole hill and all the walks on it were the private property of the convent, and that I was a trespasser! Imagine being pursued by such a word even in the Himalayas! Whether they had legal right on their side I know not. They certainly had might, in point of numbers, whereas I was alone and heavily laden, so that there was no use in disputing the question, or in attempting to point out to these irascible and illogical women that the path whereon we stood would in a very few minutes land me at home. I could not well get past them, as they might have given me a rapid impetus down the khad, so there was nothing for it but to return half a mile or more, and descend to the high road, whence all view of the snows was effectually shut out by the very hill whereon those sour and selfish old maids were taking their eventide constitutional. I need scarcely say that such rare lack of courtesy dispelled at once, and for ever, all romantic illusions concerning the meek and holy sisters, and that my future visits to the hill-top were so judiciously timed as to avoid further acquaintance with them, though I am bound to add that I heard them highly spoken of by sundry Protestant mothers who had intrusted their daughters to their charge.

The weather became daily more and more cloudless, and we did pity the victims of that arbitrary law which compels all working bees to return to the plains before the 15th of October. Then all the hill-stations seem to empty, as if by magic, within a couple of days. It certainly is a strange regulation, as the hills are just then at their most perfect phase, while the plains are still simmering in sultry heat, and many a half-recovered invalid finds out too quickly that he has only returned to this purgatory to lose all that he had gained.

It is said that Massourie and Landour are very much healthier than the military stations round Simla, where cholera, dysentery, and fever have a full share of victims. Here, as in all the hill stations, the gay season begins in April, when the rhododendrons are in their glory, and continues till the end of September, in one unceasing round of picnics, archery parties, and every variety of evening gaiety, which, as a general rule, have the superlative advantage of early hours. All October and November the climate is simply heavenly, and the sky cloudless. Then in December comes the snow, when the residents flee down the hill to Dehra, where it has very rarely been known to follow them.

Unlike the houses at Simla, all those here are built like the bungalows of the plains, only one storey high, with pillared veranda of white plaster on stonework. But all alike are perched on artificially level sites. It is the fashion of many people to decry Massourie as being ugly compared with Simla. I cannot say I thought so. Moreover, a sweeping assertion declares that there are no trees here. Here again I can only imagine that they use the word to denote cedars only (just as we in Scotland understand salmon, by the term fish). For though in bygone years all deodars were ruthlessly cut down, as a ridiculous sanitary measure, there still remain rich masses of rhododendron and Indian oak, where troops of brown monkeys and grey langours disport themselves right merrily; while the especial peculiarity of Massourie is the number of its small weeping willows. Now, all timber is so strictly preserved that it is a matter of difficulty to get sufficient firewood; and all wood for other purposes is absurdly expensive.

The hill people hereabouts are in some respects different from those among whom we have been wandering hitherto. They are said to be pure Hindoos, though here also all religious feeling seems vague and undefined. Every household has its special god or deota, to which one corner of the house is assigned.

Sometimes you may meet wild-looking men almost naked, daubed all over with yellow powder, made from the blossom of the pine-tree. These are generally returning from a curious religious dance, when a whole village goes mad for several days; men and women supposing themselves to be possessed by evil spirits, or at least pretending to be so, and going through all sorts of antics, as if they were bears, monkeys, leopards, or other varieties of wild beasts.

They have one great festival at midsummer, when the milk of three whole days is collected and consecrated to the use of the temple. On the feast day each family brings its offering. The head man of the village dips a bunch of flowers into each lota full of milk, and therewith sprinkles the image (the deota) which has been brought out gaudily dressed. All the milk is then emptied into one vessel and every one is invited to drink. The village street is strewn with flowers, and men and women are both adorned in their gayest raiment, wearing bunches of flowers.

When a Pahari dies, in this district of Garwhal, his relations shave the head and beard, and make much lamentation for ten or twelve days, during which they must abstain from all pleasant food, such as meat or ghee. They must also refrain from hunting. At the end of their time of mourning they offer a sacrifice to the spirit of the departed, and go their way. Should he, however, have died from any epidemic, such as cholera or small-pox, no public mourning is allowed. In the districts where wood is too expensive to be wasted on funeral pyres, it is customary simply to expose the dead on a hill-top, where the fowls of the air quickly dispose of him.

Hindoos though they bc, there seems to be no prejudice among these people against the re-marriage of widows, and should such a one remove the great nose-ring worn by all wives, it is a sign that she purposes seeking a second mate. Should she have no son, her re-marriage is compulsory, as by the laws of Garwhal the property of a man dying without male issue reverts to the Rajah; and the term "property" includes all female appendages. So the widow and unmarried daughters are forthwith provided with husbands, and the dower paid for them goes to the pocket of the Rajah.

The people complain in vain of this arrangement. It is said that practically the position of the very poor is abject slavery, as, owing to the amazing extent to which usury is carried, a very small debt once contracted rapidly accumulates such frightful interest, as to become a hopeless clog on the debtor, and in many cases he himself and his family are actually sold in payment of it. Children are sometimes sold to pay their parents' debts. Thus whether slavery is or is not nominally allowed, it is so virtually, and the wretched debtors have a life-long period of hard labour for their owners, though the value of their labour soon covers the amount of the original debt. The owner also pockets whatever dowers are paid for any members of the family whom he may see fit to dispose of.

Mr. Wilson, whose name is celebrated in India as that of a keen and successful sportsman, tells of one instance that came under his notice, in which a man, having broken the leg of a goat, had to borrow two rupees to pay the fine. This debt was allowed to stand over, accumulating interest till it amounted to twelve rupees, when he was seized and sold as a slave, his family and all their work being included in the bargain. The owner had actually sold one of the daughters for sixty rupees, and a quarrel about the sale of the second brought the case before Mr. Wilson's notice. If only these wretched creatures can succeed in running away, and can settle on British territory, they are of course free, but every possible difficulty is thrown in their way. Besides, the love of home amounts, in these men, to a passion, though indeed it is often anything but a "sweet" home.

Amongst all my Himalayan memories none return more pleasantly than the recollection of the early mornings at Massourie, looking down upon a sea of mist, bathed in mellow, rose-coloured light. Then as it slowly rose, a chain of islands would here and there appear, as if floating upon those white billows. These were the peaks of the low Siwalik range; none of them more than three thousand feet in height. Yet the deep gloomy ravines of those pine-clad hills have an interest lacking to many a higher range; for in their dark, mysterious solitudes have been discovered such strange and wonderful fossils as have filled geologists with delight; fossils of camels, far larger than any now extant; fossils of tortoises, crocodiles, giraffes, elephants, and hippopotami. Similar discoveries have been made in the Dehra Doon, and all these remains are on a colossal scale.

For instance, there is the gigantic land tortoise, with shell six inches thick, which measures eight feet across the back, and is upwards of twelve feet in length, while with head and tail protruded he must have been fully eighteen feet from tip to tip, and stood about six feet high. He is called the Atlas tortoise, as if to suggest the Hindoo legend which tells of that tortoise on the head of which rests the earth. It is supposed that this great creature must have existed until comparatively recent ages, that is to say, till long after the creation of man, as various old Greek travellers have recorded how both in Ceylon, on the shores of the Red Sea and of the Persian Gulf, tortoises and turtles existed so enormous that huts and boats were roofed with a single shell. Even at the present day turtles are sometimes captured which measure from four to five feet in length; such shells, raised on four sticks, make a very fair sunshade.

Besides the huge elephants, there are found remains of the Sivathere, a heavy ungainly beast, the size of a rhinoceros, adorned with two pairs of horns of different form—one pair on the forehead like those of an ox; and behind these another large massive pair, palmated and branching like those of a fallow deer, but on a gigantic scale. All these revelled in vast forests of teak and dense bamboo jungle.

Of those great forests small trace now remains, though in the early part of this century the Doon was covered with fine timber, a survival of those dense primeval forests which (from the descriptions preserved in the old Sanskrit poems) must have clothed the greater part of India at the time of the Aryan invasion. Gradually the country was cleared, but vast tracts of hill country in central India, and on the slopes of the Himalayas, remained untouched—indeed, were purposely preserved by the men of the plains as a barrier betwixt themselves and the wild mountain tribes whose incursions they had such good cause to dread.

These mighty belts of forest secured a steady average rainfall, but when under British rule the rapidly increasing population found they had no longer cause to dread their mountain neighbours, the work of de-forestry was carried on so recklessly, that broad tracts were wholly denuded, and the rainfall so seriously affected as greatly to increase the desolating droughts which result in such terrible famines. The regular timber supply was also seriously diminished by this ruthless destruction, and but for Government interference in the last thirty-five years, in rigidly preserving all such forests as still remain, the whole would ere now have vanished, and Hindoostan would be a treeless waste.

Now all is under most careful supervision of the Forest Department: the cutting of timber is strictly regulated; stringent precautions are adopted to guard against fire; some waste districts have been re-clothed by planting millions of timber trees; others by sowing tons of seeds of shrubs and forest-trees broadcast over the land. Certain forests are wholly reserved; in others the people are allowed to retain hereditary rights of pasturage and woodcutting, while throughout the whole Empire certain tracts are specially reserved to furnish fuel, with a view to possible railway extension.

It is estimated that the Reserved Forests of India cover an area of about forty-six thousand square miles, in addition to vast tracts of forest which are merely under protection. Apart from the immense good done to the whole Empire by this work of Forest Conservancy, it already increases the national revenue by upwards of 310,000*l.* annually, after paying all its own expenses, which amount to over 557,000*l.* Altogether it is a great and good work.

The great belt of dense jungle stretching along the base of the Himalayas formerly gave all this district a very unhealthy character in autumn, owing to the malaria produced by such a mass of sodden, decaying vegetable matter, so that the Terai was accounted a very dangerous camping-ground. Where, however, the country has been cleared, and fertile cornland has replaced the wilderness, the whole character of the valley has changed, so that beautiful Dehra Doon may now claim to have her old ill fame forgotten as a dream of the past.

She still, however, keeps some quiet corners, where an occasional wild elephant or bear may be found in spite of multitudinous sportsmen. Leopards, deer, and pigs there find a haven, while snipe and florikan, quail and black partridge, pheasants and pea-fowl, still abound. In the rivers are fish enough and to spare. Great mahseer that would mock our finest salmon, fish that think nothing of weighing twelve or sixteen pounds, inasmuch as some have been captured weighing a hundred pounds, and one that weighed 105½ pounds was some years ago caught at Mapoorie with rod and fly. Not bad sport!

October slipped by all too quickly. Its most marked memories are of exhilarating, bracing air, decidedly chilly in the mornings and evenings—of pink sunrises on the boundless plains—pink sunsets on the eternal snows, with foreground of dark Indian oak; and steepest banks, clothed with a waving sea of gorgeous dahlias, only relieved here and there by patches of grey rock which carry the eye upward till it loses itself in the vivid blue of heaven. Here, indeed, the lover of radiant colour may revel to his heart's content.

The very ground near these dahlia beds is rainbow-hued, being strewn with fallen petals. And every jampanee you meet, carrying his mistress out for her airing, is sure to be adorned with some of these bright blossoms.

Many of these are fine merry lads, and they carried us cheerily up steep hills, or down the deepest valleys to see waterfalls, and explore damp ravines, where on dewy banks or in dark crevices the rarest and daintiest ferns grow in wild luxuriance, their light feathery fronds weaving a delicate tracery over the black rocks. Here in the cool shade we would sometimes seek shelter during the heat of the deep mid-noon, where only a soft, subdued light came trembling through green leaves, just revealing the wonderful intricacy of all that fragile, fairy foliage, such mellow light as calms the spirit like the dim twilight of some old cathedral. Then, when the shades of evening once more called us up from this underworld, it was perhaps to see the grey mist drawn aside, revealing a far-away range of ruby and opal, while the world at our feet was one carpet of rarest emerald.

So you see Nature has done her work gloriously, and many pleasant human beings did all that in them lay to make Massourie still more delightful. And so it remains stored up amongst memory's pleasantest pictures.

CHAPTER XX.

FROM MASSOURIE TO HARDWAR.

A Sikh Tomb at Dehra Doon—Sikh Tenets and Sacred Books—Ghoorkas—Animal Sacrifices—Dripping Well—Bamboo, its many Uses—Giant Grasses—Reach Hardwar—Colour of Rivers—Floods—Town of Hardwar—Picturesque People—Sealing up Holy Water—Brass Idols—Architecture—Forest Bungalow.

WHILE rapidly driving through Dehra on my way to Massourie, I had caught glimpses of divers temples appearing through the rich foliage. There was one in particular which I felt convinced would reward a closer inspection. But as usual when I came to inquire about it, not one of the English inhabitants had ever noticed it, or indeed knew of the existence of any native building of the smallest interest, though the majority had just returned from spending the race week in the little town itself. I was further assured that there was no hotel there where I could put up with any sort of comfort.

Nevertheless I was fully resolved to halt and have a look at the place. I there found quarters more comfortable and home-like than I had met with in all my experience of Indian hotels, a house kept by a kindly family who took every possible pains to make my stay pleasant. Under their guidance I explored every nook of the pretty town. We went in and out of temples, onto roofs, into gardens, along bamboo avenues, and in fact saw all there was to see.

The large building that had first attracted my attention was the centre of interest. It proved to be a remarkably fine Sikh tomb, in fact it was that of the grandson of Nânak, the founder of the sect. This was the only specimen of their handiwork I ever had a chance of seeing, so it would have been annoying indeed to have passed it by. Its architecture is much the same as that of the great Mohammedan tombs at Delhi and Agra, and the building is on the same colossal scale. There is the same cluster of domes crowning the central building; the same tall minarets at the four corners of the great platform on which the whole is raised. The Sikhs are a sect of Hindoos with very peculiar religious tenets. The most apparent are that they allow no idols; and that they totally eschew tobacco in all forms, but allow a free use of spirits. They also eat all manner of meats: pork, fowls, and eggs, thus making themselves unclean in the sight both of Mohammedans and Hindoos; fowls being as vile in the eyes of the latter, as pork in those of the Mussulman.

Nevertheless they are as particular as any other sect in upholding the divinity of cattle, and hold that to cause the death of a cow is an offence worthy of death. This tenet was very practically exemplified in 1871, when a body of the Kooka sect made a raid on two villages just outside of Umritsur, inhabited by the town butchers, who in their lawful trade had been guilty of slaughtering cattle. To avenge this sin, the Kookas massacred the inhabitants of both villages. Much to their astonishment, they were duly brought to justice for this outrage, and twelve men were condemned to death by the Court at Lahore.

In the days of the Moguls, Umritsur frequently changed hands, and when the Mohammedans gained ground they killed cows, and smeared the Holy Fount of Immortality with their blood. When the Sikhs triumphed they slew pigs, and defiled the Mohammedan mosques with the blood of the unclean beasts!

Although the Sacred Book of the Sikhs apparently inculcates the worship of only one God, they reverence all the principal incarnations of Vishnu, whose symbols are invariably branded on the breast and shoulder of his worshippers.

The Sikhs hold that, having thus been touched with fire during life, it is unnecessary to burn the body after death. Hence they are the only Hindoos who bury their dead, and who take pleasure in erecting tombs to their memory.

(I am told that certain great Brahman saints are buried instead of being burned, but this is from a belief that owing to their exceeding sanctity they have not died, but are lying entranced. So the tomb is to them only a place of rest, to which their followers make pilgrimage.)

The word Sikh means literally Disciple, and though now applied as a national distinction of the people of the Upper Punjaub, it was originally merely the name of a religious sect founded in the fifteenth century by a high-caste Hindoo, by name Nânak. So rapidly did the new faith spread that, when Nânak died in A.D. 1539, his disciples already numbered one hundred thousand; a race bound together in a mystic commonwealth by the intensity of religious fervour and warlike temperament.

The object of the founder was to break down all barriers of caste, and to combine the best points in the faith of Hindoos and Mohammedans, that both might accept a common creed. Establishing himself as Guru or spiritual teacher, he founded a theocratic government, and embodied his teaching in a sacred book called the *Âdigranth*, which to the present day lies open before his successor, the great Guru, who receives actual worship in the far-famed Golden Temple of Umritsur. Not only are divine honours paid to the Guru, but also to the sacred Scriptures —the Granth, as they are commonly called—and which are deemed visible representatives of Hari, *alias* Vishnu. Notwithstanding the prohibition of idol worship, this sacred book is treated with exactly the same childish reverence as any other Vishnuvite idol. It is daily dressed in oft-changed precious coverings of costly brocade, and is laid open on a rich throne beneath a jewelled canopy, while attendants wait around it waving chowries. Each night it is carried in state to its sleeping quarters in another temple on the brink of the sacred tank, where it is laid by to rest in a golden shrine.

Umritsur, "the Fount of Immortality," is so called because of the exceeding holiness of the great tank, in the centre of which stands this beautiful golden temple. Here the Guru, who is a venerable old man, still holds sway, and receives the homage of his martial devotees, and their offerings of flowers and jewels, though his chief office seems to be the constant study of the sacred volume. He is surrounded by a bodyguard of *Akâlis*, who represent the concentrated essence of the Sikh faith. They call themselves the soldiers of GOD, and are distinguished by their invariable blue dress, bracelets of steel, and conical turbans. Round the waist they wear circles of sharp steel, which act, when so required, as very dangerous weapons, being thrown at a foe with unerring aim. These *Akâlis* are a turbulent lot of fanatics, and give no small trouble to the good old man, whom they nominally reverence as their spiritual superior.

The sect was at first essentially peaceful in its tenets. This state of things, however, could not be of long continuance, inasmuch as the hand of every man was against them—Hindoo and Mussulman being alike furiously opposed to a sect which had ventured to make its own selections from its neighbours' creeds. Thus the Sikhs were forced into a position of perpetual self-defence, which in the very nature of things soon became aggressive. But it was not till the accession of the great Guru Govind that the strong spirit of ambition was infused into their ranks and their military character developed. In addition to common tenets of faith, he insisted on uniformity in external matters. Hair and beard were to be unshaven; dress blue, and the use of arms habitual. He gathered his recruits from every caste and every tribe, admitting them to a perfect equality of rank; and, assuming for himself and them the title of Singh (lion), managed to infuse a wondrous spirit of unanimity, which, strange to say, has so manifested itself in outward life that from this multitude of mixed races has sprung the finest people in India, with strongly marked physical characteristics, tall, well-built, lithe and agile in action, generally dark in colour, and unmistakably warriors.

Their first struggles to establish their power were a series of desperate and hopeless enterprises, but at length, crossing the Sutlej, they forced their way to the very gates of Delhi. Repulsed by the son of Aurungzebe, they were driven back to their hills, whence, returning to the charge in 1716, they were again defeated, and the sect of Sikhs so mercilessly persecuted that for the next thirty years no more was heard of them.

Nevertheless there were certain attractive points in their creed which brought them many proselytes. For instance, one rule prescribes the maintenance of the poor members by the richer; and the latter find compensation in being allowed the free use of wine and all strong spirits—a fact which came so prominently forward at the time of our treaties with Lahore, that Sir John Malcolm said, "it was rare to see a Sikh soldier quite sober after sunset," and the most urgent political business had to wait day after day in consequence of the state of helpless intoxication of every individual concerned.

This does not seem to have lessened the warlike tendency of this fiery and turbulent sect, which next came into notice under the chieftainship of Runjeet Singh, who, having established his own supremacy in the Upper Punjaub, and accepting the course of the Sutlej as his boundary from British States, made treaties with England under Lord Auckland, whereby his kingdom was recognised as an independent State, on a footing of equality with the older Powers of India. By this treaty England secured a faithful ally and a secure boundary, up to 1839, when the Old Lion of Lahore died. It is difficult to picture the mighty old chief—the warrior whose influence kept all these aggressive spirits in check—as "a little, tottering, one-eyed old man," which is the description given of him at the time of his treaty with Lord Auckland.

After his death a desperate conflict for his throne arose among his near kinsfolk, who contrived by all the ordinary Oriental methods to secure a marvellous rapidity of succession: methods which history sums up as a bloody saturnalia; thirty-six members of the royal family having disappeared in seven years!

This cheerful process continued till the chief survivor of Runjeet Singh's dynasty was a child, the Maharajah Duleep Singh, son of a dancing-girl, who now assumed the title of Ranee, and the reins of government. The vast body of soldiery, however, having by this time realised their own power, utterly set at nought such feeble rulers, and, acknowledging no law but their own reckless will, determined on the conquest of Hindoostan, and the overthrow of the British sway.

Then followed those battles which are still matters of contemporary history; the result of which was, that to Goulab Singh, who had continued faithful to Runjeet's policy, was awarded the fair vale of Cashmere, and those precious teak-forests whence Britain now has to purchase timber at a tremendous cost—while the Maharajah Duleep Singh has been relieved of the care of his fiery subjects, and found a more secure and peaceful home among the heathery braes of Scotland, till his practice of Eastern falconry proved so grievous to the terrified grouse that he has latterly been content with southern coverts. His British home is happily beyond the reach of dangers from the fanatical rage which his adoption of the Christian faith must certainly have excited.

The Kookas, whose name has latterly become so familiar to us as being a dangerous ingredient in the undercurrent of Indian discontent, are a sect of ultra-fanatical Sikhs, founded about thirty-five years ago, near Attock, by Baluk Ram, who became their high priest. His object was to restore the Sikh religion to its original purity; and also to organise a secret political body, ready at any moment to do his bidding. This sect now numbers fifty thousand men—a brotherhood bound together by the most solemn oaths never to flinch from any work appointed them, and ready to obey unhesitatingly the commands of their superiors.

This is a long digression from the old Sikh tomb at Dehra; but I confess that the fact of this sectarian meaning of the word was to me altogether a new idea; and the notion of a *buried* Hindoo, and one moreover who had forsworn the joys of hubble-bubble in exchange for the pleasures of strong drink, threw altogether a new light on the manners and customs of the race. I spent several days here, much interested in sketching, but nevertheless envying my sister and her husband, who had gone off to

Umritsur to have a look at the great Guru in his Golden Temple —travelling, however, at a pace too rapid for my taste.

Near the tomb, which is guarded by many devout men, there is a large tank, where from morning till evening the people come to bathe. As usual, men and women are all together. Nevertheless they accomplish their bath with the modesty of perfect unconsciousness. They bring all their vessels to scour, and their clothes to wash. More especially they polish their teeth, with their wooden tooth-brushes, till you would imagine there could be no enamel left. Then they pray, and taking water in their hands hold it up towards the sun; then pour it out as an oblation. After this, they fill their brass vessels with the same water, which, although constantly running, is by this time moderately dirty, and go their way.

During the summer months Dehra is the spot where the Viceroy's bodyguard make their home. There is also a Ghoorka regiment always stationed here. These little Ghoorkas are about the finest native battalion in the British service, not by reason of their size, for it is the old story of "great goods in little bundles," but as possessing all manner of soldierly virtues; wonderful honesty, power of endurance, and a talent for making the best of things, that would do credit to Mark Tapley himself.

In addition to the accoutrements supplied by Government, each Ghoorka must provide himself with the weapon peculiar to his race, namely the kookeree, which is a very broad, sharp, and curiously curved knife, capable in skilful hands of doing wonderful execution. There is an annual festival when the Ghoorka gods must be propitiated by the sacrificing of divers animals, even (to the horror of the Hindoos) of an ox. To make the offering truly acceptable, the creature must not only be slain with one blow, but its body should be cleft right in two—no easy feat, especially with so short a weapon. To attain proficiency, therefore, Ghoorka lads try "their prentice hands" on a multitude of kids, who, on the whole, must have a bad time of it.

The kookeree, however, comes in useful in a thousand other ways, and two small knives which nestle in its sheath are handy for dinner purposes, therein answering to the little knife appended to a Highlander's dirk.

One of the points of interest near Dehra is a certain dripping rock overhanging a sheltered pool, hidden among richly wooded hills. The water, filtering through the rock in a continuous shower, has formed an incrustation of glittering stalactites, and this dripping cave in the deep wooded dell is altogether a very pretty and fairy-like retreat. Of course it is a favourite rendezvous for the Dehra world.

But the chief attraction after all is the extreme fertility of this rich valley. The luxuriance of all manner of crops, the large Government tea-gardens, or rather tea-plantations, the wealth of flowers, more especially of one beautiful plant, the *Rosa hibiscus-mutabilis*, which in the early morning is loaded with pure white blossoms, like large scentless roses, and when you look again at noon, your roses have changed from white to deepest crimson. These grew in beautiful clusters round the little church in the middle of the village.

Lovelier than all else were the rich masses of tall bamboo, which line the central street, and stretch away in a beautiful avenue, fully a mile in length, the great plumes intertwining their feathery arms in one long continuous arch, far overhead. It was especially charming to ride along this pleasant shady grove on the gentlest of elephants, which the kindness of a friend had placed at my disposal—a nice, easy way of seeing the country from an advantageous height. So we could overlook fields and streams, and count the great bamboo clumps dotted all over the valley.

It would be impossible to imagine foliage more graceful than these great isolated clumps of bamboo, which, after all, are only magnificent colossal grasses. They grow in clusters like gigantic plumes of ostrich feathers. Each reed may average four or five inches in diameter at the base, and rise to a height of forty or fifty feet, with joints two or three feet apart, fringed with long, slender leaves. The tapering canes bow their elegant, feathery heads in graceful curves and bend at every breath of wind, while the vividly green leaves quiver tremulously and incessantly.

Sometimes these beautiful reeds have been taught to whisper low, musical responses to the wooing of the breeze. The Malays call them the cane of melody, and at their bidding the mysterious forest voices blend in wild cadences like some strange Æolian harp. These people have a custom of boring holes in each joint of these hollow pipes, the holes being of divers dimensions, larger or smaller according to the girth of the bamboo, so that as the wind sighs through them it produces various notes, more or less rich and full in tone—sometimes soft and flute-like—sometimes melodious as the full swell of an organ—sometimes whistling shrill and piercing as the cry of some tortured spirit. So the winds and the grasses have their own rare music in the deep shade of these tropical forests.

In beautiful contrast with this feathery foliage rise the broad shining leaves of the giant plantain, each leaf eight or ten feet long, crowning a low stem, whence hang simultaneously the great crimson blossoms and the clusters of ripe creamy fruit, one such cluster affording a satisfying meal for several persons. It is a noble plant, and the young fresh leaf when first expanded is the loveliest, greenest, and smoothest thing you can imagine, though too soon cracked and split into a thousand shreds by the combined action of sun and wind.

If you care to build up an imaginary bamboo from a small British weed, you may get a faint idea of its pattern from the common *Equisetum*, which abounds in most of our woods. But of the loveliness of the reality nothing save sight can convey a notion. To the Hindoo of the plains it is as precious as is the cocoa-nut to his brethren on the sea-coast. The young sprouts, which must be diligently pruned so as to strengthen the main shoots, are either eaten as a vegetable, like asparagus, or else boiled with sugar and made into sweetmeats, or with vinegar to make pickles. Sometimes they are cut up small and mixed with honey; a bit of hollow bamboo is filled with this mixture, and is then coated with clay, and roasted over a wood fire till the clay splits, and a very excellent sort of sweetmeat is ready for food. In China the young shoots of the bamboo are a common article of consumption.

The bamboo supplies physic too. A decoction of its leaves is considered a very good cough-mixture. Its outer rind acts as a febrifuge. The root is an ingredient of a valuable salve, while a cooling drink is made from the young buds. It sounds like seething the kid in its mother's milk, but you may, if you choose, boil these buds in water procured from the large hollow stems, many of which contain a considerable amount of fluid, which is considered a most wholesome and pleasant beverage. This juice as well as the outer rind contains a large quantity of silica, which is obtained by burning the wood, and is believed to have wonderful powers of healing.

The bamboo is, however, too precious to be often burnt. Every conceivable thing is manufactured from it, from the light fishing-rod to the mast of the vessel, indeed the vessel itself, hull, sails, and ropes, are made from bamboo in some form. Houses are built of it, rafters and floors and door-posts. When split, it forms the sharp spears used by watchmen or hunters, and when very finely divided it forms admirable wickerwork of all sorts; matting and baskets, blinds, bows and bow-strings, arrow-shafts, reed-pens, and poles, flutes and fifes, water-wheels and buckets, water-pipes of any required length (miles perhaps, made by placing them end to end), are a very small proportion of the countless uses of this precious grass. Its joints act as oil-jars, wherein the peasant keeps his store. As an instrument of punishment its use is commonly well known, "bamboo-backsheesh" being among the endearing words of promise most frequently addressed by the Briton to his followers, for their special encouragement. The Chinese find still more varied treasures in the bamboo-mine, not the least of which is a soft white paper, with which they cover the bamboo skeletons of their umbrellas.

When I was about to leave Dehra, my landlord most wisely suggested that surely it was foolish to have come within thirty miles of Hardwar, the holiest of all Hindoo cities, and one which even bears away the palm of sanctity from Benares, and yet not to see it. Therein I fully agreed, but could not see any satisfactory way to accomplish it, as Hardwar is a purely native city, without one resident Englishman, and not possessing even a Dâk Bungalow where a tentless traveller could lodge. That difficulty, however, was soon dispelled, as my host most kindly allowed his pretty daughter to accompany me, and a very pleasant companion she proved, as well as a most useful one; for being thoroughly mistress of the language she was able to make all arrangements in the most satisfactory manner.

A gentleman in the Forest Department did much to make our way smooth, having most courteously placed at our disposal the largest, gentlest elephant in his stud, and allowed us the use of the Forest Bungalow, a roughly furnished house built for the accommodation of the foresters when on their tours of inspection. He further sent an intimation to the principal moonshee and big men of the town, announcing our approach, and laying on them strictest commands to see that no evil befell us.

So one beautiful morning we started before sunrise in doolies (a sort of canvas box-bed), each carried by six men, who walked calmly along for the whole thirty miles, with only one rest of half an hour for their poor, frugal dinner. I never saw such walkers. On our elephant rode the khitmatgar, who was to cook for us, together with all his degchis (*alias* cooking-pots) and other stores.

Our road lay along the rich wide valley, bounded on the left by the Himalayas bathed in lilac light, and on the right by the low, pine-clad Siwalik range. Soon, however, we were in the uncleared jungle, which was not very striking. Here and there was a good tree, but the general effect was of very tangled underwood. There were pretty bits, however, where delicate parasitical plants of tenderest green bind their large-leaved neighbours to the slender palms, and swing from branch to branch in light feathery festoons. And a closer look reveals an endless variety of greenery, all interwoven with bright blossoms, and sometimes a quick flash of wings gleams in the

HARDWAR ON THE GANGES.

sunlight. One lovely plant, growing in rich profusion, seemed like a wild asparagus; but each little feathery tuft of the tall plume was covered with tiny white blossoms, set at regular intervals, and each tuft was guarded by one sharp thorn.

But the beauty of the grasses was beyond telling, and their endless variety was a source of unbounded pleasure. Scarcely one common English pattern of grass was missing, but all on a Brobdingnagian scale. Jumping grass, and trembling, bowing grass; spiky grass, and tufted grass; waving grass like wild oats; silky, feathery grass. Go into our English woods and autumn fields, and count, if you can, the almost innumerable variety of these little delicate plants. Then imagine every one of these reproduced eight or ten feet high, some far higher, and add to them very many species unknown to Britain, and then you will have some notion of the Indian jungle grasses!

There are white, silky spikes like pampas grass, and tall, tossing plumes like ostrich feathers. Great, black, drooping plumes also, like the English marsh-weed exaggerated; and tall, pink, sirkee grass, whose great rosy plumes waved far above our heads as we sat on the tall elephant. The latter is, I think, the commonest of all. Imagine all of these growing together in densest luxuriance, and you will see that Indian grasses are not a feature to be overlooked.

As we drew near Hardwar, or Haridwar, that is, the gate of Hari, the Sun-god, *alias* Krishna, *alias* Vishnu, we made the cook dismount, and distribute his cooking-pots among the coolies, while we took possession of the elephant, so as to command a better view on entering the city. Here, indeed, the country is lovely. The two mountain chains almost meet, and in the intervening valley flows the broad, clear, beautiful Ganges, as yet unsullied by the filth of her worshippers, for though she has already travelled nearly 150 miles since she left her snowy cradle, her journey has lain through difficult mountain gorges, where only the very devout and physically strong can seek to do her homage. The water is clear as crystal, of the most exquisite aquamarine colour, and delicious to drink. No wonder that the people see in her the purest of goddesses, and adore Ganga, the daughter of Himarat (the Himalayas), above all their other gods.

We did congratulate ourselves on having found her in this calm, heavenly temper; had we been three months earlier we might have learned to hate her as cordially as we did the yellow Sutlej. For the colour of these rivers varies not only with the soil where they have their source, but also with the season of the year. All those which flow from the snows and glaciers are turbid in summer, and are generally clear and bluish in autumn and winter, whereas those rising in lower ranges are generally clear at all seasons. Thus the Ganges at midsummer is a rushing, mighty, muddy cataract, of twenty times the volume it has in winter, and fully a mile in width. Then, instead of the green, glassy pools and quiet reaches that so enchanted us in autumn, we should have found a boisterous river swollen with melted snows, and mud and rain, tearing and foaming along in rapid overwhelming current.

I am told that the sister stream, the blue Jumna, is invariably clear, inasmuch as she does not rise in the snow. I confess I do not understand the statement, as her birthplace, Jumnoutri, is a snow-peak as glittering as that Gangoutri whence flows the mighty Ganges. The Jumna, however, although thus cradled amid the eternal snows, is said to be greatly affected by the vicinity of hot springs.

These glacial streams contain no animal life, at all events no fish, till they have received the waters of warmer tributaries. Here, as in all rivers of the plains, one striking feature is the wide extent of shingly, sandy soil, showing how broad a space the waters sometimes cover, and also how the bed of the river varies from year to year. In fact, in passing through soft yielding sand, it makes no definite channel, so that the main stream of one year may flow a mile away from that of the previous year. Having once taken a new line of its own, it must perforce go on, rushing onward with an impetus that sweeps all before it.

Such inundations too often destroy whole villages, carrying with them all the little household treasures; to say nothing of grain, goats, sheep, and all little farm stocking, the people barely escaping with their lives; a heartrending scene too often repeated, and one which gives tremendous meaning to that Hindoo proverb which, in allusion to matrimonial quarrels, describes a wife who goes away in anger "like a river in the rains." In the plains, where the low, flat shores afford no strong boundary line to resist the fury of the advancing flood, it sometimes extends for many miles on either side of the usual bed of the rivers, so that vast tracts of land are wholly submerged, and continue so for many days. As far as the eye can reach, the country appears like one gigantic lake, dotted with tree-tops, and with the roofs of the houses whereon the wretched starving inmates cower, beholding the destruction of all their property in those seething waters, and waiting in hopeless patience for the day, perhaps far distant, when they should once more subside; or when some friendly boat shall come to their rescue, possibly too late to be of any avail.

As an example of such an inundation, I may instance that of 1866, as described by Dr. Hunter, when in a single district of Orissa, 275 square miles were submerged, for from five to forty-five days, the depth of the water averaging seven feet, but in some villages being fully ten.

"The rivers came down like furious bulls, bursting their banks in every direction. More than 412,000 people were suddenly driven out of house and home, and found themselves in the middle of a boiling ocean. Thousands of miserable families floated about in canoes, on bamboo rafts, on trunks of trees, or on rice sacks, which threatened every moment to dissolve into fragments beneath them. Every banyan tree had its rookery of human beings, while the Brahmans, from the roofs of their brick temples, looked down in safety as the flood roared past.

"The common danger disarmed all creatures of their natural antipathies. Snakes glided up to the roofs, and burrowed harmlessly in the thatch. Sheep and goats were carried away by herds in the torrent, and in a few days their carcasses came to the surface, and floated about, covered with crows and kites. But the most pitiable sight of all was the plough cattle, standing in shallow parts up to their necks, and hungrily snuffing the barren waters for food, until they sank exhausted into the slime. Ere the flood subsided, many a famished family had also sunk beneath the waters."

Of course such an inundation as is here referred to is happily an extreme case, but even the ordinary rains cause most troublesome deviations in the courses of rivers, as what is arable land one year, may be selected by the river as its channel the following year—a channel which may shortly be once more forsaken, and left as a worthless sandbank or marsh. In like manner, the field that in spring was the centre of a compact farm, may, ere the autumn, have become an island, difficult of access.

One of the most remarkable instances of erratic conduct on the part of a river was in the case of the Brahmapootra, which within the first thirty years of the present century actually changed its course two hundred miles to westward, thus completely revolutionising the condition of two great tracts of country, the ancient cities which it forsook being thereby ruined, while the poorest villages that chanced to lie on the brink of its new channel became rich and prosperous, not only on account of the great roadway for trade thus brought past their very doors, but also because of the facilities for irrigation, and the rich soil annually brought down by the overflowing waters. This mighty stream, which now unites with the eastern mouth of the Ganges, and helps to form the great delta, formerly flowed to the east of Dacca, and found its way to the sea in a wholly different direction.

This tendency to a wayward course is more or less betrayed by all Indian streams, and is the reason why our first vision of the Ganges, above Hardwar, was of wide reaches of sand, apparently extending right across the valley—sand, however, which was half covered by the tall sirkee grass, whose great pink feathers waved and quivered in the light of the setting sun. And through the faint hot haze gleamed the soft delicate outline of the hills, which an eastern poet has compared to some celestial spirit assuming visible form and crowned with sun and snow.

We rode on through the holy city, thereby acquiring unutterable sanctity, and becoming objects of envy to many a poor Hindoo in far-away districts. The town is very small, and by no means imposing, although every house we passed was more or less ornamental; indeed many are richly carved and painted; each window has its own small overhanging balcony, and some of the domestic architecture is very fine. Most of the buildings are of brick, but many are of a fine white freestone, and rise from the very brink of the sacred stream wherein they lie mirrored.

But in the middle of the main street comes the usual, odd, Eastern blending of the tawdry and the magnificent, for the most rubbishy little booths, with brown thatch, fill up each side of the road, being built up against these fine, tall houses. Of course the effect is most picturesque, and the intense depth of colouring, and rich brown shadows thus obtained are very pleasant to the artistic eye. Of course there are monkeys innumerable all over the place, careering over the roofs, running along balconies, suddenly dropping into the street to help themselves to some coveted dainty—with their babies in their arms or sitting on their backs, with their little arms round the parental necks. And in every direction squat groups of human babies far more naked than the monkeys!

The crowds who throng the street are purely Hindoo, all pursuing their ordinary avocations. Groups of women, draped in bright colours, are preparing cakes of the "sacred" fuel of the country (cow-dung) and plastering them all over the fine houses, as high as they can reach, to bake in the sun. Multitudes are provided with great baskets of flowers, lovely garlands of roses and marigolds, as offerings to the idols, but especially to the river, on which they float so gracefully. The lip of the water is generally actually lined with blossoms.

Many Brahmans are engaged all day long in sealing up very peculiar tall long-necked bottles of the thinnest green glass, filled with Ganges water, which all pilgrims must purchase from the priests only, therewith to anoint their domestic idols or to shrive their dying kinsfolk perhaps at the other end of the Empire. The peculiarity of the bottles, and the seal of the Brahman priest, are safeguards against fraud in the substitution of unhallowed water.

Even this sealing process is curious, for, instead of a little commonplace fire, the men we noticed had each kindled one end of a whole tree, and were allowing it gradually to smoulder. This, remember, was all in the open street, and the blue smoke from the fires curled upwards in a light film, blending with the warm brown tones of thatch and shadow. Each bottle is protected by a wicker case, for doubtless it has far to travel. A vast number of ecclesiastical traders devote their lives to the sale of this holy water, not only for the service of the idols, and for medicinal purposes, but also for use in British courts of justice (where it takes the place of the Bible in the administration of oaths.) So large covered baskets are filled with these thin bottles, of all sizes to suit all purses, from tiny bottles two inches long, to large ones containing about a quart. (We may be sure that the tiniest bottle is costly, by the time it has been carried a thousand miles !)

The water carriers travel in companies, each carrying two of these baskets slung from the ends of a bamboo which rests on his shoulder. The baskets are decorated with peacock s feathers and little red flags, and in each company there is apparently a leader, whose basket is more ornamental than the others, having a large arched cover with numerous little jingling bells, which tinkle as they travel.

This traffic in holy water seems to be the chief trade of the town. The only secular business of which I saw any sign was cotton-picking. Everything else was more or less in the sacred line. Many stalls were exclusively for the sale of brass idols of every sort and kind, chiefly neat little pocket idols. There were thousands of brass bells, such as are rung in the temples; incense burners, flower vases, absurd brass toys, mirrors, lotas, glass bottles of every size for holy water, while many men are wholly occupied in making basket-work cases for these. I think all the other booths were devoted to the sale of sweetmeats and beads —beads of every sort and kind and colour, ridiculously cheap, made of Ganges mud painted and gilded.

The temples lie all along the edge of the river. There are none of very striking architecture, but the general effect is nevertheless picturesque in the extreme. The domes are chiefly pyramidal, very tall in proportion to their height, almost like thick spires, and much carved. Some are short and low, and incrusted with a pattern like huge roses in stone. They are mostly overshadowed with sacred peepul trees—the abode of innumerable monkeys, who have the run of the temples and of the town; and who sit perched on roofs or balconies, inspecting the various goods offered in the market below, and, suddenly pouncing down, help themselves to whatever they fancy, none venturing to thwart the sacred animals.

Passing through the town, our road lay for about a mile beside the river, sometimes overshadowed by fine old banyan-trees and small temples. We found the pleasant little Forest Bungalow all ready for us, a secluded nest, in a compound surrounded with a hedge of tall aloes in blossom, far above which waved pink sirkee grass, which in fact was actually higher than the house. Beyond were fine trees and clumps of tall bamboo. Two bed-rooms and a large sitting-room, with sufficient furniture for all requirements, seemed to us luxury, and being very dusty, very hungry, and very tired, supper, baths, and bed, happily crowned a day of much enjoyment.

CHAPTER XXI.

IN THE HOLY CITY OF HARDWAR.

A Brave Christian—The Telegraph—The Great Canal—The Great Fair—A Terrible Catastrophe—Scorpion and Snake Bites—In the Temples—Familiarity with Idolatry—Sacred Pebbles—The Five Daily Services—Sacred Bulls in Marble or Metal—Animals associated with divers Gods—A Priest's Home—A Living Image—A Lovely Island—The Ganges from its Source to the Ocean—Shrine at Gangoutri—The Town of Kanthal—Night March through the Forest—Adventures—Nynee Tal—Almorah—Darjeeling.

VERY near the house in which we were so comfortably lodged, stands another, inhabited by the only Christian resident in the district, a clerk in the telegraph office. I believe he is an American, quiet and shy in speaking to such a *rara avis* as ourselves, but brave and plucky enough in other matters. Fancy this only Christian in that hotbed of heathenism, going bravely out to the temples at the hours of sacrifice, to preach, which, I was told, he does most eloquently. If you can imagine a solitary Hindoo explaining his views of religion at some great revival meeting in Ireland or Scotland, you may perhaps realise the situation. The people listen to his words as to a curious and pleasant story, but he told me that he had not the smallest reason to hope he had ever made one convert. Nevertheless if pleading for the Master's cause, *when that cause is unpopular*, be the truest test of discipleship, it may be that from this far-away village there shall some day be gathered one of earth's least, who shall be chief in the Master's kingdom.

How strange it did seem to find a telegraph working in this out-of-the-way place, and to know that, if need were, I could have flashed a message home by lightning! Nor is this the only wonderful proof of England's skill that has astonished the people of Hardwar. Within a stone's throw of our bungalow was the head of the great Ganges Canal, the work which above all others, not even excepting the railway, has most amazed the natives, and which will, through long ages, prove the most priceless boon to this thirsty land.

Of all India's difficult questions, that of irrigation has always proved one of the most fertile sources of trouble in a land subject to sudden and prolonged droughts, such as must inevitably destroy the growing crops, especially the rice-fields on which so many myriads are wholly dependent. This too in a country where vast districts have even now no good roads whereby to bring food from afar. Of course a frightful famine follows, such as that of which we have in several recent years received such appalling statistics; human beings dying in numbers almost incredible, while bullocks, cows, sheep, and goats have all shared the same horrible fate. And looking back a few years farther, we find that in 1833 a million and a half of human beings perished in the awful famine.

To avert such horrors as these, the Mogul emperors devoted their chief energies. Thus we hear of Feroze having made one great canal from the Chetang river to Hansi and Hissar, and he bordered his canal with trees which should give to all travellers shade, blossom, and fruit. Moreover, he made thirty great reservoirs, and fifty dams across the river, for purposes of irrigation. He also constructed roads that should open up the country, with one hundred and fifty bridges, and one hundred caravanserais for travellers. When Shah Jehan succeeded to the throne, he made a branch canal from that of Feroze which was carried by an aqueduct of masonry right through Delhi, whence watercourses diverged to supply all quarters of the town, the tanks and gardens. Akbar's chief part in this matter seems to have been repairing the works of his predecessors.

Two hundred years later these were choked up during intestine wars till they were once more restored at enormous cost by the East India Company, to the exceeding joy of the people, who went forth as to a great religious festival to meet the returning waters, and cast in their offerings of flowers.

For England was reserved the honour of devising this mighty Ganges Canal, and for Sir Proby Cautley the merit of designing it. Its first suggestion was met with utter amazement on the part of the Hindoos. To those who dwelt in distant regions, the possibility that these sacred, life-giving waters might perhaps be brought to their very doors was so astounding that they could hardly believe in it, more especially as the Brahmans denounced the undertaking as altogether impious, and declared that the great goddess Gunga would swiftly avenge herself on the rash mortals who dared attempt to divide the sacred stream, and assign to her any course save that in which it should please her to flow.

Great, then, was the interest with which they marked the vicissitudes of the work, and of course the difficulties of such an undertaking were manifold. In many places the canal is constantly endangered by the overwhelming torrents which, only during the rains, rush down from the mountains, varying their course from year to year at their own sweet will. Sometimes foundations had to be laid on the shifting sands across these vague river beds. Across one of these—the River Solani—the canal has been carried by a great aqueduct, ending in a raised embankment three miles long, thus reaching the town of Roorkee. Beyond Roorkee two long tunnels of strong masonry carry the canal below the bed of similar torrents.

But in some places the levels will not admit of either of these methods, and then comes the sorest test of engineering skill, when, by the help of mighty weirs and sluices, the flood is carried right across the bed of the canal, whose own waters are held back by great floodgates. Those who have witnessed this bridling of the mad, foaming waters, thus mightily forced back by the work of puny human atoms, speak of it as a scene of breathless excitement utterly indescribable. The raging torrent comes tearing down from the mountains in headlong career, sweeping onward with irresistible might, and bringing with it huge tree-trunks, rocks, and every conceivable variety of heavy plunder, accumulated on its way. These act as battering-rams to beat down whatever might dare to oppose its course, and as the boiling flood dashes over the canal works their very existence is often endangered.

These are a few of the difficulties with which the engineers of this wonderful canal have had to contend.

Imagine, then, what a moment of excitement that must have been when, in 1854, the mighty work was complete, and the canal opened; an excitement extending over the length and breadth of the land, as the great body of water, four times the volume of the Thames at Windsor, flowed quietly away from the mighty river into its new channel, exchanging its free wanderings over vague sands for an imprisonment in a bed of hewn stone! Then passing gently onward, on a course of four hundred miles, it supplies means of irrigation to about six hundred thousand acres, besides bringing joy and gladness to myriads of Hindoos, who went out to meet the advancing waters with wildest enthusiasm, casting thereon garlands without number, therein recognising the presence of their favourite goddess, and knowing, moreover, that henceforth they would be spared the trouble of long and weary pilgrimages to her shores. The canal that has done so much good work on its way, rejoins the mother stream at Cawnpore, its last action being to supply abundant streams of life to the Memorial Gardens, thus transforming a sea of driest dust into a peerless rose-garden with greenest turf.

The canal is entirely in the hands of Government, the farmers paying a given sum per acre, varying with the nature of their crop. Of course such grains as Indian corn, and others requiring a dry soil, pay very much less than sugar-cane or rice, more especially the latter. In fact, the "paddy fields," as they are called, require for several weeks to be kept entirely flooded. The land thus fertilised yields quick returns. The crops of barley, wheat, and divers other grains sown in October are reaped in April, while the rice and other crops sown in early summer are reaped in the end of autumn.

Thus, then, the blessed waters carry life to all this district. Wherever their influence extends there are splendid crops and healthy flocks. Where it ceases there is drought and starvation; dry beds of sand instead of green fields, cattle dying for lack of forage, poverty and misery on every hand—in many places a difficulty in obtaining even the scantiest supply of foul water. Well may the Hindoos acknowledge the priceless blessing of this pure stream.

Close to the head of the canal is a very fine bathing ghaut, long flights of wide stone stairs, recently built by the British Government to endeavour in some measure to lessen the awful crush of pilgrims who here assemble at the great annual fair. For Hardwar, being the city nearest to the source of the Ganges, is accounted well-nigh as holy as Gangoutri itself, where the river rises at the base of a mighty glacier.

Every year, therefore, pilgrims assemble from every corner of the Empire, and devote a fortnight at high pressure to religious duties. The fair must be held at the end of March or beginning of April, when Jupiter is in Aquarius, at the time of the sun entering Aries; and eager crowds await the announcement by the Hindoo astrologers as to which day and hour is shown by the stars to be specially auspicious. Then comes the awful struggle for precedence in reaching the blessed waters. The city, as I before observed, is especially sacred to the Sun-god Hari, *alias* Krishna, and is dear to the Hindoos as being the Gate of the Sun "Hari-dwar."[1]

For days before the great fair of Hardwar the people arrive,

[1] Many of their old legends tell of the great deeds of the Haricules, the lords of the race of Hari the Sun, and it has been suggested that some of these may have travelled to Egypt, and from thence have been adopted by the old Greeks, who thus originated the fables of their Sun-god Hercules. You remember that the ancient Egyptians worshipped the Sphinx as Harimukh—that is, the Sun on the horizon.

streams pouring in incessantly, and encamping on every available spot, but chiefly on the broad dry bed of the river, which at that season is very low. They bring their whole families, for all alike need to wash away their sins in that pure stream, and the vilest wickedness will assuredly be cleansed by one plunge in those cool, clear waters, provided only that the golden atonement be not lacking. Coins must be freely showered into the sacred river at the time of prayer; and the priests (who have already received their offering before allowing the pilgrim to enter the cleansing flood) are privileged to search the sands for any coins which the goddess may not think worth taking for herself.

Here, then, multitudes from north, south, east, and west, come once a year to worship—Cashmerians, Persians, Paharis, Hindoos, of every possible sect. To these are added merchants from Calcutta, Sikhs from Umritsur, horse-dealers from Dokhara, Tartars, Afghans, Cabulees, and Mohammedans of many nations, drawn thither simply by the great fair, as to a profitable market. In the first place, it is the chief horse fair of the year, and every conceivable variety of the animal is here to be found, from the sturdy ponies of Cabul and Cashmere, to the fleet Arab or heavy "Whaler," as the steed of New South Wales is commonly called.

Nor is the fair for horses only. Elephants, camels, buffaloes, mules, cows, sheep, monkeys, dogs, cats, bears, and occasionally hunting cheetahs and leopards, are among the zoological varieties here offered for sale. Every man brings whatever he has got to dispose of. There are merchants selling all manner of dried fruits; Cabul grapes in those well-known round boxes, where the grapes are laid separately in layers, packed in cotton-wool to exclude the air; sweetmeats, nuts, all manner of Indian and Cashmere shawls, woollen goods, jewels for rich and poor, precious stones unset, silvery hubble-bubble vases, together with all manner of European goods. You may even sometimes detect a case of French rouge lying beside the henna prepared for the fingers of Eastern damsels.

The holiest spot in all Hardwar is a certain ghaut, in the heart of the little town, just below a favourite temple. Here every one rushes to bathe on the great day of the festival, and often half a million of people contrive to plunge in at this consecrated spot within a few hours. Men, women, and children, as usual, all bathe quite indiscriminately. They plunge joyously in, as if thoroughly enjoying themselves in the clear rippling stream, and the women washing their long raven hair, and all coming out again, as fresh as . . . well, I cannot say as fresh as daisies! more like glossy horse-chestnuts! The richer pilgrims are led into the water, supported on either side by a venerable Brahman, who carefully takes them to the mid-stream, plunges them in thrice, silently and solemnly, then escorts them to land once more; a very grave proceeding, much in the style of the solemn three dips and out again, of the genuine health-seeker at the seaside.

The average attendance at the annual gathering is somewhere about two hundred thousand human beings. Every twelfth year, however, it increases to something very considerably over a million. For on the twelfth year it is supposed that Krishna himself revisits the earth, and is invisibly present at the great fair. Therefore the sanctity of Hardwar at that time is beyond telling. It is literally the gate of heaven, and such a concentrated essence of holiness is shed abroad as to insure the salvation of all who are present. Death under such circumstances merely means a sudden translation to a world of bliss, and it is even supposed that any Christians present would have some chance of being included!

In bygone years some very awful accidents have occurred at this time, when these observers of times and seasons, and days and hours, all struggled to reach the holiest ghaut at the very moment declared by the astrologers to be the most propitious. The most appalling scene of all was enacted at the great fair in 1820, when the concourse of people was unusually great. The crowd poured in from both sides along a broad street, from which a narrow street, diverging down a steep flight of steps, leads to the sacred bathing-place. As the hour drew nigh, the multitude pressed on more and more eagerly. New comers, not knowing the nature of the ground, and the steepness of that narrow street, still pressed more and more earnestly, struggling to force the others onwards, themselves crushed by those behind. Thus the living torrent was borne along with irresistible impetus, the crush becoming more and more awful as the immense mass of living beings became so tightly wedged as to be perfectly immovable.

Every moment the pressure became more terrific, and every attempt at extrication more utterly hopeless. At first the appalling shrieks of agony of the crushed and dying were merged in the general roar and hubbub of Hindoo voices, at all times tumultuous, and the eager worshippers in the rear still pressed on, so that it was some hours before the street could be cleared. When, at length, they began to suspect that something was amiss, and the human mass recoiled, the city presented a scene as of a dreadful battlefield. *Upwards of one thousand corpses strewed the ground!* hundreds more were maimed for life, thousands more or less injured. A terrible sacrifice indeed, to the calm, sunny goddess, whose clear, green waters flowed on unperturbed, little heeding the agonising struggles of those who sought to do her honour.

Now the bathing is all under supervision of the native police—Government servants—and their arrangements are admirable. By simply dividing the stream of pilgrims they are kept in order, their numbers regulated, and the recurrence of any accident such as this becomes impossible.

The spot which is supposed to be especially dear to Krishna on the occasion of his twelfth yearly visit is just above the great new bathing ghaut, where a stone throne is set for him on a raised stone platform between two stately Indian fig-trees, whose thick glossy leaves cast a deep, cool shadow all around. These trees are surrounded by short, very broad pillars of divers heights, whereon loathsome, naked Yogis, of varied degrees of sanctity, lie crouching or sprawling the livelong day, awaiting the offerings of the faithful. No beings could be imagined more villanously ill-favoured and repulsive than these revolting creatures, the very sight of whom always fills one with invincible disgust.

It was a source of intense satisfaction to us that at the time of our visit all these foul wretches had removed their saintly presence from beside the grand old trees, which were so close to our bungalow that we spent many pleasant hours beneath their green shadow, looking down on the glassy river. On these occasions the worthy moonshee who had received such strict commands concerning us, was sure to be hovering somewhere in our neighbourhood. He was a Mohammedan, one of the very few whose work brings them to this Hindoo city. He was a very great man indeed, and most anxious to impress us with a due sense of his own importance. More especially he was always laughing at the follies of Hindoo worship, though he escorted us to an infinite number of temples, which he would not enter, however, but gave us in charge to the priests, who made the most of their little show, just like children showing their doll-houses, and really appeared quite anxious that we should be amused thereby.

But the great moonshee had some curious little jugglery of his own, at least I hardly know what else to call it, in this faithless age which cannot believe in evident answers to modern prayer. One day, while we were sitting under the great tree, a poor woman came past, half carried by her son. She was writhing in agony, having been bitten in the foot by a scorpion. When the great man heard what was the matter, he at once knelt down on the ground muttering prayers, and taking up a handful of dust, he therewith rubbed the wound. The woman who had sunk down, almost in a convulsion, slowly came to herself, and in a few minutes arose, blessed him, and walked away, scarcely needing any support at all. We asked him what he had really done to her, and he declared that he had only prayed for her and then touched the foot.

I find that Forbes, in his "Indian Travels," has recorded a very similar occurrence which he attributes to magnetism. It was the case of a man named Lalla Bhai, who certainly had almost miraculous power in curing the bite of the most venomous serpents, and who recovered many natives when apparently on the very brink of death. On one occasion the Resident of Baroche, believing this to be all deception, determined to test his skill. One of the gardeners having been bitten by a cobra, Lalla Bhai was sent for, and asked whether he could cure the sufferer, who lay in great agony, and quite delirious. He replied that by the blessing of God he should doubtless succeed. But it was not till the man had become speechless, and the state of his pulse showed the rapid approach of death, that Lalla Bhai was permitted to approach him. He stood for a few moments in silent prayer; then commenced waving a short dagger over the dying man, without touching him. The patient still continued motionless, but at the end of half an hour his heart appeared to beat, circulation quickened; within an hour he moved his limbs and recovered his senses. By the end of the third hour his complete cure was effected, and he was sent home to his family, and in a few days recovered from the weakness occasioned by the convulsive paroxysms which, probably, would never have been so severe or of such long continuance had the counteracting influence been sooner applied.

The poor woman, whose scorpion bite had been thus strangely cured, had already departed when another poor soul came along and sank down to rest beneath the widespreading shadow of the old trees. She was utterly exhausted, well-nigh fainting; but what was that to her? for she had walked the whole way from Cashmere to worship at these shrines, and was she not now within a mile of her goal? The moonshee gave her a handful of pice, but could not resist a little playful chaff on the utility of the journey! If you glance at a map, and see how far Hardwar lies from Cashmere, you will have some notion of the weary weeks it must have cost that poor fragile woman to reach the shrine whence her prayer must so surely rise to Heaven. I wonder how many Christians would have done as much!

I must say for our bear-leader, the faithful Sadi Khan, that he obeyed to the letter the commands he had received, and did take immense care of us. Wherever we went, riding the stately elephant, he followed on another, attended by a series of "forest rangers," who relieved guard in so important a charge, so that our progress was quite imposing. Considering that we were generally out from dawn till long after sunset, I think the worthy man was probably, in his secret heart, glad of our departure. As I before said, he took us a round of innumerable temples, though he himself would not cross the idolatrous threshold, but always waited for us outside. I noticed the same thing at Benares, where we were also in charge of a Mohammedan.

I think the priests must have favoured us considerably, for they showed us all over the temples without even objecting to our boots, and seemed quite delighted to do the honours of all their hideous idols, painted and carved, their multitudinous brass bells, their brazen horns, their sacred courts all covered with elaborate carving and mythological sculptures.

This being "the slack season" for pilgrims, they had plenty of time on hand, and our visit was quite an event. Anyhow we invariably found them most courteous, gentle, and respectful; and I felt quite sorry to see them look mortified when we shrank back, declining to allow them to adorn us with neck-garlands of sweet roses, or unfragrant marigolds, from off the idol shrines. They were merely offering us the best they had to give, but the innocent flowers seemed tainted from having been offered to idols, so we always refused these gifts.

I frankly confess, however, that there is something startling in the rapidity with which one gets quite at home amongst all this paraphernalia of heathenism, and how very soon idolatry ceases to shock the mind, and becomes merely a curious study with picturesque adjuncts. Six months previously the sight of a veritable temple with its hideous idols and devout worshippers was a thing from which we shrank in shuddering pity. Now we were quite connoisseurs, and lounged from one temple to another, inspecting jewels and exquisite stone carving, and anything wonderful the priests had to show, and quite forgot to be shocked. It was all so natural and seemed so entirely in accordance with the feeling of the people!

And yet, the more I think, and see, and hear, and read about Indian mythologies, the more bewildering to me do their endless intricacies become. It is like watching the dancing of midges on a summer's evening, but then each midge is a divinity, who to thousands of our fellow men represents a great reality, to be worshipped with the most intense devotion of body, soul, and spirit. Of such midges, the Hindoo Pantheon numbers 330 millions, and records long-winded histories of many—biographies celestial or infernal, of their wives and their sons and brothers—prescribing elaborate rituals for the service of many.

From beginning to end, every detail is eccentric and grotesque, and the whole is a tissue of incoherent confusion, only to be compared to some troubled dream, wherein winds and rain, storm and tempest, sun, stars, and clouds, birds and beasts and fishes, all take active part in the ordinary life of Earth and Heaven, blending in inextricable labyrinths of sacred legends. Yet all of these are to be implicitly believed, and do in some measure influence the daily life of two hundred millions of our fellow subjects, every one of whom, in successive generations covering perhaps three thousand years (no matter to what sect he belongs), has never failed day by day to consecrate his awakening by turning to the east, to address to the rising Sun-god a prayer that he, the Divine Lord of Life, may enlighten the understanding of his servant.

Truly the Hindoo capacity for worship is extraordinary! He seems ready to deify and worship everything that can do him either good or ill—human beings noted for virtue or for vice, the animals he most dreads or most venerates—forces of Nature, stocks and stones, ghosts and goblins. He even does homage to the implements of his profession, so the fisher worships his nets, the peasant his plough, the literary man his pen and ink, the merchant his business books, the weaver his loom, the carpenter his plough. Even the conch-shell and the bell which call the worshipper to the temple at the hour of prayer each receive adoration, the bell being recognised as a goddess.

Among the multitudinous eccentricities of symbolic worship, one of very frequent recurrence is the homage accorded to certain water-worn pebbles, brought from various holy rivers. These are arranged in little metal trays, and attendant priests spend hours daily in pouring single drops of oil on each, while reciting certain prayers. A red pebble symbolises Ganesa, the god of good fortune. Here, as in Japan, a crystal symbolises the Sun, a bit of metallic ore represents the female principle in Nature, white quartz pebbles,[1] called Bāna-linga, are symbolic of Siva, but these have no value unless they have been brought from the sacred river Nerbudda, otherwise they have no indwelling deity. Krishna is represented by a black fossil ammonite called Sāla-grāma, but these likewise have no special virtue unless they have been found in the Gandakī river, and as it is not possible to prove whence a fossil has been brought, it is to be feared that frauds are sometimes perpetrated in this matter.

In some of the temples I observed dozens of oviform pebbles simply set in rows on a great metal dish, but more commonly the five above specified are arranged on a small tray, and by placing each in the centre by turns, and moving the positions of the other four, five distinct orders of ritual can be arranged, so as to honour each god in his turn. Granting any amount of symbolism, all this seemed more like a childish game than like the religion of devout men.

The ceremonies in the various temples, of course, differ somewhat; but the following description, taken from the Râs Mâlâ, of the ordinary routine in the temples of Vishnu, may serve as a fair sample of the whole. Each day there are five services. The first is at sunrise, when bells are rung in the temple, and drums and conch-shells are sounded to awaken the Dev, or god, from his slumbers. The officiating priest, having bathed, enters the temple, and swings before the idol a lamp having five or seven branches. An hour or two later the Dev is dressed in raiment suited to the season. In cold weather he wears a quilted coat, and has a lighted brazier placed near him; whereas in hot weather he is anointed with sandal-wood dust and water; clothed in fine linen, and adorned with flowers and jewels. He is then placed beside a fountain and fanned by his attendants. In the rainy season he is dressed in scarlet cloth and shawls. Then his breakfast of rice, milk, and other things, is set before

[1] Sacred white quartz pebbles are found in Celtic tombs. See *In the Hebrides*, C. F. Gordon Cumming. Chatto and Windus.

him, while his votaries perform "the sixteen acts of worship." At noon there is a third service. The Dev is again rubbed with oil of sandal-wood, or sandal-dust and water, and adorned with fresh flowers; the lamps are trimmed, incense burnt, and his dinner is set before him, after which he retires for his noonday sleep, during which perfect silence must be maintained in the temple.

At three in the afternoon the beating of a drum announces his awakening; his attendants bring in fruit and sweetmeats, and various games for his amusement. At sunset he is set on a throne; his feet are bathed, water is sprinkled over him, his mouth is washed, more sandal-wood ointment, flowers and incense are offered. He is again clothed, goes through the form of a lengthy dinner; concluding with the offering of betel-leaves, and again the branched candlestick is waved before him.

Meanwhile all the congregation again perform "the sixteen acts of worship," one of which is to walk round the temple following the course of the sun (the *deisul* of the Celts), a ceremony which some perform only once, others seven times, and some even as often as one hundred and eight times! Only think how giddy they must be! At each turn a certain formula of prayer is uttered. The number of the turns has reference to the hundred and eight most sacred names of Vishnu, for the record of which the Brahmans have adopted this for the number of beads in their oft-told rosaries.

The last of the five daily services takes place at night, when the image is supposed to sup on bread and milk, and having received the usual oblations of incense and flowers, he is undressed and put to bed, if he be movable, otherwise he is covered with shawls and quilts. And this is the daily life of Vishnu and Rama, and sundry other favourite deities!

Among the most remarkable objects in these Hindoo temples here and elsewhere, are the great statues of bulls in white or black marble or in metal. Great bulls and small bulls, adorned with precious necklaces, or garlands of gay fresh flowers.

It has often struck me as singular, that in the great Brazen Laver, which Solomon was commanded to make for the use of the Temple, the symbols selected for the adornment of that consecrated Molten

Sea should have been those which in later ages were to hold so prominent a place in the symbolism of faiths so widely spread as those of Brahma and Buddha. That huge laver, you will remember, was supported by twelve oxen of cast metal, three looking to each point of the compass, while the brim of the great sea itself was all wrought with flowers of lilies, much the same, I suppose, as the pattern of lotus or water-lily with which the throne of Buddha is invariably edged. That sea, as we all know, was broken up by the Chaldeans, and carried to Babylon as old brass.[1] It might happen that some wandering Child of the Captivity may have carried some fragment of this "lily work" still farther east.

However, without straining at such vague possibilities, it is impossible to walk through any Hindoo "ecclesiastical bazaar" without recalling the descriptions of all vessels of the Temple: the cauldrons, the pots, and the bowls, the shovels and the snuffers and the spoons, the censers, the basins, the lamps, the candlesticks, and all manner of things to be made either of gold or of bright brass which might be continually scoured. Here in the open sunlight, are stalls heaped up with all sorts of brass-work for the use of the worshippers. Incense burners and curious spoons, basins and lamps, pots and bowls, and a thousand other things of which we knew neither the name nor the use, but which the owners were continually scouring, till they gleamed in the sun.

As to the marble or metal bulls, these seem to have found a place in almost every known form of idolatry, for it is said that the worship of the sacred bull may be traced in almost all lands, beginning of course, with the Apis of the Egyptians, and the golden calf. It also existed in Persia, Rome, Greece, Tyre, and Assyria. It is said that even in Britain this faith once found a place, though I believe that such bovine images as have from time to time been dug up in this country have generally been proved to be of Roman origin.[2]

[1] 1 Kings vii. 25, 26; 2 Kings xxv. 13.

[2] Such doubtless were those thirty small stone bulls found at Burghead, in Morayshire, while making the harbour in the immediate neighbourhood of the old Roman well.

Here the images represent the mythological bull Nandi, who is ever in attendance on Siva. Most of the gods are generally represented as attended by some bird or animal, on which they can ride should it so please them. Thus while Siva usurps the symbolic bull, his fierce wife Durgâ, claims the tiger and sometimes the lion. Moreover, Vishnu was incarnate as a man-headed lion. He is also escorted by the human-headed eagle, Garunda. Varuna rides on a human-headed fish, Indra on an elephant. The ram is sacred to Agni, the buffalo to Yama, the goose to Brahma, the vulture to Sani, the white crane to Saravasti, the rat to Ganesa; the parrot to Kamadeva, and the peacock to Skanda (who is a son of Siva, and god of war). He commands the hosts of good spirits and makes war against demons. He is sometimes represented with six heads, and twelve arms, each bearing a different weapon. At other times he appears as a handsome lad, riding on a peacock—a great contrast to his ugly fat elephant-headed brother Ganesa, the god of wisdom, who is escorted by the sagacious rat.

All these, and many other animals, seem to take their place naturally in this all-embracing mythology—but the association of Christian saints with animals is more remarkable; and, as in the incomprehensible vision of Ezekiel,[1] one wonders how St. John first came to be associated with the eagle, St. Luke with the ox, St. Mark with the lion, and why St. John's immunity from poison should have been symbolised by a serpent rising from the sacred chalice.

Before coming to Hardwar I had been somewhat afraid that the people might dislike my sketching propensities in a place of such sanctity; but I found that, on the contrary, this proved a strong bond of sympathy, as the usual Hindoo interest in anything like a picture insured me every facility for my work; and so it came to pass that my pleasantest studio was the balcony of an exceedingly reverent old Brahman, whose curious, simple little household arrangements were in themselves interesting. His little mud oven in one corner of the room; his poor little cooking-pots and lotas, a rickety old bedstead, and little bags of grain, in another; while the place of honour was, of course, assigned to a hideous idol,

[1] Ezekiel i. 10.

crowned with flowers, and wet with holy water, and smeared with red paint to symbolise the offering of blood.

From that balcony I could look right up the main street, with its carved houses, its thatched bazaar, its rich lights and shadows, and the ever-changing groups of monkeys and human beings passing to and fro, or loitering in the market-place—an ever-shifting living kaleidoscope. Right before me was the great smouldering log, whereat the priests were sealing their bottles of holy water.

Just beyond sat a young Brahman perched on a table, dressed up to represent one of the gods. He was thus passing his days in a pleasant inaction truly profitable, inasmuch as almost all who went down to worship and bathe at the holiest ghaut made him some little offering. He sat on the topmost step, where every bather must leave his slippers; so that there were sometimes such piles of these heaped up, that you wondered how any man ever hoped to recover his own queer curly-toed treasures. Doubtless they were safe enough here, but at railway stations and other places, the trusting owner of anything extra smart is very apt to find that something amazingly shabby has been substituted!

Close to these steps a brisk sale of flowers was going on; and great baskets of roses and large African marigolds added to the brilliancy of the foreground. Every worshipper of the beautiful river invested largely in these, and many garlands were showered upon the waters. Multitudes of Yogis were starting on distant journeys with great jars of Ganges water in wicker cases slung across the shoulder from a bamboo adorned with peacocks' feathers. These men are almost invariably dressed in deep yellow or saffron robes, that being the most sacred colour of these worshippers of the Sun-god—just as the old Highlanders accounted it lucky, as being the colour of his rays.

Deeply interesting as were these days in the city, there were others still more pleasant, when our steady elephant carried us right through the Ganges to a large grassy island in mid-stream, where we might spend the livelong day in perfect peace. As the huge creature walked through the river, his great body made a swirl in the water like the track of a steamboat. The crossing was a very slow process, as even this half of the river was exceedingly wide, and the sensible old "Hathi" never moved his feet till he had sounded the ground before him, and made sure of safety. The only inhabitants of the green island were a set of wild-looking Yogis, intent only on their adoration of the lovely river, to which every now and then they rushed down, always jabbering the same unvarying cry, and ending with a yell. Then they once more retreated to their hut. I suppose our watch-dog considered them safe neighbours, for having once seen us safely settled, he allowed us two days of the most enchanting repose, only fetching us in the evening for an elephant ride to some place worth seeing.

When I call our island grassy, you must remember that I speak of Indian grasses, waving far overhead; tall tossing plumes and spikes, black, white, pink, or green, but chiefly pink. Part of the island was covered with low brushwood, bearing small yellow berries like little plums, of which the natives eat quantities—an example which on this occasion we followed with more pleasure than was warranted by the flavour of the fruit, its wild growth on that far-away island giving it a charm which you would well understand could you catch but one glimpse of that lovely spot, with the glassy, green river flowing so calmly by.

Indeed, Hardwar at this season had altogether a feeling of calm and repose that I found nowhere else in India. I do not, however, suppose that many who have seen the place would endorse that sentiment, inasmuch as the only week when English people come here is at the time of the great fair. Then their white tents are pitched among a thousand more, every available corner is alive with swarms of pilgrims or merchants, and all is noise and stir and hubbub; such ceaseless noise as none can fully realise who have never mingled in an Eastern crowd.

But to-day there was peace unspeakable on earth and sky: the crystalline goddess and the beautiful home of her worshippers were alike looking their very best. And, in truth, the little city as seen from the island is very fair to look upon. Each temple and stately dwelling faces the river; and clinging to its banks, the city extends in one long line of graceful pyramidal spires and domes, with porches of pillars rising from hallowed courts, and overshadowed by sacred trees, which throw their trembling shadows athwart their own fair image, reflected in the clear mirror below.

The beautiful goddess loves her own birthplace too (those snowy peaks above Gangoutri), and in her clearest, stillest pools, she reflects them faithfully, as though she would cherish the image of that pure home of her infancy ere she hurries on to receive the gross homage of myriads of worshippers, by whom her clear depths are too quickly polluted, and the loveliness of her aqua-marine waters changed into the foul yellow stream, from touch of which we in turn shrink, in her later days. The Ganges at Hardwar—the Ganges at Benares! no sweet country village, rapidly transformed into a seething, bustling, manufacturing city, with blackness of busy chimneys and horrors of chemical works, can afford a more striking contrast than does the lovely river at these two most sacred places of pilgrimage. One week later we beheld the spoilt beauty, which, having passed from city to city, had reached the very acme of fame and of pollution, and was hurrying on to that ocean whose waters would for many miles be discoloured by its filth.

The total length of that mighty stream is fifteen hundred miles, of which thirteen hundred are navigable. It is difficult for us in these days of swift railways to realise the incalculable value of such a river as the Ganges, forming a broad highway from the sea to the very foot of the Himalayas, affording a constant route for communication and traffic in a country where good roads and the art of making bridges were alike unknown till first the Mohammedan conquerors, and afterwards the English, made them for themselves.

We raise our eyes from the reflections in the clear green waters to the glittering snow-peaks. The highest of these is Gangoutri, where, at the base of the mighty glacier, lies a low ice-arch called the Cow's Mouth, whence, at a height of 13,800 feet above the sea, flows the Bhagirathi or true Ganges, in a stream which is about twenty-seven feet wide. This shortly afterwards receives the waters of the Alcananda, and the double stream enters the great plain of Hindoostan at Hardwar, and is henceforth known to us as the Ganges, and reverenced by myriads of Hindoos as the goddess Ganga. Hence she flows onward, doing her good work in fertilising the land, and receiving the loving worship of her followers, receiving moreover the waters of many tributary streams, the Jumna, the Goggra, the Goomtee, the Sone, and many others.

About two hundred miles from the sea, the delta begins to be formed—a delta twice as large as that of the Nile. In the network of waters which now interlace the country in every direction, two principal arms dispute the supremacy. The eastern, retaining the name of Ganges, mingles its waters with those of the Brahmapootra; but the western, or Hooghly, is said by the natives to be the true Bhagarathi, and therefore the most holy. Between these two lies a vast alluvial flat, nearly two hundred miles in breadth; the remaining waters, passing through a swampy, pestiferous jungle, known as the Sunderbunds, the haunt of tigers and other evil beasts, enter the sea by about twenty mouths: in short the mouths of the Ganges form a series of estuaries—a triangular network of streams extending two hundred miles along the coast.

Brahmans and Buddhists alike have strange legends concerning the source of this and other mighty streams, from dim caverns in that mysterious world of rock and ice. They tell how Siva once came down to earth on a pillar of fire; and how when he returned to heaven he converted his fiery pillar into the mythical mountain Meru, that it might for ever be to his worshippers a symbol of his divine protection and presence. This vast world-mountain, though invisible to any eye save that of faith, towers heavenward, far above the highest Himalayan summit. It is surmounted by three cones, on the greatest of which are three golden peaks whereon repose the sacred Triad.

Within the hidden recesses of this mysterious mountain, the gods prepare the Life Drink, which is the germ of all organic life. In its dark caverns dwell the Asurs or giants of the Buddhists, while their Yakas or demons roam on its surface, and around the summit are the abodes of such human souls as have attained to exalted degrees of merit.

From this sacred mountain of Meru there issues a celestial river, which flows round the invisible city of Brahma, and then discharges its waters into a mystic lake, Mansarovara. This lake is guarded by four huge rocks in the form of animals, from whose mouths issue four great rivers. The Ganges, as we have seen, flows from the mouth of the cow, which symbolises earth. The Hoangho is said to issue from that of an elephant, which is another symbol of mother earth. The Oxus flows from the mouth of a horse, symbolic of water, while the tiger, emblem of evil, vomits forth the Yenisei, which flows towards frozen deserts.

Various traditions tell how in some of the wars of the gods, the mystic peaks of Meru have been broken, and fragments thereof hurled far and wide, each becoming a centre of holiness for the land where it fell. One great rock-mass, having fallen into the sea, became the island of Lanka or Ceylon. Many other myths have sprung up concerning this invisible crown of Himla, for there is no ending to the labyrinths of Oriental fable. Nevertheless as we watch the golden sunset lighting up the great white masses of cloud, piled in fantastic form, like etherealised mountains, and dwarfing the true snows of earth, we recognise the poetic glory of that mystic Meru, which to so many millions of our fellows, represents the very throne of the Creator.

Descending once more from the ideal, we gaze on an outline well-nigh as shadowy, and quite as inaccessible, namely, that of Gangoutri, the highest snow-peak we have yet seen. It towers to a height of 22,798 feet, that is to say, about ten thousand feet above the source of the Ganges, near to which there is a small temple, holier than all others, but so difficult of access that comparatively few pilgrims venture farther than Hardwar, which is considerably more than a hundred miles short of the mark. The peak stood up so distinct and bold that we could not have guessed a quarter of that distance, but then the wonderful clearness of the atmosphere so soon after the rains brings everything close to the eye. The apparent distance is very much greater in hot weather, when a filmy haze overspreads the landscape.

In the little temple at Gangoutri there is a silver image of the goddess Ganga, in the form of a woman; also of Bhāgīrath and other local deities. A small wooden shed is provided for such adventurous pilgrims as reach this holy of holies, where they must remain for seven days. Should they chance to die of cold during this pilgrimage, it matters little, as such a death would atone for the greatest crimes of which man could be guilty. The pilgrim must accomplish the last day of his journey fasting. On reaching the shrine the Brahmans take him in hand, receive his offerings, shave his whole body, and then allow him to bathe in the icy stream, and to perform funeral rites in honour of his deceased ancestors. At the end of the seven days he may depart in peace, fully shriven, and carrying with him precious treasures of holy water, ashes of sacred cow-dung, and withered basil-leaves. The merit of having accomplished such a pilgrimage will be to him a safeguard against many of life's troubles, and will carry him satisfactorily through his subsequent transmigrations.

It appears that here, as in other lands, the poor are most rich in faith, for the pilgrims who undertake this toilsome journey are mostly of the poorer sort. It is said, however, that the number of all classes who find their way to these hill sanctuaries has greatly increased in proportion as the attendance at the great gatherings in the central provinces has lessened. Moreover, railways and good roads give facilities for travel of which multitudes gladly avail themselves.

The hill festivals here seem to be much the same as those we noticed in the Kanawur valley, the sacrifices being followed by the same mystic religious dance to the music of loud brazen instruments. The girls and the men form in two long rows, men and women *vis-à-vis*. Each line is linked together by every individual clasping his or her neighbour on either side round the waist, and for an hour at a time they go on advancing and retreating, while singing choruses. These festivals are kept up all night by moon and torchlight.

It is not only religious devotees who visit this shrine. It is a favourite hunting-ground for musk-deer, snow-bears, and burrell, or wild sheep. Sometimes the sportsmen who have come hither in search of these, have come in for more than they expected, from severe shocks of earthquake; and these have told us how, when peacefully encamped in the calm moonlight, they had suddenly become conscious of that dread trembling, when the strong foundations of the earth seemed to upheave and huge masses of rock fell with headlong crash from the cliffs overhead, and rebounding, vanished in the abyss below.

While we were basking on our pleasant island like a pair of turtles, or crocodiles, or any other creatures that love the warm sunshine and the ripple of gleaming waters, and while we were moreover rejoicing in the sweet cool breath brought down by the river from the ice-range, suddenly we beheld a most startling apparition! Something rustled in the tall grass, and brushed aside the wild plum-trees, and stalked curiously onward. We could scarcely believe our eyes. Just imagine Robinson Crusoe's feelings on seeing Friday, and then imagine ours on beholding a brace of white men taking a day's shooting on our beloved desert isle! Its romance was gone. In another second they were also gone, but we were conscious of no longer being the sole pale-faces in the district, and as we sat next morning on the Yogis' pillars beneath the great sacred banyans, we could see civilised creatures clad in common domestic broadcloth, busy photographing!

Twice in the lovely evenings the gentle old elephant Motee, "The Pearl," took us to Kanthal, a picturesque town two miles down the river, where, at the time of the great fair, the wealthy and high-caste Hindoos encamp, so as to be out of the tumult of Hardwar itself. Here are more temples, more carved houses, more gateways, great huge gateways like exaggerated bars of York; but miserable architecture, with stucco, as on the palaces of

Lucknow, instead of such carving as we had seen in the Mahommedan cities, such as Delhi and Agra.

As to the monkeys, they were literally innumerable. Every branch of every tree seemed alive with them. On houses and balconies they were perched, now swinging over garden walls, now scampering over the roofs; sometimes nursing their babies tenderly as a woman; then darting suddenly off, leaving the little one swinging on the tip of the maternal tail; sometimes carrying a baby in each arm; sometimes running on all-fours with the baby slung below and grasping the parental body. Sometimes the young one sits on the shoulder, or astride on the back; in short whatever attitudes human beings could devise seem to come quite naturally to these absurd creatures.

We passed from one shady, bowery garden to another, and in each were loaded with roses and jessamine, graceful offerings from the inhabitants. Then we took up our station on a terraced garden-wall, with turrets; a high wall rising from the river's brink, whence we could look right down into its clear green depths, far below us; or else might look up the quiet reaches and along the wooded shores, to where the city of Hardwar with its long line of temples lay mirrored in the calm aquamarine pools; and the grassy island, and the Siwalik hills (honeycombed with the cave-dwellings of the Yogis) and the Himalayas, with their ethereal peaks, which the natives call Himla, "the Palace of Snow," all were softened and blended by the mellow rose-coloured light of evening.

Soon the pleasant twilight deepened into night; faint lights began to twinkle among the black foliage. A thousand fairy flies gleamed through the darkness, now veiling, now revealing, their pale green lamps; till the whole air glittered with these "winged lights that spangle India's fields."

Presently the fire-flies seemed to be floating on the river also. These were tiny lights, set in little boats, which, launched at Hardwar, had come thus far in safety, weathering all dangers of currents and ripples, and auguring well for the safety of him whose welfare they symbolised. For still, as in the days of Lalla Rookh, the Hindoo maids or mothers launch a frail raft, a bamboo, a cocoa-nut, an earthenware jar, or some other tiny boat, wherein is placed a cluster of lamps. If these burn stedfastly till the boat floats out of sight, all goes well with the loved one. But should the little bark be caught by a sudden gust of wind, or engulfed in the darkness, then the shrinking woman with the sad gentle eyes believes that the blast of adversity will surely overcloud *his* future. And so she steals home through the darkness, heavy of heart.

We are in duty bound to believe that these lamps burn only for child or husband; lover being a relationship by no means acknowledged in a land where no maiden may choose her own lord, or even behold him, until her bridal day. We tried to make our great moonshee weave some graceful romances for us, *à la Feramorz*, but he preserved a discreet silence, for it is quite against etiquette to allude to the existence of women, and all the native men seemed invariably to shrink from any comment on feminine actions.

If we had only reached Hardwar one night sooner, we should have seen the Dewali, or feast of lamps, when the town was illuminated, and the whole river covered with little fire oracles. At Dehra, where there is no river, the people had to be content with commoner sorts of light. But in every door and every window the women placed tiny earthenware saucers of oil, with a wick, which acted as simple lamps. I think the only person who had no light, was an English clergyman in the hotel, who feared it was something idolatrous. To me it only seemed a graceful custom, so I still cherish my little Dehra lamp in memory of the Dewali.

I am told that at the Japanese feast of lanterns, small lighted lamps are sometimes thus launched on the waters; not, however, with reference to the well-being of the living, but that their fate may reveal that of the souls of friends and relations, who have passed away to the spirit-land.

Only one day more remained to us in this sweet calm spot. We spent part of it in the old priest's balcony; and his neighbours, mustering courage, came to inspect the drawing of the street, and each with immense delight pointed out his own house, and wanted to be represented at his own door. They said surely we would not go away without a picture of the sacred ghaut; and strongly advised us to stay where we were, as indeed we were sorely tempted to do. But we feared that our bungalow might be required by the forest officers who had so courteously placed it at our disposal. So, soon after sunset, we very regretfully said good-bye to our moonshee and the foresters, and the quiet little bungalow, and saw the last of Hardwar.

Once more we were in our "doolies," the canvas box-beds, with our dozen strong bearers, and a couple of extra men as "masalchees" or torch-bearers, who marched before each doolie to show the way, feeding their torches from time to time with oil from a hollow gourd. The red torchlight only made the darkness of the jungle seem more intense; while throwing a strong glare on our white canvas box-beds, and the coarse white turbans and drapery of the bearers, and falling with ruddy glow on their dark faces and glossy limbs—a fine study in browns.

There is something very strange—almost solemn—in such a night march; when the deep stillness is only broken by the measured tread of the bearers, and the deep-toned "Khaberdar," "take care!" which, uttered by the leader, is chorused by all at every difficult bit in the road. Then, too, strange voices resound through the forest; insects of every sort awaken, and by turns you hear sounds of chirping, and drumming, and whirring; some harsh, some shrill. Sometimes they seem all to join in chorus, as if to suggest something of the exuberant animal life which lies hidden under the green leaves. Then pale phosphorescent lights glimmer in the darkness, and mark the track of the so-called fire-flies, which are really luminous bettles.

Our bearers took their onward march in shorter stages than they had done in coming. They halted repeatedly, to rest and hubble-bubble; always first kindling a great bonfire, to scare away possible tigers or other noxious creatures—a precaution by no means unnecessary, as a night adventure in the forest is not desirable in reality, however thrilling to remember. My host had told me how one night, returning through this jungle on an elephant, an old rogue elephant[1] had come up and joined company, running alongside for a considerable distance. The position was one of extreme danger, and he was unarmed. Happily he chanced to have two or three boxes of lucifer matches; these he struck at intervals, and the elephant, not knowing what to make of them, was fairly puzzled, and finally turned aside, to the infinite relief of the traveller.

We heard of another gentleman whose bearers suddenly dropped him, shouting "Tiger! tiger!" and took to their heels. He too was defenceless, so he did the only thing he could. He closed both doors of his doolie—a feeble protection indeed against the tiger's mighty paw! It proved efficacious, however, for when the great beautiful creature came up, and found only a canvas-covered box, she did not quite know what to make of it, so after snuffing round it for some time, and rolling it clean over and over once or twice, she trotted back into the jungle, and was no more heard of.

It is not, however, always that these night alarms end so satisfactorily. One friend of ours had a very awful adventure on her night march from Nynee Tal, accompanied only by her English maid. She had been asleep, and awoke suddenly to find her doolie on the ground, and a great blaze of light all round her. Her maid stood by, and told her there was an alarm of wild elephants. Springing up, she saw that her coolies were encircling her with a ring of bonfires, while in the darkness beyond she could just discern the grey forms of a troop of these great wild creatures. A few paces farther was another doolie, which had likewise been stopped by the same alarm. Its occupant, a gentleman, was standing by, in a state of great agitation, holding in his hand a revolver, which he occasionally fired vaguely to-

[1] A solitary old male elephant, who had been expelled from the herd, invariably fierce.

wards the beasts, to scare them. So tremulous, however, was his hand, and so uncertain his aim, that pointing his revolver full at the unhappy maid, he shot her dead, the bullet winding the face of the lady. In the horror of the moment all crowded round the body of the poor girl, quite forgetting the fires; whereupon the elephants watching their opportunity, made a grand charge, and utterly routed the intruders. Away rushed every one helter-skelter into the forest. Happily for the lady she tumbled into a hole, and there lay quietly concealed till some hours afterwards, when, with returning daylight, the elephants retreated; and her coolies coming to search for her, they once more resumed their dreary march, carrying with them the body of the poor girl.

I am thankful to say we had no adventure of any sort, but full leisure to see how picturesque were these night fires in the dark forest; with the groups of coolies squatting round, and the tall pink grasses and sombre foliage overhead, with openings here and there through which the glittering stars looked down.

We reached Dehra in the morning, and gave full account of our pleasant gipsying. Then, having restored my pretty companion to her parents, and taken one last general look at beautiful Dehra. I resumed my southward route, to rejoin my own people on their return from Lahore. One more night of travelling, partly by gharry, partly by doolie, alone with the wild-looking (but in truth patient and gentle) brownies, and then once more a return to railways and highly-developed civilisation.

I was then sorely tempted by several pleasant invitations to Nynee Tal; another favourite hill station, and one which possesses a great advantage over its rivals in the beautiful lake, whose pleasure-boats of all sorts lend a very unwonted charm to Himalayan scenery, where any piece of water larger than the tank of the temples is rare indeed—so rare, that I for one never saw even a pond. So this blue lake is thought very precious and very lovely indeed by the dwellers in Nynee Tal, whose countless pretty bungalows, perched on the steep wooded shores, look down on those placid waters through tangled mazes of scarlet rhododendron and oak, each branch of which is matted with rich brown mosses, a soft bed of luxuriant ferns of every species.

Only the houses on the highest levels, however, can catch a glimpse of the snowy range, the grandest view of which is to be had from Almorah, a station somewhat farther in the hills, now chiefly noted as a tea-growing district; this is the village which Bishop Heber said reminded him of Chester—one long wide street, paved with slabs of slate and closed at either end by a gate. One half of the street being on higher ground than the other half, the ascent is made by a low flight of steps, up which the hill ponies walk, as easily as the Maltese donkeys do up the streets of stairs. The houses have wooden verandahs, in some cases richly carved. At one end of this long street is an old Ghoorka fort (for Almorah is near the Ghoorka frontier), at the other is a modern English fortification.

Tantalising as was the thought of a visit to Nynee Tal, I was still more sorely tempted southward by Darjeeling, which I am told is the most beautiful of all the "hill stations." It also is in the Himalayas, though fully 800 miles from Simla, and only 361 miles from Calcutta, from which indeed it can now be reached by twenty-four hours of luxurious railway travelling! This railway, which was opened in the summer of 1881, is considered to be a triumph of engineering skill, the terminus at Darjeeling being 7,690 feet above the level of the sea. Some of the gradients mount one in twenty-one feet, and there are curves of seventy feet radius. The line has been described as suggestive of "a snake winding up into the clouds."

But this travelling-made-easy had not become possible at the time of my visit, so when the friend who was to have accompanied me became seriously ill, I gave up the idea. Had we carried it out it is probable that we should have followed it up by a second winter among innumerable quaint native cities; and then such a summer in Cashmere as would have been a memory of delight for ever. And from Cashmere, a rapid run to Southern India, and a third winter spent in exploring its wonderful temples, such temples as are nowhere to be seen in Bengal! In short, there seemed no particular reason for not gliding on for years, in one unvarying summer, and ever passing from one new beauty to another!

However we just drifted along as usual, and so it came to pass that a very few days after we had paid our homage to the Ganges at its source, we awoke to find ourselves within sight of the same broad river nearly a thousand miles farther down the country, at the holy city of Benares.

CHAPTER XXII.

BENARES.

The City of Siva—Ancient History—Grotesque Architecture—Temple of Doorga—Of Ganesa—Of Maha-devah—Tables of Money-changers—Sacred Bulls and Peacocks—Sarnath, the ancient Buddhist City—Benares from the Ganges—Sale of Holy Water—Mud Idols—The Retention of Breath—A Devoutly Spent Day—The Threefold Cord—Manufactured Brahmans—Undermining by the Ganges—Of various Sunwise Turns—The Goddess of Small-pox—The Burning Ghaut—Hindoo Rosaries—Shaving—A Wedding—Zenana Mission—Eastern Women—England.

FROM Hardwar to Benares! No words can convey to any western mind the concentrated essence of sanctity conferred on the Hindoo pilgrim by visiting these two most holy cities. Such a pilgrimage would in bygone days have involved many weeks of slow and painful progress, with hardships and difficulties on every hand; and many a pious Hindoo has lived and died without being able to accomplish an act which would have loaded him with merit.

Now the swift railway has so simplified the business that in less than a week he can slip easily from one to the other; and, having worshipped the clear transparent waters of the beautiful Ganga at her source, can, a very few days later, catch his first glimpse of the wonderful city of Siva, with its thousand domes and pyramids glittering in the early light, while the yellow rays of the rising sun lend a halo and a charm to the broad stream, though its waters are now turbid and foul, polluted by the filth of myriad worshippers.

As Muttra and Bindrabund are emphatically the cities of

BENARES.

Vishnu, so is Benares especially sacred to Siva, that complex deity, who, under his title of Maha-devah, "the great God," is adored as the author of all life, while, as Siva, he is worshipped with trembling, as the dread destroyer of his own work. Thus he embodies the most varied qualities, appearing sometimes as the source of happiness, the deliverer, the blessed one,—sometimes terrible and adverse. Now he is young and beautiful, and now grotesquely hideous; now he is portrayed with one face and three eyes, and from the central eye flashes destructive fire—again he has five faces on one head. He is the patron of most respectable tradesmen and of most disreputable robbers. He is lord of the storms and of the goblins, and so comprehensive and all-embracing are his functions that his worshippers have to enumerate 1008 names and attributes when rendering him homage.

Though Vishnu is the most popular god, and most in sympathy with the human beings in whose likeness he was incarnate, the worship of Siva is more general and more apparent throughout the land. This is said to be in a great measure a matter of economy, inasmuch as the worship of Siva requires only the offering of a few sacred trefoil leaves[1] and red flowers, or a smear of red paint, with a libation of water, to a rude stone emblem,—whereas the worship of Vishnu seems to involve a temple and priests and continual offerings of food and raiment for the use of the divine doll, which must be dressed and undressed and fed, like any other great man, his attendants of course consuming the offerings. Such little trifles as flowers, perfumes, and sacred tulasi (basil) leaves must be brought as a matter of course.

Here, however, there is no question of economy in worship, for the wealth of Hindoostan has from time immemorial flowed to enrich the city of temples.

At this spot the river sweeps in a stately curve, its banks on one side rising abruptly, so that the city rises from its waters in the form of a crescent, facing the east; and the morning sun lights up each beautiful line of its strange architecture. The opposite shore of the river is flat and bare, for though the worshippers of

[1] Of the Bilva, *i.e.* the wood-apple, *Ægele Marmelos.*

Vishnu did in olden times attempt to build on the right bank a city which should rival that of Siva, their attempt failed, and the triumphant inhabitants of the ancient Kasi mocked at their ambition, declaring that whoever died in the new city of Vyas-Kasi would certainly be metamorphosed into an ass, than which no greater depth of degradation could be conceived. This threat had its weight. The city was forsaken, and only a few picturesque ruins near Ramnuggur mark its site. Here the Maharajah of Benares has his luxurious palace, but no Rajah in his senses would risk transmigration into the body of an ass; so when his last hour approaches, he is carried across the river that he may die in the sacred city, and so secure a certain and direct passport into heaven. Not only must he die there, but there also must he be cremated, as only the north bank of the Ganges has special virtue for this purpose.

The name of Benares is derived from the rivers Barana and Asi, which flow into the Ganges on either side of it. This name, however, has only been adopted for the last five hundred years, or thereabouts. Probably it was given when the worshippers of Siva rebuilt the city after their expulsion of the Buddhists.

The original city of Kasi is said to have heen coeval with Babylon and Nineveh, when it was the chief centre of Hindoo learning, and great and wise men flocked to it. Its earliest fame was in the days of the Rig-Veda, when faith was pure and monotheistic. At that time we are told that temples and places of public worship were unknown in India. In the course of ages, however, when men had learnt to worship many gods, and to multiply temples and holy places, Kasi became not merely the wisest, but also the most sacred city in the land. Hence when Buddha desired to spread his new faith, he selected Kasi as the most fit city wherein to "turn the wheel of the law."

At that time there were 700 schools and colleges in the city; the wealthiest merchants dwelt here, and great nobles and warriors assembled at all festivals in vast throngs. Treasures of all sorts were stored in the town, and the streets glittered with the gold and precious raiment of the people.

Where the ruins of the modern fort now stand, there was then a strong Hindoo citadel, commanding the junction of the rivers Barana and Ganges. Here especially, the men-at-arms assembled in force, armed with spears and scimitars, and iron-bound clubs; while the turrets were defended by archers whose arrows were six feet in length. Chariots of war, and elephants whose tusks were armed with sabres, were among the locomotive defences of the the city.

When the faith of Buddha overspread the city, his temples and monasteries grew up on every side. Of the latter upwards of thirty are known to have existed. When the reaction came, and the sect of Jains sprang up, seeking to amalgamate both faiths, a third set of temples arose, and the city became one great cluster of domes, pyramids, and pinnacles. Then came the invasion of the Moslem hordes, who, sweeping down from beyond the Indus, carried fire and sword wherever they went; and, seeking to destroy all idolatrous worship, razed to the ground a vast multitude of unholy places, without respect to their beauty, and built in their places mosques and minarets.

Once more, however, the Hindoo faith ventured to lift its head, and once more did Benares become a City of Temples; numbering fifteen hundred spires and pyramids. Yet again must Islam assert itself, and the great Emperor Aurungzebe overthrew so many of these, that the soil of the city is said to be raised to a very considerable height by their ruins. Then, on the highest and most central point in the city, he built the grand mosque that bears his name; which, placed on the verge of a steep cliff, rises sheer from the river, overtopping all other buildings. No wonder his Hindoo subjects hated him! Now, under the religious toleration of British rule, a new supply of modern temples has arisen, insignificant compared with those of the past, but numbering about fifteen hundred, while every ghaut, garden, and tree has its own especial idols and shrines besides. It has been calculated that there must be fully half a million of idols in the city, each receiving a fair share of worship! Mohammedanism is represented by about three hundred mosques.

Thus we see that every phase of faith has here reigned by turns, and even now, though the Brahmans would fain make it appear that Siva, *alias* Maha-devah, *alias* Bisewara, is *the* god of the city, multitudes of others are worshipped; and every sect into which Hindooism is subdivided has here found a home. So we pass from the temples of Siva to those of Ganesa, of Hanuman, of Krishna, Vishnu, and others without number.

As the most distinctive symbol of Vishnu, the Sun-god, is the wheel which he carries in one hand, so is Siva specially distinguished by the trisula, or trident, which is generally said to symbolise his threefold work—creative, destructive, and regenerative. One or other of these symbols, placed on the summit of a temple-spire, shows at a glance which god is therein worshipped.

Moreover, these and other distinctive symbols are branded on the breast and arms of the worshippers with a red-hot golden instrument. Only priests of a specially high order—the Bishops of Brahmanism—are competent to impress the mystic brand. Boys are thus marked at about seven years of age, and girls not till after their marriage (a proviso which, however, may not augur advanced years).

The successive waves of conflicting faiths that have swept over Benares have destroyed every magnificent ancient temple, such as still remain intact in southern India. Nowhere need you hope to find any beauty of architecture that can strike home to the heart, and irresistibly claim reverent homage for its sheer loveliness, as in the Mohammedan buildings of Agra, still less any that can compare with the grey aisles of our own glorious old cathedrals. For quaintly beautiful as are many of the great mosques and temples of India, especially in matters of detail, I doubt if throughout the length and breadth of Hindoostan there exists one building that could bear comparison with Canterbury or Westminster, even were such comparison possible.

Very few of the temples now standing in Benares date farther back than two or three hundred years, and of these few are individually striking. Their main characteristic is that of grotesqueness, with bewildering intricacy of detail, truly symbolising in stone carving the complex mythology which has given them birth. Yet though lacking in individual beauty, collectively they form groups as picturesque as they are novel to the eye of a traveller. Nowhere but in a Hindoo city do we see such freaks of architecture, such strange fancies in stone, such clusters of domes and cupolas, and odd richly-sculptured pyramidal spires, new and old, half veiled by sacred trees, or reflected in holy tanks, or in the river itself.

Of the fifteen hundred temples which now exist in the city, the greater number are clustered along the river bank. Some are of elaborately carved stone; some are painted, some are gilded, all have glittering gilt spires. Behind these rise the houses of wealthy men, with overhanging balconies, and rich gardens, with stately trees laden with scented blossoms. From the midst of these, peep the glittering cupolas of some private oratory, for not here only, but throughout the country, almost every wealthy Hindoo has his own private temple, where the "tame Levite" of the family attends to his spiritual interests. Most rich Mohammedans also have their own little mosque. Along the brink of the broad river are terraced ghauts, where, beneath huge grass umbrellas like enormous fungi, devotees rest all day in contemplation, while myriads of people come down to bathe.

The Brahmans teach that the world ever since the Creation has rested on the thousand heads of the serpent Ananta (eternity) and will eventually be destroyed. But the ancient city of Kasi the Magnificent, now known as Benares, rests securely on the three points of the trident of the terrible Siva, or, as he is generally called, Mahadéo, the great god, whose especial care it is; therefore it is that all who die within its walls are for ever blessed. Siva himself built this wondrous city, with streets of purest gold, and temples of priceless gems, and although, by reason of sin in the beholder, all may seem to be but common stone, the faithful Hindoo well knows that it is because his own eyes are blinded, and that, could he attain to perfect purity, he would indeed see this glorious city as it is. This is actually believed by multitudes who come from the far ends of the lands to make the "*Panca kosi*," or five miles' pilgrimage round the city; a sunwise turn, which may nowhere exceed a distance of five miles from the centre of the city, whose atmosphere of sanctity so pervades this charmed circle, that whoever dies within it, is transported straightway to Siva's heaven.

The protection of Siva is no mere fiction. There have indeed been times when, to punish the sins of the people, he has suffered their enemies to desolate his own sacred city; nevertheless in many ways his favour is apparent. All natural powers are propitious to the Holy City. From remotest ages, no earthquake has ever been known within the sacred circuit of five miles, though the country around has been devastated. This of itself would be proof positive, were such required, of its isolation from the rest of the earth. Though innumerable crocodiles bask on the sandbanks, or lurk in the reedy shallows, not one has ever been known to hurt any of the myriad bathers, however rashly they might plunge into the stream.[1] Hurricanes and tempests have

[1] It seems, however, that once at least Siva proved himself a careless guardian of the city. Perhaps he was asleep when that savage tiger stole into the city, and wounded a dozen of his worshippers. Here is the story, as related by the Indian papers :—

Tiger Hunt in the Streets of Benares.—On Monday, December 18th, 1871, Mr. M'Mullin, assistant superintendent of police at Benares, was surprised at being told that some wild beast during the night had seriously wounded several people in the city. He was further told that the animal was then sitting in a dark recess on the top of some steps. Going to the spot, he could plainly see two eyes glaring in the darkness. Taking a musket from one of the police, he fired, when, with a fearful roar, a huge tiger bounded from the recess and rushed down the steps. Fortunately, Mr. M'Mullin had hit him in the fore-arm, and the tiger fell into a hole. A policeman then fired at him, but missed, and the tiger, recovering himself, sprang on the policeman, mauling him severely. A large crowd was now gathered round, and a scene of the utmost confusion ensued. The tiger bounded furiously about, wounding people on all sides. Files of policemen now marched up with loaded muskets, but, unfortunately, the police were not provided with caps, and had to beat a retreat. Mr. M'Mullin rode off to cantonments to obtain assistance; he returned with some officers, and the tiger was brought to bay in a place inclosed with walls near the Raj Mandil. A well-directed volley from a number of guns at length laid low the noble animal, who was game to the last. Altogether he had wounded twelve people, one of whom is not expected to recover. No one can tell where the tiger came from, but it seems probable that he had

devastated other spots, while calm and peace enfolded the loved abode of the gods. Here, too, the rains invariably fall moderately, while the neighbouring districts are either deluged or parched with long drought.

This question of "the rains" and the consequent rise and fall of all Indian rivers, is a matter of very great moment to towns or villages situated, as is Benares, on the very brink of the flood. For the rise of one year gives the very smallest possible clue to what that of the next may be. It depends of course on the intensity of the summer rains. These begin in the mountains about the end of May; thus the inundations by the rivers begin fully a month before the rains set in on the plains. By the end of July the lower flats of Bengal are flooded in all directions, and continue till the end of August to present the appearance of large lakes, sometimes extending over many miles, and dotted with villages like islands. Early in September the waters gradually begin to subside, the sun's scorching rays making evaporation rapid, and leaving a thick deposit of rich soil. Throughout the winter months the rainfall is *nil*, so that the rivers shrink into mere streams: their size is thus as varied as their course, which is remarkably vague.

Our thorough enjoyment of our visit to Benares was greatly due to the kindness of Rajah Sir Deo Naraien Singh, one of the kindest and most courteous gentlemen I have ever had the pleasure of meeting. There was something about him that always reminded me of a courtly Prelate, in fact his benevolent countenance greatly resembled that of Pio Nono. It was with very great sorrow that shortly after our return to England we received letters from his son announcing the sudden death of the kind old man. He had received his well-earned knighthood, and the Star of India, for very great service done to the English during the Mutiny, where, to his good influence both with the

come from the Maharajah's preserves at Chuckea, crossing the Ganges at Raj Ghaut by the bridge of boats during the night. The natives are in a state of great excitement, there being a tradition that when tigers eat people in the streets of Benares, then the day of tribulation will have come.—*Pioneer.*

Maharajah and all the people, it was due, that in this hotbed of fanaticism, there was no outbreak whatsoever. Yet at that time there were in the whole Province of Benares only twenty-five artillerymen and sixty invalids to represent European soldiers, all the other troops being native regiments; while the population of the district is three times that of all Scotland. Amongst many other steps taken to secure peace, and to inspire confidence, Sir Deo quitted his own palace, and actually lived with the English Resident during the worst time of trouble and anxiety.

Throughout his long and useful life Sir Deo had always shown the same unvarying kindness to all English; and a letter recommending us to his care, called forth such genuine and cordial hospitality as is not often accorded even to old friends. For so long as we chose to remain in Benares, an English open carriage was placed at our disposal, with two, sometimes three, relays of excellent horses. A large houseboat on the river, fully manned, was always at our service from dawn till night. Also an elephant and *tonjauns* (portable armchairs) should we go into the city. Two of his own confidential servants had orders always to be in attendance to make every possible arrangement for our comfort, and to show us everything; and very needful we found their presence, for the priests and riotous beggars proved a very different lot to our peaceful friends at Hardwar.

Our first impression of Benares was literally of Pandemonium let loose. Some great feast was going on, and heathendom was in triumphant riot. Houses and temples were hung with gay stuffs, and in the streets a surging sea of human life swayed to and fro, with shouts and screams and hubbub, such as only an eastern crowd can produce. They pressed on from one shrine to another with deafening shouts, blowing horns and conches, and ringing bells, and reiterating the praises of their gods; some in holiday garb, others travel-stained, having assembled from all quarters of the empire. Every tribe and every trade were there present, with the distinctive marks of their kingdom and their profession.

Under the safe escort of the Rajah's servants, we too visited shrines and temples without number, thereby accumulating untold merit! and only wishing we had each fifty pairs of eyes to feast on the ever-varying and most picturesque throngs of human beings, and the fantastic grouping of grotesque architecture, all seen in intense light and shadow, with a vivid blue sky over all. Where the streets were broad we drove; where they narrowed we mounted the elephant. Where he could not pass, we got into the *tonjauns*, and where they fairly stuck we got out and walked, changing backwards and forwards incessantly, at the bidding of the Rajah's trusty servants. One advantage of the elephant was that it raised us to the level of the upper windows, and so from time to time we fancied that we caught glimpses of bright eyes and jewelled dames peeping out from within their curtained windows.

First we drove rapidly to the Doorga Khoond, or Mirror of Doorga, the chief temple of that amiable goddess—the guardian angel of the city. I have already told you what a bloodthirsty fiend she is, and how her temples always reek with blood of goats and buffaloes which are sacrificed at her altars. Of course a bullock must in no case be put to death, therefore the buffalo is a convenient substitute. Before her shrine, which is always heaped up with golden marigolds and other flowers, stands a stone obelisk surmounted by a dragon. At the foot of this lies a huge sacrificial sword, wherewith are slain victims innumerable to appease the rage of the insatiable goddess. She is generally supposed to come and eat their bodies, but it is whispered that the city butchers come by night to buy them from the priests, and then retail them to the vulgar public. So it may chance that the European population eat their full share of things offered to idols!

This temple of Doorga is very fine, being of elaborately carved red sandstone. Round the great tank (her mirror) are some old trees, which are literally alive with monkeys. This one temple supports five hundred of these ludicrous creatures. An old priest called them down for our amusement, when they scampered up to us in a perfect mob, and the attendant satellites of the temple showered grain among them, for which they all, from the hoary grandfather to the infant in arms, scrambled in most undignified style. Then, swinging themselves up by post and pillar, they perched on every carved nook of the temple, swarming to the topmost peak or swinging themselves up the tall trees.

We then went on from one temple to another, sometimes passing down streets so narrow that we could well-nigh touch both sides at once; between tall houses, like those in the old town of Edinburgh, six or seven storeys or more, with projecting windows, and balconies actually meeting overhead, so that the narrow street seemed arched with flying bridges, and just showing narrow peeps of bright blue sky. Houses with carved pillars; sometimes with projecting verandahs of rich brown wood, casting dark shadows, and sculptures of mythology on the walls. Most of these open into small courts, whence low doors lead into dark cool rooms. These low rooms are favourite quarters in the daytime, as they lie in cool, deep shadow, while the top storeys catch all the hot sun. But at night these have the benefit of the clear, cold starlight, while the street below is comparatively hot and stuffy.

Among the most magnificent, though by no means most frequented temples here, are those of Ganesa, *alias* Ganapatu, the subtle god of wisdom and good luck. He is the son of Siva, and is always represented as a fat Brahman, wearing the mystic thread. He sits cross-legged, and has many arms. He has, moreover, the head and trunk of an elephant, that wise beast whose sagacity afforded a ready type of wisdom. The story, however, told concerning him is that he was originally born with a human head, but having lost his own in a fight, his mother vowed to supply him with the head of the first living creature she met. This proved to be an elephant, and her son happily inherited the wisdom of the elephantine brain. In some of his temples each pillar represents the leg of an elephant, while the capitals are monstrous elephantine heads.

He is escorted by a rat—the type of sagacity; and owns two wives, who are the goddesses of prosperity and success. He is one of the popular gods whose shrine is found in every village, and who is worshipped by every schoolboy, for he is the patron of literature, and famed for good writing, so his sign must be inscribed at the top of every page.

Formerly a multitude of female infants were sacrificed to Ganesa; not a bad speculation, as daughters were expensive to dower, and the pious offering received its due reward, as the tiny life thus consecrated was sure to be eventually returned in the birth of a son, a far more acceptable article. These sacrifices in the temples were very horrible scenes, and moreover very expensive to the parents, as the priests claimed heavy fees for butchering the poor babies; consequently the majority of people found it cheaper, and quite as efficacious, to dip the little innocents into cauldrons of boiling milk!

We passed on and on, through streets and through bazaars, past shops for the sale of all eastern goods: vessels of brass, sweetmeats, raiment, toys innumerable; fruit merchants selling cocoanuts, guavas, plantains, pomegranates, pumeloes or shaddocks, loquats, limes, custard-apples, pine-apples, bringals (which are a common vegetable shaped like an egg)—all manner of good things; and here and there stalked some tall adjutant, or a great, white, Brahmanee kite, seeking what it might devour, without the smallest regard for the ever-moving, noisy throng, which passed before the eye in a confused jumble of bright colours and glittering jewels, and clear brown skins of divers shades.

What chiefly impressed us was the multitude of white-robed priests, and in truth they muster strong in this city, where no less than 25,000 Brahmans rule as absolute lords temporal and ecclesiastical, holding the 200,000 residents, and the innumerable pilgrims in most rigid bondage. As an evidence of their wealth we were told that the Brahmans alone own 8,000 horses; nevertheless begging holds a conspicuous place among their religious duties, and this, at least, is one which they fulfil *con amore*. Not only the Brahmans, but all the Yogies and Sannyasis and other varieties of holy people, and the vast swarm of idlers who always haunt every temple, beg lustily, as though demanding a right, and make the life of all visitors a burden to them. It required all the influence of the Rajah's trusty servants to steer us safely through the haunts of these rapacious harpies. As to the Hindoos, they consider it an inestimable privilege to be allowed to contribute to the necessities of these saints. They, in their turn, are charitable enough: and are said to administer the funds of the temples with wisdom, these being generally endowed by wealthy Hindoos for the relief of weary, wayworn wanderers, when, as is too often the case, sickness and misery overwhelm them.

In several temples we saw carved marble bulls, like those at Hardwar, and multitudes of the real animals walking quietly about the street, among all the people, beautiful white creatures, adorned with garlands of flowers, and having the trident of Siva stamped on their hind-quarters. They went calmly about the bazaar, eating whatever they fancied, for none dare contradict them; so one moment their noses were in some merchant's cherished sacks of grain, the next they would begin snuffing the garland of some white-robed worshipper, who would straightway take it off and present it to this living representative of his god! Thus the sacred robbers exact what blackmail they please, while the luckless owners look on in reverential awe. The Brahmanee bull is generally rather small, with the hump between the shoulders strongly developed.

We went into one large temple where the open court was full of brilliant peacocks, sacred to Skanda, one of Siva's sons, while the side aisles, if I may so call them, were divided into stalls for sacred cows, the representatives of the earth-goddess. In the mythology of Scandinavia the chariot of the same beneficent earth-mother is drawn by cows. In the centre of the court was an image of Doorga, literally buried beneath the fresh, beautiful flowers that had been heaped upon it. I could not, however, venture on a very close inspection, as I had left the rest of the party in the "ecclesiastical bazaar," and nothing would induce my Mohammedan bodyguard to cross the threshold of this idolatrous temple.

So I very quickly rejoined the others, in a bazaar whose contents were wholly brazen vessels for the use of the temples. These stalls were most tempting curiosity shops. Apart from every

A STREET IN BENARES.

species of idol, great and small, in which we were not anxious to invest, there were such endless varieties of beautifully engraven brass lotas, or pots, brass plates inlaid with other metals or of some silvery material, curious incense-burners, such as quaint figures supporting lamps, odd spoons, silvery boxes for betel-nuts—in short, all kinds of delightful curiosities, such as old Indians never think it worth while to bring home, but which are really far more characteristic than the far more costly orthodox Indian treasures which are so familiar to us all.

To see the brassworkers' quarter was especially fascinating. It was so strange to see such engraving—wondrously intricate and artistic patterns, with only a hammer and an old nail as their stock of engraving implements. The admirable results produced by these wretched appliances was a practical commentary on those bad workmen who quarrel with their tools!

The tables of the money-changers are an interesting feature of the approach to an eastern temple—the heaps of gold and silver coins and piles of shell-money, *i.e.* the white cowrie-shells, which children compare to chicken with white sauce, but in which orientals, both Egyptians and Hindoos, recognise an effectual charm against the evil eye, and which here passes current for some incredibly small sum of money. Sweetmeat stalls also abound, and some of their dainties are rather tempting. These "tables of the money-changers," and the presence of the white oxen, the flocks of tame pigeons, and the goats prepared for sacrifice, together with all the brightly-polished brazen vessels for temple use, might well have recalled a scene in another Temple, when the changers of money, and those who sold oxen and sheep and doves, were driven out by the Master. But there was an incongruity and lack of dignity in all this ecclesiastical fair which rather happily prevented the suggestion of any such comparison.

This bazaar is in the outer court of the Great Golden Temple, which the natives prize above all others. One dome, and all the pinnacles, are gilt, and glitter in the sun. There is a large group of domes and pyramids; some red, some grey, and overshadowed by sacred peepul trees. The streets and bazaars come so close round it, that it is difficult to get a good,—at least a sketchable,—view of it. My brown guardian-angel took me to an upper balcony of a house opposite, whence we could look into the court of the temple, and down on the throng of worshippers, mostly clad in white, and adorned with huge necklaces of great African marigolds. The balcony was full of men playing on every species of discordant brass instruments and shells, and we were nearly deafened, both by them, and by the insatiable and clamorous crowd of priests and beggars. This certainly was the vilest nest of orthodox Hindooism we had ever seen, and went far to efface the memory of its calmer aspect in peaceful Hardwar, beside the pure river. Here, everything seemed as foul as the sullied waters.

Beneath the Golden Dome we saw sacrificial fires burning, and devotees leaping through the flames in honour of Maha-devah, the great god. This was formerly a common custom throughout the country, just as it was on midsummer night's eve and Hallowe'en in Britain, and wherever else Baal-worship has prevailed. Here it has long been discouraged by the Government; nevertheless the rite is still greatly in favour in parts of Southern India, *e.g.* in North Arcot, where so many deaths have recently resulted from the practice, that it became a question whether a positive prohibition might not be necessary. This, however, has been deemed an undesirable interference.

Many such practices have, however, been happily checked, such as the Churuk Poojah, or Swing Worship, which is now illegal, though still occasionally practised. We chanced to see it once, and a very disgusting exhibition it was, the wretched devotee inducing the Brahmans to pass great iron hooks through the muscles below the shoulder. He was then somehow slung from one end of a bamboo, balanced on a tall pole, and swung violently in a circle in mid-air. The whole weight seemed sustained by those muscles. This agonising torture was supposed to be so pleasing to the cruel goddess Kali that her votaries used constantly to undergo it, and a very few years ago there were still hundreds of these swinging-posts always at work in Bengal. There were scores in the immediate neighbourhood of Calcutta, some even in its streets. I think that in their secret hearts the people must bless the foreign rule, which takes on itself the responsibility of prohibiting such horrors.

The priests point to the great Golden Dome, and tell you it is overlaid with thick plates of pure gold, which were an offering from Runjeet Singh to the great god Bisewara (Siva). The gold, however, has long since been removed, and common gilding is all that now glitters in the sun, and the great golden chain by which the lamp was once suspended above the altar is now replaced by one of commonest brass. Nevertheless, worshippers assemble in vast crowds to throng these courts, more especially at the time of any eclipse of the sun or moon, when the altars are more than ever loaded with flowers and sweetmeats. For Bisewara loves these, and shows a just appreciation of sugar-plums, betel, and such like. Day by day he is duly washed with water from the holy Ganges, and dressed with all solemnity, and at night he is laid away, safely wrapped up in his summer or winter raiment as the case may be—either a light shawl or a rich warm brocade.

His worshippers, mindful of his tendency to slumber, never fail to preface their prayer by ringing the bell above his shrine to arouse his attention!

Hard by is the temple of his one wife, Annapurna, variously named Pârvatî, Kali, and Doorgâ, a veiled goddess, whose face was not displayed to us heretics. True believers declare her to be of marble, with a variety of masks and faces of gold and silver changeable at pleasure, which perhaps accounts for Siva being content to have but one fair minister, instead of the Eastern allowance!

A beautiful marble well, with canopy of rich carving, is especially sacred to her, and here devout offerings are thrown, of all manner of food, of which it is supposed she eats what she requires, and gives the remainder to the poor, so everything is thrown in quite promiscuously—milk, flour, cakes, fruit, flowers—and the result is, as you may suppose, a horrible mass of putrescence, sickening to approach, and one which loads the air with the seeds of pestilence. Our Mohammedan friend looked on with an expression of unutterable loathing, and exclaimed, "Well! I am thankful my Allah does not eat and drink!" A small boy pressed forward to give us information, in excellent English. "That," he said, "is the well into which god jumped!"

The legend to which he referred is to the effect that when the Mohammedan emperor Aurungzebe destroyed the temple of Siva to build his own grand mosque on its site, the image of Siva took refuge of its own accord at the bottom of this deep well. Therefore do the endless throng of pilgrims come ceaselessly to cast in their offerings. From the invisible depths the attendant priests draw up lotas full of foully unfragrant fluid—I cannot call it water—and bestow it on the pilgrims, who therewith anoint their bodies, even drinking some of the holy liquid.

This is one of the curious points in Hindoo notions regarding cleanliness, as distinct from ceremonial purity. To drink the most sparkling water which had been drawn in a leathern bucket, or on which the shadow of a low-caste man had rested, would involve defilement; but no matter how foul is the water drawn in a correct manner from a sacred source, *that* is a desirable draught. Therefore the dirty water, in which the images of Krishna have been washed at their daily dressing, is drunk as cleansing holy water. So too in one of the Vishnuvite sects (the Vallabha) whose high priests receive actual worship in the temple; the people prostrate themselves before them, and devoutly offer flowers and incense, eagerly drinking the filthy water in which the clothes and feet of these spiritual chiefs have been washed!!

Still we went on and on, through wide streets and narrow streets, among big gods and little gods, meeting at every glance some image or symbol to remind us that in truth this is a city "wholly given to idolatry." Wherever we turned there was the same noisy throng of worshippers, the same insatiable and clamorous crowd of priests and beggars, all covered with garlands of flowers, all howling for backsheesh, and many playing on horrible musical instruments.

It was with unspeakable relief that we at length found ourselves at the entrance to Aurungzebe's Grand Mosque, with its tall minarets cleaving the sapphire sky, like fingers pointing heavenward. Slim fingers indeed, for while their height is about 147 feet, their diameter at the base is only eight and a half feet decreasing to seven and a half at the summit. It was Friday, and the hour of prayer, and the great court was full of solemn, silent worshippers. Everything about both mosque and people was of dazzling cleanliness, the brilliant sunlight showed no stain on white robes or snowy turbans, as every man knelt on his own square of the marble pavement. Everything was hushed and still, and the broad blue sky formed a meet canopy for so noble a temple. It was a very solemn and impressive scene, all the more so in contrast with the wild devil-worship that was going on in all the rest of the city.

We felt deep sympathy with Aurungzebe, though we could not wonder at the hatred with which the Hindoos behold this stately building, which to them must be a perpetual eyesore, overtopping all else in the city of their many gods, so that from its lofty minarets, his hated soldiers were wont to look down on the Hindoo bathers, to their intense annoyance. These minarets are found to have a very distressing fascination for men who are "weary of life and light," amongst them we were told of one gambler who during the "Feast of Lanterns" had lost all his money, and finally staked and lost his wife. This last straw was the finishing touch which decided the wretched man's fate.

We ascended to the top of one of the minarets, whence we commanded a magnificent view of the city, the river, all the temples, and the surrounding country. But above all, our eyes were riveted by a heap of nondescript ruins, lying about three miles north of Benares, for there we knew lay all that remained of the once mighty city, Sarnath, a city which was to the Buddhists all that Benares is to the Brahmans, for here it was that Buddha first publicly preached the newly discovered "Way of Life," and how all men might enter "The Gates of Righteousness."

Here, in the days of its glory, were thirty great monasteries, inhabited by three thousand monks. There were also eight "Divine Towers," one of which is stated to have been three hundred feet high, and adorned with most precious jewels. Amongst the innumerable statues of Buddha which adorned the city at every turn was one great copper image, representing him as the teacher, in the act of turning the wheel of the law. In this city Buddha was worshipped for upwards of a thousand years, after the Brahmans had driven his followers out of Benares. So the two great strongholds of the rival faiths flourished for many centuries within sight one of another.

At length the Brahmans seem to have been goaded out of all their usual theories of toleration, and falling suddenly on their unsuspecting neighbours, sacked and burned the monasteries, overthrew the colleges, and reduced the city to ashes, while such of the terror-stricken inhabitants as escaped the sword fled for their lives. So sudden was their flight, that they left their bread half-baked in their little mud ovens, and there it was found in very recent years, buried beneath the general pile of ruins that the fire had in some measure spared. Amongst these were numerous statues of Buddha and other images, and elaborately carved stones, but so little value was set on these precious relics of antiquity that they were carted away wholesale, and cast into the river Barana to serve as a breakwater to protect the piers of the bridge!

The multitude of carved stones of unmistakably Buddhist origin, which are built into so many Brahman houses at Benares, tell their own tale. There are capitals carved with lotus-leaves, shafts of pillars, and more especially broken umbrellas of stone, just like great mushrooms, which were once the most sacred symbol of Buddha's sovereignty. The great round tower, the ruins of which are so conspicuous even as seen from our post on the minaret, was one hundred and ten feet in height, and ninety-three feet in diameter, its top being of ancient brickwork. This, until a very few years ago, was cased with finest stonework, all carved with lotus leaves and blossoms, with figures seated therein, contemplative Buddhas floating on still waters. Now the carved stones have been removed, and there remains little more than an unsightly heap of rubble.

Descending from our high post of observation, our next halt was at a private house belonging to Maun Singh, where a great terrace of stonework acts the part of an astronomical observatory, or Man Mandil as it is called—*Man* meaning measurement, and

Mandil the globe. On the terrace are built all manner of huge sun-dials and other astronomical instruments, of solid masonry; contrivances for finding out the declinations of stars, the meridional line, and other things, also an enormous gnomon, globe, and huge stone buildings like giants' playthings, just like those we saw in the great ruins of the observatory at Delhi. All these things were elaborately explained to us by a very scientific old Hindoo, who, in the abstruseness of his calculations, had quite forgotten his raiment!

This old man is a very important person in Benares, as is the astronomer or astrologer in every community of Brahmans, for no Hindoo will do anything important without consulting the stars, and a regular astrological almanac is published for the convenience of such as cannot conveniently go in person to the astrologer, a process which is at once simpler and more economical. There were formerly some great instruments of brass belonging to this observatory, but these were removed, and are still preserved by the Hindoo Princes of Rajpootana.

Once more we plunged into the mazes of the city, into the noisy thronged streets, with their quaint architecture, their intense lights and shadows, their brilliantly coloured figures sprinkled here and there, amid a crowd of which the vast majority were clad and turbaned in dazzling light, and garlanded with flowers, while all the small boys, too young to wear the turban, were adorned with brilliant skull-caps of silk, embroidered with gold and silver.

Now we turn aside into a small dark shop. Thence we were led along dark, winding passages, till we reached a small upper room, where, at the bidding of our guide, one roll after another of priceless kincob was spread before our admiring gaze. Kincob is that marvellous silk and gold brocade for which the looms of Benares are so justly celebrated. Brocades of every brilliant hue, wrought with richest patterns of gold and silver, the most gorgeous materials you can imagine. What their price per yard was, we hardly paused to inquire, so obviously were they far beyond our reach. Not that we coveted them particularly, even as hangings, and no one but a Begum, or a Ranee, or their spouses, could wear such stuffs. Their own rich colouring harmonises all this splendour, so that dress and wearer are all in keeping, but the fair skin is overpowered by it. And nowhere is the perfect Oriental taste in colouring shown more strikingly than in this exquisite manufacture. The one standing miracle is how these natives, who can devise and execute such designs—so perfectly becoming to themselves—can ever be guilty of showing a corner of toleration for our hideous, western garb, and even occasionally of adopting it, or part of it, for their own use.

When at length we returned to rest, after the bewildering sights of the day, we found a fresh deputation of servants from the dear old Rajah, bearing trays of the most delicious sweetmeats, and fruits of all sorts. Various tradesmen soon scented us out, and brought us huge baskets of Benares toys, all carved in coloured wood, highly polished; boxes of every sort, with dozens of lesser ones fitting into one another, and all sorts of ingenious playthings. We invested in a great number, and still further increased our store of brass curiosities, though one man grinned from ear to ear when I remarked that we only wanted genuine Benares work, and that he need not take the trouble to show us Birmingham goods. I strongly suspect that every little idol in his basket was pure "Brummagem," and not without good reason, for it is currently reported that Birmingham exports an immensely large proportion of the idols of Hindoostan, and finds them a very profitable speculation !!

One might have supposed that Benares was competent to supply its own idol market, so numerous are the cunning workers in divers materials, who devote their skill to this manufacture. The potters mould images of clay for daily worship, these are always thrown into the river, so must be renewed daily. Sculptors produce more lasting idols of stone or marble, the carpenters make great wooden idols for the temples, while the workers in metal, goldsmiths, coppersmiths and brassworkers, find a ceaseless demand for their respective productions. Special value attaches to golden images of certain gods and goddesses, while for others, copper or brass or an amalgam of mercury and tin is preferred. Shitala, the goddess of small-pox, is always represented in silver, but the most sacred of all materials for the manufacture of gods is a perfect alloy produced by mixing eight metals—namely, gold, silver, brass, lead, iron, tin, mercury, and copper. I need scarcely say that as objects of art, the rudest of these hand-wrought productions, are far more interesting than the most highly finished factory work.

All that night a never-ceasing whirl of native carriages jingled past our door, chiefly little *ekkas*, those picturesque one-horse vehicles, with hoods supported by four posts, the funniest little machines, utterly unlike anything in Europe. They were all crammed with natives, men and women, in their very brightest apparel, and all chattering and laughing. It was a clear moonlight, and we would fain have followed them, for they were bound for a great native festival, when part of the town would be illuminated, and would doubtless have been most picturesque. But our watch-dogs, the Rajah's servants, were greatly scandalised by the proposition, as they vowed the fair was by no means respectable, and I have no doubt they were quite right, as we learnt subsequently, that the principal feature of the festival consisted in the free use of *shrab* and *bhang* and other intoxicating liquors, of which libations were poured over certain idols, in whose honour the night was spent in wildly licentious revelry. This is a festival only observed by certain sects.

But a real illumination at Benares would be a sight worth travelling far to see, when every line of the tall pyramidal temples is marked by myriads of small oil lamps—when fire-balloons float upward to the dark blue heaven, and down the silent stream float star-like points of glittering light produced by lighted wicks floating in little earthenware saucers full of oil, and many coloured fires shed wondrous effects of gorgeous crimson, blue or green glow, on the temples and the dense crowds of dark figures.

Our chief enjoyment of Benares certainly lay on the river, where we spent five long, and most pleasant days, from dawn till sunset. Each morning the Rajah's carriage was at our door between five and six o'clock, and a four miles' drive through palmy groves brought us to the brink of the river just ere the sun's first ray touched the city. The house-boat was always in readiness, and then we slowly rowed up the broad stream for several miles, past the marvellous piles of temples, wonderful bathing-ghauts, palaces, and buildings of every sort, which rise mass upon mass—tier above tier, from the water's edge, right up to the broad blue sky.

Every morning we came with fresh delight, each day revealing some new, curious detail that had hitherto escaped our notice. Some new spire of the thousand temples, some quaint, religious ceremony hitherto unnoticed; some new combination in the ever-changing groups of temples, pinnacles, balconies, overhanging windows in indescribable variety; green trees telling of shady gardens; pigeon roosts,—always a conspicuous feature in Hindoo cities; steep flights of stairs reaching up to the blue heaven; broad landing-places of solid stone, never two alike, but all showing endless variety of detail.

Along the water's edge are groups of huge umbrellas, thatched with grass matting and resembling great mushroom-beds, beneath whose shade squat imps that would astonish Puck himself. Others, also of matting, are covered with scarlet calico, and add one more touch of colour to the gay scene. There are bathers and worshippers without number—thousands on thousands—washing, sprinkling holy water, reading sacred books, clamouring for backsheesh, all in endless confusion; everywhere there is light, colour, motion. The blue of heaven is reflected even by the river, now alas, little better than a filthy sewer of many great cities, and the blue overhead and the blue below are blended by an incessant film of bright blue smoke, for ever rising from the burning ghaut, and from the bodies of those happy dead who have breathed their last in this city beloved by the gods, and whose ashes will soon be sprinkled on the sacred river.

The great mass of the people come to bathe at sunrise, when the ghauts are indeed a scene of wondrous animation. As usual, men and women all bathe together as a matter of course, and think no evil thereof; and the daintiest dames (who at other hours of the day veil even their eyes from the chance glance of a stranger, and are carried to the river's edge in closely curtained tonjauns, wherein, after their bath, they will again take refuge from the eyes of the vulgar), now stand revealed in the very airiest of drapery, probably only a sheet of the finest muslin—without the slightest hesitation. It is the custom of the land, and no one thinks it strange. So, at every few yards you perceive beautiful groups in bronze of most graceful bathing nymphs, such as would rejoice the heart of a sculptor, and indeed these beautiful bronzes never strike you otherwise than as statuary, and that, of a very high class, so that the faintest idea of immodesty or indelicacy never for a moment suggests itself.

All day long the washing of human beings, dead or alive, and of their clothes and their vessels, goes on unceasingly. One constant succession of new comers pour down to the river to bathe and to pray before eating: afterwards they take water in the palms of their hands, and hold it up to the Sun as an offering, or else filling a brass lota with Ganges water, they pour it out before him while they stand praying. Then falling prostrate, with their forehead in the dust, they worship in silence. Next, with infinite relish, they drink a draught of the sacred water, while the men all round are diligently polishing their teeth in the most approved style, standing knee deep in the river! They then fill their vessels with the same filthy water, which they carefully seal up, and carry home for all household purposes, while Yogis in like manner, start on pilgrimage to distant parts of India to sell the sacred fluid to the faithful for immense sums, so that the idols in the most remote districts may not lack this precious anointing.

Nor is it the idols only for whose service this holy water is required, for, as I mentioned at Hardwar, in Indian Courts of Justice it holds the place of the Bible, for a Hindoo knows of no oath so solemn as that which is sworn by the water of the Ganges, on which has been laid a branch of the sacred tulasi-shrub.[1]

On one ghaut we saw a huge gaudily-painted image of Bhim Singh, a noted giant. It was made of Ganges mud and would soon return to its pristine condition; meanwhile it lay like a

[1] The basil.

modern Gulliver among his Lilliputian worshippers. Beside it stood a little group, like a nest of ants. One was a European, and beside him a native, evidently a convert, preaching, but collecting a mere handful of listeners, who rarely paused for two moments consecutively. Various other idols, similarly fashioned of Ganges mud, adorn the neighbouring steps: and often we saw a devout worshipper fashioning a little god for himself, of mud or of cow-dung. To this he prayed most earnestly; then, when his prayer was done, he chucked it into the river, as being of no further use. Rather suggestive of the fate of a good many human idols, among worshippers of the ideal! But if you ask any educated Hindoo whether that mud image is indeed his god, he will answer that he worships an invisible Spirit, without reference to any created matter, but the use of this outward symbol is a help to concentrate his thought, which else would wander over the vast heaven.

Every morning we slowly rowed up the stream, keeping close in shore, so as to have full benefit of all the picturesque life at the ghauts, and to notice the quaint religious ceremonies of the people; and often I wished that some of our friends, with a strong turn for Ritualism, could come and see a little of heathendom, just to see what formalism can come to. It is curious enough to see the little ceremonies of an ordinary worshipper. First, he casts on the river his offering of flowers, he then rinses his mouth with holy water, never heeding the bloated corpse that bobs up and down in the stream close to him, and which may have died of some horribly infectious disease. Then he prays, while standing first on one leg, then on the other. Next he falls flat on his face, kissing the earth. Rising, he bows to the four points of the compass. Then looking heavenward, he raises his hands in supplication. He next pours out an offering of Ganges water to the sun. Perhaps he daubs his own body with Ganges mud. He washes his turban and the cloth wrapped round his loins, and goes on his way rejoicing.

But the simple ceremonial of the laity is nothing compared with the quaint means adopted by the quiet, meditative Brahmans, to stir up their own minds and increase their powers of concentrated thought. Remember what an intellectual race these high-caste Brahmans are, with their pure Aryan descent written on every lineament of their clear-cut features and high foreheads —a race whose distinctive characteristics have been evolved by fully three thousand years of hereditary self-culture, self-restraint and life-long discipline, perpetually aiming at the highest standard of ideal perfection.

Imagine thousands of these proud men with little raiment save the mystic, threefold Brahmanical cord, which to mortal eyes is only a bit of whipcord, worn over the left shoulder and under the right, but which is really a certificate of the highest aristocracy for both worlds. Picture to your mind these men sitting for hours —sometimes the livelong day, on wooden stands, or platforms, built out into the river, where, beneath the shadow of the huge grass umbrellas, they sit absorbed in silent contemplation, striving to intensify their devotion by a religious rite called *Habsidam* or *Pranayama*, *i.e.* THE RETENTION OR REGULATION OF BREATH!!!

The manner in which this is practised is to close one nostril with the first finger of the right hand, while drawing a long breath, and then reverse the process with the left hand; then, closing both nostrils, sit in silent, concentrated thought, till well-nigh suffocated; then, removing the finger first applied, breathe slowly through that nostril. It sounds like a little joke; but this nevertheless, is a most solemn act of faith. It is sometimes practised while sitting calmly gazing on the river; sometimes while standing on one leg, while adoring the sun; and is probably followed by a series of rapid grotesque prostrations and mutterings.

Similar concentration of mind is aimed at in another ceremonial wherein the devotee is required to repeat a mantra or sacred charm sixteen times while in the act of inhaling, and sixty-four times while holding the breath. By snapping the fingers ten times in different directions, during the ceremony, evil spirits are scared!

One great practical advantage of this mode of slow breathing is the prolongation of life, for, as every man is fated to draw only a given number of breaths between his birth and his grave it follows that the longer he can take about it, the longer he will live ![1]

The virtue of prolonged retention of breath is further exemplified by a man suddenly taking a header under water, and there remaining till you think he is certainly drowned. Not at all. He is only trying to work out some abstruse, metaphysical train of thought, or perhaps striving to realise to the uttermost how very great and holy is the river goddess, and how certainly she is even then washing away all his sins. He must also strive to realise the indwelling within his own heart and brain of the three-fold god whom he adores; of Brahma, Vishnu, and Siva, all of whom are symbolised by the holy and mystic word AUM which he must reverently whisper—a name as sacred to the devout Hindoo as was the title JAH to the Hebrew worshipper of JEHOVAH. Who can say that in these earnest aspirations after more perfect union with that Great Unknown Power in Whose presence within himself he so firmly believes, he may not have more than we often imagine, in common with creeds which we account more orthodox?

Strange and childish, even ridiculous, as many of their ceremonies are in our eyes, those who can speak with these men think that many among them are not so far from the Kingdom of GOD as some might fear who glance only at their myriad idols, or as they would say, symbols of faith. If it be true that "in every nation, he that feareth GOD and worketh righteousness, is accepted of Him," we little know how far some of these strange, earnest, anxious creatures may have outrun many an easy-going Christian. It was one of these men, who, speaking of his own death, said "he knew that though his body might die, his spirit could never

[1] This extraordinary method of gaining merit has been adopted by a sect of Reformed Buddhists which originated about a hundred years ago in the province of Shantung in China. They worship no images, but reverence the characters which signify Heaven, Earth, Emperor, Parent, and Teacher. They are vegetarians, and some practice celibacy. But their peculiar rite is THE PRACTICE OF HOLDING THE BREATH TILL THE DEVOTEE IS BLACK IN THE FACE, AND LIFE IS WELL-NIGH EXTINCT. SOME HAVE BEEN KNOWN TO DO THIS FOR NEARLY HALF AN HOUR!! Meanwhile they imagine that the soul has gone out into the unseen world collecting information, which, on his recovery, the devotee divulges oracularly to the congregation.

do so; because, just as he who puts off his old garments, does so only to assume better; so he who lives in GOD only lays aside his old body that he may put on a new and more glorious one." "WHAT IS THIS WORLD?" said a Brahman sage; "IT IS EVEN AS A BOUGH OF A TREE, ON WHICH A BIRD RESTS FOR A NIGHT, AND IN THE MORNING FLIES AWAY." Therefore he seeks to attain to a perfect indifference to the pleasures or pains of the body, in order that he may finally be reabsorbed into deity. Who can say that hereafter, those who have striven to walk so faithfully by such dim light as they have, may not be numbered amongst those "other sheep that are not of *this* fold"?

The devout Brahman is early at his prayers, and greets the dawn by the recital of very beautiful ancient Sanskrit hymns (we judge of their beauty from the translations by Monier Williams, Max Müller, and other oriental scholars). Then, as the sun rises, he stands to do it homage, throwing up water into the air from his united hands, or from a brazen vessel.

Believing each part of his body to be the temple of some divine person, he touches each reverently. Then follows a long prayer, during which he twists his fingers (each consecrated to a different god) into fanciful shapes to indicate different mystic symbols, such as a garland, a tortoise, a fish, &c. He ought to utter 108 prayers, and keep count of them on his rosary. This must be done secretly, his hands and rosary being covered by a cloth.

Now standing up, he invokes Mitra, the Risen Sun, and, for the good of his ancestors, he offers them homage, and repeats his own genealogy! Then follows a closing ascription of praise to the Trinity of Brahma, Rudra (*i.e.* Siva), and Vishnu; and after a final cleansing drink of (dirty Ganges) water, the elaborate morning service is over.

Its minor details are innumerable. At different points, water must be taken up in the hand with fingers straightened, now again with fingers bent, now poured on one side of the hand, now on the other.

Moreover the sacred Brahmanical thread is constantly being shifted. In acts of ancestral worship it is worn over the right shoulder and under the left. In worshipping gods it is worn over the left and under the right. In worshipping saints it is worn round the neck as a necklace.

An almost identical service must be performed at sunset.

Besides these there is a solemn form of family prayer in the house every morning. This is the Deva-puja before the domestic idols, when the worshipper (having duly placed the mystic threefold cord on his right shoulder) pours a libation of water from his hand, praying that the water thus consecrated by the virtue of his sacred thread may be accepted by such of his dead relatives as have died without leaving sons to make offerings on their behalf.

Mr. Monier Williams, who has devoted years of study to all phases of religious thought and practice in India, past and present, calculates that an orthodox modern Brahman must devote about five hours a day to the performance of his devotional routine, the chief duties incumbent on him being: 1. Ceremonial bathing. 2. Prolonged morning and evening worship. 3. Repetition of the first words of every sacred book. 4. The daily oblation of water to the lesser gods, the sages, and deceased human beings. 5. The sacrifice by fire, butter, and rice. 6. Domestic worship in the family. 7. A prolonged service before the mid-day meal. 8. Offerings of food to gods and beggars. 9. Daily visits to the temple. 10. More reading of sacred books, and frequent fasts.

To our rarely reverent western minds, which barely brook the utterance of the shortest form of thanksgiving before even one daily meal, the practice of the really orthodox Brahman in this respect certainly suggests a serious test of patience. In the first place, the Hindoo family has generally only two meals daily—the principal one at noon, and the second at sunset.

Before eating, offerings must be made to all the food-giving gods. First to the Fire which cooked the food, and which will now bear the offering to heaven. So consecrated fire is kindled with consecrated fuel in a small brazier, and sacred kusa grass having been strewn around, one of the family recites sac ed texts. He then goes through the ceremonies of sipping water and holding his breath, as in the morning ritual.

Rice is then cooked, with a running accompaniment of ancient prayers and hymns, and when the food is ready, the worshipper purifies his hands, and offers a small handful of rice to each food-god, throwing it into the fire. Then he takes ashes from the fire and rubs them on his forehead, neck, head, and shoulders, while invoking Siva in his character of Rudra, and praying him not to harm the family or their cattle, but he prays Vishnu to grant life for a hundred years with wisdom, strength, health, happiness, intellect, and other good things. The prayer is offered to Brahma the Supreme.

After this, small portions of food are arranged on the ground in a double circle, an inner circle of little rice heaps for the gods already worshipped, and an outer circle for all other gods and beings, addressing each by name (thirty-six classes are enumerated, including waters, plants, household deities, the earth, gods of the foundation of the house, good spirits and evil spirits, spirits of day, and spirits of night. Also to the four-eyed hell-dogs, Syama and Sabala.

In offering to these, he prays the lord of food to grant a blessing on the food he is himself about to eat. Then going out of his house he places portions on the ground for persons of low caste and no caste, for dogs and all other animals, and for the crows whom he summons from the four quarters of heaven. He waits a little in case some beggar may come and crave alms. Then he again washes his hands and feet, drinks a little purifying water, and re-enters the house, invoking peace upon it.

Even now he and the family cannot fall to ravenously, as they must long to do, for the ceremony is a punctiliously religious one. The men now sit on the ground, and the women of the family wait on them, on no account eating till they have finished. Again they sip water ceremoniously for purification—each from the palm of his hand. Also it is sprinkled round each green leaf, which acts as plate. They may use plates of polished metal but not of earthenware. Then a text is recited and a long grace, and then four small portions of food are laid on the ground beside each man's plate. Then at last they may eat their simple meal of cooked or curried vegetables.

Afterwards the green leaves and the portions of dedicated food are given to the cows or other animals.

Methinks a hungry Briton would find it hard to tolerate such lengthy preliminaries for even a civic festival! Nor is it easy for him to realise all the mystical ideas associated with the insignificant looking bit of cotton-twist to which such immense importance is attached by India's millions.

The said sacred thread was by all early writers on India supposed to be the distinguishing mark of Brahmans from all other castes. Now, however, it appears that *it is only the Sudras* or servile castes *who do* NOT *wear this simple badge of honour.* The military Kshatriyas wear such a cord made of hemp only. The Vaisyas, or industrial class, wear one of wool, and THE ONLY DISTINCTION OF THE THREEFOLD BRAHMANICAL CORD LIES IN THE FACT THAT IT MUST BE OF COTTON ONLY.[1] It must be made of three cotton threads, each composed of three fine threads, which must be twisted to a running accompaniment of sacred texts, while sprinkled with holy water from a sprinkler of the divine kusa grass. The cord is supposed to symbolize the three incarnations of Brahma, and it must moreover be entirely the handiwork of some parental Brahman, who must himself gather the cotton from the plant; spin and twist the mystic cord, which is the bearer's patent of nobility.

As soon as a young Brahman attains his eighth year, he is invested therewith. His eyelids are painted. He is adorned with a coral necklace and a new garment; he is anointed with oil, and made to offer solemn sacrifices to the sacred fire and to the nine planets. Various other ceremonies and religious rites of all sorts are observed. All his kindred celebrate this glad day with feasting and gladness, and the boy is henceforth admitted to all the privileges of his high estate. He now assumes the title of Dvi-ja,

[1] The Parsees of Bombay likewise wear a sacred cord of seventy-two threads of pure white wool, forming a flat cord, or "girdle," which is coiled three times round the body.

i.e. "twice-born." No matter how poor he may be, servant perhaps to some rich Sudra, or other man of low caste, it matters not; all other castes, his own master included, owe him reverence as to one intrinsically holier than themselves.

Not that all Brahmans are of equal rank. They are subdivided into so many classes that the highest is as far removed from the lowest as that lowest is from the Pariah.

The old belief in the divine right of the Brahmans, and of their mighty power as a vast united body overspreading the whole land, has melted away on a closer examination of their actual condition. It has now been ascertained that, besides their innumerable petty subdivisions, there exist in every province of India two great classes, both bearing the name of Brahman and wearing the sacred thread, yet utterly despising one another;[1] dwelling side by side, yet refusing all intercourse; never intermarrying, not eating together. Their very countenances betray the difference, one class retaining the strikingly handsome features and clear, fair skins of the old Aryans, the other being dark in colour, and stamped with the common features of the lowest castes. The only theory by which this can be explained (for the true solution has been jealously concealed by the Brahmans themselves) is, that when the Aryan conquerors took possession of the land, and found it impossible wholly to crush the aboriginal aristocracy, they invented a compromise, so as, nominally at least, to hold all power in their own hands; and so, just as the old Greeks and Romans bestowed their name and citizenship on such of their conquered subjects as could either purchase that honour "with a great sum," or else obtain it as a reward of merit, it would appear that the Brahmans, even while thoroughly despising the aboriginal races, were driven to the expedient of receiving certain of the more wealthy families into their own body by giving them their name and investing them with the sacred thread.

That this is the case is evident from the fact that the farther south you go, the lower does the type of thread-wearers become, so that in the extreme south, as in the hill-country of Central

[1] See chapter vii. p. 180.

India, whither the aboriginal tribes were driven, and where only a small proportion of the fair-skinned race followed, the pure type of Brahman is almost unknown; and the mystic thread is worn by gold and silver smiths, stonecutters, carpenters, and even blacksmiths, all of whom are, in Northern India, accounted Sudras, that is to say, quite low caste. Passing still farther south to Ceylon, it appears that the true Brahman literally does not exist, and that all who bear the name have been manufactured as a matter of expediency.

Of the possibility of conferring this dignity on one not born to it, there still exists a practical proof in the fact that the low-caste Rajahs of Travancore ARE TO THIS DAY ELEVATED TO THIS HIGH HONOUR ON THEIR ACCESSION TO THE THRONE; part of the ceremony observed being that *they must pass through the body of a golden cow*, symbolizing the cleansing of all sin, and the new birth by which they become regenerate.

But of the wholesale Brahman manufacture of olden times we find only dim legends telling how certain great princes, desirous of offering such vast sacrifices as demanded the presence of ten thousand priests, did actually collect whole tribes of the lowest of the people to the number of perhaps a hundred thousand, all of whom were duly invested with the sacred thread! In most of these legends, Krishna kindly appears to sanction this very irregular proceeding. The story, with a few variations, is told of several arbitrary monarchs reigning respectively in Oude, Orissa, and other kingdoms widely separated. Sometimes Krishna is said to have indulged in this transformation of castes for his own special amusement, as for instance, when, in one of his incarnations as a holy sage dwelling in Southern India, he caused the sea to recede from the mainland, and thus formed the level coast of Malabar, whither he retreated. Many fishermen followed him thither, but the sage wearied for the companionship of Brahmans, so he determined to raise his followers from their degraded caste to that for which his righteous soul craved. Therefore he took their nets (the very nets which had been instrumental in the destruction of animal life), and untwining them, he proceeded to manufacture an unlimited supply of cord, of the orthodox threefold twist, and therewith invested the whole male population.

It is a remarkable fact that, although the Malabar Brahmans of the present day try to hold their heads higher than the purer families who have emigrated thither in more recent days, and try to ignore their fisher origin, it is alluded to as a well-known fact by a Dutch writer who visited the coast early in the last century. Moreover, they retain many of their aboriginal customs of the worst class, herein assimilating closely to the neighbouring tribes of Nairs—a race by whom polyandry is recognised as the orthodox form of wedded life. These fisher-priests also retain one trace of their despised origin, namely, that the casting of a net and catching a fish forms part of their marriage ceremony,[1] which, however, they carefully conceal from Europeans.

One marked characteristic whereby the descendants of the manufactured Brahmans may be distinguished from those of pure Aryan blood, is by their habitual ministration at the bloodstained altars of Siva; the sacrifice of life, and indeed the recognition of Siva in his character of destroyer, being remnants of aboriginal worship, and therefore abhorrent to the true Brahman, though admitted as a matter of expediency; a compromise, whereby in olden days the aboriginal tribes might be attracted within the pale of the church.

In many districts of India large numbers of Brahmans devote themselves exclusively to agriculture, and are accordingly despised by the idler classes, who declare that in bygone ages their ancestors forsook the priestly office and gave themselves up to this degrading work. The peasant Brahmans are scattered all over the country, some work as coolies and day-labourers, some as domestic servants, many are soldiers, others even serve as local police, which is considered as very low work indeed.

In the Himalayas several distinct races are found, some of whom are shepherds, some ploughmen, others will do almost any work, even to carrying a jampan or palanquin, and a very small proportion of them seem to hold any especially priestly office.

[1] *Orissa.* By W. W. Hunter.

These hill Brahmans eat meat freely, they allow widows to re-marry and indeed will themselves marry their deceased brothers' wives!

In short, everything that can be said on the subject goes to prove that the generic term of Brahman is applied indiscriminately to innumerable totally different races, who have no pretension to a common ancestry, and who hate and despise one another with their utmost energy. Every shade of character is thus included, from the most lazy and improvident, to the most frugal and hard-working; every gradation of faith, from the most subtle and refined which the unaided mind of man can devise, down to the very grossest and most childish, is alike represented, not by individuals only, but by distinct classes, with as little affinity one for another as oil has for water—however closely they may be associated, they will never blend.

The highest grade of sanctity that the Hindoo mind can conceive is embodied in the Coolin Brahman, before whom all other men bow down in humble reverence. The highest favour that can befall any family is that a Coolin should marry a daughter of the house. Not that the family cares are thereby lightened. The damsel never leaves her father's roof, and perhaps may not behold the face of her husband from one year's end to the next, nor does he make her any allowance whatsoever. On the contrary, he has thenceforth a right to come whenever he pleases to the house of his father-in-law, and there remain as long as suits his convenience. Moreover, there is no limit to the number of families on whom he may confer this inestimable privilege.

There is no doubt that in some cases the favour really does lie in his marrying the damsel unportioned; as, to be still "an unappropriated blessing," at the age of ten years, would be a most terrible disgrace; while to marry a man of an inferior caste would be worse still; and at best, an Indian marriage is a mere bargain, heartless and soulless, so perhaps the wives of the Coolin are better off than many of their sisters, in that they are left with their own mothers instead of being made over to the tender mercies of an Indian mother-in-law and sisters-in-law, who rule the harem with absolute power.

Certainly, it must be a weary enough lot that generally awaits these much bejewelled young brides, and the sight of an eastern wedding ceremony invariably called to my mind a story, which, by the way, suggests itself pretty often in England, where woman's rights and womanly freedom of choice are so loudly asserted—a story of a farmer's wife explaining to a neighbour how admirably she had married her daughter, what endless plenishings were in her new house, how many cows, and sheep, and pigs, and poultry, to say nothing of a gig, in which to drive to market, "jist like a leddy," concluding her description with, "Ou, there's nae doubt it's a grand marriage; an' it wasna jist for ae thing." The neighbour naturally inquired what the *ae thing* might be, to which her friend at first seemed unwilling to recur. However, at last she was brought back to the point, a mere trivial drawback: "Weel, ye see, THE PUIR SILLY CRATUR CANNA THOLE [1] HER MAN!!" So I fear there may be a good many brown brides as well as white ones who *canna thole* their lords!

There are some rather amusing stories told of the way in which covetous thieves have circumvented the Brahmans whom they dared not rob. One such tells how three thieves once found out that a Brahman was coming along a certain road, carrying a goat on his shoulder. They coveted the goat exceedingly, and agreed to separate, so that each in turn should meet the holy man, and salute him with all reverence. Then they would suddenly feign disgust and dismay on perceiving that he carried on his shoulders an unclean dog instead of a goat. Assuredly the holy father must be mad. So they parted. The first came up as had been agreed, and feigned unutterable horror. The Brahman thought the poor fellow was deranged. When the second met him and did likewise he began to be somewhat uncomfortable in his own secret heart. But when the third accosted him with the same horrible exclamation, the poor Brahman believed that in very deed they spoke the truth, and that in punishment for some forgotten sin, Ganesa had in truth afflicted him with madness; whereupon, casting away the dubious animal, he fled to the temple to make atonement. Then

[1] *To thole*, to endure.

the rascals laughed among themselves, and having slain the goat, they feasted to their heart's content.

As we leisurely rowed up the stream, stopping from time to time to make careful drawings from different points, our attention was arrested by one magnificent bathing ghaut of finely hewn stone, with elaborate carving, and obviously new, which nevertheless had fairly tilted backward, as though bodily subsiding into the river. This ghaut was built by Scindia, when he had risen from his original position as a slipper-bearer, to the high estate of his later days, and had determined to eclipse all other ghauts in the holy city. But alas for

> "The little rift within the lover's lute
> That by and by will make the music mute."

It seems that a tiny streamlet trickled along the ground where the builders laid their foundation, and instead of allowing a channel for this insignificant watercourse they simply built over it. But the little rivulet was not going to be ignored; and though it worked quietly underground, it was gradually sapping the foundations of the great new ghaut, and ere the finishing stones were laid, the whole building gradually settled backward, and will probably, sooner or later, topple over altogether. This is the native version.

Of course no earthquake could have occasioned this accident, for as we already know, Siva, who carries the city on the point of his trident, has exempted it from all such. I noticed however that one of the neighbouring temples which stands *in* the river is as much off the plumb as the tower of Pisa, while other buildings half a mile up the stream have assumed much the same angle, and I am told that within the last fifty years many ghauts and temples have subsided, undermined by the current, which in the rainy season sweeps this bank with impetuous flow, submerging many of the temples along the shore. At such times some of the best swimmers glory in swimming to their accustomed temple and diving beneath the porch so as to enter and worship at their accustomed shrine. But already several of these temples on the shore have been engulfed, and assuredly others will soon follow.

As we rowed along, we noticed a vast number of pilgrims, wearily and painfully making their five-mile circuit sunwise round the holy city, sometimes wading up to their waists in deep mud, men and women alike floundering along. These were the conscientious ones. The careless and easy-going took a simpler and drier part within the boundary of the city.

In one form or another, these *Pradakshinas*, or religious tours sunwise, are as much in favour here as they ever were in the Scottish Highlands—and in this great country we find them on a very extensive scale, the most remarkable of all being those of holy rivers, from their source down the left bank to the mouth, and then crossing, follow up the right bank, and so returning to the source. This meritorious circuit of the Ganges, from Gangoutri to Ganga-Sagara and back, takes the pilgrim about six years!! A similar circuit of the sacred Nerbudda requires about three years, but that of the Godavari and the Krishna rivers can be accomplished in about two years. How much hard labour is involved in such a pilgrimage may be estimated by those who have traced great rivers to their mountain cradles!

A small domestic *pradakshina* is performed by women who sometimes make 108 sunwise turns round a sacred *tulasi*, or basil shrub, *i.e.* keeping their right shoulder towards the plant. The basil is held sacred, from having been the form once taken, either by Krishna's wife, Rukmini, or by Vishnu's wife, Ramacandra—a point of dispute between their respective worshippers. Anyhow, it is a plant endowed with mystic powers of healing, and counteracts the poison of serpents; so a tulasi shrub holds a place of honour among the household gods of almost every Hindoo home, where it is enthroned on an ornamental pedestal, and receives offerings of rice and flowers. Moreover, a plant of basil is often grown on the raised platform at the base of the pipal tree,[1] and village matrons who have no domestic tulasi shrub, come here to make their 108 turns, while repeating the 108 names of Vishnu.

From opposite Scindia's Ghaut the view is very grand, both up

[1] *Ficus religiosa.*

and down stream. Looking back we have a very fine palace of deep red sandstone, a group of temples with quaint lantern towers, that is, tall towers incrusted with projecting lamp-stands for festal occasions. Above, on a steep bank overhanging the stream, towers Aurungzebe's Mosque, and beyond lie gardens and bathing ghauts without number, and the ruins of the Old Fort overlooking the bridge of boats.

On the opposite side of the river is Ramnugger, the palace of the great Maharajah, whose boats of divers form float past us, one of them fashioned and painted like a peacock.

As you turn to look up the river you see in the foreground one cluster after another of conical-shaped towers of richly carved stone, mostly marked by the golden trident, that shows them to be the temples of Siva. Beyond his temples comes one like a Chinese pagoda. That is the Nepaulese temple. Next to this is that of the Goddess of Small-pox, *alias* the Mother of Death! Strange to say, in a country where cremation is the rule, the victims of small-pox (of all others!!) are frequently exempt from burning, from a fear lest this goddess should object to the process. It is one of the peculiarities of this strange people, that deeming all illnesses to be occasioned by demons of various sorts, they worship these as Goddess Mothers. It is said that there are no less than 140 of such recognised, all of whom require propitiatory offerings of blood of goats, swine, and cocks. One of those worshipped in Gujerat requires an annual supply of about 4,000 black kids! Many of these very unlovable "mothers" are represented nursing a young child.

For hours we lay moored off one great ghaut, that I might thence sketch the towering city, heaped up the steep hill-side, with its narrow, almost perpendicular streets of stairs running up to meet the blue sky; its fine houses and green trees, its countless temples piled one above another, and its innumerable bathing ghauts, all thronged with ever-changing picturesque groups; each item so attractive, and the whole so bewildering, that it needed a strong effort to persevere in the patient attempt to produce anything like a faithful study of the scene.

In the middle distance towers one great temple, painted deep red, and pointed all over with gold spikes, which is always half veiled by the brightest blue smoke from the burning ghaut just beyond, where I sometimes counted as many as eight or ten funeral pyres blazing at once, while the dying lay along the muddy edge of the river waiting for their order of release. How far that may be occasionally expedited by an additional dose of mud, it would be hard to say. Once there, nothing may again pass their lips save a drink of Ganges water—a few leaves of the shrub-goddess, the sacred tulasi plant, are placed in the mouth—and if death should linger too long, a little kindly mud is no great harm. Many a weary soul just crawls to the holy city to end his long pilgrimage, and attains the boon he craves; an end of all life's suffering in the one great rest for weary limbs, and a certain welcome to the longed-for heaven. What more can he desire? Are there not scores of holy Brahmans as ready to speed the dying on their way as to absolve the living, promising rest for the weary, pardon for all sin, and blessings without number in return for offerings and priestly fees? So the sick and the aged whose hour is supposed to have come, are laid on the brink of the river, and their relations wait with apparently the utmost apathy, while Pariah dogs and birds of prey watch eagerly for the moment when their horrible carnival may begin.

I am not now speaking of the burning ghaut in the city. Those who bring their relations here are probably rich enough to pay for the shelter of a *murhī*, which is a covered shed on the brink of the river, and while the dying slowly breathe their last breath on the hallowed shore, their friends repair to the wood-merchant close by, and buy as much wood as they can afford. Sometimes they can only get enough to char the body, which is then cast into the river and floats down the lazy current together with many another, in every stage of putrefaction, spreading the seed of pestilence on the quiet air. And so it comes to pass that you cannot row up the stream without your boat or your oar again and again coming in contact with an unsightly bloated mass, once human; a *something* whose late inmate has doubtless solved all the mysteries at which in his own strange way he worked so hard. The boatmen look with the utmost indifference at these common objects of the stream and shore, and giving them a shove with their oars to prevent their becoming entangled with the boat, send them on their unrestful course.

Just imagine how frightfully this system of disposing of the dead must tend to the spread of cholera and other diseases!

It is bad enough to know that the people coming from infected houses are in the daily habit of washing their clothes and all manner of vessels, at the very edge of the wells and tanks, into which, of course, the foul water is at once drained. But the rivers fare still worse, for into them are cast the very bodies wherein fever, leprosy, and cholera fiends have held triumphant revel, and wherein they still lurk, hatching fresh mischief, and sending forth other spirits as vicious as themselves in search of fresh victims.

Of course it is the usual story of poverty revenging itself on its unsympathizing rich neighbours, for in the case of the wealthier Hindoo, the funeral pyre is carefully built, and when the corpse has been washed in the river it is swathed in fair linen, white or scarlet—or still more often the shroud is of the sacred saffron colour, on which is showered a handful of vermilion paint, which is said by some to symbolize the blood of sprinkling as the atonement for sin. Sometimes the body is wrapped in cloth of silver or of gold, and is laid upon the pyre. Sweet sacred grass is then laid over it, and precious anointing oil which shall make the flame burn more brightly; and more wood is heaped on till the pyre is very high. A Brahman then brings sacred fire and gives a lighted torch to the chief mourner, who then walks thrice or nine times sunwise round the body. He touches the lips of the dead with the holy fire, then lights the pyre. Other torches are applied simultaneously, and in a very few moments the body is burnt, though the fire smoulders long.

This simple ceremony of cremation as now practised under the regulation of British law, is shorn of all the ghastly horrors which have so often been enacted at this spot, ere the burning of widows on the funeral pyre was declared illegal. I believe that about fifty years have elapsed since the last case of sati; surely the Hindoo widows, like the self-torturing ascetics, must secretly rejoice in this intervention of the infidel rulers.

There is one very curious item in this cremation ceremonial. It is supposed that in the moment of death, the soul of a bad man passes downward from the body, while that of a righteous man escapes upward through the skull. Of course, every one assumes his own dead to be bound in the right direction, so, to facilitate the upward flight, it is proper during cremation for one of the mourners to approach with a club of sacred wood to crack the skull with a well-aimed blow.

When great saints are buried, instead of being cremated, a blow from a sacred conch-shell, or from a cocoa-nut, is equally effectual.

When the body has been consumed, all the mourners come down to the river, beating their breasts and howling, and proceed to wash themselves and their clothes, and go through divers ceremonies of purification necessary after touching a dead body. On the fourth day after cremation the ashes are collected and sprinkled on the sacred river, which thus absorbs all that was mortal of its devout worshipper.

Close by a pretty ceremony is going on. A gaily-dressed family party, including every member, from the old grandfather to the youngest child, have come to the brink of the river to give thanks and offerings to the goddess Ganga, on the occasion of a boy having been shaved for the first time. Not his beard, for not the silkiest down suggests such a future decoration, but his head has been shorn of all its locks, save the small tuft allowed by his caste; and the magnificently dressed little fellow stalks along in all the conscious pride of manhood, and casts his offerings of flowers and coins and sweetmeats into the stream.

This boy was apparently about seven years of age. Small Brahmans are subjected to the tonsure when they have attained their third year, when the father sprinkles the child's head with butter and curds and warm water, and passes stalks of sacred kusa grass through the hair, with invocation to the divine grass, after which the little head is shaved, with the exception of one, three, or five locks, which are left to adorn the scalp; and very quaint henceforth is the appearance of the tiny copper-coloured mortal.

A child's religious education begins in its third or fourth year, when it is taught to repeat the formula, "Great Krishna is my soul's refuge," which it must henceforth reiterate many times a day. To aid it in this task it is invested by the ministering Brahman with the *japa mala*, or muttering beads, *i.e.* a rosary of 108 beads of tulasi-wood, *i.e.* the sacred basil. These beads typefy a selection of 108 of the most sacred names of Vishnu, taken from his full catalogue of 1,000 names and attributes—including such titles as "The Way, the Truth, the Life, the Physician, the Most Holy, the Pure One, the Auspicious, the Omnipresent."

In the same way, the little Sivite is presented with a rosary of either thirty-two or sixty-four rough berries of the Mundrāsi, or Rudraksha tree,[1] a berry probably selected from being five-sided, and therefore suggestive of Siva's five faces. This rosary is to help the worshipper in reciting the 1,008 attributes of Siva.

The shaving party have now gone on their way rejoicing, and on the platform where they stood a new group has now arrived, bearing something in a sheet. That something is a corpse, carried miles perhaps, to be washed in the holy Ganges. The mourners do their work slowly and deliberately, and the marriage party take no heed of their neighbours, for though in any other land such meetings would be deemed evil omens, here they are the common things of daily life, and excite no comment whatever. Perhaps they lend to the feast that strange incentive to pleasure which the old Egyptians sought to introduce, when at their merry festivals they handed round an exquisitely carved ivory skeleton in a small sarcophagus—and sometimes even carried in a genuine mummy—to remind the guests how short a time they had for mirth, and bid them make the most of it. Death at the feast!—a strange, piquant sauce to lend new zest to jaded appetites!

[1] *Eleocarpus Canitrus.*

Meanwhile a very gay Mahratta marriage-party has assembled on the next platform which projects as a pier into the river. The young couple are a very small boy and girl gorgeously dressed. They are so close to us that we can count every ring in the little bride's ears, nose, and toes. The tiny bride and bridegroom are tied together by a consecrated scarlet scarf, fastened to both their dresses and concealing their united hands. A priest winds the sacred cord round their necks, while reciting prayers ; water is poured out from a brass lota, also cocoa-nut juice.

For a while they sit silently gazing into the water, supposed to be making *poojah*, that is, worshipping ; and the stillness is only broken by the cries of a burying party, who pass just behind them, bearing a corpse shoulder high, which they are carrying to the burning ghaut just beyond, whence a thick cloud of blue smoke is for ever rising in the calm sunshine.

Then there is a sprinkling of rice over the young couple (just as at a London wedding), with the addition of a little red powder, and then the wedding party return home. I am told that part of the ceremony in the father's house is the kindling of a sacred fire, round which the little bride and bridegroom walk three times hand in hand, only seven steps being allowed for each circuit. Then, waxing affectionate, he puts his own arm round her neck, and again walks thrice round the sacred flame while throwing in offerings of emblematic barley and other seeds, and while the priests burn clarified butter, just as in the early Aryan rites.

Meanwhile the wedded children have said their little prayer, and have cast on the water their garlands of roses and marigolds, their handful of coins, a little grain, and some other offerings, and Ganga in return gives her blessing to their marriage.

While young life is thus beginning to work out its endless problem, one who has solved all its mysteries comes floating past, with dead eyes fixed, in horrid, lifeless stare. And the bridal wreaths of crimson and golden blossoms, which the child-bride and her little lord have just offered to the river goddess, are drawn by the eddying currents till they circle round the dead ;

and one fresh, lovely garland clings to his head as a crown. And so, swiftly and silently, life and death float together down the smooth, solemn stream—the old story, "the Spirit of Life ever weaving, the Spirit of Death ever unweaving"—just as they have done through countless ages; while new generations fill the place of those who are gone, as swiftly and as surely as fresh floods pour down from the mountains, for ever hurrying onward to the sea, yet for ever flowing in the same channel; so that the pilgrim returns, year after year, to find the same broad brimming river all unchanged.

Thus, as our boat lay moored at any spot where it might please us to halt, this stream of life flowed past us, ever varying: youth and age, sorrow and joy, life and death, in strangest combination. And all day long, mingling with the sharp cries of the white and brown kites that floated between us and the sun, or quarrelled noisily over some precious find of dainty offal, the ceaseless clang and murmur from the countless temples assailed our ears; trumpets, *sunkhs* (shells), tomtoms, and big drums mingling their horrid dissonance. Verily! it is a holy city.

It seems to me that its interest is inexhaustible, each moment presenting some strangely picturesque incident, utterly unexpected, as if that wonderful kaleidoscope never could exhaust its curious combinations. As to giving you the faintest idea of Benares by mere description, the attempt is too ludicrous!

Among the commonplace scenes of daily domestic life are the groups of veiled, jewelled women for ever passing up and down those long stairs to fill their red earthenware jars with water, which they poise on their heads, having perhaps also a child astride on the maternal side. Others are busied in scouring their brazen vessels, which gleam in the sun like burnished gold.

One small incident of parental discipline amused us considerably. A boy had been sent down to fill his great red jar, but the temptations of the river had been too much for him, and he lingered till his angry father came in search of him, and administered summary justice. The poor little wretch howled for mercy, and on being released, filled his jar, and poising it on his head, slowly ascended that long, long stair; his father following close, and administering a sharp "spank" at every step. Poor child! it was very cruel of us to laugh, but the absurdity of the scene was irresistible.

All day long boats of every description floated past us; sometimes crowding all their quaint sails—pure white, or tattered, as the case might be; multitudes of large house-boats, thatched with straw or bamboo—the sole home perhaps of a large family; others laden with grain or with cotton, and steered by enormous rudders. Little pleasure-boats of every sort and kind pass to and fro, full of gaily-dressed people, or else bearing pilgrims to the opposite shore. Sometimes men swim across, bringing with them a raft, whereon are set their milk jars. In olden days palanquins and travellers were thus floated across the river on a raft made of earthenware vessels tied together, while all the bearers swam, and lent a hand to guide the raft. Now, however, most people would prefer taking a longer round, and coming across the bridge of boats.

One pleasant feature of our days on the river was the excellent supply of fruit which was daily sent by our kind Rajah. In fact, there was always a first-rate breakfast, or rather *déjeuner à la fourchette*, ready for us at any moment when we could spare time for anything so commonplace as eating and drinking. What we chiefly enjoyed was the capital hot tea. On the last day, however, as we were finishing our breakfast, a thought flashed across us too horrible for utterance. We looked at one another in blank dismay; and every face expressed the same mute disgust. . . . . Whence had the water been drawn to fill our little kettle? Was there any room for doubt—one lingering hope that out of deference to our feelings it had been brought from some pure well? or that reverence for the great goddess Ganga had prevented her being converted into tea for unbelievers? Alas! there was no chance for such a thing. There was no doubt that we, like most of our neighbours, had unwittingly swallowed our peck of dirt—had involuntarily incorporated a very large amount of essence of Hindoo. There was nothing for it but resolutely to determine to forget the fact with all possible speed—a resolution more easily made than kept!!

Several times when we returned from the river in the evenings, the kind old Rajah came to see us, and, leaving his gold-wrought slippers at the door, would sit chatting quite happily for a good while. Of course, I could not understand him, but a little interpreting made the conversation general; and it was pleasant to watch the benevolent expression of a face that always reminded me of some saintly bishop. I confess it was a great shock to my feelings, on going to return his visit, to see that dear old face painted with streaks and caste marks, received that morning at his temple. He received us with all ceremony in a large handsome house, took us to the roof to see the view, adorned us with large silver *harrs* (necklaces of silver ribbon, plaited), and offering us *pân* (betel-nuts and cardamoms, chatted on all manner of subjects, while his confidential servants, our trusty guides and guardians, looked on with evident interest, very anxious that we should be duly impressed by everything. They were men of just the same stamp as the faithful, trusty Highland retainers of olden days—such men as we still happily find from time to time—attached old servants.

I did not venture to ask for "the house," meaning the women-kind, as I could not have talked to them; so when we had said our say, Sir Deo himself escorted us back to his own carriage, his servants looking on admiringly. The good old man was as anxious to ensure our church-going on Sunday, as all other *ploys* of the week. He knew the exact hours of morning and evening service, and insisted on sending us there in the usual state, though we ventured to plead that for so short a distance we might surely walk. So from first to last there was no end to his kindness, the remembrance of which ranks very high amongst happy memories of India.

Amongst my many pleasant reminiscences of Benares was a chance railway acquaintance with a very charming English-woman—one of the ladies of the Zenana Mission—whose life-work it is to fraternise with as many of her Hindoo sisters as care to welcome her to their homes (and these are legion), and then try to impart to them some of the commoner branches of civilised education. It is only of late years that such a thing has become possible, as hitherto learning of any sort has been forbidden to all women of good character, and a knowledge of reading, writing, singing, or dancing, has marked those damsels only who were essentially "fast." Thus, anything more dreary than the home-life of a Hindoo matron could scarcely be devised. She may cook for her husband, but may not eat in his presence; nor may she even speak to him in presence of his mother or sisters, who rule the house, in which she is but a cipher. Very few even know how to sew.

Now a new era seems dawning on these dull lives. Multitudes are gladly learning to read and write, and the "Zenana ladies" receive a cordial welcome wherever they go, and are often invited to extend their visits to new houses, of rich merchants and great men. Some, even of the influential Rajahs, have formally admitted them to visit "their house" (as they say, in order to avoid even a distant allusion to their feminine relations), and seem well pleased that their women-folk should now begin to cultivate their minds after the manner of their white sisters. Hitherto, when any one ventured to suggest such a possibility as that of allowing dark women the same freedom as white ones, the men would scout the idea, declaring that they would be utterly incapable of using it. Now little by little they seem to be admitting the thin end of the wedge, and allowing the first glimmer of light to enter into those Zenanas, in which their sons and daughters are being reared. Who can tell how this may act on the next generation?

As regards the intellect of the women of India, there have already been a sufficient number of notable examples among such as have from time to time dared to escape from the trammels of their early training, and to assert their own powers of thought and action. Some of the most beautiful hymns in the Rig Veda are ascribed to women — the Miriams of the Aryan host! The writings of Avyar, a female philosopher of the ninth century, are to this day taught in the Tamul schools, and are classed among the standard works of the land.

Moreover, as I have already had occasion to remark,[1] there seems no reason to doubt that the most intellectual of all games, which even to this day is deemed worthy exercise for the brains of our wisest men—I mean chess—was invented by an Indian

[1] See p. 156.

queen who lived two thousand years before the Christian era, in those good old days when husband and wife shared life's responsibilities, and were jointly described as "rulers of the house,"[1] and together worshipped the gods—those good days ere the Brahmans had invented the horrid rite of widow-burning, and otherwise degraded the position of women.

There are also countless instances of clever wives and mothers of princes, who have ruled the dominions of sons or husbands with readier wit and stronger arm than these chanced to own. Such was the late Begum of Bhopal, who did not scruple to lead her own armies to the field, and even to appear in council in presence of Europeans with unveiled face; a proceeding which scandalised and shocked some of her followers, though it was admitted that they rather liked the shock!

There seems every probability that an internal upheaval has even now commenced, which will greatly facilitate the work of female education in India. Four years ago a fascinating and accomplished young Brahman lady, aged twenty-two, the daughter of a learned pundit, started to travel through Bengal, accompanied by her brother, in order to hold public meetings on the education and emancipation of women in India! Here certainly was a remarkable stride, and the charming lady found great favour, and doubtless her words will carry weight on behalf of many a dull harem.

One thing, however, I am bound to say, in favour of the results of Indian guarding of women, which is, that our Hindoo sisters certainly hold a better position than those of Britain in regard to criminal statistics, for I find that whereas, for every million of women in England and Wales, 340 are in gaol, only twenty-eight per million of Indian women contrive to place themselves within the grasp of the law. Indeed, for that matter, the men too stand well as compared with ours, for whereas about 870 per million Britons find their way to gaol, only 614 Hindoos are there to be found!

Our days at Benares were over. Once again we devoted a long morning to sightseeing in the wonderful city. Then once more crossing the bridge of boats, we found ourselves in the

[1] *Dampati.*

nineteenth century, and in the stables of the great iron horse, which bore us swiftly away from a life that seemed rather like some curious dream than like the common every-day existence of myriads of ordinary mortals.

A few hours more, and we were again in Allahabad, encamped in a great tent beneath shady tamarind trees. A week later found us whirling along by rail to Bombay, halting at Nagpore "the city of the Naga," *i.e.* of the Serpent—once a stronghold of his worshippers—and likewise halting at Jubbulpore to see the far-famed marble rocks, which rise like gleaming walls on either side of the clear green waters of the Nerbudda, most sacred of all rivers. One more expedition through the beautifully wooded mountain country near Bombay and Poonah, and one long day spent in exploring the wondrous rock temple on the Isle of Elephanta, and then we bade adieu to the beautiful Indian land.

Then followed a voyage of many storms, and at length we caught our first glimpse of the white cliffs of Albion on a wild March morning, in the short intervals between sweeping snow-showers. And

> "Oh! the frosty cliffs looked cold upon me,
> All things blurred and dull and vague.
> Not a hill or stone with heart to strike a radiant colour
> Or active outline on the indifferent air!"

Cold too, and pinched, and poverty-stricken, and eminently unpicturesque looked the squalid crowd of tattered men, women, and children. Oh, so different from the brilliant sunlit throngs we had so recently left!

Many weeks elapsed ere I could shake off this first impression of Britain. Therefore, should any who have read these pages be inclined to follow in my footsteps, let me give them one solemn warning, namely, so far to extend their twelve months' wandering, as not to return to England until the summer sun has warmed these grey isles into such kindly heat and colour as may save invidious comparisons between East and West.

INDEX.

B.

I.

J.

K.

Q.

R.

THE END.